The Sixty Years' War for the Great Lakes, 1754–1814

The Sixty Years' War for the Great Lakes, 1754–1814

EDITED BY
DAVID CURTIS SKAGGS
AND
LARRY L. NELSON

Michigan State University Press

East Lansing

♾ The paper used in this publication meets the minimum requirements
of ANSI/NISO Z39.48–1992 (R 1997) (Permanence of Paper).
Michigan State University Press
East Lansing, Michigan 48823–5202
Printed and bound in the United States of America.

07 06 05 04 03 02 01   1 2 3 4 5 6 7 8 9 10

LIBRARY OF CONGRESS CATALOGING-IN-PUBLICATION DATA
The Sixty Years' War for the Great Lakes, 1754–1814 / edited by David
Curtis Skaggs and Larry L. Nelson.
p. cm.
Papers from a conference held in Sept. 1998 at Bowling Green State
University, Bowling Green, Ohio.
Includes bibliographical references and index.
ISBN 0-87013-569-4
1. Great Lakes Region—History, Military—Congresses. 2. Indians of
North America—Wars—1750–1815—Congresses. 3. Indians of North
America—Wars—Great Lakes Region—Congresses. 4. United
States—History—French and Indian War, 1755–1763—Congresses. 5.
United States—History—Revolution, 1775–1783—Congresses. 6. United
States—History—War of 1812—Congresses. 7. Great
Britain—Colonies—North America—History—Congresses. 8.
France—Colonies—North America—History—Congresses. I. Skaggs,
DavidCurtis. II. Nelson, Larry L. (Larry Lee), 1950–
F551 .S53 2001
977'.01—dc21
00-012881

Cover and book by Sharp Des!gns, Inc., Lansing, MI

Visit Michigan State University Press on the World Wide Web at:
www.msu.edu/unit/msupress

Contents

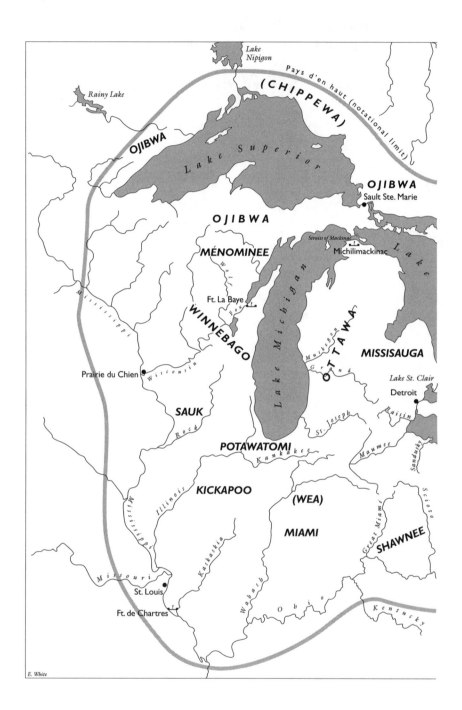

Lake Nipigon

Pays d'en haut (notational limit)

Rainy Lake

(CHIPPEWA)

OJIBWA

Lake Superior

OJIBWA
Sault Ste. Marie

OJIBWA

MÉNOMINEE

Strait of Mackinac
Michilimackinac

Ft. La Baye

Lake

WINNEBAGO

Lake Michigan

Wolf

Fox

OTTAWA

MISSISAUGA

Prairie du Chien

Wisconsin

Muskegon

Grand

Lake St. Clair
Detroit

Mississippi

SAUK

Rock

St. Joseph

Raisin

POTAWATOMI

Kankakee

Maumee

Sandusky

KICKAPOO

(WEA)

Illinois

MIAMI

SHAWNEE

Scioto

Great Miami

Mississippi

Kaskaskia

Missouri

St. Louis

Ft. de Chartres

Wabash

Ohio

Kentucky

E. White

— VIII —

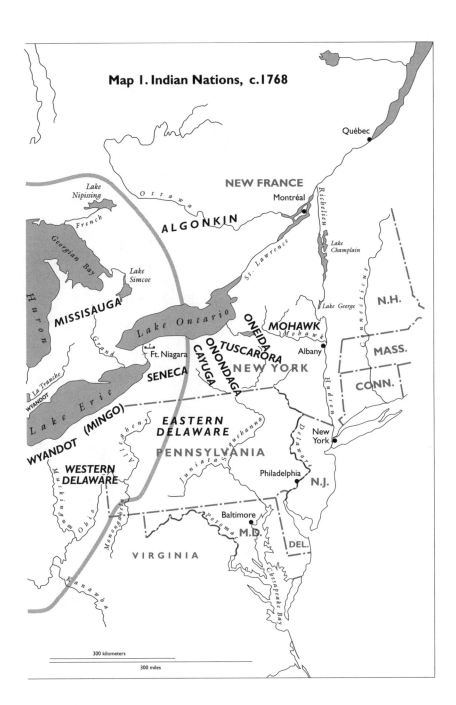

Map 1. Indian Nations, c.1768

NEW FRANCE

Québec

Lake Nipissing

Ottawa

Montréal

Richelieu

ALGONKIN

French

Lake Champlain

Georgian Bay

Lake Simcoe

St. Lawrence

Lake George

Connecticut

N.H.

Huron

MISSISAUGA

Lake Ontario

ONEIDA

MOHAWK

Mohawk

MASS.

Grand

Ft. Niagara

TUSCARORA

Albany

ONONDAGA

CAYUGA

NEW YORK

CONN.

La Tranche

SENECA

WYANDOT

Lake Erie

Hudson

WYANDOT (MINGO)

Allegheny

EASTERN
DELAWARE

Susquehanna

New
York

Delaware

WESTERN
DELAWARE

PENNSYLVANIA

Juniata

Philadelphia

N.J.

Muskingum

Ohio

Monongahela

Potomac

Baltimore

M.D.

DEL.

VIRGINIA

Kanawha

Chesapeake Bay

300 kilometers

300 miles

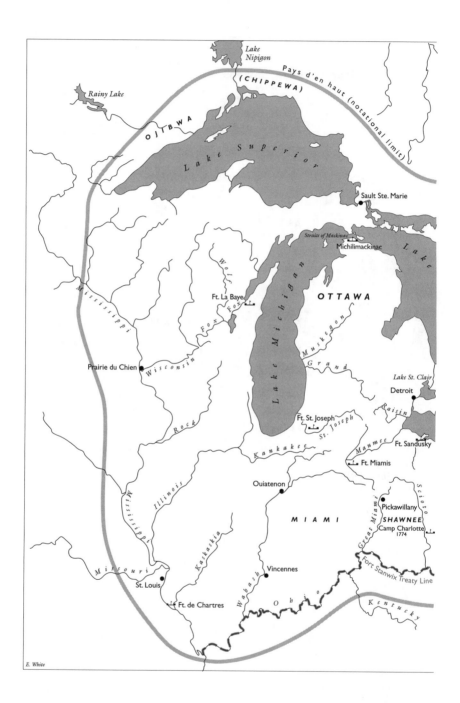

Lake Nipigon

Pays d'en haut (notational limit)

(CHIPPEWA)

Rainy Lake

O J I B W A

Lake Superior

Sault Ste. Marie

Straits of Mackinac

Michilimackinac

Wolf

Fox

Fox

Ft. La Baye

OTTAWA

Lake Michigan

Muskegon

Grand

Prairie du Chien

Wisconsin

Lake St. Clair

Detroit

Rock

Ft. St. Joseph

St. Joseph

Raisin

Kankakee

Maumee

Ft. Sandusky

Illinois

Ft. Miamis

Scioto

Ouiatenon

Pickawillany

Mississippi

M I A M I

SHAWNEE
Camp Charlotte
1774

Kaskaskia

Great Miami

Missouri

Vincennes

Wabash

Fort Stanwix Treaty Line

St. Louis

Ohio

Kentucky

Ft. de Chartres

E. White

— x —

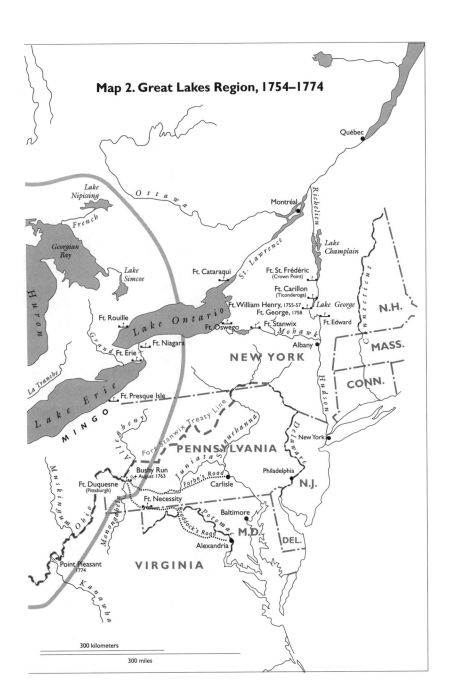

Map 2. Great Lakes Region, 1754–1774

Québec

Lake
Nipissing

Ottawa

Montréal

Richelieu

French

Georgian
Bay

Lake
Champlain

Huron

Lake
Simcoe

Ft. Cataraqui

St. Lawrence

Ft. St. Frédéric
(Crown Point)

Ft. Carillon
(Ticonderoga)

Ft. William Henry, 1755-57
Ft. George, 1758

Lake George

N.H.

Ft. Rouille

Lake Ontario

Ft. Oswego

Ft. Stanwix

Ft. Edward

Connecticut

Grand

Ft. Niagara

Mohawk

MASS.

Ft. Erie

Albany

NEW YORK

La Tranche

CONN.

Lake Erie

Hudson

MINGO

Ft. Presque Isle

Allegheny

Fort Stanwix Treaty Line

Susquehanna

Delaware

New York

Muskingum

PENNSYLVANIA

Juniata

Bushy Run
◇ August 1763

Forbe's Road

Philadelphia

Ft. Duquesne
(Pittsburgh)

Carlisle

N.J.

Ohio

Ft. Necessity

Monongahela

Potomac

Baltimore

M.D.

DEL.

Braddock's Road

Alexandria

Point Pleasant
1774

VIRGINIA

Kanawha

300 kilometers

300 miles

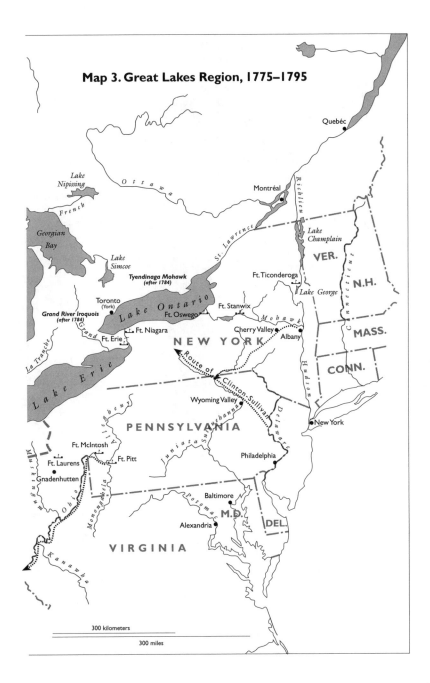

Map 3. Great Lakes Region, 1775–1795

Lake Nipissing

Ottawa

French

Georgian Bay

Lake Simcoe

Tyendinaga Mohawk (after 1784)

Toronto (York)

Grand River Iroquois (after 1784)

Grand

Ft. Erie

La Tranche

Lake Ontario

Ft. Niagara

Ft. Oswego

Ft. Stanwix

NEW YORK

Cherry Valley

Albany

Mohawk

Route of

Clinton-Sullivan

Wyoming Valley

Susquehanna

Delaware

Allegheny

PENNSYLVANIA

Juniata

Ft. McIntosh

Allegheny

Ft. Laurens

Ft. Pitt

Gnadenhutten

Muskingum

Ohio

Monongahela

VIRGINIA

Kanawha

Quebéc

Montréal

Richlieu

St. Lawrence

Lake Champlain

VER.

Ft. Ticonderoga

Lake George

N.H.

Connecticut

MASS.

CONN.

Hudson

New York

Philadelphia

Baltimore

M.D.

Potomac

Alexandria

DEL.

300 kilometers

300 miles

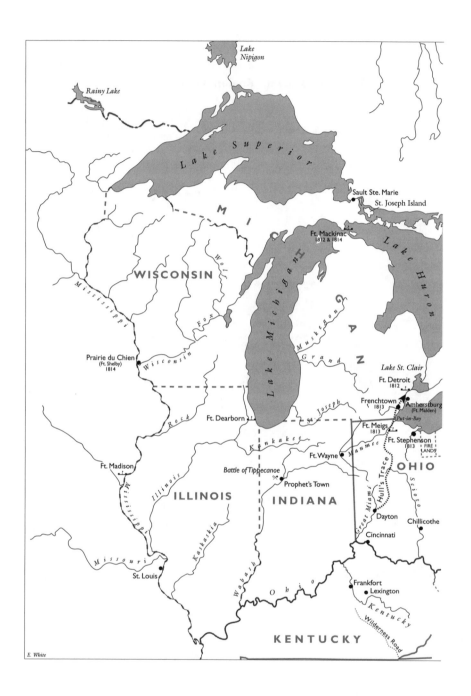

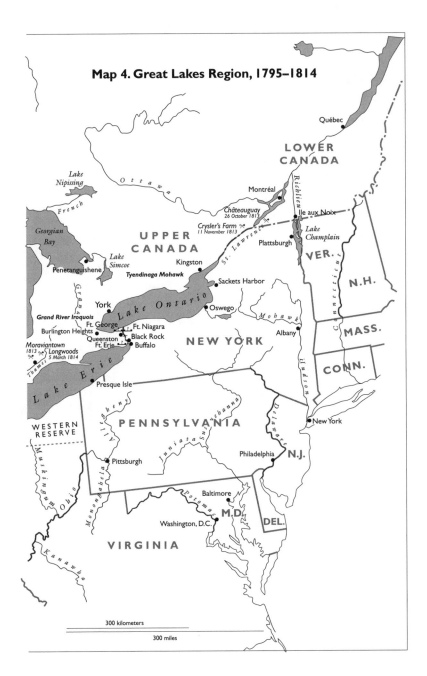

Map 4. Great Lakes Region, 1795–1814

Québec

LOWER
CANADA

Lake
Nipissing

Ottawa

French

Montréal

Georgian
Bay

Châteauguay
26 October 1813

Crysler's Farm
11 November 1813

Richlieu

Île aux Noix

UPPER
CANADA

Lake
Simcoe

Kingston

St. Lawrence

Plattsburgh

Lake
Champlain

VER.

Penetanguishene

Tyendinaga Mohawk

Sackets Harbor

N.H.

Grand

York

Lake Ontario

Oswego

Mohawk

Connecticut

Grand River Iroquois

Ft. George

Ft. Niagara

Albany

MASS.

Burlington Heights

Queenston

Black Rock

NEW YORK

Moraviantown
1813

Longwoods
5 March 1814

Ft. Erie

Buffalo

Hudson

CONN.

Thames

Lake Erie

Presque Isle

New York

WESTERN
RESERVE

Allegheny

PENNSYLVANIA

Susquehanna

Delaware

Muskingum

Juniata

Philadelphia

N.J.

Pittsburgh

Monongahela

Ohio

Baltimore

Potomac

M.D.

DEL.

Washington, D.C.

VIRGINIA

Kanawha

300 kilometers

300 miles

Introduction

LARRY L. NELSON & DAVID CURTIS SKAGGS

In the introduction to her *Atlas of Great Lakes Indian History*, historian and demographer Helen Hornbeck Tanner tells that her interest in Great Lakes Indian history began in 1963 when she was casually asked to find out what Indians had lived near her home in Ann Arbor, Michigan. That initial request began a period of protracted, original research that would eventually define much of her career, encompass the history of the entire Great Lakes region from about 1640 to 1820, and figure prominently in the work of the Indian Claims Commission. "Unwittingly," she writes, "I had been drawn into the most singularly unexplored area of Indian history in the eastern United States—the Ohio country," unexplored, she points out, because at the time the region seemed to offer little of interest for anthropologists or historians.[1]

Today, few of either profession would characterize the colonial and territorial-era history of the Great Lakes region in such a manner. Indeed, frontier and trans-Appalachian studies in general, and Ohio Valley/Great Lakes scholarship in particular, have emerged as particularly vigorous and viable fields. That renaissance is the result of the fortuitous confluence of several trends. Frontier studies seem to enjoy wide general interest, sparked perhaps in part by the coming of age of a generation raised watching the weekly adventures of Daniel Boone and Davy Crockett, and continue to benefit from strong popular interest in Native American culture and history. Advances in methodology and historiographic emphasis, including "The New Social History," ethnohistory, regional and local history, material culture studies, evolving sensibilities of race, culture, ethnicity and gender created within feminist and ethnic studies, and cross-disciplinary understandings derived from ethnography, cultural anthropology, sociology, cultural geography, and archaeology have given modern practitioners tools of unprecedented sophistication and refinement. Lastly, the renaissance profited from the first wave of scholars to enter the area, whose work convincingly demonstrated the worth of the mid-American studies. Scholarship including Helen Tanner's own cartographic insights, the genius for narrative demonstrated by Stephen Aron, David Edmunds and John Mack Faragher,[2] the chiding admonitions of Francis Jennings and Rob Allen,[3] the emphasis on cross-cultural analysis displayed in the work of Colin Calloway and Ian Steele,[4] and a brilliance for creating organizational and explanatory paradigms shown by Fred Anderson, Drew Cayton, Gregory Dowd, Michael McConnell, and Richard White,[5] to name only a few, legitimized the endeavor, defined it in terms of academic excellence and scholastic rigor, and provided the initial momentum that continues to propel the field today. We are particularly proud that several of these scholars allowed new additions to their contributions to be published in this volume.

On 18 September 1998, over 225 American, Canadian, and European scholars, secondary and primary educators, museum personnel, archivists, and a heartening number of interested lay-enthusiasts, all of whom share an abiding interest in the early history of the Great Lakes region, met for a three day conference at Bowling Green State University in Bowling Green, Ohio. Collectively they examined the long series of colonial and early national-era conflicts that swept through the region beginning in 1754 with the onset of the Seven Years', or French and Indian, War and ending at the conclusion of the War of 1812. Despite the program's militaristic theme, the conference organizers wished the participants to probe beyond the traditional focus on tactics and strategy and to assess instead these conflicts' immediate and long-term political, ideological, economic, cultural, and material consequences for the region and the two nations that emerged from the struggle. While acknowledging that these wars were fought at different times by different people for different reasons, the organizers urged the attendees to view the struggles collectively and to deal with them as parts of a single conflict, a nearly three-generation-long contest waged among European, American, Canadian, and Native peoples for suzerainty over the Great Lakes. The initial response to the organizing committee's request was encouraging and eventually the conference was constructed around forty-one papers delivered in twenty-one sessions. This book presents twenty of the best papers given at the conference and, while not intended to be a comprehensive overview, suggests the creative vitality and wide variety of topics and methodologies shaping the field today.

The first essay, by David Skaggs, sets the theme and tone for this collection. Drawing inspiration from the Greek historian Thucydides and his *History of the Peloponnesian War*, Skaggs claims that the series of wars for control of the Great Lakes region were not unconnected events, but rather a series of interrelated episodes. They were, in fact, aspects of a single conflict, what Skaggs labels the Sixty Years' War for the Great Lakes. Within this offering, he demonstrates the relationship between the disparate threads of geography, diplomacy, intercultural relations, politics, economics, tactics, and strategic concerns that eventually contributed to the geopolitical transformation of the area.

William Eccles, considered the dean of New France historians, in a broad-ranging and thought-provoking essay traces French responses to English initiatives throughout the colonial era until the end of the War of 1812, with an emphasis on those events taking place from 1663 through the conclusion of the Seven Years' War. He concludes that the clash between France and England was actually a struggle between opposing ethical and moral systems: one based on honor and deference held by the French and one based on the ruthless pursuit of ends, regardless of normally accepted concepts of civilized behavior, held by the Americans and the British. In Eccles' provocative view, the conquest of New France marked the beginning of the decline of gentility in the Western world. Dr. Eccles was widely recognized, before his death in October 1998, as one of the leading Canadian scholars of his generation. Because of his illness, Dr. Eccles was unable to attend the conference and his paper was read to the audience. This essay is his last published work. We are grateful to his family for allowing us to print it.

Charles Brodine examines the career of Colonel Henry Bouquet and reassesses the Swiss mercenary's influence on the evolution of tactics on the western border. He argues that while Bouquet was responsible for some tactical innovations, his stature as an innovator has been overestimated. This discussion of a small portion of the event we usually call Pontiac's Rebellion makes an interesting commentary on the growing body of literature dealing with warfare on the North American frontier.

Matthew Ward tackles a particularly disputatious topic, the impact of disease during the Sixty Years' War era. In a thoughtfully presented essay that examines a topic too often obscured by sensationalist rhetoric, Ward claims that disease was introduced along the western border as the direct, though unintended, consequence of British policy. Once established, the effects of endemic illness were exacerbated by widespread alcohol abuse, changes in imperial policy that required Indians to conduct trade and diplomacy at British posts, declining game reserves, the inherent hardships caused by war and dislocation, and the slow collapse of native culture.

Michael McDonnell addresses the cross-cultural politics of the Sixty Years' War period through the life of Charles Langlade, a *métis* fur trader and adventurer. McDonnell demonstrates a basic tenet of the New Indian History, namely that Native peoples were willing and capable of manipulating events for their own benefit. He places the life of Langlade (a true frontier swashbuckler about whom we need to know more) into the context of cultural mediation by explicating the kinship and economic links upon which his influence was based.

Jon Parmenter's offering advances our understandings of Iroquois Confederacy history and diplomacy. Parmenter suggests that the eastern Iroquois Confederacy maintained contact with the Ohio Valley on two different levels, a macro, or diplomatic level on which the Iroquois asserted a territorial claim to the Ohio Valley and the right to represent Indians living in the Ohio Country in negotiations with colonial officials, and a micro level articulated through the migration of Iroquois to the Ohio Valley where they became known as the Mingo. By 1754, members of the eastern Confederacy and the Ohio Iroquois had split on the question of how best to preserve their political autonomy. Eastern Confederacy members advised continued adherence to the Covenant Chain and the outward appearance of neutrality; Ohio members chose military confrontation with their enemies. Both positions, claim Parmenter, can be viewed as legitimate "Iroquois" responses to the mid– and late–eighteenth-century struggle to control the Ohio Valley/Great Lakes region.

Keith Widder explores the French contribution after the English conquest of New France. According to Widder, following the conquest British authorities considered the Interior French (those who lived with their *métis* or French families away from the European settlements at Detroit and Michilimackinac) to be their enemies. In truth, however, the Interior French were indispensable to the efforts of British traders to enter and profit from the region's fur trade. The Interior French acted in concert with British trading interests by providing French personnel to work with

English traders, by providing entree to the region's Native leaders, and by using informal diplomacy to discourage violence and solve problems of mutual concern. Widder's article does for the French living in Canada what recent scholarship has done for Native peoples, namely change our understanding of "French" from a pan-ethnic, monolithic, unified generalization to one that acknowledges a wide and complex diversity in cultures, political alignments, and economic interests.

Susan Sleeper-Smith, writing along similar lines, also examines the role of the Interior French by focusing on the life of Louis Chevalier, the patriarch of a prominent Interior French family during the 1760s and 1770s. By defining the complicated linkages that existed between trade, family, gender, economics, religion, and politics, and then demonstrating how all effected demographic change and long-term strategic concerns, Sleeper-Smith concludes by showing that Great Britain's failure to recognize or utilize the Interior French to establish hegemony within the Great Lakes region significantly compromised that nation's ability to recruit Native allies during the Revolution.

Few places west of the Appalachian Mountains were as central to events during the Sixty Years' War for the Great Lakes as was Detroit. Controlled successively by the French, British, and Americans, it was home to Native populations, military garrisons, and a large fur-trading community. Each nation developed and maintained defensive works at the town and used the site as a domestic, military, and economic base for their activities in the region. Brian Dunnigan creatively utilizes eighteenth- and nineteenth-century maps and drawings to describe the changing appearance of Detroit from 1750 to 1815.

There are few episodes during the Sixty Years' War period more disturbing than the execution of ninety-eight Christian Indians by Pennsylvania irregulars at Gnadenhutten, a Moravian mission town on the Tuscarawas (then called the Muskingum) River, on 8 March 1782. Leonard Sadosky sees the massacre as an act of rebellion by western-Pennsylvania and Virginia backwoodsmen who, angered over regional fur-trading policy and the prosecution of the war from Fort Pitt, were actually striking a blow against continental authorities and eastern élites, while at the same time demonstrating their hatred of the Natives.

Elizabeth Perkins looks beyond the legacy of intercultural violence during the Sixty Years' War era and examines a second legacy, a process of mutual discovery common to both Indians and Europeans that she calls "Ethical Extension." According to Perkins, this process begins with curiosity about one's opponents, then leads to a measure of shared comprehension between combatants, and ends with the recognition of an enemy's humanity. Perkins significantly advances our understanding of the dynamics of frontier society by her willingness and ability to integrate gender, class, regional affiliation, and nationality along with ethnicity in her consideration of "inter-cultural" relationships.

Eric Hinderaker describes the process by which liberty and power were redefined in the Old Northwest between 1763 and 1800. American settlers poured into western lands with little regard to the disapproval of either Crown authorities or Indians, undermining imperial policy and inverting traditional British understandings that held that power flowed from the top of society downward. Through this process, westerners acquired extraordinary gains, but the Ohio Indians lost any opportunity they may have had to sustain their autonomy against the new American nation.

Rob Cox combines a discussion of religion, politics, military policy, and land policy in an extremely sophisticated and subtle examination of Quaker missionary efforts to the Indians during the eighteenth and early nineteenth centuries. According to Cox, Quaker missionary initiatives during the eighteenth and nineteenth centuries were renewed and revitalized by a vision of Native peoples that mirrored their own vision of themselves, namely that of a disempowered and increasingly marginalized people who, nonetheless, held spiritual vitality and discipline as central cultural values. This shared worldview, particularly between the Quakers and the Seneca, permitted both cultures to interact and shape one another throughout the Sixty Years' War era. For Quakers, this process allowed them to recreate a sense of social and political power, establish a formal role for themselves and the society in the new American republic, and to advance the society through this sense of spiritual rebirth. Throughout the essay, Cox shows the reciprocal, mutually reinforcing nature of Seneca/Quaker interaction and places Quaker missionary efforts within the context of both protestant and Native spiritual revival.

Philip Lord Jr. successfully ties together technological, political, economic, and strategic concerns by examining the development of the Mohawk/Oneida Corridor, one of the major thoroughfares into the Great Lakes region during the Sixty Years' War era. The American improvement of this transportation rival to the Canadian possession of the much more convenient St. Lawrence Valley would allow the Yankees to compete successfully with the British and Canadians in logistically supporting their forces on the Great Lakes during the War of 1812.

Carl Benn explores how the western New York and southwestern Upper Canadian Iroquois conducted their external diplomacy during the 1812 era. Each group, although driven by a differing set of circumstances and diplomatic goals, began the war seeking neutrality. However, early American reverses caused the Canadian Iroquois to establish an active military alliance with the British. As a result, the New York Iroquois, fearful of American retaliation and believing that they had to powerfully demonstrate their friendship to the United States, declared war on their Canadian tribesmen. Benn shows that, despite being forced to deal with a declining number of acceptable options, the Iroquois made their own assessments of political and diplomatic realities, and developed foreign and domestic policies to meet their objectives within the limits of what they thought possible.

Doug Hurt examines land speculation and development in the Firelands region, a narrow strip along Lake Erie's southern shore in north-central Ohio that opened to settlement following the Revolution. Many forces pulled settlers into the Ohio Country during the Sixty Years' War era. As a result, those who speculated in land within the region often enjoyed considerable opportunities for financial gain. However, because speculators could not control national land or monetary or military policies, they also frequently met with failure. Hurt traces the impact of these forces through the career of Zalmon Wildman, a Danbury, Connecticut, manufacturer who invested heavily in lands in the Firelands region. Hurt is particularly successful in linking federal and state monetary and political policies with the region's military history and demonstrating the ability of local history to illuminate broad national trends.

Jane Errington disputes traditional claims that during the War of 1812 Upper Canadians came eagerly to the aid of their country to defend their homes and their king. Instead, she argues that a long tradition of demographic, geographic, commercial, and personal linkages among those who lived on both sides of the border caused both Americans and Canadians to see themselves as living within a shared community that spanned the international border. As a consequence of these shared interests, Upper Canadians were, at best, only "reluctant warriors" during the conflict.

David Edmunds points out that while many historians and the popular imagination have focused on Indians who opposed American expansion during the War of 1812, those Indians constituted a minority of the Native peoples living south of the international border. Many, if not most, Indians remained loyal to the United States after the outbreak of hostilities. They demonstrated that loyalty by offering military and diplomatic assistance to the republic despite hardships, danger, threats, and physical violence, often perpetrated by the very Americans whom they sought to aid. Yet, despite this assistance, these loyal Indians were removed forcibly from Ohio within two decades after the end of hostilities. Ironically, today we romanticize the actions of Indians like Tecumseh and his brother, The Prophet, while ignoring the contributions of those whom steadfastly supported the United States. As Edmunds points out, we "still prefer that Indians dance with wolves rather than plow with farmers."

Jeff Seiken reexamines the naval war on the Great Lakes during the War of 1812. The failure to gain control of Lakes Erie and Ontario during the summer of 1812 constituted a major and, ultimately costly, blunder for American forces. Seiken focuses on two questions relating to that failure: what was American policy, with respect to the Great Lakes, prior to the onset of the conflict; and, after the outbreak of the war, how did American officials amend this policy to address its earlier deficiencies? Seiken suggests that American policy prior to the conflict was formed by short-sighted indifference. Once the war began, however, energetic action by Isaac Chauncey and William Jones allowed the United States to launch a fleet capable of winning control of Lake Erie and to engage in an arms buildup on Lake Ontario, allowing the United States to establish a precarious military equilibrium, albeit at a great cost of strategic and financial resources.

Lastly, in the most inwardly penetrating of the essays presented herein, Drew Cayton observes that the events making up the Sixty Years' War for the Great Lakes have failed to generate much interest among historians despite the conflict's enormous influence on the subsequent histories of the United States, Canada, and the region's Native peoples. One reason is that these events have been overshadowed by the well-known episodes of the nation's Revolutionary era and early founding period. But much of this disinterest springs also from a vague sense of shame over the openly imperialistic aims of the war and its ultimate consequences for the region's Indians, feelings that Cayton traces back to the Federalist era. Cayton argues that the inherent ambiguities and ambivalence that framed the Sixty Years' War, the distance between what the early Republic aspired to become and what it was required to be, are the central themes that give the conflict its meaning and importance to contemporary America. Part critical history, part historiographical analysis, part contemporary commentary, and part introspective rumination,

Cayton's article shows the inter-connections between Federalist ideology, popular culture, and historiographical development in a way that stresses the internal contradictions and historical uncertainties of the events under consideration.

Collectively these essays demonstrate that the Sixty Years' War was not a period of continuous conflict or preparation for war. Instead, we find people conducting daily lives without the knowledge that soon combat would break out. They sought a variety of solutions to the problems confronting them without knowing the outcome. Imperial and republican officials, fur traders and land speculators, missionaries and prophets, Indians of various tribes and languages, Loyalists and rebels, warriors of various costume and tactical dispositions, women and men, visionaries and reactionaries, winners and losers, all sought their destiny in the North American interior between the Ohio River and Hudson Bay. The critical six decades between 1754 and 1814 determined to the present day the political, economic, ethnic, and cultural future of this continental interior.

• • •

The conference from which these articles came would not have happened without the support and assistance of many individuals and institutions. In addition to the two editors of this volume, the conference planning committee included Gerard T. Altoff, chief ranger and historian at Perry's Victory and International Peace Memorial; Ann Bowers, associate director at Bowling Green State University's Center for Archival Collections; Rachel Buff, assistant professor of history, Bowling Green State University; Edmund J. Danziger, Jr., Distinguished Teaching Professor of History, Bowling Green State University; Brian Leigh Dunnigan, curator of maps for the William L. Clements Library, University of Michigan; Donald F. Melhorn, senior partner, Marshall & Melhorn, Toledo, Ohio; G. Michael Pratt, professor of anthropology, Heidelberg College; and W. Jeffrey Welsh, associate dean and associate professor of history at Firelands College, Bowling Green State University. Many other members of the Bowling Green State University community also contributed to the meeting's success, including the BGSU Foundation, Inc., the Canadian Studies Center, the Center for Archival Collections, the College of Arts and Sciences, the Departments of Aerospace Studies and Military Science, and the Lake Erie Studies Center, housed at Firelands College, Huron, Ohio. Other support was received from the Ohio Humanities Council, the Clement O. Miniger Memorial Foundation of Toledo, the Society for Historians of the Early American Republic, the Society for

Military History, and the Toledo Blade Foundation. The BGSU Continuing Education's conference services duo, Joyce Kepke and Ann Betts, provided the glue that kept the conference from falling apart. Particular credit for supporting the conference came from the generous financial and personal support of Dr. Suzanne Crawford, Dean of Continuing Education; Dr. Donald Nieman, chair of the BGSU History Department; and the department's Policy History Program.

Three other events during the conference greatly enhanced the experience for all of the participants and many others in the region. MidAm, Inc., a bank holding company of Bowling Green, generously commissioned Dean Mosher, a historical artist from Fairhope, Alabama, to create a painting relating to the themes of the conference. The rendering, showing the dramatic moment during the September 10, 1813 Battle of Lake Erie when Commodore Oliver Hazard Perry transferred his command from the disabled *Lawrence* to the *Niagara,* was unveiled at the conference's opening and today remains on display at the Mid-American Bank headquarters in Toledo. MidAm's CEO, Edward Reiter, was particularly supportive of this endeavor: Mr. Mosher graciously allowed this painting to be reproduced on this volume's cover. The Ohio Historical Society hosted a War of 1812 living history reenactment at Fort Meigs State Memorial in Perrysburg, a few miles from the conference site in Bowling Green, that was visited by many conference attendees and thousands of others over the course of the weekend. Lastly, committee member Donald F. Melhorn worked diligently to bring the brig *Niagara,* a fully functional recreation of the American War of 1812–era flagship operated by the Pennsylvania Historical and Museum Commission, to the Port of Toledo for a four-day anchorage. In addition to receptions, concerts, tours by the conference participants, and other festivities, the visit allowed over eight thousand Toledo-area school children, their families, and other citizens to view this floating museum. Because the list would be all too long and in fear of omitting someone who should be mentioned, we wish to extend to all those who worked so hard to make this conference and its ancillary events a success, a deeply felt "thank you."

NOTES

1. Helen H. Tanner, *Atlas of Great Lakes Indian History* (Norman: Published for the Newberry Library by the University of Oklahoma Press, 1987).

2. Stephen Aron, *How the West Was Lost: The Transformation of Kentucky from Daniel Boone to Henry Clay* (Baltimore: Johns Hopkins University Press, 1996); R. David Edmunds, *The Potawatomi: Keepers of the Fire* (Norman: University of Oklahoma Press, 1978); idem, *The Shawnee Prophet* (Lincoln: University of Nebraska Press, 1983); idem, *Tecumseh and the Quest for Indian Leadership* (Boston: Little, Brown, 1984); John Mack Faragher, *Daniel Boone: The Life and Legend of an American Pioneer* (New York: Holt, 1992).

3. Francis Jennings, *The Ambiguous Iroquois Empire: The Covenant Chain Confederation of Indian Tribes with English Colonies from Its Beginnings to the Lancaster Treaty of 1744* (New York: Norton, 1984); idem, *Empire of Fortune: Crowns, Colonies, and Tribes in the Seven Years' War in America* (New York: Norton, 1988); Robert S. Allen, *His Majesty's Indian Allies: British Indian Policy in the Defence of Canada, 1774–1815* (Toronto: Dundurn Press, 1992).

4. Colin Calloway, *The American Revolution in Indian Country: Crisis and Diversity in Native American Communities* (New York: Cambridge University Press, 1995); idem, *Crown and Calumet: British-Indian Relations, 1783–1815* (Norman: University of Oklahoma Press, 1987); Ian K. Steele, *Betrayals: Fort William Henry and the "Massacre"* (New York: Oxford University Press, 1990); Steele, *Warpaths: Invasions of North America* (New York: Oxford University Press, 1994).

5. Fred Anderson, *Crucible of War: The Seven Years' War and the Fate of Empire in British North America, 1754–1766* (New York: Alfred A. Knopf, 2000); Andrew R. L. Cayton, *The Frontier Republic: Ideology and Politics in the Ohio Country, 1780–1825* (Kent, Ohio: Kent State University Press, 1986); idem, *Frontier Indiana* (Bloomington: Indiana University Press, 1996); Andrew R. L. Cayton and Peter S. Onuf, *The Midwest and the Nation: Rethinking the History of an American Region* (Bloomington: Indiana University Press, 1990); Gregory Evans Dowd, *A Spirited Resistance: The North American Indian Struggle for Unity, 1745–1815* (Baltimore: Johns Hopkins University Press, 1992); Richard White, *The Middle Ground: Indians, Empires, and Republics in the Great Lakes Region, 1650–1815* (Cambridge, N.Y.: Cambridge University Press, 1991); Michael N. McConnell, *A Country Between: The Upper Ohio Valley and Its Peoples, 1724–1774* (Lincoln: University of Nebraska Press, 1992).

The Sixty Years' War for the Great Lakes, 1754–1814: An Overview

D A V I D   C U R T I S   S K A G G S

You can blame the conference and this book on the ancient Greek historian Thucydides. His famous *History of the Peloponnesian War* written in the fifth century B.C. is not only one of the great historical treatises, but also is one of the great commentaries on the nature of political power and the way state policies are made. This great war between Athenian and Spartan empires lasted from 431 to 404 B.C. It consisted of a series of subconflicts, interrupted by shaky peace, political intrigue, and policy decisions.

For me, the greatness of the *Peloponnesian War* is not its exceptional narrative, incisive character studies, famous orations, and strategic and tactical decision analysis, but rather its attention to the broader picture of historical drama. Thucydides understood that the series of conflicts underlying the long struggle was a continuous event. It was a quest for the destiny of Greek civilization and political power in the Greek-speaking world. It is this broader reading of the great Greek historian that brought me to see the multifaceted struggle to control the great freshwater lakes and their basins that occupy the interior of North America, not as unconnected events, but rather as part of a broader sequence of episodes involving the Native Americans and Europeans of French, British, and Creole backgrounds for control of the finest bodies of fresh water in the world.

The Great Lakes world of 1750 was one of great expanses of forests and water. Interspersed with Native American villages along its major waterways were occasional small French outposts located at critical junctions—Fort Frontenac (modern Kingston, Ontario), Fort Niagara, Fort Detroit, Fort Michilimackinac, and Fort La Baye (Green Bay, Wisconsin) were among the most significant of these. Soldiers were few at these "forts," fur trading the most common occupation of the Frenchmen who dared to work their way along the many water passages that provided access to the North American interior from the major French settlements along the lower St. Lawrence River. That river, which drained all the Great Lakes, constituted the economic tie for the region with the trans-Atlantic world that lay beyond. The furs of beaver and muskrat and the hides of buffalo and deer were its principal exports.

Seventy years later we find that 1750 world dramatically changed. The political suzerainty the Native Americans and the French enjoyed was gone. Instead, sovereignty was divided between a young republic and the British Empire. Economically the centers of power were concentrated in a series of Euro-American settlements on both sides of the lakes. The southern side witnessed American migration into central New York, the Ohio Valley, and the fringes of the upper lakes. Rochester, Buffalo, Erie, and Cleveland emerged to rival the traditional centers of economic development at Oswego, Detroit, Mackinac, and Green Bay. On the Canadian side, Toronto emerged as a new emporium of Lake Ontario, displacing Kingston. Grain, not furs, became the area's most profitable export. At the center of this transformation was a conflict lasting some sixty years that changed forever the regional balance of power.

Only three of the stages in this long struggle were totally confined to the Great Lakes and the Ohio Valley—Pontiac's Rebellion (1763–65), Lord Dunmore's War (1774), and the Maumee–Wabash Confederacy War (1786–94). The other three— the French and Indian (or Seven Years') War (1754–63), the War for American Independence (1775–83), and the War of 1812–14—were part of worldwide conflicts having significant impact upon this region. The last phase—the War of 1812—was the most fiercely fought conflict ever focused on the Great Lakes region. Like the 30 Years' War and the 100 Years' War, it contains conflict, tension, peace, and renewed warfare in a variety of phases.

In 1750, the French claimed that their provinces of New France and Louisiana controlled the vast drainage regions of the St. Lawrence and the Mississippi valleys. But the Native Americans also had regional sovereignty claims that, for them, were more real than any emanating from Versailles. The Algonquian peoples of the lakes and rivers between the Ottawa and Ohio rivers felt themselves sovereign in their homelands. On the other hand, the Iroquois Confederacy, headquartered in the Finger Lakes of upstate New York, claimed jurisdiction over the Algonquians and, because of their Covenant Chain of Friendship with the British, gave that nation's ever-greedy colonial governors a claim to the trans-Appalachian west.

By mid-century these claims were being actively broached by the three most ambitious of colonies—New York, Pennsylvania, and Virginia. New York's western claims came not so much from any charter territorial grant, but rather from the Iroquois' dubious claim to suzerainty over the Algonquian region southward into modern Kentucky. Virginia asserted that her charter of 1609 gave her title to lands between her boundary with North Carolina westward to the Mississippi River and northward to the lands of the Hudson's Bay Company. Only that of the Chinese, Russian, Portuguese, Turkish, Spanish, and British empires rivaled Virginia's vast dominion. Pennsylvania's claim rested on its trade with the Ohio Valley Indians. In the midst of all these provincial designs were assertions by various private land companies for territory in the trans-Appalachian west. These included a large number of claims in the Ohio River Valley by Virginia and Pennsylvania speculators under such titles as the Mississippi Company, the Greenbrier Company, the Loyal Land Company of Virginia, the New Wales Company, and the Ohio Company.[1]

But it was the Franco-Algonquian presence that was the most dominant. In 1749, the governor-general of New France sent Captain Céloron de Blainville to reestablish their position in the Ohio Valley. He found himself opposed by Chief Memeskia at Pickawillany and reported that Indians in the Miami River Valley favored the British. Such an affront could not be tolerated. In 1752, young Charles Michel Langlade of Michilimackinac led an expedition of thirty Frenchmen and 210 Indians to Pickawillany, where they destroyed the local trading post, killed or captured several British traders there, and boiled and ate Chief Memeskia. Such a resort to terror only proved the weakness of French control of the region. Such actions alone would not stop British commercial intrusions.

Both the English and the French knew there were three keys to controlling the region. The first concerned dominance of the region's lifeline—the St. Lawrence Valley. The second demanded dominance of the straits between the lakes—Forts Frontenac, Niagara, Detroit, Michilimackinac, and Sault Ste. Marie. The third required control of the critical portages connecting the lakes with the Mississippi

Valley. Hence, French installations at Fort Miami (modern Fort Wayne between the Maumee and Wabash rivers), Fort St. Joseph (at the portage between the river of that name in southwestern Michigan and the upper reaches of the Illinois River), and Fort La Baye (which guarded the entrance to Fox River that connected with the Wisconsin).

There were two critical weak links in the French plan—the headwaters of the Ohio River and the Lake Champlain corridor. Security of the St. Lawrence lifeline demanded control of the access route into the heart of New France afforded by the Lake George–Lake Champlain–Richelieu River route between Albany and Montreal. Here they constructed Fort Carillon, later known as Ticonderoga. To cover the upper Ohio Valley, the French began building a series of forts from Presque Isle (now Erie, Pennsylvania) toward the Forks of the Ohio (modern Pittsburgh). The Virginians formulated a counterplan. Here was the focal point of the first episode in the Great Lakes War.

Leading the British into the upper Ohio Valley were a group of fur traders and land speculators led by a Potomac River planter named Lawrence Washington, Governor Robert Dinwiddie of Virginia, and the Duke of Bedford in England. These well-connected Ohio Company proprietors began in 1747 to claim lands whose ownership was in dispute with both Pennsylvania and the king of France. In exchange for building a fort at the Forks of the Ohio and settling two hundred individuals, they were to receive half a million acres stretching southward from modern Pittsburgh to Wheeling. In 1753, Governor Dinwiddie sent the recently deceased Lawrence Washington's half-brother on an expedition to warn the French not to move into this territory. Twenty-one-year-old Major George Washington's entreaties were rejected and the French began constructing Fort Duquesne at the very spot the Ohio Company was supposed to build its outpost. When Washington led a fruitless expedition to take Fort Duquesne in 1754, the Sixty Years' War for the Great Lakes began.

We need not trace the details of this first phase of the conflict, known to history as either the French and Indian War or the Seven Years' War. Two British attempts to take Fort Duquesne failed; the last one disastrously in the battle of the Monongahela, often known as Braddock's defeat. The French also picked off the one British outpost on the Great Lakes at Oswego, New York, early in the conflict.

But it was, if one may be politically incorrect, on the sixth great lake, Lake Champlain, that the French and British fought the decisive campaign for the interior waterways. The Lake George–Lake Champlain–Richelieu River route between the Hudson and St. Lawrence rivers points like a dagger from Albany to Montreal. It is ringed by a rocky, densely forested, mountainous terrain with few land routes between Lake George's southern tip and the upper reaches of the Hudson. In other words, it worked like a highway from Albany to Montreal and like a cul de sac from Montreal to Lake George. The Marquis de Montcalm, commanding French forces in Quebec, captured Fort William Henry at the head of Lake George in 1757 and sent Indian raids into the upper Hudson Valley. But his army could not march southward; the logistical complications of movement over the Adirondacks, filled with unfriendly British Americans, were too much for him to undertake. This would not be the last time that such an avenue proved a military dead-end.

Things continued to go badly for the British until late 1757 when the new British Prime Minister, William Pitt, made one of the most critical strategic decisions of modern history. Rather than concentrate his troops and sailors on the European front, he refocused the British efforts in the New World and India. In a series of brilliant strokes, Forts Duquesne and Ticonderoga fell and a naval armada brought British army forces to Quebec, where in 1759 the decisive battle for the political control of the Great Lakes was won by the British. The fall of New France was a consequence of what Professor W. J. Eccles called the "stupidity factor" in history.[2] In this case, the French depended too much on the stone walls of fortifications to defend their American empire and disregarded the need to maintain naval supremacy to preserve their control of the saltless seas of North America. The British victory on the Plains of Abraham outside Quebec was merely part of a train of victories that saw the French empire in the West and East Indies fall to the British army and the Royal Navy. In a mixed metaphor, Horace Walpole wrote that "Our bells are worn out threadbare with the ringing of victories."

But Pitt's great triumph contained fatal flaws. First, the concentration on the American and Indian theaters left his European allies to twist in the wind. They would not easily be allied with "perfidious Albion" again. His defeated foes, France and Spain, hungered for revenge for their losses. All would find the American independence movement an ideal opportunity to coordinate and exercise their anti-British sentiments. Finally, the elimination of the French menace in Canada and the Spanish threat from the Floridas relieved the colonial Americans from strategic dependence upon the British.

However, we need to concentrate on the consequences of the massive British victory and the geopolitical transformation of the Great Lakes region that resulted. The

Peace of Paris of 1763 dramatically reoriented political power in the North American interior. France ceded her vast cis-Mississippi empire to the British and the Indians lost their ability to play two European empires off against one another in their efforts to retain control of what their homeland. Remaining in the region were the Natives, the French-speaking habitants of the former New France; the Anglo-Americans from New York, Pennsylvania, and Virginia, and British government officials and merchants who moved into New France; and the Indians. Their various claims and ambitions could not be easily satisfied.

Among the Native Americans various splits arose. Initially it appeared the Iroquois Confederacy had won out since they had long been British allies. But a century of warfare along the Anglo-French frontier had taken its toll on the people of the longhouse, and the British were no longer dependent upon them for protection. Instead, the more numerous Algonquian-speaking peoples of the western Great Lakes—particularly the Miamis, Shawnees, Ottawas, Potawatomis, Sauks, Foxes, Ojibwas (Chippewas), and Menominees—now held the balance of Indian power in the region. Traditionally allied with the French, they now confronted both the military power of the British and the aggressive land-grabbing designs of the colonists of British North America.[3]

Their attitude of independence was best expressed in the words of Ojibwa Chief Minavavana, who told the first Englishman to reach Fort Michilimackinac: "Englishman, although you have conquered the French, you have not yet conquered us! We are not your slaves. These lakes, these woods and mountains were left us by our ancestors. They are our inheritance; and we will part with them to no one." Ottawa Chief Pontiac relayed his vision from the Manitou, or Great Spirit: "This land, where you live, I have made for you and not for others. How comes it that you suffer the whites on your lands? . . . I love them not, they know me not, they are my enemies and the enemies of your brothers! Send them back to the country, which I made for them! There let them remain." From such attitudes came the second phase of the Sixty Years' War, known to us as Pontiac's Rebellion. Through subterfuge, the Ottawa accomplished one of the most unusual feats of Native American warfare; they seized a palisaded fortification—in this case Fort Michilimackinac—and they almost took Fort Detroit.[4]

The British found they could not dictate to the Great Lakes tribes and they concluded the Pontiac conflict with a series of concessions. In many ways these concessions constitute the best testimony we have of the power the Indians still possessed.

The first was the Proclamation of 1763, which forbade white settlement beyond the Appalachian Mountains. It also placed all negotiations with the tribes in the hands of an imperial Indian superintendent, rather than the provincial governors. Recognized by all as a temporary measure, the British saw this proclamation as granting them breathing space before they concluded concessions from the Indians and formulated a policy for white settlement across the mountains. For the Great Lakes, it placed the region in a vast Indian country. Trying to appease both some Indians and some land speculators, in 1768 Indian Superintendent Sir William Johnson negotiated the Treaty of Fort Stanwix with the Iroquois, which opened up land in central New York and south of the Ohio River. Still reserved as Indian lands were western New York and the area north of Ohio. For the Native Americans of the Great Lakes, the maintenance of the Fort Stanwix line on the Ohio was to be the core of their diplomatic and military efforts for over four decades. What followed was a decade of peace in the region when soldiers, traders, trappers, and Natives sought to accommodate themselves to the new environment.

But even as the imperial government was trying to conclude agreements on the region's future, the Virginians and Pennsylvanians were undoing the best-laid plans from London. Following the trail through the Cumberland Gap and into the Kentucky and Cumberland valleys were Daniel Boone and the speculators of the Transylvania, Vandalia, and Indiana companies. Although their claims were south of the Ohio, they threatened to cross that river. Even more menacing to the maintenance of the Fort Stanwix agreement were the Pennsylvania and Virginia settlements in the upper Ohio Valley, which were poised to cross that river into what is now southeastern Ohio. The Shawnees refused to acknowledge the Iroquois right to cede the lands in Kentucky where they hunted. When land-hungry Virginians clashed with the Shawnee, Governor Lord Dunmore of that province had an excuse to attack into the Muskingum and Hocking valleys of Ohio in 1774. Lord Dunmore's War, the third phase of the Sixty Years' War, resulted in the Treaty of Camp Charlotte, which dispensed with Shawnee claims south of the Ohio.

In the same year, 1774, the British drafted their imperial policy for the Great Lakes region. This parliamentary enactment chartered a colony of Quebec that included most of modern Quebec, Ontario, and the United States north of the Ohio River. In many ways the law was an enlightened one, but it offended the Anglo-American colonists. First, Quebec had no legislative assembly. It would be ruled by a governor and council appointed by the Crown. Second, it tolerated Catholicism.

Third, it offended those who had aspirations to settle on the lands claimed by several colonies (particularly Virginia and New York) and by a variety of land companies. Finally, the fur traders from the English-speaking colonies found that the law required that all pelts from the region go through either Montreal or Quebec. Even though the Quebec Act acknowledged the geographic advantage of a colony focused on the ease of transport down the lakes and the St. Lawrence, few in the older British colonies recognized the logic behind the law and instead coupled it with the Coercive Acts under the umbrella of the Intolerable Acts. From a British point of view, it had one compelling, positive outcome. The Quebec Act appeased the ecclesiastical leadership of the Roman Catholic church and the seigniorial leaders of Quebec enough to keep most of *Les Canadiens* neutral during the struggle for American independence.[5]

From the Anglo-American point of view, the Quebec Act was only one of the grievances that led to the American War for Independence. But it was important enough for Thomas Jefferson to charge George III in the Declaration of Independence that the king abolished "the free system of English laws in a neighboring province, establishing therein an arbitrary government, and enlarging its boundaries, so as to render it at once an example and fit instrument for introducing the same absolute rule into these colonies."

The Great Lakes played a minor role in the dramatic worldwide conflict that began on Lexington Green. Still, we remember many of the exploits of the region—the Indian-Loyalist raids out of Niagara into the Cherry and Wyoming valleys, the destruction of the Iroquois homeland by John Sullivan's Continentals and the New York militia; George Rogers Clark's famous expedition into the Illinois Country; Indian raids deep into Kentucky; the establishment of an American outpost at Fort Laurens in southeast Ohio; the shame of the Gnadenhutten massacre; the defeat of the Sandusky expedition led by Colonel William Crawford; and the tortured execution of this one-time agent for George Washington by the Delawares abetted by a Loyalist named Simon Girty. The region had become a dark and bloody ground.[6]

The Lake Champlain corridor was a more significant actor in the struggle. In 1775, Brigadier General Richard Montgomery led an effective campaign down that waterway, seized Montreal, and surrounded Quebec. Winter proved an important ally to the British in that community and reinforcements from the home islands relieved the siege of the Canadian capital. The subsequent campaign to drive the Americans back was quite successful in the summer and fall of 1776. However, the British failed to take Ticonderoga when Benedict Arnold's small gunboat fleet delayed their advance. The next year Ticonderoga fell, but General John Burgoyne ran into the same obstacle as had Montcalm—the Adirondacks. The result was the first great American victory of the war—Saratoga.

Nonetheless, British control of the St. Lawrence meant British control of the Great Lakes and alliances with the Indian tribes of the region. Detroit became the focal center of British-Indian activities into the Ohio Valley. American efforts out of Pittsburgh and Kentucky failed to achieve significant inroads into the lands northwest of the Ohio.

But more important than the campaigns, struggles, tears, wounds, and death were the geopolitical consequences of this fourth installment of the Sixty Years' War. The British Prime Minister, the Earl of Shelburne, authorized concessions to the Americans far in excess to anything they had won on the battlefield. There were several territorial options available to the negotiators: the cession of Canada, the Ohio River line, the westward extension of the northern boundary of New York, or a line run from northern New York to Lake Nipissing and westward, which would have given virtually all of the Great Lakes to the United States, except for Lake Superior. Instead the negotiators chose the line-of-lakes boundary which divided all the Lakes (save Michigan) down their center and down the center of the rivers joining them.

From a geographic point of view, the solution may have been the worst possible. The British retained the natural outlet from the region via the St. Lawrence River. The United States secured the most natural harbors and the most fertile hinterlands. Navigational improvement of the lakes and rivers would be perpetually tied up in international negotiations.[7]

For the Indians the consequences were disastrous. Most lived south of the lakes inside U.S. territory, and yet they had secured the wrath of the Americans by siding with the British in the war. The British colonists in Canada were furious. Shelburne had betrayed them as much as he betrayed the Native Americans. The United States received what its arms had not won and the vast fur-trading country in the west had, at best, to be shared with these republican rebels. For a dozen years Montreal fur traders connived to keep outposts inside the United States at Niagara, Detroit, and Mackinac, while abetting Indian demands for the recognition of the Fort Stanwix line as the northern boundary of American settlement.

For those at Westminster these forts may have been a bargaining chip to secure concessions regarding pre-war debts and Loyalist claims. For both white and Native on the Great Lakes frontier, their purpose was to assist in the creation of an Indian barrier state between the Ohio and the lakes to protect Canada and the fur trade from the Americans and to protect the Indian lifestyle from destruction. This led to the fifth installment in the Great Lakes war—the battle for the Ohio River line between the United States of America and the largest Native American confederacy ever assembled on this continent. This phase has no name. U.S. Army Indian Wars campaign streamers label it "Miami." The designation is deceptive. Certainly Chief Little Turtle and his Miamis were at the center of it, but the coalition assembled against the army and Kentucky militiamen, 1789–94, was far broader than this one tribe. The Shawnees, Delawares, Wyandots, Ottawas, and Kickapoos joined them and British Indian agents and fur merchants spurred them on. Some call it the Old Northwest Indian War, but perhaps it is best entitled the Miami Confederacy War.[8]

Little Turtle and his allies administered two disastrous defeats on U.S. Army expeditions sent into the Maumee Valley. The first, in 1790, at Kekionga (modern Fort Wayne) saw an expedition headed by Brigadier General Josiah Harmar decimated. The second, in 1791, resulted in the crushing defeat of Major General Arthur St. Clair's forces at the battle of the Wabash (modern Fort Recovery, Ohio). This latter engagement constitutes the most significant defeat ever inflicted on the United States Army by the American Indians.

To recover from this blow, the Americans offered a carrot and stick approach. The carrot was a conference in 1793, at which the united chiefs pressed for the Ohio River line to divide the lands between the two peoples. American agents offered money (which was useless to the Natives) if the Indians would allow Americans to settle north of that river. The king of England, one chief said, "never did, nor never had a right, to give you our Country." Why, he asked, should you expect us to do anything but fight for our rights and lands against American "invasion." "We want Peace: Restore to us our Country and we shall be Enemies no longer." The Americans denied their arguments. The king of England did have the right to concede lands he controlled to the United States. The Fort Stanwix Treaty left no permanent obligation upon the new republic. If the natives would make no concession then the stick would have to be applied. And it was.

The stick was Major General Anthony Wayne's Legion of the United States. Wayne destroyed Little Turtle's confederacy in the battle of Fallen Timbers in 1794. The first consequence of Wayne's campaign was the concession of the Ohio River line in the Treaty of Greenville in 1795. But there were others. The British had deserted the Indians in 1794 when they refused to support them from their outpost at Fort Miamis in modern Maumee, Ohio; and a year later they agreed to evacuate the Great Lakes forts at Niagara, Detroit, and Mackinac in Jays' Treaty. The United States finally and fully claimed the territorial grant it had received in 1783. The direct and indirect support the British government and Canadian citizens had provided Little Turtle's confederacy embittered the Americans.

The Indians knew they had been betrayed and resented it. They now had to make a critical choice. Could they adapt their lifestyle and live on small acreages like the Euro-Americans, or would they continue to oppose the white onslaught by military means? Two camps emerged among the Natives.

One group, the accommodationists, sought to live with the whites. Betrayed twice by the British and at the mercy of the Americans, former war chiefs like Little Turtle of the Miamis, Buckongahelas of the Delawares, Black Hoof of the Shawnees, and Tarhe of the Wyandots joined this camp, along with the Yale-educated William Anderson of the Shawnees, to form a group which remained either neutral or favored the American side in subsequent struggles. One of the most notable individuals seeking a way out of the white-versus-Native dilemma was Handsome Lake of the Seneca. Also counseling moderation in negotiations with the United States was Joseph Brant, or Thayendanega, of the Iroquois, who moved his followers over the Niagara into modern Ontario. The accommodationists's problem was whether there was a possibility for a peaceful coexistence of white and Native peoples within the Great Lakes–Ohio Valley basin. There were a variety of persons of Native, white, and mixed ancestry who believed that such a peaceful option was possible.

On the other side, led by the famous Shawnee prophet Tenskwatawa and his war chief brother, Tecumseh, was the nativist faction. They controlled only a minority of the Shawnees, but were able to find like-minded allies among the Wyandots, Potawatomis, and Ottawas. To the northwest, British fur trader Robert Dickson formed alliances with the Sioux and Chippewa from his post at Green Bay. For these peoples the Native lifestyle and religion required them to seek a military solution to their differences with the United States rather than a negotiated settlement. Without active British support their efforts were doomed, as the Shawnees found out at the Battle of Tippecanoe in 1811.[9]

The American declaration of war against the British in 1812 brought on the sixth and last phase of the Sixty Years' War. For the United States, the United Kingdom, and the Native Americans the conflict presented a glorious opportunity to revise the line-of-lakes boundary of 1783.

From the outset of the war, American officials understood the most critical strategic objective. Major General Henry Dearborn and Brigadier General John Armstrong recommended a main attack via Lake Champlain toward Montreal, with secondary operations in the vicinity of Detroit, Niagara, and Kingston. Governor William Hull, of Michigan Territory, stood out most conspicuously among the earliest advocates of gaining naval dominance of the lakes. He argued that there was no way that the tiny garrisons at Detroit, Mackinac, and Chicago could defend themselves from a combined British-Indian attack. Recognizing the logistical peril of a force so far from its base of supplies, Hull queried, "how is it to be supported?" He answered his own question: "If sir, we cannot command the Ocean, we can command the inland Lakes of our country—I have always been of the opinion that we ought to have built as many armed vessels on the Lakes as would have commanded them—we have more interest in them than the British nation, and can build vessels with more convenience."

Why, if they understood the basic strategic objectives, did the Americans fail? There were numerous factors. First, a strategy focused on Montreal required a year to mobilize, equip, and train the necessary forces. It depended upon the British, Canadians, and Indians doing relatively little while the Americans prepared. This would not be the case. This leads to the second major factor—the determined opposition by British regulars and a core of Canadians (many of whom were Loyalists or their descendants) who acted with vigor and dispatch and who knew from the beginning where their vulnerability lay and how they might distract the Americans. Third was the support of several Great Lakes Indian tribes for whom this conflict represented their last chance to militarily stop the onslaught of the American pioneers into their homeland. Allied with the British, the Native Americans represented an enormous threat to U.S. settlements in the states of Ohio and Kentucky, and the territories of Michigan, Indiana, and Illinois. Finally, the relative incompetence of American military leadership resulted in a series of disasters, frustrating the achievement of the national objectives. From a strategic point of view, the Indian and British victories of 1812 in the Great Lakes region constituted a massive diversion effort that refocused much American attention to the periphery and not enough on the Canadian center of gravity along the St. Lawrence.[10]

The key to British strategy required the utilization of the Native Americans living in the Great Lakes region. Rather than await an American assault, the British and their Indian allies took the offensive. Ever since the end of the War for American

Independence, British defense of Upper Canada depended upon Indian allies. Their callous use of the Indians as a buffer to American expansion and their betrayal of the Indians when it suited imperial interests has been described by one Canadian historian as "Machiavellian in style—manipulative, cruel, and successful."[11]

A new British-Indian alliance led by the brilliant and aggressive governor-general of Upper Canada (modern Ontario) Major General Isaac Brock captured Forts Mackinac, Detroit, and Dearborn (Chicago). He and his allies threatened the whole northwestern frontier of the United States with attacks on Fort Madison, Iowa (which protected St. Louis), Fort Harrison (modern Terre Haute), Fort Wayne, and the Sandusky Valley. Although these places were not taken, the danger to the frontier was such that it diverted, for 1813, the American effort from its primary strategic objective in the St. Lawrence Valley and Lake Ontario, to concentrate on retaking Lake Erie and Detroit.

The British-Indian failures on the western Great Lakes frontier reflect a geographic problem confronting invasion from the lakes into the Ohio Valley. While magnificent water routes lead north from the St. Lawrence and the lakes into the Laurentian Shield, most waterways to the south are short by comparison. No river route southward corresponds to the Ottawa River. The largest river running into the Great Lakes, the Maumee, flows eastward from Fort Wayne toward modern Toledo, rather than toward the Ohio. Other rivers such as the Oswego, Genesee, Cuyahoga, Sandusky, St. Joseph, and Chicago penetrate only short distances into the interior. Logistically this meant that the British were at a distinct disadvantage to conduct military operations into the American Middle West. Their most ardent Indian allies were in the vicinity of the Detroit frontier, but here military operations there were the most difficult to support. Success demanded they control the Maumee River and that required dominance over the Maumee rapids near modern Toledo and the critical portage at Fort Wayne. From the Maumee they might utilize the Miami and Wabash valleys for penetration into the Ohio Country, from Fort Wayne the route down the Wabash River lay open. But the Americans secured Fort Wayne in 1812 and began erecting Fort Meigs at the Maumee rapids the following February.

Finally, any success for the British-Indian alliance required control of the lakes themselves. Although the British initially had naval supremacy on the lakes, the Americans devoted considerable energy to revising this situation. They succeed on Lake Erie in 1813 and the naval war on Lake Ontario ended in stalemate.

Moreover, even though Brock's aggressiveness refocused the American effort to the wrong arena, the British use of Indian allies embittered and united the westerners against both. Two incidents emphasize the rationale for the virulent anti-Indian sentiment.

The loss of Mackinac Island caused General Hull to order Captain Nathan Heald to evacuate Fort Dearborn. Little Turtle's son-in-law, Captain William Wells, brought fifty Miami warriors to assist in the evacuation. As a boy Wells had been taken prisoner by the Miami and adopted into the tribe. The western Potawatomis took up arms and hurried toward Chicago where they ambushed Captain Heald's small force outside Fort Dearborn. All but twenty of the soldiers were killed. Among the dead was Captain Wells. His death prompted the Miamis to change sides. The remaining soldiers surrendered. The Indians cut off Captain Wells's head, tore his heart from his body, and ate it in front of their captives. Then they killed several of the surrendered soldiers, threatened their civilian captives, and took the survivors as prisoners to various Indian villages.

News of the ambush and its aftermath affected both sides. For the western Americans, it increased their resolve and willingness to exert extraordinary effort to win the war in the West. The center of this renewed military fervor was in Kentucky. There, Revolutionary War hero Isaac Shelby, the state's governor-elect, began coordinating a major western campaign in conjunction with Indiana Territory's young governor, William Henry Harrison, and Ohio's governor, Return J. Meigs Jr. From the British point of view, the Chicago "massacre" was a blow to the credibility they had achieved at Mackinac and Detroit where Native American depredations had been curtailed. Henceforth, the British sought to have either agents or soldiers accompany all Indian raids. But the damage had been done.

The anti-Indian tendency became more intense following the mistreatment of prisoners taken in the Battle of the River Raisin (Monroe, Michigan) in January 1813. Here, Colonel Henry Procter captured a large number of Americans and withdrew from the village of Frenchtown, leaving many of them under Indian guard. The Natives executed between thirty and sixty of them (depending upon the source). The U.S. press labeled this event the "River Raisin Massacre" and "Remember the River Raisin" became an American battle cry. Procter's failure to protect the prisoners brought severe censure upon him by many of his own officers as well as his opponents. Americans were now more than ever unified in their efforts to destroy Indian power and control in the Old Northwest. For both the Long Knives and the Native Americans this would be a war for survival.[12]

Brock's victories presented the British government with the option of incorporating into their North American empire the region corresponding roughly to modern Michigan and Wisconsin. Significantly less than the Fort Stanwix line the Indians thought the British sought, Brock's attempt to make official policy what the Canadian fur-trading interests long desired destroyed efforts by diplomats to conclude by peaceful settlement the differences between the two nations. To ensure their Great Lakes lands were not lost, the United States mobilized its ground and naval forces to re-conquer what had been lost in 1812.

The successes of Oliver Hazard Perry on Lake Erie and William Henry Harrison at the Thames, which reclaimed the Old Northwest and allowed the seizure of part of modern southwestern Ontario for the United States, should not mask the strategic failure of the Americans to secure the more important Lake Ontario basin in 1813. For those conditioned to focus on the Lake Erie portion of the War of 1812, there is a tendency to misunderstand its relative importance. The key to any American hope to rectify the 1783 Great Lakes boundary lay with success in either or both the Lake Champlain and the Lake Ontario theaters.

For most of the war, the major concentration of American forces was on the Lake Ontario basin. The bloodletting on the Niagara frontier was without parallel anywhere else in the conflict. From the British victory at Queenston, 13 October 1812, (which cost General Brock his life) to the successful American defense of Fort Erie in August through September 1814, the conflict went back and forth over ground that neither side could hold for very long. By early 1814, Napoleon had been sent into exile on Elba and the British were able to send their veteran troops to protect Canada. But this was not soon enough to overcome the growing and more competent American army that emerged by the same time. The major reason for the subsequent stalemate was that neither side had continuous control of the lake itself.

The war on Lake Ontario is a most interesting example of the importance of naval supremacy. The struggle between British Commodore Sir James Lucas Yeo and American Commodore Isaac Chauncey, their officers, men, and hundreds of shipwrights requires a far more detailed study than can be made here. Each side engaged in a massive shipbuilding war, in which the size of the ship rose in a manner that reminds one of the great Dreadnought race before World War I. Eventually the British constructed the HMS *St. Lawrence*, a three-decker carrying 112 guns, more powerful than HMS *Victory* with which Horatio Nelson won the battle of Trafalgar. She gave the British command of the lake for the last months of 1814. The

Americans countered by ordering the construction of two three-deck, 120-gun vessels. These would have been the largest warships in the world. To counter this, the Royal Navy began two similar leviathans. None of these last four reached completion before the war ended. They all stayed in the stocks for years thereafter, memorials to the armaments race on Lake Ontario. Commodore Chauncey's unwillingness to risk battle unless he was sure of victory led to two years of indecision. By not losing to the Americans, Commodore Yeo achieved strategic victory and preserved British North America.

During one brief period of American naval supremacy, the United States attempted to close the Canadian lifeline along the St. Lawrence. Major General James Wilkinson, perhaps the most corrupt and incompetent senior officer in the history of the U.S. Army, led a force of seven thousand to be repulsed by eight hundred British troops at the Battle of Crysler's Farm, 11 November 1813. Seldom has the ineptness of one allowed so many to be frustrated by so few.

The final great offensives in the Sixty Years' War were on Lake Champlain. During 1812 and 1813, the traditional invasion route between New York and Canada was a backwater to the campaigns to the west. Master Commandant Thomas Macdonough engaged in a shipbuilding race with a series of British commanders. British ground troops guarded the approaches down the Richelieu River and Americans concentrated at Plattsburgh, New York. In 1813, Major General Wade Hampton commanded the one ground offensive mounted by the United States from Lake Champlain. It ended in disaster when Lieutenant Colonel Charles-Michel de Salaberry, a French-Canadian with extensive British army experience, conducted a spirited defense at the Battle of Châteauguay that October near the Canada–New York border.

With reinforcements from the Napoleonic Wars at his disposal, British governor-general, Lieutenant General Sir George Prevost, decided to conduct an offensive up the Lake Champlain corridor in the late summer of 1814. The British objective was to bring the Lake Champlain basin back into His Majesty's Empire. Prevost refused to attack a defending American force at Plattsburgh until the Royal Navy disposed of Macdonough's squadron, anchored in that village's harbor. A year and a day after Perry's victory, Macdonough fought a superior Royal Navy force with an intensity that one British sailor asserted made Trafalgar "a mere flea bite in comparison." No less an authority than Sir Winston Churchill called Macdonough's dramatic victory "the most decisive engagement of the war." Without naval superiority,

Prevost withdrew his vastly superior ground troops. But one remembers that this route had proved a dead-end to both Montcalm and Burgoyne. Along with news of the British defeat at Baltimore, knowledge of this setback contributed significantly to the decision by both sides to end the conflict at the *status quo ante bellum*.

The American version of the Peloponnesian War was over. The geopolitical division of the Great Lakes became an accepted fact and the numerous boundary disputes between the British and Americans were settled through negotiations. Navigational improvement of the lakes and rivers would be perpetually tied up in international negotiations. In all probability we will never fully develop the economic potential of the region because of the diplomatic problems inherent in such development. On the other hand, the beginnings of the Anglo-American rapprochement that dominates the world of the twentieth century followed.

The Indians residing inside the United States no longer had an outside ally. Neither accommodation nor nativism worked. The war created a powerful anti-Indian faction in the national government headed by Andrew Jackson of Tennessee, Henry Clay of Kentucky, William Henry Harrison of Ohio, and Lewis Cass of Michigan. All would become presidential nominees and two became presidents. All sought the removal the region's original inhabitants. Even though the secretary of war wrote in 1818 that the western tribes had "in a great measure, ceased to be an object of terror, and have become that of commiseration," virtually all the Indians of the region save the Iroquois, Ottawa, Chippewa, and Menominee would lose title to lands east of the Mississippi. Most would end up on reservations far from the lakes and woodlands of their native region and find themselves on the rolling hills and grasslands of eastern Kansas. The First Nations of Canada fared little better in the years that followed.[13]

For both the United States and Canada this final phase of the Sixty Years' War left lasting legacies. The Americans received a national anthem and a host of new heroes after whom counties, towns, streets, and babies could be named. A new generation of political leaders emerged who dominated national leadership for another thirty-five years. The battle of the Thames, for instance, produced a president, a vice-president, three governors, three lieutenant governors, four senators, twenty congressmen, and a host of lesser officials. It also produced the most inane campaign slogan in American history—"Rumpsey, dumpsey, rumpsey dumpsey, Colonel Johnson killed Tecumseh." Canadian nationalism, which hardly existed before the war began, received an immense boost, and a host of new heroes—real and imagined—emerged to cement the disparate groups who inhabited the Great Lakes and the St. Lawrence Valley. A Canadian generation of 1812, known there as the "Family Compact," dominated Upper Canadian politics for decades, creating a conservative bastion trying to find the place for British constitutional and parliamentary traditions within the shadow of the republican giant to their south.[14]

The Sixty Years' War left a geographically cohesive region divided politically and economically. Through its six stages, the world of 1750 had been altered dramatically. One wonders what the subsequent history of the region would have been had not the construction of canals and the inventions of the steamboat and the railroad altered forever the importance of the St. Lawrence River outlet for the region's abundant agricultural, mining, and industrial products. Technology may have done more than anything else to reduce the tensions between the United States and British North America and to contribute to the eventual creation of the longest unfortified border in the world. In the end, the manifest destiny of both the British and American empires required them to share the North American continent and the Great Lakes.

NOTES

1. Among the books best describing the origins of the French and Indian War are: Fred Anderson, *Crucible of War: The Seven Years' War and the Fate of Empire in British North America, 1754–1766* (New York: Alfred A. Knopf, 2000); Lawrence Henry Gipson, *Zones of International Friction: The Great Lakes Frontier, Canada, the West Indies, India, 1748–1754* (New York: Alfred A. Knopf, 1942); idem, *The Great War for Empire: The Years of Defeat, 1754–1757* (New York: Alfred A. Knopf, 1946); and idem, *The Great War for Empire: The Victorious Years, 1758–1760* (New York: Alfred A. Knopf, 1964–67), which are volumes 5–7 of his 15-volume *The British Empire before the American Revolution;* W. J. Eccles, *The French in North America, 1500–1783*, rev. ed. (East Lansing: Michigan State University Press, 1998); Ian K. Steele, *Guerillas and Grenadiers: The Struggle for Canada, 1689–1760* (Toronto: Ryerson Press, 1969); Francis Jennings, *Empire of Fortune: Crowns, Colonies, and Tribes in the Seven Years' War in America* (New York: Norton, 1988); Frank W. Brecher, *Losing a Continent: France's North American Policy, 1753–1763* (Westport, Conn.: Greenwood, 1998).

2. See Eccles' article in this volume, p. 37. See also, David Buisseret, ed. *France in the New World* (East Lansing: Michigan State University Press, 1999).

3. Richard White, *The Middle Ground: Indians, Empires, and Republics in the Great Lakes Region, 1650–1815* (New York: Cambridge University Press, 1991); Michael N. McConnell, *A Country Between: The Upper Ohio Valley and Its Peoples, 1724–1774* (Lincoln: University of Nebraska Press, 1992); Gregory Evans Dowd, *A Spirited Resistance: The North American Indian Struggle for Unity, 1745–1815* (Baltimore: Johns Hopkins University Press, 1992); Helen H. Tanner, *Atlas of Great Lakes*

Indian History (Norman: Published for the Newberry Library by the University of Oklahoma Press, 1987).

4. All the quotations for Native Americans used here and subsequently are found in Colin Calloway, *The World Turned Upside Down: Indian Voices from Early America* (Boston: St. Martin's Press, 1994); Howard H. Peckham, *Pontiac and the Indian Uprising* (Princeton: Princeton University Press, 1947); White, *Middle Ground;* Dowd, *Spirited Resistance;* McConnell, *Country Between.* See also Daniel Richter, *Ordeal of the Longhouse: The Peoples of the Iroquois League in the Era of European Colonization* (Chapel Hill: University of North Carolina Press, 1992).

5. Hilda Neatby, *The Quebec Act: Protest and Policy* (Scarborough, Ont.: Prentice-Hall of Canada [1972]).

6. General overviews of the Revolution in the Great Lakes region are found in Jack M. Sosin, *The Revolutionary Frontier, 1763–1783* (New York: Holt, Rinehart, and Winston, 1974) and Randolph C. Downes, *Council Fires on the Upper Ohio: A Narrative of Indian Affairs in the Upper Ohio Valley until 1795* (Pittsburgh: University of Pittsburgh Press, 1940). On the New York frontier, see Barbara Graymont, *The Iroquois in the American Revolution* (Syracuse: Syracuse University Press, 1972); Isabel Kelsay, *Joseph Brant, 1743–1807: Man of Two Worlds* (Syracuse: Syracuse University Press, 1984).

7. On peace negotiations, see especially Jonathan R. Dull, *A Diplomatic History of the American Revolution* (New Haven, Conn.: Yale University Press, 1985); Richard B. Morris, *The Peacemakers* (New York: Harper and Row, 1965).

8. On this conflict, see especially Harvey Lewis Carter, *The Life and Times of Little Turtle: First Sagamore of the Wabash* (Urbana and Chicago: University of Illinois Press, 1987); John Sugden, *Tecumseh: A Life* (New York: Henry Holt, 1997); Reginald Horsman, *Matthew Elliott: British Indian Agent* (Detroit: Wayne State University Press, 1964); Paul David Nelson, *Anthony Wayne: Soldier of the Early Republic* (Bloomington: Indiana University Press, 1985); Robert S. Allen, *His Majesty's Indian Allies: British Indian Policy in the Defence of Canada, 1774–1815* (Toronto: Dundurn Press, 1992); Larry L. Nelson, *A Man of Distinction Among Them: Alexander McKee and British-Indian Affairs along the Ohio Country Frontier, 1754–1799* (Kent, Ohio: Kent State University Press, 1999).

9. Those interested in the intra-Indian debates following the Fallen Timbers defeat should consult Anthony F. C. Wallace, *The Death and Rebirth of the Seneca* (New York: Alfred A. Knopf, 1970); White, *Middle Ground;* Dowd, *Spirited Resistance;* Allen, *His Majesty's Indian Allies;* Kelsay, *Joseph Brant;* Carter, *Little Turtle;* Sugden, *Tecumseh.* Most of these also have relevance to the War of 1812.

10. Among those books having particular relevance to the war on the Great Lakes, see George F. G. Stanley, *The War of 1812: Land Operations,* Canadian War Museum Historical Publication No. 18 (Ottawa: National Museums of Canada, 1983); Robert S. Quimby, *The U.S. Army in the War of 1812: An Operational and Command Study,* 2 vols. (East Lansing: Michigan State University Press, 1997); Wesley B. Turner, *British Generals in the War of 1812* (Montreal and Kingston: McGill-Queen's University Press, 1999); Alfred Thayer Mahan, *Sea Power in Its Relations to the War of 1812,* 2 vols. (1903; Reprint, Boston: Little, Brown, 1919); Theodore Roosevelt, *The Naval War of 1812* (1882; Reprint, Annapolis: Naval Institute Press, 1987).

11. Allen, *His Majesty's Indian Allies,* 86.

12. Particular campaigns in the Old Northwest are examined in Allen, *His Majesty's Indian Allies;* R. David Edmunds, *The Shawnee Prophet* (Lincoln: University of Nebraska Press, 1983); Edmunds, *Tecumseh and the Quest for Indian Leadership* (Boston: Little, Brown, 1984); Sugden, *Tecumseh;* Sandy

Antal, *A Wampum Denied: Procter's War of 1812* (East Lansing: Michigan State University Press, 1997); David Curtis Skaggs and Gerard T. Altoff, *A Signal Victory: The Lake Erie Campaign, 1812–1813* (Annapolis: Naval Institute Press, 1997). On the Lake Ontario theater see Robert Malcomson, *Lords of the Lake: The Naval War on Lake Ontario, 1812–1814* (Toronto: Robin Brass Studio, 1998); Donald E. Graves, *The Battle of Lundy's Lane on the Niagara in 1814* (Baltimore: Nautical & Aviation Publishing, 1993); Patrick A. Wilder, *The Battle of Sackett's Harbour, 1813* (Baltimore: Nautical and Aviation Publishing, 1994).

13. For a comparative approach to the fate of the Natives, see Roger L. Nichols, *Indians in the United States and Canada: A Comparative History* (Lincoln: University of Nebraska Press, 1998).

14. Jane Errington, *The Lion, the Eagle, and Upper Canada: A Developing Colonial Ideology* (Kingston and Montreal: McGill-Queen's University Press, 1987); Sidney F. Wise, "Upper Canada and the Conservative Tradition," in *Profiles of a Province*, ed. Edith Firth (Toronto: Ontario Historical Society, 1967).

French Imperial Policy for the Great Lakes Basin

W. J. Eccles

This article is an attempt to view this part of the world through the eyes of the French, the British, their American colonists, and the Indian nations in the seventeenth and eighteenth centuries.

In 1663, Louis XIV decided to take control of the French colonies in North America into his own hands, out of the hands of the private companies that had been exploiting them. The man placed in charge of this endeavor was the minister of finance, Jean-Baptiste Colbert. His plan was that the French should adopt England's colonial policy. The French colonies would thus provide France with the raw materials previously obtained from the Dutch.

In Canada, up to that point in time, the sole mainstay of the Canadian economy had been the fur trade. From their subsistence farms along the banks of the St. Lawrence, the young men embarked for the northwest in their birch bark canoes with loads of European goods to trade with the Indian nations for furs. Thus, every year a large proportion of the men were out of the colony for months at a time, instead of laboring to clear their land and make the colony self sufficient in food, rather than importing it from France.

Colbert was determined to put a stop to that activity. The Canadian settlers were forbidden, by decree, to leave the confines of the colony without a permit issued by the newly appointed royal officials. Instead, the western Indians were, somehow, to be induced to bring their furs to the colony to trade. It seemed a rational policy, but it failed; it was defeated by economic opportunity, geography, and sex.

First, economic opportunity: one summer's voyage to the northwest could garner a man a far greater profit than years of back-breaking labor clearing trees from a 200-acre farm. Striving to curb the proclivity of these men was as futile as attempting to bail out a boat with a fork. The Indians with their furs were in the west. The Canadians were determined to garner them. Moreover, they had the means to do it.

Second, geography: from Canada the Ottawa River led to Lake Huron, and from there to the richest fur-bearing lands, west and north—at the junction of Lakes Huron, Michigan and Superior. It was there that the Canadian traders or *coureurs de bois*—as they came to be called—established their main base, Michilimackinac. The Canadians also had the only practical means of getting there and back—the Indians' birch bark canoe.

The *coureurs de bois* who made their way to Michilimackinac then fanned out to the remote Indian villages and quickly established good relations with their hosts, mastered their languages, adopted their customs, their mores—eventually becoming more Indian than French. The Jesuit missionaries were appalled by this development. In particular, they held firmly to the belief that premarital sex was anathema. Michilimackinac they declared to be a den of gambling, drunkenness, and lechery. The Indians regarded the missionary attitude as ridiculous. Indian girls were masters of their own bodies, free to take any man who took their fancy as a lover, and this included the Canadians. The Indians considered that unions between their young women and the Canadians strengthened the trade and military alliance between them. The Jesuits, early on, strove to have the Indians adopt the French way of life, to become assimilated. As it happened, the Indians assimilated the Canadians. The result was the *métis* nation in the northwest. Colbert's "compact colony" policy had no chance of success.

During the years 1663–1700, some of the royal officials, notably the intendant, Jean Talon, and the governor-general, Louis de Buade, comte de Frontenac, both knee-deep in the fur trade for their own accounts—paid not even lip service to Colbert's orders. In alliance with some of the Montreal fur-trade merchants, a chain of trading posts was established through the Great Lakes and down the Mississippi.

Imperial rivalries in Europe had led to war—known as the War of the League of Augsburg (in America known as King William's War). War, rather than peace, was the norm in Europe. In North America the European war changed nothing. The Canadians were coping with the assaults of the Iroquois Confederacy. Hostilities were terminated with the signing in 1697 of The Treaty of Ryswick. The European powers then sought to resolve the knotty problem of the succession to the throne of Spain without war, but to no avail. Although placing his grandson, Philip, on the Spanish throne portended war, King Louis XIV did so. England, the Netherlands, and the Hapsburg Empire declared war on France, which now had to afford military protection to Spain and her American colonies.

At this point Louis made a momentous decision. In May 1701, the governor-general and the intendant at Quebec were informed: "His Majesty has resolved to establish a settlement at the mouth of the Mississippi . . . this has become an indispensable necessity to halt the advance that the English from the colony of New York have begun to make in the lands that lie between them and that river."

It was not expected that this new colony would be of much economic benefit to France in the foreseeable future. It was intended to serve as a base, an anchor, a seaport, for a series of posts to be built on the rivers from the east into the Mississippi, from the Great Lakes to the Gulf of Mexico. These garrisoned posts were to be bases to weld all the Indian nations between the Alleghenies and the Mississippi into a military and economic alliance with the French—to bar the English from the west. Were this not to be done, it was feared the English would press south and west until they threatened Mexico. The French thus found themselves committed to claiming sovereignty of the entire western section of North America from Hudson Bay to the Gulf of Mexico—at a time when the population of Canada was about 1/10th that of the English colonies and doubling each generation.

In 1702, the anticipated hostilities had erupted in Europe and would last for a decade. At the war's end little seemed to have changed on that continent; all the participants were economically exhausted. At this time there appeared to be a shift in the balance of power in North America. To end the war, France had to sacrifice some of its colonial territory to the British. The question was which territory? To relinquish any of its West Indies islands, the jewels in France's colonial crown, was unthinkable. Similarly, the French trading posts in India and the African slave trade bases had to be retained. Louis chose to trade away parts of the lands that France claimed in America. Looking at a map of the continent of his day, his decision appears ominous, but the French were very skillful diplomatic negotiators; they knew what they were doing; the British diplomats did not.

The Newfoundland fisheries were the great prize. As Louis ceded his claims to the island, his diplomats retained the right for French fishermen to fish on a shoreline stretch of land that extended along the eastern shore of the island and around the northern tip into the Strait of Belle Ile. That shoreline became exclusive French fishing ground, enabling the fishermen to take all the cod that they could on the Grand Banks. The British were determined to prevent permanent settlement on the island; the fishery had to be reserved for British seamen and also to serve as a nursery for sailors to man the Royal Navy in time of war. It was a vain attempt to stop illegal settlers from selling their catch to the New Englanders, who found it more profitable to let the settlers do the fishing and then purchase their catch. By protecting the rights of British seamen, they rendered the same service to the French.

Louis was also obliged to cede Acadia to Britain, which Britain and New England maintained comprised all of present-day Nova Scotia and New Brunswick up to the St. Lawrence, with that river marking the border between the French and British colonies. The French riposted by claiming that Acadia consisted only of the peninsula of Nova Scotia, but not Cape Breton, where they constructed the formidable fortress of Louisbourg. There the French established a clandestine but thriving entrepôt among Canada, New England, and the West Indies. Perhaps this was an early example of a North American free trade agreement.

The Hudson's Bay Company posts captured during the war had to be ceded back to Britain, but here the British overreached themselves. They insisted that the term "ceded" Hudson Bay to his Britannic Majesty be replaced by "restored," this to make explicit their assertion that they had always had the prior claim by virtue of the Company's charter of 1670 by which the king granted it title to most of present-day Canada. The French readily accepted the proposition but then later riposted by asserting that, by definition, the British could have restored to them only the territory that they had previously occupied—namely their isolated posts on the shore of Hudson and James bays. From then on the French kept the British bottled up, utilizing the Indian nations of the Great Lakes and beyond in the French alliance.

What is significant here is that the French sacrificed title to territory in the east and far north, but they retained their dubious claims to the middle west, claiming that the border between New France and the English colonies remained still the Allegheny mountain range; that France held title to the lands between that mountain range and the west by right of prior discovery, exploration and, to debatable degree, occupation. Those lands included the entire Great Lakes basin and the Ohio Valley.

To the amazement of all, the Treaty of Utrecht, after centuries of dynastic wars, was succeeded by a generation of peace between Britain and France. Both countries now had unstable monarchies. Louis XIV died in 1715; the kingdom was now to be ruled by a regent—the duc d'Orléans. The heir to the throne, Louis XV, was a sickly five-year-old. Were he to succumb, then despite the terms of the Treaty of Utrecht that barred Philip of Spain from succeeding to the French throne while also king of Spain, the French people bound by the ancient Salic Law would regard Philip as their king. Should this transpire, the War of the Spanish Succession would have to be fought all over again.

In Britain, Queen Anne died in 1714 and was succeeded by George I, the Elector of Hanover, a descendant of James I on the distaff side. He needed years of peace and stability to establish a firm hold on the throne for himself and his descendants.

During the ensuing three decades, the French in America sought to strengthen their alliances with the Indian nations in the west. They were far too thin on the ground to hope to oppose the burgeoning population of the English colonies on their own. The Canadian forces—colonial regular troops, the militia, fur traders—in the west never numbered more than a thousand, plus the odd hundred *coureurs de bois*. At their garrisoned posts throughout the Great Lakes basin, down the Mississippi and into the far west, the sovereignty that the French claimed over this territory was for British and Anglo-American political consumption only. They never dared even hint that they regarded the Indian nations as, in any way, subjects of the French Crown. Moreover, some of those nations made it plain to the French that they were on their lands only on sufferance. French sovereignty in the Indians' country never extended farther than the range of their muskets.

Moreover, the Indian nations expected the French to provide them with "presents" on every official occasion. This was the Indian custom. In fact, the presents they received when they visited a French post were little more than rent to be paid for the privilege of having a post on Indian territory. When the Indians descended on Montreal for a conference with the governor-general, an exchange of presents had to take place to open the ears of the delegates so that discussions could begin the following day. The Indians offered packs of furs or enemy slaves taken in their tribal wars. In return, they expected the French to be generous with their presents. There was little they despised more than parsimony; nor could they abide haggling or overreaching. Thus, it was that the French established relatively, if nervous, good relations with these proud peoples. As Governor-General Charles de La Boische de

Beauharnois explained to the minister of Marine: "They fear us but they do not love us." The western nations were logistically dependent on the French for a constant supply of arms, in particular muskets, gunpowder, flints, and musketballs, with which to defend themselves against their enemies for, like the European nations, they were on a permanent war footing, one nation against another.

In 1700, Antoine Laumet de Lamothe Cadillac, whose assumed title of nobility was fraudulent, had somehow persuaded the minister of Marine, Louis Phélypeaux, comte de Pontchartrain, that the French should establish a garrisoned military outpost at the narrows between Lakes Erie and St. Clair (the site of present-day Detroit), with himself in command. It was intended to be more than military base, also a farming settlement—a mini-colony. Vigorous efforts were made to have young Canadian families move there, but with little success. It was also intended to persuade the Ottawas, Hurons, Ojibwas, and Miamis to move from Michilimackinac and relocate at Detroit. With their support, the French could bar the Great Lakes basin to any invasion by the Anglo-Americans. Some of these tribesmen did so, but under Cadillac's command the project came close to ruining French imperial policy in the west. He was manifestly, by all credible accounts, completely without honor or scruples, and a coward to boot.

Eventually all manner of complaints from the Canadian officials and fur-trade merchants began to reach the minister's desk. He finally decided that he needed an impartial, firsthand report. In 1707, he appointed a very competent naval commissary, François Clairambault d'Aigremont, to go to Canada, make a tour of inspection of the posts and submit his report directly to the ministry. He arrived at Quebec in 1708 and immediately departed for the west.

His 76-page report was scathing of Cadillac. The minister, however, was reluctant to admit that he had made a mistake by appointing him in the first place. So, in typical bureaucratic fashion, Cadillac was kicked upstairs and appointed governor of the barely surviving colony of Louisiana. He arrived there in 1713, continued his habitual practices, and was recalled in 1717. There he committed the heinous crime of political incorrectness, telling the minister that Louisiana was an economic basket case. The minister still entertained great hopes for the colony. Cadillac's report was the last thing he wanted to hear. Cadillac and his son were sent to the Bastille for several months. (So ended Cadillac's American career, apart from his fraudulent crest on an American automobile.)

D'Aaigremont's report went much further than exposing Cadillac. He also recommended that the French abandon the posts they had established south of the Great Lakes, or any notion of establishing more north of the territorial limits of Louisiana. He pointed out that the furs of the Ohio Valley, owing to its warmer climate, were of poor quality. If the Anglo-Americans coveted the region, let the Iroquois Confederacy deal with them.

At Versailles, the minister did not view the Ohio Valley from the perspective of the Canadian fur traders, but from the French imperial chessboard and there it loomed large. At all costs the Anglo-Americans had to be prevented from swarming over the Alleghenies, occupying the territory to the Mississippi, and eventually pushing ever westward into New Spain. The French, therefore, proceeded to tighten their grip on the region. They established trading posts along the south shore of Lake Ontario, where they provided the Iroquois with the vital services of blacksmiths and gunsmiths, something that the Albany merchants conspicuously failed to do.

When, in 1719, the governor of New York sought to seize the Niagara passage and erect a fort there, he received little support from the provincial assembly. The Albany merchants were receiving all the beaver pelts they could market, smuggled down from Montreal; hence, they were not willing to vote funds for a distant fort that would serve no useful purpose for them.

When Governor-General Philippe de Vaudreuil at Quebec got wind of what Governor William Burnett at Albany intended, he acted swiftly. The Senecas, during the preceding war, had taken prisoner one of his officers in the colonial regular troops, Lieutenant Louis-Thomas Chabert de Joncaire.

There are two versions of what then ensued. After the customary preliminary torture (Indian boys gnawed his fingers to the bone with their teeth), he was brought before the Seneca council where it was decided he should be subjected to the customary twelve-hour torture ceremony. During their deliberations, one of the chiefs seized Joncaire's hand and thrust a mangled finger into the bowl of his pipe. At that Joncaire lashed out, struck the chief and sent him sprawling on the council fire, scorching his backside. The Senecas were so impressed by this show of spirit that they spared his life and adopted him into their nation. The highest praise the Indians had for such an act was "He is a man!" [Sorry ladies.] Now, as an adopted Seneca he was as much a Seneca as any of them, in their eyes. The other recorded version of what transpired is that a Seneca woman liked Joncaire's looks, claimed him, and the Council could not refuse her.

In any event, Joncaire remained with the Senecas until the end of the war and then returned to Canada. During his years with the tribe, he mastered the language and acquired a profound understanding of their mores, their *mentalité*. In 1720, Vaudreuil dispatched Joncaire to the Senecas to gain their assent for the construction of a post at Niagara. At a grand council meeting he was granted that permission; since he was a Seneca he could not be refused. He then swiftly mustered soldiers from the Fort Frontenac garrison and constructed the post.

Three years later he replaced the post with a palisaded fort and within a few years a massive masonry structure was erected—not as a fort but as a large, thick-walled French manor house similar to the ones the Senecas had seen on Canadian seigneuries. This was done to spare the Senecas' susceptibilities; they might well have been upset had the French erected a large fort on what they regarded as their territory. To offset this development and restore some semblance of balance of power, the Confederacy now granted New York the right to establish a trading post at Oswego, at the southeast end of Lake Ontario.

In Europe the generation of peace was drawing to a close. Once again, for dynastic reasons, Britain and France were sucked into war—the War of Austrian Succession. At its end, in 1748, France wanted an enduring peace, but the British war hawks wanted a renewal of hostilities at the earliest opportunity. The latter group with the Earl of Halifax, the wavering Duke of Newcastle, and the commoner William Pitt as its political agents, was convinced that peace was good for France but bad for Britain. During the years of peace the French economy had soared, but that of Britain had stagnated. The recent war had achieved just enough success for the British commercial class that it concluded should Britain concentrate its naval power against the French colonies, they could be captured or destroyed, leaving the British merchants to gobble up the pieces.

This aggressive policy found its counterpart in North America where the planters and land speculators of Virginia and Pennsylvania were eyeing the rich lands of the Ohio Valley. Land companies were formed in both provinces to seize and parcel out these lands to prospective settlers. That these were the lands of the resident Indian nations, and had been for millennia, meant nothing to these men. They coveted the land and the Indian peoples who had failed to cultivate it by European methods of husbandry had, thereby, forfeited their title. These tribes had to be dispossessed by one means or another and the way made for those who could make proper use of it. Anglo-American fur traders, who in some instances were agents of the land companies, had already begun to flood over the mountains and establish posts in the region.

The French in Canada and at Versailles were all too acutely aware of the danger posed by this encroachment on lands they claimed to be under French suzerainty. At Quebec, the acting governor-general, the comte de La Galissonière, took note of these dangers and recommended measures to circumvent them. He proposed that garrisoned forts be established in the Ohio Country and the Indian nations there—the Shawnees, Miamis, Delawares, and if possible the Senecas—be brought into the French alliance. In that manner the inroads of the Anglo-American pack horse traders could be blocked. In addition, in time of war the rear of the English colonies could be threatened by Canadian-led Indian war parties. Only a small force of colonial regulars would be needed to secure the bases and the supply routes from Montreal.

In the previous wars the Canadians had more than held their own against the Anglo-Americans, carrying the war into their territory time and time again. The British would have to respond to a renewal of that threat. They would have to send trained regular troops from their small army to bolster the untrained, ill disciplined, colonial militia. By 1758, the British army and marines numbered 140,000 men, whereas the French had 330,000 units of the line. Moreover, sizable elements of the British navy would have to be employed to supply the American army, hence those ships would not be available for attacks on the French West Indies, French maritime commerce elsewhere, or to blockade the French ports as they had eventually succeeded in doing effectively in the last war. In short, the role of the French in America was to be the classic one of a fortress with a small garrison to tie down a much larger enemy force.

La Galissonière's dispatch received strong support from the minister of Marine. The Anglo-American traders had to be driven out of the trans-Allegheny west. The French interpretation of the Treaty of Utrecht was still that the Indian nations were free to go to the English colonies to trade, but the Anglo-Americans could not go to them. In 1749, La Galissonière sent an expedition, led by veteran western post commander Pierre-Joseph Céloron de Blainville, to the Ohio Valley to show the flag, reclaim the region for France, and chase out the American traders. Once there he discovered that the Anglo-American infiltration of the region and their influence in the councils of the local nations was far more pervasive and dangerous than the French had imagined.

La Galissonière's successor, Ange de Menneville, marquis de Duquesne, acted swiftly. Unlike the governors of the squabbling English colonies, a governor-general of New France could mobilize Canada's entire military resources (the colonial regulars and the militia), in less than a week. The militia were well trained and long accustomed to hard living with the western fur brigades (to living off the land in the wilderness from the mouths of their muskets when need be).

In addition the French had far greater mobility, winter and summer. They had command of the St. Lawrence and the Great Lakes. Theirs was a river empire. In summer the large *canots de maitre* transported supplies to Fort Frontenac and from there a fleet of *barques* took them on to Niagara and Lake Erie. In winter, when need be, military detachments could be sent west, each man dragging a toboggan loaded with his food and equipment.

In 1753, Duquesne decided to send an expedition of two thousand men to Lake Erie to establish a route from the southeast end of that lake to the headwaters of the Ohio and build a chain of forts along it. The French pounced on any Anglo-American traders they encountered and shipped them to Quebec in chains. At this show of strength the Indian nations began to think twice before continuing to trade with the Anglo-Americans.

To his dismay, Duquesne now found himself faced with an internal Canadian problem. The Canadians opposed his policy of invading the Ohio Valley in force. The leading colonists, including the baron de Longueuil, who had served as acting governor-general before Duquesne's arrival, feared that it would incur the enmity of the Iroquois Confederacy. Infuriated, Duquesne wrote to the minister that Longueuil and his supporters "would yield all of France to the Iroquois rather than displease them."

That the Canadians had good cause to fear the consequence of Duquesne's aggressive policy had been made very plain in July 1751. When Lieutenant Chabert de Joncaire, during a grand Iroquois council meeting stated that the French would drive out the Anglo-Americans, the Iroquois responded that the French must force their allies, the Ottawa, the Christian Iroquois of Canada, and the Abenakis to quit hunting in the Ohio Valley, for that region was the hunting preserve of the Iroquois and their allies, the Shawnee and Delaware. The governor-general had to agree to this, but he warned the Iroquois that they must be blind to let the Americans have trading houses in their midst. Those same Americans, who now caressed them with rum, would whip them like their black slaves once they had seized their land. He assured the Confederacy that the Ohio Country had to be preserved as their hunting ground. All the French wanted was to see the English driven out. At a subsequent conference in October, the Iroquois assured the French that they would not allow the English to establish posts in the disputed region; but, they added, nor would they agree to the French establishing themselves there either. Their attitude was clearly "a pox on both your houses."

To return to the point made earlier: the opposition of the Canadians to the proposed invasion of the Ohio Valley. This marked the first time they had openly opposed a French government policy. They did so because, as they saw it, the policy served French, not Canadian, interests. From that point on, those interests continued to diverge. In a less severe but similar form, it resembled the problems the British military would face once their regular troops began to pour into the colonies and found themselves face-to-face with the colonial politicians and populace at large. Yet in this instance, the Canadians had to back down and obey the orders issued at Versailles. The French invasion of the Ohio Valley ensued, at a terrible cost to the Canadians—some four hundred of them left their bones there before the expedition was over.

Robert Dinwiddie, governor of Virginia and one of the leading land speculators in the colonies, responded by sending twenty-one-year-old Virginian, Major George Washington, who had no military experience to speak of, to deliver a warning to the French forces to retire from the territory that Virginia and the war hawks at Westminster claimed, on the most specious of grounds. On 11 December 1753, Washington reached the French fort, Le Boeuf, accompanied by seven men and Jacob Van Braam, who was to serve as his interpreter. Dinwiddie's orders to Washington were: "You are to act on the defensive but in Case any attempts are made to obstruct the works or interrupt our Settlements by any person whatsoever, You are to restrain all such offenders & in Case of resistance to make Prisoners of or kill and destroy them."

At Fort Le Boeuf, Washington encountered the French commandant, Captain Jacques Legardeur de Saint-Pierre, a very competent veteran soldier. Saint-Pierre received Washington graciously, studied Dinwiddie's blustering missive, took his time, and then delivered his response. He informed the governor of Virginia that he should have sent his emissary to Montreal to discuss the issue with the governor-general of New France. Under the present circumstances, he had no choice but to reject Dinwiddie's demand. Thus, having no cause to complain at the way he had been treated, Major Washington was shown off by Saint-Pierre and made his way back to Williamsburg.

Meanwhile, Dinwiddie, acting more as an agent of the Ohio Company than of Virginia, had dispatched a small, hastily mustered detachment of frontier fur traders, some thirty-three in all, led by Ensign Edward Ward, to construct an outpost at the forks of the Ohio. Before he could complete the task, Captain Claude-Pierre Pécaudy de Contrecoeur, with a sizable French force, swooped down on him and ordered him to clear out. He had no choice, but it was a long march back to Virginia. Supplies had not reached him. Contrecoeur courteously supplied him with enough for the journey. The French then began constructing their fort at the forks—predictably named Fort Duquesne.

Washington was given command of a motley collection of militia with orders to drive the French out. They managed a build a ramshackle palisaded base some miles from Fort Duquesne. It stood in a large open meadow surrounded by forested slopes that offered cover to an enemy, but at least gave the defenders an open field of fire. This base came to be named Fort Necessity.

Upon learning of this renewed Anglo-American invasion of lands claimed by the French, Captain Contrecoeur ordered Ensign Joseph Coulon de Villiers de Jumonville to deliver a summons to the invading force, with a warning that were it to be spurned: "then I shall be obliged to constrain by any means that I deem to be the most efficacious to safeguard the honour of His Majesty's arms." Note the difference in wording between this missive and that of Dinwiddie. Unlike Dinwiddie's there is no mention of "resistance," "making prisoners," "to kill or destroy them." Instead, the French threat is merely to constrain and "to safeguard the honor of His Majesty's arms." Jumonville, with another cadet and a party of thirty men departed in search of the Americans, wherever they might be. They did not find them. George Washington did. Then occurred not just a clash of arms, but a clash of cultures.

Some of Washington's few Indian scouts had detected Jumonville's party some five miles away. He set off with thirty-two of his men and the Indians. At daybreak they crept up on the French, most of them asleep under a twenty-foot overhanging cliff edge. A couple of the men were awake, stirring the embers of a fire to prepare breakfast, the men's muskets stacked nearby. Without warning, at close range, Washington's men opened fire. When the smoke cleared away, Jumonville and ten of his men were dead. One of the Canadians managed to escape and made his way back to Fort Duquesne. The surviving prisoners were then marched to Virginia, where they later complained of very bad treatment. It is significant that Washington, in his journal, makes no mention of his force having suffered any casualties.

What is one to make of this incident? Washington, when he had encountered Captain Saint-Pierre at Fort Le Boeuf, had been treated courteously and sent on his way. This time Governor Dinwiddie's orders had stated that "You are to act on the defensive . . . ," but if he were to be opposed then he was empowered to resist, taking the opposing forces as prisoners or kill them. To ambush the French in the way that he did, to open fire on sleeping men without warning, can hardly be styled acting defensively. The contrast between the way that Washington was received by Saint-Pierre and the way he treated the French party, bearing a missive similar to that which he had carried to the French is, to say the least, startling.

The French were outraged by this action. The mildest of their condemnations was that it had been a totally dishonorable act. Duquesne expected that Britain would bring the perpetrators to book and deal with them as they deserved—as common assassins. That word "honor" always figured prominently in the French documents: "personal honor," the honor of the king that had to be defended at all costs. One does not find that word in the British or Anglo-American documents. It manifestly did not exist in Washington's vocabulary.

It was a clash between the mores, the culture of the European nobility, and that of the emerging new dominant class of Britain and its American colonies, to gain one's end regardless of normally accepted concepts of civilized behavior. The end justified the means. It marked the beginning of the decline of gentility in the Western world.

That episode over with, Washington and his men returned to Fort Necessity. At Fort Duquesne the commandant, upon learning the fate of Jumonville's mission, dispatched a war party to deal with the perpetrators. The detachment—five hundred colonial regular, one hundred militia, one hundred allied Indians—was commanded by Jumonville's elder brother, Louis Coulon de Villiers. His orders were to encounter Washington's force, demand satisfaction for the murder of Jumonville and his men, and then drive them off French-claimed territory.

Much ink has been spilled over what then ensued, and there is no need to recount it here. Suffice it to say that Washington was forced to capitulate to Villiers and accept his terms. Included in the capitulation document was the admission that he was responsible for the "*assassinat*," to quote the French phrase, and which has only one meaning—assassination. Washington signed the document. He, and generations of American historians, from Francis Parkman to the latter day, have sought to exculpate him. For the French of his day there was no such equivocation. In their eyes Washington had acted as a common assassin—a man totally without honor.

The next day the Anglo-Americans began their doleful march over the Alleghenies, leaving with the French two hostages, the Dutch interpreter, Van Braam and a certain Major Stobo, as guarantors that the Virginians would repatriate the prisoners they had taken during their attack on Jumonville's detachment, a commitment that was not honored. Major Stobo, while held on parole at Quebec, demonstrated that he did not know the meaning of the words "parole" and "honor"; he pleaded ignorance during his court martial for espionage. Van Braam, on the other hand, made it plain that he knew the meaning of those terms.

Washington had fled Fort Necessity in such haste that he left his journal behind. When Duquesne read it, he was appalled. In his next dispatch to Contrecoeur at Fort Duquesne he wrote: "Nothing could be more shameful, so base or so black as the train of thought of this Washington. It would have given me great pleasure to read to his face his outrageous journal." Washington later sought to deny that he had kept a journal, but the French had it in their hands.

In the Ohio Country, meanwhile, Contrecoeur's men systematically destroyed every American trading post west of the mountains. The Indian nations now rejected all the futile American blandishments and rallied to the French. The Iroquois Confederacy chose to remain neutral and abide by the terms of the Montreal Treaty of 1700. That may well have been their biggest mistake. The French were now in tenuous control of the entire region.

At Versailles, the king and his ministers desperately striving to avoid war, played down the Jumonville affair. They fully realized that were a maritime war to ensue, they would lose their colonies. Orders were issued that the French were to remain on the defensive. The British war hawks, led by the Duke of Cumberland, Henry Fox, Lord Halifax, and William Pitt, were determined to drive the French out of Acadia, extend British territory to the St. Lawrence along its entire length, take Fort Niagara, occupy the Ohio Valley, then go on to sever Canada's Mississippi route to Louisiana. Were this to lead to war, so be it.

In October 1754, Major General Edward Braddock, given command of two battalions of regulars from the Irish establishment, was ordered to America with orders to take Fort Duquesne, while the colonial forces attacked Fort Niagara, the French forts on Lake Champlain, and those on the Nova Scotia border. He did not sail until April. On the eve if its departure, the French ambassador at London obtained a copy of Braddock's orders. The French then detached three army battalions for service in America. When the British cabinet learned of this, Admiral Edward Boscawen was ordered to take command of nineteen ships of the line and two frigates to intercept the French convoy, seize the ships, and if they gave battle, sink them. A few days later, still in time of peace, the French ambassador somehow learned of Boscawen's orders. Two weeks later two British cabinet ministers dined at his house and assured him that all such "rumors" were completely false, that no such orders had been issued.

Off Newfoundland, Boscawen succeeded in intercepting only three of the French. When Captain Tousaint Hocquart hailed the ships that loomed up in the fog, assuming them to be British, asked if they were at war or at peace, the reply was "At peace, at peace." The British ships sailed closer. Then came shattering broadsides. Two of the French ships were captured. The rest of the convoy escaped to Louisbourg and Quebec.

Elsewhere, the Royal Navy had greater success. More than three hundred French ships and eight thousand sailors were seized in English ports or on the high seas. This was a crushing blow to French maritime power. From then on the French had to make the best use possible of their few remaining ships and crews, and hire ships from the neutral powers to supply Quebec. In the final years of the war, the minister of Marine contemplated accepting offers from English ship owners to transport supplies to Canada. The French also insured their ships at Lloyd's of London, whose rates were lower than those of the French insurers. Lloyd's was also able to inform the French of the movements of the British fleets to enable them to take evasive action. In an unwitting quid pro quo, the Anglo-American colonies supplied the French West Indies with all their needs, thereby negating the Royal Navy's attempts to starve them into submission.

On land in America, the British did not fare so well. Braddock's army was destroyed at the Monongahela by a far smaller French, Canadian, and allied Indian force. The intended assaults on the Lake Champlain corridor failed dismally. Then followed three years of French military success. Rather than driving the French north of the St. Lawrence and the Great Lakes, they found themselves with their backs to the wall from unrelenting French pressure.

At the same time the northwestern nations—Ottawas, Mingos, Shawnees, Miamis, Delawares, and even some Senecas—were ravaging American settlements to within thirty miles of Philadelphia. Canadian officers of the *Troupes de la Marine* accompanied many of these war parties. Their purpose was to try to impose some sound tactical purpose on their allies, to strive to have them abstained from their usual custom of slowly burning their prisoners to death, and occasionally, devouring them. They made their food supply walk. The French, on the other hand, wanted to save the prisoners, to discover by adroit questioning the state of affairs in the enemy camp. They were as the governor-general explained to the minister of Marine, his "walking messengers."

As the intensity of these raids increased, by 1757 the governors of the more exposed American colonies began pleading for a negotiated peace—at almost any price. Reports reached the French at Niagara that the governor of Pennsylvania had offered to grant the Indians free access to traverse his province to ravage Virginia, provided that they spared Pennsylvania's territory. As Colonel Bougainville, General Montcalm's aide de camp, put it: "What can they do against these invisible enemies who strike then flee with the speed of lightning. They are the exterminating angel."

And that is exactly what they were. They were not French mercenaries. They were fighting to right too many old wrongs, for revenge, to prevent a recurrence, to drive the Americans off their lands once and for all. That was their war, fought to achieve their ends, not those of the French. Yet they had to depend on the French for logistical support: for weapons, for food supplies for themselves while raiding, and to feed their families since they could not both wage war and hunt over an extended period.

That the Indian nations would serve as independent allies of the French only as long as that support served their purposes was made clear by their gullible acceptance of the Easton Treaty, whereby they were assured that the land stripped from them by American chicanery would be restored. With that the other nations began to draw back from the French, sniffing a change in the winds of war.

To make matters far worse for the French, the Americans had assaulted, sacked and destroyed the main Great Lakes supply depot—Fort Frontenac. Without the supplies and boats there awaiting for shipment to Niagara and Fort Duquesne, neither fort was tenable. The main supply route to the west had finally been cut. The garrison at Fort Duquesne was now forced to abandon it and withdraw to Niagara.

Nearing it, they were ambushed by their ancient foes, the Mohawk, accompanied by Sir William Johnson. It was a slaughter. Few of the French survived. The British were now firmly in control of the Great Lakes. The river route down the St. Lawrence was now open to them. Worse yet, the Royal Navy had managed to transport nine thousand British regulars up the St. Lawrence, where they laid siege to Quebec.

It is here that we come face-to-face with a perhaps extraneous, hidden factor in political and military affairs that I have labeled the "stupidity factor" in history. Nowhere did it operate more effectively than during the British war for the conquest of Canada. But first, the historian has to distinguish between two categories of stupidity. There was the stupidity that was glaringly apparent to the people at the time. As anyone who has served in the armed forces of any nation, or as a professor on an academic committee knows there is nothing worse than stupidity backed up by authority. Then there is the stupidity that is discovered with the benefit of 20/20 hindsight by subsequent generations of historians.

In one particular context, an early example of French stupidity was the decision to establish an overseas colonial empire without a strong navy to protect its coasts from assault and its ships from blockade or capture on the high seas. In the seventeenth century, Cardinal Richelieu warned of this danger, but the governments of succeeding generations ignored it. Instead of creating an adequate navy, the governments of the day chose to build strong fortresses in the colonies, as was done along the Rhine frontier, and then rely on privateers to attack the enemy at sea. That proved to be a receipt for disaster in the eighteenth century; akin to the Maginot Line of a later age. In the eighteenth-century war, the Royal Navy transported armies, captured the main French islands in the West Indies, Louisbourg not once but twice, and eventually Quebec. In the latter case, military stupidity has to be equally divided between the British and the French.

At the onset of the Seven Years' War, the proclaimed British aim was to establish secure frontiers for its American colonies. With the advent of Pitt to power at Westminster these war aims changed. He, with paranoid intensity, demanded nothing less than the total destruction of the French colonial empire. For Pitt, the whole of North America had become the great prize. The key to this treasure chest was Canada; were that colony to be conquered then the continent was open, waiting to be plundered.

Yet Pitt continued the earlier policy of his predecessors in office; the policy of attacking the French on the peripheries of its American empire. A year was wasted in the siege and capture of Louisbourg. Without a navy based there, the fortress was worthless, able to do nothing for the French, serving merely as a prison for its garrison.

Meanwhile, throughout the duration of the war, the French managed to keep Canada well supplied. More supplies reached Quebec during those years than had reached it during all the years preceding in the colony's history. Every year the Royal Navy stationed its fleet off the southern coast of Newfoundland, waiting to pounce on the French convoys heading for the Cabot Strait. The French eluded them by sailing far to the north and slipping through the Strait of Belle Ile, between the northern tip of Newfoundland and Labrador, then safely up the St. Lawrence to Quebec.

That being the case, it is astounding that Pitt and his admirals did not realize that were the navy to sail early enough and station its ships well up the Gulf of St. Lawrence, then Canada could have been denied everything, staved into submission in months. This had happened in 1628–29 when David and Lewis Kirke blockaded the river. Come spring the Kirke brothers returned and Samuel de Champlain was forced to surrender Quebec. Then again, John Bradstreet's destruction of the French supply base—Fort Frontenac—led directly to the French being forced to abandon Fort Duquesne, and, subsequently, Niagara.

The following year, 1759, one of the more momentous battles in the history of the Western world occurred, and once again stupidity determined the outcome. The Royal Navy managed to get a fleet with nine thousand British regulars to Quebec. Ironically, it was preceded by a few days by a French supply convoy. Then all through the summer every British assault was beaten off. Come September, the British commander, Major General James Wolfe, determined on one last desperate assault before he had to admit defeat and sail back to Britain and ignominy.

On 13 September, at daybreak, he landed his sleepless army behind the city. They scaled the heights and lined up, not on the ridge that overlooked the fortress, but at the foot of a reverse slope. The ridge facing him hid the city from view. Governor-General Louis-Joseph, Marquis de Montcalm had twelve thousand men, plus an indeterminate number of Indian allies under his command. Ten miles to Wolfe's rear was Colonel Bougainville, with an elite force of three thousand men. Wolfe and his army were trapped. He had dug a grave for his army. Montcalm then marched his own army straight into it. The battle lasted half an hour.

Ironically, there then occurred one touch of gentility. When the French learned that the British General had been wounded, the commander of the Quebec garrison sent two surgeons to attend to him.

The following year, as three British armies descended on Montreal, where the French had mustered the remnants of their forces, the governor-general of New France was forced to capitulate. To all intents and purposes, that marked the end of the French Empire in North America. It also meant the doom of North America's Indian nations.

In Europe, meanwhile, the French were desperately striving to get Pitt to agree to a peace treaty on honorable terms, but to no avail. In October 1761, Pitt was forced from office. During the ensuing peace negotiations, Britain had to choose whether to retain Guadeloupe or Canada; of the two, Canada seemed expendable. Moreover, the far-seeing French foreign minister, Étienne-François, duc de Choiseul, was convinced that were Britain to retain Canada, thereby removing the French threat to the British colonies, they would very soon strike out for independence. Some in Britain were of the same opinion. They were not heeded.

The British then found that they had stepped into the French shoes, but they did not fit. In the Ohio Valley they antagonized the Indian nations as would-be American settlers swarmed into the Native hunting lands, and began clearing the forest for the plow, driving away the Indians' food supply. Fearing Indian reprisals, a resumption of the past wars, attacks on the invaders that had cost the lives of too many British soldiers, the government of the day at Westminster issued the Proclamation Line of 1763 forbidding Anglo-Americans west of the Alleghenies. It came too late. The Indian nations of the Great Lakes and Ohio Valley struck back in a vain attempt to drive the invaders off their lands.

Without the logistical support that the French had supplied in the previous war, their preemptive strike was doomed. They could not sustain a long campaign. The British lost five hundred men, one battalion, and some two thousand Americans were killed. Arrows skewered many of the British. Stone Age weapons opposing European firepower.

Eventually the Indian nations were ground down, but not before, on the orders of the British commander-in-chief, Jeffrey Amherst, his subordinates resorted to bacteriological warfare. When the Delawares demanded that the garrison at Fort Pitt surrender, the commanding officer responded with a "present" of blankets and a handkerchief from the fort's hospital ward. An epidemic soon spread.

Once peace was restored in the west, the British government urgently sought a means to prevent a recurrence. The colonial governments were appealed to provide both the men and money needed to police the region, to put an end to the depredations of their land speculators and the Indian traders. Those governments would have none of it. Neither men nor money nor an administrative framework were forthcoming. The men at Westminster were, therefore, forced to find a solution. It was the Quebec Act, which among other things forbade settlement by Anglo-Americans north of the Ohio River. The American land speculators, including such notables as Washington and his kin, Benjamin Franklin, and others reacted the way a dog does when its bone is snatched away.

The Quebec Act also added to the festering colonial grievances that were shortly to erupt into the War for American Independence. Ironically without the financial, logistical, and finally direct military intervention of the French—who sought only one thing, revenge for its humiliation by the British in the preceding war—the American leaders of the rebelling colonies could never have achieved their aims. But achieve them they did.

During the protracted peace negotiations the French foreign minister, Charles Gravier, comte de Vergennes, was appalled to learn that his British adversary, the devious William Petty Fitzmaurice, Earl of Shelburne, was willing to grant the emerging American republic what he had no legal or ethical right to cede—namely the west between the Alleghenies and the Mississippi. Vergennes sought to have Shelburne rescind the cession of the territory south of the Great Lakes. He wanted that region reserved for the Indian nations, whose lands, after all, they were. They were to serve as a buffer zone between the Americans and Louisiana.

The Indian nations whose lands were in dispute, treacherously ceded by Britain to the Americans, were not to be a discard of history. In May 1783, Brigadier Allan Maclean at Niagara reported to the governor at Quebec, Sir Frederick Haldimand, that the Indians were very uneasy over certain pretended boundary disputes. He stated that they regarded themselves as a free people, subject to no power on earth. Having served the king of England faithfully as allies, not his subjects, during the war with the Americans, they declared that he had no right whatsoever to grant their rights to the enemy. Maclean added: "I do from my soul pity these people."

They Americans showed them no pity. By 1840, the Indians east of the Mississippi, with the exception of a few enclaves, had either been removed to the west of the Mississippi, by one means or another, or had died in the process. (Ethnic cleansing perhaps?)

EDITORS' NOTE

Professor Eccles death precluded his providing documentation for his essay and revising it for publication. However, by consulting his *The French in North America* (East Lansing: Michigan State University Press, 1998) one will find the citations that support his arguments. The editors have retained the language, with only minor editorial changes, that Professor Eccles provided for his address at the conference.

Henry Bouquet and British Infantry Tactics on the Ohio Frontier, 1758–1764

CHARLES E. BRODINE JR.

On the afternoon of 5 August 1763, a four-hundred-man British force under the command of Colonel Henry Bouquet was on the march in the wilderness of western Pennsylvania. The Swiss colonel was bringing supplies and reinforcements to Fort Pitt, whose garrison had been under siege from hostile Indians since late June. Twenty-six miles from its objective, near Bushy Run, a large body of Native American warriors attacked Bouquet's relief column. In the desperate, two-day firefight that ensued, Bouquet's men succeeded in driving off their attackers—but not without heavy casualties. In one of his first letters written after the battle, Bouquet offered the following assessment of the action at Bushy Run: "The most Warlike of savage Tribes," he proudly declared, "have lost their Boasted Claim of being Invincible in the Woods." In the weeks that followed, his fellow officers congratulated Bouquet for the severe "thrashing" and "drubbing" he had given the natives.[1]

That British officers should crow over the result of Bushy Run is understandable, given the repeated defeats the army had suffered at the hands of native warriors throughout the spring and summer of 1763. But there is more to their comments than the expression of wounded pride. They speak to the deep frustration an entire service felt at its inability to cope effectively with a deadly and skilled opponent. For eight long years, the army in North America had had to live with the memory of Major General Edward Braddock's defeat, with the idea that regulars were no match for Indians in a wilderness fight. The victory at Bushy Run, at least temporarily, shattered the myth of Native American invincibility in the woods.

More than any other event in his distinguished nine-year career, the Battle of Bushy Run has come to define whom Henry Bouquet was and why he was important. Just as Braddock's defeat at the Battle of the Monongahela came to symbolize the bankruptcy of European tactics in the New World setting, so Bouquet's victory at Bushy Run came to symbolize the ability of the British army to adapt successfully to the demands of fighting in the American wilderness. This image of Bouquet is worth exploring both to have a clearer understanding of his military achievements and of his impact on the training and discipline of the British army in North America during the Great War for Empire.[2]

Henry Bouquet has long enjoyed a reputation as one of the most competent field officers in the king's service during the French and Indian War. Historians such as Francis Parkman, Lawrence Henry Gipson, and John Shy have praised his integrity, professionalism, and sound judgement. Yet, the one aspect of Bouquet's American service that has drawn the most comment is his role as a military tactician and frontier fighter. He has been credited by some writers with developing innovations "in drill, tactics, and equipment" that helped establish his regiment, the Royal Americans, as "the first true light infantry" in the British army. It has been said that his ideas on drill and discipline were found so sound that the rest of the army incorporated them into its formal training and exercise. Bouquet has also earned encomiums as the Robert Rogers of the British army in America and as the greatest Indian fighter that the British army produced in the eighteenth century. One writer has even pondered whether the American Revolution might not have had a different outcome had Bouquet lived to lead British troops against the rebellious colonies.[3]

While Henry Bouquet deserves accolades as a brave soldier, astute tactician, and steady battlefield commander, there is much that is wrong with this portrait of the Swiss colonel. Taken as a whole, it inadequately addresses Bouquet's early thinking on tactics and drill, especially during the Forbes Expedition of 1758. Moreover, it inaccurately attributes practices to Bouquet that he had, in fact, only expressed as ideas in print. A more reliable portrayal of Bouquet, of his ideas on tactics and drill, and of his actual training practices, is needed. This essay will attempt to address that need by examining the role of Henry Bouquet in the training and tactical discipline of the British army on the Ohio frontier from 1758 to 1764. Further, this paper will also briefly describe the drill and training of the British army in other American theaters in order to evaluate the uniqueness of Bouquet's concepts on wilderness warfare and their impact on the army in general.

Bouquet's approach to fighting in the American wilderness was shaped by his experiences as a soldier on the European continent. When he arrived in New York, in August 1756, Bouquet was a veteran of twenty years' service in the armies of Holland and Piedmont-Sardinia. Most importantly, he was a combat-tested soldier having participated in numerous battles and sieges during the War of the Austrian Succession. It is noteworthy that this experience was gained in the rugged terrain of Piedmont and northern Italy. There the young Bouquet learned first-hand the immense difficulties of waging war in mountainous country. He also had his first introduction to irregular warfare at this time, witnessing the partisan activities of the Piedmontese militia, especially their use of hit-and-run tactics. Complementing Bouquet's battlefield expertise was an extensive knowledge of mathematics and military science, gained through hours of devoted study and reading. As he was fluent in German and English, in addition to his native French, most published military treatises of the period would have been accessible to him. By experience and training, then, Henry Bouquet had a thorough understanding of the drill and tactical philosophy of the major European armies.[4]

The most fully articulated statement of Bouquet's ideas on the tactics of forest warfare appears in William Smith's *Historical Account of Bouquet's Expedition Against the Ohio Indians, in 1764*. In a section of this work entitled "Reflections on the War with the Savages of North-America," Bouquet offered a program for waging war against the Indian. Some writers have erroneously assumed that the ideas set forth in "Reflections" represent Bouquet's actual practices in the field rather than a model of warfare he had proposed. Further confusion results from the fact that Bouquet actually employed some of the ideas he discusses in "Reflections." As the organization of Bouquet's "Reflections" lends itself to an orderly discussion of his ideas on forest warfare, this paper will adopt its structure to discuss the major concepts of Bouquet's tactical doctrine and how he implemented them in the field.[5]

To know how to fight the Indian, Bouquet believed, one needed to understand his nature and his way of making war. Out of this understanding would evolve a method for defeating him. While Bouquet was contemptuous of Indians and of Indian culture, he in no way let this color his professional estimation of their abilities as warriors. Physically active, fierce in manner, skillful in the use of weapons, and capable of great guile and stealth in combat, the Indian was, in Bouquet's reckoning, a formidable opponent. Indian tactics in battle, Bouquet stated, could be reduced to three principles: surround the enemy, fight in scattered formation, and always give ground when attacked. This last principle Bouquet mistook for cowardice, not recognizing that Indian culture called for battle tactics that minimized casualties.[6]

To fight such a foe as the Indian, Bouquet deemed regular troops entirely inadequate, which may appear curious in light of the redcoats' performance at Bushy Run. Yet it was his opinion that such heavy infantry, by virtue of its training and accouterment, was not capable of fighting the faster moving, more lightly armed Indian on an equal footing, especially when campaigning in the vast American wilderness. Regulars, he said, were "too valuable, to be employed alone in a destructive service for which they were never intended." War with the Indians on these terms was always to be avoided.[7]

If regulars would not answer for service in America, what kind of force did Bouquet believe would be effective? In "Reflections," he proposed the creation of a force of light troops and light horse "raised and disciplined for the woods." He thought Americans "bred upon the frontiers" as "the fittest men for that service." Youth was critical as it was important for the soldiers to be able to endure the great fatigues of frontier campaigning. Men between the ages of fifteen and twenty would enlist for a term of twenty years.[8]

Implicit in Bouquet's remarks in "Reflections" is the assumption that Americans, temperamentally and physically, were better suited than regulars to the specialized roles called for in wilderness warfare, such as light horsemen, woodsmen, rangers, and marksmen. There is no evidence that at any time Bouquet sought to train the men of the Royal Americans in any of these forest warfare roles. In fact, given Bouquet's frequent criticism of the ineptness of veteran soldiers in the woods, his concerns about the suitability of regulars for service on the frontier become understandable. The inability of redcoats to operate without rangers or scouts was one of the reasons Bouquet was unable to follow up his victory at Bushy Run in the fall of 1763. "Without a certain Number of Woodsmen, he complained to Amherst, I can not think it advisable to employ Regulars in the Woods against Savages, as they can not procure any Intelligence; and are open to continual Surprises. Nor can they pursue at any distance this Enemy when they have routed them, and Should they have the misfortune to be defeated the whole would be destroyed if at above one day's march from a Fort." Other British officers beside Bouquet shared the notion that Americans were physically suited to the auxiliary roles assigned them by the army. But Bouquet never seems to have subscribed to the contrary notion that British soldiers and officers could be trained in woodcraft.[9]

Forest warfare also required that soldiers be "lightly clothed, armed, and accoutered." The clothing Bouquet recommended for light troops was lightweight, easily stowed, and of natural hues. It included such pieces as a hunting shirt, leggings, moccasins, and "a short coat of brown cloth." For firearms Bouquet preferred "short fusils" rather than heavier muskets, with some soldiers carrying rifles. Each man was also to be armed with a bayonet and a hatchet. The provincial troops serving under Bouquet came the closest to achieving this standard of light dress. In June 1758 Bouquet proposed to Forbes "to make Indians of part of our provincial soldiers. . . . It would only be necessary for them to remove their coats and breeches, which will delight them; give them moccasins and blankets; cut off their hair and daub them with paint and intermingle them with the real Indians. It would be difficult for the enemy to distinguish them and I believe that the impression which this number would produce would be useful to us." Forbes heartily approved of Bouquet's plan, urging him to send the best men from each provincial regiment out scouting dressed as Indians. "In this Country," the general observed, "wee must comply and learn the Art of Warr, from Ennemy Indians or any thing else who have seen the Country and Warr carried on inn itt." George Washington's Virginians adopted this Indian dress and Bouquet was pleased enough to declare that it should be the model for the expedition. Beyond the use of leggings, there is no evidence to suggest that Bouquet modified the uniform of the Royal Americans in order to dress his men as light troops. Only the Regiment's light and grenadier companies would have had distinctive dress. The grenadier company of Bouquet's First Battalion could hardly be described as lightly equipped for the woods, with each soldier carrying uniform, arms, and accouterments totaling over 60 pounds. Arms for the Sixtieth would have included the standard issue long land pattern musket, a hatchet, and a bayonet.[10]

Some of the most interesting passages in Bouquet's "Reflections" deal with the training of troops in march, maneuver, and use of arms. Here the connection between what Bouquet practiced and what he articulated as the ideal is most apparent. The two cardinal principles that underlay much of this drill were speed and open order, thus incorporating important elements of Indian battlefield tactics into that of the light troops. The type of exercise promulgated in "Reflections" included rallying and dispersing at given signals, leaping over ditches and fallen trees, learning to walk and run singly, and running "in ranks, with open files." In this last formation the men were to be taught to "wheel . . . at first slowly, and by degrees increase their speed." This difficult evolution, Bouquet wrote, was "of the utmost consequence" because it allowed one "to fall unexpectedly upon the flank of the enemy." The whole of this exercise emphasizes openness, celerity, and fluid movement, and underscores why Bouquet considered young, athletic men as the only suitable candidates for light troops. The one element of drill not discussed in this section of "Reflections" is marching formations, but from descriptions in later sections of the text, it is clear that Bouquet believed men marching in column should step either in single file or in double files.[11]

Bouquet had been applying these concepts described in "Reflections" from his earliest campaigns. In a plan he drafted in March 1757 for a campaign against Fort Duquesne, Bouquet recommended that the men "march in two files." Why Bouquet preferred this formation is revealed in a letter written the following year during the Forbes Expedition. "I have always drawn up the troops and had them march in double file, and I have found by experience that seven columns in this order have penetrated the densest thickets, and at a drum signal they have spread out and formed line of battle in two minutes, holding a very long front—with light troops and cavalry off to the side keeping up a continual fire, and the same all along the line." The journal of the Rev. Thomas Barton, a chaplain in the Third Battalion of the Pennsylvania Regiment, offers a vivid and clear description of how troops deployed into line from this double file, or two-deep formation. The troops were taken to the exercise field, Barton recorded, where "they are form'd into 4 Columns 2 Men deep, paralel to, and distant from, each other about 50 Yards: After marching some Distance in this Position, they fall into one Rank entire forming a Line of Battle with great Ease & Expedition. The 2 Front-Men of each Column stand fast, & the 2 Next split equally to Right & Left, & so continue alternately till the whole Line is form'd." Bouquet adhered to this double file or two-deep column as a battlefield tactic throughout his campaigning in Pennsylvania. It also served as an important tactical element in his expedition into the Ohio. The reason for this is clear: speed and simplicity. It allowed Bouquet to march his men in open order and deploy them rapidly in the same fashion. It could also be performed with a minimum of motions and steps—an important consideration given the poor quality of recruits and the lack of training time to instruct them.[12]

The use and handling of firearms was another important component of light troop drill and Bouquet's remarks on this topic reflect the bedrock principles upon which he trained his troops. According to "Reflections," young recruits were to "be taught to handle their arms with dexterity; and, without losing time upon trifles, to load and fire very quick." Men were also to be taught to fire from different positions: "standing, kneeling, or lying on the ground." Curiously, the practice of taking cover and giving fire from behind trees is not mentioned in this section of "Reflections," nor did that concept seem to play an important role in Bouquet's tactical thinking. His preference seems to have been to have his men take to their knees when they came under fire. For example, in his 1757 plan to capture Duquesne, Bouquet directed that when the army was attacked, the troops should drop to "their Knees." This motion would "prevent their running away," provide cover from hostile fire, and allow time for reconnoitering and for the "necessary Dispositions" to be made. There are mentions of the use of tree cover in the battle formations Bouquet used during the expedition into the Ohio, but their application was limited to use by sentries and marksmen. The majority of the soldiers were ordered "to fall on their knees" when the column came under attack, in order "to be less exposed."[13]

"Reflections" also called for recruits to practice firing at marks in order to develop skill in aimed fire. While Bouquet required both regulars and provincials to exercise at this drill, he singled out the latter group to serve as the army's marksmen. This may have been because provincials already had rifled weapons and were reckoned good shots. In his plan for the campaign sketched out in 1757, Bouquet recommended that the commanding officers of the Pennsylvania Regiments choose from among their men those "most fit" for the service of "<u>Rangers</u> & <u>marks men</u>." After the fall of Fort Duquesne he issued orders to Colonel Hugh Mercer of the Pennsylvania Regiment to select the "best marksmen" to "fire from the fort." Each sharpshooter was to have "two musketts" and a man to help him reload. Likewise Pennsylvanians provided marksmen for Bouquet's expedition in 1764. On the eve of departing into the Ohio Country, Bouquet ordered competitions held to determine the best marksmen among the Pennsylvanian troops. Cash prizes were awarded to the winners. Forty marksmen were ultimately chosen to form a body of riflemen who had special duties in battle when the army came under attack. These riflemen provided shooters skilled in hitting their target. Bouquet used them in providing covering fire for the main column and a harassing fire against the enemy. This was often best done not in line with troops but behind the cover of trees or of a fort's walls. Ironically, shortages of lead ball in both the expeditions of 1758 and 1764 prevented the men from practicing firing at marks. Instead they practiced their exercise with blank cartridges.[14]

Despite their usefulness as an arm of the army, Bouquet had no desire to turn the regulars under his command into riflemen. The reason was quite practical. Bouquet's tactics were predicated on speed and motion. A premium was placed on giving and returning fire with rapidity. It took a rifleman longer to load and fire his weapon than another man armed with a musket, fusil, or carbine. Moreover, rifles required special fine grain gunpowder to fire and the bullets had to be individually cast. In contrast, men with muskets could use pre-made cartridges speeding their rate of fire. To have most of one's troops armed with rifles would significantly reduce their rate of fire, thereby impairing their fighting efficiency and speed.[15]

One of the more important elements of Bouquet's tactical doctrine is only hinted at in his writings and letters—the use of side arms. In "Reflections," the Swiss colonel stated that each soldier should be armed "with bayonets in the form of a dirk, to serve for a knife" and with "small hatchets." Early on in the Forbes Campaign, Bouquet declared bayonets to be "a useless Arm in the Woods." Given the role that bayonet charges played in his success at Bushy Run five years later, it might be expected that Bouquet had changed his mind about their utility. But in the orderly books for the Ohio Expedition there is a directive that states "Co[ll] Bouquet recommends to the Offic[rs] to be particularly carefull that their Men do not negligently lose or abuse their Hatchets as they are the only weapons they can depend on in Attacking the Enemy after they have discharged their firearms." All the troops on this expedition were armed with tomahawks; the orderly books make no mention of bayonets. If the weapon Bouquet preferred was the hatchet perhaps it was because it could strike a more deadly blow than the bayonet. Or perhaps it was because the British exercise for bayonet was considered awkward and ineffectual. One noted drill book author declared that the bayonet drill left the attacker vulnerable to having his blow parried or to being knocked down. Since heavy firepower had been "the touch-stone of British tactical thinking" since the campaigns of Marlborough, a disregard of the bayonet would have placed Bouquet within the sphere of British battlefield doctrine. Yet while he believed in the utility of firepower, Bouquet believed just as strongly in the power of shock action, whether from a bayonet, hatchet, or battleaxe. And it was shock action that was the key element of Bouquet's tactical canon.[16]

Like any competent military commander, Bouquet recognized the importance of auxiliary forces to an army on campaign. In Europe, detachments of light troops, light horse, and irregulars served as an army's eyes and ears. In the New World, European rivals eagerly courted Native Americans to perform these duties. While Bouquet was sensible of the superior skill of forest warriors in woodcraft, he ultimately viewed them as unreliable and, therefore, undependable allies. He preferred instead to rely on a combination of woodsmen, hunters, rangers, and light horse to support the army. These auxiliaries provided valuable service in cutting roads, guiding and escorting convoys, gathering intelligence, harassing the enemy, and protecting the army from surprise. In battle, Bouquet assigned them several roles: guarding the army's flanks and rear, providing covering fire, and carrying out flanking actions. As has been noted, it was provincials not regulars who served in these auxiliary roles and Bouquet deemed their services so requisite to operations that any thought of acting without them was quickly dismissed.[17]

In "Reflections," Bouquet considered troops of light horse to be an essential component of any force that was to act in the woods against Indians. They were trained to fight on foot as well as on horseback and were expected to be expert in all aspects of horsemanship. The men were to be lightly accoutered and armed with short rifles and long-handled battle-axes. In addition, Bouquet recommended that each light horseman "be provided with a Blood-hound." What the Swiss colonel proposed was hardly new. The use of dogs in battle had a long pedigree. For centuries "Europeans bred and cultivated dogs" as "lethal weapon[s] of war." The Spanish were particularly noted for their use of four-legged soldiers as agents of conquest in the New World, employing canines to terrorize and overwhelm native peoples. Bouquet had called for the use of dogs on campaign as early as 1757, though he did not state specifically what they were to be used for. Six years later, with British garrisons in the west under Indian assault, Bouquet proposed the idea again. In a letter to General Amherst he wrote: "As it is a pity to expose good men against them I wish we would make use of the Spanish Method to hunt them with English Dogs, supported by Rangers and Some Light Horse, who would I think effectualy extirpate or remove that Vermin." The following year he made a similar proposal to the Pennsylvania Commissioners, recommending the purchase of fifty dogs from Great Britain. "A few Instances of Indians Seized and worried by Dogs," predicted

Bouquet, "would . . . deter them more effectualy from a War with us, than all the Troops we could raise." While Bouquet's ideas on incorporating dogs into a frontier fighting force never came to fruition, they are illustrative of the harsh, aggressive, and unyielding spirit that informed much of his approach to Indian warfare. That he considered Native American peoples as barbarians made such an approach appropriate and morally untroubling.[18]

One aspect of training on which Bouquet's "Reflections" is silent is the type of fire-system in which light troops were to be trained; that is, how the men were to be formed in battle, and how their musket fire was to be directed and controlled. By regulation, the British army at the time of the French and Indian War employed the platoon-fire system. By the 1750s, a competing drill known as the alternate-fire system was coming into use in the British army. This latter system offered superior advantages in speed, ease of use, and increased tactical flexibility and, by 1764, would become the army's regulation fire exercise. The alternate-fire system had two chief characteristics. First, as its name implies, musket fire was delivered from the ends or the middle of the battle line outward, in alternating fashion—first on one side than the other and so on. Second, companies became the tactical units delivering fire in line of battle. This allowed men to go into action in their parent companies with officers and men with whom they were familiar. This contributed to superior morale and discipline. Smaller fire units, platoons, could be created by splitting companies in half.[19]

Chaplain Thomas Barton's description of troops exercising in the woods during the Forbes campaign indicates that Bouquet was training regulars and provincials in the alternate-fire system. After the men have formed themselves into "one Rank entire," Barton wrote, "They are then divided into Platoons, each Platoon consisting of 20 Men, & fire 3 Rounds; the right-hand Man of each Platoon beginning the Fire, & then the left-hand Man; & so on Right & Left alternately till the Fire ends in the Center: Before it reaches this Place, the Right & Left are ready again. And by This Means an incessant Fire kept up." Entries from George Washington's orderly book, kept during the Forbes campaign, also document that the troops were being organized tactically according to the alternate-fire system. During the third week of November, as Forbes's army was preparing to make a quick march on Fort Duquesne, the order was given to subdivide the companies in each division "into as many Platoons as there are Sub[altern]s." The reason for making the division of the troops in this way was to keep the men from each company together with their officers. It was hoped this would enable "each Officer to keep their Men Calm and prevent their Throwing away their fire which they are too apt to do in a hurry."[20]

What battlefield formations did Henry Bouquet think best suited for forest combat? We have seen that in 1758 he believed in the efficacy of a single, extended battle line with the troops ranged in open order. Such a line could be formed rapidly by soldiers marching in columns of double files and was unlikely, in Bouquet's estimation, to be outflanked by the enemy. From this single rank, the troops delivered several well-timed volleys and then charged their foe while shrieking and yelling like Indians. This formation was never tested in combat, nor was it embraced by Bouquet's superior at the time, John Forbes, however elements of it were incorporated into the battle order most fully articulated by Bouquet later in his career—the hollow square.[21]

The hollow square had been in use among European armies "at least since the early seventeenth century." It was a defensive formation designed to protect infantry against attack from cavalry. As described in "Reflections," the hollow square provided a formation from which to act both defensively and offensively. Columns of soldiers marching in double and single file formed the sides or faces of the square. On a given signal, the columns designated to serve as the front and side faces of the square marched into formation. While this evolution was underway, the expedition's pack animals, cattle, reserve troops, and light horse were moved as quickly as possible into the center of the square. Once this body had been collected inside, the remaining column of soldiers, acting as the rear face of the square, marched to close up the whole. Marksmen posted behind trees off the line of march provided covering fire. Drawn up in this manner, the hollow square posed a formidable defensive challenge to any potential attacker.[22]

But Bouquet did not intend the square to be merely a static, defensive formation. He intended to attack from it as well, and he believed that the square offered the best means of striking a telling blow against a maddeningly elusive foe who refused to fight in the open. Bouquet's tactics took advantage of the Indian stratagem of surrounding their enemy. Once the square was encircled, four columns of woodsmen, accompanied by light horse and dogs, charged out from the corners of the formation until they had penetrated the Indian lines. Each pair of columns would then sweep toward the other in a wheeling motion taking the enemy warriors in flank. Detachments of soldiers defending the faces of the square would then march out to press home the attack. Soldiers were to "pursue the enemy until they were "totally dispersed."[23]

How and why Bouquet came to adopt the hollow square as a viable formation for Indian fighting is not known. James Smith, who served with the Pennsylvania troops on the Ohio Expedition, states that it was Captain Lemuel Barrett who proposed the formation to Bouquet during the Battle of Bushy Run. It is more likely, though, that the Swiss colonel contemplated using this tactical arrangement well before the action of 5 and 6 August. Bouquet's own accounts of the battle fail to mention his use of the hollow square. But another participant in the battle, Robert Kirk, a sergeant in the Seventy-seventh Regiment, has described how Bouquet formed his men into a square at Bushy Run. According to Kirk, the redcoats were unable to maintain this formation in the face of a relentless Indian onslaught and mounting casualties, so that by the end of the first day's fighting, the square was shattered. It was only by employing a *ruse de guerre* that Bouquet was able to rescue his command from its desperate situation. Feigning a retreat, he was able to lure his Indian attackers into charging his position. The surprised natives were greeted with a series of devastating volleys followed by a warmly pressed bayonet charge.[24]

Given how the British square was smashed at Bushy Run, the question is raised: why did Bouquet employ it again on his expedition into the Ohio the following year? The answer must be that he never lost faith in the efficacy of the square as a strong defensive formation. He states this much in "Reflections." He must have realized that the square failed at Bushy Run, not because it was an inherently weak formation, but because it was weakly manned. The experience of Bushy Run may have also established (or reinforced) in Bouquet's mind the potential for uniting the shock tactics he believed so necessary to fighting Indians, with the defensive advantages offered by the hollow square. The result was a strong defensive formation from which the army could act offensively.[25]

Bouquet's march into the Ohio Country in 1764 was a bloodless campaign, thus there was no further opportunity to test the Swiss colonel's tactics employing the hollow square. The reasons underlying Indian reluctance to attack Bouquet's force and "attempt another Bushy Run on a grander scale," writes historian Michael McConnell, "are not hard to identify." They include a native population weakened by disease and war, a shortage of firearms and ammunition, and the fear of starvation. The testimony of James Smith suggests an additional reason. In conversations with Indians at the forks of the Muskingum, Smith discovered that the tribesmen had declined to attack Bouquet's army because they always found his dispositions so wisely concerted as to offer no advantage to the attackers.[26]

Having sketched out Henry Bouquet's ideas and methods for training men to fight in the wilderness, it is clear that traditional interpretations of his role as a military tactician and frontier fighter are in need of revision. First, it cannot be said that Bouquet turned the Royal Americans into a light infantry regiment. This statement attributes to Bouquet an influence in the regiment's training and discipline that he did not have. In a regiment totaling four battalions, or forty companies, Bouquet rarely exercised authority over more than six companies at any one time. The authority to regulate the regiment's drill and instruction lay instead with the colonel-in-chief. For example, Bouquet's method of teaching his men to load and fire their muskets while "standing, kneeling, or lying on the ground" had actually been promulgated by the corps's first commander, Lord Loudoun, in December 1756. Bouquet's own practices also testify that he was not turning the men of the Sixtieth into light troops. He did not dress or accouter them as light troops, nor did he assign them the roles usually associated with light infantry. Instead, he assigned these auxiliary duties to provincials. The closest Bouquet came to employing the Royal Americans as light infantry was in his adherence to tactics and formations that emphasized speed and open order.[27]

It may also be said that Henry Bouquet does not deserve his reputation as a leading figure in the development of British tactical doctrine at this time. In fact, rather than leading the way, Bouquet was right in step with the efforts of his fellow officers to adapt the British army to fighting in the wilderness. From the arrival of Braddock's forces in Virginia in 1755, to the fall of New France and beyond, the British military leadership recognized the need to change the army's tactics, drill, and organization to meet the circumstances of an American war. Some of the more noteworthy practices introduced into the army at this time include: the establishment of light infantry companies, the adoption of lighter dress and arms for the rank and file, the use of the alternate fire system, drill in aimed fire, and training in bush fighting techniques. Nor was Bouquet the only officer to draft imaginative plans for conducting operations in America. James Prevost, a fellow Swiss, and founder of the Royal Americans, proposed the establishment of a body of light troops on a model very similar to that set forth in "Reflections." Where Henry Bouquet stands apart from his peers seems to be in his greater faith in the value of shock action rather than firepower in fighting Indians. His use and adaptation of the hollow square for Indian fighting is also without parallel in the army during the war.[28]

In *Toward Lexington: The Role of the British Army in the Coming of the American Revolution*, John Shy reminds us how difficult it was for the British army to campaign in the North American wilderness, how vulnerable it was to disastrous setbacks and defeats. "The forces of nature were so overwhelming" that even the most carefully laid campaigns and operations could be undone by simple bad luck. Bouquet himself understood that fortune had played a significant role in his victory over the Indians in August 1763. In numerous letters, he referred to his defeat of the native warriors as "this lucky blow." It has been argued recently that British regulars were never able to cope successfully with fighting Indians, that Bushy Run was the exception to British military experience on the frontier rather than the rule. If this is so, the Battle of Bushy Run demonstrates that one needed more than cool leadership, steady conduct, and wisely concerted tactics to guarantee victory over the Indian. One also needed a generous amount of good fortune. Perhaps no one understood this as well as Henry Bouquet.[29]

NOTES

1. Bouquet to Hamilton, 11 August 1763, *The Papers of Col. Henry Bouquet*, 19 vols., ed. Sylvester K. Stevens and Donald H. Kent, (Harrisburg: Pennsylvania Historical Commission, 1940–43), 21649:16 [hereafter cited as *PCHB*]. This edition of Bouquet's published papers will be cited only when the identified document cannot be found in the more comprehensive, letterpress edition of Bouquet's papers, *The Papers of Henry Bouquet*, 6 vols., ed. Sylvester K. Stevens et al. (Harrisburg: Pennsylvania Historical and Museum Commission, 1951–94) [hereafter cited as *PHB*]. This latter edition awaits the issuance of a microfiche supplement in order to complete the publication of the Bouquet Papers project. Adam Stephen to Bouquet, 15 September 1763; and Henry Gladwin to Bouquet, 1 November 1763, *PHB* 6:393, 445. Other officers echoed Bouquet's sentiments on the significance of the British victory at Bushy Run. "I most sincerely congratulate you," wrote Archibald Blane, "on your Compleatt Victory, as well as your good fortune in being the first Person that has ever thouroughly convinced these Rascals of their inability to cope with us." Blane to Bouquet, 18 August 1763, ibid., 365.

2. A modern expression of this opinion is offered by Douglas Leach, who states that Bushy Run represented "a clear vindication of British military discipline and valor when properly sustained in the wilderness by modified tactics based on experience." Douglas E. Leach, *Arms for Empire: A Military History of the British Colonies in North America, 1607–1763* (New York: Macmillan Company, 1973), 501.

3. See Francis Parkman, *The Conspiracy of Pontiac and the Indian War after the Conquest of Canada*, 6th ed., 2 vols. (1870; Reprint, New York: Library of America, 1991), 642; Lawrence H. Gipson, *The Great War for the Empire*, 15 vols. (New York: Alfred A. Knopf, 1936–70), 7:258; and John Shy, *Toward Lexington: The Role of the British Army in the Coming of the American Revolution* (Princeton:

Princeton University Press, 1965), 290; Edward Hutton, *Colonel Henry Bouquet, 60th Royal Americans. 1756–1765: A Biographical Sketch* (Winchester, Eng.: Warren & Son, 1911), 37; and J. F. C. Fuller, *British Light Infantry in the Eighteenth Century* (London: Hutchinson and Co., 1925), 98; James H. Silcox, "Rogers and Bouquet: The Origins of American Light Infantry," *Military Affairs* 65 (December 1985): 62–74; Kemp Malone, ". . . the greatest Indian fighter of them all," in *The Unforgettable Americans*, ed. John A. Garraty (Great Neck, N.Y.: Channel Press, 1960), 48; Lewis Butler, *The Annals of the King's Royal Rifle Corps*, 6 vols. to date (London: Smith, Elder and Co., 1913–), 1:194.

4. The best source on Bouquet's early military service is Paul-Emile Schazmann's article, "Henry Bouquet in Switzerland," published in *PHB* 1:xvi-xxiii; and Charles G. F. Dumas's "Sketch of the Life of the Late Mr. Bouquet," also printed in ibid., 1:xxiv-xvii. Additional important details can be gleaned from Beal-Emanuel May, *Histoire militaire de la Suisse, et celle des Suisses dans les différens services de l'Europe. Composée et redigé sur des oeuvrages et pieces authentiques*, 8 vols. (Lausanne, Switz.: J. P. Heubach et Comp., 1788), vols. 7 and 8. Spenser Wilkinson, *The Defence of Piedmont, 1742–1748: A Prelude to the Study of Napoleon* (Oxford, Eng.: Clarendon Press, 1927) provides an excellent treatment of the theater in which Bouquet campaigned. Bouquet was familiar with Caesar's *Commentaries* and Turpin de Crissé's *Essai sur l'art de la guerre*. He refers to the former in his "Reflections on the War with the Savages of North-America," published in William Smith, *Historical Account of Bouquet's Expedition against the Ohio Indians, in 1764* (1765; Reprint, Cincinnati: Robert Clarke and Co., 1868), 103. If he was not already, Bouquet became familiar with Turpin de Crissé's study during the Forbes Expedition of 1758. Forbes cited the Frenchman's essay as providing the model for his use of the protected advance. See Forbes to William Pitt, 20 October 1758, *Writings of General John Forbes Relating to his Service in North America* (Menasha, Wisc.: Collegiate Press, 1938), 239–40. During the eight years Bouquet spent in Dutch service prior to joining the British army, he would have had ample opportunity to build his professional library. At that time "no other region of Europe was as thickly blanketed with bookstores as the province of Holland." Jeremy D. Popkin, "Print Culture in the Netherlands on the Eve of the Revolution," in *The Dutch Republic in the Eighteenth Century: Decline, Enlightenment, and Revolution*, ed. Margaret C. Jacob and Wijnand W. Mijnhardt (Ithaca, N.Y.: Cornell University Press, 1992), 275.

5. For example, Lewis Butler and J. F. C. Fuller accept Bouquet's "Reflections on the War with the Savages of North-America" as a factual account of practices Bouquet employed in fighting Indians. Francis Parkman established Smith's authorship of *Historical Account*, and Bouquet's authorship of "Reflections." *Historical Account*, xv-xvi. For examples of the misinterpretation of Bouquet's "Reflections," see Butler, *Annals* 1:159–62; Fuller, *British Light Infantry*, 106–10; and, more recently, Hew Strachan, *European Armies and the Conduct of War* (London: George Allen and Unwin, 1983), 28.

6. "Reflections," 95–110, provides a general discussion of the Indian warrior's character. Indian maxims are listed on page 109. On the Indian's tactic of surrounding their foe, see Bouquet to Forbes, 20 August 1758, *PHB* 2:397, in which Bouquet writes: "In all the encounters in the field or in the woods, I notice that the enemy—especially the Indians—attack our flanks first and try to surround us." For another contemporary description of this tactic, see James Adair, *The History of the American Indian*. . . . (1775; Reprint, New York: Johnson Reprint Corp., 1968), 386. On the misinterpretation of the retreating tactic by whites, see Leroy V. Eid, "'A Kind of Running Fight': Indian Battlefield Tactics in the Late Eighteenth Century," *Western Pennsylvania Historical Magazine* 71 (April 1988): 150–52; and James Smith, *An Account of the Remarkable Occurrences in the Life and Travels of Col. James Smith, during*

His Captivity with the Indians, in the Years 1755, '56, '57, '58, & '59 (Cincinnati: Robert Clarke and Co., 1870), 159.

7. "Reflections," 100–1 at 101. Bouquet spoke movingly on the destructive character of frontier service on regular discipline. In requesting that the Royal Americans be allowed to winter in the settlements, he noted "That Corps having been Six years in the Woods, and their Spirit So much cast down, I would hope that a little Rest would recruit them, and make them more fit for Service in the Spring: If they are Kept here another Winter, I foresee a great desertion, and the rest discouraged will be good for nothing." Bouquet to Jeffery Amherst, *PHB* 6:438.

8. "Reflections," 111. The importance of youth in recruiting troops for light service was noted by contemporary authors on partisan warfare. According to Johann von Ewald, "young people of sixteen to eighteen years of age were those who best withstood the climate and the strain" of campaign. Johann von Ewald, *Treatise on Partisan Warfare*, trans. and ed. Robert A. Selig and David C. Skaggs (1785; Reprint, Westport, Conn.: Greenwood Press, 1991), 69. Grandmaison believed "the soldiers of light infantry, should be as robust and strong as can be procured, without regard to height." Thomas Auguste Le Roy de Grandmaison, *A Treatise, on the Military Service, of Light Horse, and Light Infantry, in the Field and Fortified Places*, trans. Lewis Nicola (1756; Reprint, Philadelphia: Robert Bell, 1777), 13.

9. Bouquet to Amherst, 24 October 1763, *PHB* 6:437. See also Bouquet to Amherst, 26 July 1763, ibid., 326; and Bouquet to James Robertson, 26 July 1763, *PCHB* 21634:225. Lord Loudoun remarked that Americans were "stronger and hardier fellows than the Indians" and that they ought to be bred up to the ranging service. Lord Loudoun to Duke of Cumberland, 22 November–26 December 1756, *Military Affairs in North America, 1748–1765: Selected Documents from the Cumberland Papers in Windsor Castle*, ed. Stanley Pargellis (1936; Reprint, Archon Books, 1969), 269. The Duke of Cumberland seconded Loudoun's efforts to encourage "the Soldiers to go out with . . . the Rangers." Cumberland to Loudoun, 22 October 1756, ibid., 251. On Robert Rogers training of British officers in ranging tactics, see Robert Rogers, *Journals of Major Robert Rogers* (1765; Reprint, New York: Corinth Books, 1961), 41–43.

10. "Reflections," 111–13 at 111, 113. Most authors on partisan warfare were in agreement that troops needed only a musket and a bayonet. See Ewald, *Treatise*, 72; Grandmaison, *Treatise*, 15; Louis de Jeney added "a light short Sabre" to the standard musket and bayonet. Louis de Jeney, *The Partisan: or, the Art of Making War in Detachment. With Plans Proper to Facilitate the Understanding of the Several Dispositions and Movements Necessary to Light Troops, in Order to Accomplish their Marches, Ambuscades, Attacks and Retreats with Success* (1759; Reprint, London: R. Griffiths, 1760), 15. Bouquet to Forbes, 21 June 1758, *PHB* 2:124; and Forbes to Bouquet, 27 June 1758, ibid., 136. Bouquet to Washington, 11 July 1758, ibid., 183; and Washington to Bouquet, 13 July 1758, ibid., 203. In 1759, the First Battalion of the Royal Americans wore green leggings with red garters. The following year they wore blue leggings trimmed in red. John Tulleken to Bouquet, 5 March 1759, ibid., 3:177; Tulleken to Bouquet, 1 March 1760, ibid., 4:478; and John Schlösser to Bouquet, 23 April 1760, ibid., 4:528. It is probable that the Royal Americans cut their coats short as did other regiments. For an example of another regiment's practices, see the obituary of Lord George Howe, in *Scottish Magazine* 20 (August 1758): 442. Light infantry companies were ordered established for every battalion in America in 1759. The only detail of the Sixtieth's light infantry uniform mentioned in Bouquet's papers states that they had no facings. John Tullekin to Bouquet, 5 March 1759, *PHB* 3:177. A fuller description of light infantry uniforms ordered by James Wolfe may be found in John Knox, *An Historical Journal of the Campaigns in North America for the Years 1757, 1758, 1759, and 1760. . . .* , ed. Arthur G. Doughty, 3

vols. (1769; Reprint, Toronto: The Champlain Society, 1916), 1:352–53. The Sixtieth's grenadier uniform is fully described in Alexander Baillie to Bouquet, *PCHB* 21648:77–78. The average weight of equipment, arms, and clothing carried by regular soldiers was 60 pounds and could run as high as 125 pounds. David Gates, *The British Light Infantry Arm, c. 1790–1815* (London: B. T. Batsford, 1987), 13.

11. "Reflections," at 114; on march formation, 128–30. Compare the phrasing in "Reflections" with Bouquet to John Reid, 15 June 1764, *PHB* 6:571, in which Bouquet writes: "The only Exercise to be practised is to march, run, & wheel in a Rank Intire with open Files." Note the reference to recruits for the Sixtieth being taught to charge in Schlösser to Bouquet, 7 April 1760, ibid., 4:513.

12. "Detail of a Proposed Expedition to Fort Duquesne," 18 March 1757, ibid., 1:52. Bouquet to Forbes, 20 August 1758, ibid., 2:397. William A. Hunter, ed., "Thomas Barton and the Forbes Expedition," *Pennsylvania Magazine of History and Biography* 95 (October 1971): 449–50. Joseph Shippen also noticed Bouquet's unique method of exercising his troops. In a letter of 15 August 1758, he wrote: "Every afternoon he [Bouquet] exercised his men in the woods and bushes in a particular manner of his own invention which will be of great service in an engagement with the Indians." Quoted in Joseph R. Riling, *The Art and Science of War in America, 1690–1800* (Alexandria Bay, N.Y.: Museum Restoration Service, 1990), 4.

13. "Reflections," 115. "Detail of a Proposed Expedition to Fort Duquesne," 18 March 1757, *PHB* 1:53. Edward G. Williams, *Bouquet's March to the Ohio: The Forbes Road* (Pittsburgh: Historical Society of Western Pennsylvania, 1975), 28. For examples of use of tree cover, see ibid., and Edward G. Williams, *The Orderly Book of Colonel Henry Bouquet's Expedition against the Ohio Indians, 1764* (Pittsburgh: Mayer Press, 1960), 18. Note in this last reference the men being ordered to lie down on the ground in case of night attack so they will "not be unnecessarily exposed." The editor of Bouquet's papers notes that Bouquet never employed full concealment as a tactic on any of his campaigns. Louis Waddell, "The American Career of Henry Bouquet, 1755–1765," *Swiss American Historical Society Newsletter* 18 (February 1981): 35. Other regiments in the army *did* take cover behind trees when they came under fire. See the testimony given at the court-martial of Henry Garman, of the Thirty-fifth Regiment. When Garman's unit came under attack in the woods, the order was given to "Tree all, Tree all." Record of a court-martial held at Fort Edward, 9 July 1757, Public Record Office, War Office 71/30. There is likewise a description in the papers of John Forbes of the troops being trained "to practise firing at Marks, and of taking their Stations behind trees." Scottish Record Office, Dalhousie Muniments, John Forbes Papers, GD 2/34/11.

14. Bouquet to Forbes, 7 June 1758, *PHB* 2:50. Provincial troops did not always outshoot the regular troops. See the comparisons between regulars and provincials shooting at marks in Blane to Bouquet, ibid., 3:167. Blane noted: "All the Pen^s [Pennsylvanians] that fire have not Riffles, nor do those that have make the best Shots." Many Americans were surprisingly inept at handling firearms. For examples of accidental shootings caused by provincial soldiers, see *The Journal of Caleb Rea*, ed. F. M. Ray (Salem, Mass.: Essex Institute, 1881), 18–21. "Detail of a Proposed Expedition to Fort Duquesne," 18 March 1757, *PHB* 1:51. Bouquet to Hugh Mercer, 26 December 1758, ibid., 2:643. Williams, *Bouquet's March*, 116–19. Note that in "Reflections," Bouquet recommends the offering of "small premiums" to make young soldiers expert marksmen. On shortages of lead in 1758, see Bouquet to Forbes, 7 June 1758, *PHB* 2:50, 675, 676, 677. On shortages of lead in 1764, see Bouquet to John Reid, ibid., 6:571; and Williams, *Bouquet's March*, 103, 111.

15. On the need for special gunpowder for rifles, see Bouquet to Forbes, 7 June 1758, *PHB* 2:50. On the need for riflemen to cast their shot individually, see Williams, *Bouquet's March*, 129.

16. "Reflections," 113. Bouquet to Sir John St. Clair, 3 June 1758, *PHB* 2:22. Williams, *Bouquet's March,* 107. A contemporary officer's opinion on the deadliness of hatchet-like weapons is printed in George A. Bray III, "Major George Scott's Provisional Light Infantry Battalion, 1758," *Military Collector & Historian* 47 (spring 1995): 26. The officer, Major George Scott, states that "The Scalping-Ax is intended to serve instead of a broad Sword, as a blow from the Ax is infinitly more dangerous to him that receives it, than two or three from a board-Sword would be, and besides this, the Scalping-Ax will be found of great use in marching through woods and Encamping." William Windham and George Lord Townshend, *A Plan of Discipline for the Use of the Norfolk Militia,* 2d ed. (Whitehall, Eng.: J. Millan, 1768), see note on pp. 14–15. William Dalrymple considered the bayonet an awkward and unnecessary weapon. William Dalrymple, *Tacktics* (Dublin: George Bonham, 1782), 14. J. C. A. Houlding, *Fit for Service: The Training of the British Army, 1715–1795* (Oxford: Clarendon Press, 1981), 261n. 10.

17. "It would be easier to make Indians of our White men, than to coax that damnd Tanny Race," a vexed Bouquet wrote to Washington. Bouquet to Washington, 14 July 1758, *PHB* 2:206. A similar observation is made in Bouquet to Washington, 10 August 1758, ibid., 351. The use of light horse was deemed so essential to the army's operations in 1759 and 1764 that special requests were made to the Pennsylvania Assembly to provide funds for the needed horse troops. See John Stanwix to William Denny, 12 June 1759, in Samuel Hazard, ed. *Minutes of the Provincial Council of Pennsylvania, from the Organization to the Termination of the Proprietary Government,* 16 vols. (Harrisburg, Pa.: J. Severns, 1838–53), 8:352–53; and Bouquet to John Penn and the Provincial Commissioners, 4 June 1764, *PHB* 6:555.

18. "Reflections," 116–17 at 117. John G. and Jeannette J. Varner, *Dogs of the Conquest* (Norman: University of Oklahoma Press, 1983), xiv. Montecuccoli reports that mounted Finnish soldiers employed dogs to disrupt enemy troop formations. Thomas M. Barker, *The Military Intellectual and Battle: Raimondo Montecuccoli and the Thirty Years' War* (Albany: SUNY Press, 1975), 126. Benjamin Franklin had suggested using dogs in "the Spanish Method" against Indians in 1755. See Franklin to James Read, 2 November 1755, *Papers of Benjamin Franklin,* ed. Leonard W. Labaree et al., 30 vols. to date (New Haven, Conn.: Yale University Press, 1959-), 6:235. Bouquet, "Detail of a Proposed Expedition to Fort Duquesne," 18 March 1757, *PHB* 1:52. The text states: "Dogs to be provided as much as possible to be Send with ye Parties." It appears from the context that the dogs were likely to be used to alert out-parties to the presence of the enemy. Bouquet to Amherst, 13 July 1763, *PCHB* 21634:215. For Amherst's response to Bouquet's proposal, see Amherst Memorandum, 16 July 1763, *PHB* 6:315. Pennsylvania Commissioner John Hughes had written to Bouquet on 11 July recommending the use of dogs against the Indians. See Hughes to Bouquet, 11 July 1763, ibid., 6:304–5. Bouquet to Penn and the Provincial Commissioners, 4 June 1763, ibid., 6:555. Michael N. McConnell discusses "the pervasiveness of Indian hating" in the wake of the Pan-Indian uprising of 1763 in *A Country Between: The Upper Ohio Valley and Its Peoples, 1724–1774* (Lincoln: University of Nebraska Press, 1992), 194–95.

19. For a succinct description of the platoon-fire and alternate-fire system, see Houlding, *Fit for Service,* 318–21.

20. Hunter, "Thomas Barton," 449, 450. Orderly Book, 20 November 1758, *Papers of George Washington, Colonial Series,* ed. W. W. Abbot et al., 10 vols. (Charlottesville: University Press of Virginia, 1983–95), 6:146, 147.

21. Bouquet to Forbes, 20 August 1758, *PHB* 2:397; and Hunter, "Thomas Barton," 450. Forbes's disposition for meeting the enemy differs markedly from Bouquet's. See "Explanation of a line of Battle," item

500, Papers of John Forbes, Charlottesville, University of Virginia, Tracy W. McGregor Library. George Washington offered a plan of battle and march that also differed from Bouquet's. Washington to Forbes, 8 October 1758, *Papers of George Washington*, 6:66–70.

22. Brent Nosworthy, *The Anatomy of Victory: Battle Tactics, 1689–1763* (New York: Hippocrene Books, 1990), 255. William Dalrymple describes the successful use of the hollow square by Russian troops at the Battle of Kahal against large numbers of Turkish cavalry. Dalrymple, *Tacticks*, 121.

23. "Reflections," 128–34 at 134.

24. James Smith, *A Treatise, on the Mode and Manner of Indian War.* . . . (1812; Reprint, Chicago: Barnard and Miller, 1948), 6. Smith reports that after the advance guard of the column was overpowered, Barrett approached Bouquet "and told him to force his men out on every direction so as to form a hollow square, and get behind trees, and if they did not do this, the army would be cut off." To which, he reports, Bouquet complied. A month after the action at Bushy Run, Captain Harry Gordon wrote to Bouquet: "You have many Times talkt of the Disposition you put in Practise, as preferring it, and I made no Doubt the Consequence would shew the Justice of your Thoughts." Harry Gordon to Bouquet, 4 September 1763, *PCHB* 21649:39. For Bouquet's accounts of the battle, see Bouquet to Amherst, 5 and 6 August 1763, *PHB* 6:338–40, 342–44. Robert Kirk, *The Memoirs and Adventures of Robert Kirk, Late of the Royal Highland Regiment.* . . . (Limerick, Ire.: J. Ferral, 1770?), 76–79.

25. "Reflections," 108. At Bushy Run, Bouquet had four hundred men, a quarter of which became casualties. In "Reflections," Bouquet called for manning a hollow square formation with 1,200 men. This was the size of his force on the Ohio Expedition.

26. McConnell, *A Country Between*, 201; Smith, *A Treatise*, 50.

27. "Detail of a Proposed Expedition to Fort Duquesne," 18 March 1757, *PHB* 1:52. Compare with Loudoun's instructions: the men "are to be taught to load and fire, lying on the Ground and kneeling." Loudoun to Battalion Commanders of the Royal American Regiment, 28 December 1756, item 2421, box 56, Loudoun Papers, Huntington Library.

28. James Prevost, "Mémoire sur la Guerre d'Amérique," *Military Affairs in North America*, 337–40.

29. Shy, *Toward Lexington*, 88. Bouquet to Hamilton, 11 August 1763, *PCHB* 21649:16; Bouquet to James McDonald, 28 August 1763, ibid., 31; Bouquet to Stephen, 30 September 1763, ibid., 72. Steve Brumwell, "'A Service Truly Critical': The British Army and Warfare with the North American Indians, 1755–1764," *War in History* 5 (April 1998): 174; and Eid, "Indian Battlefield Tactics," 166–71.

The Microbes of War: The British Army and Epidemic Disease among the Ohio Indians, 1758–1765

MATTHEW C. WARD

Between 1755 and 1815 Britain and the United States took possession of the Ohio Valley and Great Lakes region from its Native American inhabitants. That they were able to do so bears witness not only to American and European military superiority, but also to the population decline of the Indian peoples. During the "Sixty Years' War for the Great Lakes" Indian populations declined precipitously.[1] This population decline was caused not primarily by warfare but by disease. Indeed, for North America as a whole, historian Russell Thornton has argued that "warfare . . . [was] not very significant overall in the American Indian population decline."[2] The relationship between disease and Indian population decline is well documented. However, most work has focused on explaining the prevalence of "virgin soil epidemics," which swept through Indian populations in the century after first contact. By the mid–eighteenth century, the Great Lakes region and Ohio Valley were anything but "virgin soil."[3]

Between 1758, when forces under the command of Major General John Forbes occupied the forks of the Ohio River, and the final conclusion to "Pontiac's Rebellion" in 1765, the British army and the Native American population of this region came into close contact. During this period the British army itself served as a vector for a number of diseases, which it transmitted directly to the Native

American population. In addition, British military and Indian policy served to heighten the susceptibility of the Indian peoples to disease. The British army and its commanders were aware of the role it played in spreading disease. In July 1763, following the outbreak of "Pontiac's Rebellion," a frustrated Jeffery Amherst, the Commander in Chief of British forces in North America, wrote to Colonel Henry Bouquet commander of the Forty-second Regiment stationed in the Ohio Valley. He asked Bouquet, "could it not be contrived to Send the *Small Pox* among those Disaffected Tribes of Indians? We must, on this occasion, Use Every Stratagem in our Power to Reduce them."[4] A week later Amherst offered further encouragement to Bouquet, informing him "You will Do well to try to Innoculate the *Indians*, by means of Blankets, as well as to Try every other Method, that can Serve to Extirpate this Execrable Race."[5]

There is little direct evidence that the British army ever consciously used "germ warfare." In the eighteenth century, the process of disease transmission remained a mystery and while the Fort Pitt garrison may have redistributed a few blankets from the smallpox hospital in response to Amherst's memorandum, following the start of the siege most of the Indian headmen who would have accepted such gifts would have been pro-British, the group whom Amherst and other commanders would not have wanted to undermine. In addition, the attempted use of such tactics would certainly have been a two-edged sword, for disease could easily have spread back amongst the crowded ranks of the army—not to mention the colonial population. Whether, had attempts been made, they could have been successful is also open to question. The smallpox virus *Variola Major* can, under certain conditions, exist in a dried state. However, it prefers cool and dry conditions, hardly those of mid-summer in the Ohio Valley. Although the chances of its long-term survival are slight, its transmission via infected blankets is thus at least potentially feasible.[6] Such a debate over attempts to spread smallpox, however, obscures the real importance of disease. Amherst's comments reflect a direct consciousness of the important role of British army in spreading disease and the role that disease was playing in undermining Indian ability to resist the British.

In the years immediately following the British capture of Fort Duquesne in 1758, the Ohio Valley and Great Lakes region witnessed a series of epidemics, which resulted in substantial population loss and social dislocation. While records are not sufficiently detailed to reconstruct an accurate epidemic and disease profile, and attempts to identify specific epidemics must also be rather tentative, it is possible to uncover a generalized chronology. During the late spring of 1761, the Ohio towns were visited by an illness, which at first took the life of several headmen. This epidemic was almost certainly a strain of influenza, probably transmitted by British troops; indeed, the first reports of the epidemic came from British garrisons. In March, Richard Mather at Fort Venango reported an epidemic amongst the garrison, which consisted of a high fever, pain in the muscles and joints, and stiffness and fatigue. By the summer, the epidemic had spread across the region and indeed seems to have affected most of the Indian peoples of Eastern North America.[7]

In 1762 another epidemic struck, which by the late summer had become particularly fierce and had swept through most parts of the Ohio Country. Descriptions by traders suggest that this epidemic may have been typhus. The epidemic soon spread across the Great Lakes. Thomas Hutchins, who traveled through the western posts in the late summer of 1762, reported a widespread sickness across the west. At St. Joseph in August, the Potawatomi reported that "their whole Nation was afflicted with Sickness which rendered them incapable of hunting." At Ouiatenon, the Weas, Kickapoos, Mascoutens, and Piankashaws informed him that they were "very miserable . . . on Account of a Severe Sickness that has Seized almost all our People many of which have died lately and many more are likely to Die." At Lower Shawnee Town on the Scioto River he found the Shawnees and Delawares "mostly Sick, & some Dying every day."[8] Over 180 of the town's inhabitants were said to have succumbed. The epidemic also spread east to the Iroquois. At the beginning of December, a party of Iroquois headmen who traveled to Fort Pitt complained "that we have been very Sickly this Summer & fall and has Lost Several of our pople [sic]."[9]

There were also several isolated outbreaks of smallpox. During 1755 and 1756, a major smallpox epidemic had swept through Canada. Those Algonquians who served alongside the French on the Ohio or on the St. Lawrence returned home carrying the disease with them. While the epidemic does not seem to have spread much further west than Fort Duquesne, it provided a reservoir for future infection.[10] After 1759, as Indian refugees abandoned their eastern homes and moved west, sporadic outbreaks occurred across the Great Lakes. Another source for the growing epidemic was the newly established British garrisons in the west. When James Gorrell arrived at Green Bay in October 1761, the Menominee informed him that they had "Lost Three Hundred Warriers lately with the Small pox."[11] A substantial loss when, by 1768, the total Menominee population appears to have declined to only 800.[12] By the end of 1764, isolated outbreaks of smallpox had become more widespread and a general smallpox epidemic spread across the Ohio Valley, Great Lakes, and Illinois Country. Indeed, the epidemic grew so bad that some British officials claimed that during Pontiac's conspiracy headmen were "Sincerely inclined to make peace" as they were "verry much reduced by the Small Pox &ca."[13]

In 1764 another unidentified epidemic spread amongst the Ohio Peoples. Sir William Johnson, superintendent of Indian Affairs in the northern colonies, claimed that "the Shawanes lost in three Months time 149 Men besides Women & Children" suggesting a total population loss of around four hundred.[14] As population estimates place the total Shawnee population in the late 1760s at only 1,800, this epidemic was clearly a major demographic disaster.[15] The general pattern of disease in the Ohio Valley and Great Lakes that thus emerges is of four specific epidemics: influenza in 1761, typhus in 1762, and smallpox in 1763–64, followed by an unidentified illness in 1764. In addition to this there was a background level of other illnesses, most probably amoebic dysentery.

There are several explanations offered by historians as to why the native peoples of North America were so prone to European diseases, while the white colonial population was not. Native peoples, it is argued, lacked an inherited resistance to European diseases. European children inherited some resistance, but not immunity, to epidemic disease from their mothers before birth. European populations continually exposed to epidemics always possessed a substantial proportion of the population who was immune to any particular contagion limiting its spread. However, where European populations had not been exposed to viruses they remained as vulnerable as the Native American population. In 1707, for instance, a smallpox epidemic struck Iceland killing nearly a third of the population. In 1846, a measles epidemic killed over a quarter of the population of the Faeroe Islands.[16]

Another explanation for the high mortality rates is simply the provision of inappropriate treatment for a particular disease. In the seventeenth century, the Huron, for instance, treated most diseases by a combination of dieting, sweating, incisions and bleeding.[17] Such treatments would only have exacerbated eruptive diseases such as smallpox and greatly increased mortality rates. Yet another argument offered by historians is that European childhood diseases, such as chickenpox, measles, and mumps, which have a comparatively mild effect on children, have a much more serious effect on adults. As most Europeans had experienced these diseases as children they escaped the most serious effects. When Native Americans encountered these diseases as adults the effects were much more severe, and they suffered a substantially higher mortality rate. Finally, the combined effect of all these epidemics following quickly on top of one another weakened an individual's constitution until they finally succumbed to one of them.

These explanations are all plausible reasons for the high mortality rates experienced by the Native peoples in the sixteenth and early seventeenth century. However, they apply almost exclusively to "virgin soil" epidemics, the spread of a disease into a population that had no immunity at all. By 1760, the Ohio Valley and Great Lakes region were not "virgin soil." The first epidemics of European diseases may have reached the region in the 1530s and certainly had swept through the region by the 1630s, killing as many as two-thirds of the Native inhabitants. The Huron, for instance, suffered an epidemic of measles in 1634, influenza in 1636, scarlet fever in 1637, and smallpox in 1639.[18] By the 1760s, the Native peoples, thus, had over 130 years of exposure to European diseases. In addition, if the Indian peoples of the region were suffering in the 1760s from exposure to childhood illnesses, why had the epidemics not run their course earlier during 1756 and 1757, when Indian villages contained hundreds of children captured in raids on the colonial frontier?

Population studies of the native populations of other regions, in particular California, Mexico, and Peru, have also suggested a distinctive demographic pattern. Virgin soil epidemics ushered in a century of sharp population decline. However, there then followed a period of stability and even population growth.[19] If the Indian peoples of the Ohio Valley and Great Lakes had already been exposed to well over a century of European diseases, it is difficult to explain the continuing incidence of epidemics in terms of "virgin soil."

The incidence of epidemic disease in the Ohio Valley and Great Lakes in the early 1760s can, however, be explained in part by the presence of a new disease vector among the Indian peoples, the British army. The British army of the mid–eighteenth century served as a major source of disease. Many of the rank and file came from the crowded slums of British towns and cities and were carriers of a variety of epidemic diseases. Typhus, carried by lice, and dysentery and typhoid, spread by contaminated water, were very common among the ranks and spread quickly through camps and garrisons. Smallpox was endemic in nearly all of Britain's major cities and had infected over three-quarters of soldiers in infantry battalions. Contact with Native populations could easily transmit these diseases. Close contact of a more intimate kind also spread syphilis and gonorrhea.[20] The mere presence of the British army thus greatly increased the exposure of the Algonquian and Iroquoian peoples to diseases. Indeed, the presence of the British army spread diseases, which proved not only fatal to Indian populations but also to the white Anglo-American population, for American colonists had little more resistance to some European diseases than the Indian peoples. Following the posting of army units on the Pennsylvania frontier in 1757, several epidemics swept through the colony. This included a major smallpox epidemic, as well as outbreaks of typhus and dysentery. The *Pennsylvania Gazette* reported in August of that year that "There is now such a severe Sickness in these Parts (the like has not been known) that many Families can neither fight nor run away, [from the frontier raids] which occasions great Distress on the Frontiers."[21] At the same time in Virginia, Landon Carter reported "It has been a very Aguish Season. Many of my people have been ill and are dayly falling down . . . with the ague and fever."[22] These epidemics continued through 1758, but had largely run their course by 1759, although small outbreaks of smallpox continued through the early 1760s.

The army served as an even greater disease pool if units had only recently returned from service abroad. The Forty-sixth Regiment, for instance, returned straight from Havana, in Cuba, to service on the Ohio frontier. The army's contractor described them on their return as "very Sickly indeed near one half of those sent for New York are Dead and Dying Dayly by Dousens."[23] The conditions in which the troops served further increased the incidence of disease. British garrisons in the west were isolated from their supply bases and lacked fresh fruit and vegetables. Dried and salted pork formed the major component of the troops' diet. The resultant malnutrition greatly increased the incidence of disease.

Lacking fresh supplies, British garrisons in the west were overwhelmed by disease, in particular typhus and dysentery. Amoebic dysentery, caused by the parasite *Entamoeba histolytica*, was spread by the unsanitary conditions found in many of the British camps. Provincial troops, in particular, unused to camp life were reluctant to use the "necessary houses." Henry Bouquet was forced to issue explicit standing orders that "No Man [should] presume to ease himself any where near the Camp, but in the House of Office." Even when the men used the necessary houses, there were problems because they were often built too close to the camp and were allowed to overflow.[24] Dysentery seems to have been a particular problem at Fort Pitt where, according to trader James Kenny, there was nothing "but Bad Water."[25]

Typhus, spread by the human body louse *Pendiculus humanus*, also found fertile ground among the ranks of the army. The men were reluctant to shave and keep clean and had to be ordered to wash themselves and their clothes. When they did wash it was in the same springs and streams from which the drinking water was taken. Such behavior forced Forbes to issue standing orders that "Cleanliness in Camp is particularly to be taken Care of, by sweeping the Streets and Communications twice a day." Sweeping the streets was especially important as the street cleaners had to ensure "that the Camp is kept clean & free off all Dead Carcasses & Deseased Horses."[26]

The newly established British garrisons in the west thus became havens for disease. Over the winter of 1759–60, Fort Niagara was particularly sickly. Over 149 men, including the garrison's commander, succumbed.[27] At Fort Ligonier, in April 1759, Samuel Weiser reported "there are not 25 men in this Garrison that have not the Scurvy, they die fast, some have shrivelled limbs [and] can neither move back nor forwards . . . if thes[e] people must stay four weeks longer here, they will all die without Exception."[28]

The presence of this disease pool in the west was a new development as the size and composition of the British garrisons were different from the French garrisons, which they replaced. The French garrisons in the region had been smaller and generally better supplied than their later British counterparts. French supply routes were easier to maintain than British routes as the French utilized the water routes to transport supplies across the Great Lakes and down the Ohio River system whereas the British hauled most of their supplies hundreds of miles by wagon-train over the Appalachian Mountains. In winter many of the French troops were withdrawn to lessen the supply burden. Those who remained often grew most of their own fruit and vegetables, and hunted to provide fresh meat. British troops remained at post throughout the year, in part because of the difficulty of recalling troops from the far west. They also proved singularly inept at hunting and "living off the land," although there were belated attempts to encourage garrisons to grow their own fruit and vegetables.

The men who served in the French garrisons were often not European recruits, but Canadian militia who had been born in North America and were thus much less likely to be carriers of European diseases. Even if they were French, they had often already served in North America for a considerable time.[29] In contrast, the British garrisons were composed, to a large part, of regular troops many only recently arrived from Britain or the Caribbean. Even the provincial troops who served in the frontier garrisons were often immigrants. Nearly three-quarters of the men who served in the Pennsylvania Regiment, for instance, had been born in Europe, while only one in six had been born in Pennsylvania. Provincial troops were also often recruited in the colonies' ports and towns, which, while not the pools of disease of European cities, were the major centers of disease in the North American colonies. Thus, like their British counterparts, they were also often carriers of epidemic disease.[30]

After the French surrender of Canada in 1760, the British extended their occupation of the Great Lakes, taking possession of the remainder of French outposts, from Fort Venango in western Pennsylvania to Michilimackinac at the northern end of Lakes Huron and Michigan. The largest garrison was at Fort Pitt with nearly two hundred and fifty men. There were also garrisons of a similar size at Oswego on Lake Ontario and at Niagara. There was a smaller garrison of nearly one hundred at Detroit and yet smaller garrisons of between ten and twenty-five in the isolated western posts at Michilimackinac, Green Bay, Miami, St. Joseph, Ouiatanon, Presque Isle, and Venango. In addition there were several forts manned by Virginia and Pennsylvania along the Appalachian Ridge, and upper reaches of the Susquehanna Valley. This meant that by 1761 several hundred British troops were stationed in the Ohio Valley and Great Lakes. The mere presence of these troops exposed the Indian peoples to a new and much wider range of epidemic diseases than they had previously encountered and, in part, accounts for the onset of epidemics in 1761.[31]

However, it was not only the presence of British troops that increased the exposure of the Indian peoples to disease. Changes in diplomatic procedure forced Indian headmen to spend increased time in garrison posts and colonial towns. Under the French regime most diplomacy had been conducted in the Ohio villages. In the wake of the British occupation of the region Indian headmen were forced to attend a repeated cycle of conferences and treaties with the British. Many of these conferences were held at Fort Pitt, Niagara, or Detroit, but others were held in towns such as Lancaster and Easton in Pennsylvania. Not only were headmen forced to travel to colonial towns or forts for diplomatic encounters, but also the British specifically limited trade to forts. Headmen were thus forced to go to Fort Pitt or other forts to trade in addition to their attendance at conferences. Most headmen were, therefore, present in British forts, on average, on at least three separate occasions during the year. During the French regime, traders had frequently traveled to Indian towns, now Indians had to travel to British outposts, again increasing their exposure to disease.[32]

Trade also increased the susceptibility of the Indian peoples to disease in other ways. The item, which generated most problems, was alcohol. Alcohol itself has emerged as a major contributory factor to disease amongst the Indian peoples throughout the colonial period and into the nineteenth century. Many observers were very succinct about the direct links between alcohol and Indian population decline. Peter Kalm claimed that brandy killed more Indians than disease. He claimed "A man can hardly have a greater desire of a thing than the Indians have for brandy . . . I have heard them say that to die by drinking brandy was a desirable and an honourable death; and indeed it was a very common thing to kill themselves by drinking this liquor to excess."[33] Benjamin Franklin commented, after observing the drunken excesses of headmen following a conference at Lancaster, that "if it be the Design of Providence to extirpate these Savages in order to make room for Cultivators of the Earth, it seems not improbable that Rum may be the appointed Means."[34] Some Indians died directly from the impact of alcohol, from acute alcohol poisoning, and from tainted liquor, while others died as a result of accidents or alcoholic brawls. Yet others suffered long-term effects such as cirrhosis of the liver.

Although most Indians probably did not drink enough, or regularly enough, to suffer directly from alcohol-related diseases, alcohol still contributed to many other health problems. At a basic level prolonged alcohol abuse made Indian hunters less capable of hunting, which in turn contributed to nutritional deficits. In addition, alcohol itself affected the body in various ways. Modern clinical studies have demonstrated the ways in which alcohol can have a detrimental affect on the liver and the blood-supply before causing cirrhosis. Even relatively mild alcohol abuse can contribute to anemia. More serious abuse can lead to inflammation of the pancreas, which in turn can lead to diabetes. Alcohol may also have a crippling effect on the musculature, even affecting the heart muscles and causing heart failure even among individuals with no other coronary artery disease.[35]

Even moderate alcohol consumption causes a malabsorption of nutrients and vitamins, which, when added to existing nutritional inadequacy, can contribute to disorders such as pellagra. The reliance of the Indian peoples on a corn-based diet already left them exposed to the vitamin deficiency pellagra—only the combination of corn and beans, or the boiling of corn in lime rich water to produce hominy, allowed the body to absorb the niacin in the corn. Pellagra itself led to a loss of motor functions and pain in the extremities, which may have made many Indians unable to hunt or work, and have been simply dismissed by white observers as laziness.[36]

With garrisons established across the west, it was difficult for colonial authorities to distinguish between legitimate traders en route to supply the garrisons, and those seeking to trade illegally with the Indians. In addition, the construction of roads across the west facilitated the transportation of alcohol. For many western settlers the prospect of distilling part of their crop of wheat or barley, transporting it across the Appalachians, and returning with a valuable load of skins, was too alluring to resist. Traders taking supplies to army posts across the Ohio Valley soon concentrated their efforts on supplying rum and whisky to the Indians. Pittsburgh in particular became a flourishing center for the liquor trade. As early as 1760, British Indian agent George Croghan had expressed his concerns about the quantities of liquor entering the Ohio Country. Yet over the following years the trade experienced an explosive growth. Under the French regime the amount of liquor entering the Great Lakes and Ohio Country was relatively small, under the new British regime there was an explosive growth in the liquor trade.[37]

There are numerous examples of the destructive effect of liquor on the Indian peoples. At Fort Michilimackinac, for instance, the Indians begged the post's commander Henry Balfour to provide them with supplies, claiming "We have nothing to cover us as well as our Wives and Children from the Cold, and if you have not compassion for us, our ruin must be inevitable, and the next Winter will prove our last." Balfour simply said to them "you had plenty of pelletry last spring; what is become thereof. It was more than sufficient to purchase what you wanted. I well know it is not by misfortune you have become miserable. When you were at Niagara you sold your pelltry for Rum, without even buying powder, Lead, or any other Things; you are continually drunk, and then you behave yourselves not as Men, but as Beasts."[38]

The impact of the widespread availability of liquor throughout the Ohio Valley increased malnutrition and caused other mild nutritional disorders. This in turn served to increase the susceptibility of the Indian peoples to disease at the very time that their exposure was increasing. The impact of these nutritional disorders resulting from alcohol consumption might not have been so dramatic had they not occurred at a time when the Indian peoples were also facing a broader subsistence crisis. The establishment of military posts and the construction of roads across the Ohio Valley seem to have had an immediate impact on the availability of game. Supply convoys, detachments of troops, the regular mail expresses between forts, all served to scare away game from traditional hunting grounds. From 1760 onward, Indian hunters repeatedly complained of a shortage of game caused by the presence of the army. In addition to the army, hundreds of white hunters flooded across the Appalachians following the establishment of British posts in the west. An officer at Fort Burd complained in 1761, "Here Comes Such Crowds of Hunters out of the Inhabitence as fills those woods at which the Indians seems very much disturbed and say the white people Kills all there Deer."[39]

The scarcity of game was particularly significant because the Indian peoples had still to recover from the Seven Years' War. Demands by the French for support, in the form of raiding parties to attack the Anglo-American frontier, meant that Indian hunters had been unable to hunt for several seasons. In addition, from 1757 to 1759 the British had sponsored a series of raids by their Cherokee and Catawba allies against Algonquian towns on the Ohio. These raids destroyed substantial quantities of food supplies, forced hunters to remain close to their villages to protect their families, and left Indian women reluctant to venture into their fields to plant crops. Consequently, by 1759 the residents of the Ohio Valley were already facing a subsistence crisis.

The raids also had another effect causing the relocation of thousands of Native Americans who moved west. As the British began to gain the upper hand in their struggles against the French, the Shawnee and Delaware inhabitants of the upper Susquehanna and Delaware valleys became increasingly uneasy. By 1758, fearing retribution for their support of the French during the war, they had begun to move west to the Ohio Valley. As British forces began to occupy the Ohio Valley itself in 1759 and 1760, many relocated once more. In many cases these refugees abandoned their crops in the fields as they fled to a safer location. This in turn led to an increased reliance on hunting and some Indian hunting grounds close to new population centers quickly suffered from over-hunting. In addition, in their new homelands hunters were often unaware of the best locations to track game, or to build fish weirs. Hunting thus became less productive at the same time that reliance upon it increased. As Indian communities typically shared resources, by the early 1760s many Indian villages were on the verge of starvation.[40]

The flood of refugees also spread disease. Indeed, it was the movement of refugees that made the spread of typhus possible. Carrying infected lice with them, villagers transmitted the virus from town to town. The overcrowded conditions in which refugees found themselves provided an ideal breeding ground for the virus and its host. Other refugees carried smallpox from the east, or from British garrisons. Without such a major relocation of population it is doubtful whether these diseases could have spread so far, and so quickly, though the Great Lakes and Ohio Valley.

The subsistence crisis was also directly affected by other changes in British policy. With the reduction of Canada, Whitehall sought to reign in the costs of the administration of North America. As pressures to control expenditure grew, General Jeffery Amherst sought to halt the distribution of Indian gifts and presents. Instead of the British supplying goods and powder as part of the diplomatic process, Amherst argued that the Indians should "be able to supply themselves with these, from the Trader, for their furrs."[41] In the summer of 1761 he brusquely ordered Johnson "to avoid all presents in future."[42] For the Algonquian and Iroquoian peoples these gifts had been a central part of the European presence in the region for the previous half-century. The French had seen gift-giving as a central and key part of their diplomacy, and to a great extent the Indians had come to reply on such supplies in times of shortage. Now was such a time, but the British instead of generously offering gifts had instead abandoned this tradition. The change in policy caused immediate hardship. Shortly after assuming command at Detroit, Captain Donald Campbell, the new British commander at the post, wrote to Bouquet that the local Indians were "in great distress for want of Ammunition [and] were absolutely Starving."[43]

Matters grew even worse when Amherst decided, that following rumors of Indian dissatisfaction, he could "pacify" them by preventing them from acquiring any ammunition.[44] Amherst believed that by depriving the Indians of ammunition he would make it more difficult for them to execute any plot against the British. However, he did not appreciate the extent to which the Algonquians and Iroquoian peoples of the region were reliant upon European firearms for hunting. By the mid-eighteenth century, few Ohio Algonquians possessed adequate skills in using the bow and arrow. While traps could be used for hunting smaller animals, most of the meat and skins produced came from deer or other large mammals. Indian hunters also needed guns for protection against both enemy Indians—such as the southern Indians who continued to launch small raids into the region—or more importantly drunken frontiersmen. Without ammunition for their guns hunting was much more dangerous and much less productive. Amherst's policy thus had a direct and immediate impact on their ability to hunt. This came on top of an existing subsistence crisis caused by the arrival of so many refugees in the region and the lingering impact of war.

From 1758 to 1763, the Indian peoples of the Ohio Valley and Great Lakes thus faced a series of separate subsistence crises that were either directly or indirectly the result of British policy. This increased their susceptibility to disease at exactly the same moment that their exposure increased with the arrival of British army units in their midst. These units carried with them diseases that found a fertile breeding ground on the Ohio. It is the combination of these circumstances, a subsistence crisis simultaneously combined with increased exposure to disease, which explains the widespread epidemics in the Ohio Valley and on the Great Lakes in the early 1760s.

The impact of disease on Native American populations was immense. Not only did it directly undermine resistance by reducing the number of warriors that any village or nation could provide, but it also had other less direct, but equally important, effects. In non-literate societies, such as those of the Algonquian and Iroquoian peoples, disease literally destroyed culture. By killing headmen and elders who were the depositaries of their society's knowledge, epidemics destroyed much tribal knowledge before it could be passed on to younger generations. Combined with the dramatic and continuing decline in numbers, this destruction of culture also had the broader impact of undermining Indian morale. Seeing their population in continual and rapid decline while white settlers flooded over the Appalachians and appeared relatively immune to the epidemics, many Algonquians questioned their cultural and spiritual future. A very direct response to this was the first attempt to reject white contact and reassert cultural influences, and it should be little wonder that the first widespread Indian cultural revival occurred at precisely this period in the Ohio Valley. In October 1762, James Kenny, the Pennsylvania agent at Fort Pitt, reported the spread in the nearby towns of the teachings of a Delaware holy man called Neolin. Neolin argued that the Indians should reject all European influences and "learn to live without any Trade or Connections with ye White people, Clothing & Supporting themselves as their forefathers did."[45] Neolin's message soon spread across the Ohio Valley and may have played a major role in fermenting unrest prior to the Outbreak of "Pontiac's Uprising" the following year.[46]

Between 1758 and 1765, the policies of the British army and of British officials thus directly contributed to a demographic disaster amongst the Ohio and Great Lakes Indian peoples. While the resulting population decline had never been a deliberate intention of the British, British officials must have been aware of the effect their policies were having upon the native inhabitants. Indeed, Amherst's comments to Bouquet, "to Send the *Small Pox* among those Disaffected Tribes of Indians" reflect his understanding of the role of disease in the region.[47] The Indians themselves also understood this role and had no doubt whom to blame for their misfortunes. An Illinois headmen commented that "The French, our brothers, have never given us any disease, but the English have scarcely arrived, and they have caused nearly all our children to die by the smallpox they have brought."[48] During this crucial period, when Indian affairs were in a state of constant flux, epidemic disease transmitted by the British army or resulting from British military policy served to undermine the capabilities of the Indian peoples. While the British army failed to win a decisive military victory over the Indian peoples in "Pontiac's Rebellion," in the long-term the power of their microbial allies was assuredly winning the conflict.

NOTES

1. Unfortunately historical sources are not accurate enough to reconstruct an exact population count. Contemporaries, such as Sir William Johnson, tended to make bold generalizations about population figures, and were principally interested in the number of warriors any village or tribe could provide.

2. Russell Thornton, *American Indian Holocaust: A Population History since 1492* (Norman: University of Oklahoma Press, 1987), 47.

3. See for instance, Alfred W. Crosby Jr., *The Columbian Exchange: Biological and Cultural Consequences of 1492* (Westport, Conn.: Greenwood Press, 1972); Henry F. Dobyns, *Their Number Become Thinned: Native American Population Dynamics in Eastern North America* (Knoxville: University of Tennessee Press, 1983); Ann F. Ramenofsky, *Vectors of Death: The Archaeology of European Contact* (Albuquerque: University of New Mexico Press, 1987).

4. [Enclosure] Amherst: Memorandum, Louis Waddell et al., eds., *The Papers of Henry Bouquet*, 6 vols. Harrisburg: Pennsylvania Historical and Museum Commission, 1951–1994), 6:301.

5. Ibid., 6:315.

6. Ramenofsky, *Vectors of Death*, 147; Russell Thornton, Jonathan Warren, and Tim Miller, "Depopulation in the Southeast after 1492," in *Disease and Demography in the Americas*, ed. John W. Verano and Douglas H. Ubelaker (Washington D.C.: Smithsonian Institution, 1992), 191.

7. John W. Jordan, ed. "Journal of James Kenny, 1761–1763," *Pennsylvania Magazine of History and Biography* 37 (1913): 154; Richard Mather to Henry Bouquet, 11 March 1761, Waddell et al., eds., *Papers of Henry Bouquet*, 5:343. Any identification of disease before the advent of modern medical techniques must be extremely tentative. Influenza seems a likely culprit as there was probably an influenza epidemic in 1761 across North America. Dobyns, *Their Number Become Thinned*, 19.

8. Journal and report of Thomas Hutchins, 4 April–24 September 1762, in *The Papers of Sir William Johnson*, 14 vols., ed. James Sullivan et al. (Albany, N.Y.: University of the State of New York, 1921–1965), 10:526–29.

9. "George Croghan's Journal, April 3, 1759 to April 1763," ed. Nicholas N. Wainwright, *Pennsylvania Magazine of History and Biography* 71 (1947): 432; "Journal of James Kenny," 172.

10. D. Peter MacLeod, "Microbes and Muskets: Smallpox and the Participation of the Amerindian Allies

of New France in the Seven Years' War," *Ethnohistory* 39 (1992): 42–64.

11. Journal of James Gorrell, 12 October 1761–14 June 1763, *Papers of Sir William Johnson*, ed. Sullivan, 10:702.

12. Helen Hornbeck Tanner, ed., *Atlas of Great Lakes Indian History* (Norman: University of Oklahoma Press, 1987), 66.

13. Journal of Indian Affairs, 11–26 March 1765, *Papers of Sir William Johnson*, ed. Sullivan, 11:660.

14. Journal of Indian Affairs, 1–3 March 1765, *Papers of Sir William Johnson*, ed. Sullivan, 11:617.

15. Tanner, *Atlas of Great Lakes Indian History*, 66.

16. Ramenofsky, *Vectors of Death*, 161.

17. Bruce Trigger, *Natives and Newcomers: Canada's Heroic Age Reconsidered*, (Montreal: McGill-Queen's University Press, 1986), 254.

18. Trigger, *Natives and Newcomers*, 229–30. For the possibility of sixteenth-century epidemics see Dobyns, *The Number Become Thinned*, 313–20.

19. Henry F. Dobyns, "Estimating Aboriginal American Population: An Appraisal of Techniques with a New Hemisphere Estimate," *Current Anthropology* 7 (1966): 414; Daniel T. Riff, "Contact Shock in Northwestern New Spain, 1518–1764," in *Disease and Demography in the Americas*, ed. Verano and Ubelaker, 265–73.

20. Sylvia R. Frey, *The British Soldier in America: A Social History of Military Life in the Revolutionary Period* (Austin: University of Texas Press, 1981), 41–45.

21. *Pennsylvania Gazette*, 18 August 1757; Thomas Lloyd to James Burd, 8 October 1757, Shippen Family Papers, Historical Society of Pennsylvania, Philadelphia [hereafter HSP], vol. 3.

22. Jack P. Greene, ed., *The Diary of Landon Carter of Sabine Hall, 1752–1778*, (Charlottesville: University Press of Virginia, 1965), 165.

23. Plumsted and Franks Co. to Bouquet, 6 October 1762, Waddell et al., eds., *Papers of Henry Bouquet*, 6:115.

24. Orders, Carlisle, 5 July 1758, Orderly Book of Joseph Shippen's Company, 1758, Shippen Family Papers HSP; Orders, 2 July 1759, Orderly Book of Capt. Thomas Hamilton's Company, Cumberland County Historical Society , Carlisle, Pennsylvania.

25. James Kenny to Israel Pemberton, 1 August 1759, Papers Relating to the Friendly Association, 3:247, Quaker Collection, Haverford College, Haverford, Pennsylvania.

26. Orderly Book of Captain Thomas Hamilton's Company, 30 September 1759; Henry Bouquet Orderly Book, 3 July 1758, Waddell et al., eds., *Papers of Henry Bouquet*, 2:662; Orders, Carlisle, 5 July 1758, Orderly Book of Joseph Shippen's Company, 1758, Shippen Family Papers; George Washington's Orderly Book, 22 September 1758, 24 November 1758, W.W. Abbot and Dorothy Twohig eds., *The Papers of George Washington, Colonial Series*, 10 vols. to date (Charlottesville: University Press of Virginia, 1983–), 6:32, 156–157.

27. William Eyre to Jeffery Amherst, 18 May 1760, Amherst Papers, Public Record Office, London, W034/21,.

28. Samuel Weiser to Conrad Weiser, 1 April 1759, Conrad Weiser Papers, HSP, 2:151.

29. For a discussion of French garrisons, see W. J. Eccles, *France in America*, rev. ed. (East Lansing, Michigan State University Press, 1990), 116–19; Guy Frégault, *Canada: The War of the Conquest*, trans. Margaret M. Cameron (Toronto: Oxford University Press, 1969), 61–63.

30. Matthew C. Ward, "An Army of Servants: The Pennsylvania Regiment during the Seven Years' War," *Pennsylvania Magazine of History and Biography* 119 (1995): 75–93.

31. Return of Garrisons at Detroit and Dependent Posts, 8 November 1761, Jeffrey Amherst to Bouquet, 2 March 1762, Capt. Simeon Ecuyer to Bouquet, 2 June 1763, Waddell et al., eds., *Papers of Henry Bouquet*, 6:30, 50–51, 202.

32. George Croghan on Proceedings with Iroquois at Lancaster, April & May, 1757, Penn Mss.: Indian Affairs, HSP, 3:5–9; Samuel Hazard, ed., *Minutes of the Provincial Council of Pennsylvania* [spine title, *Colonial Records of Pennsylvania*] (Harrisburg, Penn..: Theophilus Fenn, 1838–53), 7:498, 8:690–91; For French policy, see Richard White, *The Middle Ground: Indians, Empires, and Republics in the Great Lakes Region, 1650–1815* (New York: Cambridge University Press, 1991). For trading at Fort Pitt, see for example Samuel Lightfoot to Israel Pemberton, 22 April 1759, 19 June 1759, 4 July 1759, Papers Relating to the Friendly Association, 3:103, 183, 191.

33. Quoted in Peter C. Mancall, *Deadly Medicine: Indians and Alcohol in Early America* (Ithaca, N.Y.: Cornell University Press, 1995). Mancall provides the most detailed discussion of the relationship between alcohol consumption and disease.

34. *Autobiography of Benjamin Franklin*, in J. A. Leo Lemay, ed., *Benjamin Franklin: Writings* (New York: The Library of America, 1987), 1422.

35. Mancall, *Deadly Medicine*, 5–6.

36. Jane E. Buikstra, "Diet and Disease in Late Prehistory," in *Disease and Demography in the Americas*, ed. Verano and Ubelaker, 88.

37. George Croghan to Horatio Gates, 23 May 1760, James Burd: General Orders, 8 October 1760, Waddell et al., eds., *Papers of Henry Bouquet*, 4:572, 5:62.

38. Henry Balfour's Conference with the Indians, 29 September 1761, Sullivan, ed., *Papers of Sir William Johnson*, 3:543–44

39. Angus McDonald to Bouquet, 25 October 1761, Waddell et al., eds., *Papers of Henry Bouquet*, 5:840.

40. Conference held at Fort Pitt, 6–12 April 1760, Sullivan, ed., *Papers of Sir William Johnson*, 3:215.

41. Jeffery Amherst to Sir William Johnson, 22 February 1761, Sullivan, ed., *Papers of Sir William Johnson*, 3:345.

42. Jeffery Amherst to Sir William Johnson, 9 August 1761 Sullivan, ed., *Papers of Sir William Johnson*, 3:515.

43. Capt. Donald Campbell to Henry Bouquet, 23 December 1760, Waddell et al., eds., *Papers of Henry Bouquet*, 5:196.

44. Jeffery Amherst to Sir William Johnson, 9 August 1761, Sullivan, ed., *Papers of Sir William Johnson*, 3:515.

45. John W. Jordan, ed., "Journal of James Kenny, 1761–1763" *Pennsylvania Magazine of History and Biography* 37 (1913): 171.

46. For the influence of Neolin's teaching on Pontiac, see Milo Milton Quaife, ed., *The Siege of Detroit in 1763: The Journal of Pontiac's Conspiracy and John Rutherfurd's Narrative of a Captivity* (Chicago: Lakeside Press, 1958), 8–16.

47. [Enclosure] Amherst: Memorandum, Waddell et al., eds., *Papers of Henry Bouquet*, 6:301.

48. Desmazellieres to Dabbadie, 14 March 1764, *Collections of the Illinois Historical Library* (Springfield: The Trustees of the Illinois State Historical Library, 1915–40), 10:236.

Charles-Michel Mouet de Langlade: Warrior, Soldier, and Intercultural "Window" on the Sixty Years' War for the Great Lakes

MICHAEL A. McDONNELL

In 1752, Governor Duquesne of New France described Charles-Michel Mouet de Langlade (1729–circa 1801) as "very brave, to have much influence on the minds of the savages, and to be very zealous when ordered to do anything." Thus, at age thirty-three, Langlade earned his first commendation for his crucial role as cultural intermediary between French imperial officials and many of the powerful Indian nations and villages of the *pays d'en haut*, or Great Lakes Region. After the British supplanted the French, he played the same role, and served at once as both Indian warrior and colonial soldier, for different imperial masters. British Governor Sir Guy Carleton later wrote that Langlade was "a man I have had reason to be very much satisfied with and who from his influence amongst the Indians . . . may be [of] very much use to His Majesty's affairs."[1]

Langlade, a synethnic trader from Michilimackinac, was, throughout his long life, a leader of Native Americans from the *pays d'en haut*, an officer in the French colonial regular troops, later an agent in the British Indian Department, and finally, touted as the "Father of Wisconsin." Langlade's importance stemmed not just from his direct, sustained, and influential role in most of the major conflicts over the period 1750–1800, but also from his ability—in imperial eyes—to mediate between colonial officials and the Native Americans of the Great Lakes and to bring large numbers of Indian auxiliaries to the battlefields of the Sixty Years' War, or at least keep them neutral. Langlade, manipulating and capitalizing upon his mixed French and Ottawa Indian blood—and important social and kinship ties to both groups— was indeed of "very much use" to imperial officials.

Yet as much "influence" as Langlade may have had over the Ottawas and other Indian nations in his sphere of influence, he was also clearly valuable to his Indian community and allies. For Langlade was used explicitly by the Indians in times of both peace and war not only to garner more trade, but also to strengthen the Indians' alliance with the European powers, to consolidate and expand power within the villages of the *pays d'en haut*, to bring mediation and peace to the region, and in creating opportunities for the Indians to cover their dead with new raids, new captives, and new gifts from imperial officials. From the moment that his father, Augustin, was allowed to marry his Ottawa wife, Domitilde, sister of the chief Nissowaquet, Langlade was carefully groomed and manipulated as one who would not so much have "much influence" over the Indians, but one who would be of "much use" to them. The astute Captain Arent DePeyster wrote in 1777 that Langlade "wants looking after; he is strictly honest, but . . . can refuse the Indians nothing they ask."[2]

Thus, by looking at Langlade as a cultural broker of the "middle ground" of the *pays d'en haut*—or even as a product or tool of that middle ground—we can begin to unravel a very different picture of Indian-European relations in the region. Such a viewpoint challenges more traditional notions of the role of Native Americans during the Sixty Years' War. Indeed, explored in this manner, Langlade's life serves not just as a mirror reflecting imperial ambitions, rivalries, and policies, but also as window, through which we can begin to glimpse the complex Native American world of the *pays d'en haut* during the major conflicts that engulfed the region over the latter half of the eighteenth century.

In the first place, Langlade's career as a soldier and warrior makes for a fascinating study of the role of an intercultural participant and mediator in the "Sixty Years' War for the Great Lakes" and is worth sketching, at least in brief, from the imperial perspective.[3] Langlade was the son of Augustin Mouet de Langlade, a prominent French trader, and Domitilde, an Ottawa Indian and sister of Nissowaquet—or La Fourche—a prominent chief of that tribe. Charles began his wartime career at the early age of ten when he accompanied his uncle Nissowaquet on a successful war party down the Mississippi against the Chickasaws. Here he gained great prestige among the Ottawas, defeated twice previously by the Chickasaws, who believed that he must have a special protecting spirit, or Manitou. On this expedition, too, Langlade might also have been impressed with the French colonial regular troops, or *troupes de la marine,* with which the Ottawa war party wintered in preparation for the campaign. At the same time he consolidated support among his Native American kin and allies, Langlade began formalizing his ties with the French. He enrolled in the colonial regulars as a cadet by 1750. [4]

Langlade's first—and probably most widely known—military expedition in the service of the colonial regulars proved to be a crucial and pivotal event in the history of the Ohio Country, and indeed, helped shape the course of the French and Indian War. On 21 June 1752, Langlade led a force of up to 250 warriors drawn from the powerful and influential "Three Fires" confederacy of Ottawa, Potawatomi, and Ojibwa (Chippewa) Indians of the *pays d'en haut* in a raid against the Miami village of Pickawillany (near present day Piqua, Ohio). The village was the headquarters of a rebellious group of pro-British and Iroquois Confederacy Miami Indians under the leadership of Memeskia (also known as La Demoiselle or "Old Briton"), a Piankashaw chief who used the strategic site of the village, which marked the convergence of several trading trails, to entertain British traders from Pennsylvania and influence other western Indians. Memeskia's recent break with the French alliance in the Ohio Valley represented a precipitous decline in French influence in that region, jeopardizing their trading network down through to Louisiana, and initiated a series of further defections amongst other tribes seeking British trade goods and alliances.

Memeskia's defiance was finally curbed by Langlade and his Indian allies, whose surprise attack came at a time when most of the Miami warriors were out hunting. After a brief skirmish, the skeleton Miami force surrendered along with five of seven British traders who were at the village. After killing and eating the heart of one of the wounded traders, Langlade also had Memeskia killed, boiled, and eaten in front of his family and village. In the aftermath of this incident, the Miamis appealed to their British and Indian allies, but no help was forthcoming and the Miamis, along with the rest of the rebellious tribes from the *pays d'en haut,* were forced to return to the French alliance in the face of this terrifying blow. Langlade's successful raid has been considered the first battle of the impending French and Indian War, though other French initiatives show that it was more generally indicative of a renewed interest in the area that would have led eventually to conflict. However, the raid was certainly instrumental in stopping the British trade offensive in the Ohio Valley and, most importantly, in securing the allegiances of most of the western tribes throughout the coming conflict. With few exceptions, the Indians of the *pays d'en haut* remained loyal to the French until the end of the French and Indian War.[5]

Langlade's role in the French and Indian War did not end there. Promoted to ensign on 15 March 1755, he and his Three Fires allies claimed to have been present at and, indeed, to have planned the ambush that led to the defeat of Edward Braddock near Fort Duquesne (Pittsburgh) in 1755. Though this story is suspect, Langlade certainly did recruit a large number of warriors to join a mixed party of seven hundred Indians led by Repentigny, Louis Herbin Jr., and Langlade who, from Fort Duquesne, launched the devastating frontier campaign against the American backcountry settlements that saw as many as seven hundred English settlers killed or captured and earned the Indians of the *pays d'en haut* the undying enmity of the Americans. One of Langlade's biographers asserts that Langlade's party were particularly brutal, so much so, that during the later Revolution, Burgoyne spread rumors of his alliance with Langlade and the Ottawas to spread fear and panic among patriot supporters in the Hudson Valley.[6]

French victories on the Pennsylvania and Virginia borders, as well as the fall of British Fort Oswego in 1756, helped lure Langlade and many of his Indian allies to Montcalm's campaign down the Champlain Valley in 1756–57. Langlade, already well-known among his mother's Ottawas and his father's Canadians, led one of the largest contingents of the 1,000 volatile warriors from the *pays d'en haut* who turned out for this campaign and was directly responsible for 337 Ottawa drawn from seven separate bands in what was later to become Michigan, including his uncle, the war chief Nissowaquet. Langlade was also probably expected to help influence the three hundred Ojibwas and Potawatomis who also accompanied the expedition as unpaid allies.

Langlade and his Indian allies were most instrumental in curbing English scouting during this campaign, particularly against Robert Rogers and his irregular forces. Together with a small force of French Regulars of the Languedoc Regiment, Langlade ambushed a scouting party of Robert Rogers' Independent companies of Rangers sent out from Fort William Henry (at the foot of Lake George) in the winter of 1756–57 to gather information on French activity at Fort Carillon (Ticonderoga). Going on the offensive in the spring of 1757, Langlade and Ottawa and Potawatomi warriors helped change the no-man's land between Fort Carillon and Fort William Henry into an area belonging to the French-allied Indians. They then formed the core of a force of five hundred Indians and fifty Canadians who launched an amphibious ambush on a flotilla of twenty-two whaleboats led by Colonel John Parker. Parker, leading five companies of his New Jersey Blues and a few New York militiamen down Lac Sainte Sacrement (Lake George) to destroy a sawmill and take prisoners, had his retreat cut off by Langlade and his force. Only 30 percent of the expedition made it back to Fort William Henry, while about one hundred men were shot, drowned, or hunted down in the forests where they tried to hide. Another one hundred and fifty became prisoners. Only one Indian warrior had been slightly wounded. The skirmishing and Indian patrols on this campaign helped keep the British in the dark about French plans and strength and sealed the fate of Fort William Henry. After hearing of the fate of Parker's expedition, Lord Loudoun, the commander of the British forces, announced, "I look upon that Place and Garrison, as lost, with the whole Troops there." After the fall of the fort, Langlade was posted amongst his Indian allies by a worried Montcalm specifically to try to curb potential Indian hostilities toward the British soldiers who were allowed to march away by the terms of the surrender. The anger of the Indians over the loss of promised booty and scalps, however, overcame any influence Langlade may have had and the result was the "Massacre" at Fort William Henry romanticized, of course, in James Fenimore Cooper's *Last of the Mohicans.*[7]

Later that year, perhaps because of his services in the summer campaign, Governor Pierre de Rigaud, marquis de Vaudreuil, made Langlade second-in-command at Michilimackinac. However, he was soon back in service in the eastern theater, where he helped gather and lead a large contingent of Indian auxiliaries at the siege of Quebec in 1759. It has been asserted that it was Langlade and his allies who first encountered the detachment sent by British General James Wolfe to reconnoiter up the Montmorency River on 26 July, and had the reinforcements he had requested of Levis arrived in time, they would have repelled the foothold gained by the British. At any rate, Langlade did take part in the Battle of the Plains of Abraham when he and the Indian auxiliaries took cover in the woods on the front and left of the British during the battle, inflicting the only casualties, including Wolfe, on the British side. Despite losing two half-brothers during the battle, Langlade stayed with French General François-Gaston Levis' army after the surrender of Quebec.[8]

The following year, in Montreal, he was promoted to lieutenant and then ordered out of the town before its surrender to Amherst. He was to escort his Indian allies back to Michilimackinac as well as find a safe passage for two companies of deserters from the Royal American Regiment. A courier dispatched to Langlade a few days after he left Montreal informed him that the town had surrendered. Upon learning the news of surrender, the commander at Michilimackinac deserted the post, and Langlade— choosing to take his chances with the British—was left to surrender the fort, which he finally did in September 1761. As his biographer notes, "Langlade, who had opened the war with his attack on Pickawillany, closed the conflict with the surrender of Michilimackinac."[9]

Langlade, like many other Canadians, seemed to adjust quickly to life under his new colonial masters and his record of service on the payroll of the British was almost as distinguished as that under his former colors. A test of allegiances was not long in coming. As Pontiac's Uprising became general in 1763, Langlade warned the British commander of Michilimackinac, George Etherington, of the danger the fort was in. However, the warning went unheeded and the post was seized by the Ojibwas under Minweweh and War-Chief Madjeckewiss. Etherington and William Leslye, destined for sacrifice at the stake, were rescued by Langlade at great personal risk. While he could not save the family of Alexander Henry, the elder, Langlade did ultimately save Henry himself and managed to get the survivors back to Montreal with the aid of his Ottawa allies and family.[10]

After the uprising, Langlade moved his permanent home to La Baye (Green Bay, Wisconsin) where he and his father had already established a flourishing trading post. Here he was able to live peacefully for a number of years with his now grow-ing family. It was in Wisconsin that Langlade had perhaps his most lasting influence, where his prominence among the early settlers earned him and his father the title of "Fathers of Wisconsin," and their name on a county and town.

Langlade's military days were not yet over, as he saw considerable service in the American Revolution. Indeed, the British—like the French before them—depended on Langlade and others like him, as guides and interpreters. In return, the Indian department offered lifetime positions and pensions for its employees and their wid-ows. As the War for Independence intensified, the British relied ever more heavily on their allies. Promoted to captain in the Indian department, Langlade helped raise Indian auxiliaries to defend Montreal in 1776. With Luc de la Corne and at least one hundred Ottawas and other western Indians, Langlade joined British General John Burgoyne in the summer of 1777 on his ill-fated campaign down the Champlain Valley. Though most of Burgoyne's Indian allies left early in the campaign, Langlade was able to convince his followers to stay until after the Battle of Bennington. It may have been Langlade and his allies who were responsible for the killing of Jane McCrea on 27 July 1777, news of which spread quickly throughout the colonies and England and brought New Englanders in droves to the American army gathering under Gates.[11]

Returning west in 1778, Langlade was asked to gather an Indian force to aid Henry Hamilton against rebels at Vincennes led by George Rogers Clark, though poor communications rendered his help late and ineffective. In 1780, Langlade also led an unsuccessful expedition with his Indian allies into Illinois Country to assist in the attack on Spanish St. Louis. After that expedition, Langlade was made captain of the militia in Green Bay, and stayed there during the rest of the war. Though he remained out of the war from that point onward, his son, Charles Langlade Jr. seemed set to take his place. He and La Fourche took part in one last campaign of the Revolution in 1782. They joined Captain William Caldwell in Piqua to defend against a rumored attack by George Rogers Clark and participated with other frontier militia and Indians in the revenge torture and death of American Colonel William Crawford. Langlade Jr.'s party moved into Kentucky and unsuccessfully besieged a small fort at Bryan's Station, five miles north of Lexington, stirring up backcountry hostility further. This led to a confrontation with Daniel Boone's militia, in which Boone's son and seventy other militiamen died.[12]

After the Revolution, the elder Langlade retained his position in the Indian department and returned to his life of trading, though he came close to being tarred with the brush of scandal. At Michilimackinac in 1780, an attempt was made to replace Langlade and his nephew Charles Gautier de Verville because a quarrelsome Lieutenant Governor Patrick Sinclair thought them to be "men of no understanding, application, or steadiness." Gautier was later dismissed from his position as storekeeper and interpreter for embezzlement from the British storehouse on Mackinac Island and Langlade was found to have received some of these goods. However, the high estimation Langlade was obviously held in by most British officials may have been responsible for his continued service. He and other Indian agents proved useful after the war particularly in trying to curb inter-Indian warfare in the *pays d'en haut* and in regulating trade and gift-giving. Langlade also returned to trading, but never seems to have profited as well as he did before the Revolution, leading to his scheming with Gautier to pilfer supplies.[13]

Langlade may also have been saved from the ignominy of a trial in Montreal for his part in his cousin's plan by one last expedition. After learning of John Graves

Simcoe's determination to stop Anthony Wayne's expedition and force the Americans to negotiate a neutral Indian territory, Langlade once again volunteered his services. Ignoring the embezzlement charges, Simcoe asked Langlade to assemble a militia company at Green Bay. Before he could act, however, Wayne attacked a mixed war party near Fort Miami on 20 August 1794. The British refused to aid their Native allies and the Indians were forced to sue for peace at Fort Greenville.

Langlade was in his sixties when the Americans finally took over the British Fort Mackinac by the terms of the Jay's Treaty. He retired from trading, though he continued to serve as Indian agent and militia captain, making occasional trips to Mackinac, St. Joseph's Island, and Toronto. His sons and grandsons served as British partisans in the War of 1812. Langlade himself finally died in Green Bay in 1802 after a two week illness, by which time, if not before, he had become generally known amongst the Indians of the *pay d'en haut* as Akewaugeketauso, the soldier chief, or as also translated, "he who is fierce for the land."[14]

• • •

Langlade's life, as interesting a story as it is, highlights some important questions that allow us to move beyond a simple retelling of a remarkable tale. Indeed, Langlade's life raises a number of provocative issues and questions about cultural identity and allegiances. Even after reconstituting a significant part of his life in an extensive biography, the man and his motivation remain an enigma. Other questions arise concerning the permeability of the supposed hardening racial lines. And, though the remarkable extent and range of Langlade's participation and activities in the Great Lakes region may have been atypical, how representative was his role in terms of individuals, Native Americans, and other groups "negotiating" their way through the shifting sands of inter- and intra-imperial diplomacy, trade, and warfare during this period? How representative was Langlade of the importance and influence of intercultural mediators in the interactions of Native Americans with the French, British, Canadian, and American presence? Certainly the ease in which he moved among the various Indian, French, and English cultures he encountered was more typical of the fluid nature of cultural boundaries in eighteenth-century colonial North America that historians are now beginning to rediscover.[15]

Ultimately, Langlade was a living product of the *pays d'en haut*, who also played an important and influential role in maintaining that middle ground, particularly when negotiating and mediating inter-tribal and inter-imperial relations. But this role also helps to illumine the nature and importance of the Amerindian contribution to shaping the contours of European life in America. One of the best ways we can approach this issue is by asking what seems to be a rather simple question—*how* was Langlade able to maneuver his way with seeming ease through both the labyrinth of the Great Lakes Algonquian world and through the shifting sands of intra-imperial and inter-imperial relations? A significant part of the obvious answer is that he did so by "networking"—both on his behalf by his father and by Charles Langlade himself—in the arenas of trade, kinship, and imperial politics and diplomacy.

Langlade was one of the many "Interior French" as the English called them who were "long-term residents" and often descendants of traders whose fathers had married Native women. Susan Sleeper-Smith has written that the western Great Lakes fur trade "encouraged intermarriage, both 'marriage in the manner of the country' as well as marriage sacramentally sanctioned by missionary priests." The fur trade was "embedded in the social dynamics of indigenous society. . . . Marriage integrated French traders into indigenous kin networks and insured access to furs."[16] Most of these French and *métis* lived in Native American villages and were often adopted and/or had acquired Indian names. Langlade may have been one of those referred to by a newly arrived British officer at Michilimackinac who described the French at the post as those who have been "in these upper Countrys for these twelve, twenty, or thirty years, [and] have adopted the very principles and ideas of Indians, and differ little from them only a little in colour."[17]

For example, Langlade's own father, Augustin, had successfully begun the kinship "networking" that would stand Charles in good stead. Augustin, inheriting neither status nor property, moved from Trois-Rivieres on the St. Lawrence and entered the fur trade at Michilimakinac after contracting to escort a traveler west to the Post of the Miami (near Fort Wayne, Indiana) in 1726. In doing so, he may have drawn on the support of his brother's father-in-law, who had served as an officer in the construction of Forts du Buade and Michilimackinac. When he married Domitilde, an older Ottawa Indian, he married into an existing Indian kinship network in the thriving Ottawa village at Michilimackinac, consisting of 180 warriors and perhaps as many as five hundred individuals. One of Domitilde's brothers, "a respected chief," died in the siege of the Sauk and Fox village at Green Bay in 1733 under de Villiers and Repentigny. He was replaced by another of Domitilde's brothers, Nissowaquet, or La Fourche (and variously known as Nosawaguet, Sosawaket, and Fork), who would later come to be known by some as the "Great Chief of the Ottawas," and who generally led his village until his death in 1797.[18]

But Augustin Langlade also married into an extensive trading family. Domitilde's first husband was Daniel Villeneuve, a former trader, with whom she had six children. Of the three sons of this first marriage, at least two were fur traders, one was an interpreter, and two died at the battle of the Plains of Abraham fighting with Charles Langlade. Though little is known about the third son, he apparently had two children with Indian women, supposedly slaves. Three daughters from this marriage also made productive and close alliances for the Langlades through their marriages. One married a commercial explorer, another married Pierre du Souligny, who served under Langlade during the French and Indian War. The third married a soldier, Claude Germaine de Vierville, whose eldest son, Claude Charles, became a close companion and partner of the younger Langlade for most of their lives. Augustin capitalized on this network to establish himself as a middleman between French suppliers and Indian and French traders at Michilimackinac, and then opening up trading posts on the east side of Lake Michigan, at Grand River (now Grand Haven, Michigan), and on the west, at La Baye (Green Bay).[19]

Charles Langlade, born into this richly complex family, continued this tradition. Though the details are unclear, the young Langlade first had a liaison with Angelique, reported to be a *panis* or Indian slave with the Ottawas in the later 1740s, or early 1750s. Though Langlade's biographer and other sources suggest that this was a fleeting relationship, it was at least formal enough for Governor Duquesne to comment on it in passing in his commendation of Langlade for his actions at Pickawillany. Duquesne noted that Langlade had "married a squaw." They had a son, also named Charles, who was sent to the College de Montreal to be raised and educated.[20] Whatever the extent of the relationship and the reason for its end, Langlade then formally married Charlotte Ambrosine Bourassa on 12 August 1754, daughter of René Bourassa, a prominent fur trader at Michilimackinac, and his second wife Marie Catherine Leriger de la Plante. Bourassa, the son of a trader and in turn the father of two active traders, was well integrated into the economic and social life of the post.[21]

Such networks served Langlade well and he continued to develop and draw upon them throughout his career. In the Revolution, for example, Langlade's use of his networks of Indian allies and among his Indian allies may have been crucial. The British appointed him superintendent of Indians and a commander of the militia in the

Green Bay region. The Menominee and other Indian tribes in the area, like Langlade and unlike some of their neighbors, fought for the British during the Revolution. Interestingly, and perhaps not coincidentally, one of the chiefs of the Menominee was one Carron, who was probably Claude, or Glode, the son of Carron the elder, or "Vieux Carron" who, together with many of the at least two hundred warriors supposed to belong to the Menominee in 1777, took part in the defense of Quebec. "Vieux Carron" was actually a French *métis,* who came to the Bay region as an agent of the Langlades. He married into the tribe, gained influence, and even became a "speaker" for the head chief. He and some of his sons were frequently referred to as "chiefs" and were integral to war operations and councils. One of his sons, Tomau (Thomas), seems to have been virtually head of the Menominee from near the end of the eighteenth century until his death in 1818.[22] Langlade may have drawn upon the Carrons for aid in influencing the Menominee to side with the British, and to join him on British-inspired campaigns. Thus Langlade, like his father, was able to use these contacts and networks profitably in both warfare and trade.

Indeed, Langlade seemed to do reasonably well in the highly competitive and often literally cut-throat arena of trade as well. By the time Charles came of age, his father Augustin had already opened trading posts at La Baye and at Grand River. Charles, probably in return for his early service in the French and Indian War, was given a monopoly of the trade on the Grand River in 1755, where he continued to trade until 1793. And both Charles and his father made Green Bay their home after 1763 and continued to trade profitably at that site as well, both legally and at times illegally.

Simultaneously, Langlade was able to draw upon these networks to enhance his standing and usefulness to both the French and British empires. He drew upon his "influence" with the Ottawas and other Indians in the region in times of war, bringing hundreds of warriors to the imperial battlefields and campaigns of the Sixty Years' War for the Great Lakes, and winning for himself military advancement, great acclaim, trust, and subsequent trading rights, as well as lifetime pensions from the French and then the British governments. If the number of times he was called upon for help from these colonial officials was not sufficient proof of their need of him, he was also directly commended by both. Governor Duquesne of New France and British Governor Carleton were simply the most prominent colonial officials to publicly praise Langlade.[23]

Most recent accounts agree with these contemporary assessments and see the "interior French"—men such as Langlade and his father—as crucial intermediaries between European colonial officials and the Indians of the *pays d'en haut*. As such, they were vital in the creation and maintenance of French imperial ambitions and, in many ways, the missing ingredient in British policy. Yet if we end the story there, we are in danger of acting as myopically as did most of those colonial officials who praised Langlade as being useful in serving their own imperial ends. Indeed, focusing on his life in this way obscures the true meaning of Langlade's significance, by overemphasizing Langlade's contribution to French and British imperial ambitions.

In this version of the story, the Native Americans of the region become mere subsidiary actors, coming when summoned by the influential Langlade. Too often, but less so recently, Native Americans have been mere secondary actors on the stage of European rivalries, entering when asked, leaving when required, and playing a role that seems, particularly, in retrospect, foreordained and dependent.[24] But Native Americans, especially those in the *pays d'en haut*, were writing their own scripts at the same time. Indeed, their participation in the Sixty Years' War for the Great Lakes must be seen not so much as a supporting act, but as a concurrently running play in itself, which overlapped with that of the Europeans' in an entangling, complex way. Thus, Langlade's life is useful as a "window" through which to understand the role and importance of the other side of the middle ground.

To do this, we have to take a more imaginative leap of perspective, and view Langlade as his Ottawa friends and family might have done. Initial alliance between Langlade's father and his mother, for example, may have been at least as much, if not more, a product of the Ottawas' desire to create a reciprocal social and economic tie that would bind the village more closely with the nearby trading post of Michilimakinac, than Augustin's ambitions or even love. As Sylvia Van Kirk has written, "through marriage, many a trader was drawn into the Indian kinship circle. In return for giving the traders sexual and domestic rights to their women, the Indians expected reciprocal privileges such as free access to the posts and provisions." There is ample evidence, she asserts, that Indian women and their kin networks "actively sought fur trade husbands."[25] The birth of Charles Langlade might not then have been heralded so much as the birth of the one who would come to have "much influence" over the Indians, but rather of the one who would be of "much use" to the Indians.

Such an interpretation is reinforced by the "use" of young Langlade on the raid into Chickasaw country early in his life. Langlade's biographer speculates that his uncle, Nissowaquet, and the young boy colluded in an adventurous spirit to have the boy accompany the war party. But the circumstances leading up to the request for young Langlade suggests there may have been other reasons for his inclusion. After Bienville's disastrous expedition against the Chickasaw and Natchez in 1736, a second attack was planned for 1739 that called for the use of the Indians of the *pays d'en haut*. Understandably reluctant to join the French given the previous fiasco, La Fourche hesitated when called upon to join the new expedition by Pierre-Joseph de Céloron de Blainville, at Michilimakinac. According to legend, La Fourche fasted in his lodge and appealed for a message to guide him. One week later he returned and gave his support to the expedition but on condition that the ten year old Charles Langlade join them. While not discounting the value of La Fourche's vision, the chief must have also seen that Langlade would serve as an excellent hostage, or at least security, for the safety and alliance of the Ottawas with the French, and a guard against the reckless use of the Indians during the campaign.[26]

Certainly, Nissowaquet was not afraid to use his alliance with the French to the best advantage. After the expedition against the Chickasaws in which Langlade participated in 1740, the Ottawa at Michilimackinac announced that they wanted to move to a different site, perhaps as far away as the Muskegon and Grand rivers, claiming that the soil was growing weak around Michilimackinac. Such an announcement, coming immediately after giving their help to the French and one year after the Huron-Petun at Detroit split into two factions with some moving south to Sandusky which alarmed the French, may have been at least partially politically inspired. Fearing the loss of influence over their immediate allies, no less than the governor of New France, Marquis Charles de Beauharnois de la Boische, sent an urgent message asking them to reconsider. As a result, Céloron spent an entire winter with the Ottawa, urging them to stay closer to the fort. He promised them gifts, including brandy, help in rebuilding their village, and a meeting with the governor in Montreal after they completed the new community. The site ultimately settled upon was L'Arbre Croche on the shores of Lake Michigan several miles south and west of Michilimackinac. Nissowaquet and the other village chiefs had turned a simple move into a political and economic coup.[27]

At other times, Langlade seems less an agent of empire than a pawn of the wily Ottawa. Though Langlade probably colluded with the Ottawa in most instances, often events appear beyond his control. The entire story surrounding the events of the fall of Michilimackinac during Pontiac's Uprising seems suspect, for example; a carefully stage-managed event in which Langlade, but especially La Fourche and his

Ottawa kinsmen rode into the scene at the right moment and saved the day. From the start, Langlade appeared to know of the plans to attack the fort in 1763. Though he attempted to warn the commander, he and Nissowaquet must have had their own back-up plan in the event. Indeed, though Langlade thoroughly ignored pleas for help from the hapless trader Alexander Henry who was only a competitor to Langlade and inconsequential to the British, Langlade strode out of the fort in the midst of the attack and seized the officers Etherington and Leslye as they were being prepared to be burned, daring the Ojibwas to stop him. Soon after, the Ottawas from L'Arbre Croche arrived, overpowering on their way to the fort a group of Ojibwas who were canoeing down Lake Michigan with their prisoners. They seized control of the fort and the other prisoners unopposed by the Ojibwas, who outnumbered them. To appease the Ojibwas, Nissowaquet returned some of the prisoners, but then immediately ransomed them back. He and the Ottawas then left for their village, where Nissowaquet, against the council of the Menominees and the Ojibwas whom he had invited to L'Arbre Croche, insisted that they escort the British officers and garrison whom they had "saved" to Montreal, rather than back to Michilimackinac.[28]

Nissowaquet was no fool. In Montreal, he was greeted with gratefulness and gifts of medals, gunpowder, rum, and other trade goods. One early report said that "the Officers and Traders can not say enough of the good Behaviour of those Ottawas and Genl. Gage is resolved to use and reward them well for their Behaviour." In addition, for his services during the uprising La Fourche obtained large quantities of trade goods and at least one slave; he also later received a chief's commission, a medal, and the undying gratefulness of the new British regime. La Fourche was thereafter able to manipulate this alliance effectively. In the end, Langlade got what he wanted as well, receiving public praise from both Leslye and General Gage for saving the day and he secured the safety of the Green Bay trading permit he had received from Etherington shortly before the uprising. This, despite the fact that the British traders at the post had accused Langlade of plundering their goods. They also accused Augustin Langlade of encouraging the Menominee at Green Bay to join in the uprising and seizing British goods.[29]

One of the fruits of this new Ottawa-British alliance was the friendship of Langlade's old adversary, Robert Rogers, the new commandant of Michilimackinac. Convinced enough of Nissowaquet's loyalty, Rogers obtained for him and the Ottawas presents of clothing, tobacco, and rum over the next few years, arguing that the chiefs of the Ottawas "take most of their time in serving the English, & keeping peace, among all the Nations." When Rogers was charged with treason in the winter of 1767–68, rumors flew that Nissowaquet would return from wintering at Grand River and help Rogers escape. Though angry, Nissowaquet did not attempt a direct confrontation, but rather kept rumors alive that other Indians were about to attack and promised to support and protect the British. At a conference in August 1768, he told the British that "as Long as you remain here you and your Garrison Shall always Sleep in Safety, that we will watch over you, And If any bad news is hered amongst any of the Villages you shall be informed of it Immediately as we are a check to all the Nations, whose harts are not True to the English." From the moment the British arrived, Nissowaquet maneuvered to make himself and his village indispensable to the British, and therefore the most valuable, as they had been to the French. He succeeded to a great degree. In addition to the British praise Nissowaquet received for, and on behalf of his village, one Indian agent also called him "the richest Indian I ever saw." His nephew, Langlade, played no small part in helping him achieve this status.[30]

When looked at from the other side of the imperial equation, the nature and extent of Langlade's "influence" over the Indians becomes a bit clearer. Most of the time Langlade brought warriors into the field it was because they wanted to be there. The hundreds who flocked to join Montcalm in the campaign of 1757 with Langlade were part of a larger movement of warriors from the *pays d'en haut* who had been driven, at least in part, by tales of the fighting and plunder of Oswego in 1756. News of that triumph, according to imperial officers, "created a sensation in the western country . . . a great number of Indians appeared full of ardour to come next season to hit the English."[31] At a council at Montreal in December, where Governor Vaudreuil tried to encourage recruiting for the next years' campaign, the Ottawa and Potowatomi warriors apparently chanted their enthusiasm in a war song, telling the French: "Father, we are famished; give us fresh meat; we wish to eat the English."[32] Many were curious to meet with the newcomer Montcalm, "this famous man who, on putting his foot on the ground, has destroyed the English ramparts."[33] Langlade could only capitalize on this enthusiasm.

The contrast with the more critical following year could not be more pointed. In the face of a new assault under the vigorous leadership of Pitt, the French hoped that they would once again be joined by the Indians of the *pays d'en haut,* but it did not happen. Partly sated by the captives and plunder begotten from the siege of Fort William Henry and partly paralyzed by a new sweep of smallpox, the Indians of the pays d'en haut held back from joining the French campaign just when they were needed most. Though early reports related that the Indians from Michilimackinac at least "seem to be satisfied with the campaign [of 1757] and with us," by early March 1758, Bougainville noted that news from St. Joseph River and Detroit dated 4 January was much worse, as "the Indians who came to the army during the last campaign have lost many people from smallpox." They expected the French to cover their dead: "Their custom in such a case is to say that the nation which called upon them has given them bad medicine. The commanders of the posts must dry their tears and cover the dead. . . . It is a mourning which will cost the King dearly." And by May, the situation was growing severe: "Great unrest among the Indians of the Far West." The "Ottawas have evil designs. The Potawatomis seem indisposed. Finally [the relations of] all these nations [with us] are on the decline." Bougainville and other French officials were not clear about the reasons, apart from the "great loss" they had suffered from the smallpox, but he also wondered whether it was "the bad medicine the French have thrown to them," or "the great greed of the commanders of the posts and their ignorance of Indian customs?" But the British were also responsible for the turn of sentiment. Johnson, attempting to exploit any possible divisions in the French camp and especially the poor conditions throughout New France owing to supply problems, immediately went to the Five Nations to garner their support. Soon after, it was reported that "the English have sent a wampum belt to all the nations, and they make them the finest offers." In the face of Indian reluctance to once more help the French, Langlade was powerless to do anything more. He stayed at home in Michilimackinac in 1758 along with the rest of the Indians of the pays d'en haut.[34] A more multi-sided interpretation of the French and Indian War would then also help explain the turnaround in Indian attitudes the following year when almost a thousand warriors joined in the defense of New France in a losing cause. The Indians may have been more desirous of covering the many dead from the previous years' epidemic with potential captives from the invading British than worried about the fall of Quebec.[35]

Even on a more direct and immediate level, Langlade's influence as a cultural go-between was limited. During the height of the alliance, the French could pay heavily for any imbalances in the arrangements and diplomacy of the middle ground. Langlade, even if he had wanted to, could not control the temper of the Indians gathered at the siege of Fort William Henry. The "massacre" after the surrender of the fort was the fruit of weeks of protracted progress and deteriorating relations between Montcalm and his Indian allies. Prior to the capitulation, Montcalm had already begun to lose control over the Indians with him because he had, in their eyes, become too absorbed with the European style campaign, and neglected to consult with the Native chiefs. Montcalm expected trouble. Just before signing the articles of capitulation, Montcalm held a council with all the chiefs, informing them of the surrender, the motives for the terms offered, and asked their consent and their "promise that their young men would not commit any disorder." The chiefs "agreed to everything and promised to restrain their young men." But after the fort was turned over to the French, the situation deteriorated rapidly, and the Indians also "could not be stopped from entering and pillaging" in the entrenched camp. Bougainville reported that "everything was done to stop them, consultation with the chiefs, wheedling on our part, authority that the officers and interpreters attached to them possessed." "We will be most fortunate if we can avoid a massacre," he predicted with some accuracy.[36]

In the end, Langlade's "influence" was only as strong as his reciprocal relationship between the Indians and the French, or the British. When either side was reluctant to uphold their part of the alliance, whether because of devastation through smallpox, inter-tribal politics, cost-cutting or indifferent imperial officials, Langlade could do little but watch out for himself. Langlade's life, therefore, and his waxing and waning influence over the Indians serves as a barometer for imperial relations with the Indians of the *pays d'en haut*. For example, when the British began to think more seriously about calling upon the western Indians for help in their conflict with the American colonists, they reaped the poor harvest of years of indecision and unwillingness to deal with the Indians as sovereign nations. And just as Richard White has shown that the power of the village chiefs had eroded significantly in these years of neglect, so too had Langlade's. In 1777, Arent DePeyster, the British commander at Michilimackinac, called upon Langlade to help recruit one thousand Indians for General John Burgoyne's campaign. After months of trying, Langlade arrived from Green Bay accompanied by only sixty Menominee warriors, many of whom subsequently deserted. During the campaign, Langlade barely maintained any semblance of control over the Indians and could not stop them from deserting, especially after the battle of Bennington.[37]

He fared no better the following year, when both he and the British command in the west faced severe financial and supply problems. His nephew, Charles Gautier, left a clearer picture of why when he wrote a letter to Carleton in the form of a journal written during his recruiting trip through present-day Wisconsin. Trying to recruit from the Winnebago, the Menominee, and the Sioux, Gautier's journal devolved almost into tragic farce as he followed bands of Indians to their winter hunting grounds, mediated between them, and had to go into hiding when Spanish-influenced warriors turned against him. Soon afterward, in council at a Fox village on the lower Wisconsin, a disgruntled chief rejected with disdain his offering of a keg of rum and his warriors murmured their approval. Once again intervention by more friendly allies saved Gautier. Another trip to a Sauk village ended with a similar result when the village divided between support for the British and support for the Spanish, or "Bostonniens." After months of arduous recruiting, Gautier could only produce two hundred and ten warriors by 1 June, turning them over to Langlade at Green Bay.[38]

In the rapidly fragmenting village world of the *pays d'en haut* during the Revolution, Langlade was no more consistently successful than the British, Americans, or Spanish. In 1778 and 1779, Langlade mustered a fraction of the warriors he was requested or expected to raise, meeting resistance because of both inter- and intra-tribal resistance. Indeed, he even competed with an old friend, Daniel Maurice Godefrey de Linctot, in attempting to procure the loyalties of the Indians in the area when Clark raised the American flag in the west. Like the French authorities before him, Langlade never regained the power or influence he had with the Great Lakes' Indians before the British regime. Yet, this too, seems a result of shrewd Indian diplomacy. After Henry Hamilton's defeat in early 1779, some of the Great Lakes Indians began prevaricating. DePeyster wrote of the Sauk and Fox that the "cunning of those Indians now appears to be such that they want to lay both sides under contributions. . . . Nothing can be expected from the Indians without a strong body of Troops to lead them." The Ojibwas and Ottawas were becoming equally intolerable for their incessant demands on the British at this critical moment. DePeyster felt he was being "pulled to pieces by the Indians." In the end, Langlade's waning influence was probably at least as much a product of the less than satisfactory relations of the Indians with the British as it was a cause of it.[39]

Both Charles' and his family's influence was strongest when they acted almost as village chiefs and when they were able to uphold the European end of the reciprocal relationship. Augustin, for example, probably by virtue of his wife, quickly came to be seen as the intermediary in Michilimackinac between officials and the Ottawa nearby, often given clothing, canoes, tobacco, brandy, food, and gunpowder to distribute among the warriors. In 1745 alone, as Paul Trap notes, he distributed goods valued at nearly 3,000 *livres*. He also attended burials and other ceremonies and offered goods and gifts to cover the dead when necessary. When he and Charles took up a lease to trade in Green Bay in the volatile year of 1746, they also acted as peacemakers. Within two years of their arrival, one Menominee historian has concluded, the Langlades were able to bring peace to the region through gift-giving and arbitration.[40]

In contrast, when the British made the French Indian agents, they were no longer allowed to trade; nor did the British ever have a consistent policy in their dealings with the Indians, and the trader go-betweens. This meant not only that Langlade became more of a mercenary, but it also indicated that he was also losing the goods or influence required of an effective agent. He could offer the Indians little in direct exchange for their help. This quickly became apparent during the Revolution when Langlade supposedly asked to be sent on new expeditions for financial reasons; but he was never as successful in raising help amongst the Indians as he was before. A grand council at L'Arbre Croche in 1779 to raise a force to go against Linctot and the American rebels, for example, yielded only 200 warriors, most of whom subsequently deserted when they learned that the French had allied themselves with the Americans. The expedition was called off. A little later, Langlade was reduced to complaining to DePeyster that his pay was too meager for Michilimackinac. He and Gautier noted that they had little to offer their Indian allies and kinsmen and consequently there was a "constant run of Indians who snatch the bread out of their mouths."[41]

Langlade's life illustrates that the Ottawas and other Native Americans were not simply supporting actors, not simply mercenaries, but rather acted as part of, and on the basis of, an ever-evolving and changing reciprocal alliance with first the French, and then the British. Langlade's influence with them did not decline when they were no longer needed. Rather, it declined when the Europeans failed to uphold their end of the alliance or the Indians themselves could not uphold theirs. When Langlade failed to deliver the goods, when he was unable because of Imperial cutbacks, or changes in policy to bring what the Ottawas and others demanded, his influence clearly faded. Langlade did have some influence over the Indians, but only when he was able to offer his Indian allies presents and gifts, opportunities for plunder and honor and covering their dead, constant and continued trade, and a central place in both French and British imperial plans.[42]

Such an interpretation, followed carefully through Langlade's lifelong role as cultural broker, both supports and challenges the arguments made by Richard White and others in recent years that have asserted and emphasized the independence, autonomy, and power of the Indians of the *pays d'en haut*. Though it is clear that a crude notion of "dependency" had little validity in the region, the shifting sands of imperial alliances did have a long-term and demonstrable effect on the nations of the region. Langlade's particular importance, influence, and value *was* dependent upon the willingness and ability of both parties on either side of the middle ground to uphold, maintain, and sustain the mutual alliances that were cultivated. When Indians' interests lay elsewhere, the imperial relationship suffered and Langlade was rarely able to do much to repair it; likewise, when the British failed to maintain a consistent policy toward the alliance, Langlade's influence was at its weakest. What attention to the middle ground shows, then, is the precarious balance of the various alliances, the need to pay attention to both sides of those alliances, and finally the limits of the "influence" of even central cultural brokers such as Langlade.

All of this is not to render inconsequential Langlade's often important role as a broker between the different European empires and at least some of the Indian nations of the *pays d'en haut*. For indeed, he was obviously the right person at the right time. But it would be wrong, or at least an incomplete picture, if we only saw Langlade, as the French and British often did, as someone who had much influence over the minds of the Indians and was thus "useful" in carrying out the dictates of imperial governance. If we see Langlade as central to the "middle ground" we also see that Langlade was just as much used by the Indians as he was by empire. This observation sheds as much light upon Amerindian life and politics in the region as about imperial designs. While this paper has only begun the process of uncovering this other world, the preliminary results are suggestive. Exploring Langlade's life further promises to tell us much about the world of the *pays d'en haut*—the "middle ground" of Indians, empires, and republics—and about the fascinating story of the Sixty Years' War for the Great Lakes. For that story to be complete we must constantly look anew at all sides of the ground in the middle.

Finally, it is also worth reflecting upon the fact that Langlade's life as intercultural mediator challenges our particular, explicit focus on conflict as the defining moment of imperial relationships and the Sixty Years' War for the Great Lakes.[43] Langlade's life as an inter-cultural actor paradoxically shows that conflict may not have been the defining characteristic of social relations between the French, British,

Americans, and Natives. Indeed, the ease in which he moved in the different cultural milieu suggests that the "middle ground" may have been much more fluid, and of greater dimensions than Richard White and others have articulated. The battles of the Sixty Years' War for the Great Lakes—in which Langlade played an unflagging and not insignificant role—were crucial in defining the geo-political landscape of North America. But Langlade ultimately shows us that more peaceful cultural negotiations were also essential to the contest for empires in the *pays d'en haut*.

NOTES

1. Governor Duquesne to the French Minister, 25 October 1752, in *Collections of the State Historical Society of Wisconsin* [hereafter cited as *WHC*], 31 vols. (Madison: State Historical Society of Wisconsin, 1888–1931), 18:130; Governor Carleton to Col. John Caldwell, 6 October 1776, *Michigan Pioneer and Historical Collections*, 40 vols. (Lansing: State Printer, 1877–1929), 10:270 [hereafter cited as *MPHC*] quoted in Donald Chaput, "'Treason or Loyalty:' Frontier French in the American Revolution," *Journal of the Illinois State Historical Society* 71 (November 1978): 247; Paul Trap, "Charles-Michel Mouet de Langlade" in *Dictionary of Canadian Biography* [hereafter cited as *DCB*], 14 vols. to date, (Toronto: University of Toronto Press, 1966–), 4:563–64.

2. DePeyster to Governor Carleton, 6 June 1777, *Report on Canadian Archives, 1890*, 84–85, quoted in Chaput, "Treason or Loyalty?," 247.

3. The following sketch of Langlade's life is drawn from Michael A. McDonnell, "Charles-Michel de Langlade" in *American National Biography*, ed. John A. Garraty and Mark C. Carnes (New York: Oxford University Press, 1999), 16:24–26; Paul Trap, "Charles-Michel Mouet de Langlade" in *DCB*, 4:563–64; Paul Trap, "Charles Langlade," undated manuscript held by the Mackinac State Historic Park. Trap's pioneer work is indispensable in any account of Langlade, or of Michilimackinac during this period. Langlade's ubiquitous presence on the North American landscape in the eighteenth century is reflected in the varied collections of sources that contribute to his story. Though no single repository of his papers exists, helpful sources can be found in the Wisconsin State Historical Society, the Ontario Historical Society, the Public Archives of Canada, the Newberry Library, and the Archives Nationales. Some of his papers, and papers relating to him, have been printed in the "Langlade Papers, 1737–1800," *WHC*, 7:209–23, and throughout vols. 1–19, as well as in the *MPHC*, vols. 8–27. Accounts of Langlade's life are few and most dated. A good starting place is the biographical sketch by his grandson printed in the *WHC*, 3:195–295, together with an account by Joseph Tassé in ibid., 7:123–88, 18:130–32. There is also a manuscript at the State Historical Society of Wisconsin by Benjamin Sulte, "Origines de Langlade." By far the best single source on Langlade's full and varied life is the account given by Paul Trap in the *DCB*. More often Langlade makes cameo appearances in different histories. Some of the more important of these are Ian K. Steele, *Warpaths: Invasions of North America* (New York: Oxford University Press, 1994), who describes Langlade's role in the Pickawillany affair in detail, Richard White in *The Middle Ground: Indians, Empires, and Republics in the Great Lakes Region, 1650–1815* (New York: Cambridge University Press, 1991), and David Edmunds in "Pickawillany:

French Military Power versus British Economics," *Western Pennsylvania Historical Magazine* 58 (1975): 169–84. Langlade's subsequent role in the French and Indian War is best dealt with in Ian K. Steele, *Betrayals: Fort William Henry and the "Massacre"* (New York: Oxford University Press, 1990). John Burgoyne's *A State of the Expedition from Canada* . . . (London: J. Almon, 1780), is the best source for Langlade's role in that affair.

4. See Trap, "Charles Langlade," chap. 3.

5. For the more traditional belief in the importance of the raid, see Lawrence Henry Gipson, *The British Empire Before the American Revolution*, 15 vols. (New York: Alfred A. Knopf, 1936–70), 4:224, who asserted that the "fall of Pickawillany was in truth a momentous event in the history of the trans-Appalachian region," and George Chalmers, *History of the Revolt of the American Colonies*, 2 vols. (Boston: J. Munroe, 1845), 2:263–64, who stated that it was "the beginning of the war which was to decide the question of English or French supremacy in North America." Recent historians show that French, British and colonial plans and initiatives would most likely have led to outright conflict in any case, see, for example, Francis Jennings, *Empire of Fortune: Crowns, Colonies and Tribes in the Seven Years War in America* (New York: Norton, 1988), 50, and White, *The Middle Ground*, 223–34. Still, the raid's impact on the allegiances of many of the villages of the *pays d'en haut* has remained unquestioned. For general accounts of the raid and its context see Jennings, *Founders of America* (New York: Norton, 1993), 287–90; Steele, *Warpaths*, 179–83; Edmunds, "Pickawillany," 169–84; Dowd, *A Spirited Resistance*, 23–24; W. J. Eccles, *The Canadian Frontier, 1534–1760* (New York: Holt, Rinehart and Winston, 1969), 160.

6. See Trap, "Charles Langlade," append., for convincing evidence that Langlade did not play as decisive a role as he himself apparently later claimed, and for evidence that indicates Langlade might not have been there at all.

7. See Louis Antoine de Bougainville, *Adventure in the Wilderness: The American Journals of Louis Antoine de Bougainville, 1756–1760*, trans. and ed. Edward P. Hamilton (Norman: University of Oklahoma Press, 1990), 125–93, for perhaps the fullest account of the campaign of 1757. See also the account of the "Missionary to the Abnakis [Pierre Roubard]" in *The Jesuit Relations and Allied Documents*, 73 vols. (Cleveland: Burrows Bros., 1896–1901), 70:91–203; William S. Ewing, ed., "An Eyewitness Account by James Furnis of the Surrender of Fort William Henry, August 1757," *New York History* 42 (July 1961): 307–16; Lord Loudoun to Holdernesse, 16 August 1757, London: Public Record Office, CO 5/48, f. 277, quoted in Steele, *Betrayals*, 91.

8. See Francis Parkman, *Montcalm and Wolfe* (New York: Collier Books, 1962), 495; Trap, "Charles Langlade," chap. 6.

9. Trap, "Charles Langlade," chap. 6, p. 14.

10. The best eyewitness account of this episode is given by Alexander Henry in *Travels and Adventures in Canada and the Indian Territories, between the years 1760 and 1776* (New York: I. Riley, 1809), the relevant sections of which were published by David A. Armour, ed., *Attack at Michilimackinac* (Mackinac Island, Mich.: Mackinac Island State Park Commission, 1971). See also "Journal of Lieutenant James Gorrell, 1761–1763," in *WHC*, 1:36–48. Good starting points for secondary source accounts are Francis Parkman, *History of the Conspiracy of Pontiac, and the War of the North American Tribes Against the English Colonies after the Conquest of Canada* (New York: Book League of America, 1929), 204–33, and Howard H. Peckham, *Pontiac and the Indian Uprising* (Chicago: University of Chicago Press, 1947), 156–70. See also Trap, "Charles Langlade," chap. 7.

11. Burgoyne, A State of the Expedition from Canada. But see also Brian Burns, "Massacre or Muster? Burgoyne's Indians and the Militia at Bennington," Vermont History 45 (summer 1977): 133–44.

12. Trap, "Charles Langlade," chap 9, p. 18–22.

13. White, Middle Ground, 402; Trap, "Charles Langlade," chap. 10.

14. Trap, "Charles Langlade," chap. 10.

15. The literature on cultural brokers, mediators and boundaries is extensive. Certainly White's Middle Ground is a good place to start. Other recent studies that provide excellent introductions to this topic include Margaret Connell Szasz, ed., Between Indian and White Worlds: The Cultural Broker (Norman: University of Oklahoma Press, 1994), Andrew R. L. Cayton and Fredrika J. Teute, eds., Contact Points: American Frontiers from the Mohawk Valley to the Mississippi, 1750–1830 (Chapel Hill: University of North Carolina Press, 1998), and Larry L. Nelson, A Man of Distinction among Them: Alexander McKee and British-Indian Affairs along the Ohio Country Frontier, 1754–1799 (Kent, Ohio: Kent State University Press, 1999).

16. "'The French and Indian are so much connected that if you disoblige one . . . the other take part,'" quoted in Susan Sleeper-Smith, "English Governance in the Great Lakes, 1760–1780," International Seminar on the History of the Atlantic World, Working Paper no. 97–17, summer 1997, 3. See also Sylvia Van Kirk, Many Tender Ties: Women in Fur Trade Society, 1679–1870 (Norman: University of Oklahoma Press, 1983); Van Kirk, "The Custom of the Country: An Examination of Fur Trade Practices," Essays on Western History: In Honour of Lewis Gwynne Thomas, ed. Lewis H. Thomas (Edmonton: University of Alberta Press, 1976), 49–68; Jennifer S. H. Brown, Strangers in Blood: Fur Trade Company Families in Indian Country (Vancouver: University of British Columbia Press, 1980).

17. Turnbell to Gage, 5 July 1772, Papers of Thomas Gage, William Clements Library, University of Michigan, Ann Arbor, quoted in Sleeper-Smith, "English Governance," 3.

18. Trap, "Charles Langlade," chap. 1, pp. 18–19, 28–29, chap. 3, pp. 1, 4, 14; David A. Armour, "Nissowaquet," DCB, 4:582–83.

19. Trap, "Charles Langlade," chap. 1, 18–19, 28–29.

20. See Jennings, Empire of Fortune, 49n.; Trap, "Charles Langlade," chap. 3, pp. 11–12, 17.

21. David A. Armour, "René Bourassa, dit La Ronde," DCB, 3:77–78. One of his sons, René, married the daughter of Jean-Baptiste Chevalier in 1744.

22. Felix M. Keesing, The Menomini Indians of Wisconsin: A Study of Three Centuries of Cultural Contact and Change (Philadelphia: American Philosophical Society, 1939), 86–87, 88.

23. See Trap, "Charles Langlade," chap. 4, p. 12; Trap, "Charles-Michel Mouet de Langlade," in DCB, 4:563–64; Jennings, Empire of Fortune, 49.

24. For example, the story of the raid on Pickawillany before imperial allegiances became too convoluted seems incomplete upon close inspection. Most commentators on the raid, and there are many, rarely move beyond the benefit the raid had in terms of the French empire. None, it seems, of the numerous sources who report the participation of Langlade and over two hundred and fifty Ottawa and Ojibwa Indians at Pickawillany attempt to explain why these warriors, and not others or anyone at all, came to the aid of the faltering French alliance when they did. Even Richard White, in his careful and detailed analysis of the shifting tribal and village alliances and conflicts of the pays d'en haut fails to consider what Langlade and his allies were doing there—they literally "emerged from the woods surrounding Pickawillany," struck the Miami, and melted back into the forest with their captives. See White, Middle Ground, 228–31. For other narratives which lack an explanation, see Jennings, Founders of America,

287–90; Jennings, *Empire of Fortune*, 49–50; Steele, *Warpaths*, 179–83, and Edmunds, "Pickawillany," 181–84. White details a series of killings and retaliations for killings among a number of nations and villages in the Great Lakes area in the months immediately preceding Langlade's raid, but nothing which seemed to impinge directly on Langlade and the Indians at Michilimackinac. Yet by the logic of White's own arguments, it is unlikely that Langlade and the Native warriors were there simply to do the bidding of French officials. Indeed, it seems that the raid came as much of a surprise to many French officials as it did to the unfortunate La Demoiselle. At the time of the raid, Governor Duquesne was busily assembling a French force to strike the rebel Indians at Pickawillany himself. See, White, *Middle Ground*, 231, 234. If the raid was seen as part of the reciprocal and patriarchal alliance between the French and the villages of the *pays d'en haut*, it becomes more intelligible, but not completely. Langlade and his Indian allies may have been fulfilling their side of the obligations owed to the French for their gifts, trade, and mediation in the Great Lakes region, but in that particular moment when the French felt that their alliance was deteriorating rapidly, the Indians of Michilimackinac need only have expressed their support and perhaps sent aid to the gathering French army to have elicited a grateful response.

25. Sylvia Van Kirk, "The Role of Native Women in the Fur Trade Society of Western Canada, 1670–1830," *Frontiers* 7 (1982): 76, 77.

26. See Trap, "Charles Langlade," chap 3, pp. 4–7.

27. See the records of the protracted negotiations in *WHC* 17:374–75 and *passim*. See also Trap, "Charles Langlade," 20; White, *Middle Ground*, 192–96.

28. Armour and Widder, eds., *Attack at Michilimackinac*, 49–70; Parkman, *History of the Conspiracy of Pontiac*, 204–33; Peckham, *Pontiac and the Indian Uprising*, 156–70; Trap, "Charles Langlade," chap. 7.

29. Armour, "Nissowaquet," *DCB*, 4:582–83; "Journal of Lieutenant James Gorrell, 1761–1763," in *WHC*, 1:36–48; Trap, "Charles Langlade," chap. 7, pp. 7–19, 19–21; Capt. Daniel Claus to Sir William Johnson, Montreal, 6 August 1763, in *WHC*, 18:257.

30. Armour, "Nissowaquet," *DCB*, 4:582–83.

31. See Bougainville, *Journals*, 59; Steele, *Betrayals*, 78–79.

32. *Documents Relative to the Colonial History of the State of New York*, ed. Edmund B.O. Callaghan and Berthold Fernow, 15 vols. (Albany: New York State Archives, 1856–87), 10:499–518, esp. 512, and 553–63, quoted in Steele, *Betrayals*, 79.

33. Bougainville, *Journals*, 66, 113–17, quote on 115.

34. Ibid., 193, 197, 201, 204; Trap, "Charles Langlade," 5:22, 28–29; Andrew J. Blackbird, *History of the Ottawa and Chippewa Indians of Michigan* (Ypsilanti, Mich.: Ypsilantian Job Printing House, 1887), 9–10.

35. As Daniel K. Richter has pointed out, at least for the Iroquois, replacing or covering the dead was not confined to those lost in battle or through murder, but extended to any kind of death, even from small-pox. "War and Culture: The Iroquois Experience" *William and Mary Quarterly* 40 (October 1983): 532.

36. Bougainville, *Journals*, 149, 150–51, 163–64, 165, 170–71. See Steele, *Betrayals*, for the most complete and sensitive account of the "massacre."

37. White, *Middle Ground*, 315–412; Burgoyne, *State of the Expedition*.

38. See Trap, "Charles Langlade," chap. 8, pp. 1–19; Barbara Graymont, *The Iroquois and the American Revolution* (Syracuse, N.Y.: Syracuse University Press, 1972), 150–56; Milo Milton Quaife, ed., *Wisconsin: Its History and Its People, 1634–1924*, 4 vols. (Chicago: S. J. Clarke Publishing Co., 1924), 1:285–87; Gautier's Journal, *WHC*, 11:100–11.

39. For he was not alone, as Susan Sleeper-Smith has shown other interior French throughout the *pays d'en haut* relocated to the west side of Lake Michigan in the face of more or less hostile British agents and officials after French capitulation, and gradually, without their intermediary presence, support for the new British regime dwindled, most often to at least neutrality. Sleeper-Smith, "English Governance," 14; Trap, "Charles Langlade," chap. 9. For DePeyster, see David A. Armour and Keith R. Widder, *At the Crossroads: Michilimackinac During the American Revolution* (Mackinac Island, Mich.: Mackinac State Historic Parks, 1978), 96.

40. Keesing, *Menomini Indians of Wisconsin,* 71–72; Trap, "Charles Langlade," chap. 2, p. 9.

41. See Armour and Widder, *At the Crossroads,* 98; Trap, "Charles Langlade," chap. 9, pp. 5–11. The British failed to grasp that the alliance was or should be anything more than a *quid pro quo* arrangement despite the French example and despite the warnings of many prominent colonial Indian agents. Even the sensitive DePeyster often failed to recognize that there was more to the Indian relations than an exchange of gifts and presents for warriors. During the Revolution he wrote, in the same letter that he began to worry about the waning influence of Langlade in gathering warriors, that the "Weenippigoes & Menomies . . . know they are not to have goods sent amongst them unless they strike the enemy. Should they also misbehave I hope you [will] see the necessity of curtailing the presents." Keesing, *Menomini Indians of Wisconsin,* 89; DePeyster to Haldimand, 13 August 1779, in *WHC,* 18:393–94.

42. See White, *Middle Ground,* for the best account of the nature of the different alliances.

43. See, for example, Keith Widder, "The French Connection: The Interior French and Their Role in French-British Relationships in the Western Great Lakes Region, 1760–1775," in this volume, which emphasizes the economic roles of the Interior French in maintaining empire.

The Iroquois and the Native American Struggle for the Ohio Valley, 1754–1794

JON W. PARMENTER

Until recently, few historians bothered much with the history of the Ohio Indians. Older paradigms of writing Native American history focused on what scholars deemed to be "important tribes," such as the Cherokees, the Sioux, or the Iroquois.[1] Looking into the Native American towns of the eighteenth-century Ohio Valley, these earlier researchers found a confusing medley of Indians scattered in multinational settlements and living in ways that appeared "disorganized" in comparison to the image of evidently larger, more geographically and politically "stable" Indian nations in the documentary records. Rather than analyze the evident chaos in the Ohio Valley, a previous generation of historians contented themselves with following the opinions of some eighteenth-century Anglo-American observers who dismissed the Ohio Indians as "a mixed, dirty sort of people" or, more harshly, as "the scum of the earth."[2] Fortunately, ground-breaking studies completed in the last decade by Richard White, Michael McConnell, Gregory Dowd, Colin Calloway, and Eric Hinderaker have significantly improved our understanding of the Ohio Indians.[3] Today, the Ohio Valley is correctly seen as one of the most important arenas of eighteenth-century Native American history.

This essay focuses on what at first glance might appear an "old" question—the role played in the Ohio Valley by one of those ostensibly "important" Indian groups, the Six Nations of the Iroquois Confederacy. Although the Iroquois were directly involved in diplomatic negotiations and warfare in the Ohio Valley until 1794, their Ohio experience has not been closely analyzed. This essay contends that eighteenth-century Iroquois contacts with the Ohio Valley took place on two different levels: a "macro" diplomatic level through which the Iroquois asserted a territorial claim to the Ohio Valley, as well as the right to represent the Indians resident in Ohio in negotiations with colonial powers, and a "micro" level represented by the migration of their own people to the Ohio Country where they became known as "Mingos." Through a closer look at these two levels of interaction and the often complicated relationship between them, we may obtain a clearer picture of what the struggle for the Ohio Valley meant to Iroquois people during the second half of the eighteenth century.

Who were the migrant Iroquois living in the Ohio Valley who eventually became known as the "Mingos?" The Mingo are perhaps best known to us from literary sources. James Fenimore Cooper's Hawkeye referred to hostile Iroquois as "Mingos,"[4] and Thomas Jefferson's account of Logan the Mingo's famous 1774 speech became an example of "Indian eloquence," which American schoolchildren recited by memory for generations.[5] Historians generally assert that the word "Mingo" is an Algonquian term of reproach, meaning "stealthy," or "treacherous."[6] Described variously as "a detached band of Iroquois,"[7] "offshoots of the Iroquois,"[8] "independent splinter groups of the Six Nations,"[9] or as "defectors from the League,"[10] historical consensus on these "Iroquois renegades"[11] to date notes their "poor organization,"[12] living in "roving bands"[13] in the Ohio Country as a means of "freeing themselves from the hegemony of the Iroquois federation."[14]

Like all generalizations, however, these brief descriptions of the Mingos warrant closer scrutiny. Iroquois migration to the Ohio Country began in earnest after the harsh winter of 1740–41 led many to areas southwest of Iroquoia in search of game. In 1743, French traders from Detroit discovered a settlement of several hundred Indians on the Cuyahoga River (in the vicinity of modern Cleveland), which included members of all constituent nations of the Iroquois Confederacy (although mostly Senecas and Mohawks), along with some Delawares, Mohicans, St. Francis Abenakis, and Ottawas.[15] Their location on Lake Erie's southern shore provided them with better access to game as well as to eager traders from Detroit and Pennsylvania. The migration of the Iroquois to the Ohio Valley was not a movement of intact "tribes," or "villages," but of smaller social units: village fragments, families, even individual hunters, who reconstituted themselves into multinational, even multiethnic villages upon their arrival in their new homelands.[16] Exchanging geography for time, the Iroquois migrants settled in comparatively unoccupied territory and began hunting, trading, and entertaining offers for alliance from the French and the English.[17] Dependent on European goods, the migrant Iroquois relocated to the Ohio Valley for improved hunting and trading opportunities, which also had underlying political purposes.[18]

Given the shift from subsistence to market-driven economies among Indian peoples in eastern North America during the eighteenth century, the young men, who did the bulk of hunting for the market, required ready access to hunting grounds. By assuming a greater role in the redistribution of goods obtained through the fur trade, young Iroquois men attained greater influence in their communities and challenged traditional patterns of leadership and authority by older men. The Ohio Iroquois migrants represent an excellent example of this phenomenon. Their relocation also differed markedly in character from the "refugee" populations resettled in the Upper Susquehanna Valley under the auspices of Iroquois and English colonial authorities during the eighteenth century.[19] The Ohio migrants moved freely, of their own volition, and without direct supervision.

Our first accurate glimpse into the demography of the Ohio Iroquois appears in the 1748 population estimate made by Pennsylvania Indian Agent Conrad Weiser. Out of a total of 789 "fighting men" Weiser tabulated for the Ohio Valley, 307 are identifiably ethnic "Iroquois."[20] This number of viable adult males could suggest a total population of Ohio Iroquois consisting of anywhere from 600 to 1,500 persons.[21] We have no way of knowing the exact number of Ohio Iroquois, but when these estimates are compared to the population figures for the Confederacy Iroquois during the mid–eighteenth century, it seems reasonable to suggest that the Ohio Iroquois population represented approximately 10 to 15 percent of that which remained behind in traditional Iroquois homelands in what is now Upstate New York.[22] When combined with the rest of the migrant Delawares, Shawnees, and other Indian groups in the Ohio region, the Ohio Iroquois constituted part of a body of Indians, which then New York Indian Agent William Johnson described in 1750 as "double the number" of the Iroquois Confederacy.[23]

The presence of such a large population of migrant Iroquois in the Ohio Valley alarmed English colonial officials. Pennsylvania Governor James Hamilton worried, in 1750, that the Confederacy Iroquois leadership, by "suffering their young men to go and settle in those distant parts, give rise to a new Interest that in a little time must give them Law instead of taking it from them."[24] Concerned over the susceptibility of the Ohio Iroquois to overtures from the French at Detroit and the obvious negative implications for the tenuous English claim to the Ohio Valley, Anglo-American nego-tiators constantly exhorted the Onondaga Council (the governing body of the Iroquois Confederacy) to recall their young men from the Ohio Country. When the Confederacy leaders consistently neglected or failed to do so, colonial officials assumed that the Six Nations had "lost control" of their young men, and expressed grave concern over what they regarded as the decline of Iroquois authority in the Ohio Valley. Subsequent historians of the Iroquois have adopted the view of their English sources uncritically, and the argument of the Confederacy Iroquois being unable to arbitrarily direct their "dependents" in the Ohio Valley[25] has contributed to an overall consensus among historians of an Iroquois decline into diplomatic impo-tence and insignificance after roughly 1730.[26]

Yet criticism of the Iroquois Confederacy for having "lost control" over their Ohio migrants assumes that the Iroquois leadership actually possessed that control in the first place. This assumption is incorrect. Indeed, the very nature of Iroquoian social organization militates against the idea. The Iroquois eschewed coercion, valued and asserted the autonomy of individuals and their immediate locality whenever possible, and relied on the persuasive authority of consensual decisions of the Onondaga Council for upholding a sense of unanimity among the constituent nations of the Confederacy.[27] Once we penetrate the thick veneer of clearly interested assertions by English colonial officials in the documentary sources, the evidence supporting the idea of the Iroquois control over their Ohio population becomes very ambiguous. For example, in November 1747, the Ohio Iroquois lit their own council fire with Pennsylvania officials, which colonial authorities interpreted as a declaration of inde-pendence from the Onondaga Council.[28] Later, in 1750, Conrad Weiser stated his belief that the Ohio Iroquois "took measures" from the Onondaga Council,[29] but his words here are fuzzy and should not be considered evidence of the Ohio Indians tak-ing orders. More likely, Weiser's opinion indicates that the Ohio Iroquois made an appraisal of the Confederacy's decisions before making their own. Finally, Michael McConnell's research suggests that the Ohio Indians (encompassing the migrant Iroquois, Delawares, and Shawnees) regarded the Six Nations' role as advisory in nature ("the door to their country"), by which they received intelligence and infor-mation about the colonial population, rather than one of overlordship.[30]

Eighteenth-century colonial observers regarded Iroquois migration to the Ohio Valley as a zero-sum game. Both French and English authorities assumed that any dispersion of the Iroquois would weaken the Confederacy, and ultimately result in a defection of these potential allies to the enemy. As the European rivalry for the Ohio Valley intensified after 1748, we find in both French and English documentary sources repeated exhortations to the Iroquois to "live together in their towns" and to recall their young men from their "lawless life" in the Ohio Valley.[31] Yet, from the perspective of the Iroquois, migration of their people to the Ohio Valley did not necessarily represent an irretrievable loss. On the "micro" level, migration provided their young men with access to hunting grounds and offered a means of resolving factional dispute in Iroquois villages by providing the discontented with an opportunity to leave.[32] On the "macro" level, these migrations extended Iroquois contacts with other European and Indian groups and restored to the Iroquois the liberating unpredictability of apparent political fragmentation.[33] To argue that the Iroquois Confederacy did not exert effective control over their Ohio migrants attributes statist political concepts to the Confederacy that it did not possess. What the Iroquois leadership could and did do was to remain in contact with their migrant population, creating a nexus of communications and a network for intelligence-gathering which the Confederacy nations wielded as a means of retaining a prominent position for themselves in the diplomacy of northeastern north America from 1754 to 1794.

On the eve of the Seven Years' War in North America, the Confederacy and Ohio Iroquois diverged on the question of preserving their rights in the Ohio Country. The Confederacy Iroquois counseled continued adherence to the Covenant Chain alliance with the Anglo-American colonies and attempted to preserve an outward appearance of neutrality. The Ohio Iroquois found themselves in the midst of hostilities and chose to act directly. Each path represented a legitimately "Iroquois" attempt to maintain the Six Nations' connection to the Ohio Valley. Each path had advantages and drawbacks, but the two divergent approaches enhanced the options available to all Iroquois people in responding to the increasingly complicated diplomatic situation in eastern North America after 1754.

In 1753, the Ohio Iroquois "Half-King," Tanaghrisson, while often characterized as being sent out by the Onondaga Council to "supervise" migrant Iroquois warriors and "socage tribes,"[34] ignored the advice of the Confederacy and attempted to warn out the French expeditionary army constructing a chain of forts in the Ohio Valley.[35] Tanaghrisson claimed in his arguments to the French in 1753 that the Ohio Country belonged to the Iroquois warriors living there and that "the chiefs who look after public affairs are not its masters."[36] These arguments put Tanaghrisson at odds with the official Confederacy policy of neutrality in the Anglo-French conflict and tied his followers closely to the English, who themselves hoped to gain the assistance of the Ohio Iroquois in removing the French. Ohio Iroquois leaders accompanied Virginia Major George Washington on his unsuccessful diplomatic mission to French Fort Le Boeuf in November 1753, participated in Washington's ambush of Jumonville in May 1754, and shared in his humiliating surrender of Fort Necessity to the French in July 1754.[37] Following the defeat of the English, an unknown number of the Ohio Iroquois, including Tanaghrisson and Scarouady, the supposed "viceroys" of the Confederacy in the Ohio Valley, withdrew to Pennsylvania. Scarouady later became an important agent of Sir William Johnson among the Confederacy Iroquois. Those Ohio Iroquois who remained behind became known as "Mingos."[38]

Scarouady himself cogently pointed out to Pennsylvania officials in 1755 the impossibility of remaining neutral for those who lived "in the woods";[39] and by that year, the Mingos joined in a nominal alliance with the French. They played a key role in recruiting warriors from the Great Lakes Algonquian tribes for the French base at Fort Duquesne, participated in Braddock's defeat,[40] and then fought what they considered their own war, with French supplies, driving back the Anglo-American frontier in order to preserve the integrity of their Ohio hunting grounds.[41]

The 1758 Treaty of Easton, negotiated directly by the British with the Ohio Indians, established a settlement boundary line at the Allegheny mountains, and promised the resumption of trade in exchange for the Indians' withdrawal from active support of the French.[42] After neutralizing the Indian allies of New France, the British, with well-timed assistance from Confederacy Iroquois warriors, completed the conquest of Canada in the campaigns of 1759 and 1760. Following the victory in the Seven Years' War, the Six Nations watched Sir William Johnson, British Superintendent of Indian Affairs in the Northern Department, set up rival confederacies to the Anglo-Iroquois Covenant Chain at Montreal and Detroit. The Mingos, along with most Indian groups in the Upper Ohio/Great Lakes region, resented the failure of their British allies to live up their promises after 1758 and joined with the western Algonquian in Pontiac's War of 1763. Mingos participated in the capture of Forts Venango, Le Boeuf, and Presque Isle in June 1763, laid siege to Fort Pitt, and assisted their Seneca kin in an especially bloody assault on a British wagon train near Fort Niagara in September 1763. Yet the British reinforcements that reached Detroit in October 1763, and ultimately put an end to Pontiac's siege, came overland unopposed through Confederacy Iroquois territory to Oswego and then traveled by water to Detroit.[43]

Outraged over the participation of the Ohio Indians in Pontiac's War, and over the failure of the Iroquois Confederacy to prevent it, or even to assist in suppressing the widespread attacks on the British presence in the west during the summer of 1763, Sir William Johnson spent four years after 1764 pursuing an agenda of bolstering and extending the Confederacy's apparent "control" over the hostile Ohio nations. In February 1764, a few Confederacy warriors joined an expedition led by mixed-blood interpreter Andrew Montour against the Geneseo Seneca/Delaware village of Kanestio. Montour's force burned the town, but the results of the "engagement" reflect something other than a military thrashing imposed by the Iroquois: one Delaware killed, and forty-one others taken prisoner.[44] Meanwhile, the Mingos continued hostilities on the Pennsylvania and Virginia frontiers, fighting with the Delawares and Shawnees until Henry Bouquet's expedition arranged for a truce in November 1764. Johnson planned punitive treaties for the Ohio Delawares and Shawnees, but, in a candid letter to General Thomas Gage, he explained why he would not follow that route with the Mingo. While admitting that the Confederacy had no more real control over the actions of the Ohio Mingos than they did over their migrant population of "Caughnawagas" living in the Canadian mission villages, Johnson determined to take upon himself a renewed campaign to return the Mingos to their respective towns. He could not treat with them as an entity in their own right, since to do so would amount to formal recognition of their independent status, which would seriously compromise the image of Confederacy authority in the Ohio Valley he required for chastising the Delawares and Shawnees.[45]

In the spring and early summer of 1765, Johnson concluded two punitive treaties with the Delawares and Shawnees in which each nation acknowledged the right of the Iroquois Confederacy to determine the boundaries of their territory.[46] Ignoring the advice of New York's lieutenant governor (and Iroquois authority), Cadwallader Colden, to check the Six Nations' "ambition of having the lead everywhere,"[47] Johnson exploited the boundary negotiating authority exacted from the Ohio Indians in 1765 at the 1768 Treaty of Fort Stanwix. Here Johnson obtained his revenge on the Ohio Indians for their decision to side with the French in 1755 and for the carnage of Pontiac's War. A handful of Mingo, Delaware, and Shawnee delegates attended the treaty, but only as observers. They witnessed Confederacy Iroquois delegates "insisting" on their right to cede their hunting grounds south of the Ohio River (in modern Kentucky, between the Kanawha and Tennessee rivers) to the crown and endured several lectures from Johnson on the evils of "wandering," "rambling," and "scattering or settling amongst other nations." The final insult came at the conclusion of the treaty when Johnson bestowed presents valued in excess of £10,000 on the Confederacy Iroquois as compensation for the Ohio land cession, while sending off the Mingo and other Ohio delegates with £27 worth of goods.[48] From the standpoint of the Confederacy Iroquois, the 1768 Fort Stanwix Treaty represented a success. The land cessions contributed to their prestige, sustained their position as crucial allies of the Crown, and allowed them to shed responsibility for what was becoming a violent and troublesome region, while still preserving (on paper) the right to hunt there. Yet the Fort Stanwix cessions also put the Confederacy Iroquois in dangerous dilemma. Their credit with the British now rested explicitly on their ability to "control" the Ohio nations, while any influence they hoped to retain with their kinfolk living in the Ohio Valley depended on their ability, through cooperation with the British, to preserve the boundary line and to prevent settler encroachment on hunting grounds.[49]

The Mingos had little faith in boundary lines after witnessing the unabated influx of settlers and "long hunters" into the Ohio after 1765,[50] and even the Confederacy Senecas regarded Anglo-American visitors to their country with suspicion, concerned that they might be there to "make a survey" of their lands.[51] After 1768, the Mingos and Geneseo Senecas (the westernmost community of Senecas in Confederacy territory) joined with Ohio Delawares and Shawnees in denouncing the Fort Stanwix Treaty and in rejecting explicitly the right of their "elder brothers" of the Confederacy to make land cessions without consulting them.[52]

The Ohio Indians' resistance took several forms. In a series of "congresses" at the Ohio Shawnee town of Scioto, from 1770 to 1772, the Ohio Indians attempted to lay the groundwork for their own wide-ranging confederacy by making peace with longstanding enemies, such as the Cherokees, and the Miamis, Kickapoos, and Mascoutens of the Wabash River. Unable to keep the Scioto congresses secret from Johnson, Confederacy emissaries infiltrated the 1771 and 1772 meetings to gather intelligence, to assert their right in arranging the 1768 boundary line, and to try and recall the Mingos.[53] George Washington's former Ohio Iroquois escort, Kayahsota, in collaboration with Johnson and other Indian Department officials at Fort Pitt, endeavored from 1765 to 1774 to relocate the "scattering Mingos" to Confederacy towns, but they consistently rejected his overtures.[54] Beyond the diplomatic sphere, leaders like Geneseo Seneca headman Gaustrax[55] found many willing adherents among the Mingos, Delawares, and Shawnees to a position of militant resistance to encroachment on the Kentucky hunting grounds. After 1768, the Mingos became notorious for plundering traders, for boycotting official negotiations with British authorities, and especially for their horse thefts and attacks on settlers' livestock. Stealing horses might appear today an insignificant tactic, but it averted the potential consequences of killing large numbers of settlers outright, and the loss of these draft animals often spelled disaster for would-be frontier settlers since it crippled their ability to transport produce and supplies.[56]

By April 1773, Confederacy Iroquois leaders advised Johnson that they could no longer account for the actions of the Mingos.[57] Nevertheless, Johnson called on the Confederacy the next year to mediate the frontier crisis, which arose from the May 1774 murders of members of Mingo headman Logan's family into a declared war on the Ohio Shawnees and Mingos by Virginia's expansion-oriented governor, Lord Dunmore. The Mingos and Shawnees sought active assistance from the Confederacy Iroquois, but received only warnings not to attack the Virginians. Despite the Scioto congresses, the Mingos and Shawnees had no help from any other Indian nations in Lord Dunmore's War. They fought a fierce pitched battle with the Virginians at Point Pleasant (in modern West Virginia) in October 1774, after which the Shawnee headman, Cornstalk, signed a peace treaty with Dunmore, which confirmed the 1768 boundary line and represented the first direct cession of Ohio lands by Ohio Indians. The noted Mingo Logan did not attend Dunmore's treaty, but sent a message acquiescing to the peace in a style at once mournful and defiant.[58]

Uninterested in attempts by the Americans to secure their neutrality in the Revolutionary War and unwilling to follow the Confederacy's prescribed neutrality, militant Ohio delegates, including Mingos, traveled to the Cherokee town of Chota in May 1776. At Chota, they urged the Cherokees to join their "common cause" of defending their hunting grounds from American encroachment and stated their preference to fight and "die like men," rather than "dwindle away by inches."[59] The speech encouraged many young men of the Cherokee under Dragging Canoe to split with the accommodationist leadership of the old men, and to migrate away from their home villages, where they became known as Chickamaugas. Historians have noted the collapse of "tribal" structures of authority during the Revolutionary era,[60] and groups like the Mingos and the Chickamaugas certainly represented the vanguard of this important change. Yet we need also to consider the reasons for these migrations away from established centers of authority and to examine carefully the militants' goals before dismissing them as reckless, suicidally violent incendiaries.

Similar to their experience as French allies during the Seven Years' War, the Mingos came to play a key role as British "allies" during the Revolutionary War, recruiting warriors from many different nations, and using British supplies to pursue their own agenda of rolling back the frontier settlements. The Mingos scoffed at the efforts of Cornstalk's Shawnees to remain neutral and mocked them with the epithet of "big knife People," normally reserved for the hated Virginians.[61] Ignoring the American treaty at Pittsburgh, in October 1776, the Mingo continued their raids into Kentucky. Fearful of reprisals against his own people for the actions of the Mingos, Cornstalk complained of their actions at the conference and berated the Confederacy Seneca delegates for failing to control their "banditti" Mingo relatives.[62]

The Mingos continued hostilities for the remainder of the Revolutionary War. Describing the Mingo settlement at Pluggy's Town in 1777, American Commissioner George Morgan noted "a Banditti of the Six Nations of every tribe," and he urged Congress to procure a delegation of prominent Confederacy headmen to come to Fort Pitt and chastise the Mingo "horse thieves and robbers." Morgan believed that the Mingos of Pluggy's Town amounted to only eighty men, but he noted that they had gained followers by intermarriage with the Delawares, Shawnees, and Wyandots, and by "assuming the Air and Authority of the Six Nations Council."[63] Morgan's description provides us with a glimpse into the methods and motives of the Mingos as they continued to take a leading role in the Ohio country, seeking allies from all sources to assist in their efforts to protect their hunting grounds from the continuing influx of settlers. By sticking resolutely to their policy of unyielding resistance, the Mingos hoped to set an example and encourage unity among their Ohio Indian neighbors. By keeping an "open door" policy, the Mingos welcomed Confederacy Iroquois dissidents and provided an alternative to the official Confederacy line until 1777, when the Six Nations abandoned neutrality and fought on opposing sides in the Revolutionary War. All but the Oneidas and Tuscaroras eventually sided with the British. From 1777 to 1783, the paths of the Mingos and most of the Confederacy Iroquois enjoyed a brief period of relative convergence.

The rejection of the myth of the "Iroquois empire" by United States Indian commissioners in post-1783 treaty negotiations has led to an exaggerated image of Iroquois demise, much as the promotion of the myth by the British prior to 1783 created an exaggerated image of Iroquois hegemony in the Ohio Valley.[64] Neither the

Confederacy Iroquois nor the Mingos folded their tents after the American Revolution, but their respective agendas for coping with the threat of American expansion diverged once more.

In September 1783, Mohawk war leader Joseph Brant, born forty years earlier to migrant Mohawk parents at Cuyahoga, met with Ohio Mingos, Delawares, Wyandots, Shawnees, and the Ottawas, Ojibwas, and Potawatomis of Detroit at Sandusky. Brant transmitted British Superintendent of Indian Affairs John Johnson's proclamation of peace with the United States. He also secured a preliminary agreement of the western tribes to a union of all the nations as a means of defending their rights and interests against the Americans.[65] At the October 1784 Treaty of Fort Stanwix, however, Mohawk leader Aaron Hill and Seneca headman Cornplanter lost their argument with the American commissioners, who denied the right of the Six Nations Confederacy to represent the Ohio Indians in any peace treaty, and rebuffed their efforts to preserve the 1768 Fort Stanwix boundary line. Convinced that the Indians shared in the British defeat, the United States Congress determined to exact land cessions from the Indians as an indemnity for their hostilities during the Revolutionary War.[66] The Americans dictated similar terms to the Ohio Delawares and Wyandots in the 1785 Treaty of Fort McIntosh and to the Ohio Shawnees in the 1786 Treaty of Fort Finney.

The Mingos did not agree with the notion that the 1783 Treaty of Paris sanctioned an American conquest of their lands and their location in the Ohio Valley provided them with ample opportunities to express their sentiments. After 1784, the Mingos, along with hostile elements of other Ohio nations, as well as some Chickamaugas "loaned" by Dragging Canoe, continued their war against white settlement. These were the "angry young men," who ignored treaties, followed transitory residence patterns, and traveled over great distances fighting American expansion by any means available to them in an attempt to preserve their traditional hunting lifestyle. For example, the settlement known as "Mingo Town" (modern Zanesfield, Ohio) served as a base of operations for 150 Mingos and 80 Chickamauga warriors from 1785 to 1786. The Mingos' and Chickamaugas' hostilities coincided with commencement of American surveys of lands north of the Ohio River, and continued until General Josiah Harmar's army destroyed their town in October 1786.[67]

Unlike his Mingo confederates, Joseph Brant believed that the day for violent resistance had passed, and that the Indians' only hope in facing the United States lay in presenting a united diplomatic front. Back from a visit to England, Brant revived the "Western Confederacy" in 1786, recommending value of unanimity to the western Indians at conference at Brownstown (near Detroit) in November and December 1786. Here Brant succeeded in getting the Ohio delegates to make a basic agreement of unity, to demand the restoration of the 1768 boundary line, and to require the unanimous consent of the Western Confederacy for any cession of land to the United States. At the end of the conference, the Western Confederacy drafted and sent a letter to Congress, repudiating the treaties negotiated from 1784 to 1786 and demanding that new treaties be negotiated with the Western Confederacy as a whole. After 1786, Brant went to great lengths to convince the Ohio Indians that he was not attempting to assert any hegemony on the part of the Iroquois Confederacy over their lands, stressing instead the common interest and ownership of all members of the Western Confederacy to Ohio hunting grounds.[68]

Denial of a hidden Confederacy agenda underlying his diplomacy was comparatively easy for Brant since a united Iroquois Confederacy no longer existed after 1784. "Confederacy" council fires burned at both Buffalo Creek, New York, and at Grand River in the British province of Upper Canada. While the Grand River Iroquois enjoyed relative peace and quiet on their British-granted lands, those who remained in New York came under unrelenting pressure from individual speculators, as well as state and federal authorities, all jockeying for jurisdiction over their remaining territory.[69] In order to avoid trouble with neighboring American state and federal authorities, Cornplanter's Senecas, along with some neighboring Delawares and Wyandots, failed to support the Western Confederacy, preferring to follow the terms of the 1784 and 1785 treaties. The rift with the westerners widened in 1787 when Cornplanter signed a 999-year lease of Seneca territory to New York land speculators. By 1788, Brant could get no support for the aims of the Western Confederacy from the Senecas.[70]

The combination of Brant's diplomatic approach with the Western Confederacy and the ongoing, violent resistance of the Mingos and other Ohio Indians began to have some impact on the thinking of American policymakers. After ratification of the Northwest Ordinance of 1787, Secretary of War Henry Knox rejected the post-1783 "conquest" theory and instructed Indian Commissioners to pay the Indians for lands acquired in treaties negotiated between 1784 and 1786 (an oblique recognition of the irregularity of those agreements). The two subsequent treaties signed at Fort Harmar in 1789 included payments to the Six Nations and Ohio Indians for ceded lands, but did nothing to alter the boundaries dictated in the 1784–1786 treaties.[71] This less-than-halfway measure angered the vast majority of the Ohio Indians and had a critical effect in weakening the position of the advocates of negotiation among the Western Confederacy. Many more leaders and warriors became sympathetic to the position of the hostile Mingos, Shawnees, and Miamis, who had avoided those treaties, and who had vowed to prevent American settlement north of the Ohio River.[72] Frontier raids accelerated again in 1789, forcing the federal government to send out armies to the Ohio Valley in 1790 and 1791, both of which the Ohio Indians destroyed.

In a dramatic about-face from the arrogance demonstrated at Fort Stanwix in 1784, federal authorities appealed to the Six Nations in the aftermath of St. Clair's devastating November 1791 defeat. Knox had no illusions that the Iroquois could arrange peace on behalf of the hostile Western Confederacy; but, in 1792, he considered their assistance in mediating the standoff essential. For his part, Brant doubted that his own influence extended so far with the Western Confederacy as national authorities hoped. He also worried that the lure of newly promised American annuity payments would draw off a significant proportion of the Western Confederacy, and feared that the trip to the American capital would ruin his reputation among the militants.[73] Nevertheless, the invitation to Philadelphia represented a significant opportunity for Brant, Red Jacket, Cornplanter, and other accommodation-oriented Iroquois leaders; and they made their case for what they considered to be the best interests of the Western Confederacy in person before the leaders of the American Republic.

The Ohio Indian leadership had other ideas. When Iroquois delegates arrived at the multinational town of The Glaize (near modern Defiance, Ohio) in September 1792, the local Shawnees contemptuously threw the documents the delegates presented, which contained the American peace message, into a fire.[74] The Shawnees then upbraided Seneca speaker Red Jacket for negotiating with the Americans and for failing to provide warriors for the 1790 and 1791 campaigns. Confident as a result of their recent military successes and bolstered by the timely arrival of a number of Chickamaugas to the conference (who announced similar military success in the South against the United States, and strongly urged continued resistance), the Shawnees recalled the Six Nations' abandonment of them in 1768, 1774, and 1784 and scorned Iroquois suggestions for compromise with United States.[75] At a key point in the conference, Ohio Delaware speaker Painted Pole produced papers captured from St. Clair, which indicated American intentions to instruct the Ohio Indians to take up agriculture, if they succeeded in forcing them to sign a treaty. Nothing aroused the fear and anger of the young men more than the prospect of being reduced to "labor like beasts of burden," and this public relations disaster for the United States virtually eliminated the viability of compromise as an option among the Ohio Indians.[76] Yet the Iroquois sought to preserve their role as mediators after their disappointment at The Glaize. They hoped that peace would be restored gradually under their auspices, so that the United States would continue the solicitous behavior they demonstrated in 1792.

In this light, we can understand the reasons for Brant's resentment of the parallel efforts of Mohican leader Captain Hendrick Aupaumut to broker peace with the Ohio Indians.[77] Unfortunately for Brant, the Ohio Indians in 1793 remained assertive after their 1790–91 military victories. Angry at the non-participation of the Iroquois Confederacy in their campaigns, and with strong encouragement from Upper Canada's Governor John Graves Simcoe, they rejected Brant's counsel on the compromise boundary line established at Muskingum in 1793, insisting on the Ohio River boundary line negotiated in 1768. Brant and other Six Nations representatives refused to countersign the Ohio Indians' response to the Americans, and the Western Confederacy disintegrated.[78]

The determined refusal of the Ohio Indians to negotiate guaranteed them a visit from Anthony Wayne's well-trained army in 1794. Western Confederacy warriors, including some Mingo, but without any official allotment of men from the Confederacy Iroquois nations, engaged Wayne at Fallen Timbers on 20 August 1794, and lost the battle.[79] News of Wayne's victory at Fallen Timbers prompted the Iroquois to negotiate the 1794 Canandaigua Treaty with the United States. [80] The Western Confederacy signed the Treaty of Greenville in 1795, which included an extensive land cession, represented by some historians as a far worse bargain than they might have obtained with a compromise boundary in 1793.[81] Yet, from the standpoint of a Mingo warrior in 1793, compromise with the Americans made no sense at all. To the minds of Confederacy leaders like Joseph Brant, negotiating with the Americans from a position of strength in 1793 represented the Western Confederacy's best, indeed, their only, hope. The separate treaties signed by the Confederacy Iroquois and their Ohio allies and relatives in 1794 and 1795 marked the end of any official Iroquois diplomatic connections to the Ohio Valley.

The history of the Iroquois relationship with the Ohio Valley from 1754 to 1794 could be told with equal validity as a triumph of adaptability and endurance, or as a tragic decline into insignificance and exile. Both stories would be equally true, and equally false, because they are equally selective. The fullest, truest story of the Iroquois connection with the Ohio Valley incorporate both the significant losses the Iroquois experienced and the limited victories the Indians obtained.[82]

Iroquois association with the Ohio Valley on a "macro" level, facilitating the Confederacy's pursuit of a "communications empire," and on a "micro" level of providing hunting grounds for young Iroquois men became two separate paths after 1754. Tension often existed between Iroquois individuals involved in different ways with the Ohio: Mingos resented the presumption of Confederacy headmen to speak for them, while Confederacy leaders grew frustrated with months of careful diplomacy undone by Mingo raids on frontier settlers. Yet neither side "gave law" to the other, and the flexibility of having two different options available with regard to the Ohio Valley proved of key importance in sustaining the Iroquois connection with that region until 1794. Neither approach by itself would have been sufficient. As hostile enemies and as diplomatic mediators, Iroquois affiliated with the Ohio Valley remained constantly on the minds of their French, British, and American rivals for effective occupation and control of that territory. They could be courted or hated, but they could not be ignored.

In some ways, the Ohio Valley provided a Turnerian frontier "safety-valve" for the Iroquois Confederacy in that the Mingos' movement to "free land" played a key role in maintaining social integrity among the Iroquois as a whole. Yet we must also bear in mind that a degree of "push" accompanied the "pull" of their people into the region. Even as the Iroquois population grew more dispersed from 1754 to 1794, the Ohio Valley provided them with opportunities to convert their widespread residence pattern into effective political influence. It was no accident that the political rhetoric and diplomatic forms of the Six Nations became the standard idiom for conducting Indian negotiations during second half of the eighteenth century.[83] Communication links with the Ohio Country conferred the authority of information and organization on the Iroquois Confederacy, and preserved their "macro" diplomatic significance as late as 1792. After 1783, the Iroquois never turned as a whole against the United States, but enough of their people in the Ohio Valley contributed to an eleven-year period of resistance that forced the Americans to re-evaluate their Indian policy and made treaties, albeit imperfect and costly ones, the solution, rather than the outright conquest or eradication of Iroquois culture.

NOTES

1. James Clifton, "The Tribal History—An Obsolete Paradigm," *American Indian Culture and Research Journal* 3 (1979): 81–100. A notable exception is Randolph Downes, *Council Fires on the Upper Ohio: A Narrative of Indian Affairs in the Upper Ohio Valley until 1795* (Pittsburgh: University of Pittsburgh Press, 1940).

2. Richard Peters to Thomas Penn, 24 October 1748, Penn Papers, Official Correspondence 4:163, Historical Society of Pennsylvania. Cf. Paul A. W. Wallace, *Conrad Weiser: Friend of Colonist and Mohawk, 1696–1760* (Philadelphia: University of Pennsylvania Press, 1945), 269–70.

3. Richard White, *The Middle Ground: Indians, Empires, and Republics in the Great Lakes Region, 1650–1815* (Cambridge, Eng.: Cambridge University Press, 1991); Michael McConnell, *A Country Between: The Upper Ohio Valley and Its Peoples, 1724–1774* (Lincoln: University of Nebraska Press, 1992); Gregory Dowd, *A Spirited Resistance: The North American Indian Struggle for Unity, 1745–1815* (Baltimore: Johns Hopkins University Press, 1992); Colin Calloway, "Beyond the Vortex of Violence: Indian-White Relations in the Ohio Country, 1783–1815," *Northwest Ohio Quarterly* 64 (1992): 16–26; idem., *The American Revolution in Indian Country: Crisis and Diversity in Native American Communities* (Cambridge, Eng.: Cambridge University Press, 1995); Eric Hinderaker, *Elusive Empires: Constructing Colonialism in the Ohio Valley* (Cambridge, Eng.: Cambridge University Press, 1997).

4. See "Preface to the 1826 edition," in *The Last of the Mohicans*, ed. John McWilliams (1826; Reprint, New York: Oxford University Press, 1994), 5.

5. *Notes on the State of Virginia*, ed. William Peden (New York: Norton, 1954), 63.

6. James Mooney, "Mingo," in *Handbook of American Indians North of Mexico*, ed. Frederick Webb Hodge, 2 vols. (Washington, D.C.: GPO, 1907–10), 1:867; George W. Knepper, "Breaking the Ohio Boundary: The Western Tribes in Retreat," in *The American Indian Experience: 1524 to the Present*, ed. Philip Weeks (Arlington Heights, Ill.: Forum Press, 1988), 83.

7. Mooney, "Mingo," 867.

8. White, *Middle Ground*, xi.

9. Helen H. Tanner, "The Glaize in 1792: A Composite Indian Community," *Ethnohistory* 25 (1978): 19.

10. William N. Fenton, *The Great Law and the Longhouse: A Political History of the Iroquois Confederacy* (Norman: University of Oklahoma Press, 1998), 12.

11. Downes, *Council Fires*, 45.

12. James L. Swauger, "The Mingo," *Pennsylvania Archaeologist* 19 (1944): 64.

13. William A. Hunter, "History of the Ohio Valley," in *Northeast*, Vol. 15 of *Handbook of North American Indians*, ed. Bruce G. Trigger (Washington, D.C.: Smithsonian Institution, 1978) [hereafter cited as *HNAI*], 592.

14. Randall Buchman, "Who and Where Were the Historic Indians of the Ohio on the Eve of the Revolution?" in *The Historic Indian in Ohio*, ed. Randall Buchman (Columbus: Ohio American Revolution Bicentennial Advisory Commission, 1976), 5.

15. Erminie Wheeler-Voegelin, "Ethnohistory of Indian Use and Occupancy in Ohio and Indiana Prior to

1795," in *Indians of Ohio and Indiana Prior to 1795*, 2 vols., ed. Erminie Wheeler-Voegelin and Helen H. Tanner (New York: Garland, 1974), 1:266–67; William C. Sturtevant, "Oklahoma Seneca-Cayuga," *HNAI*, 537.

16. White, *Middle Ground*, 187–89; McConnell, *A Country Between*, 18–20; cf. Hinderaker, *Elusive Empires*, 28n. 46, who argues that McConnell overestimates the communal and tribal cohesion of the Iroquois migrations.

17. For contacts with the French, see "Memoire de Robert Navarre sur le poste de François Seguin," [1743], Paris: Archives Nationales, Archives Coloniales, Series C11A (microfilm copy in National Archives of Canada [hereafter cited as AC, C11A]), 79:ff. 48–52; "Paroles des chefs de la rivière blanche (Canantechiariron et Araguindiague) à M. de Longueuil, 1744," AC, C11A, 81:ff.41–42. For contacts with the English, see Nicholas Wainwright, *George Croghan: Wilderness Diplomat* (Chapel Hill: University of North Carolina Press, 1959), 5–7.

18. Hinderaker, *Elusive Empires*, 52–53, 70.

19. Laurence M. Hauptman, "Refugee Havens: The Iroquois Villages of the Eighteenth Century," in *American Indian Environments: Ecological Issues in Native American History*, ed. Christopher Vecsey and Robert Venables (Syracuse, N.Y.: Syracuse University Press, 1980), 128–39.

20. Samuel Hazard, ed., *Minutes of the Provincial Council of Pennsylvania*, 16 vols. (Harrisburg, Penn.: T. Fenn, 1838–53) [hereafter cited as *MPCP*], 5:351. Cf. Pennsylvania trader George Croghan's estimate of 730 "Six Nations" earlier in 1748, ibid., 289. Weiser's estimate is more precise in delineating national affiliations.

21. Dowd, *Spirited Resistance*, 79, follows the traditional practice of considering "warrior" estimates as 20 to 25 percent of the total population. Cf. McConnell, *A Country Between*, 22, who employs a ratio of 50 percent for Ohio warrior population estimates.

22. Cf. Elisabeth Tooker, "The League of the Iroquois: Its History, Politics, and Ritual," *HNAI*, 421, table 1, "Iroquois Population Estimates By Fighting Men, 1660–1779."

23. *MPCP*, 5:481.

24. Hamilton to George Clinton, 20 September 1750, George Clinton Papers, Ann Arbor: University of Michigan, William L. Clements Library [hereafter cited as WLCL]. Cf. E. B. O'Callaghan and Berthold Fernow, eds., *Documents Relative to the Colonial History of the State of New York*, 15 vols. (Albany: Weed, Parsons, and Co., 1856–87) [hereafter cited as *NYCD*], 6:593–94; *MPCP*, 5:463.

25. A virtually unbroken line of argument can be traced back to statements like that of Sir William Johnson, who, in a November 1763 letter to the Lords of Trade, described the "declining state of the Six Nations," from 1749 to 1754, stemming from supposed English "neglect" of their interests, which rendered them, in Johnson's view, unable to cope effectively with the advance of the French into the Ohio Valley. Johnson's assessment should be seen in light of his efforts to strengthen his own claim to authority over the Six Nations by denigrating the efforts of his rivals on the Albany Commissioners of Indian Affairs during the very period (1749–1754) they replaced him in the management of New York's Indian affairs. For Johnson's letter, see *NYCD*, 7:573. The argument can be followed in Wheeler-Voegelin, "Ethnohistory of Indian Use and Occupancy," in *Indians of Ohio and Indiana*, ed. Wheeler-Voegelin and Tanner, 1:324; Francis Jennings, *Ambiguous Iroquois Empire: The Covenant Chain Confederation of Indian Tribes with English Colonies from Its Beginnings to the Lancaster Treaty of 1744* (New York: Norton, 1984), 308; Sturtevant, "Oklahoma Seneca-Cayuga," 537; Hinderaker, *Elusive Empires*, 28. McConnell, *A Country Between*, 4, 247, argues that the Ohio Valley was never a central concern for the Iroquois Confederacy as a whole, but was confined largely to Seneca, and as the Ohio increasingly became a theater of conflict, the Confederacy proved more reluctant to be drawn into the violent, volatile

region. McConnell contends that the involvement of the Iroquois in the Ohio Valley after the early 1750s was largely rhetorical, until the 1768 Treaty of Fort Stanwix. Cf. White, *Middle Ground*, 189n. 4, who points out that the distance of Mingos from their home villages deprived them of their voice in councils.

26. See Richard Haan, "The Problem of Iroquois Neutrality: Suggestions for Revision," *Ethnohistory* 27 (1980): 324–27; Jennings, *Ambiguous Iroquois Empire*, 363–65; Daniel K. Richter, *The Ordeal of the Longhouse: The Peoples of the Iroquois League in the Era of European Colonization* (Chapel Hill: University of North Carolina Press, 1992), 271, for clear statements of this hypothesis.

27. For an overview, see Fenton, "Northern Iroquoian Culture Patterns," *HNAI*, 309–16.

28. *MPCP*, 5:145–52; McConnell, *A Country Between*, 67–76.

29. *MPCP*, 5:518.

30. *A Country Between*, 247–48.

31. For French exhortations, see *NYCD*, 10:206, 232–36; For similar remarks made by the English, see 15 June 1754 entry, "Minutes of the Albany Commissioners of Indian Affairs, 1753–1755," ms. in Native American History Collection, WLCL; *NYCD*, 6:856.

32. Dowd, *Spirited Resistance*, 45, 66, notes the importance of out-migration as a means of maintaining community harmony. Cf. James Axtell, *The Invasion Within: The Contest of Cultures in Colonial North America* (New York: Oxford University Press, 1985), 284.

33. James Axtell, *The European and the Indian: Essays in the Ethnohistory of Colonial North America* (New York: Oxford University Press, 1981), 111–12; Hinderaker, *Elusive Empires*, 76.

34. Lois Mulkearn, "Half-King, Seneca Diplomat of the Ohio Valley," *Western Pennsylvania Historical Magazine* 37 (1954): 65. See also Hunter, "Tanaghrisson," in *Dictionary of Canadian Biography*, 13 vols. to date, ed. George W. Brown et al. (Toronto: University of Toronto Press, 1966-), 3:613–15.

35. *NYCD*, 6:796–97.

36. "Conseil Tenu par des Tsonnontouans venus de la Belle Rivière," in *Papiers Contrecoeur et Autres Documents Concernant le Conflit Anglo-Français sur l'Ohio de 1745 à 1756*, ed. Fernand Grenier (Quebec: Presses Universitaires Laval, 1952), 53–58.

37. Donald Jackson and Dorothy Twohig, eds., *The Diaries of George Washington*, 6 vols. (Charlottesville: University Press of Virginia, 1976–79), 1:130–61; Marcel Trudel, "The Jumonville Affair," *Pennsylvania History* 22 (1954): 371; J. F. Fausz, "'Engaged in Enterprises Pregnant with Terror': George Washington's Formative Years Among the Indians," in *George Washington and the Virginia Backcountry*, ed. Warren R. Hofstra (Madison, Wisc.: Madison House, 1998), 125–31.

38. *MPCP*, 6:130, 140, 160–61; Downes, *Council Fires*, 45, 197.

39. Quoted in Paul A. W. Wallace, *Conrad Weiser*, 389.

40. Paul E. Kopperman, *Braddock at the Monongahela* (Pittsburgh: University of Pittsburgh Press, 1977), 266–72; Dowd, *Spirited Resistance*, 25–26.

41. *MPCP*, 6:782; White, *Middle Ground*, 246; McConnell, *A Country Between*, 120; Matthew C. Ward, "Fighting the 'Old Women': Indian Strategy on the Pennsylvania and Virginia Frontier, 1754–1758," *Virginia Magazine of History and Biography* 103 (1995): 297–320.

42. *MPCP*, 8:174–223; McConnell, *A Country Between*, 132; Hinderaker, *Elusive Empires*, 144.

43. McConnell, *A Country Between*, 187.

44. *NYCD*, 7:625, 628–29. See also Jon Parmenter, "Pontiac's War: Forging New Links in the Anglo-Iroquois Covenant Chain, 1758–1766," *Ethnohistory* 44 (1997): 630. Cf. James Merrell's assessment of the attack on Kanestio, "The 'Cast of His Countenance': Reading Andrew Montour," in *Through a*

Glass Darkly: Reflections on Personal Identity in Early America, ed. Ronald Hoffman, Mechal Sobel, and Fredrika Teute (Chapel Hill: University of North Carolina Press, 1997), 39.

45. James Sullivan et al., eds., *The Papers of Sir William Johnson*, 14 vols. (Albany: University of the State of New York, 1921–65) [hereafter cited as *WJP*], 11:399–403; ibid., 4:624.

46. *NYCD*, 7:718–41, 750–57. Mingo delegates attended the second conference with the Shawnees, but only to issue a promise to return to their home villages, which they promptly disregarded.

47. *The Colden Letterbooks*, 2 vols. (New York Historical Society *Collections* [vols. 9–10], 1877–78) 2:19–20.

48. *NYCD*, 8:111–37, (see 132–34 for discrepancy in presents); *WJP*, 6:512, 569–70; ibid., 12:627–29, 633–35, 648, 665–68.

49. McConnell, *A Country Between*, 251–52, argues for the 1768 Fort Stanwix Treaty as a success for the Confederacy. Cf. Dorothy V. Jones, *License for Empire: Colonialism by Treaty in Early America* (Chicago: University of Chicago Press,1982), 94–95; Anthony F. C. Wallace, *The Death and Rebirth of the Seneca* (New York: Knopf, 1969), 123. Johnson's motives at Fort Stanwix are explored in Peter Marshall, "Sir William Johnson and the Treaty of Fort Stanwix, 1768," *Journal of American Studies* 1 (1967): 149–79.

50. *WJP*, 11:791–93.

51. October 1767 entry in "The Diaries of Zeisberger Relating to the First Missions in the Oho Basin," ed. Archer B. Hulbert and William N. Schwarze, *Ohio Archaeological and Historical Quarterly* 21 (1912): 16.

52. *WJP*, 12:406–8, 822.

53. Jones, *License for Empire*, 104–6; McConnell, *A Country Between*, 267; Dowd, *Spirited Resistance*, 43–45; Fenton, *Great Law and the Longhouse*, 561. News of the post-1768 coalition-building among Ohio Indians did prompt a crackdown on western land speculation by British authorities, manifested clearly in the 1774 Quebec Act. See Woody Holton, "The Ohio Indians and the Coming of the American Revolution in Virginia," *Journal of Southern History* 60 (1994): 453–78.

54. *WJP*, 12:1034–35, 1039, 1046; Wheeler-Voegelin, "Ethnohistory of Indian Use and Occupancy," in *Indians of Ohio and Indiana*, ed. Wheeler-Voegelin and Tanner, 2:108–13.

55. Paul A. W. Wallace, *Indians in Pennsylvania* (1961; Reprint, Harrisburg: Pennsylvania Historical and Museum Commission, 1993), 175.

56. Wheeler-Voegelin, "Ethnohistory of Indian Use and Occupancy," in *Indians of Ohio and Indiana*, ed. Wheeler-Voegelin and Tanner, 2:258n. 17.

57. *NYCD*, 8:369.

58. Downes, *Council Fires*, 171–72; Wallace, *Death and Rebirth*, 123–25; White, *Middle Ground*, 357–58; Dowd, *Spirited Resistance*, 45; McConnell, *A Country Between*, 275; Turk McClesky, "Dunmore's War," in *The American Revolution: An Encyclopedia*, 2 vols., ed. Richard L. Blanco (New York: Garland, 1993), 1:492–97; Fenton, *Great Law and the Longhouse*, 580.

59. Kenneth G. Davies, ed., *Documents of the American Revolution, 1770–1783*, 21 vols. (Shannon, Ire., 1972–82), 12:202–3; Dowd, *Spirited Resistance*, 49.

60. Hinderaker, *Elusive Empires*, 209; White, *Middle Ground*, 379.

61. Reuben G. Thwaites and Louise P. Kellogg, eds., *The Revolution on the Upper Ohio, 1775–1777* (Madison: State Historical Society of Wisconsin, 1908), 15.

62. Downes, *Council Fires*, 197; Gregory Schaaf, *Wampum Belts and Peace Trees: George Morgan, Native Americans, and Revolutionary Diplomacy* (Golden, Col.: Fulcrum, 1990), 161–96.

63. March 1777 letter of George Morgan, quoted in Wheeler-Voegelin, "Ethnohistory," 2: 232; Thwaites and

Kellogg eds., *Revolution on the Upper Ohio*, 236–39, 247–48; cf. Schaaf, *Wampum Belts and Peace Trees*, 143–60.

64. J. David Lehman, "The End of the Iroquois Mystique: The Oneida Land Cession Treaties of the 1780s," *William and Mary Quarterly* 47 (1990): 525.

65. Isabel T. Kelsay, *Joseph Brant, 1743–1807: Man of Two Worlds* (Syracuse, N.Y.: Syracuse University Press, 1984), 38–45, 345–46; Robert S. Allen, *His Majesty's Indian Allies: British Indian Policy in the Defense of Canada, 1774–1815* (Toronto: Dundurn, 1992), 62; Calloway, *Crown and Calumet: British-Indian Relations, 1783–1815* (Norman: University of Oklahoma Press, 1987), 14; White, *Middle Ground*, 433; Jones, *License for Empire*, 135–36.

66. "Treaty of Fort Stanwix in 1784," Neville B. Craig, *The Olden Time*, 2 vols. (Pittsburgh, 1846–48), 2:419–20, 423–24, 428. Cf. Jones, *License for Empire*, 152.

67. Wheeler-Voegelin, "Ethnohistory," 2:283–86; Dowd, *Spirited Resistance*, 95; Peter D. James, "The British Indian Department in the Ohio Country, 1784–1795," *Northwest Ohio Quarterly* 64, no. 3 (1992): 84; Alan S. Brown, "The Role of the Army in Western Settlement: Josiah Harmar's Command," *Pennsylvania Magazine of History and Biography* 93 (1969): 168–69.

68. Kelsay, *Joseph Brant*, 401–3, 410; White, *Middle Ground*, 442–43.

69. Barbara Graymont, "New York State Indian Policy After the Revolution," *New York History* 57 (1976): 438–74; Lehman, "End of Iroquois Mystique," 528–47.

70. Downes, *Council Fires*, 302–3; Kelsay, *Joseph Brant*, 415–16.

71. Robert F. Berkhofer, Jr., "Americans Versus Indians: The Northwest Ordinance, Territory Making, and Native Americans," *Indiana Magazine of History* 84 (1988): 90–108; Bernard W. Sheehan, "The Indian Problem in the Northwest: From Conquest to Philanthropy," in *Launching the "Extended Republic": The Federalist Era*, ed. Ronald Hoffman and Peter J. Albert (Charlottesville: University Press of Virginia, 1996), 202–5.

72. Allen, *His Majesty's Indian Allies*, 71.

73. Katharine Turner, *Red Men Calling on the Great White Father* (Norman: University of Oklahoma Press,1951), 3–27; Kelsay, *Joseph Brant*, 470–71.

74. Lehman, "End of the Iroquois Mystique," 524–25.

75. Kelsay, *Joseph Brant*, 478–80; Allen, *His Majesty's Indian Allies*, 78–79.

76. James, "British Indian Department," 88; Wallace, *Death and Rebirth of the Seneca*, 164; Tanner, "The Glaize in 1792," 33; Reginald Horsman, *Matthew Elliott: British Indian Agent* (Detroit: Wayne State University Press, 1964), 86–91.

77. Alan Taylor, "Captain Hendrick Aupaumut: The Dilemmas of an Intercultural Broker," *Ethnohistory* 43 (1996): 445.

78. Horsman, "The British Indian Department and the Abortive Treaty of Lower Sandusky, 1793," *Ohio Historical Quarterly* 70 (1961): 183–219; Allen, *His Majesty's Indian Allies*, 79–80; James, "British Indian Department," 89–90.

79. Allen, *His Majesty's Indian Allies*, 82–83.

80. Kelsay, *Joseph Brant*, 515; Fenton, *Great Law and the Longhouse*, 625–704. At Canandaigua, the United States returned 1,600 square miles of territory ceded in 1784 back to the Senecas. See Jones, *License for Empire*, 179.

81. Sheehan, "Indian Problem in the Old Northwest," 209.

82. I derive this concept from Taylor, "Captain Hendrick Aupaumut," 452.

83. Jones, *License for Empire*, 35.

The French Connection: The Interior French and Their Role in French–British Relations in the Western Great Lakes Region, 1760–1775

KEITH R. WIDDER

French-speaking people played a vital role in the dynamic and often turbulent world of the western Great Lakes following the British conquest of Canada in 1760. Historians, however, have not always adequately analyzed the diversity of the French, who were anything but a homogeneous group. A full understanding of the complicated relationships between French and British requires an answer to the question—who were the "French"?[1] Only after determining who made up this group can we begin to comprehend how French-speaking and English-speaking people related to each other in the complicated society that revolved around the fur trade. This article focuses on the Interior French, who lived with their mixed Indian or French families away from the European settlements at Detroit and Michilimackinac, in a region that encompassed much of what became the Northwest Territory and parts of the Canadian provinces of Ontario and Manitoba. They made their living in the fur trade.[2]

The following discussion argues that the Interior French, who appeared to the British military as their implacable enemy, were indeed indispensable to the efforts of British traders to enter and profit from the fur trade of the western Great Lakes. (Although it is beyond the scope of this essay, the Interior French also played a vital role in the successful efforts of the British military to keep the western Great Lakes

British during the American Revolution.[3]) Violence perpetrated by Frenchmen and Native people against English traders and intense rivalry between French and British traders often marred evolving relationships among members of all three groups, particularly in the late 1760s. But the new reality that the British brought to the western Great Lakes after their conquest of Canada forced the French and the British to get beyond their centuries-old rivalry and work together in the western Great Lakes. British relationships with the Interior French were tense, fluid, and, at times, intensely disagreeable. Whether they liked it or not, the British had to do business with the Interior French, and they did. The Interior French, after all, held the keys to the trade—their kin and trading alliances with the Native people.[4]

A brief comment on the identity of the British is needed for it is their words and deeds that illuminate the presence and behavior of the Interior French, almost all of whom were illiterate. In November 1760, the British military and British merchants arrived in Detroit and, by late 1761, they had established their presence at Michilimackinac, Green Bay, Fort St. Joseph, Fort Miamis, and Ouiatenon.[5] The military extended British "sovereignty" to the western Great Lakes as they took possession of French settlements and required French inhabitants to take an oath of allegiance to the British king. During the first two years officers and representatives of the Indian Department,[6] hoping to enlist the support of Indians, held councils with the Native people at Detroit and throughout the region.[7] Merchants and traders coming from Albany and Montreal appeared on the scene seeking access to the riches of the fur trade controlled by Native and French inhabitants of the region.[8] By 1763, English, Scottish, Scotch-Irish, Irish, and Jewish people had settled in the western Great Lakes.

Delineating the identity of the French is more complicated than portraying that of the less numerous British.[9] English documentary accounts about the "French" frequently refer to the behavior of French-speaking people without making distinctions between different French-speaking groups. In many instances, however, the context of a letter, journal entry, or business ledger leaves little doubt that the French being discussed can be identified. They may be French-Canadian or French civil authorities living in Canada, the military, or Quebec or metropolitan based merchants. When the identity of the French can be determined with clarity, useful analyses of their dealings with British counterparts can be made.

Determining the identity of the French in the western Great Lakes, where many French men and some French women had lived and worked among the Indians for

decades by 1760, often requires a very critical reading of documents.[10] Correspondents used the term "French" to refer to any of several subgroups of French-
speaking people: French living in Canada; traders and *engagés* who traveled
between Montreal and the upper country; settlers living at Detroit, Michilimackinac, and other smaller hamlets in the region; or the Interior French. Frequently,
British letter writers called the people from all of these groups Canadians. (Today,
some scholars use the name French Canadians.) References to the "French" could
also mean French traders from New Orleans or Illinois working in the Mississippi
River Valley, inhabitants of the Illinois Country and Louisiana, or French military
forces.

To further complicate matters, as members of French subgroups worked together
in the trade and built diplomatic alliances with the Native people, they created a
larger French identity that included all French-speaking people including those with
multiethnic heritages. As a result, when the British used the term "French," they frequently left the impression that they were commenting on the French in North
America as a single group rather than on one of the smaller French entities.

On top of the tangled mix of French subgroups in the real world, British officers
routinely blamed the "French" for their difficulties with Indians and obstacles that
British merchants encountered in the fur trade. Since officers in the field, generals
at headquarters, and ministers in London all viewed the French as their longstanding enemy, post commandants found that they could absolve themselves of culpa-
bility and gain a sympathetic hearing from their superiors when things went awry
by blaming the "French."[11] But many of the French of the western Great Lakes were
not the same people with whom the British had been waging war for decades. Even
though both British officers and traders came to understand the diversity of the
French-speaking population in the western Great Lakes, still they often referred to
the French as if they were a monolithic group in their correspondence.

The term "French" carried one more connotation that muddies the understanding of the French presence in the western Great Lakes. Some Indians and French-
speaking people harbored hopes that the French king would send an army to liberate
them from their British occupiers. From time to time rumors to this effect spread
throughout the region inflaming anti-British feeling and rhetoric while alarming
British officers.[12] Although the likelihood of a French army appearing in the western
Great Lakes was almost nil, the power of the belief in its possibility kept alive mutual
French-British suspicions.

From the time British traders first came to Michilimackinac and Detroit they had employed French-speaking people to help them carry on their business, but they discovered that not all French spoke with the same voice. At Michilimackinac in September 1761, Alexander Henry hired "Canadian interpreters and clerks" to carry his goods far to the west, and James Stanley Goddard engaged Canadian clerks to trade his merchandise to Indians in Wisconsin.[13] When the local Odawa[14] threatened Henry if he did not give them his wares, Jacques Farley urged him to comply, but Henry's assistant, Etienne Campion, advised otherwise. Henry deduced that Farley hoped to discourage his entrance into the trade in order to preserve French dominance. Undaunted, Henry, Goddard, and Ezekiel Solomon refused the Odawa demand as they welcomed the arrival of British troops.[15]

The next year at Detroit, James Sterling, who was building a far-flung trading network, found that it was "rare to get a Frenchman here that can be depended on or intrusted with Goods" to take to Miamis and Ouiatenon.[16] But three months later, Sterling sent two bateaux filled with merchandise under the care of "Mr Foucher a French man" to Sault Ste. Marie to establish his business in the Lake Superior country.[17] Sterling's acceptance of the reliability of a Frenchman to carry out this assignment may be explained in part by the fact that, initially, the British were more favorably received by the French at Sault Ste. Marie. Jean-Baptiste Cadot, the leading French-Canadian trader at the Sault, accepted the British and helped to create a far friendlier environment for British traders than was true along the Miamis [Maumee] and Wabash rivers, where French-speaking inhabitants exhibited strong anti-British feelings.

British officers in the field recognized that the French had a special relationship with the Indians in the western Great Lakes; they also viewed the French living in the region as part of the enemy who had contested with Great Britain for European hegemony in North America for over a century. In April 1762, Captain Donald Campbell, commandant at Detroit, told his colonel, Henry Bouquet, "The french Inhabitants and Indians are soe much connected that if you disoblige one of them, the other takes Part."[18] At Michilimackinac, Lieutenant William Leslye confided to General Jeffery Amherst, commander in chief of the British Army in North America, that the French had "great influence with the Indians," and spread false stories intended to undermine the British presence in this region and to prepare the way for a French force to replace the recently arrived British army.[19] In March 1763, Edward Jenkins complained to Major Henry Gladwin, commandant at Detroit, that the

French influence over the Native people was so great that the English had little or no chance to carry on a profitable commerce at Ouiatenon, and they told the Indians that a large French army coming from the Mississippi would soon dislodge the British.[20]

Accounts of British distrust of the "French," however, often masked evolving partnerships between the Interior French and British traders. Nowhere is this more evident than in British proposals to deport the "French" from the West. A critical analysis of this deportation frenzy, which raged in 1767 and 1768, not only tells much about the Interior French, it also reveals how British rhetoric painted a very incomplete, often erroneous picture of the "French."

British anger with the "French" after the War of 1763 induced General Thomas Gage, Amherst's successor, to suggest to Major Gladwin that "it would be best to rout those villains out of all the small posts, and that Michillimackinac will be the better for being thinned of those vile Inhabitants."[21] On 31 August 1764, Colonel John Bradstreet ordered Captain William Howard to send all of the French inhabitants at Michilimackinac, except Charles Langlade and Jacques Farley, to Detroit after Howard had re-garrisoned the fort.[22] (The Chippewa had taken Fort Michilimackinac from the British on 2 June 1763.) Howard, however, found no reason to expel the fort's residents, and after administering oaths to them, he determined that they were fit to remain. Howard's evaluation of these French people after meeting them personally contrasted sharply with Gage's opinion, formed in faraway New York, that they were "a most Vile Sett" and "Trash."[23] Captain's Howard's defiance of Bradstreet and Gage ended most talk of deportation for several years.

Responding to proposals by Major Robert Rogers at Michilimackinac and Captain George Turnbull at Detroit in early 1767, Gage searched for a strategy to remove the "French" from the western Great Lakes region. A close look at the Gage and Turnbull correspondence in 1767 and 1768 reveals that the real target of their deportation scheme was the Interior French. Gage and Turnbull had no chance to oust them from their homelands, but their attempt to devise a plan serves as a lens through which we may glimpse a largely invisible people often unknown by name.

From the perspectives of Gage and his junior officers, close ties between the Interior French and their Indian kin and trading partners both worked against the interest of British merchants and the military's efforts to control the behavior of the Native people. Benjamin Roberts complained from Michilimackinac that "bad French men amongst the foreign Indians," thwarted the plan of Sir William Johnson, superintendent of Indian Affairs for the Northern District, to restrict the fur trade in the northwest to Michilimackinac.[24] Roberts blamed the Interior French for stirring up Indian opposition to the British in order "to keep the trade amongst themselves." He then told Gage that "we Shall have no peace from them [Indians], "'till the French are brought from thence [the interior]."[25]

In the face of official British antipathy, the Interior French had no intention of surrendering their persons to British officials at Detroit, Michilimackinac, or any place else. The only people who possessed the power to throw them out of the country were the Indians, and they were not about to turn against their own kin and trading partners. Even though Gage suggested that the Chippewa be employed to drive the French from interior settlements, Turnbull lamented that he lacked the influence with the Indians to convince them to wage war on the Interior French.[26]

A series of murders during the winter of 1767–68 demonstrated the volatility and complicated nature of the evolving relationship between English traders and the Interior French, as well as the important roles played by the Native people in this process. After Turnbull and Gage learned of these crimes, they turned up their deportation rhetoric. The violence began when some Potawatomis murdered two British traders, a man named Rogers, near Fort St. Joseph, and Frederick Hambach, near the post at Miamis. These two incidents showed how intertwined the Interior French at St. Joseph's were with the Potawatomis and how, at the same time, some French worked in the British interest. Confronted by British suspicions, Louis Chevalier, a longtime resident at St. Joseph, and several other Frenchmen pleaded that they had no part in Rogers' death. They claimed that the Potawatomis told them that they had killed Rogers because "they would not suffer an Englishman among them," a condition upon which they had made peace with the English. Some time after the murder, the perpetrators came to Chevalier's house demanding that he inform Turnbull of their act, that they had more plans to disrupt the English, and that they intended to find Hambach at Miamis and kill him.[27] On 19 January 1768, the Potawatomis murdered Hambach in his house at Miamis. Since Chevalier was deeply in debt to Hambach, the British were convinced that the Frenchman was behind Hambach's death.[28]

Upon learning of Hambach's death, Lieutenant Jehu Hay called together traders at Detroit, who had agents working at Miamis, to devise a strategy to protect their employees that contrasted sharply with a policy of deportation. It was agreed that representatives of the Detroit traders would seek safety under the protection of "two or three frenchmen." In addition, Hay sent letters and wampum to Mini Chesne (Mini or Leopold Chêne), who served as interpreter to the Ottawas, to convince the Ottawas at Miamis to prevent the Potawatomis from doing further violence against Englishmen trading in the area. He also sent a belt, with a speech, asking Petit Gree (Le Petit Gris), an important chief of the Miamis, to stop the Potawatomis from stealing Hambach's goods.[29] Hay sought to counteract Potawatomi hostilities, possibly, even probably inspired by some Interior French, through diplomacy with the Native people and by employing Frenchmen to support British traders.

The murder of James Hill Clark at the Maumee River, on 1 March 1768, throws even more light on how uneasy and tenuous the evolving relationship between British merchants and the French could be. Clark, Samuel Kennedy, and Philip Boyle had come from Albany to trade at the Maumee. Boyle had hired a Canadian, Jacque Maiet, as a servant, but it is not known whether Maiet was a resident of the post at the Maumee or Detroit. A few days before Clark's murder, Maiet and Boyle had argued over Boyle's refusal to supply the Frenchman with liquor. Maiet and some of his fellow Frenchmen found another source of supply, and they drank to excess and had become argumentative while at Mini Chesne's house located along the Maumee River. When the party of English traders approached Mini Chesne's house, Maiet raced out "with a Hatchet in his hand Calling out has any Englishman any thing to Say here this Night." Clark took the hatchet away from Maiet before the Frenchman ran into the woods as Clark yelled "take Care of the Rascal." A short time later Maiet returned to the house and shot Clark dead.[30]

While the extant evidence relative to Clark's death leaves many questions unanswered, it does allow for some relevant observations. First, the longstanding rivalry, even hatred, between the French and British was alive and well in the interior and too much liquor brought deeply rooted attitudes to the surface that could have fatal results. Second, the circumstances of Clark's murder reveal that although the French congregated among themselves in the interior, not all of them approved of Maiet's deed, for Lewis Chattilon and Mini Chesne promised to secure Maiet. The apprehension of Maiet by Canadians was necessary to reestablish their credibility among their English employers. If the Interior French wanted British goods, they could push their challenge to the newcomers only so far. While many of the Interior French may have wished for a return to the days of French hegemony in the western Great Lakes, reality dictated that they learn to do business with the British. This incident also shows that although British traders entered the interior accompanied by French employees, they still had to be very careful in their relationships with the French wherever they found them. Clearly, each French inhabitant acted in his own way, but any generalization that characterized them all as being "vile" was untrue.

In contrast to the deadly incidents of early 1768, Louis Chavalier, Pierre Detailly, and a man named Bernard or Beausoleil demonstrated how complicated relationships between the Interior French and the British were when they acted with charity toward Edward Stuard, a British soldier, and his wife, in May 1768. Some Potawatomis had captured the Stuards near Fort de Chartres and walked them all the way to St. Joseph where, according to Stuard, the three Frenchmen "spar'd no pains to Redeem us out of their hands and us'd us with great humanity, and cloath'd us." Chevalier then used his influence with the Indians between St. Joseph and Chartres to arrange safe passage back to Illinois for the Stuards. Chevalier's good deeds in this instance, however, did not relieve the British military's suspicions of him.[31]

In the aftermath of violence committed against British traders, Gage shared his plans for the Interior French with Turnbull and Sir William Johnson. Gage ordered Turnbull to keep merchants at Detroit from supplying Chevalier and "any others settled in the Indian Villages" who traded where Englishmen could not go without risking their lives. The general also hoped that Chevalier could be brought to Detroit or Michilimackinac to answer for his alleged crimes. In addition, Gage wanted Hay to exploit rivalries between different Indian groups in order to encourage bands who were favorably disposed toward the British to "chastize" pro-French Indians, particularly the Potawatomi of St. Joseph.[32] Furthermore, Turnbull entertained an unrealistic hope of employing Indian parties to attack and scalp any Interior Frenchman who refused to voluntarily move from his village.[33]

British merchants who hired Frenchmen to trade for them increased Gage's frustration with the Interior French and reaffirmed their role in the trade. There was no way that British merchants would stand for deportation of the Interior French. The British traders understood that the French served as their entrée to the riches of western fur trade and they had no qualms over engaging French traders to take their wares to the interior. French traders working out of Michilimackinac or Detroit who had retained family and business ties with Montreal had been trading with the Native people for years through the Interior French. The British entrepreneurs' primary concern was to make money and if they needed to turn to the French in Canada at Detroit or Michilimackinac, or in the interior to help them turn a profit, they did so without a wince. In 1767, in defiance of the policy confining the trade to Michilimackinac and Detroit, 121 canoes went from Michilimackinac carrying goods to be exchanged for furs. Of the five British traders who sent canoes to St. Joseph, only Isaac Todd put an Englishman in charge of his party.[34] While Todd's man Rogers suffered death, the French employees of the other British traders seem to have gone about their business without incident. The Interior French and the Native people welcomed English goods if they received them from French hands. Displeased by the British traders' concern for "present gain," Gage complained they "continuously employed French Commissary's or Agents, whom they have trusted with Goods for them to Sell at an Advanced price in the Indian Villages."[35]

Sir William Johnson also cast about for an effective means to dislodge the Interior French, but he, like British traders, hoped to employ French inhabitants at Detroit to further British interests in the western Great Lakes. Johnson was intrigued by a plan put forth by Lieutenant George McDougall that called for McDougall to lead a party of Detroit militia to remove "the French from amongst ye Indians." Johnson reasoned that Frenchmen from Detroit could bring in "their own Renegadoes" without upsetting the Indians. He also believed that if a British officer commanded a contingent of French forces, the Indians would deduce that they, too, must obey the British.[36]

In the real world of the western Great Lakes in the late 1760s, however, the importance of the fur trade far outweighed the desires of Gage, Turnbull, Johnson, and others to deport the Interior French. While some of the Detroit and Michilimackinac French may have helped to arrest a few troublesome characters in the interior, it is inconceivable that they would have turned against their own kin. The British military's and Indian Department's schemes to deport the Interior French amounted to no more than hallucinations brought about by a desire to wish away a group of people whom they neither liked nor trusted but could not live without. Both British *and* French-Canadian traders depended upon the Interior French to make the trade work and the needs of the trade ultimately determined relationships between French- and English-speaking people in the western Great Lakes— not decisions at Whitehall, New York, or Johnson Hall.

Clearly the Interior French were a force to be reckoned with, but how did they come into being? The answer to this question throws more light on who they were and why they occupied such an important place in the social and economic structure of the western Great Lakes in the 1760s and 1770s. George Turnbull, expressing his bewilderment over the rendezvous of five hundred or six hundred "Vagabonds" at Michilimackinac in June and July 1772, described the Interior French as people who had "been in these upper Countrys for these Twelve, Twenty, or Thirty Years. Who have adopted the very Principles and Ideas of Indians, and Differ from them only a Little in Colour."[37] Furthermore, they spoke the languages of their Indian kin and trading partners.[38] Some of the Interior French had fled to the Indian villages in order to escape responsibility for large debts.[39]

Writing in the early 1850s, William Warren noted that the "main body of the French traders and common voyageurs" married Chippewa women with whom they raised large families who continued to live in the Lake Superior country. Warren goes on to say:[40]

> These Frenchmen, as a body, possessed an unbounded influence over the tribes amongst whom they resided, and though they did not openly aid and advise them in the strenuous efforts that they continued to make even after the French as a nation had retired from the field, to prevent the occupation of their country by the British, yet their silence and apparent acquiescence conduced greatly to their noble and protracted efforts headed by the great Algic leader Pontiac.

Warren knew of what he spoke. His mother was Mary Cadot; her mother was the daughter of White Crane, "the hereditary chief" of the Chippewa village at La Pointe. Her father was Michel Cadot, a prominent French-Chippewa trader, whose mother was Athanasie, the daughter of "a chief of the A-waus-e clan" of Chippewa.[41] Warren acquired a vast knowledge of his Chippewa heritage from tribal elders, upon which he based his book *History of the Ojibways* in 1851.

Peter Pond's story of "Old Pinnshon" expands our understanding of the origins of the Interior French and how they became useful to the British. While stationed with the French army in Illinois (probably Fort De Chartres), Old Pinnshon deserted by taking a boat up the Missouri River where he joined French traders working among the Mandan. The Canadian traders "took him into thare Sarvis til the Hole Cuntrey Was Giveen up to the English and he then Came in to thare Sarvis."[42] In 1773, Pond encountered Old Pinnshon at the portage between the Fox and Wisconsin Rivers, where Jonathan Carver had met him in 1766. Old Pinnshon had learned several Indian languages, which enabled him to serve as an interpreter for British traders who came to sell their goods to Native people living in the upper Mississippi

River Valley and further north.[43] For Carver, Pond, or other British men seeking to establish trading partnerships with Indians, Old Pinnshon and others like him were a godsend, not an enemy.

French Canadians, who took up permanent residence at settlements that depended upon Detroit, formed a segment of the larger, regional Interior French community. Seven men identified as "Capucin, Lorain, La Motte, Pot de Vin, Bartholomé, Bergeron, and Richardville" had "been settled among the Miamis and Ouias from fifteen to twenty years, except Pot de Vin who has been settled as long at Detroit." Sir William Johnson was concerned that none of these men held "passports," which meant they were beyond official British supervision. Guy Carleton, governor of Quebec, knew the identity of each of these men except for Capucin, who lived among the Miamis but had assumed a fictitious name "to conceal that of his Family."[44] Captain Turnbull undoubtedly was referring to these persons, and others, who were beyond his reach when he accused "French fugitives" at Miamis, St. Joseph, Ouiatenon, and Vincennes of "doing everything in their Power to Poison the Minds of the Indians."[45]

Although not as visible as their male partners, French-Canadian women linked the Interior French to Canada. For example, in May 1742 the wife of a "man named La Chine" went from the post at Miamis to Quebec to plead with Governor-General Charles de La Boische de Beauharnois to allow her husband to trade at Miamis. Captain Jacques Legardeur de Saint-Pierre, post commandant, had kept La Chine out of Miamis, charging that he was "a very bad subject who has Been Chased away from all the posts where the officers have not put up with his insults." Appealing to Beauharnois not to accede to La Chine's wife's wishes, Saint-Pierre suggested that La Chine could be much more productive if he moved back to Quebec. But Saint-Pierre identified a very important motivation for Canadians to live in the interior away from French authorities. He suggested that the La Chines' fondness for "debauchery" kept "them in these parts Without even worrying about providing the slightest Upbringing to their Children."[46] Freedom from the restraints of government and church appealed to the Interior French.

In order to understand fully the Interior French we must also recognize the power exercised by women who were the daughters of French men and Native women living in the region. They connected French and later British traders with their Native kin networks. Marie Madeleine Réaume L'archevêque Chevalier's career at Fort St. Joseph demonstrates how important she was to the life of that community. Marie was the daughter of an Iliniwik woman and Jean-Baptiste Réaume, who engaged in the fur trade and later served as interpreter at the post at St. Joseph, and also at Green Bay. After Marie's first husband Augustin L'archevêque, an Illinois trader, died, she married Louis Chevalier, a son of a prominent Michilimackinac family, at St. Joseph in 1752. Their marriage formed a highly effective trading partnership. Louis supplied the goods and Marie distributed the merchandise through her extensive kin network that reached to Illinois, Detroit, and Michilimackinac. Louis Chevalier derived considerable prestige and influence from his marriage to Marie, whose capacity to meet the needs of her own people was enhanced by Louis's ability to get goods from the trading establishment at Montreal. Small wonder that the only way British traders could do business with the Potawatomi and other Indians at St. Joseph was by working through French-speaking men and women who lived there.[47]

The state of affairs in the western Great Lakes frustrated British officials who found it impossible even to control the behavior of licensed traders. George Turnbull, while at Michilimackinac, summed it up quite well in 1771:[48]

> The Trade of the upper Countries is going into confusion very fast. The Immense Quantitys of Rum Imported from Albany Debauches the Indians and makes them unfit for Hunting, and there are many Traders from Montreal who Take out Passes for the Interior Parts of the Country, of Course they don't think themselves Obliged to come nigh the Fort, they supply all the Fugitives who dare not show their Faces at a Fort, and Dayly Increase their Numbers.

Turnbull's remarks spelled out how powerless he was to establish the kind of order in the interior which he believed should exist. Albany and Montreal traders (many of them British) used rum to defraud the Indians, some brazenly ignored the supervision of the post commandant and, perhaps worst of all, they gave goods to the Interior French. To make this point, Turnbull lamented:[49]

> Two days ago one Mr Guillaume Passed this Fort in the night with four Canoes for St Joseph. I cannot help observing that if such things are Permitted Commanding Officers cannot be Supposed to answer for what happens in their Districts as such Proceedings is Flying in the Face of all authority.

Yet, it was this outwardly lawless behavior that perpetuated the way the fur trade had functioned for decades and enabled British merchants to participate in it successfully.

The British military could not prevent any French subgroup from participating in the trade. Gage complained to Carleton in October 1767 that the Interior French, the French from Detroit, Canadian traders, and the Illinois French, "all ramble over the Country without restraint, holding Conferences with each other, planning mischief by exciting Savages against us, and carrying on illicit trade."[50] Seven years later Peter Pond felt at home during a rendezvous at Prairie du Chien, where a large number of French from New Orleans, Illinois, Michilimackinac, and the interior met many Indians prior to departure for their wintering grounds.[51] English traders, such as Pond, saw nothing illicit about coming together with their rivals to take part in an exercise that brought together all of the essential players in the trade. It mattered to no one at Prairie du Chien whether or not General Gage approved of his or her actions.

An analysis of the account listing traders who left Michilimackinac in 1767 shows that British merchants employed French traders, many of whom had traded out of Michilimackinac for years, to take their goods throughout the western Great Lakes. Alexander Henry, Alexander Baxter, Forrest Oakes, John Porteous, and others sent their merchandise to Green Bay, St. Joseph, Lake Superior, and points beyond each of these destinations in canoes under the direction of men named St. Germain, Bartie, Menard, and Richotte. Undoubtedly, these French veterans of the trade worked closely with the Interior French who served as a conduit to the Native people who exchanged furs for things procured by English capital. Ten years later, British entrepreneurs secured over 90 percent of the trade out of Detroit and 65 percent out of Michilimackinac.[52] Even though British merchants gained financial control of the trade, they continued to be dependent upon the French, especially the Interior French, to increase and maintain their places in the trade. The fact that some of the Interior French continued to stir up anti-British sentiments throughout the western Great Lakes barely fazed British traders. The benefits of a functioning, profitable trade far outweighed the risks of violence.[53]

The Interior French lived in a very complicated world that British traders understood far better than did the military officers at Detroit and Michilimackinac or their superiors in New York. The merchants willingly accepted the risks of employing the Interior French to trade goods to their Indian kin and trading partners. The record clearly establishes that the Interior French committed acts of violence against the British and encouraged Native people to do the same. While no trader welcomed violence against himself or one of his employees, it was a cost of doing business.

Peace in the western Great Lakes depended upon a functioning fur trade that met the needs of the Native people and the Interior French. At times the military began to grasp this reality, but they never got beyond their anti-French biases to understand sufficiently how such a motley group of people as the Interior French could have so much influence in determining the course of events in the western Great Lakes during the 1760s and 1770s. Fortunately for the military, the British trading establishment appreciated the vital role played by the Interior French, as English, Scottish, Scotch-Irish, Jewish, and Irish merchants integrated British capital into the fur trade. By so doing they joined both the Interior French and Native people to the British in a way that preserved the social order of the western Great Lakes and ensured that the economy of the region remained sound after the War of 1763, and throughout the American Revolution.

NOTES

1. I have put quotation marks around the word "French" at places in the narrative where I wish to emphasize that the French were either referred to, or perceived to be, a monolithic group.

2. A number of recent works have greatly expanded our knowledge and understanding of the importance of the French contribution to the history of the western Great Lakes region and the Illinois Country in the seventeenth and eighteenth centuries. Richard White, *The Middle Ground: Indians, Empires, and Republics in the Great Lakes Region, 1650–1815* (Cambridge: Cambridge University Press, 1991) is the first major work analyzing French activities in the western Great Lakes since Louise Phelps Kellogg, *The French Régime in Wisconsin and the Northwest* (Madison: State Historical Society of Wisconsin, 1925). The works of Joseph L. Peyser have expanded the horizons of our comprehension of the integral relationships between Indians and French-speaking people: *Letters from New France: The Upper Country, 1686–1783* (Urbana: University of Illinois Press, 1992); *Jacques Legardeur de Saint-Pierre: Officer, Gentleman, Entrepreneur* (East Lansing/Mackinac Island: Michigan State University Press and Mackinac State Historic Parks, 1996); *On the Eve of the Conquest: The Chevalier de Raymond's Critique of New France in 1754* (East Lansing/Mackinac Island: Michigan State University Press and Mackinac State Historic Parks, 1997); and R. David Edmunds and Peyser, *The Fox Wars: The Mesquakie Challenge to New France* (Norman: University of Oklahoma Press, 1993). Michael N. McConnell, *A Country Between: The Upper Ohio Valley and Its Peoples, 1724–1774* (Lincoln: University of Nebraska Press, 1992) and Eric Hinderaker, *Elusive Empires: Constructing Colonialism in the Ohio Valley, 1673–1800* (Cambridge: Cambridge University Press, 1997) have contributed fresh interpretations of the French in the Ohio Country. Carl Ekberg, *French Roots in the Illinois Country:*

The Mississippi Frontier in Colonial Times (Urbana: University of Illinois Press, 1998) and Tanis C. Thorne, *The Many Hands of My Relations: French and Indians on the Lower Missouri* (Columbia: University of Missouri Press, 1996) push the study of the French further into the interior of North America. Daniel H. Usner, Jr., *Indians, Settlers, & Slaves in a Frontier Exchange Economy: The Lower Mississippi Valley Before 1783* (Chapel Hill: University of North Carolina Press, 1992) tells much about the French experience in colonial Louisiana. All of these books build on such earlier works as W. J. Eccles, *France in America* (New York: Harper and Row, 1972) and *The Canadian Frontier, 1534–1760* (Albuquerque: University of New Mexico Press, 1969); Dale Miquelon, *New France, 1701–1744: "A Supplement to Europe"* (Toronto: McClelland and Stewart, 1987); and Cornelius J. Jaenen, *Friend and Foe: Aspects of French-Amerindian Cultural Contact in the Sixteenth and Seventeenth Centuries* (New York: Columbia University Press, 1976).

The scholars cited above are all quite aware that the French were a diverse group of people whose relationships with each other, Native people, and other Europeans were very complicated. They analyze the diplomatic, military, religious, commercial, and social roles played by French-speaking people in the western Great Lakes and neighboring regions. The literature informs us of the antagonism that existed between missionaries, traders, and military officers, the official condemnation of the *coureurs de bois*, rivalries between traders, jealousies among the officers, familial relations formed by French traders and Native women, etc. After the French defeat in the French and Indian War, however, the focus of the historiography of the western Great Lakes is on the British and their relationship with the Native people. Consequently, the French are relegated to a position in the wings of the historical theater after 1763. But French-speaking people not only continued to live in the region, they acted out crucial parts in the drama of real life between 1763 and 1783. Their marginalization by historians has led to the perception that the primary significance of the French during these years was little more than serving as a thorn in the side of the beleaguered British. A thorough understanding of the French and their relationships with the British and Native people must begin with an analysis of the sub-groups who formed the larger group the "French."

3. For a detailed discussion of the role played by people dependent upon Michilimackinac in the American Revolution see David A. Armour and Keith R. Widder, *At the Crossroads: Michilimackinac During the American Revolution* (Mackinac Island: Mackinac Island State Park Commission, 1986) and Widder, "Effects of the American Revolution on Fur-Trade Society at Michilimackinac," in *The Fur Trade Revisited: Selected Papers of the Sixth North American Fur Trade Conference, Mackinac Island, Michigan, 1991,* ed. Jennifer S. H. Brown, W. J. Eccles, and Donald P. Heldman (East Lansing/Mackinac Island: Michigan State University Press and Mackinac State Historic Parks, 1994), 299–316.

4. Jacqueline Peterson's focus on the *métis* in "Many Roads to Red River: Métis Genesis in the Great Lakes Region, 1680–1815," in *The New Peoples: Being and Becoming Métis in North America,* ed. Jacqueline L. Peterson and Jennifer S. H. Brown (Lincoln: University of Nebraska Press, 1985), 37–72, and "The People in Between: Indian-White Marriage and the Genesis of a Métis Society and Culture in the Great Lakes Region, 1680–1830" (Ph.D. diss., University of Illinois-Chicago, 1981) clearly demonstrates the centrality of the French in the western Great Lakes. For an intriguing account of how kinship worked at Fort St. Joseph, see Susan Sleeper-Smith, "Furs and Female Kin Networks: The World of Marie Madeleine Réaume L'archevêque Chevalier," in *New Faces of the Fur Trade: Selected Papers of the Seventh North American Fur Trade Conference, Halifax, Nova Scotia, 1995,* ed. Jo-Anne Fiske, Susan Sleeper-Smith, and William Wicken (East Lansing: Michigan State University Press, 1998), 53–72. Gary Clayton Anderson, *Kinsmen of Another Kind: Dakota-White Relations in the*

Upper Mississippi Valley, 1650–1862 (Lincoln: University of Nebraska Press, 1984), 29–76, gives an interesting account of evolving relationships between Europeans and the Dakota between 1670 and 1800.

5. Dietrich Brehm, "Lieut[nt] Brehm's Raport [sic] to His Excellency General Amherst, of a Scout going from Montreal by la Galette, round, part of the North shore to Lake Ontario to Niagara, from thence round the South shore of Lake Erie to Detroit up Lake S[t] Claire and part of Lake Huron returning by land to Fort Pitt," 22 February 1761, Papers of Jeffery Amherst [hereafter AP], W.O. 34/49, 21–24, Public Record Office [hereafter PRO], Kew, Surrey, England, and "Report to His Excellency Sir Jeffery Amherst Commander in Chieff of His Majestys Forces in North American etc: etc: etc. of the Lakes, Creeks, and Roads, seen in going round the Frontier Posts of Canada, with a Detachment, first Commanded by Major Gladwin and latst by Cap[t] Henry Balfourt," 6 April 1762, AP, W.O. 34/102, 20–23.

6. The Indian Department helped to create British North American Indian policy, and its superintendents carried out that policy. Sir William Johnson served as superintendent of the Northern District from 1755 until 1774, and John Stuart headed the Southern District from 1762 until 1779. For a recent analysis of Stuart's career see J. Russell Snapp, *John Stuart and the Struggle for Empire on the Southern Frontier* (Baton Rouge: Louisiana State University Press, 1996).

7. "Proceedings at a Treaty held at Detroit by Sir William Johnson Bart, with the Sachems and Warriors of the several Nations of Indians there assembled," Sir William Johnson Minutes, 6: 17 February 1761–17 October 1763, 92–128, Indian Records, RG 10, Series II (micro reel C-1222), National Archives of Canada (NAC); Henry Balfour, "Speech delivered to the Indians of Nations living in the Environs of Michilimackinac, at said Fort the 29th September 1761," *The Papers of Sir William Johnson* [hereafter cited as JP], 14 vols., ed. James Sullivan et al. (Albany: University of the State of New York, 1921–62), 3:537–45; and William L. Jenks, "The 'Hutchins' Map of Michigan," *Michigan History Magazine* 10 (1926): 358–73.

8. Accounts of the first wave of British traders to enter the fur trade at Michilimackinac and Detroit include Milo Milton Quaife, ed., *Alexander Henry's Travels and Adventures in the Years 1760–1776* (Chicago: Lakeside Press, 1921); and James Sterling, "Letterbook," William L. Clements Library [hereafter cited as WLCL], University of Michigan, Ann Arbor. See also, Walter S. Dunn, Jr., *Frontier Profit and Loss: The British Army and the Fur Trade, 1760–1764* (Westport, Conn.: Greenwood, 1998).

9. Estimating the population of different groups of people living in the western Great Lakes region is difficult and any figures will be imprecise. I think it is safe to say that several thousand French-speaking people lived in the region in the 1760s and 1770s. It is unlikely that the British civilian population exceeded 500 or 600 in 1775.

10. I have chosen not to use the term *métis* in this essay even though I have used it before for the same time frame. There has been considerable discussion among students of the Great Lakes during the eighteenth century as to whether or not the *métis* existed as a distinguishable group before the early nineteenth century. It is a debate that probably cannot be satisfactorily resolved because people who claimed both a Native and French heritage played such complicated roles in a world where relationships among people of Indian, French, British, Spanish, and later American extraction reached in countless directions. But it is these relationships that explain how the people lived, worked, and died in the western Great Lakes region. It was commonplace for an Interior French person to have simultaneous, fluid relationships with people of several Native groups and more than one European group. In the highly charged social and political environment of the western Great Lakes, the political loyalty of the Interior French

shifted easily and often depending on how it affected their relationships with trading partners, Native kin, or the overall state of the fur trade. While the Interior French may have functioned as a distinct group, their close ties with their Native families and French traders probably caused some of them to perceive of themselves as both Indian and French. I do not think we know enough of how the Interior French thought to formulate any generalizations regarding their self-perception. Consequently, historians are left with the challenge of interpreting the experience of people who in essence defy a neat ethnic label. But at the same time scholars need to communicate to their readers that the *métis* or Interior French or whatever term they use to distinguish people of mixed Indian and French heritage from others cannot be viewed simply as Indians or French. The difficulty in arriving at a suitable term to name people of mixed Native-French heritages is evident in Thomas H. Johnson's review of Tanis C. Thorne's book *The Many Hands of My Relations: French and Indians on the Lower Missouri.* He suggests that perhaps the term "Francophone Native Americans" be used to refer to people of "mixed French and native ancestry," *Journal of American History* 85 (June 1998): 213–14. This term may be as good as any of the others.

11. For example: On 16 September 1762, Lieutenant William Leslye, at Michilimackinac, blamed many of his troubles on the French, "I am of oppinion there is some Damn Rascalu ffrench who spread a great dale of News ammongst the Indians, & tell a great many storys to our disadvantage, . . . & till then I look upon the ffrench here as much if not more dangerous that the Indians, not from their force but from their great influence with the Indians & their hopes of seeing the Country soon in the hands of its late Masters, . . ." Leslye to Amherst, AP, W.O. 34/49, 116–17. On 8 July 1763, Major Henry Gladwin, at Detroit, told General Jeffery Amherst:

> therefore, from this, and other circumstances I conclude that the french are at the bottom of this affair [the Indian capture of Michilimackinac and the siege of Detroit], in order to ruin the british merchants, and engross the trade to themselves, . . ." AP, W.O. 34/49, 196–99. On 28 August 1767, Captain George Turnbull, at Detroit, informed General Thomas Gage, "The Bearer of this Mᵣ Maisonville Sets out immediately for Philadelphia and I Believe proposes going to New York. He has been Employd by Mᵣ Croghan for some years past with the Miamis and Ouyaehtanons. He tells me that numbers of our troops at the Illinois Desert and got over to the Spanish Side, and that there is Little Harmony between the Inhabitants and Colonel Reed it is very difficult to prove any thing against these fellows as every common french man has cunning enough for a Jesuit. But from the Descourses of these french Inhabitants, every where I am much afraid they will bring the Indians to an Open Rupture with us."

Thomas Gage Papers [hereafter cited as GP], American Series (AS), 69, WLCL. For a discussion of ideological assumptions of British officials serving in North America between 1760 and 1774, see Kerry A. Trask, "To Cast Out the Devils: British Ideology and the French Canadians of the Northwest Interior, 1760–1774," *American Review of Canadian Studies* 15, no. 3 (1985): 249–62.

12. Gregory Dowd, "The French King Wakes Up in Detroit: Pontiac's War in Rumor and History," *Ethnohistory* 37 (summer 1990): 254–78; and John Parker, ed., *The Journals of Jonathan Carver and Related Documents, 1766–1770* (St. Paul: Minnesota Historical Society Press, 1976), 122.

13. Quaife, ed., *Alexander Henry's Travels*, 46–47; James Gorrell, 25 March 1762, "Journal of the Proceedings of Lieut. James Gorrell from the day he took Post at Fort Edward Augustus (or La Bay) being the 14th of October 1761 to June 1763," Sir William Johnson Minutes, 7:5–11.

14. The Little Traverse Bay Band of Odawa are descended from this group of Native people. Since the Little Traverse Band uses the spelling "Odawa," I also use it when referring to them. Later in the article, I use

the word Ottawa when referring to Ottawa people who lived south and east of the Straits of Mackinac.

15. Quaife, ed., *Alexander Henry's Travels*, 50–3.

16. James Sterling to James Syme, 8 June 1762, Sterling, "Letterbook."

17. Sterling to John Duncan & Co., 5 September 1762, Sterling, "Letterbook."

18. Donald Campbell to Henry Bouquet, 26 April 1762, Henry Bouquet Papers, ADD MSS 21648:122–23, reel 11, British Library, London.

19. William Leslye to Jeffery Amherst, 16 September 1762, AP, W.O. 34/49:116–17.

20. Edward Jenkins to Henry Gladwin, 28 March 1763, AP, W.O. 34/49:202.

21. Thomas Gage to Gladwin, 28 March 1764, GP, AS, 16.

22. John Bradstreet to William Howard, 31 August 1764, GP, AS, 23.

23. Gage to Bradstreet, 15 October 1764, GP, AS, 25.

24. Benjamin Roberts to Gage, 10 July 1767, GP, AS, 67.

25. Roberts to Gage, 17 July 1767, GP, AS, 67.

26. Gage to George Turnbull, 13 July 1767, GP, AS 67.

27. John Hay to George Croghan, 19 February 1768, in Croghan to Gage, 14 April 1768, GP, AS, 76.

28. Turnbull to Gage, 23 February 1768, GP, AS, 74.

29. Hay to Croghan, 19 February 1768. For a brief account of Le Petit Gris's role in Henry Hamilton's march to Vincennes in 1778, see White, *The Middle Ground*, 373–74.

30. Samuel Kennedy, 26 March 1768, Deposition, and Daniel Wheeler, 24 March 1768, Deposition, in Turnbull to Gage, 10 April 1768; Turnbull to Gage, 10 April, GP, AS, 75.

31. Edward Stuard and his wife, in Richard Mahieu to Turnbull, 28 May 1768, GP, AS, 76.

32. Gage to Turnbull, 2 May 1768, GP, AS, 76; Gage to William Johnson, 2 May 1768, JP, 12:486–87.

33. Turnbull to Gage, 23 May 1768, GP, AS, 77.

34. "An Account of the Number of Canoes gone out Wintering from the Post of Michilimackinac, Including the Names of Traders and those that are Bail for them. Allso [*sic*] the Value of their Goods and where they are found," C.O. 42/14, 98A, PRO.

35. Gage to Guy Johnson, 29 May 1768, GP, AS, 76.

36. W. Johnson to Gage, 13 October 1768, GP, AS, 82.

37. Turnbull to Gage, 5 July 1772, GP, AS, 112.

38. Croghan to W. Johnson, 12 July 1765, JP, 11:836–41.

39. Beamsley Glazier to Gage, 4 October 1768, GP, AS, 81.

40. William W. Warren, *History of the Ojibway Nation* (1885; Reprint, Minneapolis: Ross and Haines, 1970), 195–96.

41. Theresa Schenck, "The Cadots: The First Family of Sault Ste. Marie," *Michigan History* 72 (March/April 1988): 37; Warren, *History of the Ojibway Nation*, 10–11.

42. Peter Pond, "The Narrative of Peter Pond," in *Five Fur Traders of the Northwest*, ed. Charles M. Gates (St. Paul: Minnesota Historical Society, 1965), 38.

43. Parker, ed., *The Journals of Jonathan Carver*, 83.

44. Guy Carleton to W. Johnson, 27 March 1767, JP, 5:520–24.

45. Turnbull to Gage, 20 May 1767, GP, AS, 65.

46. Jacques Legardeur de Saint-Pierre to Charles de La Boische de Beauharnois, 27 May 1742?, and Beauharnois to Saint-Pierre, 22 July 1742, in Peyser, trans. and ed. *Jacques Legardeur de Saint-Pierre*, 54–55.

47. Sleeper-Smith, "Furs and Female Kin Networks," and John M. Gram, "The Chevalier Family and the Demography of the Upper Great Lakes," 30 June 1995, unpublished paper in the Research Library, Mackinac Island State Park Commission, Mackinac City, Michigan.

48. Turnbull to Gage, 12 May 1771, GP, AS, 103.

49. Turnbull to Gage, 12 June 1771, GP, AS, 104.

50. Gage to Carleton, 5 October 1767, GP, AS, 71.

51. Pond, "Narrative," 44–46.

52. "An Account of the Number of Canoes gone out Wintering from the Post of Michilimackinac," and "Consolidated Returns of Indian Trade Licenses, 1777–1790," Canada MSS G, NAC.

53. Gage to W. Johnson, 31 March 1773, GP, AS, 117; R. B. Lernoult to Gage, 24 September 1774, GP, AS, 123.

"Ignorant bigots and busy rebels": The American Revolution in the Western Great Lakes

SUSAN SLEEPER-SMITH

Engjand's attempt to govern the western Great Lakes, following the conquest of Canada, proved far from successful. Neither Native people nor their French fur-trader kin were receptive to the English. Pontiac reminded England that the French, not the Indians, lost the recent war. Many English officers often displaced blame for the uprising on French fur traders and, consequently, believed that their ability to control the region rested on removal of the people they disparagingly called the Interior French. But the French were not removed and those English officers who sought the cooperation and assistance of the Interior French proved more effective in garnering the support and assistance of Native people. English officers who blatantly disregarded the social processes of fur-trade society compounded the problems associated with fighting the revolutionary war and proved unable to recruit Indian warriors.

The Interior French were usually the descendants of French fur traders and Indian women. Kin networks of mixed ancestry descendants not only paralleled and extended but also further complicated the kinship structure of indigenous society. Most of these Interior French remained involved in the western Great Lakes fur trade and served as cultural mediators between their indigenous kin and New France officials. Those English officers who blatantly disregarded the intermediary role played by the Interior French not only found their orders ignored but also endangered the lives of English traders who attempted to trade among the Indians. The complexity and diversity of this social landscape was apparent at many of the smaller fur-trade posts. This essay relies on the L'archevêque-Chevalier kin network, who married among the St. Joseph Potawatomi of southern Lake Michigan, to show how the Interior French and their Native kin either frustrated or facilitated English governance. Ultimately, kin networks affected the ability of the English to elicit the assistance of Great Lakes people in their struggle against the American rebels.

Our story begins on Christmas Eve in 1772, just before midnight, when the irate Detroit commandant Henry Bassett sent a hastily written letter to General Gage requesting permission to attack the renegade French at old Fort St. Joseph, almost two hundred miles to the west. The story unfolded earlier that evening when a frightened and weary Cornelius Van Slyck arrived in Detroit after a harrowing, weeklong journey along frozen Indian trails. He had narrowly escaped death.

> . . . Mr. Van Slyck, a considerable trader of this place, is just arrived from St. Joseph, the Potawatomi Indians attempted murdering him and three servants about Ten Days since. He had one killed and another wounded so ill that he left him in the house and of course is put to death, the third was a Frenchman who made his escape to the fort . . . Mr. Van Slyck had received a slight wound in his face and with utmost difficulty had got here, he tells me that it was the fault of some French traders that are settled there. I'm informed there's a certain (Louison Chevalier) a very bad man, that is married to a Squaw and encourages these murders. I'm told that this is the third time within three years.[1]

By the spring, Gage had not responded to Bassett's request to march on St. Joseph and "root out these villains." Once again, Bassett wrote to Gage and he included Potawatomi testimony to affirm the truth of Louis Chevalier's attack on Van Slyck. He even took the precaution of appending to his letter "a true copy of the Indian signatures."

> *Pitchbaon:* . . . you are not mistaken with respect to Louison Chevalier, for immediately after the bad Indians had struck the blow, and Mr. Van Slycke was fled he encouraged the Indians to go back and plunder, they said they were afraid as they had seen Mr. Van Slycke loading his guns (Louison Chevalier) then told them that

he was fled and that they must go and plunder, that there were a great deal of rum and goods left. We secured twenty blankets, three barrels of powder, three bags of ball, and one barrel of rum, etc., and etc.: all which we kept for Mr. Van Slycke and delivered them to him when he returned. But Louison Chevalier and all the French people there plundered as well as the Indians, but he was the worst of them and could have saved all the goods if he would as there were two bateaux lying close by the House to carry them away, and we have reason to believe for his behavior that he encouraged the Indians to strike the blow, he nor the rest of the French have not returned the things they plundered for they sold us of the rum this spring.[2]

Bassett never received permission to attack Fort St. Joseph.[3] To Gage, it must have seemed foolish for a commander at a wilderness post to venture almost two hundred miles into Indian lands in defense of a fur trader. Bassett, like many of his fellow officers, distrusted men with French names[4] and considered the French who lived among Great Lakes people to be "the outcasts of all Nations, and the refuse of Mankind."[5]

Longstanding English animosity toward the French clouded the judgments of commanders such as Bassett. At western outposts it was not readily apparent who were allies and enemies, a dilemma aggravated by the numerous French who lived in Native American villages. English Francophobia was worsened by the ethnic, national, and racial diversity of this region and hasty judgments about "good and bad" characters could have disastrous consequences. Officers like Bassett, whose assessments routinely relied on nationality or ethnicity, transformed the French into the most despised of Great Lakes inhabitants. Bassett identified Louison Chevalier as Interior French and, for this reason, accepted what he usually considered "unreliable" Indian hearsay as proof of bad behavior.

By the time the English took control of the western Great Lakes, the kinship ties that bound Frenchmen to Native people spanned generations. Mixed ancestry descendants often blended seamlessly into Native society. They were often adopted and acquired Indians names, although some retained their French names. The western Great Lakes[6] fur trade had encouraged intermarriage, both "marriage in the manner of the country" as well as marriage sacramentally sanctioned by missionary priests.[7] The exchange of trade goods for peltry was not the simple exchange process of a market economy but was embedded in the social dynamics of indigenous society. The best furs were reserved for kin and allies. Marriage integrated

French traders into indigenous kin networks and ensured access to furs. The Interior French, even the more recent arrivals, bore a strikingly similar appearance to their Native kin. As one Michilimackinac officer remarked ". . . they have been in these upper Countrys for these twelve, twenty, or thirty years, [and] have adopted the very principles and ideas of Indians, and differ little from them only a little in colour."[8]

The blending of French and Native peoples represented one small part of the larger demographic changes that began in the seventeenth century when Native people from the east were pushed westward, first by the Fur Trade Wars and later, by colonial settlement. Abenaki, Sauk, Huron, Neutral, Shawnee, and Delaware were adopted into more populous nations like the Potawatomi, Odawa, and Miami. Even Creek and Chickasaw, captured during wars, lived among Great Lakes people. Nations like the Illini had raided slaves from among the western Pawnee and thus the word *panis* became synonymous with slave. *Panis* were shipped from Montreal to the Caribbean, while others were traded at New Orleans for African American slaves. However, many *panis* were adopted, and they married among Native people. Fur-trade communities also had significant slave populations. By 1750, Kaskaskia, near present-day St. Louis, included 1,000 French residents, 300 black slaves, 60 *panis*, and 800 Kaskaskia Indians who lived in adjacent villages. A 1762 census for Detroit indicates that 65 of the approximately 900 people living near the fort were African American slaves. Three years later, the nearly equal ratio of male to female slaves resulted in a doubling of that population.[9]

In the western Great Lakes, kinship defined identity rather than either race or ethnicity. During this socially dynamic time period, identity was a complex issue dependent on kin networks, residential and occupational patterns, and cultural orientations. Louis Chevalier's identity was rooted in his wife's kin network, rather than in his nationality. Chevalier was born to French fur-trade parents and had been raised at Michilimackinac, but at age forty, when he moved to St. Joseph to marry Marie Madeleine Réaume L'archevêque, an Illini woman, he was incorporated into her household and became part of her kin network. Marie Madeleine was a forty-one-year-old widow with four daughters who had lived and traded among the Potawatomi for over forty years. At age forty, she bore Louis Chevalier's son, Louison, and it was then that Chevalier moved from Michilimackinac to St. Joseph and joined a household typical of those involved in the fur trade. Generally Catholic and matrifocal, the women processed peltry, produced an annual agricultural surplus, and manufactured such items as snowshoes, which were integral to the fur trade. Marriage to Madeleine gave Louis Chevalier acceptance into the kin networks of the St. Joseph River Valley fur trade, an entrée denied the Chevalier family for over twenty years. When the English arrived to take control of Fort St. Joseph, their son was almost twelve years old and Louis had lived at St. Joseph for over a decade. In the eyes of English officers, Chevalier was a French fur trader while the woman to whom he was married was mistakenly dismissed as inconsequential.

By the time of the American Revolution, Louis and Madeleine had constructed a familial kin network that joined the St. Joseph community to every fur-trade post in the western Great Lakes. The marriages of Madeleine's youngest daughters solidified kinship ties to the Chevalier family and to the even larger fur-trade community in Montreal. Louis' younger brother married one of Madeleine's daughters, while another daughter married Louis' Montreal trading partner. Madeleine's two oldest daughters and their fur-trader husbands moved to Illinois Country, one to Fort Pimiteoui (now Peoria) and the other to Cahokia. Madeleine had a sister who lived at Green Bay, as did Louis. Louis Chevalier had sixteen siblings; his brothers had married among the Winnebago, while his sisters lived at Detroit and Michilimackinac. Louis himself had been married, first to an Odawa woman; his son of that marriage was an important headman among his mother's people.

A fictive kin network that evolved under the umbrella of Catholicism further extended this familial kin network. Most French families had moved to Detroit during the 1750s, a time at which no resident priest was available at the settlement. Madeleine became the most important lay practitioner and used Catholicism as a socially integrative tool to weave together the diverse people of this increasingly indigenous fur-trade community. Indigenous people, as well as slaves, were baptized at the St. Joseph mission church. Marie Madeleine appeared repeatedly as a godparent, as did Louis. Even L'archevêque Chevalier kin returned there, when missionary priests were present, to baptize their children.

These familial and fictive kin networks had a sympathetic correspondence with the networks of indigenous society. Initially, English attempts to impose order on this kin-related world differed from those of their French predecessors, who had exercised minimal control over the region and relied on traders and their kin networks, rather than the military, to thwart intrusion by foreign traders. Intermarriage ensured a continued French presence despite the English victory at Montreal.

The lands that fell into English hands proved too vast and financial resources proved too limited to establish an effective military presence. Former forts, even when manned by English troops, never equated with effective control of the western Great Lakes. Fort St. Joseph was typical of many smaller French forts that were built throughout the western Great Lakes. There were no barracks for military personnel and the soldiers resided in nearby houses.[10]

Visually, it was often difficult to distinguish the French dwellings from those of the Indians. Extended French families lived together in one house; some inhabited *poteaux en terre* French style buildings, while others lived in log cabins or indigenous style longhouses. At Fort St. Joseph, the Potawatomi lived in similar dwellings, and one of the Potawatomi medal chiefs lived in a framed house.[11] Although residence patterns often separated the French from the Potawatomi, this mixture of housing styles complicated the outsiders' attempt to readily discern social divisions, since French and Indians often lived with or next to each other. Mixed ancestry descendants, adopted and integrated into clans, lived among the Indians. Native Americans separated from their indigenous kin often lived in French households, as did *panis*.

Posts like St. Joseph were the crossroads of the trade and, there, socially diverse communities of Native people and the Interior French produced an agricultural surplus sufficient to supply transient fur traders and manufactured goods for the trade, such as snowshoes and canoes. Valuable canoe space transported trade goods from Montreal; they rarely carried an extensive food supply or such bulky items as snowshoes. Western posts had a settled agricultural appearance with extensive acreage under cultivation, usually controlled by the matrifocal households of Native women. Oxen were used to plow the fields and to draw French carts that carried hay for dairy and beef cattle. There were chickens, pigs, and even fruit orchards that supplemented more traditional sources of food. Indian ponies roamed the nearby woodlots and carried people and peltry overland. While the tending of horses and the trapping of furs was primarily a male pursuit, the processing of furs and the control over agricultural resources remained a female responsibility.

In the St. Joseph River Valley, Native women easily incorporated the rich cereal and grain crops of European society into their own diet.[12] French fur traders proved to be reluctant agriculturalists, but they were able instructors. During the early eighteenth century, Native women produced an agricultural surplus that fed fur traders as well as warriors commissioned to fight on behalf of European forces. For instance, before she married Louis Chevalier, Madeleine Réaume L'archevêque supplied the Fort St. Joseph commandant with the wheat, oats, and corn he needed in the French fight against the Chickasaw. Like their French predecessors, the English also depended on an indigenous agricultural surplus to supply military operations in the western Great Lakes.[13] Historians rarely emphasize the role that agricultural produce played in the fur trade, but there were both local and export markets for chickens, cattle, oxen, and horses. Traders shipped boatloads of corn, *makuks,* and barrels of maple sugar, as well as furs, to Michilimackinac, Detroit, and St. Louis; eighteenth-century traders were brokers of foodstuffs and furs.[14]

At the end of the French and Indian War, when Captain Joseph Schlosser assumed command of Fort St. Joseph, he arrived unprepared for the community that he encountered. Schlosser found himself in the middle of a prosperous fur-trade community, rather than a military post. His lack of familiarity with Native customs was further hampered by Amherst's order that terminated presents to the Indians. Schlosser had nothing of significance for the ritual exchange of gifts that established the bonds of friendship and sealed alliances with Native people. Schlosser and his soldiers were unwelcome at Fort St. Joseph.

The English presence in the Great Lakes reinforced fears about the appropriation of Native lands. Fur traders who arrived with the military further magnified the English threat. England's pronouncements of "sovereignty" over the land, coupled with continuing streams of Native refugees from the east, troubled people in the western Great Lakes. British officers were emphatically reminded that they had defeated the French, not the Native people.[15]

Pontiac's Rebellion proved a vivid reminder of who controlled the western Great Lakes.[16] Garrisons at St. Joseph, Ouiatenon, Miami, Sandusky, La Boeuf, Venango, and Presqu'Isle were easily captured by Pontiac and his followers.[17] Only Detroit withstood attack, and it remained under protracted siege, from May to October 1763. Although Pontiac's Rebellion lasted for only six months, it was clear that there would be no retribution for Native insurgency. Sir William Johnson, the Superintendent for Indian Affairs of the Northern Department, wrote to Gage that ". . . our Misfortune [is] that the Indians know too well their own Strength, and that it is not in the power of the English alone to punish them effectually. . . ."[18]

Unfortunately, Pontiac's Rebellion also intensified the Francophobic attitude of many English officers, especially when English officers were killed by the Indians. At Fort St. Joseph, Schlosser and twelve of his men died; two were taken prisoner and later ransomed at Detroit. Gladwin, under siege at Detroit, displaced blame for the uprising on the greed of the French traders, ". . . the French are at the bottom of this affair, in order to ruin . . . British merchants, and engross the trade to themselves."[19] Even Thomas Gage believed that the French behaved "[i]n a scandalous and seditious manner."[20] Many officers advocated forced removal of the Interior French. Major Gladwin believed that "those vile inhabitants at the outposts ought to be removed, and sent where they can't return."[21] The same remedy was proposed by George Turnbull, who told Gage, "As to removing the French inhabitants between this [place] and the Mississippi, it would be a very great, and necessary piece of service."[22]

The peace that Pontiac signed was a victory for indigenous sovereignty. The Proclamation of 1763 restrained the movement of European colonists into the western Great Lakes. More importantly, it restricted land sales to English traders at the larger posts, such as Detroit and Michilimackinac, and thwarted the type of large land grants that caused continual havoc in the Ohio River Valley.

Pontiac's short but effective uprising also dramatically reversed the direction of fur-trade policy in the western Great Lakes. The English attempted to restrict the movement of fur traders into Native villages. They envisioned that the fur trade would operate as it did along the eastern seaboard where Native people transported furs to the posts. In New York, for instance, the trade was confined to inside the Albany and Oswego forts. Johnson's Plan of 1764 adapted this model of the eastern fur trade to the west. Major forts became central to the exchange process and, consequently, all legal trade was to take place only at Michilimackinac and Detroit.[23]

Inadvertently, England set in motion policies that left the western Great Lakes in the hands of Native Americans and their French kin. Instead of becoming less dependent on the French, the English became increasingly dependent on those people whom they most distrusted. Under the French, it had been unnecessary for Native people to make long journeys to sell peltry. Fur traders lived in the villages and others arrived in the spring, when trade goods were sent upcountry by the Montreal merchants.[24] The restriction of trade to two locations meant that the Interior French continued to trade at wintering grounds, or in Native villages, while the English traders who did the same were engaged in illegal activity. At former posts, like Miami, Ouiatenon, or Fort St. Joseph, English traders were rarely welcome. Those who poached risked their lives. In the spring of 1766, two English traders were murdered near the River Rouge. Lt. Campbell, then commanding at Detroit, reported to Gage that "it was the Potawatomis of St. Joseph that committed the Murder, and that two of them were the Chief's sons of that tribe . . . I have since put a stop to any trade with that nation, until they deliver up the Murderer, though I suspect it will not have the desired effect."[25]

English traders pleaded with Johnson to rescind the restrictions on the fur trade and complained that they would lead to "the total ruin of that Valuable Branch of Commerce, the lessening of his Majesty's Revenue and the Consumption of British Manufactures more especially the Woollen; besides depriving the Merchants of the necessary Remittances."[26] Fur exports to England actually declined for the four years that the Johnson Plan remained in effect.[27] In March 1767, the newly appointed governor general, Sir Guy Carleton, lobbied for an elimination of the Johnson policy, and the next year, the policy was rescinded.

The Johnson Plan had hampered English fur traders but bolstered the fortunes of the Interior French. Four years of fur-trade restrictions firmly established the Interior French as the middlemen of the trade. They continued to engage in an illegal trade, wintered with their indigenous kin, and collected the season's peltry. They established new merchant connections, at St. Louis and New Orleans, and this encouraged the export of furs to the south, rather than north to Michilimackinac and Detroit.[28] With the dissolution of the Johnson Plan, these Frenchmen proved willing to carry English trade goods, but often unwilling to accommodate intrusion by English traders. Those traders who trespassed into Native villages and wintering grounds south of Lake Michigan faced dire consequences. In the fall of 1767, an English trader named Rogers arrived in the Kankakee River Valley, where the St. Joseph Potawatomi wintered. He was killed and his merchandise disappeared. Two English traders, whom Louis Chevalier had hidden in the basement of his house during Pontiac's Rebellion, were also murdered. In January 1768, Frederick Hambach attempted to sidestep Chevalier, trade directly with Native people, and was murdered by several Potawatomi. Cornelius Van Slyck was fortunate when he escaped with his life.[29]

The English suspected Louis Chevalier, but they were unable to remedy the situation and protect their own traders. Louis Chevalier and his kin network controlled access to furs in the St. Joseph River Valley. They willingly secured trade goods from English merchants, but were unwilling to tolerate English encroachment in the exchange process.[30]

It was difficult to penetrate the kin networks that controlled the western Great Lakes fur trade. Five to six hundred French traders arrived at Michilimackinac each summer to exchange the peltry of their kin networks for trade goods.[31] They readily accepted English goods, but rarely returned with English traders aboard their bateaux and canoes.[32] English trade goods were substituted when they proved less expensive or when the flow of French or Spanish trade goods into the western Great Lakes was interrupted. But the conveyors of those trade goods remained remarkably unchanged. In 1767, over 85 percent of the men identified as Michilimackinac traders were French, while English merchants posted security for over half the canoes. The personnel of the fur trade in the Lake Michigan area and south along the Mississippi River Valley were primarily drawn from the Interior French and their Native allies.[33]

Pontiac's Rebellion and the Johnson Plan ensured that the Interior French were not displaced by English fur traders. Kin networks remained intact, reinforced the interdependence of the Interior French on their Native kin, and drew both societies closer together. Those English traders who successfully penetrated the trade were generally experienced fur traders. They secured entrance into the Great Lakes trade through marriage into French families or to Native women. John Askin, a Scots-Irish trader seasoned in the New York trade, entered the Michilimackinac trade when he married in "the manner of the country" an Odawa woman at the nearby Native village of L'Arbre Croche. At Detroit, he also married Marie Archange Barthe, whose father had traded there since the 1740s.[34] James Sterling entered the trade by marriage to Angélique Cuillerier, who was the daughter of an Indian interpreter. She was considered, ". . . used to trade from her infancy, and is generally allowed to be the best interpreter of different Indian languages."[35] Although there are other examples, the English primarily integrated themselves into the western Great Lakes trade as suppliers, rather than traders. The English proved far more successful in opening the trade of the Canadian Northwest, which was unencumbered by established kin networks. These rich fur-trade lands of the Canadian Northwest eventually opened new avenues of interaction for the Interior French and English fur traders. The Great Lakes French and their Indian allies became the *engagé, voyageurs,* and canoemen for English traders, in a region where furs promised to be a valuable resource.

Unfortunately, by the time of the American Revolution, the Francophobia of many English officers had intensified, their prejudices inflamed, first, by Pontiac's Rebellion and, subsequently, reinforced by the treatment that English traders received at the hands of the Interior French. Distrust of the Interior French proved increasingly problematic. Bassett left Detroit in 1774, but was replaced by men who believed that the French were "the most worthless and abandoned Fellows in the Provinces" and men without education, honesty, or sentiment. When the American Revolution broke out, Rogers called the Interior French "ignorant Bigots and busy Rebels;" and Lernoult, Bassett's immediate successor, condemned them as "Rebels to a man."[36]

Blinded by their dislike for the French, English officers often neglected their most influential resource for recruiting military manpower during the revolution. Although many Iroquois fought on behalf of the English, there was never equivalent support among the Algonquian-speaking people of the western Great Lakes. The enlistment of Native warriors on behalf of the English required diplomatic management of the Interior French and their Native allies. Those officers who relied on the Interior French to secure Native American loyalty demonstrated the effectiveness of such tactics.[37] Major Arent Schuyler DePeyster, the commandant at Michilimac-kinac, exerted considerable influence in this face-to-face world because he effectively utilized Louis Chevalier. DePeyster focused increased attention on Fort St. Joseph and made no attempt to regarrison the post, but relied on Chevalier to relay messages, secure allegiances, and raise warriors. To do this required the assignment of English trade goods to Chevalier, who then redistributed those goods in established rituals that solidified alliances and successfully solicited Potawatomi warriors.[38]

DePeyster appreciated the tremendous influence the Interior French exerted and believed that kin networks, like the Chevaliers, exercised control over more than just the St. Joseph River Valley. He wrote to General Haldimand, "Mr. Chevalier at St. Josephs holds the pass to Detroit and . . . [t]his gentleman is so connected with the Potawatomis that he can now do anything with them having lived upwards of thirty years at that Place."[39] DePeyster cultivated Chevalier's friendship and increasingly relied on him to meet with the Potawatomi. DePeyster provided Chevalier with the gifts distributed at Native councils. DePeyster even used Chevalier to distribute presents as far west as the Sioux and as far north as the Winnebago.[40] Through Chevalier, DePeyster succeeded in curtailing Native support for the Americans in Illinois Country following George Rogers Clark's conquest of Cahokia.[41] Chevalier raised warriors from both the Potawatomi and the Miami to fight on behalf of the English.[42] When Henry Hamilton sought warriors to recapture Vincennes, Chevalier arranged for him to meet with the Potawatomi at St. Joseph.[43] In return, DePeyster encouraged General Haldimand to entertain Chevalier's Odawa son when he was in Montreal. He wrote, "[a] Young Indian named Amable at present at Montreal is his son" and encouraged him to provide, "Some mark of distinction."[44] It was these visible signs of friendship that earned Chevalier's support for the English cause. He wrote to Haldimand that "the marks of distinction which you have shown to Amable, give me confidence and confirm me in the resolution which I have already taken . . . I do my best to give my opinion conformable to the good of the state and acknowledge the great honor you have heaped upon me."[45] Eventually, DePeyster even enlisted Amable as a lieutenant in the English forces.[46]

English officers who acted out their French prejudices and attempted to eliminate or reduce the influence of the Interior French produced disastrous results, as evidenced by the events which transpired in the St. Joseph River Valley in 1780. DePeyster's successful approach to Native affairs was in sharp contrast to that of his successor, Patrick Sinclair. DePeyster was appointed to the Detroit post in 1779 and Patrick Sinclair was appointed to Michilimackinac, of which St. Joseph was a dependency. Although Chevalier and the Potawatomi transferred their loyalty from Michilimackinac to DePeyster at Detroit, Chevalier's allegiance to DePeyster angered Sinclair. Anxious to retain Potawatomi loyalty, DePeyster wrote to Haldimand and justified his communications with Chevalier. "The St. Joseph's Indians have a constant intercourse with this place, they come here on horseback, in four or five days, sometimes in great numbers, whereas they seldom, or ever, go the Post of Michilimackinac, except when sent for. . . . If Captain Sinclair thinks I encroach upon his Government I will freely give him up one half of my command, provided Your Excellency thinks it will be for the good of His Majesty's Service—which is the sole object I have to view."[47]

At Detroit, DePeyster also discovered that his predecessor had alienated French residents by placing almost five hundred, or one-fourth of the population, under arrest as suspicious persons.[48] French alienation from the English cause was further magnified by the events that then transpired in the St. Joseph River Valley. While DePeyster worked to earn the trust of the Interior French, Sinclair advocated the removal of the Interior French. Governor Haldimand, unaware of Sinclair's intention, reassured him that St. Joseph remained a Michilimackinac dependency. Haldimand had previously ordered the removal of fur traders, whose loyalty was questionable, from living among the Indians, and Sinclair used this pretense to forcibly remove the French from Fort St. Joseph in 1780.[49]

Sinclair implemented the removal policy long espoused by many English officers. Sinclair's Francophobia focused on Louis Chevalier, whom Bassett vilified as that "very bad man." Unfortunately, the new commandant did not fully appreciated the highly complex and intertwined allegiances of kin networks and the ways in which kinship loyalties could frustrate even his clearest directive. Sinclair relied on a Michilimackinac trader, Louis Ainssé, to transport the French from St. Joseph to Michilimackinac. Ainssé was Louis Chevalier's nephew, his sister's son, and although he followed Sinclair's directive to remove the French, he was, more importantly, bound by his kinship loyalties. He dutifully completed a census of the St. Joseph inhabitants, boarded his French relatives and their neighbors in six canoes, and led the convoy to Michilimackinac.[50] Ainssé simultaneously left the community in the firm grasp of the Chevalier kin network by not removing the Indian offspring of Louis and Marie Madeleine.

Sinclair's Francophobia severely jeopardized England's ability to exert control over the river valley lands south of Lake Michigan. His replacement of Louis Chevalier with English traders incited the same type of violence that transpired during Pontiac's Rebellion. Blatant disregard for the social dynamics of kinship frustrated Sinclair's attempt to rid the region of the Interior French. Shortly after English traders arrived in the St. Joseph River Valley, an invading force from Illinois Country attacked them. It was a makeshift militia composed of Madeleine's kin network, thirty men from Cahokia, headed by the American husband of Madeleine's daughter, led the first unsuccessful raid.[51] In early December 1780, the invaders overpowered the English traders, loaded the contraband on packhorses, burned what they could not carry, and set fire to storehouses and buildings. Lieutenant de Quindre, then the English Indian agent for St. Joseph, arrived shortly after the Cahokian departure. He pursued and overtook them, killed four men, wounded two others, and captured seven of the party from Cahokia.[52]

Undeterred by failure, Marie Madeleine's relatives organized a larger force several months later and launched it from Illinois Country, under the Spanish flag. Madeleine and Louis' Indian son, thirty-year-old Louison Chevalier, was the expedition's guide and interpreter. The Potawatomi reckoned the number to be "one hundred white people and eighty Indians led by Sequinack and Nakewine."[53] Historians' estimates are lower: perhaps sixty-five men, some from St. Louis and others from Cahokia, and a large Indian contingent. Louis Chevalier's negotiations with the Indians allowed them to effectively surprise the English traders. On 12 February 1781, St. Joseph was plundered anew. Chevalier seized the English trade goods and divided them among the Potawatomi. This devastatingly effective attack burned a large supply of corn, which had been set aside by the English for their planned attack on St. Louis. The invaders were gone when Lieutenant de Quindre arrived, but the Potawatomi, on this occasion, refused to join him in pursuit of the raiders.[54]

DePeyster, anxious to correct the problems caused by removal, summoned the St. Joseph Potawatomi to council in March 1781. They provided plausible explanations of why they had been unable to prevent the attack on the English traders. DePeyster was told that, "They came to St. Josephs at a time that all the Indians were yet at their hunt, excepting a few young men who were not sufficient to oppose one hundred white people and eighty Indians." No mention was made of Louison Chevalier's role in the attack and DePeyster, either unknowing or discreetly diplomatic, failed to mention his name. DePeyster strenuously warned the Potawatomi about alliances with the Spanish and the Americans. He repeatedly spoke of the American greed for land, but this accomplished very little. DePeyster knew that the Potawatomi had harkened to the voice of the Spanish from the silver that they wore, bracelets and gorgets decorated with southwestern turquoise.[55]

Even the most lavish quantity of presents failed to regain the loyalty of the St. Joseph Potawatomi. Councils were held throughout the Great Lakes, but to no avail. Many of the Interior French, treated harshly by English officers, had relied on their kin networks to relocate to other more friendly Native villages and fur-trade settlements. With their loyalty continually called into question by men like Patrick Sinclair, many Interior French settled on the west side of Lake Michigan, in Green Bay.

DePeyster proved unable to "delicately manage" the Native people of the western Great Lakes without the aid of the Interior French. The warriors previously provided by the Potawatomi dwindled to insignificance and the English found themselves being lectured by Native people about the folly of warfare. The St. Joseph Potawatomi openly admonished English officers and urged them to lay down their weapons against the Americans.

I am surprised my father, that you are come to disturb the peace which reigns in our lands. I am pleased to see you with the pipe of peace which you offer us today instead of the tomahawk. . . . I confess to you that the red pipe presented to a party of my nation has been a poison to them as fatal as that of a venomous animal, this smoke has obscured the beautiful light and painted the shadow of death. . . . I have the same thing to say to [you] my father, change thy plans, renounce they projects which have been formed with neither prudence nor wisdom, if you are stubborn and despise my councils you will perhaps repent, believe me my father and go no farther. . . .[56]

Insensitive treatment rendered the Interior French unwilling allies and the Potawatomi a neutral nation. DePeyster found that the numerous councils held directly with the Indians were futile.[57] By 1782, DePeyster reported to Haldimand that Great Lakes people were fickle allies in the war against the colonials.

> I have wrought hard to endeavor to bring them to it, [better discipline] but, I find it impossible to change their natures. I assemble them, get fair promises, and send them out, but once out of sight the turning of a Straw may divert them from the original plan. If too severe with them, upon such occasions they tell us we are well off that there are no Virginians in this Quarter, but such as they bring here against their inclinations.[58]

In the western Great Lakes, many Native people found it advantageous to remain neutral. Over time, and because of the fur trade, many Native communities had become increasingly agricultural. Indians had much to lose if they sided with the English, and the Americans burned their houses and fields, destroyed their orchards, and killed their livestock. There were no means to protect agricultural villages left vulnerable by the departure of warriors.

The American Revolution revealed changes in Native society that had evolved over the course of the eighteenth century, when the presence of a market for agricultural produce, as well as for furs, lent stability to fur-trade communities in the western Great Lakes. The rhythm of daily life in the St. Joseph River Valley was that of an agricultural community. This was also true of other former French posts, where, as an adjunct to the fur trade, abundant harvests produced sufficient surplus to feed both the residential and transient fur-trade populations. While some historians contend that the fur trade spiraled Native society into demise, there was not a decline in either the quantity or quality of peltry during the eighteenth century in the western Great Lakes.[59] More importantly, the American Revolution failed to disrupt the trade. Instead, the market for furs and foodstuffs remained stable and even expanded. The Michilimackinac trade remained viable during the revolutionary period because England kept the St. Lawrence River open.[60] The Interior French who moved west of the Mississippi, particularly to St. Louis, provided an additional marketplace.

The tendency toward Native neutrality resulted from England's failure to accurately assess the consequences that warfare entailed for indigenous agricultural communities. Most English officers failed to see Indians as more sedentary than nomadic. Once George Rogers Clark occupied the nearby Illinois Country, any community that sent warriors to fight against the Americans left their settlements vulnerable to attack.

Following the Seven Years' War, Indian enthusiasm for war was further dampened by England's failure to sufficiently expend the human and financial resources required to win Native support. Although effective military control was established over the St. Lawrence River Valley, Whitehall refused the resources necessary to establish control of the Mississippi River Valley. This longer and more expansive waterway from the Great Lakes to New Orleans required a greater financial and military outlay. Even climate worked against English control; the Mississippi was navigable twelve months of the year, while freezing temperatures closed the St. Lawrence River during the winter months. England's military was dwarfed by the expansiveness of the region inherited from France.

English control of the western Great Lakes was further compromised by Spanish control of New Orleans. This strategically important city was the communications center and market outlet for both the lower and upper Mississippi rivers. Its importance was enhanced by the eighteenth-century emergence of St. Louis as a collection point for furs.[61] The Mississippi proved a viable fur-trade highway because short portages at the Fox, St. Joseph, and Miami rivers drew the western Great Lakes into its confluence. The Mississippi's southward flow facilitated the transportation of furs. At the conclusion of the Seven Years' War, Gage acknowledged the increased importance of New Orleans as a fur-trade market.[62] The trade, he said, would "always go with the stream . . . either down the Mississippi or the St. Lawrence."[63] New Orleans proved problematic for the English when, as Gage pointed out, higher peltry prices drew furs in that direction.[64]

England established forts on the eastern shores of the Mississippi, as their French predecessors had done, but they were of limited value. Many forts were similar to St. Joseph, but others, more martial in appearance, lacked an adequate military presence; indebtedness from the Seven Years' War limited English expenditures. In addition, Whitehall often enforced policies of economy and entrenchment on colonial administrators, thus increasing dependence on Native people.

England failed to surmount the hurdles posed by geography and limited military resources when they proved unable to diplomatically employ the Interior French as cultural negotiators with Native people. Sinclair's forced removal of the

L'archevêque-Chevalier kin network demonstrated his naïveté about the complex way in which the web of kin relations structured society in the western Great Lakes. Numerous English officers distrusted the Interior French and they often inadvertently found themselves in opposition to the established social order. The smaller forts that lined the perimeter of former French lands had social, rather than military, significance. It was there that kin networks became increasingly important, as expenses were reduced and outposts were staffed with minimal numbers of military personnel. The French relied on fur traders who had married among Native people to maintain a French presence, and in times of war, to recruit their kin and allies to fight on behalf of the French. Kin networks maintained order across the continent's vast interior landscape. It was these social barriers that thwarted England's effective control of the North American interior. The evolution of these networks, stimulated by the fur trade, gave the Interior French an established presence that was foolhardy to ignore. Patrick Sinclair understood the power of these networks when he remarked, "The Canadians I fear are of great disservice to the Government but the Indians are perfect Free Masons when intrusted with a secret by a Canadian most of them being much connected by marriage." It was unfortunate for the English that Sinclair, like other officers, often treated the Interior French with paranoid distrust.[65]

NOTES

1. Henry Bassett to Thomas Gage, 24 December 24, 1772, *The Papers of Sir William Johnson*, 14 vols., ed. James Sullivan et al., eds. (Albany: University of the State of New York, 1921–65), 8:672–73.

2. Speech of Four Indian Chiefs, 22 May 1773, *Johnson Papers*, ed. Sullivan, 8:803–6.

3. For a detailed description of Fort St. Joseph as a military post under the French, see Dunning Idle, "The Post of the St. Joseph River During the French Regime, 1679–1761" (Ph.D. diss., University of Illinois, 1946). Information on the fort can also be found in Ralph Ballard, *Old Fort Saint Joseph* (Berrien Springs, Mich.: Hardscrabble Press, 1973); Gérard Malchelosse, "Genealogy and Colonial History: The St. Joseph River Post, Michigan," *French Canadian and Acadian Genealogical Review* nos. 3–4 (1979): 173–209; Mildred Webster and Fred Krause, *French Fort Saint Joseph: De La Poste de la Riviere St. Joseph, 1690–1780* (St. Joseph, Mich.: privately printed, 1990).

4. Major Henry Bassett arrived at Detroit in 1772 and served as commanding officer at Detroit for two years, until 1774. For a list of Detroit commandants, see Nelson Vance Russell, *The British Régime in Michigan and the Old Northwest, 1760–1796* (Northfield, Minn.: Carleton College, 1939), 292.

5. Bassett to Haldimand, 29 April 1773, *Historical Collections: Collections and Researches Made by the Michigan Pioneer and Historical Society*, often catalogued as *Michigan Pioneer and Historical Collections*, 40 vols. (Lansing: Michigan Historical Commission, 1877–1929), 19:297 [hereafter cited as *MPHC*].

6. The western Great Lakes includes present-day Indiana, Illinois, Michigan, Wisconsin, parts of Minnesota, and Ohio.

7. Marriage in "the manner of the country," or marriage à la façon du pays, combined both Indian and European marriage customs. These unions, although not always permanent, were neither casual nor promiscuous. For information on how these marriages were institutionalized in the fur trade, see Sylvia Van Kirk, *Many Tender Ties: Women in Fur Trade Society, 1679–1870* (Norman: University of Oklahoma Press, 1990), 3–6; and Sylvia Van Kirk's "The Custom of the Country: An Examination of Fur Trade Practices," in *Essays on Western History*, ed. Lewis H. Thomas (Edmonton: University of Alberta Press, 1976), 49–68; and Jennifer S. H. Brown, *Strangers in Blood: Fur Trade Company Families in Indian Country* (Vancouver: University of British Columbia Press, 1980), 51–110.

8. Turnbull to Gage, 5 July 1772, Papers of Thomas Gage, Ann Arbor: University of Michigan, William L. Clements Library [hereafter cited as Gage Papers, WLCL].

9. The original of the 1762 census is from the Burton Historical Collection, Detroit Public Library [hereafter cited as BHC]. A 1768 census taken by Philip De Jean was enclosed in a letter dated 23 February 1768 from the Detroit Commandant George Turnbull to General Thomas Gage, the original is in the Gage Papers, WLCL. The census completed by Governor Henry Hamilton listed 78 female slaves and 79 male slaves. For Michigan censuses, see Donna Valley Russell, ed., *Michigan Censuses, 1710–1830, under French, British, and Americans* (Detroit: Detroit Society for Genealogical Research, 1982); Charles R. Maduell Jr., comp., *Statistical Series, II, Illinois Census Returns, The Census Tables for the French Colony of Louisiana From 1699 Through 1732*, in *Collections of the Illinois State Historical Library*, 34 vols. (Springfield: Illinois State Historical Library, 1907–59), 24:ix–xxix,150–63; *MPHC*, 10:446.

10. The last effective commandant at Fort St. Joseph, François-Marie Picoté, Sieur de Belestre, was appointed in 1747. He was rarely present; well known as a peace negotiator, he made frequent and extended appearances in Detroit and Montreal. In 1757, the stepson of the governor general of New France, Marquis de Vaudreuill, was the last commandant, but Louis de Varier stayed fewer than two years. He left by 1759. Ballard, *Old Fort Saint Joseph*, 25–26.

11. The house was constructed shortly before the British took over Fort St. Joseph. The post interpreter, Pierre Deneau dit Detailly, submitted a claim for 1,000 *livres* for building a house for a medal chief. Certificate, St. Joseph, 30 April 1760, Paris: Archives Nationales, Series M, v⁷, 345:99. Archives Nationales, Colonies are microfilm, transcripts, and photocopies housed in the Canadian Archives and in the Library of Congress. The original documents are in the Archives of the Department of the Marine and the Colonies, in the Archives of the Department of War, and in the Royal Library at Paris.

12. Marest to Germon, *Lettres Edifiantes et Curieuses* (Paris, 1829–32), 226.

13. In 1777, 150 head of cattle were driven from Illinois eastward to Michigan to supply the troops garrisoned at Detroit. Hamilton to Germain, 14 July 1777, Canadian National Archives, Q, XIV, 94, Ottawa; Russell, *British Régime in Michigan*, 120.

14. A *makuk* or *makuck* was an Indian basket woven to hold maple sugar. These baskets generally held fifty pounds of sugar. Burnett to Messrs. Innes and Grant, Sandwich, Canada, May 31, 1801, Wilbur M. Cunningham, *Letter Book of William Burnett, Fur Trader in the Land of Four Flags* (n.p.: Fort Miami Heritage Society of Michigan, 1967), 143; *History of Berrien and Van Buren Counties, Michigan* (Philadelphia, 1880), 39.

15. W. J. Eccles, "Sovereignty Association, 1500–1783," *Canadian Historical Review* 65 (December 1984): 475–510.

16. Howard Peckham, *Pontiac and the Indian Uprising* (Princeton, N.J.: Princeton University Press, 1947);

Ian K. Steele, *Warpath: Invasions of North America* (New York: Oxford University Press, 1994), 237–42; Charles E. Cleland, *Rites of Conquest: The History and Culture of Michigan's Native Americans* (Ann Arbor: University of Michigan Press, 1992), 134–43; Richard White, *The Middle Ground: Indians, Empires, and Republics in the Great Lakes Region, 1650–1815* (New York: Cambridge University Press, 1991), 269–314; Gregory Evans Dowd, "The French King Wakes Up in Detroit: Pontiac's War in Rumor and History," *Ethnohistory* 37 (summer 1990): 254–78; idem., *A Spirited Resistance: The North American Indian Struggle for Unity, 1735–1815* (Baltimore: Johns Hopkins University Press, 1992); Jon William Parmenter, "Pontiac's War: Forging New Links in the Anglo-Illinois Covenant Chain, 1758–1766," *Ethnohistory* 44 (fall 1997): 617–54.

17. For a description of these events at St. Joseph, see Joseph L. Peyser, ed., *Letters from New France: The Upper Country, 1686–1783* (Urbana: University of Illinois Press, 1992), 215–16; Ballard, *Fort St. Joseph,* 44–46.

18. Johnson to Gage, 3 May 1764, Gage Papers, AS, 18.

19. Gladwin to Amherst, 8 July 1763, Gage Papers, W.O. 34/49, 196–99.

20. Instructions for Col. Bradstreet, 2 April 1764, enclosed in Gage to Bradstreet, 2 April 1764, Gage Papers, 16.

21. Gladwin to Gage, 7 June 1764, Gage Papers, 19.

22. Turnbull to Gage, 25 September 1767, Gage Papers, 70.

23. Jack M. Sosin, *Whitehall and the Wilderness: The Middle West in British Colonial Policy, 1760–1775* (Lincoln: University of Nebraska Press, 1961), 73–78. Johnson's Plan was referred to as "Plan for the future management of Indian Affairs."

24. Carlton to Shelburne, 2 March 1768, Ottawa, Canadian Archives, Q, V, pt.i, 383.

25. From Lt. Campbell Commanding at Detroit to Gage, 10 April 1766, Newberry Library, Ayers Manuscript Collections, no. 308, Chicago, Ill.

26. There are numerous examples of these petitions, Canadian Archives, Q, VIII, 133.

27. Beaver pelts exported from Canada in 1764 totaled £17,259 and, by 1768, exports had decreased to £13,168. Clarence Edwin Carter, *Great Britain and the Illinois Country, 1763–1774* (Washington, D.C.: American Historical Association, 1910), 94. Carter calculated the annual value of furs exported from the colonies to Great Britain as follows: 1764, £28,067/18; 1765, £27,801/11; 1766, £24,657/0; 1767, £20,262/2; 1768, £18,923/18.

28. Croghan wrote Gage that the furs worth £80,000 in 1767 were being shipped to New Orleans. Croghan to Gage, 16 January 1767, Shelburne Papers, WLCL.

29. Turnbull to Croghan, 1 March 1768, and Jehu Hay to Croghan, 19 February 1768, in Croghan, 14 April 1768, Gage Papers, AS, 76; and Turnbull to Gage, 23 February 1768, Gage Papers, AS, 74. Also see Fr. Hamback Account against Louis Chevalier, 1763, in William Edgar Correspondence and Papers, MS., William Edgar, R2, 1750–1775, BHC.

30. From Lt. Campbell Commanding at Detroit to Gage, 10 April 1766, Ayers Manuscript Collection, 308, Newberry Library, Chicago.

31. Turnbull to Gage, July 5, 1772, Gage Papers, WLCL.

32. A description of British merchant involvement in the fur trade is described by Harry Duckworth in "British Capital in the Fur Trade: John Strettell and John Fraser," in *The Fur Trade Revisited: Selected Papers of the Sixth North American Fur Trade Conference, Mackinac Island, Michigan, 1991,* ed. Jennifer S. H. Brown, W. J. Eccles, and Donald P. Heldman (East Lansing: Michigan State University Press, 1994), 39–56.

33. "An Account of the Number of Canoes gone out Wintering from the Post of Michilimackinac, Including the Names of Traders and those that are Bail for them. Also the Value of their Goods and where they are bound," Charles E. Lart, ed., "Fur-Trade Return, 1767" *Canadian Historical Review* 1 (1920): 351–58.

34. *The John Askin Papers*, 2 vols., ed. Milo M. Quaife (Detroit: Detroit Library Commission, 1902), 1:12–13.

35. 26 February 1765, Sterling Letter Book, BHC; *Askin Papers*, 1:47n. 29.

36. Lernoult to Haldimand, 26 March 26, 1779, *MPHC*, 10:328.

37. Captains Turnbull and Campbell, despite their occasional anti-French rhetoric, also proved more skilled at handling Indian affairs in the Great Lakes. Russell, *British Régime in Michigan*, 79.

38. Traditional societies operate in what Marcel Mauss has described as a gift economy. The obligation to give, to receive, and to reciprocate is explained by Mauss in *The Gift: The Form and Reason for Exchange in Archaic Societies* (1954: Reprint, London: Cohen and Cohen, 1970).

39. S. DePeyster to Gen. Haldimand, 15 August 1778, *MPHC*, 9:368.

40. Louis Chevalier to Major Arent S. DePeyster, 15 September 1778, *MPHC*, 19:352–53.

41. Mr. Chevalier to Major DePeyster, 20 July 1778, *MPHC*, 10:286–87.

42. To Mr. the Captain Langlade and the Lieut. Gautier from A. S. DePeyster, 26 October 1778 [Arent Schuyler DePeyster], *Miscellanies by An Officer*, ed. J. Watts De Peyster (Dumfries, Scotland: C. Munro, 1813), Appendix LXXII, No.III.

43. Louis Chevalier to Gen. Frederick Haldimand, 28 February 1779, *MPHC*, 19:375–76; Major Arent S. DePeyster to Gen. Frederick Haldimand, 29 May 1779, *MPHC*, 19:425–26; From Mr. Chevalier Unaddressed, 13 March 1780, *MPHC*, 10:380–81.

44. A. S. DePeyster to Gen. Haldimand, 15 August 1778, Haldimand Papers, *MPHC*, 9:368–69.

45. Louis Chevalier to Gen. Frederick Haldimand, 29 February 1779, *MPHC*, 19:375–76.

46. DePeyster to Sinclair, 12 March 1780, *MPHC*, 9:581.

47. DePeyster to Haldimand, 1 October 1780, Haldimand Papers, *MPHC*, 9:615–16.

48. Survey of the Settlement of Detroit Taken 31st March, 1779, *MPHC*, 10:311–27; Russell, *British Regime in Michigan*, 84.

49. Keith R. Widder, "Effects of the American Revolution on Fur Trade Society at Michilimackinac," in *Fur Trade Revisited*, ed. Brown, Eccles, and Heldman, 307.

50. Mr. Ainssé to Lieut. Gov. Sinclair, 30 June, 1780; Memorial of Louis Joseph Ainssé, 5 August 1780, *MPHC*, 13:55–62, 10:434–38.

51. Jean Baptiste Hamelin led the raid along with Tom Brady. Hamelin family members frequently served as godparents for St. Joseph children, "St. Joseph Baptismal Register," Rev. George Paré and M. M. Quaife, eds., *Mississippi Valley Historical Review* 13 (1926–27):, 235–36.

52. John Francis McDermott, ed., *Old Cahokia: A Narrative and Documents Illustrating the First Century of its History* (St. Louis; St. Louis Historical Documents Foundation, 1949), 31, 128; Webster and Krause, *Fort Saint Joseph*, 123; Idle, "Post of St. Joseph," 182, 188; Malchelosse, "St. Joseph River Post," *French Canadian and Acadian Genealogical Review*, 204–5; George Paré, *The Catholic Church in Detroit, 1701–1888* (Detroit: Gabriel Richard Press, 1951), 47.

53. Indian Council: At a Council held at Detroit, 11 March 1781, with the Pottewatimies from St. Joseph, Terre Coupé and Couer de Cerf, *MPHC*, 10:453–55.

54. The attack was led by Eugène Pouré dit Beausoleil. The number of men who accompanied him varies in different historical accounts. Descriptions of the attack on and destruction of Fort St. Joseph include

A. P. Nasatir, "The Anglo-Spanish Frontier in the Illinois Country during the American Revolution, 1779–1783," *Illinois State Historical Society Journal* 21 (October 1928): 291–358; Clarence W. Alvord, "The Conquest of St. Joseph, Michigan, by the Spaniards in 1781," *Michigan History* 14 (1930): 298–414.

55. Indian Council, 11 March 1781. *MPHC*, 10:453–54.

56. Necessary Part of the Councils Held by Mr. Bennet with the Potawatamies at St. Joseph, 3 August 1779, *MPHC*, 10:349–50.

57. Russell, *British Regime in Michigan*, 85.

58. DePeyster to Haldimand, 26 January 1782, *MPHC*, 10:548.

59. Calvin Martin, "The European Impact on the Culture of a Northeastern Algonquin Tribe: An Ecological Interpretation," *William and Mary Quarterly* 31 (January 1974): 7–26.

60. Widder, "Effects of the American Revolution on Fur-Trade Society," in *Fur Trade Revisited*, ed. Brown, Eccles, and Heldmand, 304nn. 17, 18; Ida Amanda Johnson, *The Michigan Fur Trade* (Lansing, Mich., 1919), 78–101.

61. Tanis C. Thorne, *The Many Hands of My Relations: French and Indians on the Lower Missouri* (Columbia: University of Missouri Press, 1996), 68–97.

62. Carleton to Johnson, 27 March 1767, *MPHC*, 10:222–24.

63. E. B. O'Callaghan, ed., *Documents Relative to the Colonial History of the State of New York*, 15 vols. (Albany, N.Y.: Weed, Parsons and Co., 1856–87), 2:486 [hereafter referred to as *NYCD*].

64. Gage to Shelburne, 22 February 1767, Charles Clarence Carter, ed., *The Correspondence of General Thomas Gage with the Secretaries of State, 1763–1775*, 2 vols. (New Haven, Conn.: Yale University Press, 1931) 1:121–22; National Archives of Canada, Dartmouth Transcripts, 1765–1775, Ottawa, 61–62; O'Callaghan, *NYCD*, 2:485.

65. DePeyster to Haldimand, June 1779, *Collections of the State Historical Society of Wisconsin*, ed. Lyman C. Draper and Reuben G. Thwaites, 31 vols. (Madison: State Historical Society of Wisconsin, 1854–1931), 11:131–32.

Fortress Detroit, 1701–1826

BRIAN LEIGH DUNNIGAN

Of the many places that figured in the Sixty Years' War for the Great Lakes, none was more consistently near the epicenter of events than Detroit. Although the city is today more likely to be remembered for its significance to industrial, automotive or entertainment history, Detroit was a well-established agricultural and commercial center by the outbreak of the Seven Years' War. As such, it sheltered a military garrison and resident populations of European colonists and Native Americans that would actively participate in all the conflicts of the coming six decades. During these years, Detroit was controlled successively by France, Britain, and the United States. Each nation developed and maintained the defenses of a miniature, wilderness fortress town and used the place as a base from which to support their interests in the Great Lakes and Ohio Valley. The War of 1812 proved to be the last conflict to directly involve Detroit. Thus, the conclusion of the Sixty Years' War coincided with the waning of the town's significance as a military center and the beginning of its rapid growth as a nineteenth-century city.

Detroit's consistent importance derived largely from its location astride the water corridor connecting Lake Erie with the three Great Lakes above. The settlement also lay in close proximity to the Maumee-Wabash river system and the diverse groups of Native Americans who populated Ohio, Indiana, and Michigan. The town's traders dominated the southern margin of the fur trade and, from 1760, Detroit became the heart of British power in the Great Lakes. It was the place from which Virginian incursions into Kentucky and the Illinois Country were opposed during the American Revolution, ultimately with enough success to ensure that the post and the lakes themselves were under British control at the cessation of hostilities. During the thirteen years after 1783, Detroit became the focus of American ambitions and animosity toward the defiant Indians of the Northwest and the British who continued to occupy posts granted to the United States by the peace treaty. For more than two decades, American frontiersmen perceived Detroit as a base from which hostile Indians were supplied and to which prisoners of the unrelenting frontier war were carried. Incorporated into the United States in 1796, Detroit and its fort played an early, albeit disastrous, role in the War of 1812. For thirteen months during 1812–13, Detroit was again a goal for United States military forces until recaptured in the aftermath of the Battle of Lake Erie.

In addition to its military significance, Detroit was a place of commerce and settlement for several groups of people. These populations were introduced to the vicinity when the French established the post in 1701. Canadian colonists formed one segment. Many of the Detroit settlers, however, were Native Americans, enticed by the French to reoccupy the straits in order to present a barrier to English penetration of the Great Lakes. By the onset of the Sixty Years' War, the local population had stabilized to include the French settlers and four native groups, the Huron, Ottawa, Potawatomi, and Ojibwa. Each had its own village and agricultural lands, and each lived more or less in harmony with the others. This balance of population would soon be disrupted, first by Pontiac's War and then by the American War of Independence. By the end of the century, the Native American groups had moved to more distant locations on the Detroit River, or in the Michigan interior, and the Francophone Canadian colonists had been supplemented by British and American merchants and landowners.[1]

Throughout these six decades of conflict, the fortified village of Detroit, supported by its nearby farms and Indian populations, served a purpose akin to the fortress cities of Europe. It was a military base, depot, and place of refuge. The town was dominated by a garrison and its fortifications with all the attendant inconvenience to the civilian population. Detroit was laid out and guarded by soldiers, expanded under considerations of military necessity, and governed by army officers.

The use of land was regulated by the commandants, and inhabitants were taxed to support the garrison and maintain the town's defenses. The soldiers offered security in time of peril, but their presence was also sure to place the townspeople in the line of fire, as occurred during Pontiac's siege of 1763 and William Hull's disastrous opening campaign of the War of 1812.

This article describes and defines the constantly changing appearance of the post of Detroit during the period of the Sixty Years' War for the Great Lakes. The visual documentation presented here is part of a project to compile an iconography of Detroit from its founding in 1701 until 1837, by which time the last restraints of fortification had been removed and the city had assumed the core of its modern configuration.

The Detroit of the Sixty Years' War is entirely foreign to us today, having been swept away first by disaster, as the town burned in 1805, and then by relentless nineteenth-century growth that removed any landmarks beyond the post-fire street plan and whatever archaeological fragments remain. Even before such wholesale transformations, eighteenth-century Detroit was a constantly changing place, its form and appearance influenced by the perishable nature of its construction and the plasticity of the stockade surrounding its streets and houses. Aside from innumerable repairs to its constantly deteriorating fortifications, the town of Detroit, or its defenses, were significantly altered no fewer than sixteen times during the first 125 years of its existence. Ten of these major expansions or modifications occurred during the sixty years of conflict for the Great Lakes.

Detroit was altered for reasons other than deterioration and expansion. Increasingly sophisticated needs of defense and the accommodation of military garrisons stimulated many of the changes. At first, the potential hostility of the native peoples was the overriding consideration, one justified by the events of 1763. After 1775, the possibility of attack by colonial or European-style forces became equally important. It was only the disappearance of both of these perceived threats that concluded the era of fortress Detroit.

By 1754 and the commencement of the Sixty Years' War for the Great Lakes, the Canadian and Native American settlements of Detroit had been in existence for more than half a century. Antoine de la Mothe Cadillac took possession of the narrowest point of the upper part of the Detroit River on 24 July 1701.[2] His goal was to establish a French colony and to attract Native American groups to settle near his post. Cadillac and his settlement had a rocky start. The founder ultimately left

America in disgrace. The colony survived, however, despite accident, neglect, friction between groups, and the difficulty of establishing a European agricultural community at such a distance from the center of New France. The most severe test came in 1712, when the French garrison and their Indian allies battled the Fox Indians who had briefly, though contentiously, joined Cadillac's enclave. By 1754, the upper stretch of the Detroit River between the River Rouge and Lake St. Clair accommodated substantial villages of Potawatomi, Huron or Wyandot, and Ottawa, as well as the farms of French or Canadian settlers on both sides of the water. An Ojibwa settlement was located somewhat farther away at the northern end of Lake St. Clair.[3] The stockaded "French Fort" of Detroit, which, by 1754, had already been altered or expanded at least five times, contained about one hundred houses, a church, a guardhouse, and a newly constructed storehouse and bakery, all surrounded by a stockade with four tiny bastions.[4] Since about 1717, this fortified town had assumed a roughly rectangular plan around a main east-west thoroughfare, named for Ste. Anne, with three parallel streets and a number of narrow cross streets.

Fighting between French and English colonial forces in the Ohio Valley in the spring of 1754 signaled the opening of the long struggle for the Great Lakes. The security of the French posts there, particularly Detroit and Michilimackinac, was of sufficient concern for Lieutenant Gaspard-Joseph Chaussegros de Léry to be dispatched from the Ohio. Léry found the stockaded village little changed from an earlier visit in 1749, at which time he had carefully mapped the fort and the countryside. He and the commandant agreed that the place was "not able to defend itself," and the latter made it clear that he intended "to have some work done there."[5] Just how much work soon became apparent as Léry found himself directing a project, unauthorized by Quebec, to not only renew the stockade but to alter its walls into a more substantial six-bastion trace. Léry soon experienced the frustration of undertaking such work when the source of material was a levy on the reluctant inhabitants. Each proprietor was ordered to provide four fifteen-foot stockade pickets for every *arpent* (French acre) of river frontage held. Although this meant only twelve logs for most landholders, the engineer and the commandant spent the winter alternately cajoling and threatening the populace to comply. The work had not been completed when Léry departed in March 1755.[6] Later French and British commandants would experience similar difficulties in enforcing this traditional community responsibility.

Unfortunately, no plan of Léry's 1754–55 fort is known to survive. Accounts by English prisoners make it clear that it was an insubstantial fortress, and the

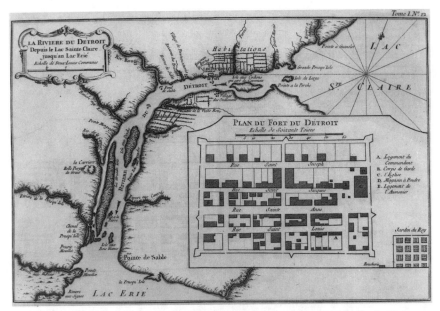

A plan of Detroit was first published in Jacques-Nicolas Bellin's *Le Petit Atlas Maritime* of 1764. His engraving is based on maps and plans drawn by Lt. Gaspard-Joseph Chaussegros de Léry, the younger, in 1749 and reflects the appearance of the fortified town prior to enlargement in 1752. Courtesy of the William L. Clements Library, University of Michigan, Ann Arbor.

stockades were already beginning to rot by 1757.[7] This state of affairs became of greater concern as the war turned against the French and Canadians in 1758. The new commandant who arrived in that year, Captain François-Marie Picoté de Belestre, was destined to be the last officer of New France to govern Detroit. Late in 1758 and early in 1759, he undertook to rebuild the defenses and expand the village at its western end.[8] This effort was in vain, however. The surrender of New France in September 1760 was followed, late in November, by the arrival of Major Robert Rogers leading British troops. After some short-lived posturing on the part of Belestre, Detroit changed hands without incident.[9]

Among the items surrendered with Detroit was a plan of the fortified town from which British engineers, beginning with Lieutenant Diedrich Brehm, derived drafts of their own. The Detroit of 1758–68 is, thus, well documented, and the trace of Belestre's walls survived for a decade to serve a British garrison during the long siege by Pontiac's warriors. The British made no alterations to the virtually new fortifications, utilizing the few government buildings and continuing the French practice of quartering troops in houses rented from the townspeople. One disadvantage

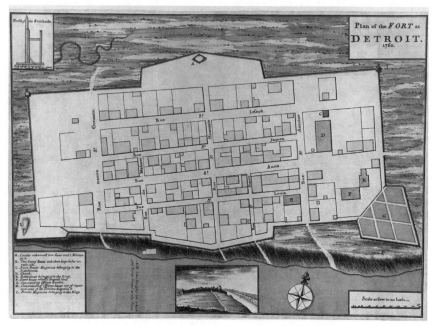

Diedrich Brehm depicted Detroit as the British found it in December 1760. The town had grown to both the east and the west since 1749, and the trace of its walls was a result of Belestre's improvements of 1758–59. These fortifications would serve the British through Pontiac's siege and would not be substantially altered until about 1768. Brehm's composition was probably based on a French plan and includes, at the bottom, the first known view of the town. Courtesy of the Burton Historical Collection, Detroit Public Library.

of this was that the troops were spread throughout the enclosure. As well, government-owned buildings were located at widely separated points around the town. In addition to the stockade and a few blockhouses, the garrison had control of a storehouse and bakery on a military square facing the church at the east end of Ste. Anne Street. A house for the commandant was located in the next block to the west, at the corner of St. Louis and St. Antoine streets. The guard house, formerly adjacent to the west gate of the 1754–55 fort, had been isolated by Belestre's 1758 expansion to a spot two blocks from the nearest gate. The garrison powder magazine, established in the area of Belestre's expansion, was located in a bastion at the extreme southwestern end of the fort.[10] The defenses were thus sprawling and the garrison badly scattered.

The summer of 1763 witnessed the first major attack on Detroit since the Fox battle of 1712, and the anticipated deficiencies of the post were realized, although the vigilant garrison was never in serious danger of losing the place to assault. In addition to the scattered nature of quarters and stores, the presence of a commanding height across a small creek just north of the stockade became a concern for the garrison. This was corrected by the construction of a pair of "cavaliers" or small blockhouses, on the hill, and other advanced defenses were established and maintained outside the west end of the fort.[11]

Pontiac's siege inspired no substantial changes to the fortifications themselves, aside from construction of the advanced blockhouses on the hill. Internally, however, the events of 1763 influenced a consolidation of garrison quarters that would influence Detroit for the next fifty years. When Belestre expanded the stockade to the west in 1758, the area of the town had been increased substantially, although little of this new ground was occupied. It is possible that British authorities were considering this space as a location for barracks as early as 1761.[12] It was not until the arrival of Colonel John Bradstreet's relief army in 1764, however, that military development began in the western end of the stockade in an area that would for many years thereafter be known as the "Citadel." Barracks for men and officers were laid out by Lieutenant John Montresor in September 1764, and construction was soon underway.[13]

Work on the quarters and storehouses within this barracks yard continued through 1766, although it was not until the end of 1767 that General Thomas Gage could report that "At the Detroit, the Garrison has contracted their Defences, and formed a kind of Citadel separate from what is called the Town; which it in great Measure commands."[14] The greater part of the officers and men and the critical stores of the garrison, including the powder magazine, were now concentrated in a segregated area where attack by either an outside force or the inhabitants themselves could be resisted more effectively.

Completion of the Citadel, defended at first by a variety of small blockhouses and batteries around the perimeter of its stockade, marked the beginning of a period of simplification of the trace of the town walls. With the garrison securely ensconced in its own compound, the distinctive bastions on the north wall and southeast corner of the town soon disappeared, as stockade lines were straightened in those areas and flanked by additional small blockhouses. This phase of Detroit's structural development is the most poorly documented of all by maps or plans, with only vague descriptions and intelligence reports known from the late 1760s until the 1780s. But it was with these defenses that the garrison and inhabitants of Detroit faced the uncertainties of the American Revolution.

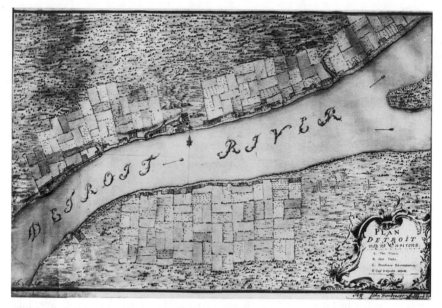

The Detroit settlement of Pontiac's siege was depicted by Lt. John Montresor in the fall of 1763. Its stockaded town, surrounded by outposts established the previous summer, sits amidst *habitant* farms and Indian villages. Courtesy of the William L. Clements Library, University of Michigan, Ann Arbor.

The events of 1775 rapidly isolated the Great Lakes posts. Rebellion in Massachusetts cut off Detroit from the Boston headquarters of Commander-in-Chief General Thomas Gage, and thereafter Detroit's official communication was with the governor of Quebec. The capture of Montreal by the Americans soon severed even this avenue of contact. By the summer of 1776, however, communications were reestablished, and Detroit's new lieutenant governor, Henry Hamilton, could report that the place was in "a tolerable state of defence at present, against Savages, or an Enemy unprovided with Cannon." The stockades were new and defended by eleven blockhouses, while the Citadel had been strengthened by a ditch and fraizing.[15] Otherwise, the place remained much as it had been since the late 1760s.

Circumstances would soon force the defenders of Detroit to employ more sophisticated means to counter the growing threat posed by rebel incursions into the country west of the Appalachians. The invasion of the Illinois Country and the occupation of Vincennes by George Rogers Clark and his Virginia troops in 1778 brought the war, for the first time, in dangerous proximity to Detroit. Governor Hamilton countered by retaking Vincennes, but his initial success was reversed in February 1779, when the small British expeditionary force was in turn cornered by Clark and forced to surrender.

By the time disaster overtook Governor Hamilton, the troops left behind in Detroit had taken action to render the place much more secure. The elevated land commanding the north side of the stockaded town and Citadel had been recognized as a problem since Pontiac's siege of 1763. In Hamilton's absence, Captain Richard B. Lernoult improved the defenses of Detroit by constructing a substantial earthen redoubt on the high ground to shelter the garrison and command the town. Work commenced in November 1778 and continued through the winter.[16] The British garrison, assisted by many of the inhabitants, dug ditches and erected an earthen field work with four half-bastions, a type of construction more than capable of resisting any sort of artillery likely to be brought against it. On 3 October 1779, the new fortification was named for Lernoult.[17] This distinctive structure would remain the keystone of Detroit's defenses until 1826.

For the balance of the American War for Independence, Detroit consisted of two separate fortified enclaves: the stockaded town, with the strengthened barracks complex of the Citadel at its western end, and Fort Lernoult, dominating the hill to the north. This phase of Detroit's development is also very poorly documented by graphic material, the only evidence being a spy sketch given to the American commandant at Pittsburgh, who passed it on to General George Washington. Although crude and requiring some interpretation, it accurately represents the main features of the British post seen by the many prisoners carried there from Kentucky during the later years of the Revolution.[18]

Students of the American Revolution in the West are most likely to be familiar with the plan of Detroit incorporating Fort Lernoult and the town in one sprawling enclosure. Resembling a giant triangle with the fort at its apex and the Detroit River forming the base, this plan was achieved during 1782–83 under the direction of Major Arent S. DePeyster. The modifications were made by simply removing the pickets of the stockade that formed the north, or land, side of the town of Detroit and relocating them to connect the blockhouses at the northwest and northeast corners with Fort Lernoult.[19] Not only did this greatly improve security by integrating the two fortified areas, it also provided a covered communication from the Citadel to the fort. The stockades also protected a new, stone powder magazine constructed at DePeyster's orders during 1782.[20] Most of the newly enclosed area, long the site of the garrison's vegetable gardens, retained its former use and also provided a spacious

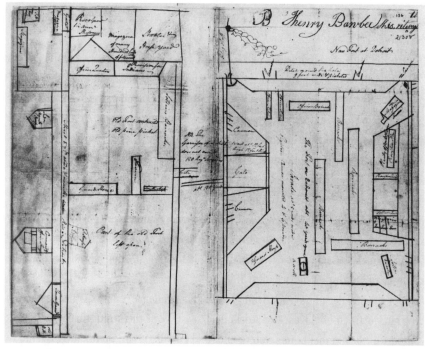

No formal plans survive to show fortified Detroit in the period from 1765 to 1784 save this rough sketch presented by one Henry Bawbee to the American commander of Pittsburgh in 1780. It was subsequently forwarded to Gen. George Washington. Despite its crude appearance, the plan conveys reliable information on the new Fort Lernoult (right), the Citadel (top left), and government buildings in the town itself (bottom left). Courtesy of the Library of Congress, George Washington Papers.

drill field, the "Esplanade," for the troops. At the same time, the stockades were removed from the waterfront of the town, a development for which DePeyster was criticized but which allowed proprietors to extend their lots to the water's edge.[21] The river front stockade was later re-erected in 1788–89, and further strengthened with blockhouses and batteries.

The conclusion of the war brought an order for all work to cease on the British fortifications around the Great Lakes. Negotiators in Paris had drawn a boundary line between British Canada and the new United States that placed Detroit and the other posts on the American side. Within a year it was apparent that these forts would be retained indefinitely, however, so Detroit continued to be the forward point of British influence in the Great Lakes. While the Ohio Indians strongly resisted the flood of American settlers flowing into their country, the British garrison had strong incentive to keep up their defenses, even making substantial improvements at times of increased tensions when American expeditions marched against the Indians in 1790, 1791, and 1794. The design of Detroit otherwise remained as it was at the close of the American War for Independence.

During the Indian wars of the 1790s, there were actually three primary areas of garrison activity in Detroit, with government property literally bracketing the civilian buildings of the town. To the north, Fort Lernoult provided the chief defense in the event of an attack by the U.S. Army. Its earthen walls and half-bastions could oppose a respectable train of siege artillery. The west end of the town was bordered by the Citadel, containing storehouses and comfortable, permanent quarters for officers and men. Between the Citadel and the fort stood the main powder magazine, and the river side of the Citadel connected to the "King's Wharf" where naval vessels could moor to discharge cargo. The southeast corner of town was also an important government precinct, containing a guardhouse, gardens, the Indian council house, and "Government House," the residence of the commandant until the structure burned in 1790. Adjacent and just beyond the east wall of the town was a naval yard where government vessels were constructed and maintained.[22]

Detroit changed hands for a third time on 11 July 1796, when Captain Moses Porter and a detachment from Anthony Wayne's army took possession as the British withdrew across and down the river to establish Fort Malden at Amherstburg. Important though this political change was, it had virtually no impact on the appearance of Detroit. Of greater significance was the fact that the opposite riverbank had become the territory of a potential enemy. Detroit's chief defense rested on Fort Lernoult (not officially renamed "Fort Detroit" by its new occupants until 1805), but the fortification was best suited to guard against a land attack. "There is a small regular work back of the town," wrote Ebenezer Denny in 1799, "but it's lost to appearance & covers only the side next itself. It seems to have been designed for a retreat for the commanding officer."[23] The town lay between the fort and the enemy, and the complaint that the river could not be adequately covered from the ramparts would be a regular one until the end of military occupation.

American authorities also increasingly voiced a concern that had been heard since the earliest days of British occupation. Anthony Wayne was among those who noted that "The Town—is a crowded mass of wooden or Frame buildings—& therefore subject to a general Conflagration—either by accident—or from design . . . the Citadel, barracks Stores &c within it must share the same fate from

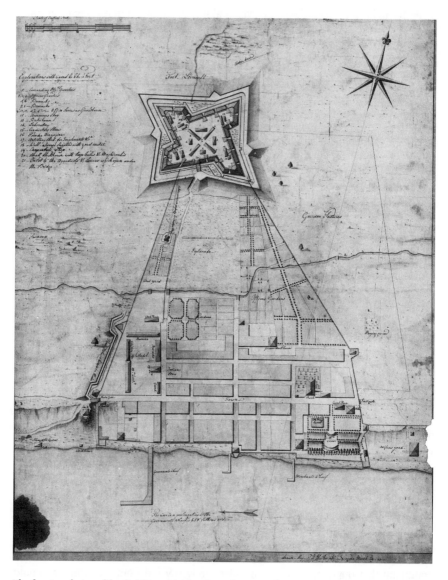

The finest rendering of fortified Detroit is that drawn by Maj. John J. U. Rivardi in 1799 for Maj. Gen. Alexander Hamilton. It neatly summarizes the many changes made to the fortifications since the 1760s. Fort Lernoult (top) was originally constructed as a separate fortification in 1778–79 and not connected to the town until 1782. Rivardi served at Detroit in 1796–97, and his plan represents the place as found by the Americans in 1796. Courtesy of the William L. Clements Library, University of Michigan, Ann Arbor.

their contiguity & inflammable Materials, of which they are Composed."[24] On 11 June 1805, these fears were finally realized when a "general Conflagration" reduced the entire town to "a heap of ruins, consisting of naked chimnies and cinders." Only Fort Detroit, the stone powder magazine, the shipyard, and one blockhouse survived the inferno.[25]

The greatest part of eighteenth-century Detroit was thus wiped away just as the town was about to become the capital of the newly created Michigan Territory. Territorial Governor William Hull arrived on 1 July to be greeted by a scene of devastation, but also an opportunity to improve the town. Most important was a new street plan, which, it was hoped by the secretary of war, would allow the area between the fort and the river to be cleared of obstructions.[26] The inhabitants forestalled this sound idea, however, and had begun to rebuild even before Hull arrived. The governor was at least able to impose an improved and innovative street plan, based on two broad avenues (east–west Jefferson and north–south Woodward). These formed the beginning of Judge Augustus B. Woodward's concept of a city laid out in an unending series of hexagonal units connected with broad avenues. Hull then exchanged government land east of the fort to extinguish many claims in the old town. Nonetheless, many private structures were reestablished between the fort and the river.[27]

The priorities of rebuilding meant that, for the next two years, Detroit would be without the security of a stockade for the first time in its history. Fort Detroit and its garrison provided substantial protection, of course, but it was not until the *Cheasapeake-Leopard* crisis of 1807 and the threat of war with Britain that a new stockade was erected around the town. This was accomplished during the summer of 1807 by detachments of local militia. The new street plan required the enclosure of a much greater area and caused the stockade to be extended farther to the east. The new town plan also gave the stockade a clumsy configuration, difficult to protect from the fort. For this reason, large blockhouses were constructed in the northeast corner of the stockade and at the east end of Jefferson Avenue. Defense of the west end of town rested on the fort and on an "old" blockhouse that had survived the 1805 fire and now stood in the middle of Jefferson Avenue, some distance within the stockade.[28]

The crisis stimulated further improvements. Substantial repairs were made to the fort during 1808, and new barracks were constructed in the old Citadel compound on the foundations of the former British buildings destroyed in the 1805 fire.

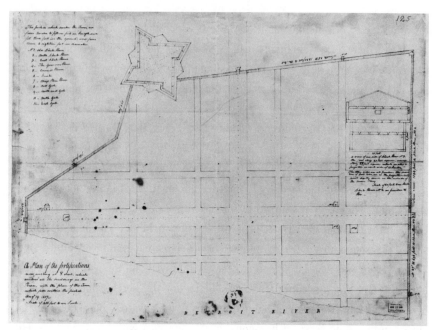

The town of Detroit was not re-fortified immediately after the catastrophic 1805 fire. It was not until the *Chesapeake-Leopard* incident of 1807 raised border tensions that Gov. William Hull ordered a stockade constructed to enclose the new and larger street plan. The widest streets represent modern Woodward and Jefferson avenues. Most of this stockade had been dismantled before the outbreak of the War of 1812. Courtesy of the Library of Congress.

The new structures of the Citadel included an officers' quarters and a single barracks where, as in the British occupation, the garrison could be more comfortably accommodated than within the cramped interior of Fort Detroit.[29] The re-establishment of the Citadel also made the government more aggressive in asserting its claims to the military reserve and access to the river. Surveys of government property and the erection of a large brick storehouse on the riverbank were accomplished in 1809.[30]

Despite the scare of 1807 and the considerable effort expended to restore the walls of Detroit's civilian quarter, it was not long before these defenses were considered redundant. By the spring of 1810, citizens were removing stockade timbers, and Governor Hull was disinclined to stop them because the defensive wall had mostly been erected on private property. Hull, fearful that the valuable timber would be consumed for firewood, ordered most of the stockade taken down and the pickets stored for use in a future emergency.[31]

When the real crisis came in 1812, Detroit could rely on only its earthen fort and the pickets that surrounded the Citadel and connected the southwest corner of the fort with the river. Governor Hull was absent during the winter of 1811–12, as U.S. relations with the Indians and Britain deteriorated. Responsibility for the security of Detroit fell to Captain John Whistler who was instructed to repair the fortifications and, later in the winter, to erect batteries in the town to bear on the Canadian shore.[32] Plans by American officers are not known to have survived from this period, if indeed any were drawn, but there is good data from intelligence maps prepared by British officers. They show a repaired and renewed Fort Detroit, and a town undefended by traditional stockade walls.[33]

The only additions to Detroit's fortifications during the 1812 campaign were three batteries constructed within the town between the fort and river. These were sited atop the riverbank to compensate for the obstruction of the fort's cannon by part of the town. The labor of constructing them proved to be in vain for, much to the frustration of General Hull's officers and despite the powerful 24 pounder cannon mounted in these positions, "he allowed the British to erect a Battery immediately opposite . . . without ever firing a gun to prevent them."[34] The British crossed the river and intimidated the aging American general into surrendering. Detroit thus passed into British hands on 16 August.

The wartime British garrison had few resources to devote to the fortifications of a town that was poorly located for active participation in this new conflict. Holding Detroit now depended more upon retaining naval control of Lake Erie. A garrison was placed in Fort Detroit, and the public buildings were maintained; however, the defeat of the British squadron in September 1813, and the landing of General William Henry Harrison's army near Fort Malden, rendered the place untenable. On 27 September, British troops set fire to the public buildings, including those in the Citadel and the fort, and withdrew up the Thames River.[35] Troops from Harrison's army reoccupied Detroit two days later.

By the autumn of 1813, Detroit was a war-weary and impoverished community, suffering from the effects of the disruption of agriculture and commerce and a year of hostile military occupation. It could offer the new garrison little in the way of resources, although a substantial body of troops was still in need of housing, particularly since all the barracks had been destroyed. The soldiers sheltered under tents or in abandoned houses while they constructed temporary huts.[36] The focus of their work was the immediate area of the fort, re-christened for Isaac Shelby of Kentucky.[37]

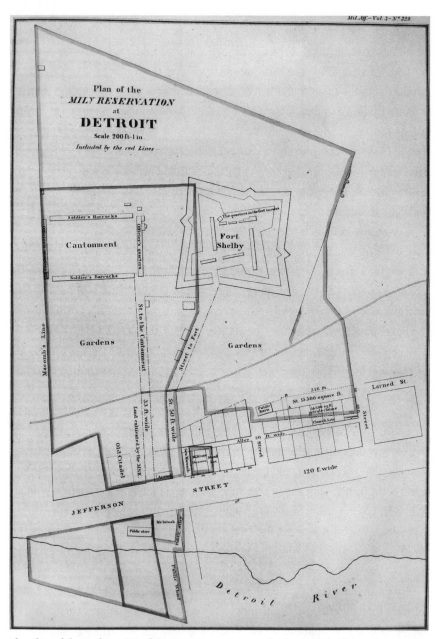

Plan of the
MILY RESERVATION
at
DETROIT
Scale 200 ft-1 in.
Included by the red Lines

Soldier's Barracks

Cantonment

Soldier's Barracks

Officer's quarters

Fort
Shelby

The quarters in the fort to cross

Macomb's Line

Gardens

St to the Cantonment

Street to Fort

Gardens

33 ft. wide
Land cultivated by the MSK.

St. 50 ft wide

Old Citadel

310 Ft.
St. 15.500 square ft.

Public
store

Church Lots

Larned St.

Street

Alley

20 ft. wide

120 ft. wide

STREET

JEFFERSON

McIntosh

Public store

Public Wharf

Detroit River

The military defenses of Post–War of 1812 Detroit were concentrated at the west end of the growing town. Fort Shelby was maintained until 1826, supplemented by the barracks of the Cantonment and the arsenal and public storehouse properties facing each other across Jefferson Avenue. This plan shows the military reserve as it was about 1820. Courtesy of the William L. Clements Library, University of Michigan, Ann Arbor.

Detroit ended the war in this condition and, for the next decade, continued as an active military post supporting Fort Mackinac and the new establishments at Sault Ste. Marie, Green Bay, and the upper Mississippi River region. There was never again an attempt to enclose the town with fortifications, and, indeed, it rapidly began to burst its bounds in every direction. The army reasserted its rights to the public lands, including the all-important access to the river between the Citadel property and the brick storehouse. A large square of log barracks and officers' quarters, dubbed the "Cantonment," was constructed in the autumn of 1815, just to the west of Fort Shelby. It was designed to shelter as many as seven hundred men, but these were usually troops in transit to other northwestern posts.[38] In 1819, the Ordnance Department erected a substantial stone arsenal on part of the old Citadel property and developed the surrounding land for a storekeeper's house, gardens, and shot and wood yards.[39] Like the Cantonment, it primarily served as a depot for distributing military equipment elsewhere.

Despite restoration of the military precincts of Detroit, it was increasingly apparent that Fort Shelby and nearby structures had outlived their usefulness. Removal of the military structures was under serious consideration by 1825. In January 1826, the civilian authorities in Detroit petitioned Congress for the land still retained as a military reserve and for the removal of the potentially hazardous stone powder magazine. Their request was justified by the assertion that the "growth of the city has now almost entirely encompassed the military works and the public reservation for military purposes, hence the utility of those works, either for offensive or defensive purposes has absolutely ceased."[40] The army was in agreement, aside from insisting that the arsenal and storehouse should be retained as a "place of deposit" for military stores needed by other posts on the lakes.[41] On 27 May 1826, nearly 125 years after the first French soldiers arrived on the shores of the straits, Fort Shelby was evacuated by its garrison. The land was turned over to the City of Detroit and, in the spring of 1827, the remaining stockades around the fort were removed as workmen began leveling the ramparts.[42]

This was the end of fortified Detroit. A new post would later be constructed some distance down the river at Spring Wells (Fort Wayne), but never again would fortifications and a military garrison be an integral, even dominant, feature of daily life in Detroit. Such had been the case throughout the Sixty Years' War for the Great Lakes, and military necessity had controlled the development of the place throughout that time.

NOTES

1. See Helen H. Tanner, *Atlas of Great Lakes Indian History* (Norman: University of Oklahoma Press, 1987), 39–47.

2. Cadillac's account of founding the settlement is translated in Cadillac to the Minister of Marine, 25 September 1702, *Michigan Pioneer and Historical Collections*, 40 vols. (Lansing: Michigan Historical Commission, 1877–1929), 33:133–51 [hereafter cited as *MPHC*].

3. Gaspard-Joseph Chaussegros de Léry Journal, 27 July1749, *Rapport de l'Archiviste de la Province de Québec pour 1926–1927* (Québec: L.-Amable Proulx, 1927), 344–45.

4. "Plan du Fort du Detroit . . . ," 6 August 1754, by Joseph-Gaspard Chaussegros de Léry. Musée de la Civilisation, L-58, Fonds Verreau, manuscrit O 94. See also John Pattin's account, 1754, *Wisconsin Historical Collections*, 31 vols. (Madison: State Historical Society of Wisconsin, 1855–1931), 18:145–46.

5. Sylvester K. Stevens and Donald H. Kent, eds., *Journal of Chaussegros de Léry* (Harrisburg: Pennsylvania Historical Commission, 1940), 68.

6. Ibid., 68, 95.

7. Beverly W. Bond Jr., ed., "The Captivity of Charles Stuart, 1755–57," *Mississippi Valley Historical Review* 13 (1926–27): 78.

8. Deposition by Francis Navarre, 23 June 1766, Thomas Gage Papers, vol. 53, William L. Clements Library, University of Michigan, Ann Arbor, Michigan [hereafter WLCL].

9. Robert Rogers, *Journals of Major Robert Rogers* (London: J. Millan, 1765), 229.

10. "Plan of the Fort at Detroit 1760" by [Diedrich Brehm], Burton Historical Collection, 977.4D4–1760-P695, Detroit Public Library, Detroit, Michigan [hereafter BHC].

11. Franklin B. Hough, ed., *Diary of the Siege of Detroit in the War with Pontiac* (Albany: J. Munsell, 1860), 38; "Plan of Detroit with its Environs," [1763], by John Montresor, WLCL.

12. The space is shown cleared of buildings in "Plan of the Fort at De Troit," 18 August 1761, by William Brasier after [Diedrich Brehm], which was drawn for Gen. Jeffery Amherst. Advertised in Sotheby's catalog of 4 July 1967. Current whereabouts are unknown.

13. G.D. Scull, ed., "The Montresor Journals," *Collections of the New-York Historical Society for the Year 1881* (New York: New-York Historical Society, 1882), 288.

14. Gen. Thomas Gage to the Earl of Shelburne, 10 October 1767, *The Correspondence of General Thomas Gage with the Secretaries of State, 1763–1775*, 2 vols., ed. Clarence Edwin Carter (New Haven: Yale University Press, 1931), 1:153.

15. Lt. Gov. Henry Hamilton to the Earl of Dartmouth, 29 August 1776, *MPHC*, 10:265.

16. David Lyster to George Moorehead, 4 February 1779, *George Rogers Clark Papers, 1771–1781*, ed. James Alton James (Springfield: Illinois State Historical Library, 1912), 101; Lt. Col. Mason Bolton to Gov. Frederick Haldimand, 12 February 1779, *MPHC*, 19:373.

17. Logbook of the Sloop *Welcome*, 3 October 1779, Alexander Harrow Papers, BHC.

18. "New Fort at Detroit . . . Old Fort contracted . . . Part of the old Fort left open," [1780], by Henry Bawbee, George Washington Papers, vol. 159, Library of Congress [hereafter LC].

19. Lt. Col. Arent S. DePeyster to Haldimand, 1 October 1784, *MPHC*, 20:262–63.

20. Capt. Henry Bird to Brig. Gen. J. Watson Powell, 13 August 1782, ibid., 10:625–26.

21. DePeyster to Haldimand, 1 October 1784, ibid., 20:262–63.

22. See "Plan of the Town of Detroit and Fort Lernoult," 1 August 1792, by [William Adye?], Simcoe Map Collection, F 47–5–1–0–11, Ontario Archives, Toronto; [Plan of Detroit], 29 March 1799, by John J. U. Rivardi, WLCL. For a detailed account of Detroit from the perspective of an Indian prisoner, see Oliver M. Spencer, *Indian Captivity: A True Narrative of the Capture of the Rev. O.M. Spencer by the Indians, in the Neighbourhood of Cincinnati* (New York: B. Waugh and T. Mason, 1835), 126–32.

23. Ebenezer Denny to Josiah Harmar, 20 December 1799, Harmar Papers, vol. 18., WLCL.

24. Anthony Wayne to Sec. of War James McHenry, 29 September 1796, Anthony Wayne Papers, Historical Society of Pennsylvania, Philadelphia, Penn.

25. "The Conflagration of Detroit," *National Intelligencer*, 6 September 1805.

26. Sec. of War Henry Dearborn to Gov. William Hull, 23 July 1805, *The Territorial Papers of the United States*, 27 vols., ed. Clarence Edwin Carte (Washington, D.C.: Government Printing Office, 1934–54), 10:23–24.

27. Hull to Sec. of State James Madison, 3 August 1805, *MPHC*, 31:524.

28. "A Plan of the fortifications now erecting at Detroit . . . Augt. 19. 1807," LC.

29. Capt. Samuel T. Dyson to Dearborn, 1 October 1808, *MPHC*, 40:268; Col. Henry Burbeck to Col. Jacob Kingsbury, 1 April 1809, Jacob Kingsbury Papers, L5: 1807–9, vol. 12, BHC.

30. "Map of the Military Ground at Detroit . . . 13th April 1809," by Aaron Greeley, Washington, D.C.: National Archives, RG 49, Michigan, 1 [hereafter NA]; Kingsbury to Sec. of War William Eustis, 1 September 1809, Kingsbury Papers, L5: 1810–11, vol. 13, BHC.

31. Hull to Kingsbury, 10 November 1810, Kingsbury Papers, L5: 1809–11, vol. 17, BHC.

32. Hull to Eustis, 6 March 1812, *MPHC*, 40:363.

33. See [Plan of the town and fort of Detroit], 20 May 1812, Gano Papers, Cincinnati Historical Society, MSS G198c, vol. I. Accounts of events at Detroit in the summer of 1812 make it apparent that the north and east sides of the town of Detroit were not fortified. At least three other plans of the former Fort Lernoult survive, all by British or Canadian authors.

34. Capt. John Whistler to Kingsbury, 5 January 1813, Kingsbury Papers, L5: 1812–13, vol. 20, BHC. The only plan known to show these batteries is [Plan of Detroit], by [William Evans?], 977.4D4-[1812?]-D4, BHC.

35. Maj. Gen. Henry Proctor to Maj. Gen. Francis de Rottenberg, 23 Oct. 1813, *MPHC*, 15:427.

36. Brig. Gen. Lewis Cass to Sec. of War John Armstrong, 28 October 1813, ibid., 40:542; Account of a soldier, [October 1813] quoted in Silas Farmer, *The History of Detroit and Michigan*, 2 vols. (Detroit: Silas Farmer and Co., 1889), 1:283–84.

37. See "Sketch map of Fort Shelby, June 7th, 1814," by Xymmybn M. Cmbol, New York Public Library, Ms Division.

38. Maj. Samuel Brown to Sec. of War A. J. Dallas, 30 August 1815, Letters Received, War Department, RG 107, NA; Brig. Gen. Alexander Macomb to Sec. of War W.H. Crawford, 14 December 1815, ibid.

39. Capt. Rufus L. Baker to Col. Decius Wadsworth, 30 October 1819, RG 156, Letters Received, NA. These developments are shown in "Map of the Military Reservations of Detroit," ca. 1820, by Philu B. Judd, RG 49, Michigan, 30 (1), NA.

40. Mayor John R. Williams to Congress, 23 January 1826, *American State Papers, Military Affairs* (Washington: Gales and Seaton, 1860), 3:303.

41. Maj. Gen. Alexander Macomb to Sec. of War James Barbour, 17 April 1826, ibid., 302–3. The arsenal and storehouse properties were given up by the army and sold in 1832, although the ordnance facility could not be completely transferred to the new arsenal at Dearborn until the spring of 1834.

42. Farmer, *The History of Detroit*, 1:225.

Rethinking the Gnadenhutten Massacre: The Contest for Power in the Public World of the Revolutionary Pennsylvania Frontier

LEONARD SADOSKY

And it came to pass in those days, that the devil entered into Colonel Williamson (who lived fifteen or twenty miles west of us) and stirred him up, to raise a company of men, to go against a town of friendly Indians, chiefly of the Delaware tribe, and professing the Moravian religion, who had taken no part with the hostile Indians, and who lived on the waters of the Muskingum.

—*Capt. Spencer Records, in an autobiographical narrative, 1842.*[1]

[U]pon the whole I find that it will be Impossible to git an Impartial and fare account of that affair . . . it is really no wonder that those who have lost all that is near and Dear to them go out with determined revenge, and Exterpation of all Indians.

—*Dorsey Pentecost, Esq., in a letter to President Moore of the Pennsylvania Executive Council, 9 May 1782.*[2]

I hear nothing of what is going on in any other part of the world. There never was, nor I hope will there ever be such a wretched, villainous place as this. I do not remember any part of my life spent in so little purpose as at present and so exceedingly disagreeable to myself.

—*Brig. Gen. William Irvine, Commandant of Fort Pitt, in a letter to his wife, 29 May 1782.*[3]

In early 1782, the town of Pittsburgh and the garrison of Fort Pitt together formed one of the westernmost redoubts of the American Revolution. Although the October 1781 victory of General George Washington, Admiral the Count de Grasse, and General the Count de Rochambeau at Yorktown had all but ended the American War for Independence, the armed conflict still raged on the western slope of the Appalachian Mountains. Great Britain and its American Indian allies remained a formidable threat to the Pennsylvanians and Virginians who had settled in the Ohio Valley during the 1760s and 1770s. In response, the Continental Army centered its defensive strategies of the American states' western frontiers on the men inside the battlements of Fort Pitt. Yet, as the winter of 1781–82 dragged on, it became increasingly clear to many that the greatest danger to the Continental garrison at Pittsburgh was not from British soldiers at Detroit or Wyandot warriors at Sandusky, but from the very western Pennsylvania farmers they had been charged with protecting.[4]

In February and March 1782, the Revolutionary War in western Pennsylvania turned into an outright and open rebellion against the Continental Army. This rebellion took on various forms and had many causes.[5] Disaffection with the garrison at Fort Pitt began years beforehand, as a result of the command of Colonel Daniel Brodhead. Order in the greater Pittsburgh area was tenuous when William Irvine took command in late 1781; with his departure in January 1782 on a trip to Congress, that order quickly collapsed. Rumors of mutiny circulated in early February 1782. Hostility toward the Fort Pitt garrison and Continental Indian policy finally erupted in violence in March 1782. Washington County militiamen attacked, killed, and burned an entire village of neutral, Christian Indians with ties to the Continental commandants. Many of these same militiamen were part of a Washington County group that then attacked and killed a small band of Delaware Indians with Continental commissions. Finally, these men threatened to kill the acting commandant of Fort Pitt, Colonel John Gibson. Although Irvine's return in late March quelled the disturbances, order continued to remain tenuous.[6]

For most historians, the central event in this extended period of rebellion was the destruction of the Delaware village of Gnadenhutten on 8 March 1782, an event that has come to be known as the Gnadenhutten Massacre. The massacre has figured prominently in several recent histories of the Revolutionary frontier and Indian-white relations, but it has yet to be put in its appropriate context. Thomas Slaughter describes the massacre as a product of "frustration" on the part of the western Pennsylvanians, and it was but one of many events that prefigured the Whiskey Rebellion that was to follow.[7] For Richard White, the massacre was prime evidence of an omnipresent, almost pathological, feeling of "Indian-hatred" that permeated the society of the American frontier.[8] Although the descriptions of the Gnadenhutten Massacre offered by these and other historians are generally accurate, their explanations of the massacre are unsatisfactory. Too often, historians have

either seen the massacre as a sidebar to the story of frontier development, or more often, as simply another event in the well-worn meta-narrative of Indian-white relations that has usually stressed white violence and Indian victimization. Given recent study of Native American societies and the communities of the Anglo-American frontier, a deeper understanding of the origins of the Gnadenhutten Massacre is now possible.

The 1970s and 1980s saw the appearance of a body of historical literature describing both the experiences of Native Americans and the development of Anglo-American frontier communities, albeit in relative isolation from one another.[9] In the

1990s, authors such as Stephen Aron, Eric Hinderaker, and Alan Taylor built on these earlier writings and wrote highly nuanced frontier histories that stressed the continuities between the first contacts, the contests for empire, and the ultimate projects of state-building.[10] In his 1997 synthesis of political history, social history, and the New Indian History, *Elusive Empires*, Eric Hinderaker argues that from the moment Europeans entered the Ohio Valley through the nineteenth century, they were involved in the project of creating empires. European imperial aspirations were achieved initially through commercial exchanges. These "empires of commerce" were replaced in the middle of the eighteenth century by empires rooted in territorial claims and alliance structures that had political, military, and commercial bases. Finally, the American Revolution saw the emergence of a vision of empire based on "land and liberty." The development and expansion of the American republic was grounded not simply in the traditional ideology that justified an expanding nation-state, but also in an intellectual and legal framework that celebrated private property and personal independence. The various and changing relationships between Europeans and Natives throughout these two centuries were rooted in these changing conceptions of empire.[11]

What Hinderaker calls the "Empire of Land and Liberty" was fully elaborated in an earlier Alan Taylor essay, "Land and Liberty on the Post-Revolutionary Frontier." In his formulation, the Revolution revealed a diversity of aspirations between the three groups who had an interest in the frontier: white farmers who settled in the West, white elites both in the East and West, and American Indians. The Indians of the Ohio Valley desired to maintain their dispersed world of villages in which women engaged in agriculture and men engaging in hunting, war, and politics. White settlers attempted to create a world of freehold farms, in which every adult white male had the opportunity to realize personal independence and patriarchal control. White elites saw the importance the West would have in the new Republic and sought to maintain the allegiance of western communities to Congress and the eastern states while upholding the rule of law and providing an environment that would ensure orderly political and economic development.[12]

It has been too easy to see the relations between frontier farmers and frontier élites as dichotomous. These farmers have been traditionally portrayed as proto-Jeffersonians who sought only to engage in subsistence agriculture and protect hearth and home from an array of outside forces, while frontier elites have often been portrayed as nascent capitalist robber barons engaged in widespread land speculation, the promotion of tenancy, and encouraging the encroachment of the market.[13] Recent scholarship has punched holes in nearly all these myths. Tenancy was not as widespread nor as permanent in most locales as some historians have thought; landholders of all persuasions engaged in various types of speculation; frontier farmers were just as likely to embrace the market and the consumer goods it offered, as they were to lament the debt and dependency that often accompanied it.[14] Natives, too, were as liable as not to insert themselves into white market relationships, embrace white religion, and contract political alliances with white polities.[15] Occupying the same position in space, each of the three groups was forced to interact with the others. In doing so, each sought to maximize the advantages for itself while simultaneously maintaining the viability of a particular vision of how the world was supposed to work. The Gnadenhutten Massacre occurred in this atmosphere of competing visions, similar to that which Taylor's essay described.

Divisions between whites on the frontier mirrored the societal divisions elsewhere in North America. In the middle of the eighteenth century, the Anglo-American world was divided into two distinct social orders, the gentry and the common people. In observing both Britain and America, historians with such diverse ideological backgrounds as E. P. Thompson and Gordon S. Wood have seen the gap between "patricians" and "plebeians" as the crucial division in eighteenth-century society.[16] Even as Americans struggled to define the meaning and extent of their revolution, many American elites steadfastly clung to beliefs of patrician distinction. The Fort Pitt commandants were such men, and their cultural backgrounds and assumptions would condition their responses to the challenges to their authority. Similarly, Anglo-American traditions of revolt and resistance would inform plebian actions as the two sides engaged in an extended debate over the proper policies of engagement toward American Indians.

The manner in which these competing perceptions manifested themselves becomes clearer through a detailed examination of the events themselves. Primarily, this essay is a retelling of the narrative of the Gnadenhutten Massacre. However, unlike earlier descriptions, which have focused on the massacre exclusively, this account begins with the assumption of command of Fort Pitt by Colonel Daniel Brodhead in the spring of 1779 and follows events through the massacre to the spring months of 1782. Through these years, Natives, plebian farmers, and patrician officers all voiced various interests and jockeyed for political and military power. The essay will simultaneously proceed to elaborate the factors that divided the

Continental officers from the Pennsylvania farmers. The division was twofold. On one level, there was a straightforward dispute between officers and the militia over how, if at all, to incorporate Native peoples into the defensive strategies for the Western Department. On another level, there was a vast and unspoken social and cultural divide between the two groups. The officer corps and the militiamen were separated by differences in wealth, upbringing, and education—in short, by the fundamental social tensions of eighteenth-century Anglo-American society. It was this multifaceted divide between two groups of men and their relation to a third group that spawned a contest for power on the frontier that, in the end, culminated in massacre and rebellion.

The roots of the conflict between Continental Officers and western Pennsylvania farmers had their origin in the social and cultural divisions that were part and parcel of life in the eighteenth-century Anglo-American world. Yet these social tensions would not have erupted into violence had there not been a dispute over proper policy toward the Native American communities of the Ohio Valley. Initially, relations between the Fort Pitt commanders and the residents of the Upper Ohio Valley were cordial. From the lowliest subsistence farmers, to the relatively wealthy few who had brought slaves to the Upper Ohio and speculated in huge tracts of land, the vast majority of the Virginians, Pennsylvanians, and Continentals believed in the righteousness of the Patriot cause and desired American independence from Britain. Yet the question of how to achieve this desired end remained an open one.

Since the time Europeans penetrated the interior, Native Americans had been trading partners, allies in diplomacy, and occasionally, enemies in warfare. British success in the Seven Years' War had rested upon alliances with the Iroquois and other Native groups, while the continued viability of Pittsburgh itself after the war depended upon trade with the Ohio Valley and Great Lakes Indians.[17] With independence, a divide emerged. Some on the frontier believed that the best manner in which to achieve success on the western front was to imitate the policies that had worked so well for the British during the last war, and for the French decades before that. Indian traders in Pittsburgh and the Continental Officers at the fort acknowledged that the villages and tribes to the far west and north were irretrievably in the British orbit. But, they believed that by cultivating Indian alliances with nearby tribes, such as the Delaware, the patriot cause would be provided with intelligence, some warriors, and a buffer zone to protect the new westernmost farming settlements from hostile raids. Punitive expeditions and raids were still quite useful, but they were only to be directed against hostile groups and targets whose destruction was tenable, given the dearth of troops and supplies. These men believed that policies that had worked so well throughout the entire eighteenth century did not need to be abandoned.

The farmers who had come from Pennsylvania and Virginia to settle the Upper Ohio disagreed. They saw the trade that maintained the alliance with the Delaware as a drain on the small supply of materiel that could be better used to defend their homes. Marauding Natives still crossed into the western townships, despite the alliance with the Delawares. Popular sentiment consistently favored the massing of men in huge expeditions that could, in theory, sweep through the Ohio Country, destroy Sandusky and Detroit, and ensure peace on the frontier. The model, both spoken and unspoken, was the 1778–79 expedition of George Rogers Clark that conquered Vincennes and Kaskaskia.[18] Indeed, Clark himself was one of the main advocates for an expedition to Detroit through 1780 and 1781.[19] The desire for aggressive warfare could not be placated. When expeditions were countenanced, they usually turned into dismal failures (such as William Crawford's abortive attempt to destroy Sandusky in the spring of 1782), but in response, popular sentiment was usually for yet another expedition.[20]

The popular antipathy toward commerce and diplomacy with Indians became manifest at several points during the years leading up to the Gnadenhutten Massacre. One of the first was the popular uproar that resulted in the removal of Colonel Daniel Brodhead. The struggle to remove Brodhead from his command reveals not only the vast personal distance between him and the surrounding populace, but also the divergent conceptions of Indian policy and civil-military relations among the inhabitants of the Pennsylvania frontier and among elite Continental officers.

Daniel Brodhead commanded Fort Pitt through the middle of 1781. Militarily, his record was mixed. His 1779 expedition to support John Sullivan's invasion of Iroquoia saw the destruction of some villages, but not to the extent Brodhead had originally hoped, and a rendezvous with Sullivan quickly became untenable.[21] He attempted to maintain the Americans' fragile alliance with the majority of the Delaware villages, in what would become eastern Ohio. Brodhead took the acts of alliance-building and treaty-making seriously, and was rewarded by the Delawares with the name of one of the great Delaware chiefs, "Maghingua Keeshoch," or the Great Moon, as a sign that, in Delaware eyes, he was an "Upright Man."[22] Despite Brodhead's sincerity in his efforts to maintain Delaware loyalty, the pull of the

British post at Detroit proved too strong. The Continental's alliance with the majority of the Delawares collapsed.[23] In the spring of 1781, Brodhead launched a retaliatory expedition, which destroyed the main Delaware village, Coshocton.[24] But for the western Pennsylvanians who were subject to Indian raids, this was not enough. Brodhead's earlier Indian policies, financial dealings, and disregard of local institutions and customs had all made him suspect. Letters and petitions were dispatched to the Pennsylvania Executive Council, to the Continental Congress, and to General Washington. All of them called for the removal of Daniel Brodhead from command of the Western Department.[25]

Pittsburgh resident Alexander Fowler penned the first set of accusations against Brodhead in a letter to Pennsylvania Executive Council President Joseph Reed. Fowler offered a picture of a "contemptible situation," in which the Commandant had lost all legitimacy in the eyes of those around him. "Colonel Brodhead has not only rendered himself universally obnoxious to the people," Fowler asserted, "but also to many of his officers, who have refused for these twelve months to dine or associate with him." Not only Brodhead, but also the "indians and quarter masters" were "equally objects of the people's jealousy and aversion."[26] In alleging "corruption" on the part of Brodhead and his quartermasters, Fowler offered a common critique of the quartermasters and commissaries of the Continental Army.[27] But what separated Fowler's accusations, was his observation that at the heart of this "contemptible" and "disgraceful" situation was the fact that the Indians and quartermasters were "indulged" like nowhere else.

> An indian trade is carried on in this department on principles hitherto unknown to even our enemies in their lost and corrupt state. Under the auspices of our Commandant his harlot [the Deputy Quarter Master] purchases furs and peltries from the savages which are paid for with liquor, salt &c from the commissaries store and sold for cash: and though this trade must be allowed to be snug, safe and profitable yet it is degrading , is unworthy of imitation and ought to be reprobated.[28]

In the same letter, Fowler went on to assert, "Indians have not only been countenanced but public criminals screened through base and interested motives." In his equation of Indians with "public criminals," Fowler indicated a latent hostility to commerce with the Indians. Although he asserted that Brodhead's Indian trade was worse that the British version, his language gives the impression that he would have been unsatisfied with the existence of any networks of exchange. For Alexander Fowler, it was a trade "unworthy of imitation."[29]

Brodhead would have most certainly disagreed with this assessment. Shortly after he took command of Fort Pitt, he acknowledged that a policy of engagement with Indians was necessary for the post's survival as he relied on "intelligence from the Delawares" to monitor the "movements of the Enemy."[30] Delaware soldiers were vital also, as they accompanied Brodhead's troops in his expedition to the Seneca homeland in 1779.[31] Any charges of financial misconduct were certainly unfounded. After one set of negotiations, Brodhead made it clear to his superiors that the Delawares were "poor wretches . . . quite destitute of clothing," and that they needed Continental largesse or else these potential allies would be forced to "submit to such terms as our enemies may impose on them." Brodhead observed that it would be best to make arrangements to "receive their peltry in exchange for [any] goods furnished," as "the Public cannot meet with a loss but must reap a certain profit."[32] What the western Pennsylvanians considered corruption, was in Brodhead's mind simply a diplomatic necessity that also made good financial sense. These differences in perception over a question so fundamental as Indian policy inevitably distanced the Continental commandant from the majority of the populace.

However, some of the distance between the commandant and the communities around Fort Pitt was not merely a product of a policy dispute. The son of a wealthy Bucks County merchant and landowner, Brodhead's correspondence makes it clear that he saw himself living in a world apart from the farmers around him.[33] Within months of taking command of Fort Pitt, Brodhead was embroiled in a controversy with Pittsburgh residents over the proper bounds of Fort Pitt. He complained to Timothy Pickering that the "inhabitants of this place are continually encroaching on what I conceive to be the rights of the Garrison and which was always considered as such when the Fort was occupied by the King of Britain's troops." Brodhead wanted Congress to delineate a parade ground, and reacquire some "Block-houses . . . which are part of the strength of this place," but which were "occupied and claimed by private persons."[34] Months later, no action had been taken. In a haughty, patrician tone, he again asked Pickering to consult Congress to clarify the situation. "The Inhabitants on this side of the Alleghany Hills profess a great law knowledge, and it would be exceedingly disagreeable to me to be pestered with their silly Courts."[35] Brodhead apparently seized at least one of the out-buildings, as Edward Ward kept trying to sue Brodhead in the Yohogania County court from January 1780 through

May 1781.[36] Brodhead held aristocratic, patrician pretensions in the midst of a revolution against monarchy and aristocracy. Given this psychic distance that Brodhead fostered between himself and the population he was charged to protect, it is little wonder his actions were perceived in such an ill light.

The calls for Brodhead's removal were heeded, and General Washington ordered that he relinquish command in May 1781. Brodhead thus turned command of Fort Pitt over to Colonel John Gibson, and left for Pittsburgh for Philadelphia.[37] Brodhead's impolitic handling of militia relations and the public stores in the Western Department ultimately handicapped Gibson's attempt to support George Rogers Clark's planned expedition to the Indian towns near Sandusky and Detroit.[38] Brodhead then returned from the East in August, claimed his May orders were unclear, and attempted to regain command at Fort Pitt.[39] A power struggle between Gibson and Brodhead ensued, with Brodhead first arresting Gibson, and then General Washington ordering Brodhead to once again concede his command.[40] Simultaneously, legal action was taken against Brodhead in the civilian court of Pennsylvania's Westmoreland County.[41] This contest for power had been a tumultuous one, but Brodhead's departure from the Greater Pittsburgh region in October should have ended the turmoil.

Yet the unrest on the Pennsylvania frontier continued. In late August and early September, while Brodhead and Gibson battled for control of the Western Department, reports circulated through Washington and Westmoreland counties that a large body of Indian warriors from Sandusky had massed at a set of Delaware towns in the Tuscarawas-Muskingum Valley. Brodhead had knowledge of the developments, but the disarray among the Continental Officers at Fort Pitt inhibited a response.[42]

These villages on the Tuscarawas River, Gnadenhutten, Salem, and Schoenbrunn, were unique entities in the world of the revolutionary frontier.[43] They had been founded by missionaries of the pietist Church of the United Brethren, commonly referred to as the Moravian Church. The villages' populations were composed entirely of Native Americans who had converted to Christianity and a few white missionaries, mostly of German ancestry, who ministered to them. The War for American Independence placed the Moravian villages in a precarious position. They found themselves almost directly between the Anglo-American farming communities of western Pennsylvania, and the numerous British-allied Native villages of the Great Lakes Basin. Caught in the middle of this geopolitical vortex, the Moravian Delawares attempted to placate both sides in order to maintain their neutrality. The Moravian towns often provided a way station for British-allied Indians raiding the Pennsylvania farms, while Moravian leaders, such as the Reverend John Heckewelder and the Reverend David Zeisberger, provided intelligence to the Continental commanders at Fort Pitt.[44]

In November 1781, David Williamson, a farmer and colonel in the Washington County militia, led a small body of men to the Moravian towns. They found Salem, Schoenbrunn, and Gnadenhutten to be largely deserted. The large military force Brodhead had heard about was a large band of warriors under the Wyandot chief Half-King. These British-allied Indians had marched to the Moravian towns, had taken the missionaries and the villagers prisoner, and escorted them to the Sandusky area. The missionaries were (correctly) suspected of supplying the Continental army with intelligence.[45] As a result, although Williamson's men did not find hundreds of Moravians or warriors, they did manage to capture a few Indians that were residing at the mission towns. The militia brought them to Fort Pitt. The commandant, upon hearing that they were from the Christian Indian towns, promptly released them. The fact that the Indians' release was soon followed by attacks against farms on the western edge of Washington County raised the ire of many of the County's residents.[46]

The new commandant of Fort Pitt and commander of the Western Department was Brigadier General William Irvine. He had taken command upon his arrival in Pittsburgh in early November. Irvine's initial correspondence with the commander-in-chief revealed a desperate situation. The troops of the garrison cut a "deplorable" figure, the public stores of food and ammunition were nearly exhausted, and Fort Pitt itself was in a state of disrepair. The remaining complement of the Fort Pitt garrison was not very large and few of the militia could be counted on by the Continental command. Irvine struggled to enforce discipline and enact measures that would economize the usage of the public stores.[47] However, in attempting to supply and pay the various militia units, the lack of stores severely curtailed his options. Thus, the majority of the residents of the greater-Pittsburgh region remained disgruntled. In January 1782, Irvine left Fort Pitt to consult with Congress, and John Gibson once again commanded the garrison.[48] The situation then deteriorated rapidly.

For the next two months, until Irvine returned, the rumble of mutiny and rebellion was heard from inside the walls of Fort Pitt, to the town of Pittsburgh, and through the foothills of Washington County. In early February, citing lack of pay and no provision for clothing, the enlisted men at Fort Pitt threatened mutiny against

the officer corps.[49] At nearly the same time, a raiding party from Sandusky, probably of Wyandots and Mingos, entered the western townships of Washington County.
They attacked and raided several blockhouses, killing some Pennsylvanians and
taking others prisoner. Ostensibly desiring to recover the prisoners, the men of
Washington County mustered into a militia unit in the latter part of February in
order to pursue the Indians. Again under the command of David Williamson, almost
two-hundred militiamen from Pennsylvania's Washington and Westmoreland counties and Virginia's Ohio County gathered in a stretch of bottomland on the eastern
bank of the Ohio River. Crossing the Ohio, Williamson led his men over the wooded,
frozen foothills of the Ohio Country and into the valley of the Tuscarawas and
Muskingum rivers.[50]

In contrast with the picture of desolation Williamson's men had encountered in
November, the Moravian towns were bustling with activity in the late winter months
of 1782. By the middle of the winter of 1781–82, the Moravians had been in forced
exile near Sandusky and Detroit for over five months. Provisions for all of the captives were in short supply, and the Wyandot chief, Half-King, allowed some of the
Moravian Indians (but not the missionaries) to return to the towns on the
Tuscarawas to gather the corn they had left standing in their fields. In February,
almost one hundred Moravians returned to their homes and began reaping the harvest they had sown months before.[51] The peaceful diligence with which they went
about their labor was shattered in early February, as a Sandusky raiding party
stopped in the villages on their way to Pennsylvania. In the last week of February,
these warriors came back through the village warning the Moravians that they
would probably be pursued. Some villagers were worried, but the majority reasoned
that since the Americans knew they were Christians, and since they needed to finish
gathering their corn, they would return to Sandusky only when the entire harvest
was gathered.[52] It was a fatal miscalculation.

On 7 March 1782, the two hundred-odd men of Williamson's expedition made
their way along the Tuscarawas River as they approached the village of Gnadenhutten. The front rank of this mass of men spotted a young Delaware man. Without
warning, a gun fired. The bullet from one of the militiamen's Pennsylvania rifles had
found the Delaware man's arm. He collapsed to the ground. As the militia came upon
him, he begged for his life, saying he was Joseph Shebosh, the son of a white
Moravian missionary. Another gunshot echoed through the frozen woodland, and
Shebosh was dead. One of the Pennsylvanians took out his hunting knife and, with

dispatch, cut the hair, skin, and tissue from the top of Joseph Shebosh's cranium. A scalp had been taken. Leaving the corpse, the militiamen looked up the river.[53] Gnadenhutten lay just over the horizon.

The men and women of Gnadenhutten were still busy gathering their corn when the militia entered their village. The men from Washington County initially appeared non-threatening. They warned the Moravians that they were in danger and promised to take them to Fort Pitt and safety, just as the previous Williamson Expedition had done. The villagers had still hoped to rejoin their brethren near Sandusky, but, upon reflection, they acquiesced, and began to prepare for the trip to Pittsburgh. They sent messengers to the village of Salem to have the other Moravians come to Gnadenhutten and prepare for a journey east. The villagers then turned over what weapons they had to the Pennsylvanians.[54] Although the Washington County men knew that this was a village of Christian Indians, much seemed odd to them. As members of the expedition moved about the Gnadenhuttens' cabins, they observed that the Delawares were using axes, pewter bowls, pewter spoons, teakettles, and cups. They observed also that their horses were branded and other articles were stamped with letters. Surely, they reasoned, these goods were evidence that these Indians had engaged in the plunder of Washington County, or at least were friendly with those who had. Williamson and his men then accused the Delawares of theft and murder.[55]

With the arrival of the villagers from Salem, ninety-eight Delaware men and women, both children and adults, were at the mercy of David Williamson. Accounts vary as to what transpired next. Detailed contemporary testimonials of the events in Gnadenhutten are lacking. Brief sketches, informed by rumor and word-of-mouth, were relayed in correspondence among the extended community of Moravian missionaries, but no actual members of the expedition would speak of the events in their immediate aftermath. A few of those involved offered testimony decades later in order to procure pensions or to satisfy the queries of antiquarians. The most detailed records of the Gnadenhutten Massacre, and the ones which modern historians have come to rely on the most, are those of the historians of the Moravian Church. These historians lived on the frontier and spoke with the survivors of the massacre. Although particulars vary from source to source, the documents taken all together present a fairly coherent picture of Gnadenhutten's final day.[56]

What emerges from the extant documents is a disturbing image of violent actions that were as cold and calculated as they were brutal. In light of the material items found in the village, many of the militiamen argued that the Indians should not be taken prisoner, but should be killed on the spot. Not all of the men were in agreement. As the day grew short, Williamson apparently convened a council of war and put the question to a vote of the men. Some accounts record that the men were equally divided on the question, others state only about one or two dozen stepped forward to advocate sparing the Moravians' lives. Whatever the final tally may have been, majority rule prevailed. The men, women, and children of Gnadenhutten and Salem were informed that they were to be put to death. Initially they protested, but as they became resigned to their fate, they asked for some time to prepare themselves spiritually for their journey. Rather than packing for Pittsburgh or Sandusky, they now anticipated a journey to Heaven.

> [T]hey kneeled down, offering fervent prayers to God their Saviour—and kissing one another, under a flood of tears, fully resigned to his will, they sang praises unto him, in the joyful hope, that they would soon be relieved from all pains, and join their redeemer in everlasting bliss.[57]

Those militiamen who did not wish to participate in the killing left the village. But plenty of Pennsylvanians and Virginians remained to enact the sentence of death. Still singing, still crying, the male Moravians were separated from the women and children, and led to two separate houses. Then, one militiaman seized the mallet of Gnadenhutten's cooper from one of the houses and began striking the men on head with it, one by one. After the first man had killed fourteen, he called for another to take his place. All the Indians were struck, then scalped. Finally the militiamen set the houses afire. Amazingly, two young boys managed to survive the slaughter—one by hiding silently in a cellar, the other by feigning death amidst the pile of corpses in one of the "slaughter-houses." They both escaped, made their way to Sandusky, and their testimony became the basis for the accounts of Moravian historians George Loskiel and John Heckewelder.[58]

Leaving the burnt-out shell of Gnadenhutten in the distance, Williamson's expedition made their way back into Washington County several days later. At this time, violence against Delaware Indians continued. William Irvine recorded that, "On [the Expedition's] return, a party came and attacked a few Delaware Indians, who have yet remained with us, on a small island close-by this garrison [known then as Killbuck's Island]."[59] The militiamen killed two Delawares commissioned as captains, "made prisoners of a guard of continental troops," and finally "sent Colonel [John] Gibson a message that they would scalp him."⁶⁰ This last act of rebellion occurred just days before Irvine's return from the East, and he reported that soon after his arrival, the troops were "again reduced to obedience."⁶¹

Taken together, the wanton slaughter of the Moravian Indians at Gnadenhutten and the Delaware in the Continental service provide evidence of the inability of the majority of western Pennsylvanians to countenance either a position of Indian neutrality or of an alliance with certain Indians. There were several reasons for this. Heckewelder reported that during the initial encounter at Gnadenhutten, the relative prosperity of the Moravian villages caused many of the Pennsylvania farmers to balk. He wrote, "[T]he number of horses and other property which [the Moravian Indians] possessed, was an object with these murders, who concluded, that 'when they killed the Indians, the country would be theirs; and the sooner this was done, the better!'"⁶² The farmers' belief that the Moravian Delawares' neutrality was untenable was confirmed in a narrative written by Washington County resident Spencer Records. In his old age, Records could not recall that many supported the massacre at Gnadenhutten, and he himself was appalled by it. But support was there. Records wrote that a "poor old dirty Scotchman," James Greenlee, was able to excuse the event. "Owh mon, its a weel cum don thing, for they suppurted the other Injuns as tha cum and gaad," Greenlee was alleged to have said.⁶³ Although Records stated that these sentiments won Greenlee "no applause from his neighbors," this recollection, combined with Dorsey Pentecost's initial record of widespread silence in the massacre's aftermath hint that there was some support for the destruction of Gnadenhutten.⁶⁴ At the least, these accounts confirm that many western Pennsylvanians simply could not support or even believe in Moravian neutrality. Furthermore, many of the same men evinced their hostility toward the prospect of Indian allies when they killed the Delawares who formed the Continental guard on Killbuck's Island and then made threats against the Indians within Fort Pitt.

Equally important in this light are the threats made against Colonel John Gibson. Unlike Daniel Brodhead and William Irvine, who left homes in Eastern Pennsylvania to take their post at Fort Pitt, John Gibson had lived in and around Pittsburgh since the close of the Seven Years' War. Before the Revolutionary War broke out, he was a Justice in Virginia's Yohogania County Court. Given that Gibson was such a constant presence in the world of the Upper Ohio, one might initially assume that the local populace would be more sympathetic to his command.

But Gibson did not live the life of a backcountry farmer. A young officer in the 1758 Forbes Expedition, Gibson settled in Pittsburgh immediately after the war and entered the Indian trade. Late in 1763, during Pontiac's Rebellion, Indians, likely Delaware, captured Gibson. As was often customary, he was adopted into an Indian family and was reported to have taken an Indian bride. The next year he was released and returned to Pittsburgh.[65] He still was an active Indian trader, and maintained a marriage with a Native woman.[66] Land records also hint that he may have been involved in land speculation. In Washington County alone, he held title to 1,000 acres of land, which set him far above the vast majority of those who did the killing at Gnadenhttuen.[67] (See tables 1 and 2.) Rather than serve as a voice for local interests with the Continental commanders, as an authority figure, land speculator, and Indian trader, Gibson epitomized everything the region's farmers despised. In the wake of the threatened scalping, William Irvine observed that, "A thousand lies are propagated against him. . . . The whole is occasioned by his unhappy connection with a certain tribe, which leads people to imagine, for this reason, that he has an attachment to Indians in general."[68] In attacking John Gibson, along with the commissioned Delawares at Killbuck's Island, the men of Washington County attacked the policies of Indian trade, alliance, and coexistence that formed the centerpiece of the Continental commanders' western strategy.

TABLE 1. WEALTH AND MILITARY SERVICE IN WASHINGTON COUNTY, EARLY 1780S
*Number of Identifiable Williamson Expedition Members in Each Decile
of Washington County Landholders ; Including Non-landholders*

Decile	Acreage of Decile	Number of Expedition Members in Decile
1	0– 69	15
2	70– 99	0
3	100–109	9
4	110–149	2
5	150–199	6
6	200–249	8
7	250–299	2
8	300	9
9	301–399	2
10	400–4700	5

TABLE 2. WEALTH AND MILITARY SERVICE IN WASHINGTON COUNTY, EARLY 1780s

Comparison of Williamson Expedition Members Against Township Norms[80]

Township	Number of Adult Men		Median Acreage Held		Median Estate Value in Pennsylvania (£)	
	Total	Expedition	Twp. Total	Expedition Members	Twp. Total	Expedition Total
Bethlehem	279	2	125	40	17	17
Cecil	288	23	200	150	56	77
Donegal	165	8	250	225	82	102
Hopewell	233	33	200	200	78	89
Nottingham	216	3	150	64	96	32
Peters	303	1	181	150	103	150
Robinson	201	2	300	300	45	39
Smith	156	12	300	200	112	88
Somerset	150	7	150	100	62	57
Strabane	191	18	200	100	92	190
Others	945	2	N/A	N/A	N/A	N/A
Washington County	3127	185?	200	150	N/A	85

Exceedingly conscious of his surroundings, William Irvine provided the most illuminating discussion of Continental-Militia-Indian relations. The last in a long line of Revolutionary Fort Pitt commandants, Irvine was determined to not become a victim of the political pratfalls that had handicapped, and in some cases almost killed, his predecessors. Fortunately for the historian, on several occasions Irvine revealed his inner thoughts and feelings about the situation in the West in his correspondence with his wife, Anne. Just weeks after he returned to Pittsburgh and learned of the violence of February and March, he observed that "The general and common opinion of the people of this country is that all Continental officers are too fond of Indians." Irvine hoped, "however, to be an exception," as the people around him did not "yet harbor this opinion, and I am sure they never shall reasonablely." He believed he had "given some convincing proofs" to assuage local suspicions that he might be friendly to Indians.[69]

Like Daniel Brodhead, Irvine seemed to feel he was in a world apart during his years at Fort Pitt. Upon his arrival, he was shocked to observe a "country . . . laid waste," but the region still held some excitement as an exotic new place. Sounding like something of a tourist, he informed his wife that John Gibson had talked of sending her "an Ohio pike, by way of curiosity, for [her] . . . to dine on."[70] But the thrill quickly wore off. By May, Irvine described western Pennsylvania as "the most wretched and miserable vile hole ever man dwelt in. . . ." He struggled to maintain his deportment and civility. "My time is employed in the best manner I can think of," he wrote, and he this time "riding, walking. . . . at others, gardening."[71] "We even have a pack of hounds and go frequently a hunting," he also reported.[72] Maintaining his garden was particularly important. "I assure you we have a pretty good garden, such as would pass with you as tolerable," he explained to Anne, "How elegant our peas are—thick and fine!"[73] But for all of Irvine's attempts to cultivate gentlemanly pursuits, there was no escaping the "wretched, villainous place" that surrounded him. Relations with the militia and residents of western Pennsylvania occupied the majority of Irvine's time and energy.[74] The rebellion of February and March 1782 revealed that the maintenance of order in the public world needed to be a constant preoccupation.

In the wake of the Gnadenhutten Massacre, Irvine did all he could to prove that he was unlike previous commandants, and consistently attempted to demonstrate that he would not extend any special privileges or considerations to Natives. Irvine acknowledged that any situation where there was a "combination of Regulars and

Militia, the business will be complicated, and [there will be] a diversity of interests."[75] In such situations, Irvine realized that the Commandant needed to avoid any appearance of partiality. For example, in early April, he granted Captain Uriah Springer's request to lead a "small party of [allied] Indians and soldiers to go against an Indian town." Upon the discovery that one of the Indians of the party was a traitor, the "rest of the Indians of the party" requested that Irvine make an example of him. The Commandant obliged, telling his wife, "I ordered him instantly put to death."[76] In July, an Indian suspected of raiding a Westmoreland County blockhouse was captured while begging on the streets of Pittsburgh. Rather than utilize the system of military justice, Irvine quickly turned him over to the local justices of the peace.[77] Even the manner he spoke of such things in public was guarded. Immediately after the Gnadenhutten Massacre, he cautioned his wife against discussion.

> Whatever you private opinion of these matters may be, I conjure you by all the ties
> of affection and as you value my reputation, that you will keep your mind to your-
> self, and that you will not express any sentiment for or against these deeds;—as it
> may be alleged, the sentiments you express may come from me or be mine. No man
> knows whether I approve or disapprove of killing the Moravians.[78]

In both his actions and words, Irvine struggled to maintain an appearance of impartiality. His ability to command the Western Department depended on his ability to command and persuade those outside Fort Pitt and the Continental service. This required him "to gain the confidence and esteem of the people." In order to achieve that end, "they must be convinced that no partiality, favor, or affection to any color will be shown by me."[79] More than any of his predecessors and contemporaries, William Irvine realized that the Pennsylvania frontier was a place where the wielding of public power depended upon the successful reconciliation of the competing interests and emotions of settlers, Indians, and Continental Officers.

The causes of the Gnadenhutten Massacre were complex. The communities of western Pennsylvania were sharply divided between a few Indians, even fewer Continental officers, and a large number of farmers. These three groups were divided both by the social and cultural structures of eighteenth-century society, as well differences of opinion regarding Indian policy and the proper defensive posture for frontier warfare. By themselves, neither one of these factors was sufficient to cause the rebellion which occurred in February and March 1782. Yet together, an adversarial and hierarchical social structure combined with a potent public policy debate to produce a combustible situation. Commandants Daniel Brodhead and William Irvine were patrician, autocratic outsiders in a world that valued independence, liberty, and patriarchal authority. Given the anti-aristocratic nature of the American Revolution, the commandants found themselves in a position that offered enormous potential to offend the local populace. The militiamen of Washington County wanted a change in how the Continental commanders made use of the enormous public powers granted them. Violence against the Continental army's Native wards, and threats against its officers were a brutal, but effective way to achieve these ends. Daniel Brodhead's inability to heed the signs of popular discontent resulted in his removal from office and set into motion a series of events culminating in massacre and rebellion. Conversely, William Irvine's ability to listen to the language of violence and threats in which the populace expressed it allowed him to bring the Revolutionary War on the Pennsylvania frontier to a peaceful conclusion.

NOTES

Many thanks are needed. This article began as a master's thesis, under the direction of Andrew Cayton at Miami University. His assistance was invaluable in so many ways. Important as well were the suggestions of Jack Temple Kirby, Jeffrey P. Kimball, and Peter Onuf. Thanks go also to Michael Thompson, Hedda Lautenschlager, Johann Neem, Brian D. Schoen, Jennifer Creger, Kristen Mathieson, and Allyson Dunn for their help with various drafts. Of course, I am appreciative of the love and support of my mother, Jo-Ann Robb Sadosky, my sister Jennifer, my grandparents, and the rest of the Robb and Sadosky families.

1. Spencer Records, "The Narrative of Captain Spencer Records," in *Further Materials on Lewis Wetzel and the Upper Ohio Frontier,* ed. Jared C. Lobdell (Bowie, Md.: Heritage Books, 1994), 56–57.

2. Dorsey Pentecost to President Moore, Pittsburgh, 9 May 1782, *Pennsylvania Archives,* ed. Samuel Hazard (Philadelphia: Joseph Severns & Co., 1854), 9: 541–42.

3. William Irvine to Mrs. Irvine, Fort Pitt, 29 May 1782, Draper Manuscripts, Madison: Wisconsin Historical Society, 2AA32.

4. From straightforward narratives describing the war's various campaigns and battles, to discussions about the relationship between warfare and society as a whole, the literature discussing the war of the American Revolution is vast. For descriptions of the events of the War, and discussions of the some of the basic military issues involved, the reader may consult Howard H. Peckham, *The War for Independence: A Military History* (Chicago: University of Chicago Press, 1958); Don Higginbotham, *The War of American Independence: Military Attitudes, Policies, and Practice, 1763–1789* (New York: Macmillan, 1971); Higginbotham, ed., *Reconsiderations on the Revolutionary War, Selected Essays*

(Westport, Conn.: Greenwood Press, 1979); John Ferling, ed., *The World Turned Upside Down: The American Victory in the War for Independence*, (New York: Greenwood Press, 1988); Jeremy Black, *War for America: The Fight for Independence, 1775–1783* (New York: St. Martin's Press, 1991).

Much of the scholarly treatment of the War of the Revolution has been focused on the institution of the Continental Army and the role it played in the subsequent formation of American military and political institutions. Important recent works of this vein include Charles Royster, *A Revolutionary People at War: The Continental Army and American Character, 1775–1783* (Chapel Hill: University of North Carolina Press for the Institute of Early American History and Culture, 1979); James Kirby Martin and Mark Edward Lender, *A Respectable Army: The Military Origins of the Republic, 1763–1789* (Arlington Heights, Ill.: Harlan Davidson, 1982); E. Wayne Carp, *To Starve the Army at Pleasure: Continental Army Administration and American Political Culture, 1775–1783* (Chapel Hill: University of North Carolina Press, 1984).

Melding the traditional concerns of military and political history with more recent insights into social history, scholars have sought to integrate the story of the War for Independence into the intellectual framework that has seen the American Revolution as a fundamental societal transformation. For example, see Ronald Hoffman and Peter J. Albert, eds., *Arms and Independence: The Military Character of the American Revolution* (Charlottesville: University Press of Virginia for the United States Capitol Historical Society, 1984); Steven Rosswurm, *Arms, Country, and Class: The Philadelphia Militia and the "Lower Sort" during the American Revolution, 1775–1783* (New Brunswick: Rutgers University Press, 1987); Don Higginbotham, "War and Society in Revolutionary America: The Wider Dimensions of Conflict," in *American Military History*, ed. Thomas L. Connelly (Columbia: University of South Carolina Press, 1988); John Shy, *A People Numerous and Armed: Reflections on the Military Struggle for American Independence*, rev. ed. (Ann Arbor: University of Michigan Press, 1990).

Discussions of the Revolutionary War in the trans-Appalachian region have been traditionally less numerous, but recent scholarship has begun to redress this imbalance. For accounts of the Revolution in the West, see Charles Perkins Abernathy, *Western Lands and the American Revolution* (New York: Appleton-Century, 1937); Edward G. Williams, *Fort Pitt and the Revolution on the Western Frontier* (Pittsburgh: Historical Society of Western Pennsylvania, 1978); Thomas P. Slaughter, *The Whiskey Rebellion: Frontier Epilogue to the American Revolution* (Oxford: Oxford University Press, 1986), 28–45; Colin G. Calloway, *The American Revolution in Indian Country: Crisis and Diversity in Native American Communities* (Cambridge: Cambridge University Press, 1995); Eric Hinderaker, *Elusive Empires: Constructing Colonialism in the Ohio Valley, 1673–1800* (Cambridge: Cambridge University Press, 1997), 185–225.

5. Any attempt to find a single label for these episodes of popular unrest and violence in Western Pennsylvania is problematic, at best. While certainly part of the overall framework of social unrest and transformation of the American Revolution, the actions against the Continental Army were not, of themselves, a revolution. That is to say, this article will demonstrate that the social unrest on the Pennsylvania frontier ran with the main currents of the American Revolution, rather than against them. See Alan Taylor, "'To Man Their Rights,' The Frontier Revolution," in *The Transforming Hand of Revolution: Reconsidering the American Revolution as a Social Movement*, ed. Ronald Hoffman and Peter J. Albert (Charlottesville: University Press of Virginia, 1996), 231–57.

Describing the Gnadenhutten Massacre and related unrest as a 'rebellion' emphasizes that it was a local phenomenon, a local contest over the power and ability to define what the revolution would mean in one particular community. Yet, still the term must be used carefully. The Washington County militiamen were not 'primitive rebels' such as Eric Hobsbawm described, engaged in an unconscious and unspoken collective action against the forces of capital and modernization. See Eric J. Hobsbawm, *Social Bandits and Primitive Rebels: Studies in Archaic Forms of Social Movement in the Nineteenth and Twentieth Centuries* (Glencoe, Ill.: Free Press, 1959). If these actions fit within any established pattern of rebellion, it is that of agrarian rebellion. Just as the tripartite dichotomy that this essay will illuminate presages the division described by Alan Taylor's "Land and Liberty" article, the actions of the Washington County militiamen are quite similar to other backcountry agitations and rebellions of the Revolutionary Era. For example, see Alan Taylor, *Liberty Men and Great Proprietors: The Revolutionary Settlement on the Maine Frontier, 1760–1820* (Chapel Hill: University of North Carolina Press for the Institute of Early American History and Culture, 1990) and Michael A. Bellesiles, *Revolutionary Outlaws: Ethan Allen and the Struggle for Independence on the Early American Frontier* (Charlottesville: University Press of Virginia, 1993). Of course, as Thomas Slaughter has argued, the unrest during the War prefigured the conflict that ultimately resulted in the 1790s. See Slaughter, *Whiskey Rebellion*, especially pages 28–89.

Just as the revolt that surrounded the Gnadenhutten Massacre presaged other revolutionary conflicts, it also built upon traditions of rural unrest and collective action that were long part of the history of the British Isles. Elements of the social unrest in western Pennsylvania are quite consistent with histories of English agrarian rebellion and popular protest. For eighteenth-century analogues see in particular E. P. Thompson, *Whigs and Hunters: The Origin of the Black Act* (New York: Pantheon Books, 1975) and Douglas Hay, "Poaching and the Game Laws on Cannock Chase," in *Albion's Fatal Tree: Crime and Society in Eighteenth-Century England*, ed. Hay et al. (New York: Pantheon Books, 1975).

6. These events will be discussed and cited in detail below. For brief summaries of the events described, one may consult the introductory matter to the following documentary compilations. Louise Phelps Kellogg, ed., *Frontier Advance on the Upper Ohio, 1778–1779*, State Historical Society of Wisconsin Collections, vol. 23 (Madison: State Historical Society of Wisconsin, 1916); Kellogg, ed., *Frontier Retreat on the Upper Ohio, 1779–1781*, State Historical Society of Wisconsin Collections, vol. 24 (Madison: State Historical Society of Wisconsin, 1917); C. W. Butterfield, ed., *Washington-Irvine Correspondence: The Official Letters Which Passed Between Washington and Brigadier General William Irvine and Between Irvine and Others Concerning Military Affairs in the West from 1781 to 1783* (Madison: David Atwood, 1882) [hereafter cited as *WIC*], as well as and James H. O'Donnell, "Frontier Warfare and the American Victory," in *The World Turned Upside Down*, ed. Ferling; and Williams, *Fort Pitt and the Revolution*.

7. For Slaughter's account of the Gnadenhutten Massacre, see *Whiskey Rebellion*, 75–78.

8. Richard White, *The Middle Ground: Indians, Empires, and Republics in the Great Lakes Region, 1650–1815* (Cambridge: Cambridge University Press, 1991), 387–96.

9. The number of histories of American Indians was but a trickle in the 1960s; it became a torrent by the early 1990s. Key work in the 1960s was done by Reginald Horsman and Francis Paul Prucha. See Horsman, *Expansion and American Indian Policy, 1783–1812* (East Lansing: Michigan State University Press, 1967); idem., *The Frontier in the Formative Years, 1783–1815* (New York: Holt, Rinehart, and Winston, 1970); Prucha, *American Indian Policy in the Formative Years: The Indian Trade and Intercourse Acts, 1790–1834* (Cambridge, Mass.: Harvard University Press, 1962). The 1970s and 1980s saw the rise of the methodologies of ethnohistory and literary criticism. Some of the most influential works of this period include Francis Jennings, *The Invasion of America: Indians, Colonialism, and the Cant of Conquest* (Chapel Hill: University of North Carolina Press for the

Institute of Early American History and Culture, 1975); Robert F. Berkhofer, *The White Man's Indian: Images of the American Indian from Columbus to the Present* (New York: Alfred A. Knopf, 1978); Bernard W. Sheehan, *Seeds of Extinction: Jeffersonian Philanthropy and the American Indian* (Chapel Hill: University of North Carolina Press for the Institute of Early American History and Culture, 1973); James Axtell, *The European and the Indian: Essays in the Ethnohistory of Colonial North America* (New York: Oxford University Press, 1981). Key 1990s works include: James Hart Merrell, *The Indians' New World: Catawbas and Their Neighbors from European Contact Through the Era of Removal* (Chapel Hill: University of North Carolina Press for the Institute of Early American History and Culture, 1989); Daniel H. Usner, *Indians, Settlers, & Slaves in a Frontier Exchange Economy: The Lower Mississippi Before 1783* (Chapel Hill: University of North Carolina Press for the Institute of Early American History and Culture, 1992); Daniel K. Richter, *The Ordeal of the Longhouse: The Peoples of the Iroquois League in the Era of European Colonization* (Chapel Hill: University of North Carolina Press for the Institute of Early American History and Culture, 1992).

10. See Stephen Aron, *How the West Was Lost: The Transformation of Kentucky from Daniel Boone to Henry Clay* (Baltimore: Johns Hopkins University Press, 1996); Alan Taylor, *William Cooper's Town: Power and Persuasion on the Frontier of the Early American Republic* (New York: Alfred A. Knopf, 1995); Hinderaker, *Elusive Empires*.

11. Hinderaker, *Elusive Empires*.

12. Alan Taylor, "Land and Liberty on the Post-Revolutionary Frontier," in *Devising Liberty: Preserving and Creating Freedom in the New American Republic,* ed. David Thomas Konig (Stanford: Stanford University Press, 1995), 81–108.

13. This dichotomy is laid out in a very straightforward manner by Michael Allen in "The Federalists and the West, 1783–1803," *Western Pennsylvania Historical Magazine* 61 (October 1978): 315–32.

14. The best examples are Taylor's *Liberty Men* and Elizabeth A. Perkins, "The Consumer Frontier: Household Consumption in Early Kentucky," *Journal of American History* 78 (1991): 486–510. For a summary of the current literature on the market in rural early America, see Richard L. Bushman, "Markets and Composite Farms in Early America," *William and Mary Quarterly* 55 (1998): 351–74.

15. White, *Middle Ground,* 94–141, 315–65, and Hinderaker, *Elusive Empires,* 46–77. For Native adoptions of white religious themes, see Gregory Evans Dowd, *A Spirited Resistance: The North American Indian Struggle for Unity, 1745–1815* (Baltimore: Johns Hopkins University Press, 1992).

16. See E. P. Thompson, "The Patricians and the Plebs," in *Customs in Common: Studies in Traditional Popular Culture* (New York: The New Press, 1993), 16–96, and Gordon S. Wood, *The Radicalism of the American Revolution* (New York: Alfred A. Knopf, 1992), 24–42.

17. White, *Middle Ground*; Hinderaker, *Elusive Empires*.

18. For a recent treatment of Clark's expedition to Kaskaskia and Vincennes, see Andrew R. L. Cayton, *Frontier Indiana* (Bloomington: Indiana University Press, 1996).

19. Thomas Jefferson to George Washington, Williamsburg, 10 February 1780, Kellogg, ed., *Frontier Retreat,* 133–34.

20. Irvine to Washington, Fort Pitt, 11 July 1782, *WIC,* 126–28.

21. For Brodhead's account of the 1779 expedition, see Brodhead to Washington, Pittsburgh, 16 September 1779, "Letters from Col. Daniel Brodhead," in *Pennsylvania Archives,* first series, vol. 12, ed. Samuel Hazard (Philadelphia: Joseph Severns & Co., 1856), 155–58 [hereafter cited as "Brodhead Letterbook"]. See also Joseph R. Fischer, *A Well-Executed Failure: The Sullivan Campaign Against the Iroquois, July-Septmeber 1779* (Columbia: University of South Carolina Press, 1997).

22. Delaware Chiefs to Brodhead, Fort Pitt, 9 April 1779, Kellogg, ed., *Frontier Advance,* 282.

23. Heckewelder to Brodhead, Salem, 26 February 1781, Kellogg, ed., *Frontier Retreat,* 337–39.

24. See correspondence in Kellogg, ed., *Frontier Retreat,* 376–82.

25. Alexander Fowler to Joseph Reed, Pittsburgh, 29 March 1781, Memorial of Pittsburgh Inhabitants, [April 1781], Petition of Pittsburgh Inhabitants, [April 1781], Kellogg, ed., *Frontier Retreat,* 356–70.

26. Alexander Fowler to Pres. Joseph Reed, Pittsburgh, 29 March 1781, Kellogg, ed., *Frontier Retreat,* 356–60.

27. Carp, *To Starve the Army at Pleasure,* esp. 99–135.

28. Alexander Fowler to Pres. Joseph Reed, Pittsburgh, 29 March 1781, Kellogg, ed., *Frontier Retreat,* 356–60.

29. Ibid.

30. Brodhead to Washington, Pittsburgh, 22 May 1779, "Brodhead Letter-book," 113–15.

31. See Brodhead to Lieutenants of Counties, Pittsburgh, 17 July 1779, Brodhead to Washington, Fort Pitt, 31 July 1779, Brodhead to Washington, Pittsburgh, 16 September 1779, "Brodhead Letter-book," 137, 146–48, 155–58.

32. All quotes from Brodhead to Timothy Pickering, Pittsburgh, 22 November 1779, "Brodhead Letter-book," 190.

33. Brodhead's father, Daniel Brodhead II was a merchant in Albany, New York. He moved his family to Brodhead Manor in Bucks County, Pennsylvania, in 1737, a year after Daniel III was born. The elder Brodhead was a justice of the peace in addition to being an extensive landholder. "Daniel Brodhead," *Dictionary of American Biography,* 21 vols. (New York: Charles Scribner's Sons, 1937–44), 2:62–63.

34. Brodhead to Timothy Pickering, Pittsburgh, 27 June 1779, "Brodhead Letter-book," 133.

35. Brodhead to Pickering, Pittsburgh, 22 November 1779, "Brodhead Letter-book," 190.

36. "Proceedings in case of *Edward Ward v. Daniel Brodhead,*" Jan. 1780–May 1781, Virginia District Court, Yohogania County, *Papers of the Continental Congress,* microfilm edition, Washington, D.C.: National Archives, M247, roll 56, vol. 8, 284.

37. Washington to Brodhead, New Windsor, 5 May 1781, Kellogg, ed., *Frontier Retreat,* 395. See also note on that same page.

38. See correspondence in Kellogg, ed., *Frontier Retreat,* 416–21.

39. Brodhead to Washington, Fort Pitt, 19 August 1781, Draper Mss. 3HH, 102–5.

40. Brodhead to Washington, Fort Pitt, 6 September 1781, Washington to Brodhead, Head of Elk, 6 September 1781, Draper Mss. 1HH, 131, 155.

41. Brodhead to Mr. Galbreath, Fort Pitt, 14 October 1781, Draper Mss. 3HH, 147–48.

42. Brodhead, circular letter to County lieutenants, 7 September 1781, Draper Mss. 3HH, 134–35.

43. The river on which Gnadenhutten, Salem, and Schoenbrunn were located is today known as the Tuscarawas River, a tributary of the modern Muskingum. However, contemporary correspondents uniformly referred to both of these rivers as the "Muskingum." In order to avoid confusion, the river is referred to throughout this article as the Tuscarawas, except in direct quotations, where original spellings and usage are retained.

44. The most recent exploration of the activities of the Moravian missionaries in the Delaware communities of Pennsylvania and Ohio in the late eighteenth century is Earl P. Olmstead, *Blackcoats Among the Delaware: David Zeisberger and the Ohio Frontier* (Kent, Ohio: Kent State University Press, 1991). For a more general discussion of the difficulties Indian communities faced during the Revolutionary War, one may wish to consult Calloway, *American Revolution in Indian Country,* 26–64.

45. John Heckewelder, *A Narrative of the Mission of the United Brethren Among the Delaware and Mohegan Indians* (Philadelphia: McCarty and Davis, 1820); George Henry Loskiel, *History of the Mission of the United Brethren Among the Indians in North America*, trans. Christian Ignatius LaTrobe (London: The Brethren's Society for the Furtherance of the Gospel, 1794).

46. See C. Hale Sipe, *The Indian Wars of Pennsylvania: An Account of the Indian Events, in Pennsylvania* (Harrisburg, Penn.: Telegraph Press, 1931), 639.

47. Irvine to Washington, Fort Pitt, 2 December 1781, *WIC*, 72–82.

48. William Irvine Order Book, Fort Pitt, 15 January 1782, *WIC*, 85.

49. John Finley to Irvine, Fort Pitt, 2 February 1782, Draper Mss. 1AA, 160–61.

50. Joseph Doddridge, *Notes, On The Settlement and Indian Wars, of the Western Parts of Virginia & Pennsylvania, From the Year 1763 Until the Year 1783 Inclusive . . .* (Wellsburgh, Va., 1824), chap. 31.

51. Heckewelder, *Narrative*, 280–310.

52. Ibid.

53. Ibid., 313.

54. Ibid., 313–17 ; Loskiel, *History*, pt. 3, 177–79.

55. Heckewelder, *Narrative*, 317.

56. In addition to William Irvine's correspondence, contemporary second-hand accounts of the Massacre include Dorsey Pentecost to President Moore, Pittsburgh, 8 May 1782, *Pennsylvania Archives*, first series, vol. 9, 540–41 and Relation of Frederick Lineback &c., 31 March - 5 April 1782, *Pennsylvania Archives*, first series, vol. 9, 524–25. Several veterans' depositions transcribed by Lyman Copeland Draper mention the massacre, see Draper Mss. 6ZZ47–107. The massacre is also mentioned in the 1842 narrative of Spencer Records, see "The Narrative of Captain Spencer Records," in *Further Materials on Lewis Wetzel*, ed. Lobdell. Joseph Doddridge was only a child in 1782, but the Massacre figures prominently in his history of the frontier, *Notes, On The Settlement and Indian Wars*. Writing in the late nineteenth century, Consul Wilshire Butterfield described the massacre somewhat sympathetically in his *An Historical Account of the Expedition Against Sandusky Under Col. William Crawford in 1782Y* (Cincinnati: R. Clarke & Co., 1783), in addition to the extended discussion available in the foot-notes of *WIC*. The Moravian histories are Loskiel's *History* (1794), and Heckewelder's *Narrative* (1820).

57. Heckewelder, *Narrative*, 318–19.

58. Ibid., 313–17 ; Loskiel, *History*, pt. 3, 177–79.

59. Irvine to Washington, Fort Pitt, 20 April 1782, *WIC*, 99–109.

60. Irvine to Mrs. Irvine, Fort Pitt, 12 April 1782, *WIC*, 343–46. The composition of this party is difficult to ascertain, although Irvine's letter indicates they came from the Chartiers Creek region of northern Washington County. These northern townships drew the vast majority of the identifiable members of the Williamson Expedition. (See table 2.)

61. Irvine to Washington, Fort Pitt, 20 April 1782, *WIC*, 99–109.

62. Heckewelder, *Narrative*, 318.

63. Records, "Narrative," 57.

64. Pentecost to Moore, Pittsburgh, 9 May 1782, *Pennsylvania Archives*, vol. 9, 541–42.

65. For a biography of Gibson see Charles William Hanko, *The Life of John Gibson, Soldier, Patriot, Statesman* (Daytona Beach, Fla.: College Publishing Co., 1955) and "John Gibson," *DAB*, vol. 4, pt.1, 253–54.

66. John Nevill to George Rogers Clark, Woodville, [Pennsylvania], 14 April 1782, Draper Mss. 52J18.

67. "Washington County Supply Tax" in *Pennsylvania Archives, Third Series*, vol. 22, ed. William H. Egle

(Harrisburg: William S. Ray, State Printer, 1897), 701–82.

68. Irvine to Mrs. Irvine, Fort Pitt, 12 April 1782, *WIC,* 343–46.

69. Irvine to Mrs. Irvine, Fort Pitt, 12 April 1782, Draper Mss. 2AA21.

70. Irvine to Mrs. Irvine, Fort Pitt, 14 November 1781, *WIC,* 340.

71. Irvine to Mrs. Irvine, Fort Pitt, 1 May 1782, *WIC,* 346.

72. Irvine to Mrs. Irvine, Fort Pitt, 2 December 1781, *WIC,* 341.

73. Irvine to Mrs. Irvine, Fort Pitt, 1 May 1782, *WIC,* 346.

74. "I am heartily tired and almost worn down with people coming daily for protection and assistance," ibid.

75. Irvine to Col. Cook, Fort Pitt, 28 March 1782, Draper Mss. 1AA166–67.

76. Ibid.

77. Irvine to Mrs. Mary Willard, Fort Pitt 21 July 1782, *WIC,* 384–89.

78. Irvine to Mrs. Irvine, Fort Pitt, 12 April 1782, *WIC,* 343–48.

79. Irvine to Mrs. Irvine, Fort Pitt, 12 April 1782, Draper Mss. 2AA21.

80. The composition of the Williamson Expedition was measured in the following manner. Louise Martin Mohler of the Washington County Historical Society and Washington County genealogist Raymond Martin Bell have identified, from various sources, 185 men who were part of the Washington County Militia during the first week of March, 1782, the time of the Gnadenhutten Massacre. Estimates have placed the number of men in the expedition between one hundred-fifty and two hundred men, so this list may be a few names short. See Louise Martin Mohler, "The Massacre at Gnadenhutten, 1782: Washington County's Day of Infamy." (Washington, Pa.: Washington County Historical Society, 1984). Of this number, it was possible to discern the residences of fifty-eight of these men, and by examining extant tax records, the nature of the property that they held. Those names were checked against the state supply tax list of 1781–82 in the *Pennsylvania Archives, Third Series,* vol. 22, ed. William H. Egle (Harrisburg: William S. Ray, State Printer, 1897), 701–82. Mohler and Bell were able to identify townships of residence for 114 of the men on their list. The fifty-eight names identified were the ones actually found on the rolls of the township given on Bell and Mohler's list. If a name appeared more than once on a township's roll, it was eliminated from consideration.

Sources for tables 1 and 2. The fifty-eight names amount to about 37 percent of the names on the list. This available, although unscientific, sample of the Williamson Expedition reveals that the men who marched to Gnadenhutten to be a relative cross-section of rural Washington County in the early 1780s. The names are analyzed as an aggregate in tables 1 and 2 through comparisons with the findings of R. Eugene Harper. They show that: (a) the material circumstances of these members of the Expedition square well with the averages for their townships, and (b) the bulk of the expedition was drawn from four contiguous townships: Cecil, Hopewell, Smith, and Strabane, all in the north-central portion of Washington County. The median landholding size tends to be marginally lower than that of their neighbors, while their estate values tend to be slightly higher. Countywide, the Expedition's medians tend to approximate median figures for the entire taxable population. In his study of the region's economic and social structures, Harper concluded that most western Pennsylvanians held enough land at this time to earn a subsistence, but not much more. See Harper, *Transformation of Western Pennsylvania,* chapters 2 and 3. Harper divided the Washington County landholders into ten groups of equal numbers of individuals. Only five of the sample considered here (around 9 percent) held over four hundred acres of land. Only two of the sample held slaves.

While most of the expedition members were not living in abject poverty, few enjoyed anything approaching affluence. Earning subsistence from the land in western Pennsylvania was a difficult prospect that was only exacerbated by the uncertainties brought about the war. It is also worth noting that a substantial number (about 22 percent) held no land whatsoever. Whether they were sons awaiting inheritance or tenants are impossible to determine. Likely, the group contained numbers of both.

War as Cultural Encounter in the Ohio Valley

ELIZABETH A. PERKINS

In his 1827 memoir, Kentucky migrant and former militia captain Daniel Trabue described the treaty negotiations at Fort Greenville as an impressive and colorful affair. The summer of 1795 had brought together Major General Anthony Wayne and his United States Legion with members of the confederacy of western Indians they had defeated one year before at the Battle of Fallen Timbers. Their parlay formally ended a long and bloody contest (1774–94) over the permanence of the Ohio River as a boundary between Indian and Anglo-American settlement. As part of the military posturing that went on at such ceremonial occasions, Daniel Trabue recalled that General Wayne "Did often Muster and perrade his men," who fired their muskets and cannon to (what Trabue naively assumed was) "the astoneshment of the Indians." The regulars, in Trabue's estimation, "cut a Marshal appearrince" and were "very well Disipblind,"—praise, indeed, from a member of the notoriously *ir*regular Kentucky militia.[1]

Yet it was the more pacific scenes of this sprawling tableau that Trabue recalled most minutely. He witnessed the emotional reunion of Indian captives Stephen and Abraham Ruddle with their aging father Isaac, which was complicated by Stephen's refusal to give up the Indian wife who accompanied him. The Ruddle sons, who had been taken prisoner some eighteen years before at their father's fort on the Licking

River, appeared at the treaty grounds as fully acculturated Indians. Isaac Ruddle was literally knocked off his feet at his sons' introduction, collapsing and crying out with dismay "My cheldrin is Indians!" Over the next few days, Trabue served as an intermediary between the elder Ruddle, his sons, and their Indian families, giving one adopted brother a shirt and advising "Old Riddle [sic] he ought to give stephen's wife something," after she was overlooked in the distribution of new clothing. Trabue minced no words in describing the Indian woman's appearance, calling her "Old, ugly, black looking." Nevertheless, he helped to replace her "Old smoked blankit" with a new calico outfit, and noted her pleasure in the gift. As he interacted further with the family, Trabue came to understand why Stephen so stoutly refused to trade his wife "for no woman in the world." Indeed, after she single-handedly rounded up her party's scattered horses, traveling for two or three days and a distance of forty miles to do so, Trabue decided that the Indian woman "was worth all the rest of the company together."[2]

A frank conversation with an old Indian chief marked the climax of Trabue's Greenville memoir. As the formal negotiations dragged on, the two men "agreed to walk out some distance and set Down and talk about the Despute between the Indeans and white people. This chief said to me, 'You big Captain. Me big Capt. too. What Do you want to take Indian land from them for?" After sparring good-naturedly over the role of the British king in promoting the late hostilities, the two men turned to the question of religious sanction. The Indian expressed his belief that "the Great Spirret made all the people—the Indean and the white people. He made all the land and it was the Great sperrit's land. And it was rong [sic] for Indian or white man to say it was his land." Trabue countered: "You got land enough left, and as the Great sperrit made the land for white folks as well as Indean, what make you Mad about it?" The chief replied that "the truth was the british give them Rum and tell them the white people will never stop untell they take all the land from them." Trabue denied this intention, as it was not his own, and their conversation ended amicably. As is so often the case, two individuals achieved a measure of mutual understanding that continued to elude their two peoples.[3]

I quote from these Greenville vignettes at length because Trabue's reactions are so plainly at variance with the image of the hot-headed, Indian-hating, Kentuckian of popular (and even scholarly) literature. History, with its constantly shifting inter-pretations, has played a cruel trick on men like Daniel Trabue. The erstwhile heroes of Boonesborough and Blue Licks are now history's heavies: "Indian haters" who freely sank their hatchets into the heads of friendly Shawnee chiefs; men who, in historian Richard White's words, "wished to obliterate the middle ground" of cultural accommodation on the Anglo-Indian border. The interpretive problem is, of course, twofold: Anglo-American actions, whitewashed in the past, seem all the more horrific when viewed forthrightly; Native American perspectives, once opaque in history, sear the conscience with the shock of discovery. The result is inversion: victors become the vanquished in the court of historical opinion.[4]

My purpose in this essay is to challenge this zero-sum game head-on. I will not sugarcoat: there was enough blood spilled in the war for the Ohio Valley to give every one of us pause. More broadly, the dispossession of North America's indigenous population is a blot on the national record that cannot be explained away. But to take this great human tragedy seriously does not, I think, require that we overlook the ambiguities of even the darkest moments of this encounter. Even as the "middle ground" of Anglo-Indian military parity crumbled away in the Ohio Valley, opportunities for human contact and communication were still being created. Because many of these were the experiences of ordinary people who did not write for posterity—Daniel Trabue is the exception here—we have inherited principally the simplified public stories that were meant to secure American national claims or to titillate the readers of the antebellum penny press. There is, I would argue another legacy of the war for the Ohio Valley: a process of mutual discovery.[5]

Curiosity about, comprehension of, and even empathy for opponents complicates the image of the Indian-hating frontiersman. Traces of these variant emotions can be found in the rich oral lore recorded by western collectors such as John Shane and Lyman Draper, in autobiographies such as Trabue's, and in the missionary accounts and captivity narratives where we can hear (faintly) native American voices. To be sure, ferreting out moments of understanding during wartime requires reading against the grain. Long-rehearsed stories of Indian attack and white retaliation (or the reverse) were the stock and trade of backwoods raconteurs, and form the bulk—the vast bulk—of extant narratives. But collected together and viewed as a whole, seemingly ephemeral exchanges reveal a pattern of cross-cultural communication, ranging from insights into one another's dietary habits to the frank exchange of political or spiritual views. In rare instances, the granting of ethical status to one's opponent challenged even the conduct of war.

Concurrent with and fueled by the American Revolution, Anglo-American expansion beyond the Appalachians reached the Kentucky Country in the 1770s.

Colonizers constructed the first frontier outposts, called stations, in 1774, and occupied them continuously beginning in the following year. In effect, we must view the so-called settlement of Kentucky as a military occupation. Disgruntled Shawnee, Delaware, and Iroquois villagers living along the Ohio River refused to recognize the questionable cession of their Kentucky hunting lands by the terms of the Treaty of Fort Stanwix in 1768. Native Americans continued to assert their claims with customary subsistence activities and forays against the fortified white settlements. Anglo and African American migrants to Kentucky, whose numbers grew from a few hundred souls to over 73,000 residents in 1790, retaliated with both state-sanctioned and extra-legal raids of their own, taking captives and destroying Indian villages north of the Ohio River. It is in the context of this confused intermingling of rival claimants to the Ohio Valley that we can discover evidence not just of animosity, but also of curiosity about one's opponents.[6]

Well into the nineteenth century, aging Kentucky militiamen recalled minute details about Indian material possessions and cultural practices, suggesting just how acute their interest in their opponents' lives once had been. Campaigns against the Shawnee towns north of the Ohio River offered glimpses of Native American daily life—even as the curious marauders burned the cornfields and looted the cabins they discovered. On Clark's Campaign against New Chillicothe in 1782, for example, militiaman William Clinkenbeard marveled at the horse paths that ran between the Indian towns. As he later told interviewer John Shane: "Prettiest, levellist, straightest paths I ever saw. Could have been made no straiter. Level as this floor." Entering a hastily abandoned Shawnee cabin, Clinkenbeard stopped to sample boiled dumplings that still steamed in a tray; but he found that an absence of salt made the Indian dish unpalatable to his taste. On another occasion, as he took part in an ill-provisioned raid against Old Chillicothe, Clinkenbeard admired the Shawnee sugar-making camps and survived off the bounty of the Indian planting fields: "Not as big corn as ours," he remembered. "We would have suffered, had it not been just in roasting ear time. Also got a few Irish potatoes there." For militiamen, plundering held out not only economic incentives, but also functioned as a primitive data-gathering exercise. After a campaign north of the Ohio River in 1779, Josiah Collins's company took two days to divide its loot, including "one squaws gown, in which were 1100 silver broaches." Discovering an Indian hunting camp on another foray, Robert Jones took their kettle off the fire, retrieved their blankets from a tree, and loaded all the hunters' possessions into his own canoe. His haul included, he remembered, "a moccasin tied up full of powder, lots of beads—suppose there was not less than a peck—, looking-glasses, paint bags, & c." These details, I should emphasize, were being recalled for western collector John Shane some sixty years after their occurrence.[7]

Returning Indian captives found themselves celebrated, not only for their brush with danger, but also for the eyewitness accounts of Indian life they could convey. Some former captives, like Dr. Knight, were so beset by the curious that they ultimately referred their neighbors to their published accounts. Others, like Shawnee captive Benjamin Allen, must have told their stories many times, alternating thrilling descriptions of capture, torture, and escape with more prosaic details about food, clothing, and leisure activities. Allen, like many captives, commented at some length on Indian food preparation techniques, suggesting that finding something palatable to eat was a common concern for those crossing cultural boundaries. The sixteen-year-old Allen was well satisfied on this score, as his Shawnee captors served him several different dishes of stewed or dried buffalo meat, one of which he termed "elegant." The young captive was also impressed with his glimpse of Shawnee woodcraft, recalling how the Indians constructed rafts to cross over the Ohio River: "surprising how quick they would cut off a log with those tomahawks, and peel Linn bark to tie [it] with." At the end of his three-week captivity, Allen could describe Shawnee dining customs ("only ate of nights, though might eat all night if you chose"), Shawnee clothing (Don't know where they got those calico hunting shirts. . . . Had something round their heads, too. One had something like silk on his head"), and Shawnee musical tastes ("When I woke, the Indians had a gourd with shot in it; were holding it to their ears and rattling it, at the same time singing, 'Hee ho yoh! he ho yoh!' They called it fine music").[8]

Nor was such curiosity a one-way cultural street. Several of John Shane's informants remembered instances of Native Americans taking significant risks in order to investigate the burgeoning white settlements in Kentucky. In the early 1780s, two young women were ironing on the second floor of a log house on Lexington's main street. As Elijah Vaughn told the story, the young women, glancing out of the window, "saw some curiously wrapped up persons pass down the street." Only later did the women realize they had actually seen Indians on the main thoroughfare of the town, which was by that time the largest white settlement west of the Appalachians. After passing out of Lexington, the Indians later "did mischief and got some prisoners. The prisoners afterwards related that the Indians told them

they had passed through the town as spies, and had seen these two young women."
When the traveler Needham Parry visited Kentucky's new state capital in 1794, he
found that other Native American tourists had preceded him. As Parry recorded in
his diary, Frankfort had "an elegant State house erecting. . . . A fine stone building
[which] will take 1368 panes of glass to fill the windows and above the doors." Parry
noted that he "went through every part of it, and up in the steeple, for which I paid
a quarter of a dollar. . . . And they told me that the Indians were in this town and
state-house, last spring, in the night time, but did no harm." (And, presumably, paid
no quarter). Anglo-Americans found that their personal possessions, too, were of
interest to curious warriors. Near Danville, a Mrs. Kirkham delayed the capture of
her family when she "at once made up with the Indians and . . . showed them her
silk dresses and whatever would amuse them."⁹

Over time, personal experiences and public lore resulted in a measure of shared
comprehension between combatants. Communication was the first difficulty to be
overcome; simple pantomime was probably the most frequently used means of con-
veying one's intentions. John Graves, for example, recalled chasing a company of
four Indians that had stolen horses in his neighborhood. "The one I shot, it broke his
back. . . . He took out his tomahawk and gave it to me to kill him, and I tomahawked
him." This signal must have been widely understood in western warfare, as another
man overtook an attacker in a field, "and as he was unwilling to answer any
inquiries, and made sign to be tomahawked," he, too, was killed. Non-verbal signs
also communicated peaceful intentions. When a party of Indians took three captured
children to the Shawnee council house at Piqua to determine their fate, "the squaws
made motion to them . . . not to be afraid, they wouldn't kill them." Often, a few simple words supplemented the language of gesture, as strangers struggled to communicate. Upon his capture by a company of Kentuckians, the peace-seeking Shawnee
chief Moluntha "patted on his breast and said "King." On another occasion, a
Wyandot warrior greeted the black slave he intended to capture with a cheery
"Howdy do?" A few residents of the Anglo-Indian border region became fluent con-
versationalists. A neighbor of James Harrod recalled that "Harrod had . . . lived
among [the] Delawares. Could talk their language." Another man claimed that
Black Wolf, a Mingo warrior, "could talk English very well. But only talked when it
suited him. Was raised about Pittsburgh."¹⁰

Black Wolf's caution in appearing to understand English was well warranted.
When the Shawnee captive Moluntha was brought before the officers of Logan's

Campaign in 1786, Col. Hugh McGary asked if he had commanded at Blue Licks in 1782. The old chief nodded and smiled, although he probably did not understand the question. McGary, according to a witness, "said 'damn you, I will show you Blue-Lick play,' and just tomahawked him." The battle at Blue Licks had been the worst military disaster suffered by the Kentucky militia, and McGary undoubtedly still smarted from the personal blame he earned for precipitating the attack that killed some seventy Kentuckians in a bloody ambush. When McGary had yelled words to the effect that "all that are not cowards follow me," he had not realized that a much larger Wyandot army commanded by Capt. William Caldwell lay in wait. This time, for killing the Shawnee prisoner Moluntha in cold blood, he was broken of his officer's commission. As one of John Shane's informants later commented: "McGary was a creature without consideration. Was by nature a savage."[11]

Repeated encounters between Indians and Anglo-Americans built up a store of lore—of perhaps questionable accuracy—which helped to interpret the actions of strangers. Kentuckians, for example, believed that Indian raiders usually went about their business in groups of four, that they traveled by scattering on both sides of a trail, and that they would not burn a white man while it thundered. Indians, in turn, shrewdly estimated the monetary value of a captured black slave, accused whites of preferring to kill rather than to take a prisoner, and feared that even friendly gestures might hide ulterior motives. When Cuthbert Combs' father offered to dose a sick Indian with cream of tartar, "the Indian refused to take the preparation till the family, and then the interpreter, had first tasted it." Undoubtedly, misperceptions and suspicions clouded the process of mutual comprehension. Yet efforts to communicate across the cultural divide continued throughout the long years of warfare. When nine-year-old Archibald Hamilton was to be returned to his white family after a two-year captivity with the Shawnees, "his mother squaw took him and dressed his hair in Indian fashion with bear's oil, and told him to go home and tell his people she had treated him well." Many years later, Hamilton's son continued to honor the memory of the Shawnee woman who had cared for his father.[12]

Recognition of an enemy's humanity was the final—and most troublesome—step in the process of mutual discovery that took place in the Ohio Valley. At risk, of course, was the very premise of the war: that Indians and Anglo-Americans could not coexist within the same geographic region. Some of the crosscutting loyalties at work in this time are fairly well known. During the Revolutionary War, for example, the Delaware chief White Eyes sided with the Americans against the British, while the Girty brothers fought for their adopted Indian communities against their former countrymen. White captives refused to return to their birth families, or, like the Ruddles, returned with new families—Indian families—of their own. We know less about the actions of anonymous men and women whose lives are recorded by John Shane. Mentions of the deserter from Logan's Campaign (1786), who warned the Shawnees of the army's approach, or of the Kentucky woman who, for many years afterward, used to cry and say how sorry she was for her long-dead Shawnee captors, are no more than tantalizing fragments. Nor has the public censure of Hugh McGary been widely publicized; indeed, his striking down of the prisoner Moluntha in cold blood has been left to stand for the behavior of all Indian-hating Kentuckians.[13]

And finally, as we contemplate the murder of Moluntha, there is another prisoner story that we should also consider: the refusal of Kentucky troops to kill the Shawnee war leader Blue Jacket. John Hanks served in the militia company that captured this noted war captain during a horse-stealing raid; he recalled, for John Shane, the events that surrounded the Indian's eventual escape. After Blue Jacket's capture, the inevitable debate began over what to do with the prisoner. "There was a little Irishman in company, named Jim Wilson, who was the only man . . . that would kill a prisoner," Hanks recalled. Sensing the mood of the others, Hanks "went up to [the captain and] said it looked like murder to kill that man. He turned round and said 'Jim Wilson don't shoot him.' I knew I had touched his feelings." Indeed, instead of killing Blue Jacket, the members of the militia troop proceeded to get drunk with him. Hanks visited the party during the night and found that "Frank Jones, of the Cross Plains, who was half drunk, had Blue Jacket on his knee." A few days later, after another drunken party, the Shawnee leader escaped. Hanks told this story openly and with a certain amount of pride. Unlike Hugh McGary's experience, no public censure seemed to follow the men responsible for this military lapse.[14]

In short, what we can see at work in the late eighteenth-century Ohio Valley is a process—albeit halting and incomplete—of "ethical extension," the granting of ethical status to one's enemies. Although the philosophical roots of moral universalism go back at least to the Stoics of ancient Athens, it was in eighteenth-century Europe that the process of "ethical extension" most visibly expanded the circle of moral relevancy outward from the individual and kin group to include all of humanity. Historians have assumed that while America's leaders of the Revolutionary generation incorporated this new Enlightenment view of mankind into their Indian policy, retrograde westerners continued to regard their opponents as "violent savages" worthy of extermination. The candid and rueful stories collected by John Shane, or told by Daniel Trabue, suggest that the national moral dilemma of Indian dispossession cannot so easily be solved by casting blame on regional scapegoats. Indian humanity was more than just a theory to the generation of men and women that seized the Ohio Valley.[15]

NOTES

1. Chester Raymond Young, ed., *Westward Into Kentucky: The Narrative of Daniel Trabue* (Lexington: University Press of Kentucky, 1981), 139. For a suggestive analysis of the drama surrounding this treaty negotiation, see Andrew R. L. Cayton, "'Noble Actors' upon 'the Theatre of Honour': Power and Civility in the Treaty of Greenville," in *Contact Points: American Frontiers from the Mohawk Valley to the Mississippi, 1750–1830*, ed. Andrew R. L. Cayton and Fredrika J. Teute (Chapel Hill: University of North Carolina Press, 1998), 235–69.

2. Young, ed., *Westward Into Kentucky*, 139–42. Trabue's richly detailed narrative figures in several recent publications. See Elizabeth A. Perkins, "Distinctions and Partitions amongst Us: Identity and Interaction in the Revolutionary Ohio Valley," in *Contact Points*, ed. Cayton and Teute, 205–34; Marco Sioli, "Huguenot Traditions in the Mountains of Kentucky: Daniel Trabue's Memories," *Journal of American History* 84 (March 1998): 1313–33. On the capture of the Ruddle [or Riddle] sons, see J. Winston Coleman, *The British Invasion of Kentucky* (Lexington: University Press of Kentucky, 1951).

3. Young, ed., *Westward Into Kentucky*, 143–44. The classic literary depiction of the brotherhood of all soldiers is Erich Maria Remarque, *Im westen nichts neues* [All Quiet on the Western Front] (Boston: Little, Brown, and Company, 1929).

4. Reginald Horsman, *Race and Manifest Destiny: The Origins of American Racial Anglo-Saxonism* (Cambridge: Harvard University Press, 1981), 111; Richard White, *The Middle Ground: Indians, Empires, and Republics in the Great Lakes Region, 1650–1815* (Cambridge, Eng.: Cambridge University Press, 1991), 383. For a more nuanced view of Ohio Valley settlers, see John Mack Faragher, *Daniel Boone: The Life and Legend of an American Pioneer* (New York: Henry Holt, 1992); Stephen Aron, *How the West Was Lost: The Transformation of Kentucky from Daniel Boone to Henry Clay* (Baltimore: Johns Hopkins University Press, 1996). I have previously explored several of the themes addressed in this essay in *Border Life: Experience and Memory in the Revolutionary Ohio Valley* (Chapel Hill: University of North Carolina Press, 1998).

5. The eighteenth-century Ohio Valley has recently attracted significant scholarly interest. In addition to those authors already cited, see Gregory E. Dowd, *A Spirited Resistance: The North American Indian Struggle for Unity, 1745–1815* (Baltimore: Johns Hopkins University Press, 1992); Ellen T. Eslinger, "The Great Revival in Bourbon County, Kentucky" (Ph.D. diss., University of Chicago, 1988); Craig Thompson Friend, "Inheriting Eden: The Creation of Society and Community in Early Kentucky, 1792–1812" (Ph.D. diss., University of Kentucky, 1995); Eric Hinderaker, *Elusive Empires: Constructing*

Colonialism in the Ohio Valley, 1673–1800 (New York: Cambridge University Press, 1997); Douglas R. Hurt, *The Ohio Frontier: Crucible of the Old Northwest, 1720–1830* (Bloomington: Indiana University Press, 1996).

6. For an expanded discussion of these events, see Perkins, *Border Life,* 7–39.

7. John D. Shane [hereafter JDS] interview with William Clinkenbeard, ca. 1840s, Draper Manuscripts, 11 CC 65–66 (microfilm edition, 1980, reel 76), State Historical Society of Wisconsin [hereafter cited as Draper MSS]; JDS interview with Josiah Collins, 1841, DM 12 CC 66; JDS interview with Robert Jones, 1842, Draper MSS, 13 CC 157.

8. JDS interview with Marcus Richardson, ca. 1840s, Draper MSS, 12 CC 127; JDS interview with Benjamin Allen, ca. 1840s, Draper MSS, 11 CC 71–72.

9. JDS interview with Elijah Vaughn [inserted within interview with William Niblick], ca. 1840s, Draper MSS, 11 CC 84; Needham Parry, diary [1794], [copy by JDS], Draper MSS, 14 CC 3; JDS interview with Mrs. Sarah Graham [d. 1844], Draper MSS, 12 CC 47.

10. JDS interview with Col. John Graves, ca. 1845, Draper MSS, 11 CC 123; JDS interview with Jarvis Brummagin, ca. 1840s, Draper MSS, 12 CC 78; JDS interview with Alexander Hamilton, ca. 1840s, Draper MSS, 11 CC 291; JDS interview with Isaac Clinkenbeard, ca. 1840s, Draper MSS, 11 CC 3; JDS interview with Josiah Collins, 1841, Draper MSS, 12 CC 109; ibid., Draper MSS, 12 CC 97; JDS interview with John Crawford, ca. 1840s, Draper MSS, 12 CC 160. On communication in early America, see James H. Merrell, "'The Customes of Our Countrey': Indians and Colonists in Early America," in *Strangers within the Realm: Cultural Margins of the First British Empire,* ed. Bernard Bailyn and Philip D. Morgan (Chapel Hill: University of North Carolina Press, 1991), 117–56.

11. Colin G. Calloway, *The American Revolution in Indian Country: Crisis and Diversity in Native American Communities* (Cambridge: Cambridge University Press, 1995), 177; JDS interview with Isaac Clinkenbeard, ca. 1840s, Draper MSS, 11 CC 3; JDS interview with Patrick Scott, 1844, Draper MSS, 11 CC 7.

12. JDS interview with Ben Guthrie, ca. 1840s, Draper MSS, 11 CC 255; JDS interview with John Crawford, ca. 1840s, Draper MSS, 12 CC 162; JDS interview with Mrs. Sarah Anderson, Draper MSS, 15 CC 215; JDS interview with Josiah Collins, 1841, Draper MSS, 12 CC 109; ibid., Draper MSS, 12 CC 107; JDS interview with Cuthbert Combs, ca. 1840s, Draper MSS, 11 CC 80; JDS interview with Alexander Hamilton, ca. 1840s, Draper MSS 11, CC 293.

13. William Sudduth's narrative [1845], [Lyman Draper copy], Draper MSS, 14 V 7; JDS interview with David Crouch, Draper MSS, 12 CC 225–29; JDS interview with John Hanks, ca. 1840s, Draper MSS, 141. On the ambiguous identities of the Girty brothers, see Colin C. Calloway, "Simon Girty: Interpreter and Intermediary," in *Being and Becoming Indian: Biographical Studies of North American Frontiers,* ed. James A. Clifton (Prospect Heights, Ill.: Waveland Press, 1989), 38–58.

14. JDS interview with John Hanks, ca. 1840s, Draper MSS, 141.

15. On western savagery, see, for example, Horsman, *Race and Manifest Destiny,* 108–9; Bernard Bailyn, *The Peopling of British North America: An Introduction* (New York: Vintage Books, 1986), 112–31. On the contrasting views of Revolutionary leaders, see Bernard W. Sheehan, *Seeds of Extinction: Jeffersonian Philanthropy and the American Indian* (New York: W.W. Norton, 1973). I have borrowed the concept of "ethical extension" most immediately from the literature of environmental ethics. Environmental ethicists argue that a progressive evolution of ethical consideration has grown from a concern for self and kin group to, today (for some), a concern for animals, plants, and non-human nature in general. See, for example, Roderick Frazier Nash, *The Rights of Nature: A History of Environmental*

Ethics (Madison: University of Wisconsin Press, 1989). In thinking about the circumstances in which people recognize common humanity, I have also profited from James Q. Wilson, *The Moral Sense* (New York: Free Press, 1993), 191–221. Wilson argues that while a moral sense is innate, its astonishing expansion in the past two centuries can be attributed in some part to a western European family system that encouraged a belief in individual dignity. The historian of early America hastens to add that this sort of marriage system was also in place in most native American societies.

Liberty and Power in the Old Northwest, 1763–1800

ERIC HINDERAKER

The most familiar political legacies of the American Revolution relate to the intertwined concepts of power and liberty. In the British monarchy of the eighteenth century, power theoretically flowed from the top of society downward, from God's chosen regent the king, through his appointed noble authorities, until it finally settled in a residual form among established landowners of the realm. The Revolution, as we all know, reversed this conception of power. Revolutionary leaders assumed that power originally resided in the people—specifically, in the hands of all independent adult males. The Revolution also made guarantees of liberty a cornerstone of national principles. In particular, liberty meant to an eighteenth-century audience the right to control one's own property and to consent to its appropriation by the state. Because Parliament was not in any modern sense a representative body by the time of the Revolution, and because the colonies lacked both voice and vote in its deliberations, colonists argued that their liberties as Englishmen were infringed by Parliamentary taxes. The security of property and the importance of representative government constituted the essence of what eighteenth-century Anglo-Americans understood by the term "liberty," and one of the Revolution's primary goals was to secure those principles for posterity.[1]

Yet there is more than one way to understand the means by which definitions of power and liberty were transformed during the Revolutionary era, and events in the Old Northwest allow us to gain a broader view of exactly what was gained and what was lost in this process of redefinition. The British empire acted on its own assumptions about the meanings of power and liberty in its efforts to control the trans-Appalachian west after the Seven Years' War, as did the Ohio Indians as they labored to establish a workable equilibrium with Euro-American colonists and representatives of British government. This essay seeks to describe the process by which liberty and power were redefined in the Old Northwest between 1763 and 1800 and to consider the significance of that redefinition for white settlers and Native American residents of the region.[2]

I

Following the Peace of Paris in 1763, in which France ceded all of its claims to North America east of the Mississippi to Great Britain, British prospects in the west were transformed. The challenge of administering the vast new territory inspired conflicting visions of postwar development. From the highest levels of imperial administration to the ordinary farmers and laborers in the colonies who pinned their hopes on colonial expansion, the trans-Appalachian west presented both opportunity and danger. At the top of British government, the challenge of administering this region led to sharp conflicts among the king's ministers. Charles Wyndham, the Earl of Egremont, and Sir William Petty, the 2d Earl of Shelburne, favored a process of limited and orderly western development. To that end, they promulgated the widely misunderstood Proclamation of 1763, which traced a boundary along the entire length of Britain's seaboard colonies to separate colonial settlements from Indian lands. Originally this line was intended as a prelude to further western development. But Shelburne and Egremont were soon eclipsed in the ministry by the Earl of Hillsborough, who was convinced that expansion could only damage the empire by creating enormous new administrative burdens and depopulating more useful parts of the realm. As a result, he chose to interpret the Proclamation Line as a permanent boundary. For more than a decade, the ministry vacillated on its western policy and sent conflicting signals to its agents in the colonies.[3]

Among those agents, none was more involved in the question of western administration than William Johnson. Like Egremont and Shelburne, Johnson argued for limited, orderly expansion. He recommended that the empire settle the boundary disputes that had proliferated along the western edges of settlement, and then adopt a policy of slow, steady colonial growth regulated by publicly negotiated purchases of Indian lands. He was convinced that gradual expansion would be acceptable to the Indians, who were already accustomed to periodic sales of land, as long as reckless speculation and opportunism could be avoided. As commissioner of Indian affairs for the northern colonies, Johnson would himself be central to any such negotiations. Yet at the same time that he advocated cautious, limited expansion and public accountability, he became a secret partner in the Illinois Company, which hoped to develop more than a million acres at the confluence of the Ohio and Mississippi rivers, and worked behind the scenes on behalf of other large-scale land speculation schemes as well.[4]

Johnson's opportunism reflects the increasingly aggressive efforts of powerful men to capture large western tracts for development in the years after 1763. The Ohio, Loyal, Greenbriar, and Mississippi companies of Virginia; Pennsylvania's "suffering traders," Illinois Company, and a second Ohio Company; groups of adventurers from New England and North Carolina; and eventually a great omnibus group called the Walpole Company: all eyed western lands and jockeyed for position in the sweepstakes that seemed to be developing. Beneath these coalitions of powerful men, the ambitions and aspirations of many thousands of ordinary colonists pressed for recognition and satisfaction. All of these individuals and groups worked at odds with one another and created competing claims on western lands. But despite their differences, most shared fundamental assumptions about western development that can be tied, in turn, to prevailing definitions of power and liberty within the British Empire.[5]

Above all, the assumption that power flowed from the top of society downward informed the way that most Britons thought about the west. Imperial development always had to be justified by the benefits it conferred on the metropolis, approved by the king's ministers, and governed by leading gentlemen, who expected to control and profit from any scheme to expand the boundaries of the American colonies. Within this framework for distributing power and conferring legitimacy, an individual's liberty of action was constrained at every level by the decisions that were being made at higher levels of authority. Anyone who acted outside the framework of imperial authority was regarded, in a phrase that was applied again and again by imperial officials to ordinary settlers in the west, as "lawless banditti." In the years after the Proclamation of 1763, as every attempt to organize imperial expansion in the west eventually failed, settlers nevertheless moved into disputed territory without authorization in steadily growing numbers. Late in 1773, Major-General Frederick Haldimand lamented that a "spirit of emigration" was carrying a constant stream of families down the Ohio River from Pittsburgh as far as two hundred miles into Indian country, a pattern that he feared would "threaten a great many inconveniences." It was not only that westerners would "irritate" the Indians. More than that: Haldimand predicted that "such settlements as these, so far remote from all influence of laws, will soon be the asylum for the lawless." In this comment, Haldimand expressed a distinctive understanding of the relationship between power and liberty. Liberty could only be safely exercised within the bounds of royally sanctioned authority; westerners were only trustworthy while they were governed by the authority of law and the oversight of superiors. Nothing was so threatening to a traditional conception of social order as the prospect of large numbers of people moving beyond "all influence of laws," and dozens of officers of the British empire expended considerable energy and resources to ensure that that would not happen.[6]

Their efforts were supported wholeheartedly by the western Indians, who jealously guarded their autonomy after 1763. For decades, they had relied upon the ability to play French and British power off against each other to achieve this end. The collapse of French power generated a political crisis in the west. Indian prophets who had been preaching a gospel of cultural purification and hostility to British expansion rapidly gained ground after 1760, until their followers stretched from western New York to the Mississippi River and from the Great Lakes to the Ohio. When a war leader named Pontiac persuaded a group of Ottawas, Potawatomis, and Wyandots at Detroit to rise up against the British garrison there, he explicitly invoked the teachings of the Delaware prophet Neolin to make his point. Following their attack on the Detroit fort in May 1763, Indians throughout the west responded to the news of the uprising with attacks of their own, until by the beginning of July every British post west of Detroit had fallen. Britain's commander-in-chief, Jeffrey Amherst, was astonished at the scale of the uprisings but confident that British arms could quickly recover what had been lost. In fact, it took two long years and many lives to reclaim the western posts, but by the end of 1765 they were all in British hands once again.[7]

As Britain regained a foothold in the west, most Ohio Indians followed one of two paths in response. The first was to experiment with cultural accommodation to

Europeans. The Delawares on the Allegheny and upper Ohio were especially receptive to innovations that Moravian missionaries introduced into their communities. Even when they did not convert to Christianity, Delaware towns began to adopt European agricultural methods, outlaw alcohol, and consider educating children in the English language. The second path was closer to the one marked out by the Indian prophets of the early 1760s; it entailed militant opposition to the expansion of Anglo-American settlement and growing hostility to European culture. Despite their differences, each of these paths was intended to help preserve local autonomy. Ohio Indians uniformly sought some way to guarantee their claims to western land and to preserve a measure of economic and political independence from the British Empire.[8]

Power in the Indian communities of the Ohio Valley took various forms. In one sense, war leaders and peace chiefs competed for power as they proposed responses to local crises: peace chiefs counseled negotiation and compromise; war leaders periodically advocated violence toward an enemy. Leaders were effective only as long as they could persuade others to follow them. This kind of power was local and always shifting. Beyond the local level, many Indian communities recognized the power of outsiders to mediate conflict with other groups. The mythic figure of Onontio, the French father in that nation's Indian alliances, gained its authority through the power of mediation. In a similar way, the British empire tried to promote the Iroquois Confederacy as a mediating body in its relations with the Indians of the northeast, and often neighboring Indian groups accepted that arrangement. Just as the power of local leaders was dependent on the acquiescence of their followers, however, the power of mediators had to be accepted at the local level to be effective. Liberty, for western Indians, meant local autonomy. Leaders could not coerce their followers to follow, and the right of families, bands, or communities to go their own way always underlay the exercise of power in the Indian communities of the Ohio Valley.[9]

Despite the crisis of Pontiac's Rebellion, the interests of British officials and Ohio Indian leaders increasingly converged after 1765, brought together by concerns over western squatters. From the end of the Seven Years' War, with only a brief interruption during the uncertainty of Pontiac's Rebellion, a growing number of colonists were pressing west onto Indian lands. In part, this was a result of rising immigration levels into the colonies, which reached an all-time high in the decade after the Seven Years' War; in part it reflected the confusion and growing frustration generated by all the western land speculation schemes, which always seemed to be on the verge of offering new land to prospective settlers. Along the entire length of the

Pennsylvania, Virginia, and North Carolina frontiers, squatters began to press well beyond the western limits of colonial settlement. Their movements were unauthorized, but they were encouraged by the opportunistic behavior of key colonial leaders like John Murray, the Earl of Dunmore and governor of Virginia, who were also pushing west in anticipation of the time when they would be able to gain legitimate title to Ohio Valley lands.[10]

All of this activity was disturbing to Ohio Indian leaders, British post commanders, the Indian commissioners in America, and the leading ministers of the crown in London alike, and they all moved together to try to stop it. Although Fort Pitt was originally planted at the headwaters of the Ohio River against the will of the local Indians, it soon came to serve as an important center of diplomatic accommodation and, at least in theory, as a source of restraint on the activities of western squatters. Indian leaders repeatedly appealed to the fort's commander for help in controlling the growth of illegal settlements; in response, he warned away squatters and occasionally dispatched troops to chase off settlers and tear down their cabins. In London, both the ministry and Parliament were increasingly adamant that the officers of empire deter the migration of colonists onto Indian lands and mediate disputes to keep the peace in the west.[11]

These responses to the problem of western squatters reflect a vision of empire as a mediating, restraining force. After the miseries of Pontiac's Rebellion, British military officers and cabinet leaders were increasingly willing to cooperate with Indian leaders to ensure peace and orderly trade. As long as the empire could play this role effectively, it strengthened the hand of accommodationist peace chiefs among the Ohio Indians. From a metropolitan perspective, it began to appear that the empire could act as a fulcrum upon which the scales of justice balanced in the trans-Appalachian west. If it could keep the interests of Indians, western settlers, and colonial traders in some kind of reasonable equilibrium, it might be possible to preserve peace and mutual prosperity. But this vision was never more than a pipe dream. The number of people moving across the Alleghenies, the speed and complexity of events, and the sheer cost of such oversight in pounds sterling and manpower guaranteed that affairs in the west would remain beyond the manageable scope of Britain's imperial apparatus. The difficulties of western policy were infinitely compounded by the seaboard crisis over taxation, which deprived Britain of badly needed revenue and created more pressing problems for the crown. Eventually the ministry admitted defeat in the west and withdrew altogether.[12] In the receding wake of the British army, the Ohio Indians were left to face a rising tide of prospective settlers in a contest for western lands.

II

The outbreak of the Revolution thus coincided with a crisis in the west that was already well underway by the spring of 1775. It started with the actions of many colonists who were behaving illegally and unjustly by the standard of impartiality that British administrators hoped to uphold beyond the Proclamation Line, but it gained a powerful new impetus from the American Revolution. Revolutionary governments chose to support and advance the interests of western settlers for both strategic and ideological reasons. Strategically, all the seaboard colonies were vulnerable to British attacks in the west: the empire had forts, troops, and Indian allies to draw upon, while the frontiers of the colonies were essentially defenseless, as events of the Seven Years' War had illustrated all too painfully. So the rebellious colonies needed a counterweight to British power in the west. With only a little stretching, it was possible to justify their support in terms of revolutionary ideology, which rejected the top-down model of political authority in favor of a democratic, bottom-up vision of governmental power. The democratically organized communities of squatters presented themselves as friends of liberty and enemies of the aristocratic order that had previously smothered their ambition to open new land to settlement. But allowing this radical new conception of power to define the limits of legitimate action in the west all but destroyed any chance for a just and equitable Indian policy in the years that followed.

Settlers and Indians were already in a state of war along the Virginia and Pennsylvania frontiers in the summer of 1774, when Virginia's governor, Lord Dunmore, led a military campaign against the Shawnee Indian towns on the Scioto River north of the Ohio. The campaign was approved by neither colony nor crown, and the Indians regarded it as inconclusive, but the Virginians who participated believed that they had won the right to settle Kentucky. One backcountry resident offered a provocative explanation of the campaign when he wrote, in the fall of 1774, "When without a king, one doeth according to the freedom of his own will." This is a startling image, coming months before Lexington and Concord and more than a year before the Declaration of Independence, but it reflects the extent to which backcountry residents felt abandoned by the crown. The next summer, with Dunmore's

War behind them, squatters staked claims by the thousands in central Kentucky, more than two hundred miles beyond the Appalachian ridge. Many claimants built cabins, and hundreds cooperated to found four new towns. Despite all of the activity, though, none of them knew how to make their claims good, or whether their efforts would ever be recognized at all.[13]

This land rush had no formal connection to the outbreak of the Revolution, but the coincidental timing created an important opportunity for the new communities to gain legitimacy. In the spring of 1776, the settlers of Harrodsburg, the largest of the new towns, wrote several petitions to the Virginia Convention to challenge the claims of a proprietary venture called the Transylvania Company to their land, and to request that Virginia take the new settlements under its own wing instead. Their petitions cleverly played the strategic concerns and the ideological commitments of the Revolutionary movement off against each other. The settlers emphasized that they had a legitimate claim to Kentucky after Lord Dunmore's War because "They Fought and bled for it," but that their desire for western land had been frustrated by the "Base proceedings of a Detestible, Wicked and Corrupt Ministry to prevent any more counties to be laid off." Now, they hoped, the Virginia Convention would show more wisdom. We "cannot but observe," they warned, "how impolitical it would be to suffer such a Respectable body of prime Rifle men" to remain neutral, or worse, to fight for tyrants because Virginia failed to act when it had the chance. But if the Convention laid off new western counties, "Every obstacle would be Removed, Population [would] increase and of consequence a Barrier to the interior parts of Virginia from the Indians" would be formed. "A new source of wealth would then be opened, as Trade and Navigation under the auspices of Virginia would Flourish, in the Western World."[14]

The notion of liberty embodied in the claims of the Kentucky riflemen differed fundamentally from that of most Revolutionary leaders, who assumed that liberty of action always had to be ordered by a moral attachment to the needs of the larger community. This is what John Adams meant when he wrote that "the new Governments we are assuming, in every Part, will require a Purification from our Vices, and an augmentation of our Virtues or they will be no Blessings." The haphazard opportunism of the Kentucky settlers was more like the liberty associated with John Locke's state of nature, in which, in the absence of a clearly constituted authority, individuals are free to act according to the dictates of conscience alone.[15]

The ordered liberty of John Adams and other national leaders did not square comfortably with the natural liberty of the Kentucky settlers, which justified a highly problematic land grab in central Kentucky, but the Harrodsburg petitions nevertheless succeeded in their aim. Many of Virginia's Revolutionary leaders were sympathetic to the need to open new western lands to settlement, a process which they believed to be consistent with, even fundamental to, their experiment in republican government. Nor could they ignore the strategic significance of the new western settlements. And so, in the fall of 1776, Virginia's House of Delegates created six new counties—Kentucky, Washington, Montgomery, Ohio, Monongalia, and Yohogania—and extended its jurisdiction across the entire modern states of West Virginia and Kentucky. Western settlers who were regarded as "banditti" by the British could suddenly claim political legitimacy, while Virginia took a huge stride forward in solving its problems of western defense. Revolutionary militia units were organized in every county, which Virginia began to supply with powder, lead, and manpower. At the same time, the Continental Congress also began to look west. In 1776, it built three forts on the Ohio River and began to pour resources into them. Many Ohio Indian communities initially hoped to remain neutral in the conflict between colonies and crown, but the armed invasion of the Ohio Valley by allies of the Revolutionary movement guaranteed that, by the end of 1777, nearly every Indian group in the region was allied with Great Britain.[16]

Finally, in 1779, the Virginia House of Delegates passed two laws that created a legal framework for occupying its western lands. Though the procedures they established made it hard to file a claim and favored men with ready cash, good connections, and good information, the land laws of 1779 stimulated a rush of thousands of people into Kentucky, despite the fact that the entire region was under siege by Indian attacks. Trying their best to ignore the danger, the settlers hunkered down in rudely built forts and stations and did their best to weather the storm.[17]

War's end came at a strange time for the Ohio Indians. Though Kentucky's population had grown to perhaps 12,000 by 1783, Indian warriors dominated the valley, a fact that was driven home to the Kentucky militia in the disastrous Battle of Blue Licks in the summer of 1782. Nevertheless, in the peace agreement of 1783, Great Britain abandoned the war effort with scarcely a word about what the treaty meant for its Indian allies.[18] As the seaboard states finally enjoyed a welcome respite from years of war, the animosity between settlers and Indians in the west was just reaching full flower.

III

It is a commonplace of the historical literature on the Indian policy of the new nation to contrast the benevolent spirit of the Washington administration with the increasingly violent and expeditious Indian relations that developed in the next generation and culminated with the Removal policies of Andrew Jackson.[19] While this argument certainly has merit, I would contend that it fails to account fully for the ways in which western policies that originated in the Revolutionary War and gained shape during the Washington administration made the opportunism and violence of the nineteenth century all but inevitable. Long before Washington's rhetoric of benevolence was giving way to Jackson's rhetoric of Removal, the Continental Congress and the federal army were recasting the relationship between liberty and power in the Ohio Valley.

After the war, Congress hoped to do north of the Ohio River what it had been unable to do, except in a haphazard rearguard way, in Kentucky: to impose an ordered liberty on western settlers. Its vision was embodied in the Plan of Government for the Western Territory, drafted by Thomas Jefferson and passed in 1784, and the Northwest Ordinance of 1787. The extraordinary creativity of these statutes can hardly be overestimated. They departed fundamentally from the only existing model for imperial expansion, the actions of the European monarchies, especially Britain, during the colonial era. Those colonies were permanently distinct from and inferior to their parent states because they lay beyond the kingdom they were intended to serve. The Northwest Ordinance, by contrast, established the revolutionary and counterintuitive principle that a nation could have elastic boundaries, and extended to its hypothetical future states the astonishing concession of equal power and membership within the federal union. The liberty of future western settlers to share equally in the privileges of citizenship was balanced by the responsibility to take up lands in an ordered way that would allow Congress to plan, regulate, and profit from settlement.[20]

But imposing order on the liberty of western settlers was a notoriously difficult thing. If republican government required virtuous citizens attached to the public interest and a shared vision of national identity, most western settlers appeared to be distinctly parochial and violently self-interested. Many eastern observers compared western squatters to Indians, as best they understood them: they were always pressing restlessly beyond settled communities, they seemed indifferent to civic values, they sought isolation in rude simplicity instead of reformed manners and morals in a virtuous society. They were also rushing to take up huge new chunks of land north of the Ohio River even before Congress could organize the process, just as squatters had earlier pioneered the Kentucky land rush. This was especially worrisome to national leaders who recognized that western lands were the one significant resource of an otherwise insolvent nation. For controlled expansion and responsible self-government to emerge in the west, no less than for the financial well-being of the new republic, most easterners recognized that some degree of order would have to be imposed from above.[21]

So Congress took a hard line against the squatters north of the Ohio. Late in 1784, in its first military initiative since the Peace of Paris, Congress posted three companies of American troops under Josiah Harmar at Fort McIntosh, at the mouth of the Beaver River. Their main job was to drive off the squatters. Thousands of people had moved across the Ohio River onto Indian lands in the previous year or two until, as John Armstrong informed Harmar, there was "scarcely one bottom on the river but has one or more families living thereon." He estimated that the Miami and Scioto rivers each had already been settled by more than fifteen hundred families. Detachments from the fort repeatedly warned off settlers and burned their cabins, but most returned as soon as the soldiers had gone. In the fall of 1785, the soldiers built Fort Harmar farther downriver, but the illegal settlements continued to grow.[22]

In these same years, Congress struggled unsuccessfully to negotiate workable land agreements with the Ohio Indians. It was essential to proceed quickly, both to generate income for the government and to get out in front of the squatters. The opportunism and haste of these postwar agreements lay bare the expediency of national Indian policy in the decade after the Revolution. Though national leaders professed a desire to avoid war with the western Indians and gain territory by diplomatic means, by creating an expansive nation with elastic boundaries they made land acquisition by treaty at best a face-saving gesture, at worst a poorly disguised farce. In the treaties of Fort Stanwix (1784), Fort McIntosh (1785), and Fort Finney (1786), American Indian Commissioners sought representatives of the Iroquois Confederacy and the Wyandot, Delaware, Ottawa, Chippewa, and Shawnee nations who would sign away a large chunk of territory north of the Ohio. They neither knew nor, apparently, cared whether the particular Indian spokesmen they met with on each of these occasions had the authority to approve the agreements, and in 1786 a large gathering of Ohio Indians repudiated them all. In the wake of these flawed and failed agreements, war became the only recourse for settlers and Indians who defined their legitimate interests in fundamentally incompatible terms. Beginning in the summer of 1786, raids between the Ohio Indians and the Valley's settlers escalated once again.[23]

As violence grew, the army's role changed. Posted to control squatters, it began instead to provide military support to western settlers. Harmar sent two companies of troops to Louisville to help the Kentucky militia, while Congress summoned more troops. Soon they were posted at regular intervals down the Ohio River to guard against Indian counterattacks.[24]

These troop movements coincided with a series of land sales in the valley intended to capitalize on the Northwest Ordinance. In 1787, Congress sold millions of acres to the Ohio Company of Associates, John Cleves Symmes, and the Scioto Company. In the fall it auctioned another 72,934 acres in the first four ranges of public lands.[25] This was done despite the persistent objections of a large segment of the Ohio Indians, and thereby guaranteed that violence would escalate further. After 1787, the army's primary role was to protect settlers as they moved onto land the local Indians continued to regard as their own.

The years that followed were filled with uncertainty and terror. Indian raids challenged American settlements, and the Kentucky militia organized raids in return. Beginning in 1789, the U.S. Army followed suit. First General Harmar led a detachment against the Indian towns north of the Ohio, with disappointing results. Then, in 1791, Arthur St. Clair's forces suffered a disastrous defeat at the hands of the Indians on the Wabash River. By 1792, the Ohio Indians were the dominant military power in the valley, though not for long. Two years later, American forces under Anthony Wayne won a decisive victory at the Battle of Fallen Timbers, which ended the immediate military threat of the Ohio Indians and led to a temporary peace.[26] But that victory should not obscure the significance of this period of uncertainty and violence. It demonstrated to western settlers that local resources were insufficient to challenge the power of the Ohio Indians, and so helped to cement their loyalty to the national state.[27] That loyalty had been a crucial strategic concern to eastern leaders since the earliest days of the Revolutionary War, and had consistently led Congress to be more expedient in western policy than it might otherwise have been. By defining U.S. land claims very expansively in the Ohio Valley, and committing considerable military resources to their defense, national leaders won over the western settlers.

The settlement of the Ohio Valley has often been represented as a triumph of Revolutionary-era political values and a victory for the new American nation.[28] And indeed it was. But it was achieved only at great cost, and only by redefining the relationship between power and liberty in the west. At the end of the Revolutionary War, Congress expected to assert its power over western settlers to create an orderly pattern of limited expansion. National leaders like George Washington and Henry Knox hoped that expansion would be complemented by humane and moderate relations with the western Indians. In effect, they hoped to revive the dream of a national state that could mediate disputes between settlers and Indians. But mediation is only effective when its legitimacy is acknowledged. The Continental Congress in effect abandoned mediation as a legitimate western strategy when it armed the Kentucky settlers during the Revolution, then undermined any attempt to resume workable Indian relations by adopting a western land policy that made a mockery of Indian sovereignty. Rather than using the power of the state to impose order on the liberty of westerners, Congress and the Washington administration discovered that the only way to ensure the ascendancy of the new republic in the Ohio Valley was to turn the power of the state against the region's Indian population. This process conferred extraordinary liberties on the rapidly growing white population of the Ohio Valley, but cost western Indians any chance to sustain their sovereignty and autonomy against the expansive claims of the new American nation.

NOTES

1. Gordon S. Wood, *The Creation of the American Republic, 1776–1787* (Chapel Hill: University of North Carolina Press, 1969), and *The Radicalism of the American Revolution* (New York: Alfred A. Knopf, 1992); Bernard Bailyn, *The Ideological Origins of the American Revolution* (Cambridge, Mass.: Harvard University Press, 1967).

2. For a more detailed version of the argument presented in this essay, see Eric Hinderaker, *Elusive Empires: Constructing Colonialism in the Ohio Valley, 1673–1800* (New York: Cambridge University Press, 1997).

3. The Proclamation is in James Sullivan et al., eds., *The Papers of Sir William Johnson*, 14 vols. (Albany: University of the State of New York, 1921–65), 10:976–85. For its context, see especially Jack Sosin, *Whitehall and the Wilderness: the Middle West in British Colonial Policy, 1760–1775* (Lincoln: University of Nebraska Press, 1961), 27–28 and following. For Hillsborough, see also Bernard Bailyn, *Voyagers to the West: A Passage in the Peopling of America on the Eve of the Revolution* (New York: Alfred A. Knopf, 1986), 29–36.

4. Johnson to the Lords of Trade, 13 November 1763, in E. B. O'Callaghan and Berthold Fernow, eds., *Documents Relative to the Colonial History of the State of New York*, 15 vols. (Albany: Weed Parsons and Co., 1856–87), 7:574; [William Johnson], Advice to the Board of Trade, 1764, Cadwallader

Collection, Historical Society of Pennsylvania, Philadelphia, Box 5 [hereafter cited as HSP]; Illinois Company Articles of Agreement, 29 March 1766, and [William Franklin], "Reasons for Establishing a Colony in the Illinois," 1766, in Clarence Alvord and Clarence Carter, eds., *The New Regime, 1765–1767*, Collections of the Illinois State Historical Library (Springfield: Illinois State Historical Society, 1916), 11:203–4, 248–57.

5. Sosin, *Whitehall and the Wilderness*, 42–44, 136–46.
6. Haldimand to Dartmouth, 3 November 1773, in K. G. Davies, ed., *Documents of the American Revolution, 1770–1783*, 19 vols. (Shannon and Dublin: Irish University Press, 1972–81), 6:237–38; for the idea of liberty in the context of monarchical protection, see Richard Bushman, *King and People in Provincial Massachusetts* (Chapel Hill: University of North Carolina Press, 1985), 20–22.
7. Gregory Evans Dowd, *A Spirited Resistance: The North American Indian Struggle for Unity, 1745–1815* (Baltimore: Johns Hopkins University Press, 1991), 23–46; Richard White, *The Middle Ground: Indians, Empires, and Republics in the Great Lakes Region, 1650–1815* (New York: Cambridge University Press, 1991), 269–314.
8. Hinderaker, *Elusive Empires*, 176–83; Michael McConnell, *A Country Between: The Upper Ohio Valley and Its Peoples, 1724–1774* (Lincoln: University of Nebraska Press, 1992), 207–232.
9. See especially White, *Middle Ground*.
10. For the growth of squatter communities, see *Minutes of the Provincial Council of Pennsylvania*, 16 vols. (Harrisburg, Penn.: T. Fenn, 1838–53), 9:539; George Croghan to Samuel Wharton, 2 November 1771, Cadwallader Collection, Box 5, HSP (where Croghan estimates that "Nott less than five thousand familys" had settled illegally between the Alleghenies and the Ohio River); Angus McDonald to Hancock Taylor, 11 March 1774, Taylor Family Papers, Filson Club, Louisville, Kentucky; Robert Doack to William Preston, 20 November 1771 and 28 October 1772, Draper Manuscripts, 2QQ128, 2QQ137, Historical Society of Wisconsin, Madison [hereafter cited Draper Mss]. For opportunism among leading Virginians and Pennsylvanians, see C.W. Butterfield, ed., *The Washington-Crawford Letters* (Cincinnati: R. Clarke and Co., 1877), especially Crawford to Washington, 20 April 1771, 2 August 1771, and 15 March 1772, 18–21 and 24–25; and Washington to Crawford, 6 December 1771, 23–24; Washington to Dunmore, 15 June 1772, in John C. Fitzpatrick, ed., *The Writings of George Washington*, 39 vols. (Washington, D.C.: Government Printing Office, 1931–44), 3:85–87 and 87n; Croghan to Thomas Wharton, 11 May 1773, "Letters of Colonel George Croghan [to Thomas Wharton]," *Pennsylvania Magazine of History and Biography* 15 (1891): 434. For a more detailed treatment of these materials see Hinderaker, *Elusive Empires*, 161–75.
11. See, for example, Thomas Gage to Conway, 24 June 1766, William Johnson to Gage, 11 July 1767, and Gage to Shelburne, 24 August 1767, in Alvord and Carter, eds., *The New Regime*, 325, 582, 595. For the long struggle to impose imperial order in the west see Sosin, *Whitehall and the Wilderness*, especially 211–55.
12. This was enacted most dramatically when Gage withdrew the troops from Fort Pitt and razed the fort; see Edmonstone to Gage, 11 October 1772, Gage Papers, American Series, V, 114, William L. Clements Library, University of Michigan, Ann Arbor; and more generally Sosin, *Whitehall and the Wilderness*, 221–22.
13. Reuben G. Thwaites and Louise Kellogg, eds., *Documentary History of Dunmore's War, 1774* (Madison: State Historical Society of Wisconsin, 1905); William Doack to William Preston, 22 November 1774, Draper Mss 3QQ101; Hinderaker, *Elusive Empires*, 187–99.
14. Petitions of 7–15 June 1776 and 20 June 1776, in *Petitions of the Early Inhabitants of Kentucky to the*

General Assembly of Virginia, 1769–1792, ed. James Rood Robertson, Filson Club Publications no. 27 (Louisville: Filson Club, 1914), 36–41.

15. John Adams to Abigail Adams, 3 July 1776, quoted in Wood, *Creation of the American Republic*, 123. The term "ordered liberty" comes from David Hackett Fischer, *Albion's Seed: Four British Folkways in America* (New York: Oxford University Press, 1989), 205. My understanding of the concept as it relates to the republican ideology of the Revolutionary era has been shaped especially by Bailyn, *Ideological Origins;* Wood, *Creation of the American Republic;* and J. G. A. Pocock, *The Machiavellian Moment: Florentine Political Thought and the Atlantic Political Tradition* (Princeton: Princeton University Press, 1975). For Locke's concept of liberty in a state of nature, see John Locke, *Two Treatises of Government* [originally published 1690], William S. Carpenter, ed. (London: J. M. Dent and Sons, 1991), Book 2, chap. 2, 118–24.

16. For the new counties, see William Hening, ed., *The Statutes at Large; Being a Collection of all the Laws of Virginia from the First Session of the Legislature in the Year 1619*, 13 vols. (New York, Philadelphia, and Richmond: The Author, 1819–23), 9:257–66. See also the drafts and editorial note in Julian P. Boyd et al., eds., *The Papers of Thomas Jefferson* (Princeton, N.J.: Princeton University Press, 1950-), 1:564–76. For aid see the Order of the Virginia Committee of Safety, 27 May 1776, Draper Mss 4QQ48; Patrick Henry to General Edward Hand, 27 July 1777, Draper Mss 18J26. For the Continental Congress see Worthington C. Ford et al., eds., *Journals of the Continental Congress, 1774–1789*, 34 vols. (Washington, D.C.: Government Printing Office, 1904–37) [hereafter cited as JCC], Proceedings for 11 July 1776, 5:12; September 1776, 5:752; 8 January 1777, 7:20–22; and 15 April 1777, 7:247, 270. For Indian alliances, see Hinderaker, *Elusive Empires*, 207–12.

17. The laws are printed in Hening, ed., *Statutes at Large*, 10:35–65; on their formulation see Boyd et al., eds., *Jefferson Papers*, 2:133–167. For an assessment see especially Fredrika J. Teute, "Land, Liberty, and Labor: Kentucky as the Promised Land," (Ph.D. Diss., Johns Hopkins University, 1988).

18. Evarts B. Greene and Virginia D. Harrington, eds., *American Population Before the Federal Census of 1790* (New York: Columbia University Press, 1932), 192; Randolph C. Downes, "Indian War on the Upper Ohio," *Western Pennsylvania Historical Magazine* 17 (1934): 93–115.

19. See, for example, Francis Paul Prucha, *The Great Father: The United States Government and the American Indians*, 2 vols. (Lincoln: University of Nebraska Press, 1984), 1:35–61, 183–213. For a variant that emphasizes the role of Indian resistance in producing a moderate and humane policy see James Merrell, "Declarations of Independence: Indian-White Relations in the New Nation," in *The American Revolution: Its Character and Limits*, ed. Jack P. Greene (New York: New York University Press, 1987), 197–223.

20. "Plan for Government of the Western Territory," 3 February – 23 April 1784, *Jefferson Papers*, 6:581–617. The text of the Northwest Ordinance appears in *JCC*, 31:669–72; for a thorough account of its origins, see Peter Onuf, *Statehood and Union: A History of the Northwest Ordinance* (Bloomington: Indiana University Press, 1987).

21. See especially Peter Onuf, "Settlers, Settlements, and New States," in *American Revolution*, ed. Greene, 171–96.

22. Editor's introduction; Harmar to the President of Congress, 1 May 1785; Harmar to the Secretary of War, 1 June 1785; Harmar to Secretary of War, 12 July 1786; Armstrong to Harmar, April 1785; Harmar to Secretary of War, 22 October 1785; Harmar to Secretary, 12 July 1786, in *The St. Clair Papers: The Life and Public Services of Arthur St. Clair*, 2 vols., ed. William H. Smith, ed. (Cincinnati, 1881; Reprint, Freeport, N.Y.: Books for Libraries Press, 1970), 2:1–7, 14–15, 3–4, 11–13, 14–15.

23. For the desire to avoid conflict see Reginald Horsman, "American Indian Policy in the Old Northwest, 1783–1812," *William and Mary Quarterly* 18 (1961): 35–53. Versions of the Fort Stanwix proceedings can be found in Neville B. Craig, *The Olden Time*, 2 vols. (Pittsburgh: Dumars and Co., 1846–48), 2:404–27, and in Draper Mss 23U1–11; the text of the treaty is in Wilcomb Washburn, ed., *The American Indian and the United States: A Documentary History*, 4 vols. (New York: Random House, 1973), 4:2267–69. It was formally repudiated at Fort Schlosser on 27 March 1786; see Draper Mss 23U32–33. For the text of the Fort McIntosh treaty, see Washburn, ed., *American Indian and the United States*, 4:2269–71; for a summary of the commissioners' message see Draper Mss 23U19–21. For the Fort Finney proceedings see Draper Mss, 23U34–37. For the repudiation of all three treaties by the "United Indian Nations," see Draper Mss, 23U51–56. Violence grew especially following the Fort Finney treaty between the United States and the Shawnees in 1786, which was widely opposed by the Ohio Indians; Indian raids in the spring and summer led to a coordinated attack by the Kentucky militia. For a full and balanced account of the attack see John Mack Faragher, *Daniel Boone: The Life and Legend of an American Pioneer* (New York: Henry Holt, 1992), 251–55; and for a more general account of the period that emphasizes the collapse of mediation see White, *Middle Ground*, 413–68.

24. Harmar to the Secretary, 15 November 1786 and 7 June 1787, in *St. Clair Papers*, ed. Smith, 2:18–19, 22–23; Walter H. Mohr, *Federal Indian Relations, 1774–1788* (Philadelphia: University of Pennsylvania Press, 1933), 127.

25. Malcolm J. Rohrbough, *The Land Office Business: The Settlement and Administration of American Public Lands, 1789–1837* (New York: Oxford University Press, 1986), 10–11.

26. Arthur St. Clair to Secretary of War, 5 July 1788, in *St. Clair Papers*, ed. Smith, 2:48–49; Major Hamtramck to Harmar, 31 August 1788, in Gayle Thornbrough, ed., *Outpost on the Wabash: Letters of Brigadier General Josiah Harmar and Major John Francis Hamtramck* (Indianapolis: Indiana Historical Society, 1957), 116; Richard Kohn, *Eagle and Sword: The Federalists and the Creation of the Military Establishment in America, 1783–1802* (New York: Free Press, 1975), 104–16; Col. George Clendenin to the governor, 26 May 1792, Draper Mss 15C3 [copy].

27. Andrew R. L. Cayton, "'Separate Interests' and the Nation-State: The Washington Administration and the Origins of Regionalism in the Trans-Appalachian West," *Journal of American History* 79 (1992): 39–67.

28. The frontier thesis of Frederick Jackson Turner established one context for making this argument. For example, see John Barnhart *Valley of Democracy: The Frontier versus the Plantation in the Ohio Valley, 1775–1818* (Lincoln: University of Nebraska Press, 1953), and Stanley Elkins and Eric McKitrick, "A Meaning for Turner's Frontier: Democracy in the Old Northwest," *Political Science Quarterly* 69 (1954): 321–53. More recently the paradigm of republican ideology has facilitated thoughtful reconsiderations of the Revolutionary legacy. See especially Andrew R. L Cayton, *The Frontier Republic: Ideology and Politics in the Ohio Country, 1780–1825* (Kent, Ohio: Kent State University Press, 1986).

Supper and Celibacy: Quaker–Seneca Reflexive Missions

ROBERT S. COX

Far from home in the late summer 1803, Isaac Bonsall and the emissaries from the Philadelphia Yearly Meeting stopped for supper on the banks of the Allegheny River. Their guides, Seneca Indians from the Allegany reservation, joined them as chocolate and chicken were prepared for eating, and even without the ability to communicate easily across the language barrier, things seemed to be proceeding smoothly. "We got the Indians to roast the fowls for us," Bonsall recorded, "which they did by putting them on Sticks sharpened at each end sticking them in the Ground a little enclining to the fire." But as Bonsall's fellow missionary, Isaac Coates, was pantomiming directions about the impending barbeque, things went awry. Just as the chickens were "about done," the Indians "happened to mistake [Coates'] directions and with great avidity seized the greater part and began to tear them limb from Limb and eat voraciously."[1]

Taking place at the geographic margins of the *pays d'en haut*[2] near the end of a bitter conflict that had consumed three generations, any number of dire consequences might have followed. Anger, argument, or sulking umbrage might have ensued, but Bonsall reported that though he received only a "small share," he was "satisfied and much diverted," and he dismissed the event as an "innocent mistake of the Indians in there favour" before settling in for the night, hungry but unperturbed. Instead of staining a violent land with additional violence, Bonsall ended his supper on a comic note of bemusement and satisfaction, diversion and delight.

Although in itself, Bonsall's supper was a minor incident, even trivial, it provides a valuable point of entry into Quaker-Indian relations at the turn of the nineteenth century. While the patterns of understanding, misunderstanding, and apparent understanding it reveals are representative of intercultural exchange generally, there is an aspect to Bonsall's supper that arises peculiarly in missionary interchange, and particularly in the interchange seen involving missionaries of the Society of Friends at the turn of the nineteenth century.

While missions had been a feature of Quaker life since the 1650s, Bonsall was part of a wave of Quaker missionaries to American Indians that swelled during the 1790s, resulting in the planting of a number of missions throughout the nation.[3] While religious and economic motives were "clearly" implicated in the expansion of the Quaker missionary program at this time, a close examination of the missions to the Seneca reveals a more complex terrain, made more difficult to navigate by the imprecision of certain key terms—most importantly, the term "missionary" itself. Used occasionally by Quakers about themselves, and routinely by others to denominate Quakers such as Bonsall, missionary is a term that obscures as much as it elucidates. Unlike the more familiar missionaries of the Congregational, Baptist, Presbyterian, or Moravian churches—each of which was active in western New York at the time—Quaker missionaries never sought the conversion of Indians to Quakerism. While they shared a common religious vocabulary with other denominations, stressing the need to bring Christianity and civilization to Indians, Quakers differed significantly in their attitudes toward Indian religion and culture, as well as in their view of the relationship between missionaries and the missionized. The Quaker ministry, as Thomas Hamm has argued, was intended not for broad proselytizing, but for the "edification of those who already were members."[4]

Given that Quakers sought and expected no converts from their missions, what, then, were they doing so far from home, so near peril? What would lead a group of young men and women from Philadelphia, members of an increasingly insular pacifist sect, hundreds of miles from home into a region so recently torn by war? The impulse to invoke economics as the root underlying cause has a certain explanatory appeal, given the trade carried on between Quakers and Indians, but such an approach both undervalues religious belief and creates a false dichotomy in Quaker lives between religious and secular activity. Moreover, it leaves open the question of why the Quakers chose specifically to engage in missionary activity, why to the Indians, why at this particular time?

This article explores Quaker motivations in embarking so avidly upon the missionary enterprise during the last decade of the eighteenth century, and in the process, will examine the effect of the protracted war for the Great Lakes on two geographically marginal, but politically central peoples—the Senecas and Pennsylvania Quakers. The diffuse and often subdued contact provided by the mission and the diplomatic council created a forum in which these cultures shaped one another and, in the wake of generations of almost continual armed conflict, provided a forum for each to engage in cultural "rebirth." For Isaac Bonsall, on the eve of entering the Seneca world, the hunger he experienced as a result of a waylaid supper paled before the greater hunger for spiritual and political renewal in the New Republic.

COLONIAL QUAKERS AND INDIANS

In 1676, when George Fox, the "founder" of the Society of Friends, preached that the message of Christ was bound by neither color nor creed, he was articulating a fundamental tenet of Quakerism. The inward light, he argued while touring the American colonies, was available to "any Man or Woman upon the Face of the Earth . . . both *Turks, Barbarians, Tartarians* and *Ethyopians* . . . for the *Tawnes* and for the *Blacks,* as well as for you that are called *Whites.*"[5] Yet however important the idea of spiritual equality became for Quakers, Fox's conviction did not lead him to advocate the immediate emancipation of slaves, nor did it, once Quakers had assumed political control in Pennsylvania, immediately inspire them to formulate an official policy of justice in Indian affairs. While the proper role of Friends with respect to "African" slavery and Native Americans had been identified as major moral issues before the turn of the eighteenth century, the Society responded in a deliberate, glacially slow manner, reflective of the "divided spirit" of their meetings.[6] Trade, land acquisition, and warfare periodically spurred moral inquiry among Friends and occasionally motivated individuals to political action to curb abuses. Between 1679 and 1719, preparative and monthly Quaker meetings cautiously agreed to ban the sale of alcohol to Indians—beginning when the Burlington (N.J.) Monthly Meeting concluded that the sale of liquor to Indians was "not consistent with the honor of truth"—but for over half a century, the formal, structural evidence of Quaker concern over relations with Indians was elusive, at best.[7]

Despite decades of contact and conflict between colonists and Indians, it was only when the French and Indian War brought both moral and political issues to a head for Quakers that the first signs of formal organization in response to Indian affairs emerge. In brief (the story having been told so often), following the outbreak of war, Quaker members of the Pennsylvania Assembly were drawn into a three-way struggle, pitting the renascent pacifism and desire for moral purity on the part of some of their religious countrymen against the hawkishness of their political opponents in the Proprietary party, and the accomodationism of Friends in England. While this conflict was bound up in, and helped catalyze, a religious "reformation"—a refining, revision, and revitalization of Quaker social and spiritual life—it also resulted in the resignation of a majority of Quaker assemblymen and the serious impairment of Quaker political power in the province.[8]

As war raged and religious Friends squabbled with their more secular kinsmen, Quaker interest in Indian affairs crystallized into institutional form. In 1757, a group of reformist Quakers (among those leading the revitalization of the Society) formed the Friendly Association for Regaining and Preserving Peace with the Indians by Pacific as an unofficial body, lying outside of the jurisdiction of the Yearly Meeting.[9] Drawing together the politically active elite of Quaker Philadelphia, and drawing support from other pacifist sects in Pennsylvania, "these meddling people" sought to foster peace by inserting themselves as intermediaries between Indians and the hawkish provincial government.[10] Given the suspicion they engendered among government and Indians alike, the opposition of the Proprietary party and white frontiersmen, and the divisions that erupted among Friends, one might surmise that the opportunities for the success of the Friendly Association were limited. Indeed, by most measures, they counted few political successes, and none unalloyed.

The most apt encapsulation of the experience of the Friendly Association, both politically and spiritually, may have been their much-publicized connection with the Munsee. In 1760, a delegation of Delaware Indians visited Philadelphia that included the Munsee chief, Papunhank, already known for his powers of prophecy and preaching, and for his influence at the town of Wyalusing.[11] To Friends' ears, Papunhank's address at council reverberated with the Quaker concept of waiting on the light, and his pleas for peace, temperance, and spiritual discipline struck a chord with members of the Friendly Association, engaged as they were in promoting these issues as they related to the purification and cultural revival of the Society of Friends. Significantly, Papunhank declared himself receptive to the ministry of Quakers. "When I left home," he claimed, "I resolved not to speak to the Quakers—but hearken & hear what they would say to me—and since they have spoke to me I hear'd a Voice say to my Heart the Quakers are right—it may be a wrong Voice, but I believe it is a right Voice." He suggested cautiously that if "the Goodness" remained with him, he would visit the Quakers again, and if his feelings continued to grow, he hoped to be "joind in close fellowship with them."[12]

To religious Quakers like the members of the Friendly Association, Papunhank's personal history further seemed the perfect illustration of spiritual renewal. At one time a drunkard, Papunhank had experienced visions while grieving over the death of his father and, discovering his prophetic powers, carried his personal quest for reform to the other Munsee. In his visionary state, one Quaker recorded, Papunhank's

Eyes were turned to behold the Earth & to consider the Things that were therein—and seeing the Folly and Wickedness that prevailed—his sorrows increased—then his Mind was turned from beholding this lower World—to look towards him that created it & strong Desires were begotten in his Heart for a further Knowledge of his Creator—Nevertheless the Almighty was not yet pleas'd to be found of him—But his Desires increasing he forsook the Town—and went to the Woods in great Bitterness of Spirit—the other Indians missing him & fearing Evil had befallen him—went from the Town in search of him—but could not find him—at the end of five Days it pleased God to appear to him to his Comfort to give him a sight of his inward State—and also an Aquaintance with the Works of Nature—for he apprehended a Sense was given him of the Virtue & Nature of Several Herbs Roots Plants & Trees &c and the different Relations they had to one another that Man stood in the nearest Relation to God of an Part of the Creation it was also at this time he was made and he was made sensible of his Duty to God and he came home rejoicing & endeavour'd to put in Practice what he apprehended was required of him.[13]

This epiphany led Papunhank to reject war, abstain from alcohol, and seek spiritual renewal through temperate living and meticulously observed ritual adherence; it led him to turn away from the metaphorical solitude of the woods toward the strong bonds of society—all features that Friends could immediately comprehend in their own terms. Papunhank's visions, his "sight of his inward State," his pacifism, and even the cosmic significance of plants translated easily into Quaker concepts, as surely as they were grounded in Indian experience. In short order, Papunhank became a favorite subject of the Friendly Association and Quakers more generally.

Yet Papunhank never became a Quaker. For several years, he kept his denominational options open in order to operate in a syncretic middle ground, the better to employ both Moravians and Quakers as pillars of support.[14] In his willingness to incorporate elements of Christian belief into a syncretic but fundamentally Indian cosmology, and in his skillful negotiation of distance from whites, Papunhank conformed to many aspects of the model of nativist prophecy described by Gregory Dowd, though there is less evidence for an interest in pan-Indian unity on his part than for other nativist prophets. Still, his prophecy may be seen as much as a strengthening of Delaware religion, as an accommodation to Christianity.[15] For Quakers, Papunhank's religious predilections were not an issue. They never sought to convert him, believing, along with the Quaker minister, John Woolman, that "there were children of God under all church systems," Indian as well as white.[16]

In August 1761, members of the Friendly Association traveled to Easton to attend a government council with the Indians, and again encountered Papunhank. At this council, English missionary Susannah Hatton addressed the Munsee in terms hearkening back to George Fox: "she recommended them to the inward Monitor setting forth what an excellent priviledge it was to be favoured with it, & that it was freely offered to people of All nations, Colours, & Denominations."[17] Hatton's acknowledgment of the racial politics of religious belief and the politics of councils provided an avenue for her inspiration, but as the spirit took her, the course of her message meandered. "After some time," according to one witness, "her service was turned more towards the whites, the Interpreters left off & she preached the Gospel in the demonstration of life & with authority."[18] The facility with which a sermon to the Indians transformed into a sermon to whites, with Indians barred from understanding by language and the willing silence of the interpreter, suggests that Hatton's mission to the Indians was somehow implicated in a mission to whites. Hatton slipped between systems of meaning and (through the translator) through linguistic systems, but her message was said by Quakers to find its mark on both audiences. The message was so affecting to whites that even the "Governour acknowledged . . . it was the truth," and when Hatton circulated among the Indians at the end, shaking hands in Quakerly fashion, the Indians were said to be "much affected & wept exceedingly . . . [she] owning to them as our brethren and sisters, she said they were so by creation, and trusted some of them would be so by regeneration."[19] At some level, both Indian and white audiences experienced an isometry of response, a renewal of the direct experience of the divine that Quakers considered the hallmark of their religion: whatever they heard, both Indians and whites responded with emotion, and whatever else she intended, Hatton clearly intended her message for both.

Regeneration, however, would have to wait. When Pontiac's War ignited the region from Detroit to Pennsylvania in 1763, the Friendly Association found itself in a dire predicament. Non-Quakers assailed the Friends for their pacifism, their motives, and their fitness for public office, and criticized them not only for ignoring Indian cruelty, but also for aiding and abetting it.[20] A nearly apoplectic David Dove harangued the Quakers for their "gross partiality to Indians":[21]

> When their King and Country call them to Arms, they plead Conscience, and will tell thee, with a pious Air, and meek Countenance, "they would rather perish by the Sword than use it against the Enemies of the State"—But if any of their Fellow Subjects become obnoxious to their mild and peaceful Rage, by opposing any of their arbitrary Measures, we see the Quaker unmask'd, with his Gun upon his Shoulder, and other warlike Habiliments, eagerly desiring the Combat, and thirsting for the Blood of those his Opponents.[22]

Saved from the Indians by the Paxtons, Dove argued, Quakers rewarded their saviors by taking arms against them. "No Excommunications now for taking up Arms!" he intoned sarcastically, "Behold the Meeting-House converted into a Place of Arms!"[23] Already accused of stalling the war effort, the Quaker assemblymen were accused of hypocrisy and virtually of treason. Members of the Friendly Association felt the pressure intensely. At the height of the trouble, Israel Pemberton complained that it was "very unpopular to say the least in fav[or] of ye Indians cause," and even while recognizing that the Indians were clearly in "defence of their Country," he advised the Friendly Association that "silence is safest when we cannot be Instrumental for good."[24] By 1765, the Association had lapsed into dormancy and most religious Quakers had withdrawn from public office, concentrating on the purification of their Society and the strengthening and disciplining of their increasingly insular culture and religion.

Quaker writers, however, did not surrender their pens. With vigor, they engaged in an innovative historiography, valorizing Quakerly treatment of Indians. Characteristically, they opted not to overlook improprieties in their past conduct, but rather they crafted an image of a saintly and just William Penn, uniformly fair in his dealings with Indians, to use as a spiritual cudgel against the Proprietary party and as a goad to purification. Typical of Quaker revisionist historians was Halliday Jackson, a writer and missionary to the Seneca, who argued that the corruption of Quaker commerce with Indians occurred only after Friends had become "mostly excluded from the proprietory agency to which the management of Indian affairs had been chiefly committed," an unintended, but felicitous double entendre.[25] In this view, relations with Indians in Pennsylvania soured only after Quakers were deprived of political power. Confessing to wrongs such as the Walking Purchase of 1737, Quakers pointed to their attempts at atonement, and argued that the abiding love between Indians and their "Brothers Onas" and the consistency of Quakerly justice were models of the political success of pacifism. In their contrition, Quakerly misdeeds, as well as Quakerly justice, distinguished them from their political adversaries.

Few outside the Society were persuaded, and during the two decades that followed, things deteriorated further for Quakers in public life in Pennsylvania. While Quakers were criticized during the French and Indian War and their influence on provincial affairs waned, the Revolution was calamitous. During the Revolution the membership bled, as non-pacifists were disowned (expelled) or left of their own accord, and Friends suffered schism in the form of the non-pacifist Free Quakers.[26] Worse, many observant Friends who survived the revolutionary violence and intimidation with their lives intact found themselves in the 1780s with their finances shattered and their political power virtually extinguished. It is no coincidence that the most enduring images of Quakers during the Revolution are those who left the church to fight (e.g. Nathanael Greene, Josiah Harmar) or those who were exiled from Philadelphia and imprisoned, their estates confiscated. At this political, social, and religious nadir, Quakers began to escalate their efforts on the behalf of Indians, finding in Indians a means of reconstituting a vestige of social and political power, of establishing a formal role for themselves and their Society in the new American public sphere, and at the same time, finding a way to further the revitalization of their Society.

In 1784, Anthony Benezet recalled the memory of Papunhank while discussing the American massacre of the Moravian Indians at Gnadenhutten in March, 1782.

"We cry out against Indian cruelty" he wrote, "but is any thing which Indians have done (all circumstances considered) more inconsistent with justice, reason, and humanity, than the murder of those Moravian Indians; a peaceable, innocent people, whose conduct, even when under the scalping-knife, evidenced a dependence on Divine Help for support, as much becoming Christians, as their sufferings in support of their religious principles, and their fidelity to the government had before manifested them to be our special friends."[27] In reflecting on Indians, Benezet saw a mirror of the Quakers themselves: a spiritually committed people dispossessed of power, wronged by an aggressive new government from which they were excluded. In Indians, he found a voice for Quakers in the new American Republic.

THE BEGINNINGS OF QUAKER MISSIONS

In 1790, the Seneca chief, Cornplanter, visited Philadelphia to convene directly with George Washington, and in the process, incidentally initiated a new, formal phase of Quaker involvement in Indian affairs. During the visit, Washington suggested that the Quakers might be willing to assist the Senecas in learning "good habits," by providing teachers and other support. A skilled diplomat, wielding the threat of warfare should negotiations break down, Cornplanter pursued every avenue that promised the retention of their lands and autonomy, and in May 1791, he wrote the Philadelphia Yearly Meeting for educational and technological assistance.[28] The Meeting quickly agreed. Following a well-established pattern of personal exchange, they offered to support three Seneca boys in Philadelphia to teach them to read, write, and become conversant in white culture. The presence of Cornplanter's son, Henry O'Bail, among the three suggests the importance attached to this exchange.[29]

But as in the 1750s, it was the Midwestern military crisis that catalyzed a more profound reaction, this time resulting in an institutional response by Friends that had a broader and longer lasting impact than any exchange. The hostilities in Ohio in 1791 delayed the Quaker response to Cornplanter, and by the time the Meeting was prepared to act, the federal government had already appointed a non-Quaker, Waterman Baldwin, to teach among the Senecas. Persistent, the Quakers continued to send representatives as semiofficial observers to Indian councils, as they had often done in the past, and they remained active, and mostly ineffective, in petitioning the government for justice in treating with the Indians.

What differed in the 1790s was that the Society now actively sought an *official,* governmentally sanctioned role in Indian affairs, rather than the tenuous, quasi-official advisory and monitory role they had long fulfilled, and they now responded with the full bureaucratic weight of their Yearly Meetings. As early as 1793, the Philadelphia Yearly Meeting addressed a circular letter to the Indians of the northwest to encourage industry, sobriety, sedentary agriculture, and peace, and to inquire whether any nations or tribes wished assistance in attaining these goals. In line with their new approach, Friends issued the circular only after obtaining the endorsement of Secretary of State Timothy Pickering, a copy of which was prominently appended.

While awaiting response, the Yearly Meeting labored steadily. In September 1795, in bureaucratic fashion, they established a permanent committee within the Yearly Meeting to oversee Quaker relations with Indians—their first structural response to Indian affairs. Comprised in part of former members of the Friendly Association, this committee immediately began to raise funds for "missions" to the Indians, and sought federal support for the project of "civilization." Quaker lobbyists, including Warner Mifflin, were sent to apprise Pickering, Washington, and other politicians of their intentions and to drum up support. Just as significantly, the Committee began to lobby other Yearly Meetings to take up the cause of Indian rights. As paradigmatic members of the circum-Atlantic community—with ties of kinship, commerce, and creed throughout the Atlantic world—the project was eventually extended into nearly every corner of the globe darkened by British or American imperial influence.[30]

From the outset, whether by plan or happenstance Quakers pursued two different tacks in assisting Indians: one seeking formal ties with the federal government and using public finances, the other seeking federal approval, but neither money nor oversight.[31] Whether acting as agents of the government or independently, Friends took pains to ensure that the government was aware of, supported, and acknowledged their efforts.

The first response to the Friends' circular letter of 1793 came from the Oneida, Stockbridge, and Brotherton Indians, many of whom were thought by Quakers to be far along in their "advanced towards civilization," thanks to the labors of Presbyterian missionaries.[32] After conferring with the Oneidas at the Treaty of Canandaigua in 1794 and confirming that they retained the support of the secretary of state and superintendent of Indian affairs, the Quakers opened a mission in March 1796.[33]

Although short-lived, the Oneida mission was significant in formulating a model for nearly all of the later missionary efforts of Quakers. Consistent with their belief that "God speaks to all men regardless of outward religion," they eschewed openly seeking converts, and to a degree, even proved tolerant of Indian religious beliefs.[34] Their "great object," according to a letter of support written by Timothy Pickering, was not "to teach peculiar doctrines, but useful practices": instead of sowing religious seeds, they sowed seeds of grain, issued tools and farming implements, established model farms, provided instruction in the agricultural and manual arts (blacksmithing and carpentry for men; spinning, weaving, and knitting for women), and taught academic skills such as reading and writing in English.[35] Young Oneida men were selected to reside with Friends on their model farm for six months to learn farming. Providing room and board, the Quakers expected the men to work five days a week and to conform to a routine of temperance, punctuality, and diligence, and at the end of the period, they were provided with "stuff for one cloth coat, 2 shirts, one pair cloth leggons, 5 bushels of wheat, 10 bushels of potatoes," along with other goods, if they continued to practice what they had learned after they had returned to the reservation.[36] Some children, boys as well as girls, were brought to Philadelphia for even more intensive, more controlled, schooling.

The Oneidas, however, were highly selective in what they chose to adopt from the Quakers. Men and women readily accepted some aspects of the program, but rejected others outright, and dithered on yet others. Many men subscribed to Quakerly pleas for temperance and strong marital bonds, but an equally large number resisted working in the smithy, dodged school, or refused to learn English. Women took readily to learning certain domestic skills, such as spinning and weaving, but along with many men, many resisted the Quakers' plans to move men into the fields and women out. In 1798, the Oneida could find only one young man willing "to come out of his own mind to learn farming," the others, the chiefs reported were "gone out fishing."[37]

While the missionaries reported steady progress, they failed to achieve one of their primary goals, to instill the idea of "distinct property," and they labored under the burden of a "manifest coldness and inattention" from some suspicious Oneidas, along with the "ungrateful whispering" that the Quakers intended to take Oneida lands.[38] Under the circumstances, the missionaries withdrew, arguing self-servingly that they had left the Oneidas in a condition in which they were now able to assist themselves.[39]

In the Midwest, Quaker missions followed the officially sanctioned course, perhaps because of the fearful realities of life in the Midwest.[40] Even after Fallen Timbers had demonstrated the lack of British resolve to assist their Indian "allies," the Midwest remained a volatile place. The fear of Catholic conspiracy in the Mississippi and Ohio valleys in 1795–96 left the Washington administration cringing at the prospect of renewed Indian resistance, and as the specter of Victor Collot stalked the frontier and Jacobins skulked in Louisiana, nervous military commanders alerted Secretary of War James McHenry that at Niagara, the French were "insinuating themselves among the Indians to prevail on them to act both against the British and Americans," that the Spanish "had sent agents into all the Indian nations," and that the Baron de Carondelet had invited the Indians to prepare for a joint French-Spanish war against the Americans and British.[41]

With such uncertainty looming, the federal government eagerly authorized the Quakers, Moravians, and Presbyterians to carry missions to the Indians in the hope of pacifying and stabilizing the region. In 1802, William Kirk, of the Baltimore Yearly Meeting, established a mission to the Shawnees and Wyandots in Indiana, receiving money, equipment, and supplies directly from the federal government for distribution. Kirk's mission proved an immediate but expensive success. Old Smoke, Black Hoof, and other accommodationist Shawnee chiefs welcomed the Quakers as bolsters to their authority in their internecine struggles with nativist chiefs, such as Tenskwatawa and Tecumseh.[42] Equally important, the Quakers promised to be useful in the intermediary role they set for themselves, interceding on the Shawnees' behalf to ensure the receipt of annuities, which they were owed. "The Quakers," they asked pointedly in one letter, "I hope you will pay attention to this my speech as you promice and when you receive it take it to our Father the President and Secretary of War and have everything put straight."[43] Shoring up the political aims of one faction of Shawnee chiefs and providing material benefits for the people in the form of tools, food, and services, Quaker popularity was ensured.

Unfortunately for the mission, the divisions among the Shawnees made Kirk's activities just as unpopular with some chiefs as they were popular with others, and divisions among federal representatives proved even more troublesome. Kirk earned the particular enmity of the Indian agent and would-be power broker, William Wells, who viewed the Quakers as infringing on his base of power. Although John Johnston, a rival of Wells's, reported that the Shawnees were "very solicitous to have the settlement continued, the mills completed, and Mr. Kirk to return and reside with them"—adding that "the settlement bears the marks of industry and on the whole does him much credit"—Wells's creative attacks and masterful rumor mongering damaged Kirk's reputation.[44] The news that Kirk had contracted a "disease the ofspring of vice," for example, had spread so far that Johnston found it necessary to protest to his superiors that it was "totally without foundation."[45]

The Shawnee chiefs, too, pressed the relationship with Kirk to the hilt. In May 1809, they rejected the Quaker offer assistance "on account as they say of Friends not furnishing Horses to work as well as men." The agent at Fort Wayne, however, suggested that Shawnee dissatisfaction could be traced to another Wells rumor. "The real cause," he asserted, was the report, "industriously spread," that Friends were "paid for their services, out of a grant made by Government to the Indians, and that this has been the case from the commencement of their labours in this country."[46] None of Kirk's protestations to the contrary quelled Shawnee suspicion.

The situation had deteriorated far enough by January 1809, that Secretary of War Henry Dearborn relayed word through the Stockbridge emissary, Hendrick Aupaumut, that Wells was to be superseded.[47] But this heartening news proved cold comfort to the Quakers. The combination of Wells's disinformation and Kirk's poor accounting and overexpenditure had taken its toll. Kirk was dismissed. For a decade thereafter, Quaker involvement with the Shawnees lay dormant.[48]

MISSIONS TO THE SENECA

In 1798, when the Indian Committee of the Philadelphia Yearly Meeting finally returned to the Allegany Senecas, they used their experiences among the Oneidas, rather than the Shawnees, as a model, obtaining government approval, but rejecting financial or diplomatic support. In fact, en route to visit the Senecas for the first time, the first missionaries obtained *two* additional letters of support from James Wilkinson, military commander in Pittsburgh, one addressed to whites, the other to the Senecas.[49]

The centerpiece of the Quaker program remained an initial disbursal of tools and farming implements, a combination of vocational and academic education, and the establishment of a grist mill and model farm—located initially at Genesinguhta, up river from Cornplanter's town, and later at Tunesassa on land adjacent to the Allegany reservation purchased by the Quakers from the Holland Land Company.

The missionaries presented themselves as role models for Quaker principles, for what, in a myopic way, they felt ought to define the future for the Senecas, should the Senecas agree. Through example and exhortation, they urged the Senecas to indus-try, private property, sobriety, strong marital bonds, and a stronger nuclear family; they wanted to end spousal violence, and spark a shift toward patriarchal, rather than matriarchal, relations within the marriage, family, and society. As they had at Oneida, they also preached self-sufficiency among the Senecas or, in other words, sought to avoid Seneca dependence upon external aid from any source. They agreed, for instance, to have a plough made at Niagara only if the Senecas retrieved it them-selves, adding "we did not expect to do much for them but would do a little and then they must help themselves."[50] Similarly, John Pierce informed the Senecas in 1801 that the Quaker brought along to teach blacksmithing would rather teach the Seneca men "how to do it for themselves, so that when he [the smith] should go away they might be able to do their own smith work without being beholden to any body."[51]

As frequently noted, the Quaker program was strongly marked by white pre-conceptions about the proper ordering of gender relations. Women were instructed primarily in domestic skills, while (in contrast to normative Seneca patterns) men were taught farming, and the social transformations unleashed by changes in agri-cultural practices had dire consequences for women in Seneca society.[52] In a gender system traditionally predicated on a complementarity of men's and women's roles, in a culture in which women were responsible for the bulk of food production, and in which strong social and religious values were attached to agriculture, the Quaker plan to remove women from work in the fields entailed a comprehensive shift in women's social roles. Ironically, the Quakers, known in white society for relatively egalitarian views on gender, catalyzed a shift in Seneca gender relations toward increased inequality. Quaker adherence to concepts of private property, the nuclear family, and patriarchy promised to change Seneca culture just as dramatically.

Yet in practice, Seneca men and women were as highly selective in what they chose to adopt from the Quakers as the Oneidas had been, rejecting or resisting ele-ments of Quaker teaching they found unpalatable. While they readily took an inter-est in animal husbandry and in Quaker vocational schools (taught in the Seneca language), the academic school languished, and there was strong and effective resistance to notions of private ownership of land. It would be a mistake to attribute too much influence to the Quaker missionaries, or to acknowledge too little agency among Seneca men and women.[53]

For their part, Quakers performed their most tangible service for the Senecas as mediators and allies in their struggle with the Ogden Land. The Treaty of Canandaigua had ostensibly guaranteed the Senecas undisturbed sovereignty over their remaining lands, which were distributed in two large reservations near centers of white population—Buffalo Creek and Tonawanda—and several smaller, more remote, less valuable reservations, including Cattaraugus and Allegany, on which Cornplanter resided. So it stood on paper. But after acquiring preemption rights from the Holland Land Company in 1810, the aggressive Ogden Land Company tried every avenue available, from bribery to coercion, lures to threats, patient persuasion to belligerent lies, to evict the Senecas from their lands.

The primary means to achieving this end was mapped out by Thomas Ludlow Ogden, the legal mind behind the Company. Ogden's strategy relied upon the assertion that the Senecas held the land by "*Possession* merely" and, therefore, had no right to transfer title to anyone other than David A. Ogden, the owner of preemption rights and thus "the legal Proprietor."[54] Having asserted this "fact," the Ogdens laid out a host of reasons why the Senecas should remove, dandling forth the claim that the president wished them to do so, that they had heard him exclaim "that the *Hunter* must yield to the *Civilized* State; and that the existence of Indian Tribes in their collective or national character in the midst of White Population, is inconsistent with the Interests of both." The president, the Ogdens added, had "*gratuitously* offered" them a sizable tract on the Arkansas River, "where the Lands are good and the Climate fine, with the option however of locating elsewhere if more agreeable." In the world of the Ogdens, the Senecas would find a new world at the west, better than the old, with the promise of removing yet again if they should wish to do so.

The Ogdens paired such inducements with visions of the evils that might befall the Seneca should they remain in New York. It was "a melancholy Fact," they noted, that near Buffalo, where the Senecas came into closest contact with whites, they had become "more depraved" than any other Indians. "They have lost the virtues of the Savage State and have adopted all the low vices of our lowest Classes of Society. Their Men are Drunkards and their Women Prostitutes."[55] The reservations at Buffalo Creek and Tonawanda produced the greatest debauchery, according to the Ogdens, and even relatively remote Cattaraugus and Allegany would eventually descend to the depths, given enough time.

Alternatives were available. Legally, the Ogdens insisted, the Indians had only two choices: to leave voluntarily for the west, selling their lands only to the Ogden

Land Company, or degrade themselves in New York. In the interests of humanity, the Ogdens advised the former course, but offered a compromise: "to concentrate them on one of the reservations they now occupy."[56] At Allegany, one of the smaller and least valuable reservations, the Senecas could remain far from whites, and be ministered to and administered more efficiently. There, according the Thomas Ludlow Ogden, "the Efforts of the Pious and Benevolent may be advantageously exerted and a fair Experiment will thus be made of the Practicability of imparting to this unhappy Race the Benefits of Christianity and Civilization."[57]

This apparent overture to the Quakers (among other missionaries) suggests one of the faces the Ogdens presented to their white opponents, that of the concerned fellow-laborer in the good works of mankind. When cajoling and reasoning failed to bring the Quakers and other missionaries to their point of view, however, the Ogdens did everything possible to cow or bowl over the opposition, and they became particularly irate at Quaker truculence. In 1819, Thomas Ogden advised David to have "caution & reserve" in his discussions with the Friends: "Their rule is to hear everything and to commit themselves to nothing."[58]

As a body, the Quakers continued to aid the Senecas in resisting the Ogdens' efforts for decades. On the surface, the Ogdens' strategy of identifying the evils that might befall the Indians in contact with whites seemed promising, for these were precisely the evils that Quakers recognized in American society, and precisely those that they worked to expunge from their ranks. But in adopting this line, the Ogdens merely reinforced the Quakers' sense of a need for self-purification by *staving off* white society, including the Ogdens, facing the evil, yet standing apart. During the 1790s, the Quakers were increasingly identifying themselves in opposition to mainstream society while striving to create and maintain their own unique identity, and the Ogdens were inadvertently providing the Quakers with more reason to do so. After a bitter struggle of almost thirty years, the Ogdens finally managed to snare some of the most valuable Seneca lands, but the resistance of the Seneca, aided by the Quakers, enabled the majority of Senecas to remain in New York on lands that had traditionally been their own.

The mutuality of support between Quakers and Seneca was not easily won. Entering the Allegany Reservation, at a time when rivalry was developing between Cornplanter and Handsome Lake for political primacy, the Quakers nimbly sidestepped committing firmly to either faction. In retrospect, the success of their missionary program sprang largely from the isometry of Quaker notions of Seneca progress with Handsome Lake's own program for religious and social renewal. Handsome Lake's teachings and prophetic career have been so thoroughly mapped by Anthony F. C. Wallace and later historians as to require no further expansion here, except to recall that his teachings shared a great deal in common with the Quaker program, including admonitions against the use of alcohol, an emphasis on the nuclear family and patriarchy, and sedentary agriculture. Above all, it was his ability to appropriate (or independently derive) such Quaker concepts and add to and redefine them in Seneca terms that made the Quaker program available and palatable to the majority of Senecas. Thus, paradoxically, it was the revitalization of Seneca religion that triggered the success of the Quaker missionary program.

The interaction of a self-catalyzed Seneca religious renewal and a similar process taking place among Quakers, was not coincidental. Both Quakers and Seneca engaged in a process of religiously inspired self-renewal, which was partly, but not wholly, "nativistic" in orientation; in both cases, renewal encompassed as much innovation and adaptation as it did a return to traditional belief. Handsome Lake, for example, introduced ideas of divine judgment, heaven, and hell into Seneca religion, but did not significantly alter the traditional ritual calendar. On the Quaker side, the increased importance attached during the last decades of the eighteenth century to the peace testimony, endogamy, and to Quakerly dress and speech are, if not innovations, at least a significant intensification of existing Quakerly practice. For both Senecas and Quakers, doctrinal and social innovation was framed within a traditional religious language, making it palatable to a wide range of people, though no less revolutionary. For those involved, the respective revivals spurred one another, neither inspiring the other, but operating as co-facilitators, fellow travelers, kindred spirits.

REFLEXIVE MISSIONS

Given the reception of the Quaker program among the Senecas—a pastiche of acceptance and rejection, with religious conversion a non-issue—one might inquire what it was that these missionaries gained for their efforts. While some, like Jacob Taylor, Joel Swayne, or Joseph Elkinton, lived for years at Genesinguhta and Tunesassa earning a livelihood and calling, many others, like Isaac Bonsall, John Pierce, John Philips, or William Allinson, ventured among the Senecas only for brief periods. In discussing individuals like Bonsall or Allinson, not to mention the many other men and women Quaker missionaries, historians have focused almost exclusively on the (brief) period of their lives spent among Indians, and in so doing, have potentially missed out on the meaning of these visits within the contexts of Quaker lives, and overlooked an opportunity to explore the dynamics of the missionary endeavor.

In 1803, the Philadelphia Yearly Meeting elected to relocate its model farm away from Genesinguhta, to distance themselves from the tension growing between Cornplanter and Handsome Lake, and purchased almost 700 acres of the Holland Land Company for the new site. Isaac Bonsall, a member of Uwchlan Meeting near Philadelphia and a weighty figure on the Indian Committee, was appointed to the committee dispatched to report on the reservations at Allegany, Cattaraugus, and Tonawanda. During this trip, Bonsall carefully recorded his observations for the Yearly Meeting in a journal, yet significantly, his report on the Seneca occupies fewer than half of the pages. The other half is consumed by discussions of visits among Quakers in Ohio. On the trip to and from Allegany, Bonsall's delegation visited dozens of meetings and hundreds of Quakers, revivifying the social, religious, and cultural networks that had been strained by distance and time.

After leaving Cattaraugus, Bonsall and Nicholas Waln, Jr., parted from their associates and proceeded to Ohio to visit the sixty families at Middleton meeting, where he enjoyed "an open time of communication." This was followed by a trip to Springfield meeting (twelve families where "the Gospel Spring was much closed up"), to Mahoning (five families whom Bonsall encouraged "to attend to that which would make up to them the loss of friends and otherwise bless them"), to Joshua Dickson's house for a meeting with six people, to New Garden (fifty families), Middleton Monthly, Salem (thirty families), Cross Creek (nine families), and meeting after meeting thereafter. Near the end of October at Short Creek, Bonsall visited the family of his deceased wife Mary, and on 2 November, he visited his own brother Edward near the aptly named Plainfield.[59]

Bonsall's and Waln's tour was not merely social. At Miami Monthly Meeting on 13 November, Bonsall "had sundry things to offer relative to the design of Meetings for Descipline and the benefit resulting from a due regard being had to the rules and regulations adopted by the Society." Later, he turned to secular matters, conferring with members of four monthly meetings to draft a petition opposing the state's militia law on the grounds that it violated their constitutionally protected right to freedom of conscience.[60] Continuing to the Great Miami River, Bonsall approvingly noted how some southern Quakers had removed to the Ohio Valley to avoid the taint of slavery, suggesting that "they had been brought from that Land of Darkness to this of greater liberty and freedom by the same power that caused Israel to leave Egypt for the Land of promise and wished them not to do as Israel had done to sing the Lords praise on the banks of Deliverance and afterward forget his Works."[61] In relocating to Ohio, the southerners had fulfilled the will of God, confirmed their moral worth, and demonstrated zeal for their faith.

At each stop, Bonsall carefully recorded the spiritual state of the meetings he attended, whether they were "open" (to the light) or "closed," zealous or lax, whether the people were prepared or unprepared. At Waynesville, he measured an astoundingly large buttonwood tree, 43 feet in circumference, and attended a meeting at which he criticized the minds of the people as "too much outward," prompting him to admonish them "to promote a more deeply inward attention to that which would make them more solid and give them the essence of Religion."[62]

In short, throughout his travels, Bonsall engaged in an uninterrupted series of visitations with Friends and an active effort to protect, restore, purify, and revitalize Quakerism, Quakerly discipline, and Quakerly social and family relations on the frontier, where it was most threatened by geographic mobility and social atomism. His careful attention to statistics—recording the number who attended meetings, the size of trees, and the productivity of the fields—his notes on the spiritual openings and closures at meetings, and his participation in meetings for discipline and support for secular, legal, and political issues involving Quakers all suggest how intensely he was involved in the project of missionizing to the Society itself. As an outgrowth of missionizing the Indians, Quakers renewed themselves and their communities and ritually re-incorporated isolated members scattered far from the nerve center in Philadelphia in a perambulation of the Quaker ambit.

Nor was Bonsall unique in the self-consciously reflexive objective of his mission. The delegations sent by the Yearly Meeting typically included a mix of energetic young missionaries and those with experience as traveling ministers to Quaker meetings. Thus, the first delegation to the Senecas in 1798 included "two of the Ancients of the congregation," Joshua Sharpless and John Pierce.[63] Pierce had already spent time among the Oneida, while Sharpless was an experienced public Friend whose first wife had preceded him as a minister. For a year before being dispatched "to assist in forming a settlement among the Indians, for their improvement in agriculture, and more of a civilized life," Sharpless engaged in an intensive round of visitations to meetings in New Jersey, monitoring their spiritual state, encouraging Quakerly discipline and practice.[64]

Such a balance between ministry to Indians and to Quakers was almost always struck, even for individual missionaries. When sent to the Senecas in 1801 to engage in discussions with Handsome Lake and Cornplanter, Pierce also sent explicitly "under a prospect of meeting some of the friends in Upper Cannada; and joining them in a visit to friends in that Country"—the importance of his role with the Senecas did not preclude visitation to northern Friends.[65] In terms that echo Bonsall, Pierce recorded attending "solid" meetings, and exhorting Friends to heed "the necessity of nearer acquaintance with, and more faithful adherence to the gift of divine grace in the heart." Just as important, he served to adjudicate both a dispute over a new meeting house at Black Creek and over the proper disciplining of a wayward youth in Pelham Monthly Meeting, a meeting he found "much out of order."[66] Like Bonsall, Pierce was both disciplinarian and meta-disciplinarian, concerned as much with structuring the discipline of the meeting as disciplining its youth.

As the missions became better established, the network of relations they helped establish grew increasingly complex and served to further the ties the missionaries sought to foster. Thus Joseph Elkinton, who was to become a long-term teacher at Tunesassa, consulted at length with Bonsall before undertaking his work, and Philips relied upon the translating skills of missionary Jacob Taylor when he arrived at Tunesassa. On one occasion, William Allinson reported that he and Thomas Stewardson were shown to quarters near Catawissa Creek at the house of Benjamin Sharpless, who was not only the relative of missionary, Joshua Sharpless, but the brother-in-law of Isaac Bonsall.[67]

Nor was it surprising to find John Philips traveling with Bonsall in 1806, stopping off to visit Pierce, and using the occasion to contemplate the meaning of missions and the frontier in Quaker experience. After staying at the isolated farmhouse of Quakers John and Mary Bell one night, and visiting Pierce and the family of Francis and Mary King the next, Philips attended a religious meeting. In the silence of meeting, he was overwhelmed with a sense of spiritual and emotional isolation. Mary Bell had had to travel three miles on foot to attend, having no horse to carry her, and although the meeting seemed "a Dull time" at first, Mary's words brought home the importance of ministry to Quakers. Some Quakers, she said, "were in the Wilderness in Every Respect," spawning a wave of "great simpathy" in Philips for the children of Francis and Mary King, who faced the double threat of spiritual and geographic isolation. Despite Bonsall's best efforts, Philips concluded "upon the whole I Could not believe their settled there was in Divine wisdom."[68]

For most, however, the missionary circuit was a gathering experience, a revival of faith and a reincorporation of the distant members of the Society into the community and under the disciplinary scrutiny of the Meeting. Halliday Jackson, one of the most influential of all Quaker missionaries, represented this symbolically in his highly crafted narrative of his first journey to the Senecas in 1798. Jackson chose to frame his journey with accounts of attending Quaker weddings in the wilderness. On the way to Jenechshadago, he and his companions attended the meeting and "put our names to the writeing," joining in the consensus of the meeting that both endorsed and authorized the wedding as valid, and he concluded his narrative with his return home to discover that his "kinsman," Jacob, had married, with Jackson taking part in the wedding feast.[69] Quaker weddings, in particular, are of the community, approved by the consent of all members attending the meeting, and—increasingly at the turn of the nineteenth century—carefully monitored.

While the wedding was an apt metaphor for Jackson, it formed an ironic contrast with the life of William Allinson, whose experiences reveal yet another facet of Quaker missionary activity. Allinson's dealings with Indians contain striking parallels with Bonsall, Pierce, Jackson et al., but the insight provided by his diary reveals that Allinson's odyssey was internal, personal, and spiritual as much as it was external and social. The disciplining and purification of Quakerism was waged internally as well as externally, and the struggle to renew the Society from within occupied as much of Allinson's time as his struggle with the challenges of constructing a religious life in the new Republic.

An elder in the Burlington Meeting, and a member of a family that spawned a number of religiously motivated social reformers, Allinson's business pursuits often took back seat to his regular round of visits to adjoining meetings, to attendance at monthly and yearly meetings, and to his duties as a supporter of the Westtown School—not merely an educational institution, but an institution dedicated to the transmission of Quaker ideals.[70] On numerous occasions, Allinson was called upon to approach members of the Society who deviated from the discipline of the meeting or who were lax in attendance. He was remembered by his sister as a man devoted to Quakerly testimonies, and as "a useful member in Meetings for discipline, dear in discernment and clothed with Christian Charity in treating with Offenders—yet firm and uncompromising when the honour of the cause of Truth was at stake."[71]

Allinson, who so often served as the disciplinary arm of the Society, also looked outward. He was an ardent abolitionist, a temperance advocate; and, on numerous occasions, he visited local African American families, regardless of denomination, not to convert them, but "with a view to assist, Encourage, & as ability might be afforded, advise." In a typical instance, he tended to a black man suffering from whites, though the man was a professed member of the Methodist church.[72] In Quaker spiritual geography, to search outward in charity was to search inward in discipline.

In March 1805, Allinson and two colleagues were sent on one of these charitable missions to the local prison to assist the Stockbridge Indian chief, Hendrick Aupaumut, imprisoned for a debt of $34. Upon interviewing Aupaumut, Allinson and his two associates agreed to cover the debt, "but deferd it for more enquiry." At the same time, they agreed to secure the release of an African American man accused of stealing a gallon of molasses. "Such Business affords an Opp[ortunit]y of seeing the Difference in Mankind . . . ," he wrote, "We are all Brethren by creation & if we are endeavouring to keep alive in the Truth which is pure, peaceable, easy to be entreated, full of Love & good Fruits we shall on such occasions be led to enquire & conclude in the secret of our own minds, 'who made thee to differ from another, or what hast thou that thou hast not received?'"[73] In Aupaumut, Allinson may well have recognized an affinity at another level. Both Aupaumut and the Quakers sought to establish themselves as promethean figures in an effort at self-perpetuation. The Stockbridges were metic figures among the Oneidas with whom they lived, and Aupaumut did his best to parlay this status into a role for himself as intercultural broker, just as the Quakers were attempting to do.

When Allinson returned to prison the next day, he found Aupaumut "pleasant & conversable," and his visit was enlivened with stories of Aupaumut's embassy to the western Indians in 1803. After his release was secured, Aupaumut regaled Allinson with a particularly pointed story of an Indian man he had met at the west:

An Indian Hunting about 50 miles from their settlemt saw at the root of a large Tree which was blown up something like a Plant of Indian Corn & taking care of it thro the season he was rewarded in the fall with 3 fine Ears which were carried to their settlemt & proving to be a kind entirely new to them & finer than they before had, a council was held over them where the seed could come from—in which it was concluded that the Good Spirit had sent it for the Indians benefit, whereupon it was decreed that those 3 Ears should be planted & tended by their choisest & best Young Women which being done & the crop produced very good it was distributed to the Different Families & neighbouring Tribes & they now have it in great Plenty.[74]

Whether Allinson recognized the significance within the Indian symbolic universe of the number three (possibly referring to the "three sisters" of corn, squash, and beans) or of enjoining women to tend to the care of the food crops, Aupaumut's story of renewal struck Allinson so forcefully that he (uncharacteristically) recorded it at length.

Nor did Allinson's interest wane as the stories of renewal continued that supper. That evening, Aupaumut related what he had heard of three prophets—a Shawnee man, a Seneca man, and a Delaware woman—each of whom represented a story of Indian revitalization, mixing various degrees of Christianity with Native religions. The first account involved a "seriously disposd" Shawnee man who had "for some years withdrawn much from the society of the other Indians."

one morn[in]g according to his accustomed practice he rose & set out toward his Hunting Ground where he had a Cabbin at which he spent much time—but on the way was arrested with extreme sickness & puking of Blood—in this situation he appeard to himself to expire & then to be carried to the Upper Regions—here he was told to take a view of his past life—which on doing he found he could see clearly the Various Periods & transactions—he was then led to look at his Nation, the Indians of the Shawanees Tribe, & to extend his View to past ages—he did so & all appeard plain—their antient warriors, Chiefs, & noted men some of whom had been dead for One Hundred Years, yet whose names had been handed down by tradition, passd in review before him and their Crimes appeard great & dreadful to behold as did those also of the present Generation, particularly their Drunkenness—he was told that for all this Wickedness they should be cut off & their Tribe become extinct if they did not repent & amend—having lain in this situation from morng till near night, he was permitted to return to the Body, but the Vision remained fresh on his mind & very Impressive—when he returnd to the Town he informd the Indians what he had seen & been told respecting them—some treated it lightly, but his Words were so effectual with many that they entirely refraind from Drinking & numbers of these Hendrick said continue their Integrity & live sober religious lives.[75]

Aupaumut had also heard of a Seneca prophet (possibly Handsome Lake) and a Delaware woman prophet who

> was taken Ill & as her Friends thought, Died, & when they were assembled to bury her she rose up & told her Husband that she was permitted to return to Life to communicate something to him which she wishd to do before but could not—it was that when she was buried he must take the care of their Children himself to bring them up, & not, according to the Indian Custom, commit them to her female relatives without further thought of them himself—she impressd the same also upon her said Relatives & they with her Husband promisd that it should be so—she then told him that he must leave off Drinking & become religious—that when the Days of mourning for her were ended he must remove with his Children to the Moravian settlement (which was some miles distant from thence) & join the Moravians— there live in religious fellowship with them & bring up their children in the same way—to all which Hendrick said he was obedient.[76]

There is a certain irony in hearing Aupaumut, caricatured as the quintessential accommodationist, relaying stories that bear the hallmarks of nativist prophecy to a man engaging in a parallel effort at accommodationism, though coming from the other side of the power spectrum. The black drink purgative in the Shawnee prophet's story, the prophet's dissolute past, and the visit to world of the dead in a place reminiscent of hell are all common elements. The message conveyed by the Delaware woman bears a surprising similarity to the teachings of Handsome Lake, particularly in its emphasis on switching from matriarchal to patriarchal relations and from extended to nuclear family. But while the irony of Aupaumut's situation was undoubtedly lost on Allinson, there is no doubt that he grasped the central message of cultural preservation through religious renewal. Looking at Aupaumut, Allinson was impressed. "Those things he [Aupaumut] related in a solid manner as if he believd they were designd in mercy for the awakening & reclaiming the Indians."[77]

What impressed Allinson most in the Indians whom he visited—in prison, in Philadelphia, or in Allegany—and what he most longed to find in his own meetings, was their spiritual vitality and spiritual discipline. In his own life he found ample reason for concern on these points. In terms that echo Bonsall's reports of meetings in Ohio, for example, Allinson excoriated the young men of Byberry for being "like

Bullocks unaccustomed to the yoke," and closer to home, his brothers James and John seemed to teeter on the brink of succumbing to the lures of worldly dress and comportment. Allinson was led to confront his brothers on several occasions regarding their "increasing Deviations in dress & Pursuits," and he concluded that Samuel was "in great Danger of being carried away by the Prince of the Power of the air."[78]

Yet Allinson's greatest challenge in spiritual self-discipline lay still closer than his Society or family: the burden of celibacy. A bachelor at thirty-eight, Allinson found his relations with women (or lack thereof) a tribulation. He could only reproach himself when "transgress[ing] the boundaries of true sobriety" in the presence of some "lively young girls," having been prompted into levity, "which wounded my Peace,"[79] and after demurring from approaching the parents of a woman for whom he had harbored feelings for over three years, he indulged in revealing self-reproach:

Alas! while writing I am ready to Despair of ever arriving here,—my strippings & Plungings must be greater than I have known, and my obedience & Faith greater than they have been, or most assuredly I never shall exceed (spiritually) the stature of a Dwarf.[80]

Allinson explained his reticence about marriage in typically Quaker terms, by saying only that he sought "internal Evidence to discover how long it is right to stand still & when it will be safe to move," and hoped that he could avoid temptation while awaiting the evidence. His struggle with loneliness and celibacy was also a struggle with his spiritual state and fears for a failure of self-discipline, and these mirrored the struggles he saw taking place in Quaker society and that he carried to the Senecas.

On the evening prior to leaving Philadelphia to visit the Senecas in 1809, Allinson found that his apprehensions for what lay in store could be assuaged only by the ministrations of his friend and spiritual confidant, George Dillwyn. Dillwyn, he wrote, "had this comfortable Language":

'They shall not go forth in haste, nor go by flight, but the Lord shall be their Reward'—this encouraging passage, respecting the chosen People, he said had been afresh brought to his remembrance and he applied it to our then expected undertaking—he also told me that when out committee were got together I might deliver them his Love & say, that 'his Heart was with the willing in Israel.' On bidding my Friends farewell they were brought very near to me and a precious Evidence accompanied that we loved another.—These feelings and Expressions arose at seasons as Encouragement, and with some comfortable experiences from time to time were as Brooks by the way, assisting to bear some trying dispensations which were permitted my cup being mingled with alloy, I hope for my Instruction and furtherance in the Christian Path.[81]

Allinson's journey to the Senecas was a metaphorical one as well as spiritual, a journey into religious trial and a spur to faith, a renewal of religious belief and Quaker social bonds. In the Seneca, he saw and hoped to mold an image of himself in reformation: temperate, industrious, peaceful, reinvigorated in faith and sense of community, and relevant to the identity and political process of the new State.

The quixotic missions of Friends were carried out neither for purely altruistic nor purely ulterior motives, but arose out of a Quaker perspective on the world of human relations, goaded by the course of national events and the maelstrom of violence in the Midwest, and impelled by the internal politics of the Society and the self. One might not wish to go so far as to argue that the Indian prophets and their religious innovations motivated the Quaker rebirth, but it seems likely that Quaker missionary activity provided a means of furthering the self-purification and renewal of the Society of Friends, while providing them with a clear identity in the public sphere of the new Republic that was tenable within their moral cosmology. At the end of the long route to the Senecas, the Quakers found a disempowered people, increasingly marginal to the mainstream of white American society, who were nevertheless struggling to purify and re-imagine themselves in spiritual and public life. As together, the Senecas and Quakers sought renewal, each led the other to themselves.

NOTES

1. I am most grateful to Jon Parmenter, Rachel Onuf, John Shy, Maceo Onuf, David Skaggs, and the archivists at the Clements Library, the Quaker Collection at Haverford College (QCHC), and the Friends Historical Library, Swarthmore, for their comments and assistance.
2. Isaac Bonsall, Journals, 1:9, American Travel Collection. William L. Clements Library (WLCL), University of Michigan, Ann Arbor.

3. *A Brief Account of the Proceedings of the Committee, Appointed in the Year 1795 by the Yearly Meeting of Friends of Pennsylvania, New-Jersey, &c. for Promoting the Improvement and Gradual Civilization of the Indian Natives* (Philadelphia: Kimber, Conrad and Co., 1805); *A Brief Account of the Proceedings of the Committee, Appointed by the Yearly Meeting of Friends Held in Baltimore for Promoting the Improvement and Civilization of the Indian Natives* (Baltimore: Cole and Hewes, 1805); Halliday Jackson, *Civilization of the Indian Natives* . . . (Philadelphia: Marcus T.C. Gould, 1830).

4. Thomas Hamm, *The Transformation of American Quakerism: Orthodox Friends, 1800–1907* (Bloomington: Indiana University Press, 1988), 8; see also David Brion Davis, *The Problem of Slavery in the Age of Revolution, 1770–1823* (Ithaca: Cornell University Press, 1975). Until the 1970s, Quaker reform was most often considered to arise out of a religiously based sense of the "likeness among all persons," however, several recent works have demonstrated the divisions within the Society over motives, the nature and pace of reform, and the degree to which the movement to purify the society from within, rather than reform, per se, might have been the real motive. Jack Marietta has offered the view that the move to purify the Society by withdrawing from the mainstream went hand in hand with an intensification in commitment to social reform: only by withdrawing from society, he suggests, could Friends obtain the necessary perspective to critique society effectively. See Marietta, "Egoism and Altruism in Quaker Abolition," *Quaker History* 81 (1993): 1–22; Jean R. Soderlund, "On Quakers and Slavery: A Reply to Jack Marietta," *Quaker History* 81 (1993): 23–27; idem., *Quakers and Slavery: A Divided Spirit* (Princeton: Princeton University Press, 1985); Gary B. Nash and Soderlund, *Freedom by Degrees: Emancipation in Pennsylvania and its Aftermath* (New York: Oxford University Press, 1991); Barry Levy, *Quakers and the American Family* (New York: Oxford University Press, 1988); Frederick B. Tolles, *Meeting House and Counting House: The Quaker Merchants of Colonial Philadelphia, 1682–1763* (New York: Norton, 1948); also useful are Richard Bauman, *Let Your Words be Few: Symbolism of Speaking and Silence Among Seventeenth Century Quakers* (Cambridge: Cambridge University Press, 1983); James Walvin, *The Quakers: Money and Morals* (London: John Murray, 1997).

5. George Fox, *Gospel Family Order, Being a Short Discourse Concerning the Ordering of Families, Both of Whites, Blacks and Indians* (London: s.n., 1676), 13–14, 16. Fox argued for the emancipation of slaves after a limited number of years of labor, with the emancipated to receive appropriate compensation, and with limits imposed on the slave trade.

6. Soderlund, *Quakers and Slavery.*

7. Ezra Michener, *A Retrospect of Early Quakerism* . . . (Philadelphia: T. E. Zell, 1860), 308; Society of Friends. Philadelphia Yearly Meeting, Records book, 1683–1719, American Philosophical Society, Phladelphia.

8. Jack Marietta, *The Reformation of American Quakerism* (Philadelphia: University of Pennsylvania Press, 1984); Marietta, "Conscience, the Quaker Community, and the French and Indian War," *Pennsylvania Magazine of History and Biography* 95 (1971): 3–27; Tolles, *Meeting House and Counting House.*

9. Theodore Thayer, "The Friendly Association," *Pennsylvania Magazine of History and Biography* 67 (1943): 356–76; see also Marietta, *The Reformation of American Quakerism*, Merle Deardorff and George S. Snyderman, "A Nineteenth-century Journal of a Visit to the Indians of New York," *Proceedings of the American Philosophical Society* 100 (1957): 582–612.

10. Richard Peters to William Johnson, 23 October 1762, Misc. Manuscript Collection, American Philosophical Society, Philadelphia.

11. For more on Papunhank, see Amy C. Schutt, *Forging Identitites: Native Americans and Moravian Missionaries in Pennsylvania and Ohio, 1765–1782* (Ph.D. diss., Indiana University, 1995), esp. chap. 3, where he is referred to as Johannes Papunhank; Richard White, *The Middle Ground: Indians, Empires, and Republics in the Great Lakes Region, 1650–1815* (Cambridge: Cambridge University Press, 1991), 264, 279–82, where he is listed alternately as Papoonhoal (a Minisink) and Papounhan (Munsee); and Greg Dowd, *A Spirited Resistance: the North American Indian Struggle for Unity, 1745–1815* (Baltimore: Johns Hopkins University Press, 1992), where he is referred to as Papoonan (Munsee). Munsee and Minisink were occasionally used interchangeably in the eighteenth century. In two manuscripts at the Clements Library documenting Quaker meetings with Indians at Philadelphia, 1760, and Easton, 1761, the "Delaware" religious leader is referred to as Papoonhoal (Minisink) from Mahackloosing and Papunhank (probably Munsee, though not specified as such) from Queheloosick (=Mahackloosing = Wyalusing, etc.).

12. Unidentified author, *An Account of a Visit and Conference with Some Indians Mostly of the Minnisink Tribe*, [1760, copy ca.1770], Quaker Collection, Haverford College [hereafter cited as QCHC].

13. Unidentified author, *An Account of a Visit*; see also *An Account of a Visit Lately Made to the People Called Quakers in Philadelphia by Papoonhoal, an Indian Chief, and Several Other Indians, Chiefly of the Minisink Tribe* (London: S. Clark, 1761), the early part of which bears some resemblance to the Clements manuscript. Additional Quaker material on Papounhan is included in Anthony Benezet, *Some Observations on the Situation, Disposition, and Character of the Indian Natives of this Continent* (Philadelphia: Joseph Crukshank, 1784).

14. Papunhank's changing religious convictions are murky, although it appears that after about 1763, he was most closely identified with the Moravians and was baptized by Zeisberger. See Schutt, *Forging Identities;* Woolman, *The Journal and Major Essays of John Woolman*, ed. Phillips P. Moulton (New York: Oxford University Press, 1971). Whether an exclusive identification as "Moravian" is warranted remains a topic for further research.

15. Dowd, *Spirited Resistance.* The centrality of pan-Indian resistance, however, varied among prophets, and individual prophets varied on occasion with respect to how much they might stress unity and in the form and tactics their resistance took. While Papunhank may represent an end member in the continuum of "nativist" prophecy, for any individual, resistance might appear more "accommodationist" or more "nativist," narrower or broader, depending on the context.

16. Woolman, *Journal and Major Essays*, 127.

17. Unidentified Quaker woman, *Some Account of a Visit Divers Friends Made to the Indians at the Time of the Treaty of Easton, Taken by One of the Company as Follows*, 4–12 August 1761. Quaker Collection, WLCL.

18. Ibid.

19. Ibid. See also references to Papounhan in the journal of John Woolman, *The Journal and Major Essays*, who visited Papounhan in company of David Zeisberger in 1762.

20. Among the more pointed pamphlets exchanged during the Proprietary-Quaker party conflict are William Smith, *A Brief View of the Conduct of Pennsylvania, for the Year 1755* (London: R. Griffiths, 1756); Nicolas Scull, *Kawanio che Keeteru, a True Relation of the Bloody Battle Fought Between George and Lewis, in the Year 1755* (Philadelphia: William Bradford, 1756); Lover of King and Country, *The Christian's Duty to Render to Caesar the Things that are Caesar's Considered* (Philadelphia: B. Franklin and D. Hall, 1756); David James Dove, *The Quaker Unmask'd; or, Plain Truth* (Philadelphia: Andrew Steuart, 1764) . Among the relatively few tracts to support the Quaker position are *An Apology for the*

People called Quakers, Containing some Reasons for Their Not Complying with Human Injunctions and Instructions in Matters Relative to the Worship of God . . . (Philadelphia: Joseph Crukshank, 1757), and Charles Thomson, *An Enquiry into the Causes of the Alienation of the Delaware and Shawnese Indians from the British Interest* . . . (London: J. Wilkie, 1759).

21. Dove, *The Quaker Unmask'd*, 8.

22. Ibid., 9–10.

23. Ibid., 10.

24. Israel Pemberton to Joseph Phipps, 15 January 1763, Quaker Collection, WLCL.

25. Jackson, *Civilization of the Indian Natives*, 6.

26. See Religious Society of Free Quakers Records, American Philosophical Society; Samuel Wetherill, *An Apology for the Religious Society, Called Free Quakers* (Philadelphia: Richard Folwell, 1781). Significantly, the Free Quaker Wetherill also mobilizes Quaker-Indian relations as a lash to apply to his orthodox brethren: recalling David Dove, he takes the Quakers to task both for their hypocrisy in defending the Indians against the Paxton mob and for turning a blind eye to the violence implicit in their actions after the fact—implicitly contrasting that situation with the situation during the Revolution in which many of those who became Free Quakers were censured and disowned for similar "defensive" action.

27. Benezet, *Some Observations on the Situation, Disposition, and Character of the Indian Natives*, 34–35.

28. When visiting the Seneca on a surveying expedition during the summer of 1794, John Adlum discovered a bellicose Cornplanter threatening war should negotiations fail. In a dramatic performance at a brag dance, Cornplanter made a gift of moccasins to Adlum, suggesting that he might use them when they next met in combat. Adlum to Timothy Pickering, 31 August 1794, John Adlum Papers, Schoff Revolutionary War Collection, WLCL. Also Donald H. Kent and Merle H. Deardorff, "John Adlum on the Allegheny: Memoirs for the Year 1794," *Pennsylvania Magazine of History and Biography* 84 (1960): 265–324, 435–80.

29. Quaker missions of the 1790s have been discussed at length in Christopher Densmore, "New York Quakers among the Brotherton, Stockbridge, Oneida, and Onondaga, 1795–1834." *Man in the Northeast* 44 (1992): 83–93; Diane Rothenberg, "The Mothers of the Nation: Seneca Resistance to Quaker Intervention," In *Woman and Colonization: Anthropological Perspectives*, ed. Mona Etienne and Eleanor Leacock (New York: Praeger, 1980); Richard Bauman, "An Analysis of Quaker-Seneca Councils, 1798–1800," *Man in the Northeast* 3 (1972): 36–48; A. F. C. Wallace, *Death and Rebirth of the Seneca* (New York: Knopf, 1970); Robert F. Berkhofer, "Faith and factionalism among the Senecas: Theory and Ethnohistory," *Ethnohistory* 12 (1965): 99–112; S. V. James, *A People Among Peoples* (Cambridge: Harvard University Press, 1963); Levinus K. Painter, "Jacob Taylor: Quaker Missionary Statesman." *Bulletin of the Friends Historical Association* 48 (1959): 116–27; George S. Snyderman, "Halliday Jackson's Journal of a Visit Paid to the Indians of New York (1806)." *Proceedings of the American Philosophical Society* 101 (1957): 565–88; Deardorff and Snyderman, "A Nineteenth-century Journal of a Visit to the Indians of New York"; Jackson, *Civilization of the Indian Natives*.

30. E.g. Society of Friends, *Information Respecting the Aborigines in the British Colonies* (London: Darton and Harvey, 1838); Daniel Wheeler, *Effects of the Introduction of Ardent Spirits and Implements of War, Amongst the Natives of some of the South-Sea Islands and New South Wales* (London: Harvey and Darton, 1843); Society of Friends, *Facts Relative to the Canadian Indians* . . . (London: Harvey and Darton, 1839); and many others.

31. The formal role of Quakers as government agents reached its peak in 1869, when the Grant Administration officially designated the Society of Friends to oversee all Indian agencies.

32. William N. Fenton, ed. "The Journal of James Emlen Kept on a Trip to Canandaigua, New York, 15 September to 30 October 1794 to attend the treaty between the United States and the Six nations," *Ethnohistory* 12 (1965): 313. Emlen added that Quakers, "exempt from those heavy ecclesiastical expenses which are the effects of an hireling Ministry," ought to be able to do just as well in promoting progress.

33. Densmore, "New York Quakers among the Brotherton, Stockbridge, Oneida, and Onondaga"; Deardorff and Snyderman, "A nineteenth-century journal." See also John Pierce Journal, [July 1798], QCHC. For Quaker accounts of attending the Canandaigua Treaty, see David Bacon Journal, 1794, QCHC; Jonathan Evans, "A Journal of the Life, Travels, and Religious Labours of William Savery . . ." *Friends Library* 1 (1937): 325–69; William N. Fenton, "The Journal of James Emlen Kept on a Trip to Canandaigua, New York," *Ethnohistory* 12 (1965): 275–342.

34. Bauman, "An Analysis of Quaker-Seneca Councils," 44. Typical of the mixed reaction by Quakers to Handsome Lake's teaching was John Pierce, who noted approvingly that "a temporary reform, at least" had taken place among the Seneca with respect to drinking, "in part through his influence," however, he criticized Handsome Lake for his witchcraft accusations and for retarding the progress in agriculture due to the "very frequent meetings, councils, dances &c. and the general ferment of the Indians minds." John Pierce Journal, 13 September 1801, Society of Friends, Philadelphia Yearly Meeting Indian Committee (PYMIC) Records, QCHC.

35. Pickering to Jasper Parish, 15 February 1796, PYMIC Records, QCHC.

36. Pierce Journal, 25 June 1798, PYMIC Records, QCHC.

37. Ibid.

38. Ibid.

39. Deardorff and Snyderman, "A nineteenth-century journal'" Densmore, "New York Quakers among the Brotherton, Stockbridge, Oneida, and Onondaga." The relatively new Indian Committee of the New York Yearly Meeting later supported missionary work among the Oneida, becoming aligned with the Pagan, as opposed to Christian, faction during tribal disputes in the early nineteenth century.

40. Donald F. Carmine and Luther M. Feeder, "Message of Pennsylvania and New Jersey Quakers to Indians of the Old Northwest," *Indiana Magazine of History* 59 (1963): 51–58; R. David Edmunds, "'Evil Men Who Add to Our Difficulties': Shawnees, Quakers, and William Wells, 1807–1808," *American Indian Culture and Research Journal* 14 (1990): 1–14; Francis Paul Prucha, *American Indian Policy in the Formative Years* (Lincoln, Neb.: University of Nebraska Press, 1970). See also Society of Friends, *Memorial of Evan Thomas, and Others, a Committee Appointed for Indian Affairs, by the Yearly Meeting of the People called Friends, Held in Baltimore* (Baltimore: s.n., 1802), a anti-liquor tract reprinting a speech of Little Turtle, as translated by William Wells; Society of Friends, *A Brief Account of the Proceedings of the Committee, Appointed by the Yearly Meeting of Friends, Held in Baltimore, for Promoting the Improvement and Civilization of the Indian Natives* (Baltimore: Cole & Hewes, 1805).

41. James McHenry notes, 26 October 1797, James McHenry Papers, WLCL. See also Anthony Wayne to McHenry, 29 August 1796 and 30 September 1796, also McHenry Papers and letters in the Wayne Papers, WLCL. See also Crayon Cossé Bell, *Revolution, Romanticism, and the Afro-Creole Protest Tradition in Louisiana, 1718–1868* (Baton Rouge: Louisiana State University Press, 1997); Kimberly Hanger, "Conflicting Loyalties: The French Revolution and Free People of Color in Spanish New Orleans," *Louisiana History* 34 (1993): 12–23. For British reluctance to assist the Indians in 1792, see the letters of George Hammond, Simcoe Papers, WLCL.

42. Edmunds, "'Evil Men Who Add to Our Difficulties.'"

43. Fort Wayne Indian Agency Letterbook, 10, 11–12 April 1809 WLCL.

44. Ibid., 15 April 1809.

45. Ibid., 6, 15 April 1809.

46. Ibid., 12, 16–17 May 1809.

47. Ibid., 21, 30, January 1809.

48. Edmunds, "'Evil Men Who Add to Our Difficulties.'"

49. See Joshua Sharpless Journal, 1798, PYMIC Records, QCHC.

50. Bonsall Journal 1, 30. WLCL.

51. John Pierce Journal, 1801,. PYMIC Records, QCHC.

52. Rothenberg, "Mothers of the Nation," 65. See also Marilyn Holly, "Handsome Lake's Teachings: The Shift from Female to Male Agriculture in Iroquois Culture. An Essay in Ethnophilosophy," *Agriculture and Human Values* 7 (1990): 80–91; and more generally, Carol Devens, *Countering Colonization: Native American Women and Great Lakes Missions, 1630–1900* (Berkeley: University of California Press, 1992). Rothenberg argues that the Quakers carried out a program that, had it succeeded, might have resulted in "social and cultural genocide." Such a view both overstates Quaker influence upon the Seneca and underestimates the agency wielded by Seneca, male and female, in shaping social change. Furthermore, Seneca gender roles had begun to shift dramatically prior to the arrival of the first "missionaries," with males—traditionally providers of game and participants in warfare—complaining vociferously of a shortage of game due to white encroachment and the reservation system. Certainly the opportunity to wage war, another male role, was severely curtailed. Considering the traditional complementarity of gender roles in Seneca culture, it seems fair to argue (as Quakers did) that women's roles would have changed, with or without the Quaker presence. For an analysis of the impact of (Moravian) missionary activity on gender roles among missionized Indians—at odds with Rothenberg—see Amy Schutt, *Forging Identitites.*

53. Wallace, *Death and Rebirth of the Seneca.* Opened in 1798, the academic school was irregularly attended at best, and was closed for over a decade in favor of bringing selected children to Philadelphia. A school was not firmly established at Tunesassa until 1822, remaining in operation until 1940. Hugh Barbour, "City Philanthropists and Social Concerns, 1787–1857," in *Quaker Crosscurrents: Three Hundred Years of Friends in the New York Yearly Meetings,* ed. Hugh Barbour et al. (Syracuse: Syracuse University Press, 1995).

54. Thomas Ludlow Ogden to Bishop Hobarts, 14 December 1814,. Ogden Family Papers, WLCL.

55. Ibid. See also the legal opinion by John Sergeant addressed to Mr. Harrison and Tracey of Buffalo, 2 April 1819. Ogden Family Papers, WLCL.

56. Thomas Ludlow Ogden to David A. Ogden, 24 April 1818, Ogden Family Papers, WLCL.

57. Thomas Ludlow Ogden to Bishop Hobarts, 14 December 1814, Ogden Family Papers, WLCL.

58. Thomas Ludlow Ogden to David A. Ogden, 29 March 1819, Ogden Family Papers, WLCL.

59. All references in Bonsall, Journal 3, October and November, 1806, WLCL.

60. Bonsall, Journal 3, 13 November 1806. The law required participation in the militia, violating the Quakers' testimony of non-violence, and levied a fine on those who refused service.

61. Ibid., 22 November 1806.

62. Ibid., 26 November 1806.

63. Anthony F. C. Wallace, ed. "Halliday Jackson's journal to the Seneca Indians, 1798–1800," *Pennsylvania History* 19 (1952): 122.

64. Joshua Sharpless Journal, Sharpless Family Papers, QCHC.

65. John Pierce Journal, 1801, PYMIC Records, QCHC.

66. Ibid.

67. Joseph Elkinton Journal, 1809–15, QCHC; William Allinson to Mary Allinson, 10 September 1809, Allinson Family Papers, QCHC.

68. John Philips Journal, 1806, PYMIC Records, QCHC.

69. Wallace, "Halliday Jackson's Journal." See also Jackson's diaries, QCHC.

70. Allinson was a member of the General Committee of Westtown School from 1814–1817. Archives, Westtown School. Additional information on Allinson is located in the Allinson Family Papers, QCHC.

71. Mary Allinson: "Some Account of my beloved brother William Allinson, more especially respecting the latter months and closing scene of his Life" 15 October 1814, QCHC.

72. Allinson, Journal, WLCL, 186–87.

73. Ibid., 191–92. On Aupaumut, see Alan Taylor, "Captain Hendrick Aupaumut: The Dilemmas of an Intercultural Broker," *Ethnohistory* 43 (1996): 431–57; and Jeanne Ronda and James P. Ronda, "'As They Were Faithful': Chief Hendrick Aupaumut and the Struggle for Stockbridge Survival, 1757–1830," *American Indian Culture and Research Journal* 3 (1979): 43–55.

74. Allinson, Journal, WLCL, 193–94.

75. Ibid., 194–95.

76. Ibid., 195–96.

77. Ibid., 196. The work of Alan Taylor and others on Aupaumut suggests that accommodationism might, in some cases, represent a strategy for cultural preservation. In this view, the strategic distance between the accommodationism of an Aupaumut and the nativism of a Tenskwatawa is far less, though the tactical distance remains great.

78. Allinson, Journal, WLCL, 41.

79. Ibid., 158.

80. Ibid., 172.

81. Ibid., 265–66.

The Mohawk/Oneida Corridor: The Geography of Inland Navigation Across New York

P H I L I P   L O R D   J R .

Two hundred years ago, New York State stood at the crossroads of westward migration; spanning the distance that separated the Atlantic Ocean from the Great Lakes. Across this interval passed innumerable merchants and settlers as the new nation took advantage of a natural gateway to the West in the decades following the American Revolution.

For many students of the early republic, the singular significance of this inland waterway in the history of North America is all but lost. For them the representative image of the pioneer, moving westward to occupy his wilderness homestead, is of a lonely man on horseback or a family piled into an ox cart or wagon with all their possessions; struggling along the muddy and rutted trails that sliced through the virgin forest.

But, in the 1790s, and for the century preceding, the rural roadways of the Northeast were often a poor choice for travel, even on horseback. In 1797, one traveler reported, "The traveling in the Country in the spring and fall of the year is very unpleasant, as your horse is often from his knees to his body obliged to founder on through mud and mire, owing to the depth and richness of the soil, its uncultivated state and the want of proper roads."[1]

Instead, in the late eighteenth century, the pioneer, standing on the west bank of the Hudson River at Albany, elected to use an inland waterway network to breach the Appalachian Mountain barrier and gain access to the rich lands located on the fringes of the Great Lakes.

This was an era when water-borne transport represented the only effective method of movement across the northeastern region of North America, and the desire to connect the Atlantic Ocean with the Great Lakes through inland navigation remained a constant. This was a priority during the colonial wars of the mid and late eighteenth century, when the efficiency of strike and counter strike depended on the swift movement of armies between these domains of political power and population. The players may have changed; French versus British, British versus American; and the motives may have shifted—trade and exchange, attack and defense, commerce and market development—but the geography never did. The goal remained one of moving through the interior between the great ocean and that cluster of vast inland seas that sat in the American heartland nearly half the way across the continent.

Two liquid avenues for this connection presented themselves, but only one was available to the Americans two hundred years ago. The St. Lawrence, perhaps in every way the superior passageway into the interior, was always in the hands of the "enemy." So the Mohawk/Oneida corridor became, by default, the American highway west. Prior to the era of turnpikes and improved interior road networks, which did not begin in Upstate New York until the eighteenth century had virtually ended, the pioneer used the Mohawk/Oneida navigation corridor to gain relatively easy access to the frontier. Thanks to an accident of nature, which eons ago broke a passage through the Appalachian and Adirondack mountain barriers, this linked network of natural rivers, streams, and lakes provided a nearly level water route across the entire 150 miles separating the Great Lakes from the Hudson/Atlantic navigation.[2]

We can best comprehend the quality of the Mohawk/Oneida navigation by tracing the journey west as it would have occurred in the years just after the Revolution. In that time, a pioneer migrating west, newly arrived in Albany and hungry for land, a merchant anxious to ship merchandise to the expanding western settlements, or a military commander supplying essential provisions to the garrisons along our western frontier, faced an inadequate and severely restricted transportation network.

Direct access to the upper Hudson River was rarely a problem. Ocean going vessels arriving in New York harbor could often continue up the river, which was a

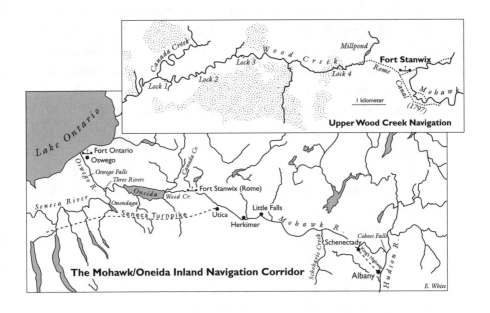

The Mohawk/Oneida Inland Navigation Corridor

tidal estuary to several miles above the port at Albany; or cargo and passengers could transfer into smaller river sloops to execute the 150-mile journey up river.

Once in Albany, the traveler could continue a few miles further north, and enter the mouth of the Mohawk River, a waterway that reached deep into the western interior. But navigation into this river was blocked almost immediately by the Great Cohoes Falls. So monumental was this obstruction that not even a canoe portage had been established here during the eighteenth century. Instead, anyone interested in going west had to disembark at the wharf in Albany and hire a wagon for overland transport across 16 miles of pine barrens to Schenectady, the actual foot of the Mohawk River navigation. This land route, established in the 1600s as "The King's Highway," provided a direct and effective alternative to the impossible direct water passage until the opening of the Erie Canal many decades later.[3]

Once at the old harbor in the Binnekill, a slack-water sprout of the powerful Mohawk, one would buy or hire a small bateau—the pick-up truck of the eighteenth century—to navigate up 58 miles of the river to the portage at Little Falls. This passage would require the boatmen to force their bateau over fifty-seven rapids or "rifts." These rifts were formed by the outwash of numerous intersecting streams, which unloaded their contents of gravel and debris each year with the spring freshets driven by meltwater and heavy rains. From a detailed river survey made in 1792, we know that many of these rifts were less then knee deep in a channel where a 6-foot depth of water was considered the norm.[4]

At Little Falls the river flowed down through a steep bedrock gorge, as pictur-esque as it was frustrating to the navigators. Within that gorge, blasted through by the glacier eons before, lay a rapid just over a mile long with a fall of water in excess of 40 feet. The channel was strewn with huge boulders, rendering any sort of navi-gation fruitless. Thus a portage had to be made, and throughout the eighteenth cen-tury, save for the final few years, this portage, a mill, a house, and a trading post were all that existed at Little Falls, which derived its name from being a lesser ver-sion of the Great Falls at Cohoes.[5]

In the latter half of the eighteenth century, when bateaux passed on the river instead of canoes, teamsters were paid to cart the cargo, and the boat, overland to the top of the falls, where the craft would be relaunched and reloaded, to traverse the upper Mohawk to Fort Stanwix at Rome, some 38 miles and twenty-two rapids fur-ther west.[6]

Interestingly, the upper Mohawk, above Little Falls, was generally less obstructed than the lower. This in part was due to the narrowness of the channel, and the tendency, therefore, to have the river flush itself clear of the debris.[7] Lower down, where the channel was very broad and the water shallow, this debris accu-mulated to form the many rifts and shoals. It is important to note that navigation in this system was not so much frustrated by the violent rush of water normally asso-ciated with the term "rapids," but rather by the extreme shallowness of the channel, where in the most placid of situations, the mere lack of depth could ground a loaded boat repeatedly. With water depths on the average rift at 18 inches or less, the crews of grounded boats often went over the side and, walking on the gravelly bottom, pushed and dragged their overloaded vessels up through this series of maddening obstructions.[8]

At Fort Stanwix, now the City of Rome, the Mohawk turned north and could no longer serve a westward course. Here boat and baggage would again be lifted from the river and dragged across a 2-mile portage to be deposited into the almost waterless channel of Wood Creek, a tiny stream running west from Rome, and narrow enough

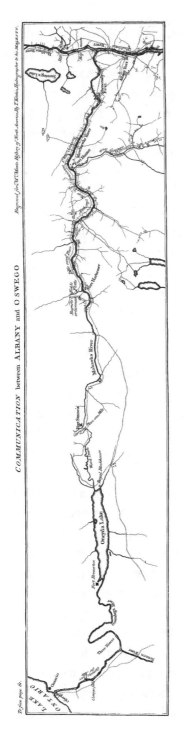

This late eighteenth-century British map shows the network of inland waterways that connected the Upper Hudson River at Albany with the Great Lakes at Oswego. Reproduced from Thomas Mante, *The History of the Late War in North America* (London: W. Strahan and T. Cadell, 1772). 61. Courtesy of the New York State Library.

at the landing to jump across. Because of the continuing shallowness of this tiny stream for miles below the landing, extending the portage would bring little relief.

The landing at the west end of the old Oneida Carrying Place stood in the shadow of the long-abandoned Fort Newport from the French and Indian War. In concert with Stanwix and its predecessor at the east end of the portage, Fort Williams, these military establishments guarded the carrying place first established by the British and witness to the passing and re-passing of hundreds of military bateaux during the French, British, and American expeditions of the eighteenth century.

The situation here, for the navigators, was never easy. Often the water was so low late in the year that only the empty boat would be launched at the landing, while the cargo and passengers were trucked on west several miles further to deeper water downstream. Unable to float their craft away from the landing, empty or full, boatmen would walk a short way upstream to negotiate with a miller, who had, at a very early date, impounded the waters of Wood Creek in a pond. A release of water from his dam would, with luck, carry the bateau 5 miles further down to the junction of Canada Creek. From here, in an average season, one could navigate the remaining 18 miles to Oneida Lake.[9]

The boatmen followed a log-choked, shallow stream, at times so twisting one could pole a boat a mile by water to advance only 30 feet by land.[10] Wood Creek passed through a wilderness that was essentially uninhabited, even into the early nineteenth century, where the trees along the banks provided a claustrophobic tunnel effect for most of the journey[11] and where the mosquitoes were legendary. Then it was out into Oneida Lake, across that 20-mile lake usually by night rowing along the north shore, to avoid the often-dangerous winds, then out into the Oneida River and down to the junction at Three Rivers. From here the pilots of small boats could elect to travel up the Seneca River to the salt springs at Onondaga Lake and on up to Seneca Lake, Cayuga Lake, and points west; or they could choose, as most did, to go down the Oswego River to Oswego and the Great Lakes beyond.

As they progressed west of Oneida Lake, boatmen met with only moderate additional difficulty. One point still to be dealt with, for those passing down to Oswego and Lake Ontario, was the so-called "Falls of the Onondaga," or Oswego Falls, at what is now Fulton on the Oswego River. Here a bedrock ledge ran completely across the river, except for a very narrow gap near the center. Boatmen sometimes unloaded their craft and ran them down empty;[12] at other times, both boats and cargo were portaged around the obstacle, which never was much improved until by-passed in the canal age some forty years later. From this point, boats rushed down through a series of navigable rapids to the harbor beneath the cliffs at Fort Ontario, the gateway to the Great Lakes.[13]

This tortuous route was the only highway west of any consequence in the late-eighteenth century, and it was this transport corridor that presented itself to President Washington, who personally inspected the route after the war. He saw it as the only viable connection between the head of Atlantic shipping and the Great Lakes for the emerging nation. The improvement of this international water route from Schenectady to Oswego became a goal of the new federal government.

Within the decade this improvement had become the mission of the Western Inland Lock Navigation Company, a private company created by the New York State Legislature in 1792. Presided over by retired Revolutionary War General Philip Schuyler, of Albany, New York, this company sold stock to help raise capital for what was, in that time, a very tenuous venture. The company employed, what was then, still experimental engineering to create an integrated system of natural waterways, improved natural waterways, and new artificial waterways—New York State's first canals—in the closing years of the eighteenth century and during the first couple of years of the nineteenth century.[14]

This period of transition, between natural water navigation and the completely detached and artificial canal navigation to be created in the 1820s, can be seen to pivot around the year 1798, precisely two hundred years ago. There was a qualitative difference in inland navigation along this route before and after this date, both in terms of infrastructure and the vehicles that were able to use it.

The effect of this decade of navigation improvements and canal building, from 1792 to 1803, can best be understood by repeating the boat voyage just described between Schenectady and Oswego, but this time as it would have occurred in the year 1804, at the end of the construction phase of the company, and just before the Embargo of 1806.

After making the prerequisite dusty trip through the sand dunes and ridges of the Albany Pine Bush, this time in a stage coach rather than the rough wagons of a decade before,[15] one could now depart the Schenectady harbor in a Durham Boat, twice the size of a bateau and able to carry seven times the cargo—the 18-wheeler of the river boat era. These boats were poled by a crew of five or six men, using 18-foot-long iron tipped poles with wooden shoulder buttons; walking or clawing their way along cleated boards that ran the full length of the hold on either side of the

This early image shows the method of running a Durham boat upstream through one of the V-shaped rock "wing dams" built by the Western Inland Lock Navigation Company in the 1790s in the Mohawk River to overcome the shallows of several rifts. Note the men standing in knee-deep water dragging the boat through the narrow gap in the dam. The boat in the foreground is a large bateau. This scene was observed and recorded in 1807 on the Mohawk River. Reproduced from Christian Schultz, *Travels on an Inland Voyage . . .* (London, 1810). Courtesy of the New York State Library.

boat. Steering was accomplished by a 23-foot-long sweep, which served to pivot the flat-bottomed boat into alignment, acting more like a lever than a rudder.[16]

Too large and heavy to lift easily out of the water for portaging, these craft depended on a continuous and relatively deep channel to navigate successfully. Whereas the little 3-handed bateau could move its ton and a half of cargo in less than 16 inches of water, and could move itself empty on little more than a heavy mist, the Durham boat, with its 10 to 12 tons of cargo, needed 2 feet of clear channel when loaded. But even at the great length of 60 feet, it could pass empty over a rift on only 5 inches of water. It was the ideal large capacity river boat for this navigation, and perfectly suited for the canals and locks built along the way by Schuyler's company, with its square profile, flat bottom and straight, parallel sides.

The voyager leaving the harbor at Schenectady, in 1804, more easily passed the fifty-seven rapids of the lower Mohawk because some of them had been deepened by the navigation company in the late 1790s, with plowed out channels or long V-shaped rock dams. General Schuyler modeled these dams after the fish traps used, first by Native Americans and later by white settlers, to capture migrating eels and other fishes. Constructed on the shallows of rifts with rocks gathered from the rift itself, these great Vs, still being employed today in the eel fisheries of the Delaware River, gathered the water into the apex as it ran downstream, forcing fish into the baskets attached in the gap.

Even though they leaked profusely, it was noted that the water was deeper within the V than outside, and Schuyler had several of these dams built in the Mohawk to provide a deepened water passage over the shallow rifts. The most notable of these wing dams was near Amsterdam. Constructed near the mouth of the Schoharie Creek, the paired V-dams, the deflecting wing dam at the upstream end, and the retaining wall built parallel to the bank represent a structure that can be seen as a static prototype of the true canal locks to come decades later.[17]

In addition to these improvements to the natural channel, and 58 miles upstream, the mile long "Little Falls Canal" replaced the portage at Little Falls. Begun in 1793 and completed in 1795, this canal was equipped with five locks. It is the first true canal created in New York and among the oldest in North America. The structure allowed boats to pass the falls without unloading or portaging, reducing the delay from days to hours. The engineering employed in building this was that of millwrights and carpenters; for, although blasting powder was used to cut the channel through the bedrock of the Little Falls gorge, no hydraulic cement nor adequate building stone was to be had, and so within the rock cuts locks of wood, caulked with oakum and tar like an inside-out ship's hull, were created.[18] These eventually leaked and rotted, and so all had to be rebuilt in 1803, with recently discovered stone and newly developed mortar.[19] Most of the guard lock of this canal survived into the twentieth century, and remnants can still be seen.

The completion of this canal opened up the entire Mohawk River to continuous navigation, and this permitted boats to evolve from the small, portable bateaux, which could be portaged around the falls, to the larger Durham boats. With the arrival of larger, heavier boats, a channel that was adequate for the smaller bateaux began again to present pressures against navigation. So it was that, a short distance westward near Herkimer, two previously ignored rapids that had become troublesome for these larger boats by 1797, were bypassed in 1798 by the mile-long "German Flatts Canal."[20] This was the first of Schuyler's canals to use stone masonry in its locks, and archeological remains can still be seen of one of the locks, much of the canal bed, and sections of the massive earthen deflection walls protecting the canal from the river in floodstage.

And further to the west at Rome, the head of Mohawk navigation, the "Rome Canal" was built in 1797 to bypass the 2-mile portage at Fort Stanwix. Here, a brickyard was established and the locks at the east and west end of this canal were built of oversize native bricks,[21] many of which survive in archeological sites today. The bed of the canal itself still survives beneath a curving alleyway, just behind the Burger King parking lot in the City of Rome. Because this canal crossed the summit lands that separated the eastward flowing Mohawk from the westward flowing Wood Creek and waters beyond, a feeder had to be built to refill the canal as the opening and closing of the locks drained away the water.[22]

After passage through the Rome Canal, a Durham boat could smoothly enter Wood Creek where four timber locks, built in 1802 and 1803, raised the normally shallow stream into a series of navigable pools.[23] With the advent of larger boats, the shallows of the upper end of Wood Creek, above its junction with Canada Creek, had represented an almost impossible passage.

Even the lower section of Wood Creek now presented major problems for the heavily laden Durham boats coming east out of Oneida Lake, often with cargoes of salt from Onondaga Lake (now Syracuse). In this period many accounts exist of boats being forced to unload two-thirds of their cargo at the lower end of the stream to then undertake three arduous journeys up to the Rome Canal in order to pass their cargoes successfully down into the Mohawk navigation.[24]

Passing down the twisting channel of Wood Creek, a Durham boat would take advantage of thirteen short canals cut across necks of land in 1793. These tiny cuts are some of the oldest artificial waterways in North America. The first works completed by the new canal company, they were executed in a wilderness using hand tools and oxen transported by boats to the sites. These cuts shortened the passage to Oneida Lake by 6 miles!

The method used for creation of these mini-canals was simple in concept, yet extraordinarily difficult in practice. Where a particularly sharp or inconvenient loop of the creek existed, workers would first clear-cut the virgin forest along a line that traversed the neck. These trees would be stockpiled for later use and the massive stumps would be grubbed up. A narrow ditch, perhaps 10 feet deep and not much wider, would be excavated across the neck along the cleared land. Once completed, the upstream end of the old channel would be dammed with the logs cut from the clearing, and when the next freshet or heavy rains came, the water, forced into the ditch, would rapidly erode it to the general dimensions of the rest of the stream and the navigation channel would be thus realigned.[25]

It is perhaps of interest that where the old ox-bows of the original channel still can be found, abandoned by the stream during the summer of 1793, they are often less than 3 feet deep, whereas the modern banks of Wood Creek are often 10 or 15 feet deep in the same location, revealing the erosional impact of deforestation during the nineteenth century. But even with this improvement, and with the cutting down of much of the marginal forest that had prevented towing paths to be created along the banks of the stream, passage was still obstructed by sunken logs and overhanging trees—the same conditions that had plagued this stream since the early 1700s, resulting in the name "Wood Creek." Additionally, there were sandbars built up along the way, often grounding boats that were not lightly laden.[26]

The Company never exercised its option to undertake improvements west of Wood Creek, partly due to lack of resources, but also because the natural waterways to the west presented a relatively manageable navigation. So one proceeded on to Oswego from here much as one had done for generations before. And, although the Company continued until bought out in 1820 for the construction of the Erie Canal, they apparently initiated no new projects after 1804, the year when General Schuyler died.[27] We can say, therefore, that it was 1798, precisely two hundred years ago, after the three short canals at Little Falls, Rome, and German Flatts were opened, and the several associated improvements in the Mohawk River and Wood Creek had all been completed, that was the watershed of this revolutionary enterprise. These improvements to the inland waterways, and the others created in 1799, 1802, and 1803, stand as evidence of the dramatic and unprecedented accomplishments of the Western Inland Lock Navigation Company.

Just eleven years after it was chartered, and fifteen years before construction of the Erie Canal was even begun, this company had converted an obstructed and interrupted navigation good only for small, portable bateaux, into a continuous, deepwater channel through which large Durham boats could pass relatively unimpeded, and did so at a time when American canal engineering was still experimental. Had these improvements, which included our first real canals, not been in place by 1803, our history as a state and nation might have played very differently.

Foremost in the minds of the federal government at this time was the security of the western national boundaries, recently established along the margins of the Great

Lakes. Ready access to the gateway port at Oswego, and the availability of rapid transport of men and supplies between New York and Oswego, meant the difference between a consolidated defense and one more tenuous. The unfortunate experiences of the wars of the previous fifty years were still fresh in the minds of these planners. Many of them, including General Schuyler of New York, had experienced first hand the rigors of trying to efficiently haul an inland army to the battle lines of the west in tiny bateaux through narrow and twisting waterways, interrupted by time-consuming portages, riddled with often impassable shoals, and choked with debris that required constant removal.

Now, as they looked to the continuing threats posed by aggressive maneuvering by the British on the northwestern frontier, these men saw an open avenue to Lake Ontario for the huge Durham freighters, running swiftly through the improved channels and new by-pass canals of the inland navigation company.

Of course anything that improved military transport served the needs of the civilian population as well. Because of the capacity of this new inland waterway, settlement of the western territories was accelerated. Even though the extension of the eastern turnpikes westward from the center of population in the lower Mohawk Valley was well underway by 1800, travelers' accounts suggest the majority entering the American Continent at New York harbor chose to continue their journey westward by boat.[28] Even at the juncture of river and land travel at Utica, as many chose passage to the rich Genesee country via the navigation to Oswego and Lake Ontario as did by the newly completed Genesee Turnpike. During the first decade of the nineteenth century, the viability of these early western communities depended as much on river freighters as on freight wagons for the promise of easy shipment of farm produce to market downriver and the return of merchandise upriver to the frontier.[29]

However, as the frontier moved further west, and further from the harbors at Schenectady and Albany, the Canadian port at Kingston began to attract American shipping, particularly for the marketing of potash—the new settler's first cash crop. This was certainly true for those who located along the margins of Lake Ontario and up into the Genesee Country south of what is today Rochester. But it was also becoming true for settlers well inland around the Finger Lakes of New York, who shipped down the Seneca River. It was easier to run down the Oswego and into Lake Ontario to Canadian markets, than to undertake the tortuous nine- or ten-day voyage down to Schenectady via Wood Creek and the Mohawk. Distance to market translated to cost, as boatmen's daily wages mounted up with each mile added to the journey.

But this improved inland waterway provided a back door to the Canadian ports and international shipments coming and going on the St. Lawrence, creating an outlet for New York State merchants during the embargo and the related prohibitions against trade via New York harbor in 1806, 1807, and 1809. As a result, fleets of Durham boats from the Mohawk Valley, managed by New Yorkers, emerged in Canadian waters at the east end of Lake Ontario and the Upper St. Lawrence.[30] And during the strife that would erupt into the War of 1812, military supplies were more effectively shipped to the Great Lakes fleets and frontier garrisons in the Durham boats, which now passed along this network of waterways. Even with the improvements of western roadways, land transport was still arduous and unpredictable, and the Navy Department relied on these large river freighters to move supplies, ordnance, and personnel from the navy yard at New York City to the port at Oswego late in 1812, and during 1813 and 1814.[31]

During the first twenty years of the nineteenth century, as turnpikes were improved and land transport became more reliable, river traffic across New York began to decline. The establishment of strategic forwarding terminals, such as the City of Utica at the head of the Seneca Turnpike built in 1800, provided easier access to the western territories with a greatly truncated navigation.[32] While in the 1790s, one reached the lands lying along the southwestern edge of Lake Ontario by going up the Mohawk to Rome, then down Wood Creek to Oneida Lake, then out the Oneida River to the Oswego River, down that river to Oswego, and then along the south shore of Lake Ontario; in the early 1800s, one could leave the boat at Utica and take to the land route by horse, wagon, or stage coach.

To accommodate this new pattern of travel, an express passenger boat service using converted Durham freight boats was established between Schenectady and Utica after the War of 1812. Travelers could take a relatively quick two-day voyage upriver to the landing at Utica, which was the eastern terminus of the Genesee Turnpike.[33] By this land route they could continue on west across the tops of the Finger Lakes and into the fabled Genesee Country, some 100 or more miles west of Utica, and nearly 50 miles west of the harbor at Oswego. And, they could accomplish this without the obstructions of the upper Mohawk River, the delay and expense of passing the Rome Canal, the extreme difficulty of the twisted channel of Wood Creek (not to mention the gigantic mosquitoes), and all the perils of the river rapids, the frustrations of low water, and the lack of riverside hospitality along the Oneida and Oswego rivers.[34] So long as the stagecoach team placed one foot in front of the other, the traveler could be certain of a safe and timely arrival at any point along these new and improved highways.

This loss of competitiveness of the waterways with the land route in the early 1800s led many Mohawk Valley boatmen to seek work for themselves and their Durham boats in the forwarding trade on the St. Lawrence River, running the rapids that separated the lake schooner transport of the Great Lakes docked at Kingston and Prescott from the ship transport on the lower St. Lawrence below Montreal. And Durham boats began to emerge in Canada in this period on several other rivers, such as the Rideau navigation.[35] The completion of the Erie Canal in 1825 sealed the fate of the inland waterways and ushered in a "new" era of artificial waterways—the Canal Age. However, the roots of this age are to be found in the time when Durham boats and bateaux passed along an integrated network of improved natural rivers, streams, and lakes, linked together by New York State's very first canals two hundred years ago.

And, just as the engineering, which underpinned the canal age of the second quarter of the nineteenth century, did not rise abruptly without precedent in this earlier quarter century of transition, so our understanding of how the capacity and development of water transport systems influenced the events of the Great Lakes region needs to be fine tuned to the details of the Mohawk/Oneida navigation and the chronology of its evolution as a corridor of international transport.

NOTES

1. J. A. Graham, *A Descriptive Sketch of the Present State of Vermont* (London: H. Fry, 1797), 161.
2. Nobel E. Whitford, *History of the Canal System of the State of New York* (New York: Brandow Printing Co., 1906), 1:15–18.
3. Elkanah Watson, *History of the Rise, Progress, and Existing Condition of the Western Canals* (Albany: D. Steele, 1820), 25–26.
4. Philip Schuyler et al., *The Report of a Committee Appointed to Explore the Western Waters. . . .* (Albany: Barber and Southwick, 1792), 3–7.
5. Simon Desjardin and Pierre Pharoux, "The Castorland Journal," trans. Franklin B. Hough, A7009, Box 84, Franklin B. Hough Papers, Albany: New York State Library, 50–51 [hereafter cited as NYSL].
6. Philip Schuyler, *Second Report of the Western Inland Lock Navigation Company - 1798.* Buffalo Historical Society *Publications* 13 (1909): 200.
7. Desjardin and Pharoux, "Castorland Journal," 53.
8. Jeptha R. Simms, *The Frontiersmen of New York* (Albany: Geo. C. Riggs, 1882), 1:351. Also, Desjardin and Pharoux, "Castorland Journal," 114–15.

9. Schuyler, *Second Report*, 201. Also Desjardin and Pharoux, "Castorland Journal," 61. Also Augustus Porter, *Narrative of the Early Years in the Life of Augustus Porter* (Buffalo: Buffalo Historical Society, 1848), 278–80.

10. "Extracts From the Vanderkemp Papers," Buffalo Historical Society *Publications* 2 (1880): 68. Also Watson, *History of . . . Western Canals*, 34–35.

11. Desjardin and Pharoux, "Castorland Journal," 62–63.

12. Christian Schultz, *Travels on an Inland Voyage . . .* (1810; Reprint, Ridgewood, N.J.: The Gregg Press, 1968), 35–37.

13. Ibid., 37–38.

14. Whitford, *History of the Canal System*, 1:31–47.

15. George R. Howell and W.W. Munsell, *History of the County of Schenectady, NY from 1662 to 1886* (New York: W. W. Munsell and Co., 1886), 49.

16. John Sanders, *Centennial Address Relating to the Early History of Schenectady . . .* (Albany: VanBenthuysen, 1876), 245–48. Also Schultz, *Travels on an Inland Voyage*, 5–6, 34–35.

17. Philip Lord, Jr. "The Wing Dams at Snouk's Rapid: A Proto-Lock on the Mohawk River." *The Bulletin—Journal of the New York State Archaeological Association*, no. 106 (fall 1993): 5. Also Schultz, *Travels on an Inland Voyage*, 7–8; Jonathan Pearson, *A History of the Schenectady Patent* (Albany: Joel Munsell's Sons, 1883), 423.

18. Duke de la Rochefoucault Liancourt, *Travels Through the United States of North America, The Country of the Iroquois, and Upper Canada in the Years 1795, 1796, and 1797*, 4 vols. (London: R. Phillips, 1799), 2:45–47.

19. William W. Campbell, *The Life and Writings of De Witt Clinton* (New York: Baker and Scribner, 1849), 44–45.

20. Philip Schuyler and William Weston, *Report of the Directors of the Western and Northern Inland Lock Navigation Companies . . . Together with the Report of Mr. William Weston, Engineer* (New York, 1796), reprinted in Buffalo Historical Society *Publications* 2 (1880): 173–74. Also Campbell, *Life and Writings of De Witt Clinton*, 48.

21. Whitford, *History of the Canal System*, 1:43–45.

22. Schuyler, *Second Report*, 202–3.

23. Campbell, *Life and Writings of De Witt Clinton*, 58.

24. The Scriba Papers, DE10521, vol. 29, NYSL, Albany, New York.

25. Desjardin and Pharoux, "Castorland Journal," 64–66.

26. Watson, *History of . . . Western Canals*, 33.

27. Philip Schuyler, Canal Papers, New York Public Library, New York.

28. The Durham Project Research Archive, New York State Museum, Albany, New York.

29. Orsamus Turner, *Pioneer History of the Holland Purchase* (Buffalo: Geo. H. Derby & Co., 1850), 330–34.

30. William Canniff, *History of the Province of Ontario* (Toronto: A. H. Hovey, 1872), 140–42.

31. Jeff Seiken, "'To Obtain Command of the Lakes': The United States and the Contest for Lakes Erie and Ontario, 1812–15," in this volume and personal communication with Mr. Seiken.

32. M. M. Bagg, *The Pioneers of Utica* (Utica, N.Y.: Curtiss and Childs, 1877), 93–188.

33. Pomeroy Jones, *Annals and Address Relating to the Early History of Schenectady . . .* (Albany, 1876), *Recollections of Oneida County* (Rome: Author, 1851), 500–1.

34. Sanders, *Centennial Address*, 248. Also Bagg, *Pioneers of Utica*, 22.

35. Elkanah Watson to Thomas Eddy, Letter Report on Status of Inland Navigation, 27 November 1800, Elkanah Watson Papers, GB 13294, NYSL.

36. Canniff, *History of the Province of Ontario,* 142–43.

Iroquois External Affairs, 1807–1815: The Crisis of the New Order

C A R L   B E N N

When historians study Aboriginal participation in the War of 1812, they usually focus on the people in the Old Northwest—the Shawnee, Ottawa, and others—who still exercised a considerable degree of independence from Euro-Americans, and who had not yet been forced off their lands or confined to reservations. Largely ignored is the story of the Six Nations Iroquois, most of whom lived well within the Euro-American side of the "frontier" and who, for the most part, occupied reservations and tracts after losing most of their territory in previous decades, mainly as a consequence of the Patriot victory in the American Revolution.[1] To understand the Natives' role in the Sixty Years' War more completely, we need to examine how the Iroquois in western New York and southwestern Upper Canada (now Ontario) conducted their external affairs within the limitations of the new order in the years after the *Chesapeake* Affair of 1807.[2] Such an exploration provides insight into how these people of the early reservation period exercised what freedom they could in foreign relations, for their own self-preservation.[3]

The primary questions that Euro-Americans asked about the Six Nations in the months leading up to the American declaration of war in 1812, were: would the Iroquois fight, and if they did, whose part would they take? The Six Nations asked themselves those same questions and a third: why should they participate in the white peoples' strife? As the clouds of war rolled across the horizon, peace chiefs tried to persuade their people to seek shelter from the coming storm in neutrality.

The issues had been simplest for the Six Nations in New York. Confined to reservations within the boundaries of their ancestral territories, retention of their land was tenuous enough in the face of aggressive settlement, unscrupulous speculators, and unsympathetic governments without inviting military reprisals. Moreover, peaceful relations with the United States were necessary to ensure that they would continue to receive the annuities and gifts they needed to help maintain their standard of living because the new plow agriculture of the Euro-Americans had not been adopted by enough Iroquois to replace older but no longer viable forest and farming subsistence patterns.[4] They could not contemplate allying with anyone but the United States, despite their own unhappy legacy of American-Iroquois relations and America's ongoing animosity toward Native peoples, as demonstrated so clearly at Tippecanoe in 1811.[5]

Fortunately, the Americans simplified the issue because they told the Iroquois that they did not want Aboriginal allies. Just after the outbreak of war, the government's agent to the Six Nations, Erastus Granger, informed them that America's warriors were so numerous that they soon would overwhelm the outnumbered redcoats across the border on their own. Not needing Native help, Granger advised them to stay home, cultivate their fields, and take care of their property.[6] Neither kindness nor generosity motivated Granger's advice. Rather, he assumed that the only options the Iroquois considered were either neutrality or an alliance with the British. Therefore, at the same moment he asked them to remain quiet, he threatened the already insecure tribespeople. Granger claimed that if they took up arms against the United States, then the Americans would take away their territory; and the British, sure to lose Canada in the coming months, would have no land to give them, as they had back in 1784 when they had offered them refuge on the north shores of lakes Erie and Ontario. Once that happened, Granger told them, the Six Nations could expect no mercy, but, "deservedly," would be "cut off from the face of the earth."[7] Perhaps some of the people who listened to Granger's speech remembered similar words he had spoken at the distribution of their annuities in 1808, when war seemed likely following the naval confrontation between the *Leopard* and the *Chesapeake* in 1807: "If we go to war with Great Britain, and you join them, destruction will follow."[8]

The antagonism behind Granger's threats was indicative of American suspicions that Indian Department agents in Canada had deployed their diplomatic skills to pull the Iroquois in New York into the British orbit.[9] Fear tore through the border in 1812 as a result of this anxiety, and settlers on the American side of the Niagara Frontier fled at the outbreak of hostilities because they expected the Six Nations to join their old British allies and fall upon the isolated farms of the western part of the state. What the Americans did not comprehend was that the King's agents exercised little influence over Iroquois external affairs. Rather, the tribespeople made their own assessments of geopolitical realities and developed foreign policies to fulfill their objectives within the limits of what they thought was possible. Across the border on the Grand River north of Lake Erie, for instance, Crown officials, in an effort to recruit the Six Nations, told them that the Americans wanted to take their land away from them. However, the Iroquois had good reasons to be suspicious of what the King's men said, in light of the disasters of 1783 and 1794 when British diplomats ignored Aboriginal needs in the treaties that had ended the Revolution and had resolved subsequent frontier tensions between the two Euro-American powers.[10] Experience and logic also told them that the apparently irresistible expansion of the United States probably would continue with the conquest of Canada occurring in due course. If British North America fell, they did not want to forfeit their homes by fighting on the losing side. Hence, many of them had opted for neutrality at the time of the *Chesapeake* Affair.

As Anglo-American relations degenerated toward war after 1807, most of the peace chiefs in New York embraced a two-point policy to protect their people and landholdings. They agreed not to take to the warpath for either side, and they decided to counter British attempts to win over other tribes.[11] The chiefs knew they had to do something to prove their good intentions toward the United States, and they believed their security could be enhanced by keeping other Natives out of the impending conflict, because the Americans had a history of using Aboriginal resistance to push friendly as well as belligerent Natives off lands coveted by white settlers. Internally, this policy also responded to the pacifist sentiments that had taken hold of those Iroquois communities where the prophet Handsome Lake exercised his greatest influence.[12]

The Iroquois in New York decided to direct their primary diplomatic efforts at the Grand River community. Unanimity did not exist among the Iroquois who lived along the Grand. Instead, British, American, and Neutralist parties vied for the support of the unaligned majority. Even within the British party, there seem to have been some who found themselves torn between their attachments and a rational assessment of American might. The Six Nations from New York thought they might be able to solidify Neutralist opinion by undermining the legitimacy of the tract's British party, and thereby secure the safety of both themselves and their Canadian relatives, win American goodwill, and, in the process, strike a pose that clearly differentiated the Iroquois from the predominantly Algonquian western tribes, whose animosity toward the United States already had led to hostilities.[13]

In early June 1812, shortly before the outbreak of war, a deputation of Iroquois from the American side of the border traveled to what was supposed to have been a secret council to strengthen the Grand River's Neutralist party.[14] (As it was, the Iroquois in New York had been sending "private messages" for some time to support neutrality.) The delegates repeated the arguments the Americans had used to persuade them to remain at peace: the British cause was hopeless because of the gross imbalance of strength in favor of the United States; furthermore, there was no reason to support the British, given their abandonment of the Aboriginal nations in 1783 and 1794.[15] Captain Strong, a Seneca chief, warned the people of the Grand to be mindful of the King's "smooth mouth," which he would use to "deceive" them to their peril. He informed his audience that his people had "determined to take no more notice of the King" and invited the Grand River Iroquois to unite with their relatives in New York because they had no reason to align themselves with either white power.[16] Another Seneca, Little Billy, added, "We know that neither of these powers have any regard for us. . . . Why then should we endanger the comfort, even the existence of our families, to enjoy their smiles only for the Day in which they need us?" To the probable agreement of many of those listening, Little Billy recommended that they "sit still" at home "unhurt & unobserved by the enraged Combatants."[17]

During the two days it took the Grand River people to formulate a reply to the delegation from New York, there were numerous debates over what they should do and opportunities to mold opinion by spreading rumors of how quickly the Americans would overrun the British colony.[18] Some discussions were simple. In one, an Indian Department official, who had found out about the council and attended the proceedings, dismissed American might with impatient disdain saying, "The United States talks loud, brags, and has a great mouth."[19] Others were more sensitive, such as the exchange between the leader of the British party on the Grand

River, Mohawk chief John Norton, and two Seneca chiefs from New York. The Senecas told Norton that they viewed him with "apprehension and suspicion" since they feared he would persuade his people to take up arms because of his support for the British without considering the terrible consequences that might ensue from such an action. Drawing upon their prophetic heritage, one of them told him that the "gloomy Day, foretold by our ancients" had arrived, in which the independence and glory of the Iroquois had disappeared. The Six Nations now lived precariously between two powerful but identical nations who could crush them out of existence when they pleased.[20] They counseled that the best policy was pacifism similar to what they had seen the Quakers pursue during the American Revolution. In reply, Norton told the Senecas that the Iroquois in New York had no choice but to be neutral because the Americans surrounded their reservations, making it impossible for them to join their natural allies, the British. However, for those in Canada, fighting alongside King George III was the honorable route, because he had been generous in giving them protection within his dominions after the Revolution. Moreover, armed resistance to American expansion was the only viable course since other responses simply did not work, as witnessed by the murders of Natives who had attempted to follow nonviolent models, such as had occurred in the Ohio Country at Gnadenhutten, in 1782, when revolutionaries massacred ninety-six pacifist Delawares in their church.[21]

When the council met in formal session to hear the Grand River answer, the tract's Neutralist party withdrew from the proceedings. This move undermined the legitimacy of the militant policy of the British party, which was to prevail, at least officially, and at least for the benefit of the Indian Department agents on the scene, although everyone understood what the departure of so many people meant. (While most residents of the Grand River may have expected an American victory, they had to show some support for the King's cause so long as Canada remained British—something the neutralists could let the British party do for them because Iroquois politics allowed for the utilization of an extremely wide diversity of opinion.)[22] The pro-British speaker for the Grand River repeated Norton's arguments and dismissed fear of American strength by expressing a providential theology that it was the Great Spirit who determined events, not the earthly might of temporal powers. He warned the people from New York that the American call for neutrality probably was a fraud, just as it had been in the Revolution when the rebels persuaded the Oneidas to embrace a non-aligned posture at first, but then made them take up arms against the other nations of the Iroquois Confederacy. Remembering that event, he encouraged the people in New York to restrain their young men from joining the Americans because the Grand River people would "be ashamed of our Tribes" if any fought alongside "the common enemy of our race."[23] Another Grand River speaker expressed his resentment toward the visitors because they had not moved to Canada after the Revolution, but instead had fallen under American domination. He told them that they had "broken with us, with Great Britain and with Indians," that if they listened to the Americans, they would be "destroyed and made slaves like the Negroes," and that, ultimately, the United States would deceive them, stop paying their annuities, and take their lands from them. That was not the fate he wanted. He declared proudly: "The President wants you to lie still and hold down your heads. But I am a Mohawk. I will paint my face and be a man and fight Yankees as long as I live."[24]

The council ended in apparent disunity as the visiting delegation, at least outwardly, failed to achieve its objective. Asserting that friendship between the Iroquois in New York and in Upper Canada had ended—presumably for the sole benefit of the Indian Department agents on the scene—the people from New York went home. However, they knew British support among the Grand River population was frail, and they had used their time in Canada effectively to help the cause of the dominant Neutralist party on the tract.[25]

About three weeks after war broke out, another delegation from New York again tried to persuade the British party of the Grand to accept neutrality. This group met the Grand's representatives at Queenston on the Niagara River, because the British commander in Upper Canada, Major-General Isaac Brock, would not allow them to go to the tract where they might gather intelligence and sow further discord. Brock also seems to have tried to control the meeting by calling on John Norton to pick reliable people to accompany him in Queenston.[26]

The emissaries from New York took a more conciliatory approach than they had at the previous council, in order to convince the British party that Iroquois interests would be served best if they abandoned their position and joined the neutralists. One delegate was Arosa, a Seneca, who tried to sway opinion by speaking of the miseries and destruction of war and the tragedies of fighting old friends. He concluded with an almost pathetic plea, which seems to have been designed to appeal to Grand River understanding of the differences between themselves and the Iroquois in New York: "remember, we are in the power of the Americans, & perhaps when you shall have spread Destruction through their Ranks, they will change their Language, and insist upon us to join them:—they may compel our young Men to fight against their kindred,—and like devoted animals,—we shall be brought to destroy each other."[27] (Perhaps the delegates from New York at that moment were thinking about a speech given a few days earlier by Erastus Granger. He had suggested, in contrast to his earlier stance, that, while the United States did not need Iroquois support, two hundred warriors could enroll in American service, if they gave up their "cowardly" way of war and conformed to American military standards.)[28] Arosa also conveyed the respected views of the matrons who favored peace: "Listen to the words of our Mothers, they are particularly addressed to the War Chiefs, they entreat them to be united with the Village chiefs and to have a tender regard for the lives and happiness of their women and children and not to allow their minds to be too much elated or misled by sentiments of vanity and pride."[29]

A Grand River delegate countered by speaking of the need for a pan-tribal defense against the Americans, noting that the western tribes had been forced to take up arms to protect their families and that it was impossible for the Iroquois "to remain unconcerned spectators at the destruction of our Brethren." However, he then contradicted himself by suggesting that his people would not venture outside Canada. This inconsistency perhaps reflected some sort of consensus reached between the opposing interests on the Grand before Norton's delegation traveled to Queenston, in which people agreed to defend their lands if necessary, but not join the western tribes operating in American territory.[30] Another member of Norton's party was an Onondaga chief, who noted that the separation of the Iroquois in New York and Canada meant that they now had distinct destinies. Since the Grand River people had sought King George's protection when "overhung by the power of the Americans," they would have to share their fate with the King's forces, whether it was the "Shout of Victory" or "the Grave." He finished by commending the decision of the people in New York to remain quiet since they could have no interest in the American cause and regretted the coming separation between the two Iroquois groups.[31] Arosa's party then re-crossed the Niagara River to the United States.

Despite Brock's attempt to control contact between the Six Nations in Upper Canada and in New York, unobserved individuals slipped back and forth across the border with little difficulty. There can be no doubt that the tribespeople in New York recognized how weak the British party was on the Grand River. By early July at the latest, the Americans also knew about the plight of the British party, the existence of an American party, and the probability that the majority of people on the Grand favored neutrality, having been informed of these details by a Grand River Delaware, Pitris. Another who probably spied for the United States was Mohawk chief Henry Tekarihogen, who worked as an interpreter for the British Indian Department, despite his leadership of the American party.[32]

Armed with this information, American officials were poised to strike a fatal blow against the British party. They made their move at about the same time the leaders of that party were away from the Grand in Queenston. On 12 July 1812, an American army commanded by William Hull began the invasion of Canada when it crossed from Detroit into British territory. A proclamation from Hull quickly reached the Grand telling the Six Nations that their lands and rights would be guaranteed if they stayed peacefully at home. Along with this news came word that the tribes in the Detroit area had decided to remain neutral rather than join the other nations of Tecumseh's alliance against the United States. These fragments of intelligence, manipulated by the American and Neutralist parties, destroyed much of the already vulnerable pro-British sentiment on the Grand River. For those inclined to mistrust the British because of the events of 1783 and 1794, the one major reason for war—the protection of their homes—probably did not exist, contrary to what the King's representatives had claimed. Additionally, their Aboriginal neighbors immediately to the west had concluded that neutrality was in their best interests, despite the potential for them that military success might lead to the creation of an independent Native refuge in the Old Northwest. These people presumably assumed that a homeland was a mere dream since Britain soon would lose the war. Their views resonated well among the residents of the Grand as the overwhelming majority of them refused to join Isaac Brock on his march against William Hull.[33]

Thus, what we see by July 1812 was a large degree of success by the Six Nations of New York in keeping both their own people and the Grand River Iroquois out of the coming war. Standing aloof from the impending contest made considerable sense because everyone expected the war to be short and to result in the conquest of Canada. For the Iroquois, a short conflict in which they would not participate held out the promise of allowing them to retain their lands as well as provide an opportunity to try to make the victors realize how their diplomacy and neutrality had facilitated the American cause. Furthermore, if the war was short, the peace chiefs might be able to keep the warriors safely at home, which, if hostilities were to drag on, might prove to be exceedingly difficult.[34] Despite common expectations of a quick and decisive American victory, however, the United States failed to overrun Canada. The British and western tribes, contrary to expectation, won a number of strategic victories early in the struggle, including the capture of Mackinac and Detroit, which demonstrated that they were a formidable force. The Detroit region tribes entered the war, and, ultimately, the King's forces and their Aboriginal allies proved capable of defending Canada against the United States.[35]

The early victories of 1812 led the majority of Iroquois in Canada to enter the conflict alongside the British by August of that year. Other factors influenced the decision as well. These included the increased authority of the Grand River's Anglophile party arising from the British successes, cultural traditions that required young men to fight, fear that a lack of support for the King might weaken their hold on the Grand River if the British defended the province successfully, and a growing realization that an American conquest probably would lead to the loss of their lands.[36]

With their Canadian-resident relatives allied to the British, the Iroquois in the United States found they could not continue to be neutral. They had to take a stand that was absolutely different from that of the Six Nations across the border. Therefore, in 1813 they declared war on the Canadas.[37] That they did this stems also from a variety of other reasons, such as the need of young men to express their warrior spirits and a corresponding desire by more mature leaders to ensure that this expression took place on behalf of the United States so as not to endanger Six Nations security in New York. Other reasons included increased American attempts to recruit warriors after their initial wartime disasters, and concern that the Senecas might lose some of their territory on the front lines as a result of the fighting. But, fundamentally, the Iroquois in New York believed that they had to show that they were good friends of the Americans to deprive the Americans of an excuse to use the war to take their lands from them.[38] Furthermore, the nature of Aboriginal warfare, in which war chiefs exercised so much influence over how their men would be deployed alongside their white allies, held out the promise that they could minimize the human costs of supporting the Americans simply by withdrawing their people from potentially bloody actions. (In the end, the Six Nations of New York suffered fairly light casualties, although they inflicted heavy losses on their Canadian-resident relatives at the Battle of Chippawa in 1814, whereupon both groups of Iroquois, for the most part, withdrew from the war.)[39]

What is the key lesson we can draw from Iroquois external affairs in this period? For people living within the confines of reservation society, surrounded by powerful polities with little interest in their future, Iroquois external affairs could be exercised within a very limited range of options. Up to the fall of Detroit, neutrality was the best alternative, and it was the one pursued by the majority of Six Nations people. Yet, from the debates over what they should do, we see how clearly many Iroquois understood the grim choices facing them. Afterward, belligerency became the preferred option for the Six Nations. Within the limits of the new order, Iroquois external affairs were driven, as they had been in more autonomous times, with the clear objective of protecting their own best interests, which in 1812 consisted of maintaining positive relations with the white powers that controlled their future in order to retain as much of their remaining land base and independence as possible.

The War of 1812 was the last time that the Iroquois were able to pursue such policies. After 1815, on both sides of the border, the massive influx of land-hungry settlers, supported by governments unsympathetic to Native interests and which no longer depended on Aboriginal military and diplomatic support because of the great population shifts of the period, simply shunted their old allies aside whenever their interests conflicted with those of the Six Nations.[40]

NOTES

1. The Iroquois consisted of the Mohawk, Oneida, Onondaga, Cayuga, Seneca, and Tuscarora nations. In 1812, many Delawares and other peoples lived among the Six Nations. For Iroquois history in the 1775–1812 period, see: Carl Benn, "The Iroquois Nadir of 1796," in *Niagara—1796: The Fortress Possessed*, ed. Brian Leigh Dunnigan (Youngstown: Old Fort Niagara Association, 1996), 50–58; William N. Fenton, *The Great Law and the Longhouse: A Political History of the Iroquois Confederacy* (Norman: University of Oklahoma Press, 1998); Barbara Graymont, *The Iroquois in the American Revolution* (Syracuse: Syracuse University Press, 1972); Graymont, "New York State Indian Policy after the Revolution," *New York History* 57 (1976): 438–74; Isabel Thompson Kelsay, *Joseph Brant 1743–1807: Man of Two Worlds* (Syracuse: Syracuse University Press, 1984); and Anthony F. C. Wallace, *The Death and Rebirth of the Seneca* (New York: Knopf, 1969).

2. The British warship HMS *Leopard* fired on the USS *Chesapeake*, thus crippling the American vessel and forcing her captain to strike his colors. Then, a boarding party removed four sailors from the American ship, who were thought to be deserters from the Royal Navy. Although the British government repudiated the *Leopard*'s actions, the incident underscored how badly Anglo-American relations had deteriorated, which ultimately led to the outbreak of war in June 1812.

3. The only book-length study of the Six Nations during the conflict is Carl Benn, *The Iroquois in the War of 1812* (Toronto: University of Toronto Press, 1998). There also are three academic articles available: Arthur C. Parker, "The Senecas in the War of 1812," *New York History* 15 (1916): 78–90; George F. G. Stanley, "The Significance of the Six Nations Participation in the War of 1812," *Ontario History* 55

(1963): 215–31; and Carl Benn, "Iroquois Warfare, 1812–1814," in *War along the Niagara: Essays on the War of 1812 and Its Legacy*, ed. Arthur Bowler (Youngstown, N.Y.: Old Fort Niagara Association, 1991), 60–76. In addition, there are three collections of primary documents with competent introductions to the topic: Charles Murray Johnston, ed., *The Valley of the Six Nations: A Collection of Documents on the Indians Lands of the Grand River* (Toronto: Champlain Society, 1964); Carl F. Klinck and James J. Talman, eds., *The Journal of Major John Norton, 1816* (Toronto: Champlain Society, 1970); and Charles M. Snyder, ed., *Red and White on the New York Frontier: A Struggle for Survival; Insights from the Papers of Erastus Granger, Indian Agent* (Harrison, N.Y.: Harbor Hill Books, 1978).

4. Communication to the House of Representatives, 13 June 1812, in Walter Lowrie and Matthew St. Clair Clarke, eds., *American State Papers: Indian Affairs*, 4 vols. (Washington, D.C.: Gales and Seaton, 1832), 4:797.

5. American forces under William Henry Harrison attacked the predominantly Shawnee community of Tippecanoe on the Wabash River as a pre-emptive strike against the alliance that Tecumseh and his prophet brother, Tenskwatawa, were organizing to protect the frontier tribes against American expansion. Traditionally, the Americans claimed victory, but historians recently have questioned that assertion.

6. *Public Speeches Delivered at the Village of Buffalo, on the 6th and 8th days of July, 1812, by Hon. Erastus Granger, Indian Agent, and Red Jacket, One of the Principal Chiefs and Speakers of the Seneca Nation* (Buffalo: S. H. and H. A. Salisbury, 1812), 13–14; cf. Little Billy's speech, June 1812, in Klinck and Talman, *Journal of Major John Norton*, 290.

7. *Public Speeches*, 13–14. The settlements created after 1783 in Canada were the Tyendinaga Tract, in eastern Ontario near modern Belleville, and the Grand River Tract to the west, near modern Brantford. Tyendinaga had about 250 people (largely Mohawk) in 1812, and Grand River had 1,900 from all Six Nations (along with Delawares, Nanticokes, Tutelos, and some others). Another 3,400 Iroquois lived within the Seven Nations of Canada at Kahnawake and Kanesatake (both near Montreal), and at Akwesasne (on the modern New York–Ontario–Quebec border). The Seven Nations communities had been created during the French Régime. Approximately 3,800 Iroquois lived on thirteen reservations (exclusive of Akwesasne) in New York and on the Cornplanter tract in Pennsylvania. The Ohio Country was home to the Mingos and Sandusky Senecas, two tribes, totaling 550 people, that were formed in the eighteenth century, largely by Iroquois immigrants from New York. (For more data, see Benn, *Iroquois in the War of 1812*, 195–200 and maps on xii and xiii.)

8. Erastus Granger to the Six Nations, September 1808, in Snyder, *Red and White*, 38.

9. Colin G. Calloway, *Crown and Calumet: British-Indian Relations, 1783–1815* (Norman: University of Oklahoma Press, 1987), 58, 61; Frederick Houghton, *History of the Buffalo Creek Reservation* (Buffalo: Buffalo Historical Society, 1920), 160; and Parker, "Senecas in the War of 1812," 81.

10. Robert Hoops to Major Van Campan, June 1812, in Benson J. Lossing, *Pictorial Field Book of the War of 1812* (New York: Harper and Brothers, 1869), 400.

11. Klinck and Talman, *Journal of Major John Norton*, 285–86; Red Jacket's speech, 13 February 1819, in *American State Paper: Indian Affairs*, 4:804; and Wallace, *Death and Rebirth of the Seneca*, 287–88.

12. The main academic work on Handsome Lake is Wallace, *Death and Rebirth of the Seneca*.

13. Klinck and Talman, *Journal of Major John Norton*, 286–98; and the Iroquois to William Claus, 10 October 1808, in Robert S. Allen, "The British Indian Department on the Frontier in North America, 1755–1830," in Parks Canada *Occasional Papers in Archaeology and History* 14 (1975): 70.

14. Jean-Baptiste Rousseau to Claus, 7 June 1812, in Johnson, *Valley of the Six Nations*, 193–94.

15. Klinck and Talman, *Journal of Major John Norton*, 286.

16. Captain Strong's speech, June 1812, in Snyder, *Red and White*, 47.

17. Klinck and Talman, *Journal of Major John Norton*, 289–90.

18. Ibid., 290–92.

19. Claus to the Grand River Iroquois, June 1812, in Snyder, *Red and White*, 47.

20. Klinck and Talman, *Journal of Major John Norton*, 291.

21. Ibid., 290–91; and Robert S. Allen, *His Majesty's Indian Allies* (Toronto: Dundurn Press, 1992), 58.

22. This characteristic of Iroquois politics has been explored well in Daniel K. Richter's, *The Ordeal of the Longhouse: The Peoples of the Iroquois League in the Era of European Colonisation* (Chapel Hill: University of North Carolina Press, 1992).

23. Klinck and Talman, *Journal of Major John Norton*, 290–92.

24. Grand River council memorandum, June 1812, in Snyder, *Red and White*, 48.

25. Klinck and Talman, *Journal of Major John Norton*, 291–92, et passim.

26. Ibid., 291–93.

27. Ibid., 294. This was to happen in 1813 and 1814. See Benn, *Iroquois in the War of 1812*, 138–41, 143–44, 149, 160–65.

28. *Public Speeches*, 17–18.

29. Arosa's speech, 12 July 1812, Alexander Fraser Papers, Toronto: Archives of Ontario [hereafter cited as AO].

30. Council minutes, 12 July 1812, Fraser Papers, AO.

31. Klinck and Talman, *Journal of Major John Norton*, 294.

32. Ibid., 297–301; and William Kerr to John B. Glegg, 7 August 1812, Fraser Papers, AO.

33. Isaac Brock to Lord Liverpool, 29 August 1812, Ottawa: National Archives of Canada, MG 11, Colonial Office Papers (CO 42), vol. 352, 105; William Hull to the Six Nations, 12 July 1812, in *Select British Documents of the Canadian War of 1812*, 4 vols., ed. William Wood (Toronto: Champlain Society, 1920–28), 1:359; Charles Askin's Journal of the Detroit Campaign, 24 July–12 September 1812, in *The John Askin Papers*, 2 vols., ed. Milo M. Quaife (Detroit: Detroit Library Commission, 1928–31), 2:711–13.

34. For a discussion of the tensions between peace chiefs and warriors, see Benn, *Iroquois in the War of 1812*, 12–13, 57.

35. A good native-centered history of the events in the Old Northwest is Allen's *His Majesty's Indian Allies*.

36. Benn, *Iroquois in the War of 1812*, 51–57.

37. Declaration of War, 1813, in Louis L. Babcock, *The War of 1812 on the Niagara Frontier* (Buffalo: Buffalo Historical Society, 1927), 108.

38. Benn, *Iroquois in the War of 1812*, 63–65.

39. Ibid., 53–54, 78–82, 160–68.

40. Ibid., 174–93.

The Firelands: Land Speculation and the War of 1812

R .   D o u g l a s   H u r t

After the War for American Indepen-
dence, the Ohio Country lured men and women like the sirens of Greek mythology.
Many were small-scale farmers who crossed the Ohio River as early as 1785, squat-
ted on government land and hoped for the best, either to make their claims good
through lawful purchase or to bide their time until the owners and the law required
them to move. Some were large-scale speculators who had the political connections
or the capital necessary to purchase considerable acreage from the government, such
as the Ohio Company of Associates, or Nathaniel Massie or Duncan McArthur who
acquired great tracts in payment for surveying lands. During the sixty years of
intermittent conflict that began with the French and Indian War, both British and
American officials designed policies of war and diplomacy to gain access to Indian
lands for the purposes of empire and settlement. In either case, farmers and speculators took their chances, much could be gained—independence, security, wealth—
but much could be lost—money, power, lives. The risks were great for both settlers
and speculators, especially in the Firelands of the Western Reserve, where isolation
and the War of 1812 posed special problems for those who caught the nearly conta-
gious desire for land known as Ohio fever.

The Firelands, or Fire Suffers Lands, comprised a twenty-five-mile wide, half-million-acre strip of land at the western end of the reserve. Essentially a reserve within the Western Reserve, this area had been set aside by the Connecticut legislature on 10 May 1792, to compensate residents of nine towns for their property losses to British attacks during the American Revolution. In May 1796, the Connecticut legislature incorporated the sufferers under the name of "The Proprietors of the Half Million Acres of Land Lying South of Lake Erie." Today, Erie and Huron and a portion of Ottawa and Ashland counties comprise the Firelands, and the towns of Vermillion, Huron, Sandusky, Milan, Norwalk, Berlin Heights, and New London, along with Cedar Point amusement park, are familiar to those who travel along the southern shore of Lake Erie or who vacation or live in Ohio.[1]

The settlement and development of the Firelands, however, proceeded slowly for many reasons. During the late eighteenth century, for example, the Western Reserve and its far reaches remained little known, in part, because it laid far to the north of the Ohio River, which served as the main transportation route by water to the western country. Settlers who came down the Ohio bought lands along the major rivers, such as the Muskingum, Scioto, and Miami, which linked them to the market economy tied to Pittsburgh and New Orleans. In contrast, an ice-bound Lake Erie blocked eastern traders during the winter, while the Appalachians hindered the development of an efficient road system to link the reserve to eastern markets. Moreover, goods could not be easily transported north from the Ohio River, and a major road did not link Columbus with the Firelands until 1834. As a result, until completion of the Erie Canal in 1825, settlers in the Firelands and Western Reserve did not have efficient and affordable access to market. Consequently, agricultural production for a market economy lagged behind farming practices south of the reserve. Most important, however, the danger of warfare with the Indians and British along the Lake Erie shore and the propensity of Yankee speculators to overprice their lands slowed the settlement and development of the Firelands until after the War of 1812.[2]

Indeed, from the creation of the Western Reserve and the Firelands during the late eighteenth century, the threat of war and stubborn speculators slowed settlement more so than anywhere else in Ohio. At first, the Connecticut Land Company proved particularly incapable of administering and dispersing its 120-mile, three-million-acre strip of land that extended west from the Pennsylvania border. Many potential settlers were hesitant to buy land in the Reserve because its system of government remained uncertain. The Connecticut Land Company had purchased the "juridical and territorial right" to the Reserve and the area fell beyond the jurisdiction of the Northwest Territory under Governor Arthur St. Clair. Squatters from Pennsylvania had settled and speculators claimed Reserve lands. As a result, the Connecticut Land Company could not guarantee land titles. Although Congress gained control of the Reserve on 28 April 1800, and, although on 10 July, Governor St. Clair announced its incorporation into the Ohio Territory as Trumball County, the process took time and hindered land settlement in the Reserve.[3]

Indian claims to lands west of the Cuyahoga River also helped discourage legitimate settlers from acquiring land in the Western Reserve. On 5 August 1800, Governor St. Clair reported to Secretary of State John Marshall that "There has been for a considerable time past a great restlessness amongst the Indian tribes" in and near the Reserve. St. Clair wrote that the Indians had been stealing "many horses from the white people, which is a common prelude to hostilities." Peace remained uncertain until the federal government and the tribes negotiated a land-cession treaty five years later. On 4 July 1805, the Wyandots, Delawares, Shawnees, and several other tribes ceded 2.7 million acres, including the Firelands, to the United States in the Treaty of Fort Industry, thereby temporarily solving the problem of white encroachment on Indian lands in the Firelands and the Reserve. Other problems, however, still hindered rapid settlement of the Western Reserve, and more difficulties developed that plagued company members and the speculators who bought large tracts to sell and earn a profit.[4]

Speculators, such as Zalmon Wildman, a thirty-year-old hat manufacturer in Danbury, Connecticut, were undaunted by the problems, both known and unknown, involved with acquiring lands in the Western Reserve. Wildman had considered investing in western lands for some time by the summer of 1805. The lure of Ohio lands increased in late July when he received a letter from Almon Ruggles, who had traveled extensively in the Reserve and who was known to be "well skilled in the art and mystery of surveying." Ruggles called the Western Reserve the "Garden of America," and Wildman wanted a part of it.[5]

Although the Western Reserve beyond the Cuyahoga had not been surveyed, Ruggles reported the area to be a "fine level country" with "luxuriant" timber. No rise worthy of being called a hill in Connecticut marked the landscape. Ruggles urged Wildman to buy as much land as possible, no matter the interest rate, from the Sufferers and the proprietors of the Reserve who did not want to move to Ohio or retain possession of their allotments, and to include him in Wildman's plans.

Ruggles wrote: "If you know of any Rights in the Firelands to be purchased if you have any inclination to speculate a little then you need not fear giving as high as 35 cents an acre at any rate if you will purchase." Ruggles offered to buy half of the acreage that Wildman acquired for the price and interest rate paid, provided Wildman extended credit for three years.[6]

Wildman liked Ruggles' report about the Western Reserve and, on 2 November 1805, he paid $432 for an unknown acreage. If he paid as high as thirty-five cents an acre, as Ruggles had recommended, he acquired 1,234 acres, not a large tract compared to other speculators in Ohio, but an acreage sufficient to make his investment subject to the fortunes of national and international policy, and Wildman anxious for the completion of the survey. By early June 1806, Wildman had purchased another one thousand acres for about $500. Wildman was, of course, purchasing rights to lands as yet unlocated and unsurveyed, because the Connecticut Land Company had not yet devised a plan for the apportionment of lands to its claimants or to the Sufferers. Wildman was mildly apprehensive about the financial risk, but not enough to prevent future purchases. He wrote: "I am not much in favor of people in trade buying Land but it was a favorable opportunity and I think there is a prospect of it being valuable by and by."[7]

The survey became the first of many problems that troubled both Wildman and the other investors who speculated in Reserve lands. Although the survey of the reserve west of the Cuyahoga began in the spring of 1806, the party under Maxfield Ludlow, which set the southwest corner and ran the boundary line north to Lake Erie, went too far and missed its mark by a mile due to inaccurate surveying on which their line was based east of the Cuyahoga River. Upon study of the survey, Secretary of the Treasury Albert Gallatin rejected it and ordered the work begun again. In August 1807, Ruggles received the contract from the Connecticut Land Company to locate the southwest corner of the Reserve and the Firelands and to lay-off townships five miles square with four sections per township, with the exception of the area along the lake where he was authorized to divide the townships equally.[8]

The work did not go well, and Ruggles perhaps rethought his early optimism about the speculative opportunities in the Firelands, an area that he labeled the "Great Marsh" on his plat map. At the 117th mile mark of the Reserve, Ruggles noted that "We are in danger of our lives." A mile later he wrote in his field book: "Sat a post in Hell. I've travelled the woods for seven years, but never saw so hideous a place as this." Ruggles did not complete his work until 25 May 1808, and, although he planned to finish the township survey by mid-August, he informed Wildman that "There are a number of Families on here already and a great number more waiting impatiently to have Land divided." Squatters had always moved in advance of the speculators and took their chances, and, by the late spring of 1808, they had already settled in the Firelands. Ruggles recommended that Wildman and the other owners give the squatters the first right to purchase at not more than one dollar per acre and to let them keep their improvements at no extra cost even though they increased the land's value. Ruggles knew that the prairie lands to the South proved most attractive to settlers and the Firelands, broken by marsh and wooded ravines, would be less desirable to settlers unless the owners offered land at a reasonable price.[9]

Indeed, the competition south of the Firelands and Reserve was twofold. First, speculators in the Virginia Military District and Symmes Purchase offered small tracts of land, often less than fifty acres at three to five dollars per acre. Although these prices were higher than the two-dollar-per-acre minimum for public lands under the Land Act of 1804, federal or public lands could only be purchased in 160-acre tracts at the Public Land Offices in Cincinnati, Chillicothe, Marietta, and Steubenville. No farmer could clear and cultivate that much land in a reasonable time, and only speculators could afford the $320 cost, even though buyers could pay for their lands in equal installments over four years at 6 percent interest. Other lands south of the Firelands and Reserve, then, proved more attractive in both price and acreage even when purchased from speculators. Investors in lands in the Firelands and Reserve faced stiff competition.[10]

The Connecticut Land Company and the Firelands Company accepted Ruggles' survey and, on 9 November 1808, partitioned the Firelands among the Sufferers or their heirs via a complicated drawing designed to equalize the best and the poorest lands among the holders. The speculators viewed further settlement with unbounded and unwarranted optimism. Almon Ruggles anticipated selling the 640 acres he received in payment for surveying while a David Abbott bought 1,800 acres along the Huron River. On 7 February 1809, the Ohio legislature created Huron County, which encompassed the Firelands, although it was not organized for another six years. Kneeland Townshend and David Abbot also laid out Huron, the first town in the Firelands. By 1809, then, the Firelands and the Reserve west of the Cuyahoga were ready for legal settlement. As a result in early April 1809, Wildman sold his first acreage, a 444-acre tract for two-and-a-quarter dollars per acre, slightly more than the two-dollar-per-acre price for public or Congress lands to the south and below the three- to four-dollar-per-acre rates from speculators in the Virginia Military District and Symmes Purchase. In 1810, John Beatty of New London, Connecticut, became the largest scale land speculator in the Firelands when he purchased forty thousand acres.[11]

At first, Wildman's speculative venture seemed to provide the capital gains that he sought. In early August 1809, he sold 247.5 acres at two dollars per acre for $495. Money, however, remained "Extremely Scarce" in Danbury and the Reserve for three years. The Embargo Act of 1807, designed to force the British and French to stop seizing American ships, had crippled American commerce at home and abroad, which, in turn, stifled monetary exchange between the east and the Reserve. Confronted with these problems, Wildman and the other speculators in Ohio offered their lands on time, that is, credit. Wildman customarily set the terms of one-third or one-fourth of the principal, interest, and taxes due at the end of the first year, with the remainder due in equal annual installments. Given the absence of an adequate circulating medium, Wildman and other speculators also agreed to take payment in kind, such as cattle and hogs, through his land agent, who, in turn, sold them for the best price.[12]

Other problems beside the absence of an adequate circulating currency plagued land sales in the Firelands, despite the demand for good lands. In late June 1810, Eli S. Barnum, Wildman's agent, wrote that "There has been a great many people on the Fire Lands this season, some to view and some to purchase lands, but a great many returns without buying because the land is held up at such a price." With the asking price of four dollars per acre customary, only the speculators who owned land bordering the lake near Vermillion had buyers. Moreover, because the Firelands formed the western part of the Reserve, its isolation deterred settlement. Settlers who bought land wanted access to markets and the economic gain they could earn either in cash or kind from the sale or trade of agricultural commodities. In the Firelands, no mills existed to encourage farmers to raise wheat. Cleveland, with fifty-seven inhabitants in 1810, provided only a rudimentary market for wheat raised in the Western Reserve, but its mills were a distant 60 or more miles from the Firelands. Moreover, adequate roads through the Reserve, or ports for shipping, did not exist. One traveler called an 8-mile stretch "the worst road I had yet seen in America." Speculators who asked four dollars per acre either misjudged the market or stubbornly hoped for large capital gains that demand did not yet warrant. Wildman, however, listened to the advice of his agent and offered two hundred acres for sale on the Marblehead peninsula for two dollars per acre.[13]

By the autumn of 1810, a far more serious problem than insufficient currency supply, absence of markets, or inadequate transportation posed a formidable barrier to land speculation and settlement in the Firelands. Wildman's agent reported in mid-November that the British had been secretly urging the Indians to make war against the United States. "They are," Barnum believed, "at the bottom of the Shawnee Prophet's conduct. He is hired and paid by them, and he receives his instructions how to act from the British agents." Barnum also informed Wildman that during the past summer the "back Indians," under British influence, had sent the war belt and hatchet "through all the different tribes to join them in a war against the U.S." Barnum told Wildman that, although the tribes in the Ohio Country had been peaceful, "this year all the tribes generally accepted the hatchet and smoked the bloody tobacco, which always accompanied it." Barnum expected the northwestern tribes to unite with those in Canada by the next summer and to strike at "green corn time." Barnum had gained his information from an Indian who had been present at Sandusky in July, when several tribes agreed to make war on the United States. Little land could be sold under these circumstances, and he wanted action by the federal government to destroy the British and Indian alliance before they struck the settlers on the northwestern frontier. Barnum wrote that "the Indians have had many private councils the past summer, and have been much agitated; they are insolent and saucy, more so than usual, and . . . the British have a deep laid scheme of villainny on foot, which nothing but a timely intervention of our government can frustrate." While the government dallied, Barnum intended to get "a *good Rifle* and *ammunition* and tarry for a while yet, and see the result of war talk." Barnum's report did not bode well for Wildman and the other land speculators in the Firelands or Western Reserve.[14]

In the spring of 1811, however, the northwestern Indians remained peaceful, and Barnum reported that a council of chiefs, held at Detroit, concluded with the Indians expressing friendship for the Americans. The war scare had been a false alarm. Barnum now thought that Wildman could sell his lands in the vicinity of Huron for two-and-a-half dollars per acre. Only the "fevers" that frequented the area threatened to hinder settlement. Wildman no doubt thought the crisis had passed and that capital gains on his investments would soon be realized. In mid-March 1811, Barnum reported that "The land viewers and Speculators are all viewing" along the Huron River and some were willing to pay five dollars per acre. Barnum told Wildman that "Families and travelers never were so plenty nor poured into the Fire Lands so fast as they have for a few months past, . . . if the Landholders offer their lands at a price anywhere reasonable, the Fire Lands will settle speedily."[15]

Land buyers apparently flocked to the Firelands during the spring and summer of 1811; they established the market rate, not the speculators. Although Wildman could sell his lands on the Marblehead peninsula for two dollars per acre, he wanted the principal and interest over three years, but buyers considered those terms "too short." Instead, they demanded credit terms over five years and "none shorter." With merchants at Huron and Cleveland paying a dollar per bushel for corn and wheat, five dollars per bushel for hemp seed, a dollar and a quarter per bushel for beans, and eight dollars per barrel for cider, farmers in the Western Reserve saw a profit could be earned from those lands, but they wanted adequate time to make their lands pay. If they could not obtain satisfactory terms in the Firelands or Reserve, they would go where cheaper lands prevailed. In late June, Barnum reported that "Our country is full of strangers viewing lands," some of which sold for seventy-five cents per acre. He had managed, also, to sell some of Wildman's land on the peninsula for two dollars per acre over four years, because the buyers would not accept three-year terms. Although the records do not indicate how much Wildman paid for the land or how much he sold, he probably purchased those lands for less than a dollar per acre and, thereby, made a comfortable profit. The future seemed bright and prosperous for Wildman and the other land speculators in the Firelands. In early December, Barnum reported, "no apprehensions from the Indians in this vicinity."[16]

Even so, most Ohioans believed another war with Great Britain was necessary to end the threat of Indian attacks in the backcountry. War would give the federal government the opportunity to end British encouragement of the northwestern tribes against the frontier people and destroy Tecumseh's Indian confederacy. When the Twelfth Congress declared war on Great Britain on 17 June 1812, Ohioans supported the decision. In fact, Governor Return Jonathan Meigs, Jr., had anticipated war, and, in March, he had called for twelve hundred volunteers to organize at Dayton and march north to help defend Detroit. Quickly, volunteers from all walks of life began to assemble at St. Clairsville, Zanesville, New Lancaster, Circleville, and other towns in preparation for a rendezvous at Dayton in May.[17]

In early July, Wildman, who was in the Firelands surveying his lands, wrote to his son from Vermillion that "The troops are flying in all directions to defend the Settlers on the frontiers." The heady sentiment for war among the settlers in the reserve could not be missed. Wildman observed that "not a man has been drafted in this State. They all cheerfully volunteer their services; even the generals offer to shoulder their firelocks and march in ranks." Ohioans would soon have cause to criticize generals who had more enthusiasm for war than the ability to conduct it.[18]

In the early days of the war, Ohioans viewed Canada as easy prey and the hostile Indian tribes as ordained for defeat. Wildman and the other speculators in the Firelands and Reserve proceeded with business as usual through the summer. In late July, he sold 247 acres in the Firelands for $591.67, with half due in two years and the remainder at the end of the third year, plus taxes. Wildman required "immediate settlement and permanent residence" by the purchaser. If payment could not be made on time, forfeiture included loss of all improvements. Wildman drove a hard bargain, but he remained confident that the war would bring peace to northwestern Ohio, thereby making his lands more desirable and expensive for settlers.[19]

In late August, Wildman received bad news for any land speculator in the Firelands when a Jonathan H. Patch, writing from Canfield, reported that William Hull, commander of the Northwestern Army, had surrendered his force to the British at Detroit. The war had not progress smoothly or well. Instead, disaster seemed imminent. Hull had not only been defeated at Detroit without providing much of a fight, but he also surrendered. The British sent home the Ohio volunteers and militia, and two boats carrying some of the soldiers arrived at Cleveland on 23 August. More boats carrying five hundred captives were east of Sandusky Bay and due for arrival at any time. Observers from shore saw the boats of prisoners and mistakenly reported that the British and Indians were ready to strike the Reserve and that the enemy had advanced as far as Huron with three hundred regulars and six hundred Indians. These reports put northern Ohio in a panic with volunteers "fitting out with all possible speed" to march to Cleveland for its defense.[20]

While militia and other volunteers raced to the Reserve, the settlers fled the Firelands. On 30 August, Jabez Wright, a surveyor and land agent writing from Vermillion, informed Wildman that "The Indians are now at the River Raisin and Miami plundering and stripping every family. There is not more than five families on the Firelands. Dreadful times they have had, moving off, leaving almost everything behind." He anticipated the arrival of three hundred troops that night with four thousand soon expected to meet at the Sandusky rapids for the purpose of retaking the places the settlers had fled. In the meantime, he wrote: "The Peninsula people are chiefly at this place." Morale among the settlers had plummeted, and he noted that "our atmosphere hangs fraught with dispare." Any hope for protection from these troops by the settlers in the Firelands no doubt vanished when they learned that half of the force recruited to defend Cleveland and the Reserve had been dismissed because Major General Elijah Wadsworth, who commanded these militia men, believed they were "so badly armed that it would be useless to march them to the frontier." Moreover, the undisciplined force of two hundred and fifty Ohio militia, under Brigadier General Simon Perkins, which had arrived at the mouth of the Huron River by 5 September to begin building a series of blockhouses between Huron and Mansfield, proved difficult to control, and the men stole a considerable amount of property from settlers who had abandoned their farms on the Marblehead peninsula.[21]

Wildman received another letter from Wright, dated 6 September, in which he reported that after Hull's surrender at Detroit, Colonels Lewis Cass and Duncan McArthur arrived with their repatriated men aboard boats at Sandusky and "put the whole People in an uproar." The settlers now feared the British and their Indian allies would soon attack Cleveland, and they continued to flee the Firelands. Many did not stop until they had traveled as far east as Warren, where Wright observed that "Forty waggons and carts was there at one time loaded with women and children not knowing where to go; cattle all drove that could be found, which in all was a sorrowful sight to see. Sick people not able to sit up, drove off in the night, laying in wagons." Whether the evacuation of Cleveland would be necessary no one could yet say, but there, he noted "all is confusion." The streets were crowded with a thousand armed men and uncounted number of refugees from the Firelands and the Maumee River area. Three companies of militia had marched to Huron while as many as three thousand soldiers were expected to move from the south to engage the British and the Indians at the Maumee Rapids. The surrender of Hull, he believed, was "the greatest blow that America ever had. Arnold, Burr, etc. was never half equal to Hull."[22]

Despite this bad news and no assurance that the situation would soon improve, Wright informed Wildman that the court had approved all of his petitions, that is, claims for land acquired from Sufferers. One area included 475 acres and another 805 acres. Wright had surveyed and mapped these tracts, for which he charged two dollars per mile for 15 miles of survey and five dollars for preparing the maps and completing the necessary paper work for a total of thirty-five dollars. By now, Wildman owned some 5,000 acres in the Firelands, but his prospects for selling those tracts and earning a handsome profit appeared grim so long as the British and Indians remained unconquered in northwestern Ohio.[23]

Later, Major Elisha Whittlesey, aide-de-camp for Major General Elijah Wadsworth of the Ohio Militia in the Canfield area and who also marched with two companies of light horse for Cleveland and who apparently handled some of Wildman's land purchases, affirmed the bad news for land speculators in the Firelands. Whittlesey wrote:

> We have been unsuccessful in the War thus far beyond the expectations of any man. I have never believed that Canada would conquer herself as many members of Congress asserted she would by the appearance of a small Military American force. But I did suppose that the posts on the Lakes would have been taken possession of by our troops long before this without the expenditure of much money or the loss of much blood. But instead of this having been achieved by our arms, we have lost a territory and at least five thousand citizens in arms either have been killed or taken prisoners.

Moreover, with the loss of Michilimackinac and Chicago, the Indians were "without restraint." He attributed Hull's surrender to cowardice, all within hearing distance of the Reserve. Whittlesey boarded in Cleveland on 15 August when the cannonading of Hull's troops began. "The report of the guns were distinctly heard," he observed, "but little did I suppose they were summoning me from my family and business." When Harrison became commander, however, Whittlesey believed the war in the northwest would soon take a favorable turn for the Americans.[24]

In late December 1812, Eli Barnum optimistically reported that there was "no danger on the Firelands of Indians." Still, the British had not been defeated, and everyone knew that spring would bring a new campaign against them and their Indian allies. Barnum did not expect any families to return to the peninsula during the winter, although the settlers along Pipe Creek had "mostly returned" and planted wheat. Even so, provisions remained scarce on the Firelands. Merchants, he believed, could command twelve dollars per barrel of flour, except they did not have any to sell. Corn and salt brought a dollar and three quarters and fifteen dollars per bushel respectively. Wildman now owned 5,405 acres in the Firelands with $35.13 due in taxes and few prospects for selling his lands soon.[25]

The army boosted morale in the Firelands and Reserve by mid-January 1813 when General James Winchester, under William Henry Harrison, the newly appointed commander of the Northwestern Army, began building a fortified camp at the Maumee Rapids. These soldiers needed provisions, and the settlers in the Firelands and Reserve sought to meet that market demand. At that time, Jabez Wright informed Wildman that "The roads are filled with public teams with provisions for Sandusky." With wheat bringing a dollar and a half and corn a dollar per bushel respectively, he noted that "Times are healthy." Moreover, Harrison had sent riders to Huron seeking all of the horse teams that could be hired. Everyone expected another expedition against the British. The morale of the settlers in the Firelands, however, soon plummeted again, when they learned that Winchester had led another disastrous expedition against the British that ended with the near annihilation of his army at the Raisin River to the north.[26]

Despite Winchester's defeat, Harrison continued his plans to fortify the Maumee Rapids. Although his men had completed much of the work on Fort Meigs by mid-March, and although Harrison planned to defend Sandusky, the settlers in the Firelands remained worried about their safety. Barnum informed Wildman that "The inhabitance of Huron County—the timorous part—think it doubtfull whether we can remain here the Summer coming with safety, others to the reverse of opinion, which makes in some degree a confused set of minds. The timorous is rather neglect-full and appear rather to discourage than to animate." The peninsula remained too dangerous for residence. The only good news he could convey was that the war had substantially increased the price of cattle, which, he thought would remain "very high priced as long as we have troops marching through our Country."[27]

No one, certainly not land speculators such as Wildman, expected life in the Firelands to improve until the war ended. In March, Wright could not provide any reason for optimism when he told Wildman, "The troops are at Miami Rapids and whether they will ever do anything or not God only knows." Given these bleak times, at least one settler asked Wildman to take back a tract of land he had purchased, probably on the peninsula, because the war made it too dangerous for him to live there and prevented him from raising enough crops to meet his payments. Wildman considered these transactions "troublesome holdings," and often extended the credit period or let mortgages go overdue because the land remained relatively worthless so long as the British and Indians continued to threatened northwestern Ohio. Foreclosure meant that he had to pay the property taxes and seek new buyers. If his clients retained possession of the lands he sold them, Wildman believed they eventually would be able to meet their obligations once the war ended.[28]

Wildman received better news in late May when Barnum informed him about Harrison's victory over the British and Indians at Fort Meigs earlier in the month. The settlers in the Firelands and Reserve remained "timid" and apprehensive, however, because the British might mount another campaign into northwestern Ohio. More time would be needed before they returned to their homes or until new buyers sought lands. Barnum reported: "The Calamities and Disasters which has visited our Country for the year past have almost forsaken us. The Inhabitance are greatly relieved but a very few, as yet, move on to the Fire Land. But by accounts, many are waiting to have peasable times and then will move on." For the moment, though, they waited, knowing that the British could strike again. Indeed, in mid-May, the citizens of Huron had been greatly frightened when British warships arrived to return approximately seventy prisoners taken at Fort Meigs. Before they learned the intent of the British, "great confusion," once again, spread through the settlements in the Firelands.[29]

Although the British no longer possessed the will or ability to launch a major strike against Ohio, Indians remained a threat to the Firelands. On 2 June 1813, a party of Indians seized three women and ten children along Cold Creek. Although a rescue party soon followed the trail, it found only one woman and four children who had been killed. Harrison responded to the Indian threat by sending two regiments from the south to help defend Cleveland. With Fort Meigs reinforced to the west and Cleveland strengthened on the east, farmers on the Firelands and Reserve aided their own protection by working their fields in groups and fortified themselves in block houses during the day and night. There, three or four families lived together under "very disagreeable" conditions. Danger signs appeared all around—isolated Indian attacks, an unidentified body washed ashore near the mouth of the Huron River with the "print of a tomahawk stuck in his head," and British warships off the Cuyahoga River. There, a British foraging party went ashore near Cleveland and killed an ox. After butchering the animal, they left eight dollars wrapped in the hide with a note that if the payment was not enough they would return in a few days and pay the balance. To add inconvenience to fear, by the end of June the mail from Pittsburgh to Cleveland had not arrived for two weeks. And, Indian signs were seen frequently around Sandusky Bay. Barnum believed, "If Malden is not taken soon I fear the Savages will drive the Inhabitants from the Fire Lands." Even so, Barnum reported some good news to Wildman, noting that he had been approached by three men who inquired about the price of his lands in Ridgefield Township and who wanted to make a purchase in time to make hay on it that summer.[30]

The continued threat of war and Wildman's apparent unwillingness to offer his lands at an affordable price discouraged land sales. In late July 1813, three British vessels anchored off Peninsula Point and landed an estimated six or seven hundred men together with "a great many hundred" Indians who butchered all the cattle and hogs they could find before departing. Although the estimated number of the enemy probably was exaggerated, the damage wrought and fear inflicted were not for the residents of the Firelands. The few remaining settlers in the Firelands received another fright when they learned that the British had returned on 20 July for another attack on Fort Meigs. Although this attack quickly failed, the British and their Indian allies retreated, burning several houses and making a weak foray against Fort Stephenson before returning to Canada. By mid-August, Indians could still be seen "lurking about the west part of the Fire Lands." The residents of Huron, Avery, and Pipe Creek continued to sleep in block houses, and Barnum reported that most of the inhabitants west of Huron had "moved off" the Firelands.[31]

Given the threat of continued Indian attacks or campaigns by the British, Wildman and the other speculators had little prospect of selling land in the Firelands or Reserve until the war ended. Provisions remained scarce for the settlers who stayed in the Firelands and Reserve, with some traveling nearly 80 miles to Cleveland to buy grain and flour for their families. The scarcity of food by the spring of 1814 resulted because many settlers who had livestock and grain during the previous fall "hurried it off to the army on the frontier in order to get a great price." At Fort Meigs, for example, the army paid the highest prices for agricultural produce— fifteen dollars per barrel for flour and five dollars per hundred weight for beef and pork. Other nearby camps at Upper and Lower Sandusky and Huron also needed supplies, which local farmers helped provide. In addition, heavy rains during the spring and fall destroyed many newly planted crops. Although farmers had been "bewitched to find a market" and earn needed cash, by mid-May, they had not yet received payment. Consequently, they had to buy provisions from afar at prices that exceeded those received from the army, all of which one observer considered "a very proper reward for their avericious dispositions."[32]

The War of 1812, then, became a major obstacle to the settlement of the Firelands and the Reserve. In March 1813, Simon Perkins noted "the population of the Country has not increased for the last twelve months." He believed, "at the close of the War, sales will be more frequent than they ever have been, and . . . lands will command a better price than formerly" in the Reserve. After Captain Oliver H. Perry's defeat of the British fleet at Put-in-Bay on Lake Erie, on 10 September 1813, Perkins wrote: "The success of our little fleet on Lake Erie will, I think, have the effect to remove the seat of war so far from us as to induce people from the old states to come and settle with us. We have heretofore been in such an exposed situation as to render our Country uninteresting to people who were seeking a place for a family." A year later, land agent Seth Tracy reported that the war "much retarded emigration from the Eastward." It also interrupted American commerce on the Great Lakes, further restricted the amount of currency in circulation, and hampered the efforts of land agents to collect money from settlers who had purchased their farms on credit. Settlers, who could not meet their obligations, either made a partial payment or renegotiated their debt. Wildman apparently accepted both adjustments if he believed his buyers eventually would pay the entire amount owed. But, he also foreclosed when necessary, and some speculators, such as Pierpont Edwards, had buyers who simply left their land when they fell in arrears and could not pay.[33]

When peace finally came with the Treaty of Ghent, signed on 24 December 1814, provisions in the Firelands and Reserve remained scarce and expensive with flour and pork bringing fourteen and five dollars per barrel respectively. Army spending for agricultural produce, however, essentially ceased, thereby further reducing the amount of money in circulation; only slowly did settlers, both farmers and merchants, begin to return. But Wildman still had no inclination to sell his lands quickly for less than he believed the acreage warranted. As a result, his agent reported in late July 1815, "The Fire Lands settles slow, but would be very rapid if lands were for sale, many come to buy, but not being able to buy where they want leave the Fire Lands. Some go South, some West, and some East."[34]

By early 1816, steady agricultural prices and crop failure in New England encouraged immigration to the Reserve and Firelands. At that time, Wildman traveled to the Firelands and met with potential buyers at New Haven. His agent, Isaac Mills, announced his arrival by advertising his lands as widely as possible. In the Zanesville *Muskingum Messenger*, he contended: "These lands are equal in quality to any in the country; and unquestioned title will be made by the proprietor." A year later, Barnum reported, "The settlement of the Firelands has been rapid. . . . Mills is erecting in every quarter." Other settlers rapidly purchased land in the Reserve.

Norwalk and Milan were founded soon after the war, and, in 1817, Wildman and
Isaac Mills laid out the town of Portland, which became Sandusky City.[35]

Some merchants and land speculators announced grand plans for the economic
development of the Firelands. Frederick Talley, who owned considerable property in
Venice on Sandusky Bay, advertised 209 lots and a "proportional number" of out lots
for sale at auction on 26 May 1817. He boasted that "perhaps no place in the western
waters is better situated than Venice to become a place of importance and eminence."
With "pleasant and fertile country" to the south, a good harbor, and ample mill sites,
farmers could easily raise wheat and market fifty thousand barrels of flour and salt
pork annually, all within five years. With one sawmill and gristmill already in operation near the town on Cold Creek, he envisioned a four-stone flourmill, saw and paper
mill, tannery, and distillery in operation by 1818. Talley, like other speculators, proved
perennial optimists, noting that "as soon as a regular system of transportation is
established, on reasonable terms, from New York to Sandusky Bay, the New York
Market will gain (through Venice) the trade of a large section of fertile country." Then,
with a flourish of exuberance, he proclaimed that "Capitalists, Wholesale Dealers,
Manufacturers, and all classes of useful Mechanics, particularly Carpenters, Brick
Makers, Brick Layers, Stone Quarriers, Stone Masons, are invited to participate in
opening the Town of Venice." Wildman, Talley, and the other speculators and their
agents knew that artisans and merchants, who could provide goods and services,
would attract settlers who would buy land, just as Cincinnati and Chillicothe and the
river trade drew settlers to the Virginia Military District and Symmes Purchase and
provided major local markets and access to New Orleans.[36]

Despite these opportunities, speculators had difficulty promoting and selling
land, except near the towns where schools and churches already existed, in part,
because the road system in the Firelands remained "extremely bad." As a result,
the Firelands and Reserve remained a buyers market, even though New Englanders
preferred the more expensive Reserve lands at three to four dollars per acre to avoid
settling near immigrants from Pennsylvania, Virginia, and Maryland who preferred the Congress lands at two dollars per acre and whom Whittlesey, among others, considered such a "motley society that few or no persons from New England
would settle among them." Still, while relatively few New Englanders came to buy
in the Firelands and Reserve, and while cheap lands elsewhere lured away potential settlers, neither Wildman nor most other speculators lowered their prices.
Instead, they continued to price their lands substantially above the market value of

other attractive lands, either public or private, in Ohio. Wildman in the Firelands, and Edwards in the Reserve, for example, consistently made this mistake. Both asked four dollars or more per acre for their lands, regardless of quality.[37]

Elsewhere the public lands sold rapidly, and, in 1819, Congress established land offices in eight towns, including Upper Sandusky and Defiance, to sell the newly opened Congress lands in northwestern Ohio. Federal banking policy that contracted the currency supply and falling agricultural prices, however, caused the Panic of 1819 and slowed land sales throughout Ohio. Western banks often issued paper notes for circulation that they could not back with specie. Eastern banks often rejected this currency for exchange or discounted it heavily. As a result, settlers had great difficulty acquiring money, especially negotiable paper that both speculators and outside banks would accept. Moreover, in 1817, Congress required settlers to pay for public lands in specie, U.S. Treasury notes, or notes from specie-paying banks, further draining hard money from Ohio to the east. Agricultural prices dropped soon thereafter. In February 1818, agent Tracy reported to Edwards, "it is with much difficulty . . . that current money on the Eastern banks can be procured while money is so scarce and land buyers so unable to pay their installments when they become due." Actual delivery of the money to the speculators, either by courier or by deposit in the Western Reserve Bank in Warren or the Bank of the United States in Pittsburgh, also compounded the difficulty of selling these Ohio lands. As a result, Talley's optimism proved short lived, and it collapsed with the national economy during the Panic of 1819. By June 1820, settlers and speculators in the Firelands suffered considerable financial hardship. Wildman could not be optimistic about the sale of his lands. One correspondent told him that "The times are cruel hard, business is dull; produce fetches in a manner of nothing."[38]

By the summer of 1823, however, the economy began to recover and settlers again sought property in the Firelands. In August, Wildman priced his lands near Sandusky on credit at six dollars per acre with half due at the day of sale and the remainder a year later, plus interest and taxes. Or, he offered those lands for five-and-a-half dollars per acre in cash. He advertised his holdings in the Firelands as "first quality lands near villages, grain and saw mills, county seat, public roads and mail, stores, schools, and churches." Any settler could enjoy the conveniences of nearly everything needed by purchasing his lands. Yet, Wildman's attractive offer failed for want of ready cash by prospective settlers. Few bought from him because his lands were too expensive, and he would not lower the price.[39]

R . D O U G L A S H U R T

Finally, in July 1825, Wildman's agent recommended that he price his lands in Ridgefield township at three to five dollars per acre, because at six dollars per acre he did not have much hope of selling more than enough to pay the taxes. Unless Wildman decreased the price of his lands, he reported, "I shall be unable to dispose of any land on the peninsula, all are bent for Congress lands." Indeed, the newly opened public or Congress lands in northwestern Ohio, priced at a dollar-and-a-quarter per acre for eighty-acre tracts under the Land Act of 1820, drew settlers and small-scale speculators, who could afford to pay $100 for full title. Moreover, by January 1828, settlers who sought lands now preferred to locate near the projected canals rather than in areas, such as the Firelands, where inadequate transportation still hindered the shipment of agricultural produce to market, even though Sandusky reportedly conducted $300,000 in export business annually, mostly in agricultural goods.[40]

By the late 1820s, the War of 1812 and national monetary problems, together with competition from land speculators in the Virginia Military District and Symmes Purchase and cheaper public lands to the south and west, prevented Wildman and other land speculators in the Firelands and Reserve from earning the large capital gains that they had anticipated more than twenty years earlier. With only the prospect of the continued slow settlement of the Firelands, Wildman decided to sell his nearly twenty-four hundred acres on the peninsula for the competitive price of two-and-a-half dollars per acre, except for 279 acres adjoining the bay and Sandusky City, which he planned to sell for five dollars per acre. Wildman then visited the Firelands in the summer of 1829 to survey his land and negotiate the sale of his property. During the remaining years, until his death on 10 December 1835, he sold most of his remaining land, asking as much as $1,000 for some of his lots in Sandusky.[41]

Wildman, in contrast to many of the large-scale land speculators, never achieved great wealth from his speculation in the Firelands. Usually, he priced his lands higher than the market warranted, but he remained optimistic for more than twenty years that his investment would return high dividends. In July 1829, when he decided to leave the land speculation business, he wrote to his daughter Mary in New York City from Sandusky City, "Great numbers of people pass through this place to and from the States of Kentucky, Tennessee, Indiana, Illinois, Missouri, Mississippi, Louisiana, Alabama, the territories of Arkansas and Michigan, and the Spanish possessions of Mexico, Havana etc. In short it may be truly said to be a great thoroughfare." Sandusky City also had become a thriving port with the services of nine mercantile stores, several grocers, four lawyers, three doctors, Methodist and Presbyterian ministers, three hotels, two school teachers, six boarding houses, a ship builder, watch maker, tin smith, gun smith, carpenters, barbers, and a billiard hall. Money could be made in the Firelands, but now younger men would need to do it.[42]

Although land and the market economy drew many settlers to Ohio, speculators experienced considerable risk. During the sixty years of conflict that began with the French and Indian War in 1754 and concluded with the end of the War of 1812, land speculators enjoyed considerable opportunity, just as the men and women who settled the Ohio Country did. Often they met with as much failure as success because they could control neither national land and monetary policies nor the process of war. Those who adjusted to frontier circumstances, such as Nathaniel Massie, Duncan McArthur, and Thomas Worthington, and accepted market-driven returns for their lands, ultimately prevailed and profited. Others, such as Zalmon Wildman, who obstinately kept their prices high, despite overwhelming evidence of poor transportation, insufficient markets, inadequate circulating currency, and low land values in the Firelands and Reserve, achieved considerably less success measured in capital gains from the sale of their lands. Cheaper and less-isolated lands beyond the Firelands and Reserve first met the needs of settlers in the Ohio Country.

Settlement of the frontier was not a linear, orderly process, and while speculators usually contributed to it by selling small tracts of land at affordable prices, occasionally as in the Firelands and Reserve, they hindered the settlement by overvaluing their lands and by failing to adjust to unusual conditions, such as war, poor transportation, and an inadequate currency. Economic success on the frontier was not a certainty for anyone, including land speculators. Some speculators, such as Zalmon Wildman in the Firelands, ultimately realized that circumstances beyond their control proved too daunting and the end reward never quite in sight. When Wildman died in 1835, lands in the Firelands and Reserve still sold for as little as two dollars per acre with credit of five or six years. His investments in Ohio totaled little more than $17,000, including his stock in the Mad River and Erie Railroad Company, at a time when $20,000 in earnings from land served as a mark of success. Indeed, settlement of the Firelands had remained so slow that stumps still could be found in some streets in Sandusky. Frontier settlement proved a risky business for both settlers and speculators, especially in the Firelands.[43]

NOTES

1. Thomas A. Smith, "The Firelands and the Settlement of Vermillion," in *Ohio's Western Reserve: A Regional Reader,* ed. Harry F. Lupold and Gladys Haddad (Kent, Ohio: Kent State University Press, 1988), 39–40; Harlan Hatcher, *The Western Reserve: The Story of New Connecticut in Ohio* (Cleveland: World Publishing Co., 1966), 40, 44. See also Helen M. Carpenter, "The Origin and Location of the Firelands of the Western Reserve," *Ohio State Archaeological and Historical Quarterly* 44 (1935): 162–203; Clarence D. Laylin, "The Firelands Grant," *Ohio Archaeological and Historical Society Publications* 10 (1901–2): 435–50; B. A. Hinsdale, "The Sale of the Western Reserve," *Ohio Archaeological and Historical Quarterly* 2 (1888–89): 475–87; Russell H. Anderson, "The Pease Map of the Connecticut Western Reserve," *Ohio Archaeological and Historical Quarterly* 63 (July 1954): 270–78.

2. Hatcher, *Western Reserve,* 131; Brian Harte, "Land in the Old Northwest: A Study of Speculation, Sales, and Settlement on the Connecticut Western Reserve," *Ohio History* 101 (summer/autumn 1992): 121–22.

3. Clarence Edwin Carter, ed., *The Territorial Papers of the United States,* 28 vols. (Washington, D. C.: Government Printing Office, 1934–75), 2:22–24, 549, 657–58, 3:84–85, 101, 524; Harte, "Land in the Old Northwest," 124–25.

4. Carter, *Territorial Papers,* 3:101–2; Charles J. Kappler, ed., *Indian Affairs: Laws and Treaties,* 7 vols. (Washington, D. C.: Government Printing Office, 1904–75), 2:77–78.

5. Almon Ruggles to Zalmon Wildman, 30 July 1805, Zalmon Wildman Papers, Columbus: Ohio Historical Society [hereafter all manuscript citations are from this collection]; Hatcher, *Western Reserve,* 46.

6. Almon Ruggles to Zalmon Wildman, 30 July 1805.

7. Deed, 2 November 1805; Zalmon Wildman to ?, 1 June 1806.

8. Hatcher, *Western Reserve,* 46; Thomas H. Smith, *The Mapping of Ohio* (Kent, Ohio: Kent State University Press, 1977), 141–43.

9. Hatcher, *Western Reserve,* 47; Almon Ruggles to Zalmon Wildman, 31 May 1808.

10. Carter, *Territorial Papers,* 3:89, 91; Benjamin Horace Hibbard, *A History of the Public Land Policies* (Madison: University of Wisconsin Press, 1965), 74–75; Paul W. Gates, *History of Public Land Law Development* (New York: Arno Press, 1979), 129–31.

11. Carpenter, "The Origin and Location of the Firelands of the Western Reserve," 192, 195; Hatcher, *Western Reserve,* 56, 186; Smith, "The Firelands and the Settlement of Vermillion," 40; Zalmon Wildman to Seymour Wildman, 5 April 1809; Harvey Rice, *Pioneers of the Western Reserve* (Boston, 1883), 227, 319.

12. Land Purchase Agreement with Daniel Robinson, 1 August 1809; Zalmon Wildman to ?, 1 June 1806; Thadeus Tracey to Zalmon Wildman, 2 August 1809.

13. Eli S. Barnum to Zalmon Wildman, 25 June 1810; Hatcher, *Western Reserve,* 55, 66; Eli S. Barnum to Zalmon Wildman, 13 November 1810.

14. Eli S. Barnum to Zalmon Wildman, 13 November 1810.

15. Eli S. Barnum to Zalmon Wildman, 28 January 1811; Eli S. Barnum to Zalmon Wildman, 7 February 1811; Eli S. Barnum to Zalmon Wildman, 19 March 1811.

16. Eli S. Barnum to Zalmon Wildman, 5 May 1811; Eli S. Barnum to Zalmon Wildman, 26 June 1811; Eli S. Barnum to Zalmon Wildman, 6 December 1811.

17. R. Douglas Hurt, *The Ohio Frontier: Crucible of the Old Northwest, 1720–1830* (Bloomington: Indiana University Press, 1996), 327.

18. Zalmon Wildman to Horatio Wildman, 4 July 1812.

19. Agreement between Zalmon Wildman and Joseph Ramsdel, 23 July 1812.

20. Jonathan H. Patch to Zalmon Wildman, 25 August 1812; Mary Lou Conlin, *Simon Perkins of the Western Reserve* (Cleveland: Western Reserve Historical Society, 1968), 80.

21. Jabez Wright to Zalmon Wildman, 30 August 1812; Conlin, *Simon Perkins,* 80.

22. Jabez Wright to Zalmon Wildman, 6 September 1812.

23. Jabez Wright to Zalmon Wildman, 30 August 1812.

24. Conlin, *Simon Perkins,* 80; Elisha Whittlesey to Zalmon Wildman, 16 March 1813.

25. Eli S. Barnum to Zalmon Wildman, 14 December 1812; Leonard Case to Zalmon Wildman, 29 December 1812; Conlin, *Simon Perkins,* 80–85.

26. Jabez Wright to Zalmon Wildman, 16 January 1813; Eli S. Barnum to Zalmon Wildman, 18 March 1813; Conlin, *Simon Perkins,* 86–88.

27. Eli S. Barnum to Zalmon Wildman, 18 March 1813.

28. Jabez Wright to Zalmon Wildman, 5 March 1813; Eli S. Barnum to Zalmon Wildman, 18 March 1813.

29. Eli S. Barnum to Zalmon Wildman, 24 May 1813.

30. Eli S. Barnum to Zalmon Wildman, 29 June 1813.

31. Eli S. Barnum to Zalmon Wildman, 14 August 1813.

32. Zanesville *Express,* 24 November 1813; Jonathan H. Patch to Zalmon Wildman, 10 May 1814.

33. Conlin, *Simon Perkins,* 97–98; Harte, "Land in the Old Northwest," 128.

34. Eli S. Barnum to Zalmon Wildman, 28 April 1815; *Ohio Federalist and Belmont Repository* (St. Clairsville), 7 November 1816; Eli S. Barnum to Zalmon Wildman, 30 July 1815.

35. Conlin, *Simon Perkins,* 98; Hurt, *Ohio Frontier,* 347; Hatcher, *Western Reserve,* 57, 187–88; Zanesville *Muskingum Messenger,* 18 July 1816; Eli S. Barnum to Zalmon Wildman, 12 March 1817.

36. Isaac Mills to Zalmon Wildman, 15 April 1817; Cincinnati *Liberty Hall,* 18 February 1818; Chillicothe *Scioto Gazette and Fredonia Chronicle,* 22 May 1818.

37. Conlin, *Simon Perkins,* 100–1.

38. Hurt, *Ohio Frontier,* 345; Harte, "Land in the Old Northwest," 130–31; Comfort S. Mygott to Zalmon Wildman, 6 June 1820; Comfort S. Mygott to Zalmon Wildman, 11 June 1820.

39. Zalmon Wildman to ? Morse, 2 August 1823.

40. Hibbard, *A History of the Public Land Policies,* 98; Fred S. Wildman to Zalmon Wildman, 12 July 1825; Isaac Mills to Zalmon Wildman, 5 January 1828.

41. Zalmon Wildman to Burr Higgins, 2 December 1828; Hubbard and Lester to Zalmon Wildman, 10 November 1835.

42. Zalmon Wildman to Mary Starr, 28 July 1829.

43. D. Griffiths, Jr., *Two Years in the New Settlements of Ohio* (Ann Arbor: University Microfilms, 1966), 55, 58; Hatcher, *Western Reserve,* 188; Inventory Zalmon Wildman Papers.

Reluctant Warriors: British North Americans and the War of 1812

E. JANE ERRINGTON

Come all ye bold Canadians,
I'd have you lend an ear,
Unto a short ditty
Which will your spirits cheer,
Concerning an engagement
We had at Detroit town,
The pride of those Yankee boys,
So bravely we took down.[1]

So began one of the few Canadian ballads from the War of 1812. It tells the story of the glorious Canadian victory at Detroit, of how "our brave commander, Sir Isaac Brock" together with a handful of eager, undaunted Canadian boys forced the Yankees to surrender.

Those Yankee hearts began to ache,
Their blood it did run cold,
To see us marching forward
So courageous and so bold.
Their general sent a flag to us,
For quarter he did call,
Saying "Stay your hand, brave British boys,"
"I fear you'll slay us all."

The ballad, like many others of its kind, extolled the glorious victory of a heroic and patriotic people. And the sentiments expressed in this particular campfire song have become, if only unconsciously, part of the Canadian legacy of the War of 1812. In popular culture, the War of 1812 is often characterized as the first real test of the new peoples and of their earlier decision to remain loyal to the Empire and the British King during the first American civil war, or what is more commonly termed the Revolution. In 1812, the story goes, Canadians, and particularly Upper Canadians, gallantly fought for their homes, their communities, their colony, and their King. They fought for peace, and to preserve a way of life that was inherently more "civilized" than that of the enemy from the south. The Canadian victory, first at Detroit and then of the war itself, both confirmed the justness of their cause and illustrated that Upper Canadians were willing and eager combatants who had remained true to their loyalist heritage.

But as we know, how governments and popular culture remember and extol a conflict often bears little resemblance to the nature of the war itself or the attitudes of its participants. In the case in point here, all that fought in the War of 1812 claimed and continue to claim victory. For U.S. songwriters, veterans and their families, politicians, and even historians, the War of 1812 was the second War of Independence. It confirmed the righteousness of the Revolution and illustrated the ability of the new republic and its people to defend themselves against all odds. For Upper Canadians in 1815 and throughout the nineteenth and into the early twentieth centuries, the war represented the beginning of nationhood. It illustrated the strength of a nation in arms and the innate patriotism and loyalty of the Canadian people. And for the British of course, the War of 1812, if ever mentioned, was a minor, if regrettable, campaign in their contest with Napoleon.

Yet when Stephen Miles, editor of the Kingston *Gazette*, reported in late June 1812 that the United States and Great Britain and, thus, its British colonies in North America were now officially at war, his readers, although not particularly surprised, were nonetheless dismayed.[2] Since before the turn of the century, many Upper Canadians had lived in fear that they would be forced to take up arms against friends, family, and neighbors to the south. And, for twenty years, local residents had done all they could to avoid what most considered would be an "unnatural" conflict. But it had been to no avail. Miles' announcement, and General Isaac Brock's call to arms and hasty march to Detroit brought an end to years of speculation and trepidation. Upper Canadians in 1812 did not want war. Those who in the post war period came to be characterized as "brave Canadian boys" were, in 1812, very reluctant warriors. Few, if any, were willing, as the ballad related to "go along with Brock . . . without further adieu." Indeed, throughout the three years of war, as had been the case since the colony had been created, colonial leaders lived with the knowledge that some, if not most, Upper Canadians were not only reluctant, but would refuse to fight at all. Even worse it was feared, some would join the invading forces or welcome them with open arms.

The roots of this reluctance, or what one historian has characterized as wide spread indifference, can be traced back to the time before the creation of the colony.[3] The American Revolution, it is frequently asserted, created not one nation but two. In 1783–84, as Americans debated how best to govern themselves, approximately ten thousand former residents of the old thirteen colonies began to make their way north to the British colony of Quebec.[4] This heterogeneous group of "Loyalists" was bitter and felt betrayed. They were the losers in that momentous civil war over the future of their homes; and, harassed and persecuted by neighbors and republican officials, they were now political refugees—forced to leave their homes and most of their possessions and seek asylum, as one loyalist later remembered "in the howling wilderness."[5] For some at least, their flight north across the St. Lawrence or lower Great Lakes was a confirmation of their continued allegiance to the king and to a way of life that ensured order, stability and personal liberty, (not licentiousness as they believed was now being encouraged in the new republic).[6] Yet these British loyalists were, by birth and inclination, also Americans. Although they were still British subjects, "home" was North America; and it was with this land and these people, not with the rolling hills of the British Isles, with whom they identified.

It is therefore not surprising, as one commentator noted, that, soon after the Revolution, "passions mutually subsided" on both sides of the border.[7] In 1792, local officials of the newly formed colony of Upper Canada invited American settlers to cross the border and take up land and establish businesses. With reportedly little or no "attachment to the King of Great Britain" or consciousness of the international border, thousands of restless pioneers came north, as many of their neighbors went west, to find land, to find employment, and generally to grasp new opportunities for themselves and their children.[8] By 1810, it is estimated that "loyalist element was scarcely noticeable amongst the diversity of people" who had flooded into the colony after about 1792.[9] Just before the War of 1812, Upper Canada was, demographically at least, an American colony.[10]

The geographic realities, which facilitated the movement of American pioneer farmers north, also encouraged Upper Canadians to look and travel south. Although poor and in many cases nonexistent roads and other means of communication isolated individual Upper Canadian communities from each other, the St. Lawrence River and the lower Great Lakes provided easy access north and south. Until well into the 1830s, residents in New York and the New England states were Upper Canadians' closest and most accessible neighbors. Visitors, mail, news, and information from Europe, from the United States, and even from the most eastern sections of British North America traveled fastest and most efficiently to and from Upper Canada by way of New York, Boston, or Philadelphia.[11]

The bonds forged by geography were strengthened in the early years by strong personal and professional ties, north and south. Despite the turmoil and, for some loyalists, the legacy of bitterness left by the Revolution, Upper Canadians and Americans "were still interesting objects to each other."[12] For almost all Upper Canadians before the War of 1812, the United States was their former home and remained the home of relatives and friends. A French traveler, La Rochefoucault-Liancourt noted as early as 1795, that though some "American Loyalists . . . still harbour enmity and hatred against their native land and countrymen . . . these sentiments [were] daily decreasing" and were "not shared by the far greater number of emigrants who arrive from the United States, Nova Scotia and New Brunswick."[13] Within a short time, it was reported that "the most social harmony" existed between "gentleman on the American side and those on the British side" of the border.[14] Leading loyalists like Richard Cartwright of Kingston regularly visited their old homes in the United States; merchants, traders, and farmers engaged in lucrative economic relations with associates across the border; Upper Canadians entertained American visitors in their homes; a growing number attended camp meetings and met at quarterly sessions led by itinerant American preachers; some Upper Canadian children went south to school; and a few residents, taking advantage of the regular ferry services, which by 1800 linked Kingston and Niagara and their closest American communities, crossed the border to shop or take a cure.[15] Being a resident of this British colony did not mean that even the most loyal subjects rejected their close association with their old homes. Indeed, throughout the first twenty-five years of colonial development, most Upper Canadians considered themselves part of a North American community, which spanned the border.

Upper Canada was officially and administratively a British colony, however. To gain land and to vote, settlers had to swear an oath of allegiance to the British crown and, twice annually, adult men had to muster for militia training. Moreover, there is no question that for colonial leaders, including British office holders sent by London, like Lieutenant Governors Simcoe and Gore and General Sir Isaac Brock, and members of the indigenous elite, like Richard Cartwright of Kingston, allegiance to the Empire and to the principles enshrined in the British Constitution also helped to define who and what they were.

Some historians have suggested that for these men, being Upper Canadian meant being anti-American; and that throughout the first generation of colonial development, these Upper Canadians rejected all things emanating from south of the Great Lakes. Thus, it is implied, Upper Canadians in 1812 were willing and, in fact, eager to defend their place in the Empire. Certainly, many leading Upper Canadians, like the Reverend John Strachan of York, were scornful of the republic and of its lack of order and justice. And in 1812, many went out of their way to express their willingness to take up arms in defense of their homes. However, even the most conservative and patriotic Upper Canadians could not and did not try to deny the importance of geography and shared interests with neighbors to the south.

As they began to lay the political and economic foundations of the new British colony, the Upper Canadian elite could not help but be conscious of how similar the colony was to communities south of the frontier. Upper Canadians and Americans, particularly in New York and New England, shared not only a land and people, they also shared many common concerns of settlement and of future development. Most Upper Canadians were pioneer farmers and their daily struggle for survival—clearing the bush, building homes, planting and harvesting—was a re-creation of events being pursued south of the border. As a number of commentators noted, there was little to distinguish the backwoods of Upper Canada from the frontier of the United States.[16] Upper Canadians of all economic and political stripes drew frequently on American models when considering, for example, how to build roads, till the soil, establish banks, or foster local markets. Although Upper Canada was a British province, many consciously acknowledged that the United States had much to offer residents in the new colony.

Even in political affairs, colonial leaders did not reject all things American. Although they feared the insidious influence of republicanism and democracy and often predicted the political disintegration of the United States, men like John Strachan and Richard Cartwright believed that many Americans shared their concerns. In particular, they applauded the Federalists of New England and New York for their stance in support of order against unbridled democracy. And Upper Canadians recognized that, like themselves, the Federalists wanted to maintain and increase commerce and contact across the border. Between 1800 and 1812, and indeed, throughout the years of war, leading Upper Canadians made fine distinctions between those they viewed as "good" American citizens and the policies of the American government; and they were sympathetic to the plight of those Americans who, like themselves, were suffering under the policies of rapacious republicanism.[17]

Thus, for most Upper Canadians, allegiance to Great Britain usually did not automatically conflict with their continuing sense of being part of a North American community. There were times, however, when Upper Canadians were forced to recognize the apparent contradiction of their position. The colony had been created, after all, not by amicable cooperation but out of bitter confrontation between Great Britain and the United States. Moreover, although geographic proximity encouraged a sense of community that spanned the lakes, it also provided the continuing potential for local tensions, as well as the possibility that the Great Lakes–St. Lawrence basin might once again be the theater of armed conflict between the two nations.

Between 1791 and 1812, Upper Canadians worked hard to reestablish and cement amicable relations along what was still a largely unmarked and porous border. Both prudence and personal inclination encouraged this. Most Upper Canadians lived, it must be remembered, within a few miles of the expanding and dynamic republic. More importantly, close personal and economic associations with friends and family members south of the Great Lakes would be harmed and perhaps irrevocably severed if the two governments were at odds.

It was not surprising, therefore, that just before the turn of the century, one settler in Niagara suggested that residents of the area gather together for various sporting events, to supplement the already existing "intercourse of economic, friendship and sociability between the people of the province and those in the neighbouring part of the United States."[18] Upper Canadians applauded when the American garrison showed the colony's flag and played the "British Grenadiers" on the occasion of the king's birthday. "Such acts of civility" should be encouraged, many Upper Canadians believed.[19] Upper Canadians, too, should show "a spirit of mutually liberality, candour and forbearance," for only "by preserving harmony and promoting good neighbourhood" could "friends of both nations . . . respectively increase their national prosperity."[20]

Colonial leaders also pointedly condemned those counterfeiters, smugglers, criminals, and deserting British soldiers who used the border to avoid apprehension.

"National difficulties," as one commentator termed it, erupted frequently as a result of "the mutual incursions and acts of jurisdiction and other interferences of the subject of one government within the known and acknowledged limits of the other."[21] Such acts were to be "deprecated" and Upper Canadians were cautioned to avoid "becoming habituated to mutual prejudices, jealousies, reflections, reproaches and all that process of national alienation which had, in the progress of ages, rendered the British and the French so inveterate in their hostility as to call each other natural enemies."[22]

At the same time, it is clear that many Upper Canadians never really recognized that a border existed at all—and they not only traveled back and forth at will, but after 1800 when customs duties were established, regularly avoided paying duties on trade goods. Smuggling seems to have been one of the most lucrative and accepted (if not respectable) means of doing business and it was eagerly supported on both sides of the border.[23] In the summer, "crafts of all sorts and sizes crowded the River St. Lawrence."[24] In the winter, ice conditions permitting, sleighs laden with goods made the journey. One U.S. customs officer at Sackets Harbor reported in 1809, at the height of the Embargo, "all the force I can raise is not sufficient to stop them." The smugglers "appear determined to evade the law at the risk of their lives." Indeed, he concluded, fearfully, "my life and the lives of my deputies are threatened daily; what will be the fate of us God only knows."[25]

Many Upper Canadians and Americans obviously benefited from smuggling; the embargo of 1808 and the War of 1812 only enhanced their profits. For officials on both sides of the border, however, the extensive smuggling threatened to disrupt peaceful relations between their governments. Therefore, some in the colony (a number of whom were undoubtedly losing business to the smugglers) called on Upper Canadians to stop evading the law. In the fall of 1810, for example, residents of Kingston and officials on the south shore of Lake Ontario organized a cooperative effort to apprehend smugglers. "Such instances of the reciprocation of acts of justices and liberality," one contributor to the Kingston *Gazette* remarked with approval, "were much more conducive to mutual prosperity than a state of legislative counteraction and hostility."[26] Everyone, it was believed, had a responsibility to encourage "the preservation of peace" between Upper Canada and the United States.[27]

The periodic problems that erupted along the border were, for the most part, local concerns. And various individual attempts to encourage civility and goodwill in the years before the War of 1812 seemed to be successful. Yet, it was always evident that harmony on the Great Lakes frontier did not ensure peace between the governments of the United States and Great Britain. For, although open warfare between Great Britain and the United States had ended in 1784, the Treaty of Paris had not stopped the two nations from jockeying for position on the western frontier.

In July 1794, Upper Canadians read excerpts from an Albany paper that the United States intended a "total conquest" of the west and "a reduction of the interior posts of the Upper Provinces."[28] First, American officials began to stop all boats and goods from entering Upper Canada from the south. Then, General "Mad" Anthony Wayne and a contingent of troops began to advance on British forts inside the young republic. What had sparked these actions was the U.S. government's belief that British officials were actively encouraging the Native nations of the northwest to raid American frontier settlements. Moreover, Great Britain was refusing to relinquish forts in the west. Upper Canadians watched apprehensively as imperial officials responded and most expected that war would be declared immediately. It was with considerable relief that leading colonists learned of the success of John Jay's mission to London.[29]

It was soon evident that the resolution of this controversy in 1795 did not really resolve the differences between the two governments. Between 1796 and 1800, Upper Canadians watched with interest and some concern as American neutrality was buffeted by the combined pressure of war in Europe and internal political divisions. Thomas Jefferson's victory in 1800 brought renewed fears that the United States would join France in its campaign against Great Britain. And, although those fears appeared for a time to be unfounded, the *Chesapeake* Affair in 1807 threatened once again to bring war to the Great Lakes frontier. Despite calls by Upper Canadians and Federalists in the United States for restraint, the American government sounded the alarm and made preparations for war. Upper Canadian leaders had little alternative but to call the colony to arms.

The most pressing concern of colonial leaders in 1807 and 1808, as it would be in 1812, was that the majority of Upper Canadians would be at best, reluctant combatants. Indeed, it was feared that many might refuse to fight at all. Most residents had no political or emotional attachment to the king or the British Empire. Moreover, most had only recently arrived from the United States.

Colonial leaders did what they could to cope with the situation. In a speech to the local militia in December 1807, Richard Cartwright explained to assembled men that it was the American government, and the Republicans, "that blind and misguided party," who were threatening to plunge the continent into war. The "most enlightened and patriotic citizens" of the United States realized that war would harm American commerce and "ultimately the existence of their independence." By defending themselves, Cartwright intimated, Upper Canadians were defending not only their homes, but also the interests of many of their friends and neighbors in the United States. As the official government gazette, the *Upper Canada Gazette* reported, "one congressman had even written to the president that 'we are doing no good. I fear we are about to plunge the nation into the most dreadful calamities, unnecessarily and wantonly.'" [30]

For the next four years, the Upper Canadian elites waged a pointed and increasingly assertive propaganda campaign to try to convince their readers that, if and when war broke out, settlers could and should defend their new homes against the forces of tyranny (and republicanism). By doing so, it was explicitly stated, they would be remaining true to their old homes and beliefs. Most Upper Canadians appear to have ignored such entreaties. And although international tensions continued to threaten local peace, residents continued to move back and forth across the border, and till their fields and trade.

Even in January and February 1812, when General Isaac Brock, the president of the colony warned that although "we wish and hope for peace" war was probably at no great distance and "it was our duty to be prepared,"[31] most turned a deaf ear. The members of the House of Assembly refused to pass measures to require militiamen to forswear allegiance to any foreign country; and Brock's request to suspend the writ of habeas corpus was denied. As George Sheppard has commented in his groundbreaking work, *Plunder, Profits and Paroles*, "The colonists were firm in their belief that they were not responsible for the deteriorating relationship between Britain and the United States."[32] And one colonist suggested, in a letter in a provincial newspaper that "if your [the United States] quarrel is with Britain, go and avenge yourselves on her own shores."[33]

Colonial leaders and Imperial officials were, not surprisingly, alarmed. For the next four months, the propaganda campaign to convince Upper Canadians to take up arms if need be, intensified. But, when editor Stephen Miles of Kingston announced that war had been declared in June 1812, life continued as usual for most Upper Canadians; individuals, goods, and news continued to flow across the border. More to the point, most settlers resisted calls to muster and train. Even when Brock instituted changes to the Militia Act that granted volunteers exemptions from statute labor, jury duty and personal arrest for small debts, militia quotas were rarely met. It is clear in June and July 1812, that most Upper Canadians were still reluctant to go to war. And Brock and others feared that "the great mass of people" would either flee back to their old homes or "join the American government" and work for the overthrow of the British in North America.[34]

Even once actual fighting began, the war seemed to have little direct impact on the lives of most Upper Canadians. It was only in the western portions of the colony that residents suffered property damage, men were injured and died of their wounds or disease, and families were left bereft. And although many of the militiamen in the Niagara region called out in late June and early July seemed to be willing to defend their own homes and businesses, the incident of desertion was high. Moreover, Brock predicted that "most would leave anyway once the harvest began."[35] As George Sheppard has observed, colonists' indifference to the war was striking and it was not restricted to only the "recent arrivals from the United States."[36] Both Loyalists and late Loyalists, farmers, craftsmen, and politicians tried to avoid service.

As the war dragged on, many Upper Canadians even began to resist providing supplies and support to the British cause. Although there is no question that some Upper Canadians directly benefited from the war, many others did not. Militia duty took men away from the fields and their shops; the prices of goods and services increased dramatically; and the British forces often confiscated livestock, grain and other goods when they could not purchase them. In parts of the province, Upper Canadians watched, seemingly helpless, as their farms were razed to the ground by enemy forces; war widows were often frustrated when they turned to colonial officials for financial assistance.

For most Upper Canadians, the actual conflict did little to break down their reluctance to take up arms. And for many, being thrust into the maelstrom of battle only served to foster a resentment of their own government as well as that of the enemy. As Sheppard has concluded, "while a few colonists assisted the British forces, the majority resorted to desertion or paroles to avoid serving."[37]

> Come all ye bold Canadians,
> Enlisted in the cause,
> To defend your country,
> And to maintain your laws,
> Being all united,

This is the song we'll sing;
Success unto Great Britain,
And God save the King.

It seems more than questionable that these words were truly sung by Canadians during the first months of the War of 1812. In June and July 1812, as had been the case for the previous twenty-five or so years, Upper Canadians did all they could to avoid war. Geography, personal inclination, commerce, and, to some degree, politics all encouraged these British colonists to consider themselves part of a community, which spanned the Great Lakes and the St. Lawrence basin. To find that, despite all their best efforts, war was being thrust upon them, was daunting and many, no doubt, resented this intrusion onto their lives. It is not surprising that Upper Canadians were reluctant warriors in 1812. It was only after the war was over and that memory had dimmed that these reluctant warriors could become "bold Canadians."

NOTES

1. "The Bold Canadian: A Ballad of the War of 1812," taken from Morris Zaslow, ed., *The Defended Border* (Toronto: Macmillan Co. of Canada, 1964), 303–4.
2. Kingston *Gazette*, 30 June 1812, taken from the *Albany Gazette*. Miles began, "It is pretty clearly ascertained that war with the United States is no longer to be avoided."
3. George Sheppard, *Plunder, Profits and Paroles: A Social History of the War of 1812 in Upper Canada* (Montreal and Kingston: McGill–Queen's University Press, 1994).
4. Certainly, estimates vary from 6,000 to 10,000.
5. [Richard Cartwright], *Letters from an American Loyalist in Upper-Canada*, Letter X, (Halifax, Nova Scotia: 1810).
6. See among others, Janice Potter, *The Liberty We Seek: Loyalist Ideology in Colonial New York and Massachusetts* (Cambridge, Mass: Harvard University Press, 1983) for a detailed discussion of loyalist ideology.
7. François-Aléxandre-Fréderic, duc de La Rochefoucault-Liancourt, *Travels in Canada* (1795; Reprint, Toronto: William Renwick Riddell, 1917), 44.
8. Ibid., 36. See also John Maud, *Visit to the Falls of Niagara in 1800* (London: Longmans, Rees, Orme, Brown and Green, 1826), 60.
9. Michael Smith, *A Geographical View of British Possessions in North America* (Philadelphia: P. Mauro, 1813), 82.
10. See among others, Smith, *A Geographical View*, 61, for estimates of population in the colony in 1810.
11. See Stephen Roberts, "Imperial Policy, Provincial Administration and Defences of Canada" (Ph.D. thesis, Oxford University, 1975); John Lambert, *Travels Through Canada and the United States* (London:

C. Cradock and W. Joy, 1814); John Melish, *Travels Through the United States of American* (Belfast: Jos. Smyth, 1818).

12. Robert Gourlay, *General Introduction to Statistical Account of Upper Canada* (London: Simpkin and Marshall, 1822), 115.

13. Ibid., 74.

14. D'Arcy Boulton, *A Sketch of His Majesty's Province of Upper Canada* (London, 1805; Reprint, Toronto: Baxter, 1961), 32.

15. See travelers accounts already cited and numerous references in the local papers, including *Upper Canada Gazette*, 19 April 1797; 25 September 1817; 10 February 1820; 23 June 1825. It is known that Richard Cartwright, a prominent resident of Kingston, regularly made trips south after 1800. See Cartwright, see among others, Smith, *A Geographical View*, 61, for estimates of population in the colony in 1810. Papers, Q.U.A. So too did Joel Stone, Solomon Jones Papers, Q.U.A. and Robert Hamilton (Bruce Wilson, *The Enterprises of Robert Hamilton* [Ottawa: Carleton University Press, 1984]) to name only a few.

16. Ralph Brown, *Mirror for Americans* (New York: American Geographical Society, 1903) and travel accounts previously noted.

17. I have developed these ideas extensively in *The Lion, The Eagle and Upper Canada: A Developing Colonial Ideology* (Kingston and Montreal: McGill–Queen's University Press, 1987, 1995).

18. *Upper Canada Gazette*, 31 May 1799.

19. Ibid., 27 January 1798.

20. Kingston *Gazette*, 25 September 1810.

21. Ibid., 11 October 1810.

22. Ibid., 25 September 1810.

23. In addition to numerous references in the local newspapers, for the most part condemning the practice, and in travel accounts, governments on both sides of the border were forced to try to cope with the issue. See A.L. Burt, *The United States, Great Britain and British North America* (New York: Russell and Russell, 1961); Alexander C. Flick, ed., *The History of the State of New York*, 10 vols. (New York: Columbia University Press, 1933–37).

24. Matilda Ridout, Lady Edgar, *General Brock* (Toronto: Oxford University Press, 1926), 109.

25. Report of Hart Massey, 14 March 1809, quoted in Flick, *The History of the State of New York*, 5:199.

26. Kingston *Gazette*, 2 October 1810; 6 November 1810.

27. Ibid., 6 November 1810; 11 October 1810.

28. *Upper Canada Gazette*, 10 July 1794.

29. See Burt, *The United States* for a discussion of the rising tensions before the war; and Errington, *Lion and the Eagle*, chapter 4 for a more complete discussion of Upper Canadian reaction to this.

30. *Upper Canada Gazette*, 15 October 1808.

31. Reported in the Kingston *Gazette*, 28 January 1812.

32. Sheppard, *Plunder*, 37.

33. Quoted in ibid., 36.

34. Melish, *Travels*, 485. See also discussion in Errington, *Lion and the Eagle*, chapter 4 and Sheppard, *Plunder*.

35. Sheppard, *Plunder*, 47.

36. Ibid., 74.

37. Ibid., 98.

Forgotten Allies: The Loyal Shawnees and the War of 1812

R . D A V I D E D M U N D S

For most historians, the association of Indian people with the War of 1812 conjures up images of Native American resistance. From Tippecanoe to the Thames, from Fort Mims to Horseshoe Bend, historians have concentrated upon this last, futile attempt by Native American people to solicit foreign assistance in defending their homelands east of the Mississippi. Indeed, within the past decade some scholarship has focused upon the emergence of religious and cultural revitalization as the core of this resistance, while other historians have argued that the tribespeople's attempts to form a centralized confederacy during this period was just the final stage in a much larger and more prolonged effort at political consolidation. Yet, in their focus upon the War of 1812, as in other theaters of Indian-white interaction, both scholars and the general public have concentrated attention upon those Native Americans who chose to oppose the onrushing Euro-Americans. Their Indian contemporaries who promoted a policy of accommodation have generally been ignored.[1]

The Shawnee Indians, who resided in western Ohio and Indiana during the first three decades of the nineteenth century, offer an interesting case study of this phenomenon. Unquestionably, the two Native American leaders most closely associated with the War of 1812 are the Shawnee war chief, Tecumseh, and his younger brother,

Tenskwatawa, the Shawnee Prophet. Yet most Shawnees had little association with these brothers. By 1800, over half of the Shawnee nation (approximately one thousand individuals), already were living west of the Mississippi, and most of the Shawnees still in the east (about eight hundred Indians) remained neutral or supported the Americans. Only a handful of Shawnee warriors opposed William Henry Harrison at Tippecanoe; and, in October 1813, at the Battle of the Thames, more Shawnee warriors served in Harrison's army than fought with Tecumseh.[2]

Who were these Indians and why have we forgotten them? The answer, of course, tells us as much about the parameters of our conceptualization about Indians as people, as it does about the Shawnees.

Although the Shawnees had formed the vanguard in the attacks upon Kentucky during the American Revolution, and had staunchly opposed the American occupation of southern Ohio in the years following the war, the two decades of conflict had taken a heavy toll in Shawnee lives and also had been disruptive to Shawnee society. Like other central Algonquian peoples, the Shawnee political system was essentially decentralized, and traditionally the tribe had been divided into five separate patrilineal descent groups or divisions, each concentrated in a separate town and each responsible for particular religious or political obligations. The Chalagawetha and Thawegila divisions supplied political leadership to the tribe, often competing for such prominence. The Piquas were responsible for maintaining religious ceremonies. The Kispokothas supplied war chiefs, while the Maykujays, traditionally the least prestigious of the divisions, were specialists in medicine and health. Before the American Revolution, each division had maintained a separate town, but amidst the turmoil of the of the war years, the distinct physical and cultural-political responsibilities of the groups became blurred. In 1774, many of the Thawegila people left the Ohio Valley and fled to the Creeks in Alabama; and five years later almost one thousand Shawnee, mostly members of the Kispokotha and Piqua groups, emigrated from Ohio to Missouri. After departure, the remnants of these three divisions in Ohio joined with the Chalagawethas and Maykujays people to form new villages, but since the membership of the Chalagawetha and Maykujay remained primarily in Ohio, these divisions dominated the villages and began to usurp the other divisions' former political and military functions. In response, the remaining Thawegilas, Piquas, and particularly the Kispokothas harbored a growing resentment.[3]

Dissension also emerged over the changing role of war and peace chiefs. In addition to the theoretical "tribal chiefs," supposedly supplied by hereditary Thawegila or Chalagawetha elders, the Shawnees also maintained a bifurcated political leadership composed of peace and war chiefs from the local villages. Usually men of broad experience and sound judgement, the local village chiefs mediated intra-village and intra-tribal disputes and also represented their followers in negotiations with their Indian or white neighbors. In contrast, war chiefs were younger men who had proven themselves as warriors, but whose authority usually was limited to military matters. Traditionally, members of the Kispokotha division had prided themselves in providing tribal leadership in these affairs, but each village had several successful warriors who also led local residents during periods of military crises. Prior to the Revolutionary period, these warriors had relinquished their roles as leaders once the conflict had ended.[4]

By 1795, the boundaries between these duties had blurred. Since the Shawnees remaining in Ohio had been subjected to two decades of warfare (1774–95), the position of the war chiefs had aggrandized. Besieged for twenty years, the Shawnees had remained within an almost constant state of war and had begun to rely upon their war chiefs for leadership on a daily basis. In consequence, some of the war chiefs, such as Tecumseh, although too young to serve as a traditional village chief (he had been born in 1768), had attracted a small party of younger warriors and their families, and had established separate villages. But, in 1795, the Treaty of Greenville ceded most of Ohio to the Americans, temporarily ended the warfare, and encouraged the Indians to acculturate toward the role of small yeoman farmers. Obviously, such terms were distasteful to Tecumseh, a Kispokotha, and his militant, more traditional followers, but they appealed to the war weary majority of the Shawnees.[5]

They also appealed to Black Hoof. Born shortly after 1740, Black Hoof was a member of the Maykujays (traditionally the least prestigious of the Shawnee divisions), but he had proven himself as a warrior and had fought against the Long Knives at Point Pleasant, and in Kentucky and Ohio. In 1795, he was in his fifties, a respected village chief who reflected his people's desire for peace. Unlike Tecumseh, he signed the Treaty of Greenville, and in the years following the treaty he subscribed to the government's acculturation programs. In response, federal Indian agents recognized him as the spokesperson for the Shawnees, and channeled their annuities through his village. Such bounty, however, only further alienated Tecumseh who envisioned the rival Shawnee leader not only as a Quisling, but also as an upstart Maykujay, who had radically overstepped his place within the framework of traditional Shawnee society.[6]

Discounting Tecumseh's protests, Black Hoof endeavored to lead his people down the white man's road. In the decade following the Treaty of Greenville, he visited Baltimore and Washington upon several occasions, repeatedly soliciting agricultural assistance both from federal officials, and from the Society of Friends. At first he was unsuccessful, but, in June 1807, Quaker William Kirk established a mission at Wapakoneta, Black Hoof's village, and during the following year the Shawnees embraced the missionary's acculturation programs. By June 1808, Black Hoof's people had split rail fences, erected log cabins, and planted over 500 acres with traditional crops such as corn, beans, squash, and pumpkins, but they also planted turnips, cabbage, and potatoes. In addition, they nurtured several small orchards of apples, and had acquired a herd of hogs, three cattle, and two yokes of oxen. With Kirk's assistance, they utilized federal funds to purchase farm implements, and hired a blacksmith, who established a forge in their village.[7] Construction was begun on both a sawmill and a gristmill, and American travelers passing through Wapakoneta described the Shawnees' well-groomed fields and "comfortable houses of hewn logs with chimneys." Others commented upon the Shawnees' sobriety ("a matter of surprise to those who are acquainted with Indians"), and, in the fall of 1808, the War Department received a petition from white citizens near Dayton who praised the Shawnees and commented that "We find them sober and civil . . . and look upon them as a watchful safeguard to our habitations."[8]

But Kirk was more efficient as a missionary than as an accountant. He overspent his allotment of federal funds, then failed to report his expenditures. Moreover, Kirk also became embroiled in a bureaucratic dispute with William Wells, the Indian agent at Fort Wayne, and, despite his success at Wapakoneta, in December 1808 federal officials dismissed him from the Indian service and demanded that he leave Black Hoof's village.[9]

Black Hoof, other Shawnee leaders, and even neighboring settlers protested Kirk's dismissal and federal officials eventually sent another agent to temporarily reside at Black Hoof's village, but the acculturation programs suffered from lack of consistent leadership, and Black Hoof petitioned the government for another Quaker missionary.[10]

The road toward acculturation was threatened by other pitfalls. In 1805, Lalawethika, the drunken, ne'er-do-well younger brother of Tecumseh, experienced a series of visions, which transformed the former alcoholic into Tenskwatawa, the Shawnee Prophet, whose message of revitalization spread like wildfire among the more traditional tribespeople of Indiana, Illinois, Michigan, and Wisconsin. Although the Prophet's teachings attracted few Shawnee, other tribesmen flocked to his village near Greenville, where Tenskwatawa's condemnation of acculturation and his association of the Americans with the Great Serpent and witchcraft threatened Black Hoof's commitment of cooperation with the government. In response, Black Hoof remembered the Prophet as a drunken failure, considered him to be a charlatan, and perhaps more importantly, envisioned the Prophet and Tecumseh as potential rivals for leadership among the Shawnees. In 1807, a meeting between Black Hoof and Tecumseh had deteriorated into accusations and threats of physical violence, but in 1808, when the Prophet and Tecumseh moved their village to the Tippecanoe, tensions between the two groups temporarily diminished.[11]

The Treaty of Fort Wayne rekindled the antagonisms. Negotiated between William Henry Harrison and friendly village chiefs from the Potawatomis, Miamis, and Delawares, the treaty was signed in September 1809 and ceded over 3 million acres of former Indian lands in Indiana to the United States. Although Black Hoof and other Shawnee chiefs did not participate in the agreement, Tecumseh and the Prophet angrily charged the Shawnees, Wyandots, and Senecas living in Ohio with complicity in the land cession and threatened to kill all those village chiefs who remained friendly to the Americans.[12] During the spring of 1810, Tecumseh returned to Ohio where he unsuccessfully attempted to recruit new followers among the Shawnee villages, but other followers of the Prophet proselytized among the Wyandots at Sandusky, and, although Tarhe, the leading Wyandot village chief opposed their efforts, some of the Wyandots were caught up in the religious fervor and burned three acculturated village chiefs, including Leatherlips, as witches.[13]

In response, Black Hoof's people reaffirmed their loyalty to the United States, increased their acreage of corn and potatoes, and sent repeated petitions to the Quakers asking for missionaries to return and "assist us as soon as possible" so that Shawnee children could become educated and both Indians and whites "will be more united until we all land in heaven together." Under the auspices of John Johnston, their new Indian agent, they also met with settlers in west central Ohio, where they both denounced the Prophet and assured the Americans they would warn them of the approach of any hostile Indians.[14]

But the Battle of the Tippecanoe, in November 1811, markedly increased the tensions between Indians and whites. Hostile Indians once concentrated at Prophetstown now scattered in a broad arc from Lake Peoria to Sandusky Bay, and rumors swept the Ohio frontier that the Prophet and his followers were returning to Greenville. In April, five settlers were killed along the Maumee and Sandusky rivers, and one month later another white man was murdered in modern Darke County. Federal troops marched from Greenville and erected a new blockhouse near Black Hoof's village, but in the meantime, local militia units murdered two friendly Potawatomis, stole all their property, and made prisoners of their wives and children.[15] Black Hoof repeatedly assured federal officials that his people had no part in the depredations and volunteered the service of two young warriors to serve as scouts for American military units who planned to patrol along the Greenville Treaty line, but tensions continued to increase. White frontiersmen harassed the Shawnees, and John Johnston reported that "in consequence of the late murders by the savages, armed parties of our people are out in all directions breathing destruction against the Indians indiscriminately." William Perry, the commander of the troops patrolling the treaty line, became so fearful for the safety of the two Shawnee scouts that he "sent them home, not wishing them . . . to be killed by some of the Inhabitants."[16]

News that war had been declared against Great Britain reached Ohio in June 1812, and friendly Shawnees, Wyandots, and Senecas met again with both state and federal officials, reaffirming their friendship to the Long Knives and granting permission for William Hull and an American army to march through their lands to Detroit. Both the Shawnees and the Wyandots also agreed to allow the Americans to erect a series of blockhouses at strategic locations along this route, and several Shawnees, including Logan and Captain Lewis, enlisted as scouts or interpreters to accompany Hull's army enroute to Michigan.[17]

While Hull marched to Michigan, federal officials in Ohio planned a major conference at Piqua, Ohio, as the keystone of their Indian policy in the region. Federal officials believed that, within the first few weeks after war was declared, all those Indians already committed to the British would flee to Canada. They assumed that the vast majority of the Miamis, Potawatomis, Wyandots, and Ottawas (tribes who might waver in their loyalties) could be kept neutral if the United States could demonstrate sufficient military and economic strength to overawe them. Supposedly Hull's march to Michigan and the reinforcement of the garrison at Detroit, in preparation for an American invasion of Canada, would provide the military component of such a strategy, while the conference at Piqua, where the Indians would be wined, dined, and provided with presents, would demonstrate American munificence and diplomacy.[18]

Things did not go as planned. The conference originally was scheduled to begin on 1 August 1812, but provisions and presents for the Indians were slow in arriving, so John Johnston postponed the meeting until 15 August. Meanwhile, British agents circulated rumors that the conference was an American "contrivance" designed to "lead all the men from home, then fall upon their women and children, and destroy them."[19] Yet logistical problems and rumors paled in comparison to military events in Michigan. Hull reached Detroit on 6 July 1812, but he failed to capture Fort Malden, the British post at Amherstburg, in Ontario. Meanwhile, increasing numbers of hostile warriors joined Tecumseh, and, late in July, Michilimackinac fell to the British. Afraid that Detroit could not withstand a frontal assault by his enemies, on 16 August 1812, Hull surrendered the post to the British.[20]

Black Hoof, Captain Lewis, Logan, and the Wolf were eyewitnesses to some of these events. Captain Lewis, Logan, and the Wolf had accompanied Hull to Michigan, where Black Hoof joined them. In mid-July, they met with neighboring tribes at Brownstown, a Wyandot village about twenty miles south of Detroit, and unsuccessfully attempted to keep these Indians neutral.[21] They then hurried back to Ohio, where they learned that the conference had been postponed for two weeks, and, when they assembled at Piqua on 16 August, they found that the recent American military reverses in Michigan had already had a profound impact upon the proceedings. Johnston originally had planned to meet with three thousand Indians, but only seven hundred and fifty were in attendance. In addition, most of these were from tribes or bands already firmly committed to the Americans.[22]

Disappointed by the numbers, the commissioners appointed to meet with the Indians procrastinated, hoping more tribespeople would assemble. However, late in August when the conference formally opened, Black Hoof went "out of his way to assure us of his fidelity," according to Thomas Worthington, one of the commissioners. Speaking for the loyal Shawnees, Black Hoof condemned the British for repeatedly making false promises, then abandoning the Indians, asserting that the Redcoats "viewed the Indians as they did their dogs. That when they told them to bite, they must bite," but the Shawnees "were men and would make their own decisions." The conference continued until early September, when Harrison and two thousand regulars and Kentucky volunteers arrived enroute to relieve the Indian siege of Fort Wayne. After listening to Harrison harangue the tribesmen, warning them that even the names of those Indians who opposed the United States would soon be struck from the memories of their kinsmen, the commissioners ended the conference and the Indians returned to their villages.[23]

Although Black Hoof returned to Wapakoneta, Captain Lewis, Logan, Captain Johnny, Bright Horn, the Wolf, and a handful of other Shawnee warriors accompanied Harrison to Fort Wayne, then proceeded up the Maumee Valley, where they served as scouts for Brigadier General James Winchester. During the fall of 1812, they ranged across northwestern Ohio, spying upon British troop movements and skirmishing with hostile Indians. It was hazardous duty. Not only were they at risk from the British and their allies, they also were endangered by the Kentucky militia, who routinely treated all Indians as pro-British and considered any Indian to be fair game.[24]

Such suspicions inadvertently contributed to the death of Logan. In mid-November, Logan, Captain Johnny, Bright Horn, and several other Indian scouts were ambushed by an enemy war party near the rapids of the Maumee. Although they escaped, Logan, Captain Johnny, and Bright Horn became separated from the others and were forced to spend the night in the forest before returning to the American lines. Upon their arrival in the American camp, several militiamen suggested that they had been captured and secured their release only through promises to serve as double agents for the British. Attempting to prove their loyalty, on 22 November 1812, the three Shawnee warriors proceeded on foot toward the British lines, hoping to bring in either a prisoner or scalps. Unfortunately, they encountered a mounted war party of Potawatomis and Ottawas led by Winamac, a Potawatomi war chief, and Alexander Elliott, the oldest son of British Indian agent Matthew Elliott. Taken captive, they were closely guarded, but not disarmed, and forced to proceed on to the British camp. After a march of several miles, however, their captors decided to disarm them, and the Shawnees, by pre-arranged signal, suddenly opened fire, killing Elliott, Winamac, one of the Ottawas, and wounding another. But, in the return fire, Logan received a wound in the abdomen and Bright Horn one in the leg. Captain Johnny apparently was not wounded. The Shawnees then seized the dead men's horses and raced back to the American camp where Bright Horn recovered, but Logan died of his wounds. Before his death, he requested that his children be taken to Kentucky and provided with a formal education.[25]

During December 1812, the surviving Shawnee scouts returned to their homes at Wapakoneta and Lewistown and were not present in January 1813, when Winchester was defeated at Frenchtown and the American survivors were killed at the River Raisin. When news of the "massacre" reached Ohio, local settlers burned many Shawnee cabins, stole their livestock, and physically abused several Shawnee tribesmen.[26]

To diffuse the hostility, Black Hoof and several other Shawnees joined an expedition to reinforce the American position in northern Ohio. The enlistment almost cost Black Hoof his life. En route to the Maumee, Black Hoof and the other scouts passed through McArthur's Blockhouse, a small supply post on the south bank of the Scioto, near modern Kenton, Ohio. During the evening of 25 January 1813, while Black Hoof and Captain Lewis were conferring with Brigadier General Edwin Tupper in his cabin, an unknown militiaman fired a pistol through a hole in the chinking between the logs, striking Black Hoof in the face. The bullet rendered him unconscious, passing through his left cheek and lodging in his right zygomatic arch, or opposite cheekbone. Although the wound was not fatal, the old chief was forced to remain at the post while the other Shawnees continued on to join Harrison. After a partial recovery, he returned to Wapakoneta. Tupper attempted to ascertain the identity of the assailant, but he received no cooperation from the militia, and the perpetrator was never apprehended.[27]

While Black Hoof recovered from his wound, his comrades continued on to the Maumee, where they again served as scouts for Harrison; and, in April 1813, when the British and Indians besieged Fort Meigs, these Shawnee scouts took refuge in the post with the Americans. Although Black Hoof remained convalescent, another contingent of Shawnee warriors accompanied 1,200 Kentucky militia, led by General Green Clay, who marched to Fort Meigs's rescue. Led by Blackfish, the son or nephew of the Shawnee war chief who had spearheaded the attacks upon Kentucky during the American Revolution, these Shawnees, while not pro-British, preferred to remain neutral and had enlisted in the American cause only after considerable pressure from their Indian agents. Their reluctance to risk their lives for the Long Knives was soon apparent. On 5 May 1813, when part of Clay's force led by Major William Dudley landed opposite Fort Meigs, these Shawnees were ordered to serve as flankers and to warn Dudley of any impending counter attack by the British and their allies. But Dudley's militiamen were ill-disciplined, and, instead of quickly spiking the British cannons and retreating back across the river to the safety of Fort Meigs, they lingered, pursuing small parties of hostile Indians in the forest. Tecumseh and the British counter attacked, the Shawnees led by Blackfish quickly surrendered, and most of the Americans were either killed or captured.[28] The Potawatomis and Chippewas killed some of the American prisoners. In an effort to protect themselves, Blackfish and his fellow Shawnee prisoners informed British Colonel Henry Procter that they had been coerced into service with the Americans, and, that almost all the Shawnees remaining in Ohio were loyal to the Crown, but were being held as prisoners in their villages by the Americans. Procter then offered to exchange the prisoners he had taken at Fort Meigs, if Harrison would allow the loyal Shawnees to remove to Canada.[29]

Such sentiments immediately were denied by Black Hoof and the Shawnees at Wapakoneta and Lewistown, but the misinformation spurred another series of depredations upon the Shawnee villages. In July, Harrison met with Black Hoof and other Shawnee leaders and informed them that in response to the recent rumors, "the President wants no false friends, and it is only in adversity that true friends could be distinguished." Although the government earlier had allowed or even encouraged the tribesmen to remain neutral, they now must inexorably choose between the British and the Americans.[30]

Not surprisingly, Black Hoof and the other Shawnee leaders reaffirmed their commitment to the United States, and, in September 1813, when Harrison invaded Canada, Black Hoof and a party of about one hundred Shawnee warriors landed with the American army at Amherstburg. Some of the warriors joined Duncan McArthur and participated in the liberation of Detroit, while others accompanied Harrison up the Thames Valley. On 5 October 1813, as Procter and Tecumseh made their stand, Black Hoof's warriors were ordered to accompany a small force of American regulars and to infiltrate the enemy's left flank and fire upon the British from the rear. Yet the British regulars fled so abruptly that the pro-American Shawnees had no opportunity to fire at them. American officers ordered their Indian allies not to participate in the attack upon Tecumseh's forces, since militia units would not distinguish between the friendly Shawnees and the hostile warriors and would kill all Indians indiscriminately.[31]

Following the Battle of the Thames, Black Hoof and his warriors returned to Wapakoneta, and, although Captain Lewis, Captain Johnny, Anthony Shane, Blackfish, and other Shawnees accompanied Duncan McArthur on his raid into Canada during the fall of 1814, these actions proved anticlimatic.[32] Meanwhile, as the war ended, Black Hoof and other Shawnee leaders attempted to revitalize their acculturation programs. During the war, the residents of Wapakoneta had labored mightily to keep their grist and lumber mills in operation, but early in April 1815, Black Hoof complained that because they had "devoted so large a portion of their time to military pursuits," their agricultural pursuits had suffered. Moreover, he again petitioned both the government and the Quakers, requesting schools, teachers, a blacksmith, and farm implements.[33]

Although Black Hoof, Captain Lewis, and other Shawnee leaders participated in the treaty that ended the warfare between the United States and the hostile Indians, they played only a minor role in the proceedings. Negotiated at Spring Wells (now part of modern Detroit), the treaty was signed on 8 September 1815, and reaffirmed the ties between the government and the loyal Shawnees. The Shawnee Prophet initially attended the proceedings, but withdrew in protest when federal officials informed him that his repatriation to the United States was contingent upon his subjection to Black Hoof's authority. Denouncing Black Hoof as "that Maykujay," Tenskwatawa announced that he would remain in Canada rather than follow a leader whose expertise traditionally should have been limited only to medicine and matters of health. Undoubtedly, Black Hoof and the other loyal Shawnee were pleased with the Prophet's decision.[34]

In the years that followed the War of 1812, the Quakers established another mission at Wapakoneta, and Black Hoof and the Shawnees continued to walk a precarious path toward acculturation. Yet, in the two decades after 1815, white settlement surged across the Old Northwest, and Americans eager for inexpensive land and economic opportunity soon forgot the Indians who had risked their lives and property in defense of the American cause. Native American people who once had been threats, then allies, now became anachronisms—out of time and place in the linear conception of "progress,"—and as demand mounted for their lands, Black Hoof and his people found themselves under growing pressure to remove from Ohio to the West. Devoid of political or military power, the Shawnees no longer possessed the means to defend their sole, remaining economic asset: their reservation.[35]

Meanwhile, in a particularly ironic twist of fate, those very members of the tribe whom Black Hoof and his people had labored so mightily to defeat were either lionized, or at least, given some legitimacy. By 1830, Tecumseh already had emerged as the quintessential "noble savage" and American folk hero. In an even more bizarre set of circumstances, his brother, the Shawnee Prophet, was encouraged by Lewis Cass to return to the United States where he cooperated with federal officials and worked for Indian Removal.[36]

And so, the Shawnees at Wapakoneta found themselves in the same predicament most tribes have encountered through the years: stripped of military, political, and economic power, they were forced to rely upon the fidelity of the federal government for protection. But since that government was much more amenable to pressure from the non-Indian majority, its fidelity was very marketable. There is a message here, somewhere, for modern tribal governments.

At least Black Hoof was not a party to this final humiliation. He refused to sign the treaty of 8 August 1830, in which the Shawnees at Wapakoneta ceded their lands in Ohio, and died in 1832, before his family could be forced west to Kansas. Although he remained a steadfast friend of the United States and readily subscribed to the government's acculturation or "civilization" programs, his friendship has been forgotten. Perhaps, in retrospect, his obscurity is not surprising. Most Americans still prefer that Indians "dance with wolves," rather than plow with farmers.[37]

NOTES

1. Both Joel Martin, *Sacred Revolt: The Muscogee's Struggle for a New World* (Boston: Beacon Press, 1991) and R. David Edmunds, *The Shawnee Prophet* (Lincoln: University of Nebraska Press, 1983) emphasize the role of religious revitalization in the emergence of Native American resistance. Gregory Dowd, *A Spirited Resistance: The North American Indian Struggle for Unity, 1745–1815* (Baltimore: Johns Hopkins University Press, 1992) also focuses upon Native American spirituality as a key factor in the resistance movements of this period, but argues that such spirituality also permeated political leadership, and asserts that secular and religious influence was interwoven. He also argues that Tecumseh exemplifies the logical culmination of such leadership.

2. Charles Callender, "Shawnee," in *Northeast: Handbook of North American Indians*, vol. 15, ed. Bruce Trigger (Washington: Smithsonian Institution, 1978), 634; John Johnston to John Mason, 16 March 1812, Letters Received by the Secretary of War, Main Series, M221, R. 47, RG 107, Washington, D.C.: National Archives [hereafter cited as NA]; Lieutenant Governor Sir Gordon Drummond to George Prevost, 13 April 1814, British Military and Naval Records, C Series, Vol. 683, RG 8, National Archives of Canada, Ottawa [hereafter cited as NAC].

3. Callender, "Shawnee," 623–24; R. David Edmunds, *Tecumseh and the Quest for Indian Leadership* (Boston: Little, Brown and Co., 1984), 46–47. Also see Vernon Kinietz and Erminie Wheeler-Voegelin, eds., *"Shawnese Traditions": C. C. Trowbridge's Account*, Occasional Contributions from the Museum of Anthropology of the University of Michigan, No. 9 (Ann Arbor: University of Michigan Press, 1939), xiii-xiv, 8.

4. Kinietz and Wheeler-Voegelin, *"Shawnese Traditions,"* xiii-xiv; Callender, "Shawnee," 623–24.

5. Edmunds, *Tecumseh*, 19–48, passim.

6. Thomas McKenney and James Hall, *History of the Indian Tribes of North America, with Biographical Sketches and Anecdotes of the Principal Chiefs* (Edinburgh: John Grant, 1933), 1:238–39; "Anthony Shane's Statement," Draper Manuscripts, State Historical Society of Wisconsin, Madison [hereafter cited as Draper MSS].

7. Black Hoof and others to the President, spring 1808, M221, Roll 17, 5258, NA; Kirk to Dearborn, 12 April 1808, ibid., Roll 25, 8114–15; Shawnee Chiefs to the President, 1 December 1808, ibid., 8148–50; Kirk to Dearborn, 10 December 1808, ibid., 8143–44; Kirk to Dearborn, 12 February 1809, ibid., 8157.

8. "Diary of an Exploratory Journey of the Brethren Lukenbach and Haven," 26 August–13 September 1808, Box 157, Folder 11, Moravian Archives, Bethlehem, Penn.; Citizens of Ohio to the War Department, 25 September 1808, M221, Roll 25, 8147, NA; Francis Douchoquet to the President, 4 December 1808, ibid., 8145.

9. Kirk to Dearborn, 25 December 1808, M221, Roll 9, 2888–91, NA; Kirk to Dearborn, 28 January 1809, ibid., 2897; Kirk to Dearborn, 12 April 12, 1808, ibid., Roll 25, 8115; Kirk to Dearborn, 10 December 1808, ibid., 9005; William Wells to William Henry Harrison, June 1807, in *Messages and Letters of William Henry Harrison*, 2 vols., ed. Logan Esarey (Indianapolis: Indiana Historical Commission, 1922), 1:218; Wells to Dearborn, 20 August 1807, in *The Territorial Papers of the United States*, ed. Clarence E. Carter (Washington, D.C.: U.S. Government Printing Office, 1934-), 7:469–71; Dearborn to Kirk, 22 December 1808, Shawnee File, Indiana University, Great Lakes–Ohio Valley Indian Archives, Bloomington, Ind. [hereafter cited as GL–OVIA].

10. Citizens of Dayton to the President, 30 January 1809, M221, Roll 27, 8933, NA; Chiefs and Headmen of the Shawnee to the President, 10 April 1809, ibid., Roll 24, 8053–54; Dearborn to John Johnston, 27 January 1809, Frank J. Jones Collection, Cincinnati Historical Society [hereafter CHS]; William Eustis to Johnston, Letters Sent by the Secretary of War Relating to Indian Affairs, M15, Roll 2, 437, RG 75, NA; Eustis to Johnston, 23 May 1809, ibid., Roll 2, 440–41.

11. Edmunds, *Shawnee Prophet*, 28–57, passim; Wells to Dearborn, 28 May 1807, M221, Roll 9, 2854–64, NA; Kirk to Dearborn, 20 July 1807, ibid, Roll 9, 2874–78; Kirk to Dearborn, 9 August 1807, ibid., 2880; Joseph Vance to Benjamin Drake, n.d., Tecumseh Papers, 2YY108–117, Draper MSS, Simon Kenton papers, 9BB1, Draper MSS.

12. Johnston to Harrison, 24 June 1810, in *Harrison Papers*, ed. Esarey 1:430–32; Johnston to Eustis, 3 July 1810, M221, Roll 38, 4614–15, NA; Johnston to Eustis, 25 July 1810, ibid. Also see "A treaty between the United States and the tribes of Indians . . . September 30, 1809," in *Indian Treaties, 1778–1883*, ed. Charles E. Kappler (1904; Reprint, New York: Amerson House, 1972), 101–2.

13. Wyandots to William Hull, 27 June 1810, Wyandot File, GL–OVIA; Joseph E. Badger, *A Memoir of Joseph Badger* (Hudson, Ohio: Sawyer, Ingersoll and Co., 1851), 125; J. Wetherell to Thomas Palmer, 13 October 1810, in Thomas Nuttall, "Thomas Nuttall's Travels in the Old Northwest: An Unpublished 1810 Diary," *Chronica Botanica* 14 (1951): 60–61.

14. James Rogers and Fish to the President, 29 March 1811, Records of the Secretary of War Relating to Indian Affairs, Letters Received, M271, Roll 1, 550–51, RG 75, NA; Johnston to Eustis, 27 August 1811, M221, Rol138, 4726–27, ibid.; Johnston to Eustis, 29 August 1811, ibid., 4723–25.

15. John Shaw to James Rhea, 1 March 1812, M221, Roll 48, 2772, NA; Johnston to Eustis, 1 May 1812, ibid., Roll 46, 1056; Francis Duchoquet to Johnston, ibid., 1061–62; Eustis to Johnston, 5 March 1812, M15, Roll 3, 118; William Perry to Return J. Meigs, April 30, 1812, Return J. Meigs Papers, Ohio Historical Society, Columbus, Ohio [hereafter cited as OHS].

16. Perry to Meigs, 7 May 1812, Meigs Papers, OHS; Edmund Munger to Meigs, 14 May 1812, ibid.; Citizens of Montgomery County to Meigs, 15 May 1812, ibid.; Johnston to Meigs, 22 May ibid.; Duncan MacArthur to Thomas Worthington, 7 May 1812, Thomas Worthington Papers, OHS; MacArthur to Worthington, 8 May 1812, ibid.; Perry to Worthington, 24 June 1812, ibid.; Johnston to Eustis, 21 May 1812, M221, Roll 46, 1064–66, NA.

17. "Proceedings of a Council begun and held near Urbana . . . the 6th of June, 1812," in *War on the Detroit: The Chronicles of Thomas Vercheres de Boucheville and the Capitulation by an Ohio Volunteer,* ed. Milo M. Quaife (Chicago: Lakeside Press, 1940), 197–206; "Copy of an Agreement with the Wyandot, Shawnee, and Mingo chiefs made by William Hull, June 12, 1812," Shawnee File, GL–OVIA; Hull to Eustis, 11 June 1812, ibid.; Hull to Eustis, 18 June 1812, ibid.

18. Johnston to Eustis, 21 March 1812, M221, Roll 46, 1069–70, NA; Worthington to Eustis, 24 June 1812, ibid., Roll 49, 3921–23; Circular by the War Department, 11 June 1812, M15, Roll 3, 79, ibid.

19. Johnston to Eustis, 2 July 1812, Shawnee File, GL–OVIA; Benjamin Stickney to Nathan Heald, 6 July 1812, in *Letterbook of the Indian Agency at Fort Wayne, 1809–1815,* Indiana Historical Publications, vol. 21, ed. Gayle Thornbrough (Indianapolis: Indiana Historical Society, 1961), 152; Stickney to Johnston, 7 July 1812, ibid., 156–57; Stickney to Eustis, 19 July 1812, ibid., 161–65.

20. "Capitulation for the Surrender of Detroit, August 16, 1812," *Michigan Pioneer and Historical Collections,* 40 vols. (Lansing: Michigan Historical Commission, 1877–1929), 25:332 [hereafter cited as *MPHC*]. Also see Edmunds, *Tecumseh,* 169–81.

21. Hull to Eustis, 9 June 1812, Shawnee File, GL–OVIA; Hull to Eustis, 14 July 1812, *MPHC,* 40:413–15; Hull to Eustis, 21 January 1812, ibid., 419–21.

22. Johnston to Eustis, 21 March 1812, M221, Roll 46, 1069–70, NA; James Rhea to Meigs, 19 August 1812, Meigs Papers, OHS. Also see Leonard U. Hill, *John Johnston and the Land of the Three Miamis* (Piqua, Ohio: Leonard Hill, 1957), 69.

23. Entry for 18 August 1812, Thomas Worthington's Diary, Worthington Papers, OHS; S. W. Culberton to Mr. Chambers, September 1812, in *Harrison Papers,* ed. Esarey 2:139–40; Meigs, Worthington, and Jeremiah Morrow to Eustis, 10 September 1812, M221, Roll 49, 4163–66, NA; Worthington to Eustis, 11 September 1812, ibid., 4105.

24. Harrison to the Secretary of War, October 13, 1812, in *Harrison Papers,* ed. Esarey 2:173–76; Johnston to Harrison, 23 October 1812, ibid., 186–87; Tarhe to Meigs, 28 October 1812, Meigs Papers, OHS; Edward Tupper to Meigs, 28 November 1812, ibid.; Statement by John Johnston, Tecumseh Papers, 11YY20, Draper MSS; Edward DeWar to Col. McDonnell, 19 October 1812, British Military and Naval Records, C Series, Vol. 676, 136–38, RG 8, NAC. Also see Benson Lossing, *Pictorial Field Book of the War of 1812* (New York: Harper and Brothers, 1869), 345.

25. Johnston to Henry Brown, 2 December 1812, Johnston Papers, OHS; Harrison to the Secretary of War, 14 December 1812, in *Harrison Papers,* ed. Esarey, 2:246–48. Also see Robert Breckinridge McAfee, *History of the Late War in the Western Country* (Lexington, Ky.: Worsley and Smith, 1816), 472–76; and Reginald Horsman, *Matthew Elliott, British Indian Agent* (Detroit: Wayne State University Press, 1967), 202.

26. Worthington to Eustis, 11 September 1812, M221, Roll 49, 4105, NA; Stickney to John Armstrong, 8 July 1813, ibid., 1201–6; Tupper to Meigs, 26 January 1813, Meigs Papers, OHS.

27. Tupper to Meigs, 26 January 1813, Meigs Papers, OHS; Lossing, *War of 1812,* 345–46n. 2.

28. Stickney to Jacob Fowler, 3 May 1813, Michigan Papers, University of Michigan, William Clements Library, Ann Arbor, Mich.; Richard M. Johnston to Armstrong, 4 June 1813, Shawnee File, GL–OVIA; Leslie Combs to George McLaughlin, 16 October 1863, Tecumseh papers, 6YY2, Draper MSS; MacArthur to Worthington, 22 May 1813, Worthington Papers, OHS; Lossing, *War of 1812,* 480–81, 485–86.

29. MacArthur to Worthington, 22 May 1813, Worthington Papers, OHS; Johnson to Armstrong, 4 June 1813, M221, Roll 54, 8276, NA; Report of an Indian Council, 21 July 1813, William Henry Harrison Papers, OHS; Draper's Notes, 26S114–16, Draper MSS.

30. Johnston to Armstrong, 4 June 1813, M221, Roll 54, 8276; Stickney to Armstrong, n.d., ibid., Roll 57, 1201–6; William Barbee to Worthington, 21 July 1813, Worthington Papers, Ohio State Historical Society; Harrison to Armstrong, 23 July 1813, in *Harrison Papers,* ed. Esarey, 2:494–495; Report of an Indian Council, 21 July 1813, Draper's Notes, 26S114–16, Draper MSS; John Johnston to Benjamin Drake, 24 September 1840, Tecumseh Papers, 11YY22, ibid.

31. Harrison to the Secretary of War, 27 September 1813, in *Harrison Papers,* ed. Esarey, 2:550–51; Harrison to the Secretary of War, 9 October 1813, Letters Received by the Secretary of War, Unregistered Series, M222, Roll 8, 3007–13, RG 107, NA; Lossing, *War of 1812,* 545–46, 552–54; McAfee, *History,* 389–99.

32. MacArthur to Captain Lewis, Captain Wolf, Captain Johnny, and Anthony Shane, 13 February 1815, Duncan MacArthur Papers, vol. 23, Washington, D.C., Library of Congress; MacArthur to George Izard, 18 November 1814, vol. 19, ibid.; MacArthur to Stickney, 30 January 1815, vol. 22, ibid.; John Brant to William Claus, 16 November 1814, Records of the Superintendent's Office, Correspondence, vol. 29, 1367–17368, RG 10, NAC.

33. MacArthur to the Acting Secretary of War, 15 March 1815, *MPHC,* 10:519–20; Shawnee chiefs to Johnston, 27 April 1815, M221, Roll 63, 6471, NA; Johnston to the Secretary of War, 4 May 1815, ibid., Roll 63, 6469.

34. "Journal of the Proceedings," August-September, 1815, *American State Papers: Indian Affairs,* 2 vols. (Washington, D.C.: Gales and Seaton, 1832–34), 2:17–25; Speech by the Shawnee Prophet, 1 September 1815, Records of the Superintendent's Office, Correspondence, vol. 31, 1838, RG 10, NAC; George Ironside to Claus, 23 October 1815, ibid., vol. 31, 18578–80; Harrison and Richard Graham to William Crawford, 9 September 1815, William Henry Harrison Papers, OHS. "Treaty between the United States and the . . . Indians," 8 September 1815, in *Indian Treaties,* ed. Kappler, 117–19.

35. An account of the renewed Quaker mission effort at Wapakoneta can be found in Henry Harvey, *History of the Shawnee Indians* (Cincinnati, Ohio: E. Morgan and Sons, 1855), 161–314, passim. Also see Hill, *John Johnston,* 99–137, and Edmunds, *Shawnee Prophet,* 165–83.

36. Edmunds, *Tecumseh,* 216–25; Edmunds, *Shawnee Prophet,* 165–83.

37. Hill, *John Johnston,* 113; "Treaty with the Shawnee, 1831" in *Indian Treaties,* ed. Kappler, 331–34.

"To Obtain Command of the Lakes": The United States and the Contest for Lakes Erie and Ontario, 1812–1815

JEFF SEIKEN

In the aftermath of General William Hull's surrender at Detroit in August 1812, President James Madison reflected on the disaster that had befallen the United States:

> As Hull's army was lost, it is to be regretted that the misfortune did not take place a little earlier; and allow more time, of course, for repairing it, within the present season. This regret is particularly applicable to the Great Lakes. . . . The command of [the] lakes, by a superior force on the water, ought to have been a fundamental point in the national policy, from the moment peace took place [in 1783].[1]

Madison had good reason to be rueful. In a war filled with missteps and blunders, the American failure to secure control of Lakes Erie and Ontario in the summer of 1812 has to rank as one of the costliest. The absence of an American squadron on Lake Erie allowed the British to concentrate quickly against Hull, severing his lines of communication and panicking him into surrendering his entire force of 1,600 men.[2] Although the Americans did manage to drive their opponents from the waters of Lake Erie in 1813, naval supremacy on Lake Ontario eluded them for the duration of the conflict. In the end, the stalemate on the Lake Ontario redounded to the British advantage, drawing the U.S. military into two years of fruitless campaigning on the Niagara Peninsula and foiling American plans to seize Upper Canada.

Historians have rightly viewed the Great Lakes region as the decisive theater of the War of 1812, and, over the years, scholars have studied the tactical and operational aspects of the naval campaigns on Erie and Ontario with considerable thoroughness.[3] Much less attention, however, has been paid to decision-making at the policy level. Limiting myself to the American side of the issue, this essay focuses on two questions in particular. First, what was the American policy with respect to the Great Lakes in the years leading up to the War of 1812? Second, once the United States had finally awakened to the importance of controlling Lakes Erie and Ontario, what steps did Madison's administration take to gain command of those waterways? In the letter quoted above, Madison declared that superiority on the lakes "ought to be maintained without regard to expense." But the Navy Department had limited resources to work with and had to balance the needs of the lake squadrons against the requirements of the coastal flotillas and the cruising navy. Thus, the second question can only be answered by examining the American effort on the lakes in the context of the naval war as a whole.

•   •   •

Both then and now, the hapless American General William Hull has borne a large share of the blame for the loss of his army in the opening stages of the War of 1812.[4] But the debacle at Detroit was a disaster several years in the making. The United States had long eyed Canada as a potential hostage to be taken if Britain refused to moderate its position on impressment and neutral trading rights.[5] American designs on Canada progressed to the stage of concrete planning after the HMS *Leopard* clashed with the USS *Chesapeake* in June 1807, bringing the two nations to the brink of war. In a series of meetings held in late July 1807, President Thomas Jefferson and his cabinet sketched out the details for an invasion of the province. Their plan called for a multi-pronged advance into Canada, aimed at securing four strategic points: Montreal, Kingston, the Niagara Peninsula, and British posts in the vicinity of Detroit.[6] Although war was averted, American military strategy from mid-1807 deviated little from this basic blueprint for the conquest of Canada.

Despite the central role that Canada played in its strategic calculations, the American government seemed all but indifferent to the importance of establishing a naval presence on the Great Lakes. In the July 1807 conferences, Jefferson and his advisors agreed to acquire materials to build additional gunboats for coastal defense. But no provisions were made then or later during Jefferson's presidency to provide for a naval force on Lake Erie, even though Canada's Provincial Marine maintained several armed sloops on the waterway.[7] As a result, the only public vessel on Lake Erie that Jefferson could call upon in event of war was the unarmed brig *Adams*, built by the army in 1801 for use as a transport ship.[8]

The situation was somewhat different on Lake Ontario, where the Provincial Marine also had several armed vessels. In the summer of 1808, the administration did issue orders to construct a brig there under the supervision of a naval officer. In his instructions, Navy Secretary Robert Smith specified that the craft should be "sufficiently large and armed to cope with any vessel of war now in Lake Ontario or with a small sloop of war," so he was obviously thinking of a ship that would be useful in time of war.[9] Nevertheless, the administration's principal motive in building the ship was to assist the beleaguered Treasury Department in enforcing the embargo on foreign trade on the American side of Lake Ontario.[10] As it turned out, by the time the 16-gun vessel, named *Oneida*, was ready the following April, the embargo had been repealed, and so the brig was placed in ordinary.[11]

The spring of 1809 brought not only an end to the embargo, but also a change in leadership as James Madison assumed the reins of the presidency. Yet, the turnover in the executive branch produced no shift in the government's policy of disinterest regarding the naval balance on the Great Lakes. Ironically, William Hull, in his capacity as governor of the Michigan Territory, twice wrote the War Department before 1812 about the necessity of maintaining a naval force on Lake Erie.[12] But neither letter persuaded Madison to take any positive action.

The deterioration in Anglo-American relations and the imminent approach of war in the winter of 1811–12 also failed to shake the complacency of Madison and his cabinet. In his annual address to Congress in November 1811, Madison recommended expanding the regular army and recruiting a sizable force of volunteers, obviously for the purposes of attacking Canada. But neither Madison nor Navy Secretary Paul Hamilton said anything to Congress about preparing a naval force on the Great Lakes to assist with the invasion or to strengthen the nation's military posture along the frontier.[13] The subject also did not come up on the floor of the House and Senate during the lengthy debates over the military buildup proposed by the president.

Not until Congress had been in session for over four months did the government turn its attention to the lakes. In early March, the War Department received another memorial from William Hull, reiterating his belief that a large naval force on the Great Lakes was of critical importance.[14] Toward the end of his letter, Hull perhaps fatally undermined his own argument by suggesting that Upper Canada might still fall to a joint attack from both ends of Lake Erie even without the benefit of naval support, provided the invading armies were of sufficient size. Still, even with this qualification, his message got through. As military preparations slowly got under-way in late March and early April, the administration for the first time began seri-ous discussion of building a fleet on the lakes. On 18 March, Navy Secretary Hamilton summoned one of his senior officers, Charles Stewart, to Washington to offer him command of the contemplated squadron. Hull also arrived to confer with the administration about the military situation in the Northwest. In the end, how-ever, the result was the same—complete inaction. Stewart declined the appointment and Hamilton and his counterpart in the War Office, William Eustis, concluded that it was not feasible at present to construct a naval force on the lakes.[15]

While expending no effort at all on Lake Erie, the United States was not quite so ill-prepared for the onset of hostilities on Lake Ontario. The credit for this, though, belongs entirely to Lieutenant Melancthon Woolsey of the *Oneida*, who waged a one-man campaign to ready his command for war. In 1811, Woolsey wrote Hamilton repeatedly about the *Oneida*'s need for military stores and a complete crew. He also suggested making arrangements with the owners of private merchant schooners to purchase or hire their vessels in the event of war. Hamilton rejected this advice on the grounds that the Navy Department lacked authority from Congress to make such acquisitions, but he did comply with Woolsey's request for supplies and men. Undeterred by the secretary's response, Woolsey went ahead and tried to convince shipowners to lay their vessels up on the American side of the lake during the winter to keep them out of British hands.[16] Once war was declared, Woolsey moved quickly to preserve his base at Sackets Harbor from attack with the limited resources available. Again acting on his own initiative, he took two merchantmen into service and outfitted them as gunboats. He also contacted Isaac Chauncey, commander of the navy yard at New York City, requesting guns for the purposes of arming the other American mer-chant schooners on the lake.[17] Although the *Oneida* and her two consorts could in no way challenge the more heavily armed vessels of the Provincial Marine, Woolsey did provide the Navy Department with the nucleus of a force it could build around.

War commenced on 18 June 1812, amidst general expectations for the quick and easy conquest of Upper Canada.[18] Initially, Hull's reports from Detroit were optimistic, too. He informed the War Department on 19 July that the *Adams* was in the process of being fitted for guns, after which command of the upper lakes would be his.[19] As the summer progressed and the news filtering back from the frontier grew more disturbing, however, the administration in Washington belatedly began to question its decision not to prepare a naval force on the Great Lakes. On 27 August, the day before Madison planned to depart Washington for the cooler environs of his family home in Virginia, he confided to Treasury Secretary Albert Gallatin, "The command of the lakes is obviously of the greatest importance, and has always so appeared." But by then it was too late. Hull had raised the white flag at Detroit twelve days earlier.

With Hull's surrender, the blinders finally came off. After eight years of ignoring or dismissing the strategic significance of the Great Lakes, the American government at last saw the magnitude of its error with unmistakable clarity. To their credit, Madison and his cabinet reacted swiftly and effectively to the news of Hull's capitulation. Within forty-eight hours, a new policy was in place calling for the Navy Department "to obtain command of the Lakes Ontario & Erie, with the least possible delay." Secretary Hamilton selected Isaac Chauncey, commandant of the Navy Yard at New York, to direct the naval campaign, granting him unlimited authority to requisition supplies and build or hire whatever vessels might be necessary to accomplish his mission.[20]

The story of Chauncey's appointment and his labors to reverse the naval balance on the lakes in 1812 has been told many times before and can be summarized briefly here. Most of his efforts were directed toward Lake Ontario. In the space of only a few months he succeeded in transporting hundreds of sailors and skilled shipwrights, as well as vast quantities of munitions and stores to feed the growing American naval base at Sackets Harbor. By mid-November, the corvette *Madison*, mounting twenty-six guns, was nearly complete and eight merchants' schooners had been fully armed, enabling Chauncey to report with obvious satisfaction that he was "Master of this lake."[21]

The speed and efficiency with which the United States established a strong naval presence on Lake Ontario demonstrates just how shortsighted Hamilton had been in declining to take action the previous spring. Although the logistical challenges of constructing a fleet on the frontier were indeed severe, several factors rendered the whole undertaking much less daunting than it appeared to be. First, as many historians have pointed out, the physical difficulties of moving men and equipment to the lakes were eased considerably by the network of rivers and canals that linked Lake Ontario to the city of New York.[22] And at New York, of course, Chauncey could procure with relative ease the skilled workers and shipbuilding materials he needed. Of equal importance, but often overlooked by scholars, is the second point in Chauncey's favor: New York was also home to one of the navy's largest and best-equipped shore establishments. In particular, the navy yard there was well supplied with the two crucial commodities of which the department otherwise had very limited quantities: ordnance and personnel. Over the years, the station had accumulated an arsenal of more than two hundred light and heavy cannons, as well as a considerable supply of round shot, grape, gunpowder, small arms, and other munitions. The yard's only deficiency lay in the category of carronades.[23] Yet, here, too, fortune smiled on Chauncey: Just after the war had commenced, the department directed the ship *John Adams*, armed with twenty-two 32-pound carronades, to shift her berth from Boston to New York.[24] With the cannons from the yard, Chauncey was able to arm his lake schooners rather handily while reserving the carronades for the *Madison*. Over forty guns were also shipped out to Buffalo for the squadron outfitting on Lake Erie.[25] Besides ordnance, the New York station readily answered Chauncey's requirements in terms of manpower as well. All told, Chauncey dispatched roughly seven hundred sailors and marines to the Lakes from New York, including the entire complement of the *John Adams* and most of the men attached to the yard and the gunboats in the flotilla.[26]

The ample assets of the New York station were thus vital to Chauncey's success in 1812, allowing him to extemporize a naval force on the lakes in a remarkably short period of time. He managed to do this, moreover, without straining the navy's resources or otherwise upsetting the department's planning. The departure of so many men from the gunboats did leave New York's naval defenses almost completely destitute. But, at this stage of the war, with the Royal Navy posing only a slight threat to the nation's seaports, Secretary Hamilton could afford to weaken the flotilla, especially since there were gunboat crews sitting idle in the Delaware River to take the place of the transferred sailors.[27] In 1813 and 1814, however, as the tempo of the war picked up dramatically both on the lakes and the seaboard, the Navy Department would not have anywhere near the same luxury.

American policy toward the lakes underwent no significant alteration in 1813, but Madison did make one meaningful change: He replaced Navy Secretary Paul Hamilton with William Jones, a prominent shipowner, merchant, and ex-Congressman from Philadelphia. The switch had an important impact on the subsequent course of the war on the Great Lakes. During his tenure as secretary, Hamilton had been content to leave the management of the lakes campaign entirely to Chauncey. This arrangement worked well enough on Lake Ontario in 1812, especially since Chauncey was drawing his supplies and support from a single source that he was intimately familiar with—New York City. But it would hardly answer in 1813, when the expanding scale of the American naval effort would require Chauncey to requisition men and materials from a number of quarters. Furthermore, Chauncey's progress at Sackets Harbor came at the expense of the Lake Erie establishment, which languished from lack of attention. When he first set off for the lakes, Chauncey had intended to build several brigs and gunboats at Black Rock.[28] But, preoccupied by his considerable responsibilities on Lake Ontario, this plan had fallen by the wayside and control of Lake Erie still rested firmly in British hands.[29]

The new secretary of the Navy, however, entered office intent on reclaiming the authority his predecessor had delegated so freely, and he made his presence felt at once. Insofar as the lakes were concerned, Jones' most important action was to reduce the administrative burdens on Chauncey to more manageable proportions by assuming overall direction of the building program on the frontier himself. Chauncey still retained full operational control of the fleets and remained responsible for supervising the construction and fitting out of the vessels. But Jones—with Chauncey's input, of course—took charge of determining the size and composition of the lake squadrons and directing the flow of resources to carry his decisions into effect. Jones's most immediate concern was to revive the flagging American naval effort on Lake Erie. After touring the small American establishment at the town of Erie in early January, Chauncey had resolved to construct a brig at the site. Jones approved of Chauncey's plans, but instructed him to go a step further and build a second brig as well. In the same communication, Jones also directed Chauncey to build a corvette on Lake Ontario, identical to the *Madison*.[30]

While New York continued to be the primary depot for the Ontario fleet, the cities of Pittsburgh and Philadelphia served as the main suppliers for the Erie squadron.[31] As was the case the previous fall, securing a sufficient number of shipwrights and laborers from the seacoast posed little difficulty.[32] Obtaining ordnance for the ships under construction at Erie also proved to be surprisingly easy. Foxhall's iron works in Georgetown, the department's principal source of naval ordnance, already had on hand twenty-three 32-pound carronades that had been cast at an earlier date.[33] By the middle of March, these, plus the Washington Navy Yard's entire stock of fourteen 32-pound carronades, had been loaded aboard wagons and dispatched to Pittsburgh.[34] For the new corvette building at Sackets Harbor, the New York yard once again supplied Chauncey with the guns he wanted.

Procuring crews for the new vessels was a far more difficult proposition for Chauncey and Jones. Some fifty volunteers from the brig *Argus* at New York swelled Chauncey's ranks in early spring. The newly appointed commander of the Erie squadron, Oliver H. Perry, also persuaded one hundred men from the gunboat flotilla at Newport, Rhode Island, to accompany him to the lakes. Even with these reinforcements, however, Chauncey estimated that he would need another five hundred sailors and two hundred marines by the first of June.[35] The commodore initially hoped to get additional hands by requisitioning sailors from the New York station again. But with the Royal Navy menacing the coastline in force, Jones was loath to do anything that would diminish New York's defenses. Instead, he instructed Chauncey to rely on recruiting to find sailors for the fresh-water fleets.[36] Chauncey dutifully arranged for recruiting stations to be opened at Boston and other New England seaports. The results were meager. Competition from privateers and armed traders made naval recruiting difficult under the best of circumstances.[37] Lake service was particularly unpopular among sailors because of the severe weather, sickly climate, and poor prospects for prize money.

Only after Chauncey's 1 June deadline had passed and his manpower shortages grew acute did Jones begin drafting men from other stations. The first to go were sailors from the navy's cruising vessels. The secretary was careful to pick men from ships that were blockaded or undergoing repairs at places that were not under the immediate threat of attack. Thus, he rejected Chauncey's request for the crew of the frigate *Adams,* which was based at the Washington Navy Yard, ready to respond in case the British forces in the Chesapeake Bay launched a foray up the Potomac River. But he did relent and transfer the crews of the *John Adams* and the prize sloop *Alert,* close to three hundred men in all, from New York as per the commodore's original suggestion. The frigate *Constitution* and schooner *Syren,* both of which were laid up for extensive repairs at Boston, also furnished about the same number of hands. Recruiting efforts at New York secured a further eighty or so men. Jones failed to meet Chauncey's requirements in only one area, marines. He ordered a detachment of one hundred marched up from South Carolina, but more, he informed Chauncey, could not be spared from the coastal stations.[38]

Besides doing what he could to funnel men and materials to the Great Lakes, Jones also tried to help his commanders in another way—by interdicting the supply lines of the British forces on the frontier. In the spring of 1813, he ordered the brigs *Argus* and *Hornet* and the frigate *Chesapeake* to cruise off of Nova Scotia and the Gulf of St. Lawrence in the hopes of intercepting storeships and transports bound for Halifax and Quebec.[39] Jones' strategy was eminently sound; indeed, one would be hard-pressed to conceive of a more useful mission for the tiny American cruising navy at this point in the war. But his plans came undone almost immediately. At the last minute, the *Argus* was diverted to Europe on a diplomatic mission, while the *Hornet* failed to slip past the British warships guarding the exits from New York. As for the *Chesapeake,* her captain, James Lawrence simply ignored that part of his instructions calling for him to elude the British blockaders off Boston. Instead, he sailed out of port in broad daylight and challenged the British frigate *Shannon* to a stand-up fight, which he lost.[40]

The failure of this enterprise notwithstanding, the 1813 campaign on the lakes ended happily enough for the United States. Perry destroyed the British squadron on Lake Erie in September, with the second brig ordered by Jones back in January providing the margin of victory. On Lake Ontario, however, despite a promising start, Chauncey's operations produced a far less conclusive result. For the first part of the campaigning season, the British refused to venture forth from their main base at Kingston, essentially forfeiting control of the lake to Chauncey. The commodore took advantage of the enemy's inactivity to raid the British shipyard and supply depot at York, and to assist the U.S. Army in seizing Fort George at the head of the Niagara Peninsula. But the complexion of the campaign changed dramatically when the British Admiralty decided to commit the resources of the Royal Navy to the war on the lakes. In May, Royal Navy Commodore Sir James L. Yeo arrived at Kingston to take command of the Ontario fleet. He brought with him a large detachment of officers and sailors from the Royal Navy. This infusion of experienced personnel, coupled with the completion of the 23-gun *Wolfe,* enabled the British to contend with Chauncey on far more equal terms. Chauncey still possessed the slightly superior fleet once *Madison*'s sister corvette, the 28-gun *General Pike,* was launched in June. But, through the remainder of the season, the commodore failed to bring his opponent to decisive battle, necessitating another round of shipbuilding at Sackets Harbor.

Even before Chauncey's operations in 1813 wound down to their close, Secretary Jones was already laying plans for the 1814 campaign. In mid-September, he sounded out Chauncey about the possibility of constructing three 22-gun sloops of war identical to the *Peacock*, which had been built for the navy at New York during the current year.[41] News that the British were preparing to construct more powerful vessels at Kingston, however, prompted Jones to revise his calculations about the force needed for the next round of campaigning. After some discussion, Jones and Chauncey agreed at a conference in Washington to match the British building program by constructing a frigate of the largest class and two or three other well-armed ships.[42]

In carrying this plan into effect, the Navy Department faced a reprise of the personnel problems that had plagued it the previous year. Jones once again pinned his hopes on recruiting at the eastern seaports. To encourage men to come forward, he secured the President's authorization to raise the pay and bounty of sailors who agreed to serve on the lakes.[43] But, despite Chauncey's early optimism, navy agents failed to enter anywhere near enough hands to meet his needs. As of mid-March, Chauncey reported that he had only 1,085 officers, sailors, and marines on his muster rolls, which left him 1,590 men short of the number required for the upcoming campaign.[44] With no other way to make up the deficit, Jones turned to his bluewater fleet for the second straight year. The frigate *Macedonian*, trapped in New London, surrendered her complement of sailors to the lakes, as did the *Congress* in Portsmouth, the *John Adams* in New York and the brand new sloop *Erie* at Baltimore.[45] Jones's decisions in 1814 reflected the same priorities as before: whenever possible, men were to be drafted from cruising vessels rather than the coastal flotillas.

While rounding up crews caused Jones trouble enough, finding sufficient guns to arm the new vessels turned out to be an even more formidable obstacle. Availability was less the issue than transportation. From New York City, transportation was a relatively simple matter of loading the cannon aboard river sloops and sending them up the Hudson. The difficulty, though, lay in getting the guns to New York. All of the foundries the navy did business with were located in Washington and Maryland, several hundred miles to the south. Although the department had no trouble moving guns overland an even greater distance to Erie in the spring of 1813, the situation had changed greatly by the following autumn. With the coasting trade shut down and farmers struggling to get their produce to market, Jones found it impossible to hire any wagon teams to haul the cannons north. His predicament was further complicated by the fact that it was not just Chauncey's ships that wanted ordnance. The *Peacock* at New York and her sister sloops at

Boston and Newburyport also lacked guns, while additional cannons were needed for the American squadron arming on Lake Champlain.[46]

In the end, Jones resolved his difficulties by appropriating guns from his cruising vessels just as he had commandeered their crews. At Jones' direction, the 42-pound carronades were stripped from the spar deck of the frigate *President,* which was refitting at New York in early 1814.[47] The hapless *John Adams* relinquished her guns for the second time in the war as well, while the sloop *Alert* contributed most of her armament, too.[48] Acting on Chauncey's suggestion, Jones also prevailed upon the secretary of the war to loan the navy twenty-two light 18-pounders mounted on the coastal batteries at New York harbor. He received an additional twenty-three 32-pound long guns from the navy yard and gunboat flotilla at New York.[49] Even after Jones and Chauncey had scrounged up the necessary guns, though, their problems were far from over. By the time the ordnance situation had been sorted out, winter ice closed down the inland waterways that served as Chauncey's main supply route. Rather than wait for the spring thaw, the commodore chose to send the guns by land. He quickly came to regret the decision, as the teamsters hired to haul the cannons abandoned most of them between New York and Poughkeepsie when the roads proved nearly impassable. Not until early June did the bulk of the guns dispatched from New York arrive at Sackets Harbor.[50]

Chauncey eventually succeeded in getting four new ships into the water by the summer of 1814: the 58-gun *Superior,* the 42-gun *Mohawk,* and two brigs mounting between twenty and twenty-one guns.[51] But his success carried a heavy price, leaving a significant portion of the bluewater navy prostrate. The expense, too, had been immense, requiring Jones to suspend or curtail work on two of the navy's new ships-of-the-line building on the coast.[52] Most discouraging of all, though, as far as Jones was concerned, was that there was no end in sight. While Chauncey was anxiously waiting for guns and sailors to trickle in to Sackets Harbor, Commodore Yeo had been able to leap ahead in the shipbuilding race. Drawing on the Royal Navy's deep reservoir of men and materials, Yeo launched and equipped two heavily gunned frigates at Kingston in early May of 1814, several months before Chauncey's own vessels were ready. Temporarily outgunned, Chauncey elected to remain holed up at Sackets Harbor, conceding free run of Lake Ontario to his opponent until the *Mohawk* and *Superior* were fully armed and manned.[53] Chauncey finally did venture forth with his entire squadron in August, forcing Yeo to retire to his base at Kingston. But two months later, the advantage shifted back the other way when the

British completed work on the *St. Lawrence,* a three-deck ship-of-the-line mounting a staggering total of 112 guns. Chauncey promptly retreated back to the safe confines of Sackets Harbor, and it was on this desultory if inconclusive note that naval operations on Lake Ontario ended for the Americans in 1814. Chauncey had not exactly been vanquished, but the balance of forces clearly inclined in his opponent's favor. Furthermore, Napoleon's recent defeat in Europe meant that the Royal Navy now had thousands of seasoned sailors and officers to spare, along with a vast supply of naval guns and stores to answer all of Yeo's needs.

Faced with the prospect of carrying on with the shipbuilding contest for another year on Lake Ontario, Jones weighed his options. Not only had the British increased the stakes sharply by launching the *St. Lawrence* in 1814, but it looked like they would raise the ante again by building several more ships-of-the-line over the winter. Jones consulted with Chauncey about the feasibility of constructing up to three ships-of-the-line at Sackets Harbor, mounting ninety-four guns apiece.[54] He also questioned inventor Robert Fulton as to whether it would be possible to build floating steam batteries on Lake Ontario similar to the one he was completing for the navy at New York.[55] Chauncey answered in the affirmative, while Fulton did not, apparently settling the issue in favor of ships-of-the-line.

Chauncey's reassurances did not diminish Jones' misgivings, which had been mounting steadily since the previous spring. In late May 1814, he openly expressed his doubts to President Madison about the wisdom of the administration's fixation on Canada.[56] And in the final week of October, Jones again approached Madison on the subject, this time in a lengthy memorandum advocating a complete reorientation of the nation's strategic priorities. In his view, the Navy Department simply could not match the British naval effort on the lake, especially now that the war in Europe was over. Even if the proposed ships-of-the line were built at Sackets Harbor, Jones wrote, he was at a loss to understand how the navy could possibly man them. Therefore, instead of pouring yet more men, money, and resources into the northern theater, Jones advised Madison to abandon the Great Lakes altogether. The regular army, acting in conjunction with militia detachments and volunteers, could establish a defensive cordon across the frontier, while the several thousand sailors released from the lakes could be applied to the far more important service of defending the coast and attacking British commerce.[57]

Jones's counsel was startling, and it requires little imagination to grasp why Madison rejected his advice. To admit defeat and withdraw from the Great Lakes would have dealt a crushing blow to American morale, while also quite possibly upsetting the Anglo-American peace talks in Europe. Furthermore, this move would have left Ohio and the rest of the western frontier exposed to attack and might well have led to a revival of the Indian threat in the Northwest. Yet, Jones's analysis was astute. He grasped the essential point that once Britain was free to apply the enormous manpower and material resources of the Royal Navy to the lakes, the U.S. Navy with its own very limited resources could no longer continue the shipbuilding race with any prospects of success. It was just as well that the war ended when it did, for if it had carried on for another year, Madison might have found that Jones' prognosis was all too correct. By the middle of February 1815, two of the American ships-of-line at Sackets Harbor were within a few months of completion, but it was already looking doubtful that the navy would ever find enough officers, sailors, and marines to man them. When hostilities ended, the department had on its rolls less than half of the seven thousand men required for the upcoming campaign on Lake Ontario.[58]

To conclude, we should return briefly to the questions posed at the outset. As to the first question, the answer should be fairly obvious: Prior to the War of 1812, the United States had no policy regarding the Great Lakes. Despite entertaining plans to invade Canada for a number of years, only once, on the very eve of the war, did the government devote serious attention to preparing a naval force on the lakes. But the possibility was dismissed almost as soon as it was raised. Whether due to overconfidence or simple obtuseness, American leaders in the years leading up to the War of 1812 turned a blind eye to the strategic importance of securing command of the Great Lakes.

The answer to the second question is a little less clear-cut. Certainly, once the decision was made to obtain command of Lakes Erie and Ontario, the Navy Department did follow through on the president's directive to spare no expense. During William Jones's tenure as head of the navy, he worked tirelessly to see that the American naval force on the frontier received the materials it needed. Throughout 1813 and 1814, Jones and his senior commander, Isaac Chauncey, were in perfect accord as to the building and equipping of the lakes squadrons, and only in matters relating to the manning of the vessels did they disagree. Chauncey quite naturally wanted to draw men freely from the Atlantic theater, while Jones sought to do everything possible to preserve the integrity of his forces there. Even then, when other options were exhausted, Jones proved willing to sacrifice the navy's commerce raiding capabilities to further the American effort on the lakes. The ensuing stalemate on Lake Ontario did not result from any lack of support on the department's part, but rather reflected the painful truth that William Jones recognized in 1814: that as the war dragged on, the Lake Ontario campaign was a contest the U.S. Navy increasingly lacked the means to win.

NOTES

1. Madison to Henry Dearborn, 7 October 1812, Madison Papers, Washington: Library of Congress.

2. Assessments of the exact size of Hull's force vary. Sir George Prevost, in his official correspondence, claimed to have taken 2,500 captives at Detroit, but this number is certainly an exaggeration. See John K. Mahon, *The War of 1812* (Gainesville: University of Florida Press, 1972), 50; Robert S. Quimby, *The U.S. Army in the War of 1812: An Operational and Command Study*, 2 vols. (East Lansing, Mich.: Michigan State University Press, 1997), 1:47.

3. The specialized literature on the subject is substantial. Although by no means exhaustive, the following is a list of the most valuable studies: David Curtis Skaggs and Gerard T. Altoff, *A Signal Victory: The Lake Erie Campaign, 1812–13* (Annapolis: Naval Institute Press, 1997); Robert Malcomson, *Lords of the Lake: The Naval War on Lake Ontario, 1812–1814* (Annapolis: Naval Institute Press, 1998); Max Rosenberg, *The Building of Perry's Fleet on Lake Erie, 1812–1813* (Harrisburg, Pa.: Pennsylvania Historical and Museum Commission, 1950); Ernest A. Cruikshank, "The Contest for the Command of Lake Erie in 1812–13," in *The Defended Border: Upper Canada and the War of 1812*, ed. Morris Zaslow (Toronto: The Macmillan Company of Canada, 1964), 84–104; C. P. Stacey, "Another Look at the Battle of Lake Erie," in *The Defended Border*, 105–13; Frederick C. Drake, "Artillery and Its Influence on Naval Tactics: Reflections on the Battle of Lake Erie," in *War on the Great Lakes: Essays Commemorating the 175th Anniversary of the Battle of Lake Erie*, ed. William Jeffrey Welsh and David Curtis Skaggs (Kent, Ohio: Kent State University Press, 1991), 17–29; Michael A. Palmer, "A Failure of Command, Control, and Communications: Oliver Hazard Perry and the Battle of Lake Erie," *Journal of Erie Studies* 17 (fall 1988): 7–26; Cruikshank, "The Contest for the Command of Lake Ontario in 1812 and 1813," *Transactions of the Royal Society of Canada*, 3rd ser., 10 (September 1916): 161–223; Cruikshank, "The Contest for the Command of Lake Ontario in 1814," *Ontario Historical Society* 21 (1924): 99–159; William S. Dudley, "Commodore Isaac Chauncey and U.S. Joint Operations on Lake Ontario, 1813–14," in *New Interpretations in Naval History: Selected Papers from the Eighth Naval History Symposium*, ed. William B. Cogar (Annapolis: Naval Institute Press, 1989), 139–55; Stacey, "The Ships of the British Squadron on Lake Ontario, 1812–14," *The Canadian Historical Review* 34 (December 1953): 311–23; Stacey, "Naval Power on the Lakes," in *After Tippecanoe: Some Aspects of the War of 1812*, ed. Philip P. Mason (East Lansing, Mich.: Michigan State University Press, 1963), 49–59. It is interesting, but perhaps not surprising, to note that the naval contest on Lake Ontario has generated relatively little interest among American scholars.

4. For contemporary reaction to Hull's defeat, see J. C. A. Stagg, *Mr. Madison's War: Politics, Diplomacy, and Warfare in the Early American Republic, 1783–1830* (Princeton: Princeton University Press,

1983), 207. Madison condemned Hull for leading the administration to believe that Upper Canada could be conquered without a naval force on Lake Erie. See Madison to Dearborn, 7 October 1812, and to John Nicholas, 2 April 1813, Madison Papers. Hull was subsequently court-martialed and drummed out of the army. Historians have been inclined to treat Hull with more sympathy, agreeing that he was ill-served by his compatriots in the War Department, particularly General Henry Dearborn and Secretary William Eustis. Nonetheless, most also believe that Hull helped dig his own grave, both in the planning and in the execution of the campaign. For balanced evaluations of Hull's conduct, see Quimby, *U.S. Army in the War of 1812*, 1:20–21, 46–49, and Mahon, *The War of 1812*, 52.

5. For a general analysis of American attitudes toward Canada, see Reginald Horsman, "On to Canada: Manifest Destiny and the United States Strategy in the War of 1812," *Michigan Historical Review* 13 (spring 1987): 1–24. For a penetrating discussion of the evolution of Madison's thinking on the same subject, see Stagg, *Mr. Madison's War*, 3–47.

6. See the entries for 26-28 July 1807 in *The Anas of Thomas Jefferson*, ed. Franklin B. Swivel (New York: Da Capo Press, 1970), 255–62. See also Albert Gallatin's memorandum to Jefferson, July 25, 1807, *The Writings of Albert Gallatin*, ed. Henry Adams (Philadelphia: J. B. Lippincott & Co., 1870), 1:340–53.

7. Daniel Dobbins, "The Dobbins Papers," *Publications of the Buffalo Historical Society* 8 (1905): 294–95. Nor did the subject surface in the debates over military preparations that took place in Congress during the winters of 1807–8 and 1808–9.

8. Dobbins, "The Dobbins Papers," 293.

9. Quoted in Howard I. Chapelle, *The History of the American Sailing Navy: The Ships and Their Development* (New York: Bonanza Books, 1949), 229–30. The decision to construct the brig was made in a cabinet meeting on 30 June 1808. See *Anas of Thomas Jefferson*, 265–66.

10. Defiance of, and sometimes violent resistance to, the embargo laws at the port of Oswego had grown so severe that by August 1808, Jefferson and Treasury Secretary Albert Gallatin were ready to declare the violators to be in a state of open insurrection. The governor of New York was finally compelled to bring in the militia to restore order. Serious disturbances also broke out at points along Lake Champlain, prompting the administration to order two gunboats for those waters at the same time it directed the brig to be built on Lake Ontario. For a discussion of the administration's problems enforcing the embargo on Lakes Ontario and Champlain, see Dumas Malone, *Jefferson the President: Second Term, 1805–1809* (Boston: Little, Brown and Company, 1974), 586–89, 603–4.

11. Hamilton to Melancthon T. Woolsey, 17 May 1809, Secretary of the Navy, Letters to Officers, Ships of War, Microfilm Series M-149, Record Group 45 [hereafter cited as RG 45], Washington: National Archives [hereafter cited as NA].

12. For the 1809 letter, see the reference in *Defence of Brigadier General William Hull* (Boston: Wells and Lilly, 1814), 23. For the 1811 letter, see Hull to William Eustis, 15 June 1811, *Documents Relating to the Invasion of Canada and the Surrender of Detroit, 1812*, ed. E. A. Cruikshank (Ottawa: Government Printing Bureau, 1912), 1–3.

13. For the complete text of Madison's address to Congress, see *A Compilation of the Messages and Papers of the Presidents*, ed. James D. Richardson (n.p.: Bureau of National Literature and Art, 1910), 1:476–81. See also Hamilton to Langdon Cheves, 3 December 1811, in *American State Papers, Class VI, Naval Affairs*, 2 vols. (Washington, D.C.: Gales and Seaton, 1834), 1:248–52.

14. Hull's missive arrived on the heals of a communication from influential New York Republican John Armstrong, warning the War Department of the extreme vulnerability of Detroit if the U.S. did not control Lake Erie. See Hull to Eustis, 6 March 1812, and Armstrong to Eustis, 2 January 1812, *Documents*

Relating to Detroit, 3, 19–22.

15. See the testimony of William Eustis and Peter Porter, and the deposition of Charles Stewart in *The Report of the Trial of Brigadier General William Hull* (New York: Eastburn, Kirk, and Co., 1814), 126–27 and append. 2, pp. 3–4, 7–8. See also Hamilton to Stewart, 18 March 1812, Letters Sent to Officers. At his court-martial, Hull later claimed that he departed Washington under the opposite impression—that the army brig *Adams* was to be transferred to the Navy Department and a navy agent assigned to the region as a prelude to further naval activity on the lakes. But he was clearly mistaken on the first account and may well have been speaking less than honestly. *Adams* remained within the War Department's jurisdiction, and Hull's own dispatches from the frontier clearly suggest that he believed the brig to be directly under his command. He was correct, though, about the second point. On 24 April, Hamilton commissioned Augustus Porter, of Niagara, to serve as a purchasing agent for the navy. But Porter's appointment appears to have been made solely for the benefit of Lieutenant Melancthon Woolsey, commander of the brig *Oneida* on Lake Ontario, who was then busy trying to outfit his ship. See Hamilton to Joshua Potts, Jeremiah Brown, and Augustus Porter, Miscellaneous Letters Sent by the Secretary of the Navy, Microfilm Series M-209, RG 45, NA. For Hamilton's subsequent communications with Porter regarding Woolsey, see Hamilton to Porter, 20 May, 30 June 1812, ibid.

16. Woolsey to Hamilton, 10 September, 11, 18 October 1812, Letters from Officers of Rank Below That of Commanders Received by the Secretary of the Navy, Microfilm Series M-148, RG 45, NA; Hamilton to Woolsey, 23 September 1811, Letters Sent to Officers.

17. Woolsey to Hamilton, 9, 26, 28, June, 4 July, 1812, Letters Received Below Rank of Commander.

18. Donald R. Hickey, *The War of 1812: A Forgotten Conflict* (Urbana: University of Illinois Press, 1989), 72–73.

19. See Hull to Eustis, 15, 19 July, 1812, in *Documents Relating to Detroit*, 53, 60.

20. Hamilton to Chauncey, 31 August, 1812, Letters Sent by the Secretary of the Navy to Commandants and Navy Agents, Microfilm Series M-441, RG 45, NA.

21. Chauncey to Hamilton, 23 November, 1812, Captains Letters to the Secretary of the Navy, Microfilm Series M-125, RG 45, NA.

22. The Navy Department benefited greatly from improvements made in the Schenactady to Oswego leg of the water route by the Western Inland Lock Navigation Company during the 1790s and first few years of the 1800s. The company eliminated the frequent problems with rapids and shallows by deepening the channel, building dams, and, in some cases, constructing short canals to bypass unnavigable portions. See Philip Lord, Jr., "The Mohawk/Oneida Corridor: The Geography of Inland Navigation Across New York," in this volume. According to Chauncey's confidential clerk, Samuel Anderson, who was stationed at Albany to expedite the movement of supplies westward from the Hudson, shallow-draft boats carrying from 3 to 7 tons could complete the 200-mile journey from Schenactady to Lake Ontario entirely by water. See Anderson to Chauncey, 8 October 1812, Letters Received Below Rank of Commander.

23. For the state of the New York Navy Yard, see Paul Hamilton to Adam Seybart, 10 December 1811, Letters to Congress, E-5, RG 45, NA.

24. Charles Ludlow to Hamilton, 9 July 1812, Letters Received Below Rank of Commander. The previous captain of the *John Adams*, Joseph Tarbell, had obtained the carronades from the frigate *Chesapeake*, which was laid up in ordinary at Boston before the war. See William Bainbridge to Hamilton, 16 April 1812, Captains Letters.

25. All-told, Chauncey sent 104 guns, 1,340 muskets and pistols, more than 50 tons of round shot, and over 5,000 stands of grape and canister to the lakes from the New York station. For a detailed inventory of the military and naval stores transferred from New York, see Chauncey to Hamilton, 8 December 1812 [filed after letter dated 8 December 1813], Captains Letters.

26. Chauncey to Hamilton, 26 September 1812, ibid.

27. After Chauncey's departure, the interim commanding officer of the New York station, Charles Ludlow, complained that he barely had men enough to put six gunboats into service. See Ludlow to Hamilton, 29 September 1812, Letters Received Below Rank of Commander. For the transfer of men from Philadelphia, see Alexander Murray to Hamilton, 17 October 1812, Captains Letters. Of course, the *John Adams* was also left high and dry without guns or a crew, but since she was in the process of being refitted, this was hardly a significant loss.

28. Chauncey to Hamilton, 8 October 1812, ibid.

29. Some work had been carried out modifying four American merchantmen taken into naval service at Block Rock. Four gunboats were also in the preliminary stages of building at Erie. See Chauncey to Hamilton, 1, 8, January 1813, ibid.

30. On this point, Jones anticipated Chauncey's desires exactly, for just a week earlier the commodore had written Washington seeking permission to do the same. See Chauncey to Jones, 20 January 1813, ibid.; Jones to Chauncey, 27 January 1813, Letters Sent to Officers.

31. Pittsburgh was extremely well situated, connected to Erie entirely by water save for a 14-mile portage at the end. Communications between Pittsburgh and Philadelphia, on the other hand, were considerably more tenuous. Nonetheless, there was a road running between the two and, given sufficient time, it was still quite feasible to transport large quantities of naval stores from Philadelphia to the interior. See Rosenberg, *Building of Perry's Fleet*, 11–20, 35.

32. Chauncey to Jones, 16 February 1813, Captains Letters; Jones to George Harrison, 20 February 1813, Miscellaneous Letters Sent. The carpenters from Philadelphia took much longer to arrive at Erie than anticipated, but they did get there by April, 1813. See Oliver H. Perry to Chauncey, 10 April 1813, Masters Commandant Letters Received by the Secretary of the Navy, Microfilm Series, Microfilm Series M-147, RG 45, NA.

33. From the Navy Department's records, it is not clear when or for what purpose the guns had been contracted. They may have been cast at Chauncey's request in the fall of 1812, when he had advised Secretary Hamilton to have forty-four 32-pound carronades manufactured for use on the vessels he planned to build at Black Rock. Hamilton did not acknowledge his request, but it is certainly possible he went ahead and placed the order at Foxhall's. See Chauncey to Hamilton, 26 September 1812, Captains Letters.

34. Jones to Oliver Ormsby, 25 February 1813, to Harrison, 9, 15 March 1813, Miscellaneous Letters Sent.

35. Jones to Chauncey, 5 February 1813, to Perry, 8 February 1813, Letters Sent to Officers. Chauncey to Jones, 5, 18 March 1813, Captains Letters.

36. Chauncey to Jones, 16 February 1813, ibid.; Jones to Chauncey, 27 March 1813, Letters Sent to Officers.

37. Throughout the war, the wages and bounties for navy personnel lagged far behind those offered by merchantmen and trading vessels carrying letter-of-marque commissions. Crewmen aboard privateers did not receive regular pay, but their share of the prize money could amount to upward of $100 dollars a month on a successful cruise. See Jerome R. Garitee, *The Republic's Private Navy: The American Privateering Business as Practiced by Baltimore during the War of 1812* (Middletown, Conn.: Wesleyan University Press, 1977), 127–33, 193–94. As the war progressed, Navy Department instructions to

destroy all prizes, coupled with the increasing likelihood of capture by the British, also dampened the ardor of potential recruits.

38. Jones to William Bainbridge, 7 May 1813, to James Renshaw, 14 June 1813, to Chauncey, 14 June 1813, to William M. Crane, 26 July 1813, ibid.; Jones to Chauncey, 31 May, 26 July 1813, Confidential Letters Sent by the Secretary of the Navy, Microfilm Series T-829, reel 453, RG 45, NA. Between April and July, Jones provided Chauncey with approximately 650 men for service on the lakes. Although this number exceeded the commodore's initial request for 500 men by a comfortable margin, an ugly dispute still broke out between Chauncey and Perry over the distribution of personnel. Perry accused the commodore of reserving the best sailors for his own command and of being less than forthcoming in responding to Perry's pleas for reinforcements. Perry ended up relying on volunteers recruited from local militia units and from General William Henry Harrison's army to fill out his squadron. See Skaggs and Altoff, *Signal Victory*, 76–84.

39. Jones to James Biddle, 5 May 1813, Letters Sent to Officers; Jones to Samuel Evans, 6 May 1813, to Stephen Decatur, 6 May 1813, Confidential Letters Sent.

40. Jones resurrected this plan the following spring, ordering both the *Constitution* and *Adams* to take up station in the path of British vessels bound for Canada. See Jones to Charles Stewart, 21 May 1814, to Charles Morris 9 May 1814, ibid. The results, however, were again nil. The *Constitution* failed to get clear of the blockade until December, while the *Adams,* which had put in to Savannah to refit after a lengthy cruise, sailed before Jones' letter reached her captain.

41. Jones to John Bullus, 24 August 1813, Miscellaneous Letters Sent; Jones to Chauncey, 19 September 1813, Confidential Letters Sent.

42. Chauncey to Jones, 15 November 1813, Captains Letters; Jones to Chauncey, 1 December 1813, 15 January 1814, Confidential Letters Sent.

43. William Jones to Thomas Macdonough, 17 March 1814, Letters Sent to Officers; Jones to William Bainbridge, 25 February 1814, to Chauncey, 25 February and 18 March 1814, Confidential Letters Sent. Unlike wages for enlisted personnel in the army, the pay for navy seamen was not fixed by law, but rather was left to the discretion of the Navy Department.

44. Chauncey to Jones, 9 February, 15, 26 March 1814, Captains Letters.

45. Jones to Charles Ridgeley, 4 April 1814, to Jacob Jones, 6 April 1814, to Isaac Hull, 31 May 1814, Letters Sent to Officers.

46. The saga of the secretary's ordnance woes during the fall of 1813 and winter of 1813–14 can be followed in Jones to James Beatty, 9, 13 September, 7 October, 24 December 1813, to James Riddle, 10 September, 7 October, 18 December, 1813, 3 January 1814, to John Bullus, 11 September 1813, 24 January, 21 February 1814, to George Harrison, 31 January 1814, Miscellaneous Letters Sent; Jones to Samuel Anderson, 5 October 1813, to William Bainbridge, 10, 13, October 1813, 24 January 1814, Letters Sent to Commandants and Agents; Jones to Isaac Chauncey, 7 December 1813, Confidential Letters Sent.

47. Jones to John Bullus, 10 April 1814, Letters Sent to Commandants and Agents.

48. William Jones to John Bullus, 30 November 1813, Confidential Letters Sent.

49. Chauncey to Jones, 26 January 1814; Captains Letters; Jones to Chauncey, 20 March 1814, Letters Sent to Officers; Jones to John Armstrong, 20 March 1814, Letters to the Secretary of War from the Secretary of the Navy, 1798–1824, RG 45, NA. Navy Department records are spotty in areas, so it is unclear whether all of the guns mentioned in this paragraph were actually sent on to Sackets Harbor. It is possible that ordnance from other sources may have been transferred to Lake Ontario in addition to or in place of some of the guns Chauncey specifically requisitioned.

50. Chauncey to Jones, 24 February, 4, 7 March, 8 June 1814, Captains Letters. The naval stores accompanying the guns were also delayed by the miserable state of the roads. Some 600 tons of stores arrived at Sackets Harbor in the first ten days of June.

51. "Exhibit of the nature of force of the Squadron on Lake Ontario under command of Commodore Isaac Chauncey," 15 July 1814, William Jones Papers, U.C. Smith Collection, Historical Society of Pennsylvania, Philadelphia [hereafter cited as HSP].

52. Jones to George Harrison, 19 September 1814, Letters Sent to Commandants and Agents; Jones to James Pleasants, 5 October 1814, Confidential Letters Sent.

53. Chauncey's illness in July also kept his squadron harbor-bound for several weeks. See Stagg, *Mr. Madison's War*, 402–4.

54. Jones to Chauncey, 24 October 1814, ibid.

55. Jones to Stephen Decatur, 8 November 1814, ibid.

56. Jones to Madison, 25 May 1814, Jones Papers, HSP.

57. Jones to Madison, 26 October 1814, Confidential Letters Sent.

58. Chauncey to Benjamin W. Crowninshield, 1 February 1815, Captains Letters; Crowninshield to James Pleasant, 9 February 1815, Letters to Congress.

The Meanings of the Wars for the Great Lakes

A N D R E W   R .   L .   C A Y T O N

Neither American popular culture nor American history has attached much significance to the Wars for the Great Lakes. While their importance seems obvious to scholars who devote themselves to studying various aspects of the long and episodic struggles among Indians, French, British, and Americans, most people ignore them. Even historians tend to view the wars as a series of raids and uprisings, which lead a self-contained life of their own. At best, general accounts of American History between 1754 and 1815 treat events in the Great Lakes area as precipitating factors in more important events in what Northwest Territory Governor Arthur St. Clair once called "the Atlantic country."[1] To read the history of the United States in the 1790s is to learn that the military endeavors of the United States mattered less than those of Great Britain and France. The great men of the early American republic were, and so the historians who study them are, more interested in European diplomacy than they are in frontier squabbles.[2]

Take, as an example, the reception in the "Atlantic country" of the news of the encounter between several hundred American troops under the command of St. Clair and a coalition of several hundred Indians more or less under the leadership of the Miami Little Turtle and the Shawnee Blue Jacket, on the morning of 4 November 1791. There is no need to recount the details of the battle or describe the hysteria that news of the outcome provoked in the Ohio Valley. Americans named the battle "St. Clair's Defeat," thereby depriving Indians of the mantle of victory and placing responsibility for the debacle squarely on the shoulders of the incompetent commanding general. What might be better called the Battle of the Wabash was one of the most complete military humiliations ever suffered by American armed forces. In terms of casualties, which numbered about two-thirds out of a force of 1,400, it was the greatest victory of Indians over a U.S. Army—ever.[3] Wrote Lieutenant Ebenezer Denny: "The land was literally covered with the dead."[4]

Reports of the disaster provoked what Secretary of State Thomas Jefferson called a "great sensation" in Philadelphia, the capital of the new republican empire.[5] The excitement did not last long, however. President George Washington may or may not have lost his temper—but only in private and only for half an hour.[6] In the rapidly expanding public world of newspapers, congressional debates, and private correspondence, prominent Americans discussed congressional apportionment, the creation of a Post Office, the future of Haiti, and the fate of Louis XVI with greater fervor than they devoted to the protection of the western frontiers. In retrospect, the lack of attention paid to the engagement is remarkable. News of "St. Clair's Defeat" passed through Philadelphia like a nasty summer thunderstorm, leaving people shaken but otherwise undisturbed.

The reasons for this response may be obvious. The Ohio Country was far from Philadelphia. Everyone assumed that the Americans would eventually defeat the Indians; time and numbers were on their side. Besides, they believed that the real villains were the British, who were playing Svengali to the "savages." Within four years a reorganized American army would defeat the Indians, expose the fragility of their ties with the British, and force Indian leaders to surrender their claims to much of what became the state of Ohio, thereby ending their insistence on the Ohio River as a border. St. Clair's Defeat slowly faded into relative oblivion, its fate a not unrepresentative example of the fate of most of the events in these wars.

THE SIGNIFICANCE OF THE WARS
FOR THE GREAT LAKES

The general obscurity of the Great Lakes Wars is ironic because these military actions were among the most decisive in the history of North America. Between the

1750s and the 1810s, the area was the cockpit of the continent. For Europeans and Euro-Americans, control over this region—its lakes, its rivers, its portals to the interior, its peoples—meant control over North America. On one level, the significance of the ultimate American victory is all too obvious—and horrible: the destruction of Indian communities, enormous stress on their cultures, and their removal or marginalization. It meant a slow but sure death for French settlements as well; Vincennes, Kaskaskia, and Detroit retained French names and signs of their eighteenth-century origins; but they were now American towns. By the middle of the nineteenth century—at least east of the Mississippi River—the remaining French, Indians, and *métis* had become curiosities, remnants of some pioneer period whose grandchildren were Americans.

For the British and Canadians, the American victory meant a border that hugged the northern rather than the southern shores of the Great Lakes. It left the Michigan Territory as a huge obstacle to the westward expansion of British Canada and a continuing impediment to national development, both economically and culturally. It denied Canadians access (unless they wanted to become citizens of the United States) to the fertile, well-watered lands of the Ohio and upper Mississippi valleys.

No less important, the outcome of these wars permitted Americans and their national government to focus their attention almost exclusively on expanding their southern and southwestern borders. If war in eighteenth-century North America largely revolved around a struggle for control over the northeastern quadrant of the continent (especially the Great Lakes and the Ohio Valley), war in nineteenth-century North America was about control over its southern half.

In the decades following the Sixty Years' War for the Great Lakes, Americans transformed the conquered region with a speed and a thoroughness virtually unmatched anywhere else in the history of the world. In 1876, the centenary of the United States, the Old Northwest was becoming the Middle West, a unique place in its unequivocal commitment to market capitalism and its diverse western European population. There were states as far west as Minnesota and Nebraska. Cities, such as Chicago, were among the largest in the world. Railroads and steel mills, huge acreage of grains, and small towns dominated the landscape. The Northwest Ordinance's 1787 prohibition on slavery had marked the region as a showplace of free labor and racial segregation. In 1876, there were very few African Americans in the Middle West and the vast majority of Indians had been removed. The region had played a major role in winning the American Civil War and had emerged as one of the most powerful places in the United States.

Had the Old Northwest remained in British hands, would it have been very different? Much might have been the same. But the legal structures and cultural parameters established by national governments have an often-neglected influence. The prohibition of slavery in the Northwest Territory largely defined the region. It made the Ohio River a political border as well as an economic artery; there was no reason that southern Illinois and Indiana should have been free states except that the United States said they were and that its authority legitimized the efforts of antislavery forces. Conversely, Upper Canada was literally overrun with tens of thousands of Yankees in the decades following the American Revolution. Tory exiles, who could very well have moved into Ohio or Michigan, settled Ontario, which—and many people will insist on this point—is not like Ohio or Michigan. Who knows the impact on the lives of Indians if they had lived under a British Canadian rather than an American metropolitan government?

Today, popular commemorations of the events that created the American Middle West are tailored to the needs of consumer-oriented Americans seeking diversion.[7] Outdoor pageants such as *Tecumseh!* and *Blue Jacket* attract thousands of people every summer. If, on some level, they remind audiences of the importance of the struggle for this territory, they also tend to romanticize the lives of their subjects into universal tales of love and persistence. Their stories are fables in which war serves largely to enliven the proceedings. Battlefield monuments at places such as Perry's Victory and Tippecanoe are not much more sophisticated; sometimes it seems as if these wars were important only as preludes to centuries of peace between Canadians and Americans. More often than not, responsibility for the horrendous violence is neutralized, as in the Ohio AAA *Guidebook*'s explanation that the Christian Indians of Gnadenhutten "were massacred by soldiers" in 1782. Avoiding direct mention of the Pennsylvania militiamen who committed the atrocity, the description is a masterpiece of passive voice anonymity.[8]

In 1995, I was one of several historians invited to speak at the city of Greenville, Ohio's commemoration of the bicentennial of the Treaty of Greenville. The governor of Ohio arrived, made a few comments, and departed. Then, after the historians had lowered the expectations of the crowd considerably, representatives of various Indian tribes who had signed the treaty were permitted to speak for as long as they wished. A couple spoke in measured tones about their history and their lives in

Oklahoma; one invited us to visit a new resort complex, complete with a golf course; but some of the Indians were angry and they denounced the injustice of the two-hundred-year-old treaty with fervent eloquence.

Sitting on that very hot stage for several hours was a surreal experience for a historian. I will never forget the applause the Shawnee representative received when he demanded land from the United States; large numbers of the assembled Ohioans apparently agreed with his description of their government as deceptive and unreliable. It was as if the descendants of Indians and Europeans found a source of reconciliation in their mutual revulsion at the United States. In the commemoration of the Treaty of Greenville, identification was with the Indians, who, it seemed clear, had been wronged by an insatiably greedy and grasping government.

If public commemorations define the meaning of events in public memory, then we must conclude that to the extent that the Wars of the Great Lakes are alive in the memory of Americans, they are examples of what the geographer Kenneth E. Foote has termed "a sort of collective equivocation over public meaning and social memory" when it comes to conflicts between Indians and Americans.[9] Americans are, Foote suggests, ashamed of these wars. We cannot completely obliterate them—they were too important for that—but we cannot sanctify them either. For the most part, we ignore them. Or compensate for our sense of shame by making our monuments and commemorations celebrations of reconciliation and by presenting history from the perspective of those who suffered the most.

At Greenville that night in August 1995, one of the organizers approached the moderator, television sportscaster Chris Schenkel, and asked him, as the clock ticked toward midnight, to remind a particularly loquacious speaker of time limits. To his credit, Schenkel refused to do so, asking in return how he could tell the man to stop talking, given the nature of the history he was recounting. How could we who had taken his land tell him to contain his legitimate anger to fifteen minutes? The evening, in a peculiar way, had become a kind of cathartic penance for past sins. It was as if the Americans had gathered to say: We cannot undo what our ancestors did in our name but we can listen to your grievances and agree that you were wronged.

CONSIDERING THE LACK OF REPUTATION:
THE TENDENCIES OF HISTORIANS

Such sentiments are not limited to the realms of popular culture. While the sense of shame is subtler and more sophisticated in the work of scholars who deal with the Wars of the Great Lakes, it is just as pervasive.

We know more today than anybody has ever known about the societies and cultures of the combatants, their imperial and republican designs, the ways in which they interacted and misunderstood each other, and the nature of their violent conflicts. Archaeologists have reconstructed forts; ethnologists have decoded the meanings of language and trade; military experts have detailed the workings of firearms. Most important, we are enjoying the fruits of a quarter-century of remarkable scholarship on American Indians. A virtual cornucopia of books and articles have restored the Miami, Shawnee, Potowatomi, Delaware, and many others to their rightful places as actors in an enormous and immensely complicated collision of cultures. Twenty years ago, it was possible for a very young graduate student at Brown University to write a dissertation on the Ohio Country that barely mentioned either Indians or war. Today, I could not get away with it.[10] Nor would I want to do so. Scholars have permanently transformed our understanding of what happened in the Great Lakes and the Ohio Country in the critical decades of the late eighteenth and early nineteenth centuries.

We see things differently now. These wars no longer seem as straightforward as they did fifty years ago. Historians have revitalized them by taking both the Indians and the French more seriously, by making them active players in the drama, and by emphasizing contingency, the notion that human choices made a difference. We increasingly see the events in this region as parts of a larger drama taking place throughout the western world between the middle of the eighteenth and the middle of the nineteenth centuries. We are now acutely aware of the importance of battles in Europe and on the seas, decisions made in Whitehall and Versailles. And above all, we have a deeper understanding of the cultural interactions of peoples in the interior of North America. The Great Lakes region we now interpret as a multicultural region, in which struggles were not simply for land or empire but for the power to define relationships with each other and with the world as a whole. The Sixty Years' Wars were about the making and unmaking of cultural identities; they were about the constructions of landscapes.

Historians today continue to work through the same sources as our predecessors; we offer the same anecdotes and quotations; sometimes when I reread the nineteenth-century historian Francis Parkman, I wonder what we are saying that has not already been said. Clearly, the main divergence from previous scholars is a matter of perspective, the kind of assumptions we bring to the work and through which we filter the evidence. And in recent years the most critical aspect of our collective perspective is a pronounced tendency to diminish the role of the U.S. government and its citizens.

This perspective proceeds from several angles: from Indian historians on the one hand and imperial historians on the other. In part, this hostility toward the Americans is a necessary corrective to scholarship that focused largely on the Americans; in part, it has to do with the widespread late twentieth-century American distrust of government and a pronounced distaste for cultural imperialism. In general, historians tend these days to want to aggrandize those who lost at the expense of those who won and to imagine that the world today might be better if the outcome had been reversed; such a position makes not only Indians but also Frenchmen and even British officers heroes. We are with Montcalm, not Wolfe; Hamilton, not Clark; Little Turtle, not Wayne; Tecumseh, not Harrison. We even lament the potential in the early 1800s of a British empire we scorn in the 1770s. We are romantics in our sense of loss, in our implicit argument that the ultimate American victory was not the best of all possible outcomes.

CONSIDERING THE LACK OF REPUTATION: THE SACRED CAUSE OF LIBERTY

Even if we grant that both popular audiences and scholars are ambivalent about these wars, that on some level we are ashamed of them, we are still left with the problem of why they attract so little attention in the larger scheme of American History. In large part, their obscurity follows from the fact that the history of the United States in general is not receptive to either ambiguity or unhappy conclusions. As important, it is remarkably resistant to scholars' efforts to restructure its basic outlines.

Asserting the significance of the Great Lakes Wars demands that we critique, or at least qualify, the meta-narrative of U.S. History. In contemplating the reputation of these wars, we need to remind ourselves of the obvious: that they were wars of geopolitical significance fought contemporaneously with the emergence of the most powerful nation-state in the Americas. In the grand story of American History, the American Revolution is the central event. The history of eighteenth-century North America is a story of discontinuity, a story broken not in 1760 with Great Britain's decisive victory over France and the acquisition (insofar as Europeans and Euro-Americans were concerned) of Canada and the Ohio Valley or with the United States' victory over the abandoned and hungry Indians at Fallen Timbers in 1794 or a similar victory at Moraviantown in 1814, but with the winning of American Independence from Great Britain in 1776. The most important event in the history of the United States is its creation.

Emphasizing the significance of the Great Lakes Wars, however, suggests that American Independence was not the most important event in the history of eighteenth-century North America. Instead, we might talk about events that shaped the geopolitical context that provoked that independence. From a Canadian perspective, the most important moment in eighteenth-century North America was the British conquest of the French in 1760; if you seek evidence for that statement, I direct you to the residents of the province of Quebec. From the perspective of the Miami, Shawnee, Delaware, Potowatomi, and other Indians, the critical event was their expulsion from the Great Lakes region as a result of the wars that came to an end in 1815; if you seek evidence for that statement, well, you know where to go.

These perspectives give coherence to the Great Lakes Wars as a whole; they have an interpretive arc in which actions and consequences are clearly related. The French lose; the British effort to govern and reform their expanded empire provokes rebellion from Detroit to Boston; the Americans win their independence; the British and Indian alliance proves superficial and unstable; the Indians cannot sustain a united resistance to the Americans, who overwhelm them with numbers, goods, and a revolutionary desire to not only control territory but to remake the landscape in their image. For sixty years, wars in North America were about control over the Ohio Country. They started at the forks of Ohio in 1754, and they ended in January 1815 where the Mississippi River and the Gulf of Mexico begin to merge together.

But this interpretive arc conflicts with the basic story of the origins of the United States. If the Great Lakes Wars have coherence, then the American Revolution loses its centrality, if not its significance. It is just another episode in an ongoing series of wars among empires and Indians. What George Rogers Clark shares in common with George Washington is not that they are both Americans but that they were both

Virginians who led military expeditions in order to gain control of the Ohio Valley. There is a continuity here that the American Revolution informs but does not disrupt.

A major reason why these wars have not achieved fame, then, is that they do not fit the parameters of U.S. history. As long as American historians write the history of a nation rather than the history of a continent, they will find it difficult to make a case for the significance of the Great Lakes War.

CONTESTING THE MEANINGS OF THE WARS

In short, then, these wars are problematic because they remind Americans of the fact that our history cannot be understood in isolation. They force us to confront something we do not like to consider at length: the extent to which this nation's history rests on military conquest and the extent to which its history is about power as well as liberty. No wonder, then, that we tend to pass over those wars—the Great Lakes, the Mexican, the Spanish-American, the Vietnamese—which pull the curtains and show the workings of the imperial machinery of our democratic republic. Only those events that show Americans being wronged are worthy of serious commemoration. As Kenneth Foote has written in *Shadowed Ground: America's Landscapes of Violence and Tragedy*, we honor, not just simply mark, those places and events that "seem to illustrate ethical or moral lessons that transcend the toll of lives. In essence, the victims died for a cause, and the cause, rather than the victims, spurs sanctification."[11] The Plains Indians Wars have that in Custer's Last Stand; the Spanish-American War has it in the Maine; the Mexican War even has it by stretching the Alamo into its orbit. But not the Great Lakes Wars. If there were any nobility or sacrifice, it would appear to have all been on the side of the defeated.

Or so many Americans have always asserted. There was never really a serious effort to sanctify these wars. In fact, almost from the moment they began, American leaders metaphorically swept them under the rug, hid them in the proverbial closet. The United States in the Early Republic was an inchoate nation, the identity of its citizens uncertain and controversial. Prominent Americans, eighteenth-century gentlemen who prided themselves on their civility and hoped to achieve fame on the basis of their moral character more than their achievements, had little interest in celebrating victories, or mourning defeats at the hands of Indians. Participants in the novel experiment of a huge democratic republic, they were men extremely conscious of their reputations. Their sense of history was profound. In speeches, newspaper essays, and even in private correspondence, they behaved as if someone was watching over their shoulders. Not only did they have to behave better than their former British brethren and French revolutionaries, they had to behave better than their understandings of how Romans and Greeks had conducted themselves in similar situations. To be a citizen of the United States meant participating in the highest level of civilized society.[12]

The leaders of the United States in the late 1700s and early 1800s knew exactly what they were doing to Indians and they were not proud of it. Few wanted to claim the wars; neither victories nor defeats received much mention, public or private. It was not that they were unimportant; to the contrary, it was that they were so important to prominent Americans' self-image that they could scarcely confront them. What is striking about the American reaction to the Great Lakes Wars is the failure to give them names, the unspoken recognition that there was little that was noble about them. In the Early American Republic, the difficulty in labeling battles flowed directly from the sense of shame they engendered in many leading Americans. The absence of a glorious cause bred indifference, which in turn promoted obscurity.[13]

In 1792, a few Americans tried hard to turn "St. Clair's Defeat" into something worth remembering. Eli Harris published a poem, aptly called "Defeat," in Harrisburg, Pennsylvania. It was an awful but sincere example of the cult of sentimentality that was sweeping western Europe at the end of the eighteenth century. In rhymed couplets, Harris gave the world a proto-romantic view of the battle.

> Inspir'd by grief, to tender friendship due,
> The trembling hand, unfolds the tale to view—
> A tale, which strongly claims the pitying tear,
> And ev're feeling heart, must bleed to hear.

The army met its fate in a dark wilderness, full of wild animals "And savage men" who "thirst insatiate, for revenge and blood." Indians threatened the "infant arts," which "had just begun to dawn" on a "cheerful lawn." "To check their inroads, and relieve the land,/The Great St. Clair, led out this warlike band." Harris describes scenes of torture and savagery to justify the Americans' actions. "Horror" attacks the Americans. They fight with honor, but "On every side the sons of Order fail,/And Horror soon thro' all their lines prevail." It was, of course, an "unequal conflict." What to do about the bloody outcome? Nothing, really except to place faith in God and "submit to heaven's supreme controul" so that "peace once more shall smile upon the soul."[14]

Less benign was the response of a New England poet who mourned the dead in a broadside published in Boston and Hartford in 1792. The anonymous author of "Columbian Tragedy" was more interested in sensationalism than sentimentalism, although he included plenty of the latter. St. Clair's Defeat was "Perhaps the most shocking [battle] that has happened in America since its first Discovery." Offered in honor of the many brave fallen "WORTHIES who died in Defence of their COUNTRY," the publication was also meant to serve "as a PERPETUAL MEMORIAL, of this important Event, on which, perhaps may very essentially depend the future FREEDOM and GRANDEUR of Fifteen or Twenty States, that might, at some Period, be annexed, to the AMERICAN UNION." After listing the names of the dead officers, the author wrote a history of the struggles for the Ohio Country. He referred to Braddock's failed expedition and George Washington as well and blamed again the savage Indians for their fate. What to do? Feel horrible for their families, feel pain for lost friends, learn from their sacrifice and turn to God, who would eventually lead Americans to righteous battle in which "INDIANS ALL" they would "destroy."[15]

Little in either poem—the only surviving literary tributes I have found—surprises. Both are sentimental; both look to God for answers. Neither blames Americans for what happened. The soldiers were vastly outnumbered and their enemy deceptive and dishonorable. Still, notwithstanding the very real emotion, neither author seems anxious about the outcome. Both are more sad than worried. Their faith in eventual victory is sure. The most telling point is that the second author perceived this shocking event as a threat to future parts of the American Union, not to the existence of the nation itself. St. Clair's Defeat was bad news, in other words, but it did not portend anything drastic for the Atlantic World.

That view was widely shared by leading political figures. When President Washington officially broke the news to the House of Representatives, he expressed his "great concern" over "the misfortune which has befallen the troops under [St. Clair's] command." He quickly added, however, that although "the national loss is considerable," it could "be repaired without great difficulty," a sentiment he repeated in his correspondence.[16] In subsequent debates in Congress, communications to newspapers, and private letters, there is no sense of emergency. There is, however, a strong element of doubt about the nature of Indian wars and the role of the United States in them. Much of this criticism was no doubt partisan in nature, inspired by opposition to the Washington Administration. Nonetheless, it is revealing.

Today, historians worry about reading the concerns of the present back into the past. In so doing, we may underestimate the moral acuity of the dead. The oblivion into which the Great Lakes War has sunk was essentially created in the public world of the new republic in the winter of 1792. Leading Americans were just as conflicted about the value of the wars—and what they said about the new American nation— as any of us. Many recognized what the geographer D. W. Meinig has suggested we do not like to recognize, which is that the United States in the early republic was an empire.[17] It was not a benign creation guided by some laissez-faire spirit of popular sovereignty. It was the most powerful economic, political, and military entity on the North American continent. If, in its origins, the American Revolution created a democratic republic, in its conclusion, it created an imperial government. We do not have to remind the dead of that fact; they were far more aware of it than we often appear to be. Caught between the desire for land and the need for fame, they had no language with which to explain their necessary but shameful actions.

In the debate over how to respond to the devastating news of St. Clair's Defeat, the tone of public discourse was largely established by critics of American policy toward Indians. While some continued to insist that "Whatever may be the consequences of the Indian war, the United States are not responsible for them,"[18] others were far more negative. They raised unpleasant questions and pointed out parallels and contradictions with as much outrage as any late twentieth-century historian.

"Is the war with the Indians a just one?," asked a correspondent of the *American Daily Advertiser,* going directly to the heart of the matter. "Have they not the same right to their hunting grounds . . . that we have to our houses and farms?" The writer saw a striking similarity with the experience of Americans in the eighteenth century. "Do we not commit the same offence against reason and justice in attempting to take their hunting grounds from them without their consent, that Great Britain committed against the American colonies in attempting to tax them without their consent?" At best, this American's attitude was patronizing. He wanted Indians bought off with gifts and trade and enticed with "the arts of civilization," but he also asked: "Is it consistent with honor or justice to carry on a war only for the sake of revenge? Is there any honor to be acquired by killing Indians?" Or less nobly and more bluntly, "Is national honor concerned in carrying on a war after a defeat by a herd of Indians, any more than it would be if the same misfortune had happened from a herd of buffaloes?"[19]

A correspondent of a Boston newspaper was convinced that the wars were dangerous to the pleasing prospects of the United States. He questioned whether the nation had "an indubitable right" to claim Indian land. After all, Americans had plenty of land. He denied that the war was the fault of the Indians. They had "been the aggressors" in some cases, but for the most part they had been "provoked . . . to commit depredations."[20]

Hugh Brackenridge, a resident of western Pennsylvania and the author of the picaresque novel *Modern Chivalry,* eagerly answered the questions of these critics. His arguments are familiar to us. Asserting that the Americans had a right to the Ohio Country because of the 1783 Treaty of Paris with Great Britain, Brackenridge urged Americans to defend the lives and property of its frontier citizens from "the axe of the savage," especially when it was probably "put into their hands by our late inveterate, but discomfited enemy," the British.[21] A writer from New Jersey echoed Brackenridge's comments, suggesting that comparing Indians to Americans vis-a-vis the British was like comparing "Angels and Devils."[22]

This kind of language is what we expect from Americans in this period. But the story is more complicated than one of unalloyed greed and incipient racial hatred in adequately balanced by the benevolent paternalism of George Washington and his Federalist allies. The American response to St. Clair's Defeat was ambiguous and divided. Spurred by regional and partisan issues, not to mention fiscal frugality, the sense that the war was not a just one was widespread. Ironically, in the aftermath of military humiliation, prominent Americans wondered aloud whether they were doing the right thing. If nothing else was clear, it was obvious that this cause was a base one. What glory was there in fighting to acquire territory? And, on a larger level, what exactly was *just* about *any* war in which the republic was engaged?

The call for "UNIVERSAL PEACE" that filled two columns of the *National Gazette* in February 1792 may strike us as wildly naive.[23] It was, however, very real to men and women who, even at the end of an age of enlightenment, contemplated a future of harmonious and benevolent human beings. The Indian war struck at the core of their intense sensibilities; it threatened their image of what American citizens had to be. In the essay, an outraged writer tried to refute Brackenridge's arguments. The United States had plenty of "soil"; the nation had no claim on the Ohio Country; how could the king of Great Britain "alienate what he never owned [?]"; the Indians were too primitive to have a need for property ownership; most galling was the idea that Americans should hunt down and kill Indians. "Good God!," exclaimed the horrified correspondent, "Is this our temper towards these unfortunate people: Sentiments like these have in former ages rendered man a savage to man." Now they have caused this war and "we may perhaps effect our purpose and extirpate the whole race of Indians." But at what cost? Surely, God would somehow punish Americans.[24]

"Polybius" was another sharp critic of the Indian war. He, too, argued on moral grounds, noting that there were at least two "class"es of opinion on Indians—one which "misrepresented" them as "the very dregs" of mankind, "as governed only by the most malignant passions, and deserving no treatment from civilized people, but absolute extermination" and another which spoke "of them with pity, as the off-spring of the same common progenitors with ourselves . . . and capable of being recovered to a rational and refined life" once they were settled and literate—he blamed "much of the degeneracy" on "the vices of their civilized brethren." For "in their natural state, they are possessed of virtues which do honor to human nature."[25]

Members and supporters of the Washington Administration's policy were placed on the defensive by these attacks. In essence, the critics had set the terms of the debate about St. Clair's debacle. Secretary of War Henry Knox rushed into print to offer proof of "the pacific and human dispositions of the General Government towards the Indian tribes" and blame the hostilities on a few renegade Indians, "a number of separate banditti" who were incurably hostile to the United States. Another writer defended the administration as well. Even if "it should be admitted, that our frontier people have been the aggressors," the efforts of the national government to seek peace had always been rebuffed by the Indians. Therefore, "Justice is on the side of the United States." War, moreover, is a nasty business. Once hostilities began, only "the law of force" was in effect. "Congress did what seemed to be right at that time. They had not a war to make, but they had one to carry on." In other words, the war was not a glorious cause, but an unpleasant chore pressed on them by the combined folly of Indians, their British allies, and frontiers people.[26]

Even congressmen agreed. In the debate over whether or not to raise three more regiments of infantry for the protection of the frontiers, a critic lashed out at a war "in its origin, as unjustly undertaken as it has since been unwisely and unsuccessfully conducted." After all, "depredations had been committed by the whites as well as the Indians; and . . . whites were most probably the aggressors, as they frequently made encroachments on the Indian lands, whereas the Indians showed no inclination to obtain possession of our territory." Why fight Indians with "the sword" when they might "be gained by justice and moderation? We hear much of "the sufferings of the white people," but "we hear nothing of the sufferings of the Indians." Besides, Americans did not need land west of the Appalachians. "Instead of being ambitious to extend our boundaries," government should try to control frontier peoples and consolidate them into settlements. If we did not do so, the congressman predicted, "they will keep the nation embroiled in perpetual warfare as along as the Indians have a single acre of ground to rest upon." Why waste men, money, and national reputation? The real solution was to remove the British from the posts they illegally occupied in the Great Lakes; without British encouragement, the Indians would not pose a serious threat to the American republic. If force be needed, small groups of rangers would prove more effective than large, expensive armies.[27]

Even eager defenders of the war described it as an unpleasant reality not a glorious cause. They did not speak of a "just" war against Indians with the kind of racist language that would emerge in Jacksonian America and reach a scientifically calibrated fever pitch by the end of the nineteenth century. To be sure, they asserted that the war was a defensive one forced on the American people by the depredations of the Indians. It was, however, "too late" for questions of morality and justice. The general government had to act decisively or lose both the West and the respect of its citizens.[28]

In the end, Congress failed to authorize the extra regiments, although it would soon restructure the entire military structure of the United States, creating a legion that would impose a peace on the Ohio Country. The entire debate was wrapped up in a larger political context involving growing criticism of the Washington Administration over matters of taxation and expenditures. In fact, calls for a public investigation into the causes of St. Clair's Defeat provoked a debate about separation of powers, not Indian wars.[29]

Still, the public words we have about the wars strongly suggest that, from the beginning, the biggest obstacle to the reputation of the Great Lakes Wars was a widespread perception that they were immoral. The rhetoric of critics and defenders in Philadelphia illustrates the obsession of eighteenth-century American gentlemen with distinguishing between civilization and savagery and the enlightened hope of many that the United States was progressing to a state of development in which war would not occur. Americans were supposed to be better than that; they were not supposed to stoop to the brutal business of killing people, especially not over such mundane matters as territory. If they did, if they were not any better than previous generations; if they were just like other human beings from the Romans to the French, then the republican experiment in enlightened self-government was doomed. From the perspective of American leaders, the Wars for the Great Lakes were about more than securing frontiers and acquiring land; they were also about the character of the United States and the self-image and language of its citizens. Were they the proponents of universal notions of liberty or a peculiarly Anglo-American version of imperial conquest? And if the answer was both, how did they sustain themselves psychologically and ideologically on such a slippery and elusive middle ground?

In the Early Republic, American leaders worked through their confusion and dealt with their dishonor, dishonor produced as much by fighting wars as by losing battles, in large part by focusing on the British as their real enemy. They had good reason to do so. The British, after all, were supplying and encouraging Indians to harass Americans. As important, the British were a useful enemy in that they made it easier to reconcile conquest and liberty. To fight them was to transform wars of empire into an ideological continuation of the American Revolution, in which the Indians played the roles of victims who unhappily got in the way of forces beyond their control. Harping on the British deflected attention away *physically* from the Old Northwest; it reinforced the belief that the serious business of these wars took place not between the Ohio River and Lake Huron but in the discussions between representatives of the United States and Great Britain that produced Jay's Treaty in 1794 and in the struggles of the French armies which strained the resources of Britain's overextended empire and kept it from focusing its power on the Great Lakes. Historians have just followed the lead of their sources in stressing the importance of European events over those on the frontiers. Sixty years of war for the Great Lakes have significance in the history of the United States to the extent that they can be interpreted as precipitating or prolonging the glorious cause of the American Revolution. They are worth remembering if they burnish our reputations as a people who resisted British tyranny rather than conquered Indians and who are about securing rather than destroying liberty.

Our search for reasons for the neglect of the Wars of the Great Lakes thus brings us full circle. The ambivalence and ambiguity associated with them originated not with historians but with contemporaries; it was they who set the tone that scholars emulate. From the moment they were fought, St. Clair's Defeat and other battles were sources of shame, not pride, events to be explained away rather than celebrated or mourned. No wonder then that Americans, two hundred years later, fail to accord them a great place in the history of the United States, or at least a place commensurate with their importance in defining the geopolitical boundaries of North America. No wonder then that Americans turn to the experiences of Indians for inspiration, that we celebrate not the victories of the United States but the resistance of the Miami, the Shawnee, the Delaware. No wonder that we mourn the loss of thousands of Indian lives more than we honor the remains of hundreds of American soldiers in west-central Ohio who lost their lives in the sacred cause of empire.

NOTES

1. Arthur St. Clair to Captain John Armstrong, 7 December 1791, in *The St. Clair Papers*, ed. William Henry Smith, 2 vols. (Cincinnati: Robert Clarke, 1882), 2:66.

2. See, for example, Stanley Elkins and Eric McKitrick, *The Age of Federalism: The Early American Republic, 1788–1800* (New York: Oxford University Press, 1995).

3. R. Douglas Hurt, *The Ohio Frontier, Crucible of the Old Northwest* (Bloomington: Indiana University Press, 1996), 118.

4. Quoted in Wiley Sword, *President Washington's Indian War* (Norman: University of Oklahoma Press, 1985), 184.

5. Thomas Jefferson to Thomas Mann Randolph, 11 December 1791, in *The Papers of Thomas Jefferson*, ed. Julian P. Boyd and Charles T. Cullen, 23 vols. to date (Princeton: Princeton University Press, 1950–), 22:389–90. See also, the reports in the Philadelphia *Federal Gazette*, 22, 28 December 1791, 6 January 1792; and the Philadelphia *Gazette of the United States*, 10 December 1791; James Madison to Henry Lee, 18 December 1791, in *The Papers of James Madison*, 17 vols. to date, ed. William T. Hutchinson et al., vols. 1–10 (Chicago: University of Chicago Press, 1962–91) and vols. 11–17 (Charlottesville: University Press of Virginia, 1991–), 155; Baron Von Steuben to Alexander Hamilton, 5 February 1792, in *The Papers of Alexander Hamilton*, 27 vols., ed. Harold C. Syrett (New York: Columbia University Press, 1961–82), 11:16–17; Otho H. Williams to Hamilton, 5 March 1792, in *Papers of Alexander Hamilton*, ed. Syrett, 11:108–9; Augustine Davis to Thomas Jefferson, 1 December 1791, in *Papers of Thomas Jefferson*, ed. Boyd and Cullen, 22:362–63.

6. Richard Rush, *Washington in Domestic Life* (Philadelphia: J. B. Lippincott, 1857), 65–69. According to Rush, the president's private secretary, Tobias Lear, reported that Washington received the news quietly, waiting until his guests had gone to explode. When he did, he announced, *"It's all over—St. Clair's defeated—routed;—the officers nearly all killed, the men by wholesale,"* (67). Later, Washington chastised St. Clair for allowing himself to be surprised. *"O God, O God, he's worse than a murderer! How can he answer it to his country?—the blood of the slain is upon him—the curse of widows and orphans—the curse of Heaven!"* (68). After Washington had calmed down, he swore Lear to secrecy and promised St. Clair *"full justice,"* (69).

7. For interesting discussions of commemorations and memorials in the Midwest, see John Bodnar, *Remaking America: Public Memory, Commemoration, and Patriotism in the Twentieth Century*

(Princeton: Princeton University Press, 1992); and James M. Mayo, *War Memorials as A Political Landscape: The American Experience and Beyond* (New York: Praeger, 1988), esp. 118, 123–24, 145–50. G. Kurt Piehler, *Remembering War the American Way* (Washington, D.C.: Smithsonian Institution Press, 1995) does not mention the Great Lakes wars.

8. American Automobile Association (AAA), Illinois, Indiana, Ohio: Tourbook (Heathrow, Fla.: American Automobile Association, 1996), 187.

9. Kenneth E. Foote, *Shadowed Ground: America's Landscapes of Violence and Tragedy* (Austin: University of Texas Press, 1997), 35.

10. Later published as *The Frontier Republic: Ideology and Politics in the Ohio Country, 1780–1825* (Kent, Ohio: Kent State University Press, 1986).

11. Foote, *Shadowed Ground*, 35, 10.

12. See Andrew R. L. Cayton, "'Noble Actors' upon 'the Theatre of Honour': Power and Civility in the Treaty of Greenville," in *Contact Points: American Frontiers from the Mohawk Valley to the Mississippi, 1750–1830*, ed. Andrew R. L. Cayton and Fredrika J. Teute (Chapel Hill: University of North Carolina Press, for the Omohundro Institute of Early American History and Culture, 1998), 235–69.

13. Most helpful in thinking about these issues were Philip J. Deloria, *Playing Indian* (New Haven: Yale University Press, 1998) and Jill Lepore, *The Name of War: King Phillip's War and the Origins of American Identity* (New York: Knopf, 1998).

14. Eli Lewis, "DEFEAT. A POEM." (Harrisburg, Penn., 1792), 1, 2, 3, 13, 14.

15. Thomas Bassett, "Columbian Tragedy" (Boston: E. Russell, 1792).

16. *The Debates and Proceedings in the Congress of the United States . . . Second Congress* (Washington, D.C.: Gales and Seaton, 1849), 242. Washington wrote to Charles Pinckney (17 March 1792, in *The Writings of George Washington*, 39 vols., ed. John C. Fitzpatrick [Washington, D.C.: U.S. Government Printing Office, 1931–44], 10: 225) that while he "regretted" St. Clair's defeat, he was comforted by the fact "that every public loss on that occasion may be readily repaired, except that of the lives of the brave officers and men, who fell in the conflict."

17. D. W. Meinig, "Territorial Strategies Applied to Captive Peoples," in *Ideology and Landscape in Historical Perspective: Essays on the Meanings of Some Places in the Past*, ed. Alan R. H. Baker and Gideon Biger (Cambridge: Cambridge University Press, 1992), 125–26.

18. Philadelphia *Gazette of the United States*, 3 December 1791.

19. "From the *American Daily Advertiser*," Philadelphia *National Gazette*, 9 January 1792.

20. "Boston, December 29," *National Gazette*, 16 January 1792.

21. H. H. Brackenridge, "Thoughts on the Present Indian War," *National Gazette*, 2 February 1792.

22. "Newark, February 22," *National Gazette*, 2 March 1792.

23. "UNIVERSAL PEACE," *National Gazette*, 2 February 1792.

24. "To the Editors of the NATIONAL GAZETTE," *National Gazette*, 6 February 1792.

25. Polybius, "Opinions on the WESTERN TERRITORY and the INDIAN WAR, in a series of letters to a friend, LETTER II," *Federal Gazette*, 25 February 1792. See also, Polybius, "LETTER III," *Federal Gazette*, 28 January 1792.

26. *Federal Gazette*, 9 February 1792.

27. *Debates and Proceedings of Congress*, 26 January 1792, 337, 338, 339.

28. Ibid., 345.

29. Ibid., 490–94.

About the Editors and Contributors

CARL BENN is the Chief Curator of the City of Toronto's Museums and Heritage Services. He has curated about twenty museum exhibits and has worked on eleven historic building restoration projects. He is author of *Historic Fort York, 1793–1812* (Natural Heritage, 1993), *The Iroquois in the War of 1812* (University of Toronto Press, 1998), and approximately seventy other historical and museological publications. He also teaches at the University of Toronto in the Department of History and in the Museum Studies Program.

CHARLES E. BRODINE JR. is a historian with the Early History Branch of the Naval Historical Center, Washington, D.C., where he has worked since 1987 as an assistant editor on *Naval Documents of the American Revolution* and *The Naval War of 1812: A Documentary History*. Mr. Brodine is a doctoral candidate at the University of North Carolina at Chapel Hill and is currently at work on a dissertation entitled, "The American Career of Henry Bouquet."

ANDREW R. L. CAYTON, Distinguished Professor of History at Miami University in Oxford, Ohio, is the author of *The Frontier Republic: Ideology and Politics in the Ohio Country, 1780–1825* (1986) and *Frontier Indiana* (1996) and co-editor of

Contact Points: American Frontiers from the Mohawk Valley to the Mississippi (1998) and *The American Midwest: Essays in Regional History* (2001).

ROBERT COX, a Curator at the American Philosophical Society, Philadelphia, has a variety of interests in early American history, including the history of Quaker-Indian relations, theories and practices of race, somnambulism, and Spiritualism.

BRIAN LEIGH DUNNIGAN has served as Curator of Maps at the William L. Clements Library of the University of Michigan since 1996. Dunnigan has written extensively on the history of the Niagara and Straits of Mackinac regions of the Great Lakes and, most recently, on early Detroit. His article is a result of research for *Frontier Metropolis: Picturing Early Detroit, 1701–1838,* (Wayne State University Press, 2001).

R. DAVID EDMUNDS is Watson Professor of American History at the University of Texas at Dallas. He has written extensively upon the Indians of the Great Lakes Region in such books as *The Potawatomis: Keepers of the Fire* (University of Oklahoma Press, 1978) and *Trecumseh and the Quest for Indian Leadership* (HarperCollins, 1984).

W. J. ECCLES was born in England and educated in Montreal and died in 1998. During his career, he taught at the universities of Manitoba, Alberta, and Toronto. His book *Frontenac the Courtier Governor* received the 1959 Book Award of the Pacific Coast Branch of the American Historical Association. Among his other publications are *Canada Under Lois XIV, 1663–1701, The Canadian Frontier, 1534–1760,* and *The French in North America, 1500–1783.*

E. JANE ERRINGTON is Chair of the Department of History at the Royal Military College of Canada and professor of History at Queen's University, Kingston. Her works include the *Lion, The Eagle and Upper Canada: A Developing Colonial Ideology* and *Wives and Mothers, School Mistresses and Scullery Maids: Women and Work in Upper Canada.* She is currently completing a manuscript on the emigrant experience in the first half of the nineteenth century.

ERIC HINDERAKER is Associate Professor of History at the University of Utah. He is the author of *Elusive Empires: Constructing Colonialism in the Ohio Valley, 1673–1800*.

R. DOUGLAS HURT is professor and director of the Graduate Program in Agricultural History and Rural Studies at Iowa State University. He is author of *The Ohio Frontier: Crucible of the Old Northwest, 1720–1830* (Indiana University Press, 1996).

PHILIP L. LORD JR. is Director, Division of Museum Services, New York State Museum, where he manages the Cultural Resource Survey Program. Recent research projects have focused on waterways-linked systems of transportation and technology in the Early Republic Period, roughly 1790–1830. His current research documents little-known late eighteenth- and early nineteenth-century navigation improvements on the inland waterways of Upstate New York before the Erie Canal.

MICHAEL A. MCDONNELL is a lecturer in American History at the University of Wales, Swansea. His forthcoming book, *Popular Mobilization and Political Culture in Revolutionary Virginia*, will be published by the Omohundro Institute of Early American History and Culture. He is now working on a full-length biography of Charles Langlade and the Ottawa community in which he lived.

LARRY L. NELSON received his Ph.D. in American history from Bowling Green State University. He is a site manager with the Ohio Historical Society at Fort Meigs State Memorial in Perrysburg and an adjunct assistant professor of history at Bowling Green State University's Firelands College in Huron. He is the author of *A Man of Distinction Among Them: Alexander McKee and British-Indian Affairs along the Ohio Country Frontier, 1754–1799* (Kent State University Press, 1999).

JON W. PARMENTER teaches Early American and Native American history at St. Lawrence University. He is the author of several published articles and is currently working on a book-length study of Iroquois governance and society during the eighteenth century.

ELIZABETH A. PERKINS is Gordon B. Davidson Associate Professor of History at Centre College. She is the author of *Border Life: Experiences and Memory in the Revolutionary Ohio Valley* (University of North Carolina Press, 1998).

LEONARD SADOSKY is a Ph.D. candidate in American history at the University of Virginia and holds a Master's degree from Miami University (Ohio). He was a dissertation fellow at the International Center for Jefferson Studies at Monticello, 2000–2001. He is also co-author with Peter S. Onuf of the forthcoming book, *Jeffersonian America*.

DAVID CURTIS SKAGGS is professor emeritus of history at Bowling Green State University where he taught from 1965 to 2001. His ten books include authoring *Roots of Maryland Democracy, 1753–1776* (Greenwood Press, 1973), editing *The Old Northwest in the American Revolution* (Wisconsin State Historical Society, 1977), and co-authoring, *A Signal Victory: The Lake Erie Campaign, 1812–1813* (Naval Institute Press, 1997). The later received the John Lyman Prize as the best book in U.S. Navy history for 1997 from the North American society for Oceanic History.

JEFF SEIKEN is a Ph.D. candidate in early American history at Ohio State University. He is writing his dissertation on American naval policy, planning, and administration during the War of 1812. Research on this essay and his dissertation has been supported by a Rear Admiral John D. Hayes Predoctoral Fellowship from the Naval Historical Center in Washington, D.C.

SUSAN SLEEPER-SMITH is an assistant professor in the history department at Michigan State University. She has authored articles about Native women in *Ethnohistory* and *New Faces of the Fur Trade* (Michigan State University Press, 1998). Her recent work is *Native Women and French Men: Rethinking Cultural Encounter in the Western Great Lakes* (University of Massachusetts Press, 2001).

MATTHEW C. WARD is a lecturer in early American History in the Department of History at the University of Dundee, Scotland. He is originally from Walsall, England, and has his Ph.D. from the College of William and Mary. He has published a number of articles on both sides of the Atlantic on the Seven Years' War and British military policy.

KEITH R. WIDDER was Curator of History for Mackinac State Historic Parks from 1971 until 1997. He is currently a senior editor for Michigan State University Press. His research interests focus on relationships among different groups of people living in the Great Lakes region during the eighteenth and nineteenth centuries.

Index of Places and Names

A

Abbot, David, 307
Abbott, David, 307
Abenaki people, 30, 106, 148
Acadia, 24, 34
Adams (ship), 355, 357, 360, 368n. 15, 370n. 40
Adlum, John, 271n. 28
Ainssé, Louis, 157
Akewaugekatauso (Langlade), *xii*, 3, 79–99, 101n. 24, 129
Albany, 152, 276, *279*, 281, 332
Alert (ship), 360, 363
Algonquian people, 3, 106, 110; and disease and famine, 73, 74, 75
Allegany reservation, 257, 258, 260
Allen, Benjamin, 219
Allinson, William, 259, 262, 263–68,

274n. 70; brothers, 267
Amable, 155–56. *See also* Chevalier
American Daily Advertiser, 384
Amherst, Jeffrey, 39, 46, 51, 128, 151, 230; native disease and, 64, 74, 75
Amherstburg, 177, 343, 346
Anderson, William, 11
Angelique (Native), 88
Argus (ship), 360, 361
Armstrong, John, 12, 237
Arnold, Benedict, 8–9
Arosa (Seneca), 296, 297
Askin, John, 154
Athanasie, 134
"Atlantic Country," the, 373
Aupaumut, Hendrick, 118, 255, 264–66
Avery (Firelands), 316

B

Baldwin, Waterman, 251

Balfour, Henry, 72

Barnum, Eli S., 308, 309, 310, 313, 314, 315, 317

Barrett, Lemuel, 54, 61n. 24

Barthe, Marie Archange, 154

Bartholomé, 135

Bartie, 137

Barton, Thomas, 48, 52–53

Bassett, Henry, 146, 154–55, 156, 161n. 4

Bawbee, Henry, 175, *176*

Baxter, Alexander, 137

Beatty, John, 308

Beauharnois, Charles de La Boische de, 25–26, 91, 135

Beausoleil. *See* Pouré

Bedford, Duke of, 4

Belle Ile, Strait of, 24, 38

Bellestre (Belestre, Belêtre), François-Marie Picoté de, 162n. 10, 171, 172–73

Bell family, 262

Benezet, Anthony, 250

Benn, Carl, *xv*

Bennington, battle of, 95

Bergeron, 135

Bienville, Jean-Baptiste Le Moyne de, 91

Binnekill, 277

Black Creek, 262

Blackfish, 345, 346

Black Hoof (chief), 11, 254, 339–42,

343, 345, 346–48

Black Rock, 359, 369n. 29

Black Wolf (Mingo), 220

Blainville. *See* Céloron de Blainville

Blane, Archibald, 56n. 1, 58n. 14

Blue Jacket, 222, 373

Blue Licks, battle of, 221, 235

Bonsall, Isaac, 243–44, 245, 259, 260, 263

Boone, Daniel, 85

Boscawen, Edward, 35

Bougainville, Louis-Antoine de, 36, 38, 94–95

Bouqet, Henry, *xi*, 43–55, 57nn. 4, 6, 58nn. 8, 10; 59nn. 11–14; 60nn. 17–18, 61nn. 24–25; and Campbell, 128; and disease, 64, 68, 75; and Mingos, 111

Bourassa, Charlotte Ambrosine, 88

Bourassa, *dit* La Ronde, René, 88

Boyle, Philip, 131

Brackenridge, Hugh, 385

Braddock, Edward, 4, 34–35, 44, 82, 110, 383

Bradstreet, John, 38, 129, 173

Brandt, Joseph (Thayendanega), 11, 115–18

Brehm, Diedrich, 171, *172*

Bright Horn, 344

Brock, Isaac, 326–28, 329, 333; and Hull, 312, 298; Six Nations and 296, 297; victories of, 13, 15,

Brodhead, Daniel, 188, 191, 193–96, 204, 206, 210n. 33

Brodine, Charles, *xi*

G

301n. 5, 309; in the War of 1812, 338, 340–41, 342, 347

Q

Quakers, *xiv;* as missionaries, 244–46, 251–68, 347; Papunhank of the, 246–48, 250–51, 270nn. 11, 14–15; and the Seneca, 246–68; treatment of Natives, 248–51
Quebec, 7, 37–38, 174, 361; defense of, 89; siege of, 38, 83
Queenston, 15, 296, 297

R

Records, Spencer, 201
Recovery, Fort, 10
Red Jacket, 117
Reed, Joseph, 194
Repentigny. *See* Legardeur
Réaume, Jean-Baptiste, 136. *See also* Chevalier
Richardville, 135
Richotte, 137
Rigaud de Vaudreuil, Philippe de, 27, 28
Rigaud de Vaudreuil de Cavagnial, Pierre de (governor), 83, 93, 162n. 10
Rivardi, John J., *178*
River Raisin, 311; Battle of the, 14, 314, 344
Roberts, Benjamin, 129–30
Rochester (New York), 2

Rogers (murdered man), 130, 153
Rogers, Robert, 82, 92–93, 129, 154, 171
Rome (New York), 278. *See also* Stanwix
Rome Canal, 283–84, 285, 287
Ruddle family, 215–16, 222
Ruggles, Almon, 305–7

S

Sackets Harbor, 331, 356, 357, 359, 360, 361, 363–65
Sadosky, Leonard, *xiii*
Saint-Pierre, Jacques Legardeur de, 31–32, 33, 135
Salaberry, Charles-Michel de, 16
Salem village, 196, 197, 199, 200, 260
Sandusky, 196, 197, 198, 200; and the Firelands, 309, 311, 312–15, 317–19, 320–21
Sandusky, Fort, 151
Saratoga, 9
Sauk people, 6, 87, 96, 148
Sault Ste. Marie, 3
Scarouady (Native), 110
Schenectady, 277, 281, 282
Schlosser, Joseph, 151
Schoenbrunn, 196, 197
Schuyler, Philip, 281, 282, 283, 285
Scioto (town), 112, 232
Scioto Company, 238
Scioto River, 304
Scott, George, 60n. 16
Seiken, Jeff, *xvi*

Vaudreuil. *See* Rigaud de Vaudreuil

Vaughn, Elijah, 219

Venango, Fort, 65, 70, 110, 151

Venice (Firelands), 318

Vergennes, Charles Gravier, comte de, 40

Vermillion (Firelands), 308, 310, 311

Verville. *See* Gautier

Victory (HMS), 15

Vierville, Claude Charles, 88

Vierville, Claude Germaine de (father), 88

"Vieux Carron" (Native), 89

Villeneuve, Daniel, 88

Villiers, Louis Coulon de, 33. *See also* Jumonville

Vincennes, 155, 174, 193, 375

Virginia, 3, 198, 201, 235

W

Wabash, battle of the, 10, 238, 373–74; reactions to, 382–83, 384, 385, 386, 387, 388, 389n. 6. *See also* St. Clair

Wadsworth, Elijah, 312, 313

Wallace, Anthony F. C., 259

Waln, Nicholas Jr., 260

Walpole, Horace, 5

Walpole Company, 229

Wapakoneta, 340, 344, 345, 346, 347–48

War of 1812: declared, 333; Shawnee in the, 337–38; and Upper Canada, 325–35. *See also* Brock; Detroit; Kingston

Ward, Edward (ensign), 32, 195

Ward, Matthew, *xii*

Warren (Ohio), 312

Warren, William, 134

Washington, George, 4, 8, 31, 34, 47, 52, 60n. 17, 110; and Brodhead, 194, 196; described, 390–81; and Detroit, 175, *176;* and expansion, 239, 281; Quakers and, 251, 252; and St. Clair, 374, 382, 385, 389n. 6, 390n. 16

Washington, Lawrence, 4

Wayne, Anthony, 10, 118, 177, 215, 238, 332. *See also* Fallen Timbers

Wayne, Fort, 13, 340, 341, 343

Wea people, 65

Weiser, Conrad, 107, 108

Weiser, Samuel, 69

Wells, William, 14, 254–55, 340

Western Inland Lock Navigation Company, 281, *282,* 285

Western Reserve, 303–6, 307, 308, 310, 316–21

Whistler, John, 181

White, Richard, 95, 101–2n. 24, 188, 217

White Crane, 134

White Eyes (chief), 221

Whittlesey, Elisha, 313, 318

Widder, Keith, *xii–xiii*

Wildman, Zalmon, *xv;* 305–8, 309, 310–17, 318, 319–20, 321

Wilkinson, James, 16, 255

William Henry, Fort, 5, 82–83, 94–95

Williams, Fort, 280